MAKING MICROFINANCE WORK

Managing Product Diversification

Cheryl Frankiewicz and Craig Churchill

Synergy Books India

International Labour Organization – Geneva

This work was originally published by the International Labour Office, Geneva, and is reproduced by permission.

ISBN 978-93-82059-09-7

This edition first published in India in 2014 by:

SYNERGY

Synergy Books India

(A Unit of M/s Bookwell Publications)

24/4800 Ansari Road, Darya Ganj, New Delhi - 110002 (India)

Phone : 23268786, 23257264 • Fax : 23281315

Website : www.synergybooksindia.com

Email : synergybooksindia@gmail.com
bookwellpub@gmail.com

Printed at:
Mudrak, 30-A, Patparganj, Delhi-110091

Contents

III Market Segments

IV Diversifying Successfully

Acknowledgements

There is a Chinese proverb which says, "When eating bamboo sprouts, remember the man who planted them." This book would never have been realized were it not for the ideas planted by so many other authors and the support and encouragement that we received as we attempted to weave those ideas together to facilitate more successful product diversification by microfinance institutions. We are extremely grateful to the authors and organizations who have generously allowed us to repackage and recycle their ideas and tools for this purpose, in particular:

- ACCION International
- BRAC
- CARE
- CGAP
- CHF International
- CRS
- DAI
- FINCA
- Grameen Foundation
- Handicap International
- IFAD
- IFC
- Imp-Act Consortium
- Islamic Research and Training Institute
- Kumarian Press
- Making Cents International
- MEDA
- Microfinance Information eXchange
- Microfinance Network
- *MicroSave*
- Opportunity International
- SEEP Network
- ShoreCap Exchange
- Trickle Up
- USAID
- WOCCU
- Women's World Banking
- World Bank

There are a number of other individuals who contributed to the writing of this book and the development of the training course it is meant to support. We would like to thank Rahat Uraimova, Merten Sievers and Julika Breyer for their work on draft chapters. We would also like to thank the network of ILO certified trainers and the 1,515 microfinance managers from 47 countries who attended a *Making Microfinance Work* training course in the last three years and contributed their experiences, perspective and inspiration to this work. A special thanks to the trainers in Ethiopia, Jordan, Nigeria, Uganda and the Philippines who helped us test the materials, and to Margarita Lalayan and Juan Carlos Sanchez Valda, who reviewed the book in its entirety and helped ensure the integrity of the content as well as its relevance to the target market. Henriqueta Hunguana and Bich Van Nguyen Thi also participated in the peer review process and we appreciate their contributions as well.

Since the content of this curriculum pushed our own understanding of how microfinance institutions might diversify successfully, we are deeply indebted to the individuals with specialized expertise who volunteered to review our work and help us improve it. We would like to extend a heartfelt thanks to Wafik Grais, Richard Meyer, Madeline Hirschland, Michal Matul, Jan Maes, Linda Deelan, Franck Daphnis, Mayada El-Zoghbi, Daniel Seller, Petronella Chigara, Severine Deboos, Mary Yang, Diego Rei, Henry Yan, Johanne Lortie, Judith Van Doorn, Patricia Richter, Yousra Hamed, Christine Faveri, Jennifer Denomy, and Lara Storm.

We are extremely fortunate to have had the financial support of four organizations that believed in what we wanted to do and provided the resources to make it happen: the EU/ACP Microfinance Programme, the Government of Luxembourg, the United Nations Capital Development Fund, and the Government of Italy. We greatly appreciate their contributions to the development of this book, the associated trainer materials, and the trainer network through which this course will be delivered.

We would also like to recognize the support that we have received from our local partners, who helped us to organize the pilot tests and will work with us to disseminate the course material: the Association of Ethiopian Microfinance Institutions (AEMFI), Development Alternatives Resource Centre (DARC), CentroAfin, Associação Moçambicana dos Operadores de Microfinanças (AMOMIF), Uganda Institute of Bankers (UIB), UNDP Uzbekistan, ACCION International, ASCODEV, Association of Microfinance Institutions Rwanda (AMIR), Banque Centrale du Congo (BCC), Fond de Promotion de Microfinance (FPM), Fundación Andares, GTZ Tajikistan, HGConseil, ICC Mozambique, Ministry of Finance and Economic Planning of Rwanda (MINECOFIN), National Confederation of Cooperatives (NATCCO), Pakistan Microfinance Network (PMN), Punla Sao Tao, Sanabel Microfinance Network, as well as the ILO offices in Thailand, Indonesia, Lebanon, Nepal and Viet Nam.

We would like to thank the staff at the ILO's International Training Centre (ITCILO) in Turin for their support and assistance; in particular, Matteo Montesano and Michele McClure for their work with the layout and design; and Rashmi Fioravanti, Cristiana Actis, Maura Degiovanni and Patricia Lowe for their administrative support. Thanks also to Stefanie Eicke for helping us bring the book into alignment with ILO style guidelines, and to Sahar Tieby for being both a knowledgeable sounding board and an invaluable partner during the pilot testing process. We extend our deepest gratitude to Peter Tomlinson, Director of the ITCILO's Enterprise, Microfinance and Local Development Programme, who managed the development of this course and patiently supported its evolution and our learning. We would also like to thank Bernd Balkenhol, Director of the ILO's Social Finance Programme, who generously allowed his staff time to work on this project. A final thanks to Kenneth Neufeld and Sarah Labaree, without whom we would not have been able to invest the best of ourselves in this exciting initiative.

Foreword

This course evolved from material that was originally included in the International Labour Organization (ILO)'s training package *Making Microfinance Work: Managing for Improved Performance.* In that training, product diversification was discussed as one of the strategies through which microfinance managers can improve their institution's outreach. By expanding the range of products offered, MFIs can serve more poor people, meet more of their clients' financial service needs and, as a result, make greater progress towards the achievement of their commercial and social objectives.

During pilot testing of the original training, participants requested that more time be devoted to the discussion of various product options and the management of product diversification. Rather than lengthen an already intense two-week course, the ILO responded by removing product diversification content from the original curriculum and creating a separate training course to explore that material in more depth. This book is the outcome of that decision. *Making Microfinance Work: Managing Product Diversification* is the second of three volumes in the ILO's Making Microfinance Work (MMW) series. The third volume, which will help managers strengthen their "soft skills", is slated for development in 2012. Readers can find information on all three volumes at the course web site, http://mmw.itcilo.org.

This book and the training course it supports are designed to achieve four main objectives: 1) raise awareness of the opportunities and risks that product diversification presents; 2) explore options for improving the outreach of microfinance institutions (MFIs)[i] through product diversification; 3) provide tools and strategies for managing the product diversification process successfully; and 4) encourage more proactive management of MFI product portfolios over time.

Why the ILO?

Founded in 1919, the International Labour Organization is a specialized agency of the United Nations that promotes social justice and internationally recognized human and labour rights. Its vision for the 21st century is decent work for all. Decent work embraces various aspects of daily life of the working poor – productive employment, safe working conditions, equitable access to employment opportunities, absence of child labour, abolition of bonded labour, formalization of informal enterprises, access to social protection and the right to organize (ILO, 2008).

Microfinance is an important strategy for the ILO because it contributes to the decent work agenda in a variety of ways. Microcredit and micro-leasing products provide opportunities for small investments in self-employment and job creation. Emergency loans, savings and microinsurance provide the means for poor people to cope better with risk. When microfinance is delivered through group-based models, it can provide opportunities for the poor to organize and have a voice. Some MFIs, particularly those that partner with other

i In this text, the term "microfinance institution" is used to describe a wide range of regulated and non-regulated providers of microfinance services. This includes commercial banks that have a microfinance window, non-bank financial institutions that specialize in microfinance, cooperatives and credit unions that serve the low-income market, and non-governmental organizations that provide financial as well as non-financial services to the poor.

public or private actors in pursuit of a social mission, are actively discouraging child and bonded labour, and helping microentrepreneurs to grow and formalize.

As the focal point for microfinance within the ILO, the Social Finance Programme initiated the development of the *Making Microfinance Work* training series in 2003, building on another area of ILO expertise and concern – management. The ILO has a long history of involvement in strengthening management practices as a strategy for improving labour relations and working conditions. Its International Training Centre (ITCILO) in Turin, Italy, has been developing and delivering management training curricula for more than four decades. The ITCILO brought this experience to bear when it joined forces with the Social Finance Programme to produce this book and its accompanying training curriculum.

The end result is a quality product that draws from management experiences both within and outside the microfinance industry. It incorporates the perspective of a wide range of actors, including regulated financial institutions, governments, trade unions and non-governmental organizations. The ILO's unique governance structure, in which workers, employers and governments participate equally in decision-making, puts it in a privileged position to explore how public and private sector actors can work together to expand the outreach and impact of microfinance. With this course, the ILO hopes to facilitate broader and more innovative use of financial services to help create decent work for all low-income people. The course is a natural complement to other training packages created by the Social Finance Programme and ITCILO, most notably on leasing, microinsurance and guarantee funds.

Intended Audience

Making Microfinance Work: Managing Product Diversification is designed for middle and senior managers in microfinance institutions. It is relevant for institutions that have already diversified and are looking for ways to manage their diversification more effectively, as well as institutions that have not yet diversified and are looking for guidance on where and how to begin. The course can also be useful to funders and technical assistance providers that are trying to support MFI diversification.

Ideally, this course would be taken as a follow-up to the first volume of the MMW series, *Making Microfinance Work: Managing for Improved Performance.* The first volume lays the foundation for the second by examining the principles of effective microfinance management and exploring specific performance improvement strategies that will not be explained in detail here. Readers who have not yet had access to a management training curriculum are encouraged to attend a local delivery of the first course and to use that training manual as a supplement to the material contained in this volume.

Overview of the Course

This book and the training course it accompanies are divided into four parts.

I. **Preparing for Diversification.** This introductory section helps managers understand diversification, the opportunities and risks it poses, and how MFIs can prepare themselves to diversify successfully. Chapter 1 defines product diversification and the concept of a strategic product mix. It explores the many reasons why MFIs might want to develop

new products and markets while raising awareness of the damage diversification can cause. Chapter 2 then explores how to manage product development, in particular how to manage the risks inherent in the process. It provides some guidelines for deciding whether to diversify and for screening diversification ideas. Since the desire to enter new markets is often the primary reason for an MFI's product diversification, Chapter 3 focuses on the new market development process. It explores how managers can use market segmentation to better understand and serve new types of customer.

II. **Product Options.** MFIs that wish to diversify will find they have many options to choose from. Chapters 4 to 13 discuss ten different types of products that MFIs could introduce to expand their outreach: savings, long-term savings and micropensions, microenterprise loans, housing loans, emergency and consumption loans, microinsurance, leasing, money transfers, non-financial services and grants. Each chapter explores the characteristics and requirements of one type of product using examples from MFIs around the world to illustrate variations in the way the product can be delivered. For example, Chapter 4 explores mandatory, fixed, voluntary and contractual savings products while Chapter 6 explores both group and individual microenterprise lending methodologies. The main challenges and risks associated with each product type are discussed, together with examples of the strategies MFIs have used to manage them.

III. **Market Segments.** The chapters in this section explore market segments with potential for MFI expansion. Chapters 14 and 15 begin by looking at more marginalized segments, such as disabled persons, people living with HIV/AIDS, and the poorest of the poor. The isolation and vulnerability of these groups make them difficult to reach, and this requires a different approach to targeting. Chapters 16 through 21 examine six larger and more mainstream segments: youth, women, crisis-affected communities, Islamic communities, rural areas, and small and medium enterprises. Each chapter explores why that particular segment can be challenging to serve, and discusses the products and product adaptations that can help institutions serve the segment more effectively.

IV. **Diversifying Successfully.** After exploring numerous combinations of products and services that MFIs could offer to better meet the needs of specific market segments, this fourth and final section returns to the management agenda. How can MFIs plan, organize, lead and control the product diversification process to maximize the benefits for themselves as well as their clients? Chapter 22 looks at the important role of partnerships in helping MFIs of various types to diversify efficiently and effectively. It surveys the continuum of partnerships that are being used today, and provides guidelines for making them more strategic. Chapter 23 focuses on the challenges of delivering a diverse product portfolio. It raises awareness of the issues that need to be dealt with, and provides specific suggestions for adapting the institutional culture, redistributing responsibilities, empowering staff, communicating with clients, reengineering systems and managing change. Finally, Chapter 24 examines the product portfolio management function and the activities through which MFIs can not only create but also maintain a strategic product portfolio over time.

Like the first volume of the MMW curriculum, this course addresses 24 topics, but unlike the first volume, it does not address all of them in the training room. Parts I and IV make up a core curriculum which is delivered during every offering of the course. Parts II and III, however, provide product and market options that managers can choose to explore in the classroom or on their own. Participants in each training event prioritize the chapters they would most like to discuss face-to-face. Up to seven of the 18 chapters in Parts II and III can be addressed during a five-day course. This book provides an introduction to all 18 products and markets, so managers can explore options that may not be high on their current list of priorities, or may not have been prioritized by the audience as a whole, yet may constitute promising opportunities for the future.

Once an MFI decides that it wants to develop a new product or market that is discussed in this book, it will need additional information. A survey course such as this one is limited in the amount of detail it can provide on any one topic. To facilitate follow-up research, each chapter of this text concludes with a list of additional reading material. The lists are not meant to be exhaustive, but rather to point managers efficiently in the direction of supplemental resources that are respected and, whenever possible, available on the Internet. Trainers that have been certified by the ITCILO to deliver this course are also a valuable source of information, particularly with respect to the local experts and secondary data that can support MFIs' diversification efforts. Certified trainers can be contacted via the course web site.

Acronyms and Abbreviations

AAOIFI	Accounting and Auditing Organization for Islamic Financial Institutions
ABA	Alexandria Business Association (Egypt)
ABW	Association of Business Women (Tajikistan)
ACB	Akiba Commercial Bank (Tanzania)
ACF	Asian Credit Fund (Kazakhstan)
ACH	Automated Clearing House
ACLEDA	Association of Cambodian Local Economic Development Agencies
ACP	Acción Comunitaria del Perú
ACSI	Amhara Credit and Savings Institution (Ethiopia)
ADA	Austrian Development Agency
ADEMCOL	Asociación para el Desarrollo Microempresarial Colombiano
ADEMI	Asociación para el Desarrollo de Microempresas, Inc. (Dominican Republic)
ADOPEM	Asociación Dominicana para el Desarrollo de la Mujer
AFI	Assets for Independence
AIDMI	All India Disaster Mitigation Institute
AIDS	Acquired immunodeficiency syndrome
AMC	Asset management company
AML/CFT	Anti-money laundering and combating the financing of terrorism
AMFIU	Association of Microfinance Institutions of Uganda
AMREF	African Medical Research and Education Foundation
ANED	Asociación Nacional Ecuménica de Desarrollo (Bolivia)
APA	Appreciative Planning and Action
ARC	American Refugee Committee
ART	Anti-retroviral therapies
ASA	Association for Social Advancement (Bangladesh)
ASA	Activists for Social Alternatives (India)
ASCA	Accumulating savings and credit association
ASO	AIDS support organizations
ATK	Asuransi Takaful Keluarga (Indonesia)

ATM	automatic teller machine
AVFS	African Village Financial Services
AWOFS	AIDS Widows and Orphans Family Support
BAAC	Bank for Agriculture and Agricultural Cooperatives (Thailand)
BASF	Badische Anilin- und Soda-Fabrik
BASIX	Bhartiya Samruddhi Finance Ltd. (India)
BCP	Banco de Crédito del Perú
BDS	Business development services
BMCE	Banque Marocaine du Commerce Extérieur
BRAC	Bangladesh Rehabilitation Assistance Committee
BRI	Bank Rakyat Indonesia
BSFL	Bhartiya Samruddhi Finance Limited (India)
BSP	Bangko Sentral ng Pilipinas
BWDA	Bullock-Cart Workers Development Association (India)
BWTP	Banking with the Poor Network
BZ	Beselidhja/Zavet (Kosovo)
CBCP-ECMI	Episcopal Commission for the Pastoral Care of Migrants and Itinerant People (Philippines)
CARD	Centre for Agricultural Research and Development (Philippines)
CARE	Cooperative for Assistance and Relief Everywhere, Inc.
CASHE	Credit and Savings Household Enterprise (India)
CCCP	Caixas Comunitárias de Crédito e Poupança (Mozambique)
CD	Certificate of deposit
CECAM	Caisses d'Epargne et de Crédit Agricole Mutuel (Madagascar)
CEEWA	Council for Economic Empowerment for Women of Africa
CEO	Chief Executive Officer
CEP	Capital Aid Fund for the Employment of the Poor (Vietnam)
CEREMLUX	Centre de Recherche en micro-finance à Luxembourg
CETZAM	Christian Enterprise Trust of Zambia
CFPR	Challenging the Frontiers of Poverty Reduction
CFS	Community financial services

CFW	Cash-for-work
CGAP	Consultative Group to Assist the Poorest
CHF	Cooperative Housing Foundation
CIDA	Canadian Agency for International Development
CIDR	Centre International de Développement et de Recherche (Mali)
CLM	child labour monitoring
CLM	Chemin Levi Miyo [A Path to a Better Life] (Haiti)
COO	Chief Operations Officer
CPRC	Chronic Poverty Research Centre
CRDB	Cooperative and Rural Development Bank (Tanzania)
CRECER	Crédito con Educación Rural (Bolivia)
CRM	Customer relationship management
CRS	Catholic Relief Service
CVECA	Caisse Villageoise d'Epargne et de Crédit Autogérée [autonomous village banks]
DBACD	Dakahlya Businessmen Association for Community Development (Egypt)
DECT	Dowa Emergency Cash Transfer
DEPROSC	Development Project Service Center (Nepal)
DFCU	Development Finance Company Uganda
DFID	Department for International Development (United Kingdom)
DPO	disabled persons' organization
EACID	Egyptian Association for Community Initiatives and Development
ECDI	Enterprise and Career Development Institute (Pakistan)
EDA	enterprise development agency
EFT	electronic funds transfer
EKI	Microcredit Foundation EKI (Bosnia and Herzegovina)
ELA	Employment and Livelihood for Adolescents
EMS	Educación Media Superior
E&S	environmental and social
ESMS	environmental and social management system
FAO	Food and Agriculture Organization

FCC	Fundo de Crédito Comunitário (Mozambique)
FFH	Freedom from Hunger
FIE	Centro de Fomento a Iniciativas Económicas
FINCA	Foundation for International Community Assistance
FMO	entrepreneurial development bank of the Netherlands
FOCCAS	Foundation for Credit and Community Assistance (Uganda)
FSA	Financial service association
FSD	Financial Sector Deepening Trust (Kenya)
FSM	Financial service measure
FUCEC Togo	Faitière des Unités Coopératives d'Epargne et de Crédit du Togo
FUNHAVI	Fundación Hábitat y Vivienda (Mexico)
FWBL	First Women Bank Ltd (Pakistan)
G2P	government-to-person
GDP	gross domestic product
GE	Goviin Ekhlel (Mongolia)
GNP	gross national product
GPS	Grameen Deposit Pension Scheme
GTZ	Deutsche Gesellschaft für Technische Zusammenarbeit
GXI	G-XChange, Inc. (Philippines)
GYB	Generate Your Business Idea
H	high (risk)
HIV	human immunodeficiency virus
HP	Hewlett-Packard
HR	human resources
HSNP	Hunger and Safety Net Programme (Kenya)
IADB	Inter-American Development Bank
IBD	International Business Division
IDA	individual development account
IDB	Islamic Development Bank
IDLO	International Development Law Organization

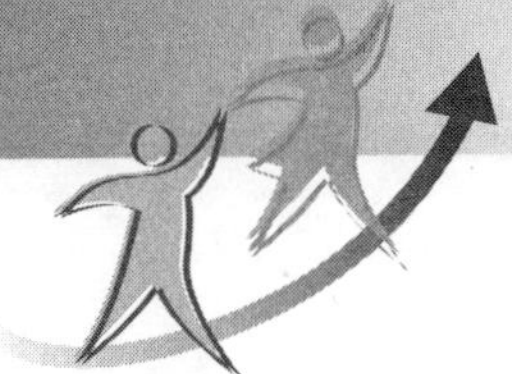

IDS	Institute of Development Studies (UK)
IDP	internally displaced person
IFAD	International Fund for Agricultural Development
IFC	International Finance Corporation
IFPRI	International Food Policy Research Institute
IFSB	Islamic Financial Services Board
IGVGD	Income Generation for Vulnerable Group Development
IIFC	Islamic investment and financial cooperatives (Afghanistan)
IIMPS	Invest India Micro Pension Services
ILO	International Labour Organization
IMAGE	Intervention with Microfinance for AIDS and Gender Equity
IMF	International Monetary Fund
ISTRAW	International Research and Training Institute for the Advancement of Women
IOM	International Organization for Migration
IPEC	International Programme on the Elimination of Child Labour
IPO	initial public offering
IRC	International Rescue Committee
IRCDS	Integrated Rural Community Development Society
ISFD	Islamic Solidarity Fund for Development
ISSIA	Initiative of Small Scale Industrialists' Agency (Uganda)
IT	information technology
ITC	Indian Tobacco Company
IYB	Improve Your Business
JCCUL	Jamaican Cooperative Credit Union League
KCIS	Kosovo Credit Information Service
KBS	Krishna Bhima Samruddhi (India)
KPOSB	Kenya Post Office Savings Bank
Ksh	Kenyan shilling
KWFT	Kenya Women Finance Trust
L	low (risk)

LEDA	Local Enterprise Development Agencies
LLC	limited liability company
LEAP	Learning for Empowerment Against Poverty
LSMS	Living Standard Measurement Surveys
Ltd	Limited
LYKOM	Linking Youth with Knowledge and Opportunities in Microfinance
M	medium (risk)
M&A	mergers and acquisitions
MABS	Microenterprise Access to Banking Services (Philippines)
MACTS	mutually aided cooperative thrift societies
MBA	mutual benefit association
MBB	*MicroBanking Bulletin*
MBP	Microenterprise Best Practices
MCO	microcredit organization
MEDA	Mennonite Economic Development Associates
MEDF	Macedonian Enterprise Development Foundation
MFI	microfinance institution
MFSP	microfinance support programme
MFT	Microdevelopment Finance Team
MIS	management information system
MIUSA	Mobility International USA
MIX	Microfinance Information eXchange
MMF	members' mutual fund
MOU	memorandum of understanding
M-PESA	M = mobile, pesa = money (Swahili)
MSE	micro- and small enterprise
MSCT	Micro Savings and Credit Trust
MSSL	Mahindra Shubhlabh Services Ltd
MSSS	Malankara Social Service Society
N/A	Not applicable
NABARD	National Bank for Agriculture and Rural Development (India)

NAD	Norwegian Association of Disabled
NBFI	non-bank financial institution
NGO	non-governmental organization
NLCL	Network Leasing Corporation Limited (Pakistan)
NMB	National Microfinance Bank (Tanzania)
NRSP	National Rural Support Programme (Pakistan)
NUDIPU	National Union of Disabled Persons of Uganda
NWTF	Negros Women for Tomorrow Foundation (Philippines)
ODI	Overseas Development Institute
OECD	Organisation for Economic Co-operation and Development
OFW	overseas Filipino workers
OIBM	Opportunity International Bank Malawi
OLC	Oportunidad Latinoamérica
PAR	portfolio at risk
PCA	personal capitalization account
PCR	poupança e credito rotativo [rotating savings and credit groups]
PDA	personal digital assistant
PEBLISA	Preventing and Eliminating Bonded Labour in South Asia
PEST	Political, economic, social and technological
PKR	Pakistan rupee
PLWHA	persons living with HIV/AIDS
PMC	product management committee
PMPC	Panabo Multi-Purpose Cooperative
POS	point-of-sale
PP	Perum Pegadaian
PPI	Progress Out of Poverty Index
PPP	purchasing power parity
PR	public relations
PRA	participatory rural appraisal
PRIDE	Promotion of Rural Initiatives and Development Enterprises (Guinea)
PRODEM	Fundación para la Promoción y Desarrollo de la Microempresa (Bolivia)

PWR	participatory wealth ranking
Q&As	questions and answers
R&D	research and development
RADAR	Rural AIDS and Development Action Research (South Africa)
RBAP	Rural Bankers Association of the Philippines
RBP	Rural Bank of Panabo (Philippines)
RCPB	Réseau des Caisses Populaires du Burkina
RD$	Dominican peso
RMC	risk management committee
RMP	Rural Maintenance Programme
ROE	return on equity
ROSCA	rotating savings and credit association
Rp.	rupees
RRA	rights, responsibilities, and advocacy
RTS	remote transaction system
S.A.	anonymous society
SACCO	savings and credit cooperative
SATM	smart automatic teller machine
SEAD	Small Economic Activities Development
SEAGA	Socio-economic and Gender Analysis
SEEDS	Sarvodaya Economic Enterprise Development Services (Sri Lanka)
SEEP	Small Enterprise Education and Promotion
SEF	Small Enterprise Foundation (South Africa)
SEWA	Self-Employed Women's Association (India)
SFCL	Small Farmer Cooperative Ltd (Nepal)
SFI	Serviamus Foundation Incorporated (Philippines)
SHG	self-help group
SIFFS	South Indian Federation of Fishermen Societies
SFL	Sisters for Life
SIM	subscriber identity module
SIYB	Start and Improve Your Business

SKS	Swayam Krishi Sangam (India)
SMART	Specific, measurable, achievable, realistic, and time-bound
SME	small and medium enterprise
SMS	Short Message Service
SPARC	Society for the Promotion of Area Resource Centres
SSB	Sharia supervisory board
SSI	survival score index
SWIFT	Society for Worldwide Interbank Financial Telecommunication
SWOT	Strengths, weaknesses, opportunities, threats
TASO	The AIDS Support Organization
Tk	Taka (currency of Bangladesh)
TLM	The Leprosy Mission Trust (India)
TPB	Tanzania Postal Bank
TRY	Tap and Reposition Youth
TSKI	Taytay Sa Kauswagan, Inc. (Philippines)
TUP	Targeting the Ultra Poor
TUW SKOK	Mutual Insurance Company of Cooperative Savings and Credit Unions (Poland)
TYM	Tao Yeu May (Affectionate Fund, Vietnam)
UGA	United Georgian Bank
UK	United Kingdom
ULD	United Leasing Company (Tanzania)
UMCOR	United Methodist Commitee on Relief
UMU	Uganda Microfinance Union
UN	United Nations
UNDP	United Nations Development Programme
UNESCO	United Nations Educational, Scientific and Cultural Organization
UNFPA	United Nations Population Fund
UNHCR	United Nations High Commissioner for Refugees
UNICEF	United Nations Children's Fund
UNIFEM	United Nations Development Fund for Women

US	United States
USA	United States of America
US$	United States dollar
USAID	United States Agency for International Development
USSD	unstructured supplementary service data
UTI	Unit Trust of India
VAT	value-added tax
VCT	voluntary counselling and testing
VDBI	Vulnerability to Debt Bondage Index
VGF	Vulnerable Group Feeding Programme
VLTCS	voluntary long-term contractual savings
VS&L	village savings and loan
VSLA	village savings and loan association
WEP	Women's Empowerment Program
WFP	World Food Programme
WHO	World Health Organization
WOCCU	World Council of Credit Unions
WORD	Women Reading for Development
WU-KG	Women's Union of Kien Giang (Vietnam)
WWB	Women's World Banking
XAC	Golden Fund for Development (Mongolia)
YAP	youth apprenticeship programme
YCO	youth charitable organization
YDF	Youth Development Foundation

I

Preparing for Diversification

Part I: Preparing for Diversification

The first three chapters of this book are designed to help MFIs plan and organize themselves for successful product diversification. Institutions that offer a very limited number of products can use this section to enhance their understanding of diversification, the rewards and risks they can expect to generate through different diversification strategies, and the steps they might need to take to diversify in a strategic and cost-effective manner. Institutions that already offer a range of products and services can use this material in other ways: to analyse their products at multiple levels and explore new opportunities for diversification, to strengthen their management of existing and new product development processes, and to identify strategies for using their diverse product mix to enter new markets or new segments within markets they already serve.

In sum, this introductory section explores the concept of diversification from a variety of perspectives, and attempts to articulate the prerequisites for success. It also encourages MFIs and the entities that support them to reflect upon their diversification efforts to date and how they might do things differently in the future to expand their outreach through ongoing product and market development.

I Preparing for Diversification

1 Understanding Product Diversification

Success (in terms of both deep outreach and institutional sustainability) will come to those organizations that best determine the perceptions, needs, and wants of the very poor and satisfy them through the design, communication, pricing, and delivery of appropriate and competitively viable offerings. ~ Kotler and Andreasen (1996)

The microfinance industry has come a long way in the last 20 years. Even five years ago, most MFIs were still focused on conquering the challenges of delivering one product – microcredit – to one market – microentrepreneurs. The success of pioneering institutions that have implemented a broader vision of sustainable financial services for the poor is now inspiring MFIs around the world to question whether they too can and should do more.

This chapter lays the foundation for discussing successful product diversification by clarifying a few important definitions and concepts. It also introduces the main opportunities and challenges that diversification can pose. It addresses the following six themes:

1. What is product diversification?
2. Why diversify?
3. The damage diversification can cause
4. Managing the challenges and opportunities
5. What is a strategic product mix?
6. Towards successful product diversification

1.1 What Is Product Diversification?

To define product diversification, one must first define **product.** For microfinance institutions, a product is a financial service that customers purchase because it fulfils a particular need. Some of the most common types of product are credit, savings, insurance, and money transfer services. Some products combine multiple financial services in one package, while others integrate financial services with non-financial services such as education, training or market linkages.

A product can be analysed at three main levels, as shown in Figure 1.1 (Brand, 1998a):

1. **Core product.** The main benefit the product is providing or the need it is fulfilling. A savings product, for example, might provide financial return, security or liquidity.
2. **Actual product.** The specific features and packaging that characterize what the customer is buying. For a passbook savings product, this would include the interest rate, minimum balance requirements, withdrawal fees, account opening form and passbook design.
3. **Augmented product.** The way customers receive what they are buying. This includes how the product is delivered and serviced: for example, the hours of operation during which customers can access their savings, the amount of time it takes to open an account, the way customers are treated before and after they open their account, and so on.

Figure 1.1 The total product

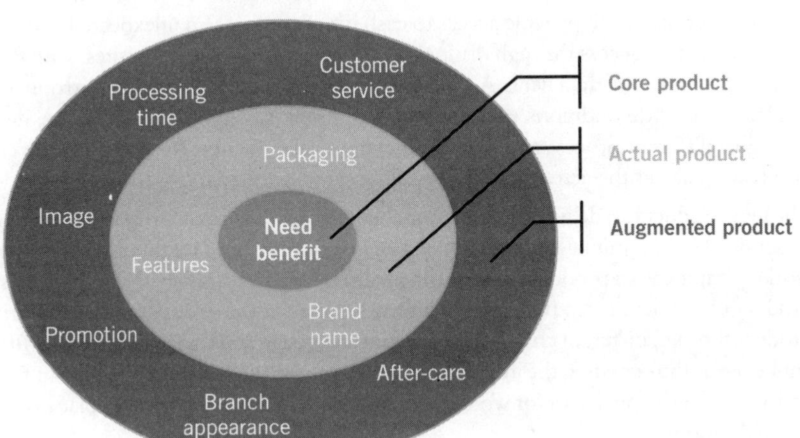

Source: Adapted from Brand, 2001.

Taking into account all three levels, the number of financial products that could be introduced into a competitive marketplace appears unlimited. Even if two MFIs were to offer two savings products that served the same basic need and had very similar features, differences in the way the two products are packaged or delivered could clearly distinguish them among customers.

Product diversification refers to the development, marketing and delivery of one or more financial (and perhaps non-financial) services that expand an institution's existing product offering. Institutions can diversify in a number of ways:

- by introducing a completely new product that has never before been seen in the market (for example, FINCA Uganda and Microcare launching a health microinsurance product in 1999);
- by introducing a product line that is new to the institution, but not to the market (for example, TSKI, a credit-only MFI in the Philippines, introducing a voluntary savings product in 2007);
- by adding a new product to an existing product line (for example, El Comercio introducing a housing loan in Paraguay to complement its existing microenterprise loan product);
- by launching a "new and improved" version of an existing product (for example, Grameen Bank introducing a more flexible "Basic Loan" to eventually replace its "General Loan").

When an MFI introduces a new product, that product can differ from existing products at any of the three levels described above:

- The new product can meet an entirely new need or deliver a unique type of benefit. For instance, a new money transfer product could enable customers to make payments in a way that existing credit, savings and insurance products cannot. In this case, diversification takes place at the core product level.

- The new product can deliver the same core benefit as an existing product, but do so through a different package of features. For example, voluntary savings and emergency loan products can both provide access to cash if a client faces an unexpected expense, but they provide that access through distinct sets of activities and prerequisites, with different costs and timing for the client. A card-based savings product could be introduced with similar terms and conditions as an existing passbook savings account, but be delivered through a different process and with distinct physical evidence. In such cases, diversification takes place at the actual product level.
- The new product can deliver the same core benefit and features as an existing product, but be serviced or communicated differently. For instance, an MFI might try to sell its existing working capital loan product to men using a different sales strategy than it uses to sell the product to women. Even if it has one internal name for the product, it could market the product through different channels, use distinct language and images, and highlight different benefits, thus creating the impression that it is selling a "working capital loan for men" and a "working capital loan for women". In this case, diversification takes place at the augmented product level.

An MFI's degree of diversification will depend not only on the number of products it offers or is perceived to offer, but also on the range of needs that its products can satisfy. Bai Tushum Financial Foundation in Kyrgyzstan, for example, has a large portfolio of loan products for livestock, crop production, trade, fixed assets, consumption, mortgages, cooperatives, small and medium enterprises, and groups of self-employed women. Bank Rakyat Indonesia (BRI)'s microfinance units offer only two loan products (salary loans and a versatile enterprise loan), but also offer three savings products and a money transfer service. It can be argued that Bai Tushum is a more diversified institution because of the number of products it offers, but it can also be argued that BRI's microfinance units are more diversified because they offer products that meet a wider array of needs.

The important question to consider is not which institution is more diversified, but rather, which diversification strategy is the right one for a particular institution at a particular point in time. As explained below, expansion of an MFI's product portfolio will not automatically create value for an institution or its clients. It is not a goal in and of itself. Product diversification can, however, play a critical role in helping an MFI achieve its objectives.

1.2 Why Diversify?

There are numerous good reasons for an MFI to diversify its product offering: to meet current customers' needs better, to increase customer loyalty, to attract new customers, to achieve a social mission, to diversify sources of income and funding, to reduce institutional risks, to increase profitability, and to be competitive. Each of these is discussed briefly in this section.

To Meet Current Customers' Needs Better

As summarized in Table 1.1, low-income clients have a need for many types of financial services. They may not require all of these services at once, and their needs will certainly change

Table 1.1 Categories and purposes of financial services for low-income clients

Category	Purpose	Financial services
1. Payments management	Receive wages or remittances, pay bills or send money	• Bank accounts • Money transfers • Foreign exchange
2. Cash flow management	Smooth income and consumption	• Liquid savings • Consumption loans
3. Investment management	Maintain and grow purchasing power of savings and other assets	• Term deposits • Housing and asset loans • Leasing • Retirement savings (or micropensions)
4. Business services	Assist business with its financial needs	• Start-up, working capital and expansion loans • Payroll services • Property and liability insurance • Venture capital investment
5. Risk management	Reduce vulnerability to economic stresses, keep money safe	• Targeted savings • Emergency loans • Life, health and property insurance • Safe deposit box

Source: Adapted from Churchill and Frankiewicz, 2006.

over time, but no microfinance institution will be able to meet all of its clients' needs through a single product. Through diversification, an MFI can offer clients more options and products that are better suited to meet particular needs. This increases product effectiveness as well as the flexibility of clients' financial management, and results in greater customer satisfaction.

To Increase Customer Loyalty

One of the best ways for an MFI to encourage existing customers to remain with the institution is to offer them a portfolio of products that remains relevant even as their needs change. Product diversification can be an important part of any institution's effort to develop a life-long relationship with clients. Children's savings accounts or apprenticeship loans could draw young people into a relationship with an MFI while microenterprise and housing loans, life insurance, or a retirement savings product could keep them in the relationship as they age. The more an MFI succeeds in satisfying a customer over time, the greater the chances of that client becoming not only a loyal customer, but also an advocate for the institution – someone who recommends the institution to friends, family, neighbours and colleagues.

Of course, the reverse is also true. Institutions that do not diversify to meet their customers' changing needs give customers no choice but to look elsewhere to have their needs met. The competitive microfinance market in Bolivia provides a case in point. BancoSol, which exclusively offered solidarity group loans for many years, was slow to develop an individual loan product for customers who were outgrowing their groups. When Caja Los Andes (now Banco Los Andes ProCredit) entered the market providing only individual loans, it easily attracted many of BancoSol's best customers because it offered what they wanted.

To Attract New Customers

Just as existing customers are enticed to remain with an institution that has a diverse product offering, new customers may be attracted by an MFI's ability to meet multiple financial needs. MFIs can also introduce new products that help them reach out to new market segments, such as savers, rural communities or migrant workers. In Bosnia and Herzegovina, EKI expanded its target market from small and medium-sized enterprises to include a poorer and more rural clientele because it believed this market segment had significant potential for growth. It developed a loan product to meet the needs of this new segment, and within two years that product came to represent 73 per cent of EKI's loan portfolio. In the same time period, EKI's total number of clients increased from 9,000 to nearly 19,000 (Szubert and Petric, 2005).

To Achieve a Social Mission

By developing additional products, institutions can be more effective at supporting the overall socioeconomic development of their clients. The Self-Employed Women's Association (SEWA) in India, for example, provides a range of services to its clients, and has tracked the benefits associated with different interventions (see Table 1.2). It has found that it is able to have a greater overall impact because of the way its multiple services reinforce each other (Chen, 2005). As discussed in Chapter 15, a growing number of MFIs are diversifying their product portfolio, often adding non-financial services to the financial services mix, to reach poorer market segments effectively.

To Diversify Sources of Income and Funding

Commission and fee-based products, such as insurance, remittances, money transfers and bill payment services, allow MFIs to generate revenue through means other than the loan portfolio. Instead of risking capital upfront to earn interest income later, MFIs can generate income upfront, either before or at the time a service is provided. The different cash flows provided by these products can aid an institution's liquidity management. They can also add to an MFI's bottom line. In 2007, 6 per cent of the revenue generated by MFIs reporting to the Microfinance Information eXchange (MIX) came from fee-based financial services; another 4 per cent came from other assets, mainly interest on investments. This may seem insignificant, yet these revenues represented at least half of all net operating income (after removing expenses) for 49 per cent of the 549 sustainable MFIs in the sample (Gonzalez, 2008).

If the products being introduced are savings products, then diversification can also broaden an MFI's sources of funding. This is particularly important if the savings products are

Table 1.2 Impact at SEWA by type of intervention

Loans and savings:

- Use of financial services is associated with increases in household income, both total and per capita.
- Use of financial services is associated with significant housing improvements and durable goods purchases.
- Borrowing and saving increase secondary school enrolment, especially of boys.
- Repeated borrowing from SEWA Bank is associated with increased expenditure on food.
- Use of loans is associated with improved ability to cope with economic shocks.

Childcare:

- Use of day care centres is associated with increases in child health and several child development indicators, notably education.
- Use of day care centres is associated with notable increases in the working hours and earnings of mothers, as well as reduction in their stress or anxiety about child care.

Infrastructure services:

- Provision of urban infrastructure – water, sanitation, electricity – is associated with improvements in health and increases in hours of work, productivity, and incomes.
- Provision of rural infrastructure – notably, water resources – is associated with increases in hours of work and in income, if the released time is invested in economic activities.

Health insurance:

- A far higher percentage of SEWA members – as many as ten times – compared with the general population have health insurance.
- Health insurance reimbursements halved the percentage of catastrophic hospitalizations (defined as costing more than 10 per cent of annual household income) and hospitalizations resulting in impoverishment.

Source: Chen, 2005.

long-term, because they can generate resources that can then be used to finance longer-term lending products such as housing loans and leasing products, which are often in demand by customers but are difficult to finance.

To Reduce Institutional Risks

Product diversification can help MFIs to reduce risk in several ways. By giving clients more tools with which to manage their financial stresses, institutions can mitigate their own credit, reputation, competition and social mission risks. As mentioned above, if different products generate income in different patterns, then diversification can help an institution ensure that it has sufficient cash on hand when needed. If an MFI is trying to provide long-term loans financed by short-term liabilities, the introduction of longer-term savings products could reduce its asset-liability risk. It can also reduce dependence on a single revenue stream. If the economy turns sour and enterprise loans are less in demand, an MFI could still generate income through other types of loans or fee-based services. In addition, by managing a portfolio of products that cater to different economic subsectors, MFIs like Confianza in Peru (see Box 1.1) can avoid the risks that come from concentrating too narrowly on one segment of the population.

Box 1.1 Loan Diversification at Confianza

Confianza is a small regulated microfinance institution in central Peru that provides agricultural loans alongside a range of rural, urban, small business, housing, and consumer loans to low-income clients. From its beginnings as an Inter-American Development Bank-funded NGO programme in 1993 until becoming a regulated microfinance provider in 1999, Confianza's loan portfolio was almost exclusively devoted to solidarity group loans for agricultural purposes. When a combination of factors, including plunging commodity prices, led to an arrears rate of over 50 per cent in 1999, Confianza was forced to make a set of swift, substantial changes in order to survive.

The MFI altered its lending methodology, instituted stricter lending requirements and monitoring, and added urban and individual loans to diversify its portfolio. Its non-agricultural portfolio flourished, yet Confianza also maintained a focus on agricultural lending (about a quarter of its total portfolio), with lending to agriculture almost quadrupling in volume over the next few years. By year-end 2002, Confianza had become financially sustainable, lending more than US$4 million annually, with a respectable arrears rate (portfolio at risk > 30 days) of less than 4 per cent and a 19 per cent adjusted return on equity.

Source: Pearce and Reinsch, 2005a.

To Increase Profitability

Expanding one's customer base and sources of income, increasing customer loyalty, generating more business volume per client by cross-selling multiple services to each customer, and lowering costs through better risk management can all contribute to greater institutional profitability. The Grameen Bank in Bangladesh, for example, increased net profits sixfold in one year – from 60 to 358 million taka (US$6 million) – as a result of reinventing its product portfolio. Researchers concluded that the improvement in performance was "related to the greater attractiveness of Grameen II's wider range of more user-friendly loan products, and to its decision to attract deposits in much greater volume, which has allowed it to expand its loan portfolio and serve many new borrowers" (Hossain, 2005).

To Improve Competitiveness

The first MFI to introduce a new product or service will differentiate itself from all other competitors. It is likely to be perceived as more innovative and more responsive, and this can result in a stronger brand and increased market share. MFIs that are not among the first to bring a product to the market can remain competitive only if they introduce a product of their own that offers at least as much value as that of the competition. XacBank in Mongolia provides a good example of how MFIs use product diversification as a competitive strategy (refer to the case study at the end of Chapter 2).

Copying a market leader's product can help an MFI retain customers, but it will not distinguish the MFI in the marketplace or enable it to gain market share. If an MFI is not the market leader, it will have to modify the market leader's design and improve upon it in some way to attract clients who did not find previous versions of the product useful, or who find the MFI's adaptation more attractive than what others are offering. In mature or highly competitive markets, even very small changes in a product's design or marketing can enable an MFI to differentiate its product and increase market share.

1.3 The Damage Diversification Can Cause

Although the potential benefits are many, product diversification will not necessarily generate returns for an institution. The introduction of a new product creates many opportunities for things to go wrong, as demonstrated by Equity Bank's experience with its consumer loan product in Kenya (see Box 1.2). Diversification could result in financial losses, reduced demand for existing products, weaker service quality, mission drift and/or damage to the institution's reputation.

Box 1.2 The Risk of Following the Competition

In the words of CEO James Mwangi, "We thought it would be a quick win." Equity Bank had a great deal of liquidity, thanks to its successful savings mobilization, and was looking for a way to use those funds profitably. Other banks already offered a salary-based loan product and Equity was under pressure to do the same. Since it offered a salary advance product, and thought it understood the salaried market fairly well, it decided not to follow the more time-consuming product development process that it had used with other products.

Equity Bank introduced a product called "Equiloan" that was very similar to other salary-based loan products on the market. From the outset, there was enormous demand for the product. It was easy to administer at low volume, so the bank scaled up quickly, reaching a portfolio of US$3.75 million within 9 months. Although Equity Bank expected the strong response, it was not fully ready for it. It underestimated the amount of staff time that would be required to complete employer assessments and to manage the employer relationships on a daily basis. Soon, one Equity employee was managing a portfolio of 5,000 clients.

It took more than three months for Equity to get into the central payment system, and it had not built a grace period into the product's design, so several months of arrears quickly piled up as customers' loan payments came due and their salaries had not yet been credited to the bank. Once an employer's salary payments had been processed, there was no easy way for Equity's management information system (MIS) to identify clients associated with that employer.

The delays in getting salaries credited, together with instances of internal and external fraud involving fake and fraudulent pay slips, masked other product weaknesses which contributed to rising portfolio at risk (PAR) levels. By July 2004, six months after Equiloan had been introduced, PAR > 30 days was 7 per cent, a level Equity deemed dangerous for a new product. Three months later, it had risen to 18 per cent.

Equity Bank had a major challenge on its hands. As Mwangi noted, "Tackling the problem when it is small is one thing; solving it when you already have a portfolio of 60,000 clients is another." Equity remapped all of the product's processes and completely reengineered how the product is delivered, paying careful attention to the risks that had been identified. It purchased and installed a new MIS and launched a major collections effort. By November 2005, it could report that 90 per cent of the delinquent portfolio was performing, although provisioning and monitoring costs associated with the product continued to be significant.

Source: Adapted from Frankiewicz, 2006.

Financial Losses

If an MFI's new product fails, the institution will lose time, energy, and money. A product can fail for several reasons:

- **Few people buy it.** Perhaps they do not like the product, or they like what the competition is offering better. Maybe they do not have a need for it, or they do not understand it well enough to be willing to purchase it. Whatever the reason, if too few people buy the product, the MFI will not generate enough income to cover the costs of developing and delivering it.
- **The product concept is well received, but the institution has difficulty delivering it.** Inadequate information systems, physical infrastructure, communication channels or risk management could result in a product not being delivered effectively, as illustrated by the Equity Bank case above. Poorly recruited, inadequately trained or unmotivated staff could also contribute to product failure, as described in Box 1.3.

Box 1.3 Product Diversification Leads to Institutional Collapse

In the late 1990s, Federal Savings, a cooperative based in Bangladesh, tried to duplicate the innovative products of *Safe*Save, which was successfully operating in Dhaka slums. However, although Federal Savings could copy the features of the product, it could not duplicate the organizational culture, or the careful management and precise reporting systems that underpinned *Safe*Save. With popular products, Federal Savings expanded rapidly, became dangerously undercapitalized, and eventually collapsed.

Source: Cracknell, 2006.

- **The product is used in an unanticipated manner.** This can subject the institution to risks that the product design does not control, as was the case with one South African bank's tractor loan. The product was very popular, but ultimately failed because the loan recipients were laid-off workers who did not understand the agricultural market. Loans were used to finance second-hand tractors, which proved difficult for customers to maintain. When tractors broke down they were gradually dismantled for parts, and without an income, borrowers could not repay their loans (Cracknell, 2006).
- **The product is priced inappropriately.** In this case, the product is well received by the market and the institution delivers it effectively, but the price of the product is initially set too low to cover its costs. Yeshasvini Trust in India had to double the premium on its health insurance product during its third year of operation in an attempt to achieve financial self-sufficiency. It lost one third of its clients (750,000 members) as a result (Radermacher et al., 2005).

Reduced Demand for Existing Products

If customers choose to buy the new product instead of a product that is already on offer, the new product will simply replace or "eat" the old one, rather than creating a new revenue stream (the phenomenon is referred to as "cannibalization"). This is what happened to the

Association for Social Advancement (ASA) in Bangladesh when it introduced the Associate Member's Savings Account. The product was an open access, voluntary savings account that could be used by members of the community who did not want to borrow. It was a relatively high-cost product that began to cannibalize the existing General Member's Savings Account because it was marketed only to existing borrowers' relatives, who were already saving indirectly through the borrowers' General Member's Savings Account (Wright et al., 2001a).

Cannibalization often occurs when a new product is added to an existing product line. If a group-lending MFI launches an individual loan product, some of the clients that used to take a group loan because it was the only option available will actually prefer and be able to qualify for an individual loan. Microenterprise lenders that introduce housing or consumption loans can face a similar situation. New products can be designed to encourage clients' transition from an old product to a new product that meets their needs more appropriately, and to cover the cost of that transition. However, existing products may begin to operate at a loss if the MFI does not foresee a certain degree of cannibalization and redistribute its resources accordingly.

Weakened Service Quality

A new product can cause damage by making it more difficult for staff to deliver an MFI's pre-existing product menu. Resources may be diverted from existing products to fuel new product development, and the old volume of business may have to be handled in less time, by fewer people, or with more limited support from back or head office staff. The quality of service provided to existing customers could suffer as a result.

The introduction of a new product could also complicate the product menu, making it more difficult for staff to explain clearly what the institution has to offer, and making it harder for clients to decide which product best meets their needs. Each time a new product is added to the mix, the volume of information that must be remembered and organized increases, and this increases the potential for confusion and errors.

Mission Drift

A fourth way that a new product can cause damage is by moving an institution away from its stated purpose or target market. This can happen if an MFI designs a new product to improve its financial sustainability and ends up serving better-off or less risky clients than it is mandated to serve. Even if an institution designs a product with its target market in mind, the product can become popular with other types of customer. For example, when some group-lending MFIs introduced individual lending to facilitate the expansion of existing (primarily female) clients' businesses, they found that the product attracted large numbers of new (primarily male) clients as well. The popularity of the product among men quickly shifted the client gender balance in institutions that existed, first and foremost, to empower women.

Mission drift can also occur if an MFI develops a new product in response to government pressure or an opportunity to access additional funds. The new product may benefit the MFI, but it may simultaneously divert resources from the institution's current strategic plan. This can result in less outreach to the MFI's target market or inadequate investment in the people and infrastructure needed to implement the MFI's core activities effectively.

MFIs that make a deliberate decision to change their mission and develop a new product as part of their strategy for achieving that new mission do not suffer from mission drift. In such cases, product development follows a change in mission; it is not product development that leads the institution away from its mission. Nevertheless, an MFI that changes its mission may still be criticized by the public for shifting its focus away from one market or purpose in favour of another, particularly if the reasons for the change are not well communicated.

Reputation Damage

Obviously, if a product fails, that failure could have a negative impact on the image of an institution. However, even a successful product can negatively affect an MFI's reputation. This can occur, for example, if staff become overworked or highly stressed as a result of the new product's introduction, and start to deliver poor customer service. Long lines or waiting periods caused by strong product demand can also frustrate customers and lead them to question the institution's ability to deliver on its promises. If an MFI begins making larger loans to small and medium enterprises, it could be criticized for abandoning the poor. Table 1.3 summarizes the main opportunities and challenges presented by product diversification.

Table 1.3 Diversification opportunities and challenges

Opportunities	Challenges
• Meeting current customers' needs better • Increasing customer loyalty • Attracting new customers • Fulfilling a social mission • Diversifying income sources • Reducing institutional risks • Increasing profitability • Improving competitiveness	• Avoiding product failure • Coping with lower demand for existing products • Reallocating resources in a way that does not harm the service quality • Communicating a more complicated product menu • Preventing mission drift • Safeguarding the institution's brand

Source: Authors.

1.4 Managing the Challenges and Opportunities

It is impossible to reap the benefits of product diversification without becoming vulnerable to its risks. Therefore, MFIs that wish to diversify must find ways of managing those risks to limit the damage that might be caused during the process of product diversification.

In general, diversification risks can be managed in the same way that all other risks are managed. The risks must first be identified, measured and prioritized. Controls must then be designed and implemented to reduce the institution's exposure to those risks as cost-effectively as possible. Afterwards, the controls must be monitored and adapted as necessary to ensure their effectiveness over time. Chapter 2 explores the risks associated with product diversification as well as some of the strategies for controlling risk during the product development process.

Successful diversification requires more, however, than the effective management of risk during the development of individual products. It also requires effective management of the product portfolio as a whole to maximize the benefits that an MFI can generate with a particular set of human and financial resources. This includes:

- making sure that the products in an MFI's portfolio work together to fulfil the institution's strategic objectives;
- coordinating product development activities so that actions taken to strengthen performance in one area do not inadvertently harm performance in another area;
- coordinating product delivery in a way that leverages institutional strengths, captures economies of scale, protects loyal customers and maximizes efficiency;
- allocating resources so that priority products get sufficient support while poorly performing products are either fixed or replaced;
- gathering, organizing and channeling information about the performance of each product to decision makers on a regular basis to facilitate timely and appropriate actions in the face of changing customer needs and market conditions.

These activities constitute the product portfolio management function, which will be discussed in detail in Chapter 24. Because of its importance, this function should be assigned to a specific group of people, ideally a product management committee, who can then be held accountable for ensuring that a strategic product mix is created and maintained over time.

1.5 What Is a Strategic Product Mix?

Ultimately, a strategic product mix is one that enables an MFI to achieve its mission. However, given limited resources and a constantly changing, competitive environment, what makes a product mix strategic is its ability to help an institution achieve short-term objectives in pursuit of a longer-term mission.

As an MFI develops, it has nine main options for growth, as summarized in Table 1.4. It can focus on selling more of its existing products to markets it already serves. It can take its existing products to new geographic areas or to different types of customers than those it has served in the past. It can modify its products for sale to existing or new markets, and it can develop new products for sale to existing or new customers (Kotler, 1999). Of course, it can also combine strategies and pursue different options for different products or product lines.

No one strategy is best. However, as Chapters 2 and 3 will explore, the risks and costs associated with new product and market development make the strategies in the upper left-hand corner of the table safer and cheaper. Thus, if MFIs can make progress towards their mission and objectives by working with their existing product(s) and market(s), it is usually wise to do so.

When the products and markets that already exist cannot meet client and/or institutional needs, then other growth options become more attractive. Institutions can scan the available options, assess their competitive strengths and weaknesses, and choose to develop a product or market that will best enable them to meet their outreach objectives.

Table 1.4 Strategy options

		PRODUCT		
		Existing	Modified	New
MARKET	Existing	1. Sell more of the MFI's existing product(s) to the same types of client and geographic areas it is already serving	2. Modify the MFI's product(s) and sell more to markets that the MFI is already serving	3. Design new product(s) that will appeal to markets that the MFI is already serving
	Geographically modified	4. Enter new geographic areas and sell existing product(s) to the same types of customer served elsewhere	5. Modify existing product(s) for sale in new geographical markets but to the same types of customer served elsewhere	6. Design new product(s) for sale in a new geographic area but to the same types of customer served elsewhere
	New	7. Sell existing product(s) to new types of customer	8. Sell modified product(s) to new types of customer	9. Design new product(s) to sell to new types of customer

Source: Adapted from Kotler, 1999.

Since resources are limited, however, and a proliferation of products has the potential to confuse staff and clients more than it helps, MFIs should find a way to focus their diversification. Some of the different approaches taken by financial service providers are described below.

- **Market segment approach.** MFIs that take this approach decide to focus on a particular market segment and develop a combination of products to meet the needs of that customer group. For example, ProMujer in Latin America is well known for its deliberate focus on women, whereas BancoEstado in Chile segmented its market into six groups (individuals, businesses, small enterprises, microenterprises, public institutions and Chileans outside the country) and offers a different portfolio of products to each. The concept and process of market segmentation will be discussed in more detail in Chapter 3.
- **Client life-cycle approach.** With this approach, MFIs aim to develop a set of products that can meet clients' needs during each stage of their lives. An institution that conceptualizes its mix in this way might include children's savings accounts, education loans, microenterprise loans, housing loans, and a long-term savings or insurance product in its portfolio. Some of the products that are designed for use early in a client's life could be "loss leaders"; in other words, they might not make a profit, but they would attract new business, build brand awareness or create affinity with the institution, which would generate revenue indirectly and over time. Hattan National Bank in Sri Lanka is serving youth sustainably through a life-cycle approach.
- **Business life-cycle approach.** This approach is similar to the client life-cycle approach, but it focuses on meeting the needs of clients' businesses as they grow in volume and assets and become more formalized over time. The Small and Micro Enterprise Project of the Alexandria Business Association (ABA) in Egypt seeks to "develop and promote

existing small and microenterprises, raise the incomes of SMEs, help the transformation of SMEs from informal to formal, and contribute to solving the problems of unemployment (ABA, 2010)." It offers seed capital, group and individual loans, as well as fee-based training, marketing and technical assistance services. Clients can access larger loans with better terms as their businesses grow, become licensed, begin paying taxes, and improve record-keeping.

- **Developmental approach.** MFIs that take this approach typically have a strong social mission and aim to support the economic and social development of their clients over time. They offer a set of products that helps people move up the socioeconomic ladder and transition out of poverty, providing safety nets along the way to prevent them from moving too far backwards in the event of a setback or crisis. The experiences of BRAC and the Grameen Bank in Bangladesh provide excellent examples of this approach (see Chapter 15).
- **Core competence approach.** Less common in microfinance, this is a popular approach in other industries and is being adopted by banks and private companies entering microfinance. To take this approach, an MFI identifies its core competence or strength relative to the competition, and chooses to deliver products and services that leverage that competence. In Mexico, for example, the third largest cement manufacturer in the world is providing financial services, but only to support the construction and improvement of housing, since this builds on its core competence. Wizzit Payments Ltd in South Africa identified technology as its core competence. Through partnerships with Vodacom, MasterCard, the Absa Group and South African Post Office it uses cellular phones, Internet, automatic teller machines (ATMs) and point-of-sale (POS) devices to deliver transactional financial services, namely person-to-person payments, transfers, prepaid purchases and retail purchases.
- **Entry and expansion (phased) approach.** With this approach, an MFI identifies a limited set of products that it delivers when it first enters a market, and other products that it introduces later. Entry-level products are generally those that are easy to manage and can generate volume and income relatively quickly. This keeps operations simple during the period of time when people are still being trained and systems are being put in place. Although institutions are often criticized for entering new markets with a credit product rather than a savings product, this is a popular choice because it generates income quickly. However, for banks that already have a licence to capture deposits, and for member-owned institutions, a simple voluntary savings product is usually the best way to go. It enables the institution to get to know the market, establish a relationship with clients, and build up a local capital base before assuming the risk of a lending portfolio.
- **Core vs. optional approach.** An MFI might decide to have a core set of products that it offers in all locations, and other products that will vary from one geographic area or market segment to another.

These approaches are not mutually exclusive. An MFI could decide to serve women (a market segment) and then develop a portfolio of products that cater to the needs that women have at different stages of their life-cycle. It could offer that portfolio of products using a phased approach, offering access to passbook savings and group loans to new clients or in new branches, and other products later.

Clearly, there are many ways to build a product mix and many product combinations that could be strategic. MFIs need to choose among the various options, keeping in mind their mission, available resources, institutional type, outreach objectives and, of course, the external environment. Since customers form their perceptions of value relative to other available options, product portfolio strategy will always have to be defined in the context of what the competition has to offer. Chapters 2, 3 and 24 provide additional guidance and tools for making the decision about whether to pursue product diversification and which product or market to prioritize for development.

1.6 Towards Successful Product Diversification

Product diversification is successful when it generates more benefits than costs, both for the diversifying institution and for its clients. The challenge, of course, is that the benefits sought by clients and institutions usually differ. Clients would like to have all their financial service needs met at a high level of quality and a low price, while institutions need to charge prices that are high enough to cover the cost of the services provided, and they do not have sufficient resources to meet everyone's needs everywhere. Choices have to be made about which services to provide to which markets and at what price.

Success lies in finding an area of overlap between what clients want and what an institution is able and willing to provide (see Figure 1.2). The more that an institution can focus itself and the spending of its resources on meeting the priority needs of the customers it wants to serve, the larger it can make that overlap. It can create more value if it can provide more of the "right kind" of benefits per unit of cost. The rest of this book explores strategies for doing this by identifying the priority needs of various market segments and developing product combinations that meet those needs.

Figure 1.2 Successful product diversification

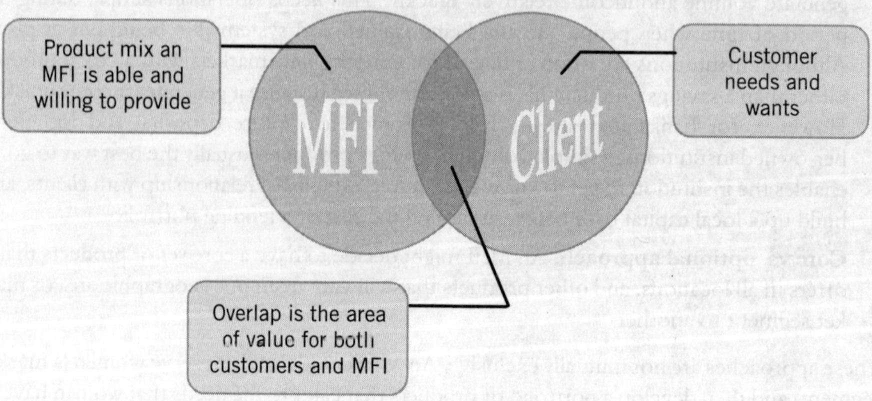

Source: Adapted from Churchill et al., 2002.

Main Messages

1. Product diversification should not be pursued as a goal in itself, but rather as a means to achieve an institution's mission and outreach objectives.
2. Although the potential benefits are many, product diversification will not necessarily generate returns for an institution.
3. Manage product development risks to limit the damage that can be caused by diversification.
4. Successful product diversification generates value for both an MFI and its clients.

Recommended Reading

- Avlonitis, G.; Papastathopoulou, P. 2006. *Product and services management* (Thousand Oaks, CA, and London, Sage Publications).
- Collins, D.; Morduch, J.; Rutherford, S.; Ruthven, O. 2009. *Portfolios of the poor – How the world's poor live on $2 a day* (Princeton, NJ, Princeton University Press).
- Helms, B. 2006. *Access for all: Building inclusive financial systems* (Washington, DC, CGAP), at: http://www.cgap.org/gm/document-1.9.2715/Book_AccessforAll.pdf
- Mahajan, V. 2005. *From microcredit to livelihood finance* (Hyderabad, BASIX), at: http://www.microfinancegateway.org/gm/document-1.9.25359/34431_file_06.pdf
- Richardson, D. 2000. "Unorthodox microfinance: The seven doctrines of success", in *Microbanking Bulletin*, No. 4, pp. 3–7 (Toronto, ON, Calmeadow, PACT Publications), at: http://www.microfinancegateway.org/gm/document-1.9.28497/2417_file_02417.pdf

2 Managing Product Development

Many companies have found that their success in product development comes more from a stream of small wins than from a one-time flood. These successes require a consistent flow of new product ideas that can be evaluated for potential commercialization, ideas that should be part of an overall product strategy… The more ideas that are evaluated in the process, the greater the likelihood of strong (rather than 'good enough') products being the result. ~ Gorchels (2003)

Six of the nine growth strategies discussed in Chapter 1 (see Table 1.4) are fuelled by product development. Three strategies involve new product development and three involve adaptations that improve the existing product offering. All six strategies depend on a flow of ideas for product innovation and an MFI's ability to identify and act on the ideas with the most potential for generating value.

This chapter focuses on the process through which MFIs can manage their product development activities effectively, both those that result in the creation of new products and those that improve the performance of existing products. How can institutions generate a consistent flow of product development ideas? How can they screen those ideas effectively to identify the ones with the greatest potential? And how can they manage the risks inherent in the process of product development so as to limit the damage that could be caused as a result of diversification?

This chapter will address these questions through a six-part discussion:

1. The product development process
2. The integration of product development
3. To diversify or not to diversify?
4. Prioritizing diversification ideas
5. Using the product development process to manage risk
6. Product development vs. product management

2.1 The Product Development Process

A considerable amount of literature has already been written to guide MFIs through the product development process. Figure 2.1 illustrates the most commonly referenced approach, which is briefly described below.

- **Stage 1: Evaluation and preparation.** Product development ideas are identified and the institution assesses not only which ideas would best help it meet its objectives, but also which ideas it is most capable of pursing.
- **Stage 2: Market research.** Customer needs and preferences, market potential, competitors, and the operating environment are all analysed to inform product design.

Figure 2.1 Product development process

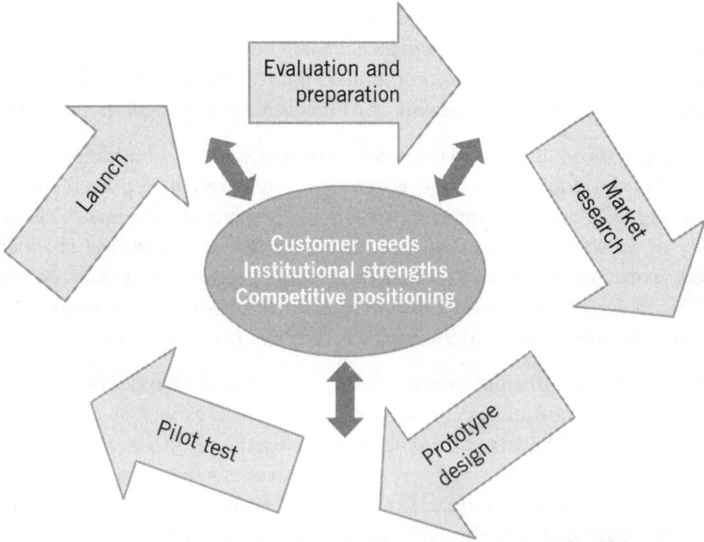

Source: Wright et al., 2001b.

- **Stage 3: Prototype design.** Market research makes it possible to define an initial concept of the new or improved product. Operational procedures are mapped, risks are identified and controlled, and cost analysis and revenue projections enable the MFI to estimate a break-even point. Eventually, the product concept is refined into a prototype that is ready for testing in the market.
- **Stage 4: Pilot test.** The prototype, or final design, is introduced to the market at a limited scale. The product is usually offered at only one or two locations for a certain period of time, and the results are closely monitored to assess both customer demand and institutional readiness.
- **Stage 5: Launch.** If the pilot test concludes that the product should be rolled out, modifications are made to the design as recommended by the pilot test, and the institution prepares to integrate the new or improved product into its ongoing operations. Staff members are trained, funds are allocated, a marketing strategy is developed, and necessary infrastructure is put into place.

Throughout this five-stage process, an MFI should gather information from its clients, staff, systems and environment to ensure that the product under development will be valuable to both the institution and its target market. The double-sided arrows in Figure 2.1 are meant to convey this regular interaction, while the circular flow of the five large arrows illustrates the cyclical nature of the product development process. Since client and institutional needs are constantly changing, successful MFIs must regularly re-evaluate, re-research, redesign, retest, relaunch and/or remove products in their portfolio to respond effectively to those changes.

2.2 The Integration of Product Development

Product development is often treated as a distinct process that MFIs embark upon only when they want to introduce a new product. This is unfortunate, because it limits MFIs' ability to identify opportunities for improving performance. Product development can be more productively thought of as an ongoing process of continuous improvement that enables an MFI to make steady progress towards the achievement of its mission, even in a competitive environment.

Successful MFIs – those oriented to the needs of their customers – have integrated much of the iterative product development process into ongoing managerial responsibilities. Information gathered during daily activities signals the need for product development, either to seize an opportunity or to correct a problem, and that information is regularly channelled to decision-makers, who then determine whether the existing product mix should be adapted and, if so, how. This integration of product development into ongoing operational activities is what facilitates the consistent flow of ideas that fuels effective product portfolio management.

As shown in Table 2.1, information gathered by managers in all functional areas of an MFI's business can signal opportunities for product development as well as competitive threats or capacity issues that might demand product development as a response. When monitoring customer satisfaction, for example, staff may gather suggestions that identify an untapped market or an opportunity to increase outreach in existing markets. They may also gather complaints or exit interview data that help the MFI understand why it is losing market share. This information could be used to improve an existing product, or to inspire product diversification, as was the case at Microfund for Women in Jordan (see Box 2.1).

Box 2.1 Ongoing Monitoring Generates a New Product Opportunity in Jordan

Faced with the launching of three new MFIs in its geographic area of operation, and the need to maintain retention rates and market share, Microfund for Women (MFW) decided to launch a parallel seasonal loan product for its active borrowers. The loan was for productive purposes and was linked to clients' need to increase their inventory to meet higher seasonal demand. The new product was designed and rolled out within 30 days of the initial conception of the idea. It was extremely successful, both from the clients' perspective (in terms of higher profit margins and the ability to repay loans) and from the MFI's perspective (in terms of on-time repayment, higher yield on portfolio and increased customer satisfaction). The experience was so successful that it was replicated by regional partners and copied by competitors; clients continue to look forward to it as an annual highlight of their relationship with MFW.

In hindsight, MFW's ability to turn a competitive threat into a product development opportunity can be attributed to its ongoing monitoring activities at various levels, which tracked changes in clients' needs, the competitive environment and the institution's position in the market. Although no formal survey indicated the need or potential demand for this product, field presence and observations, good communication channels internally (among employees) and externally (between clients and staff members) provided decision-makers with the information necessary to quickly and successfully launch the new product. It was introduced without pilot testing, but access was restricted to clients in their third cycle or more with an excellent repayment record and a business that required inventory build-up during the Ramadan season.

Source: Interview with Sahar S. Tieby, former MFW Operations Manager, 2009.

Table 2.1 Integration of product development into ongoing responsibilities

Management activity	Signals that may be observed	Implications for product development
Monitoring customer satisfaction	Customer complaints; rising dropout or desertion rate	Existing product design may need adjustment to meet customers' changing requirements; new products may be needed to make the MFI's product menu more attractive
	Customer suggestions	Untapped markets may exist and provide an opportunity for the MFI to increase outreach
Competition analysis	Declining market share	Product mix needs adjustment
	Introduction of a new product by the competition	Possible partnership opportunity; existing products may need to be adapted or a new product introduced to avoid losing market share
	News of the market's reaction to a competitor's strategy	MFI can learn from competitors' success or failure to improve its own product offering
Human resource management	Overworked staff	Could suggest larger than expected demand; product delivery processes may need to be mapped and made more efficient
	Tardiness and days lost to illness	Staff may be unhappy; changes to the product may be necessary to improve quality of work
	Staff request job enrichment opportunities	May be possible to offer additional or more complex products
Performance monitoring	Deteriorating portfolio quality; negative trends in growth or efficiency; weak performance relative to peer groups	Product design may need to be adapted to fit client needs better; bundling and cross-selling opportunities could be explored; may need to check for cannibalization or rethink allocation of resources to focus on products with competitive advantage
	Average loan size is increasing	New products may be required to reach lower-income market segments or to support the growth of successful clients
Annual business planning	Overcapacity is identified	Underutilized resources could be channelled towards product development
	New objectives or target market are introduced	New product development may be able to help achieve the new objectives
Product costing	Unprofitable product; negative trend in a product's profitability	Product design and/or delivery must change to increase revenue or decrease costs
Financial management	Regular cash shortages; MFI has difficulty meeting its loan obligations on time	New products with different revenue streams or asset and liability structures may be required
	Longer-term financing becomes available for the MFI	Longer-term products (such as housing loans) may become feasible
Managing information	Delays in reporting, data entry or programming errors	Product delivery processes need to be mapped and examined for appropriate controls
	New technologies emerge	May increase the feasibility of new products or delivery channels
Risk management	A new risk appears	Products must be adapted to mitigate the risk
	An old risk becomes weaker	May be possible to remove costly controls
Legal and regulatory compliance	Legal and regulatory changes	It may become more (or less) feasible to offer certain products; existing products may need adaptation to comply with new requirements
Internal audit	Incidences of fraud, security breaches, or lack of compliance with institutional policies	Better controls must be introduced into the product design or delivery systems

Source: Authors.

For such a system to work, however, at least three things are needed: 1) the managers carrying out the activities described in Table 2.1 need to understand that they have a role to play in product development; 2) they must want to carry out that role; and 3) mechanisms have to be created to channel the information gathered to decision-makers in a timely and useful manner.

Understanding Managers' Roles

Ongoing product development activities are the responsibility of both middle and senior managers. Middle managers quickly and frequently gather information about clients, competitors and the local environment as they are engaged in the day-to-day delivery of products. They tend to focus on current issues at the local or regional level and make the first attempt at responding to complaints, suggestions and enquiries as they arise in the field. They then forward to senior managers any issues that are not within their authority to address.

Senior managers focus on the overall business strategy, adopting a longer-term perspective than managers in the field. As part of their ongoing responsibilities, they perform regular reviews of the institution and its products, from different perspectives. For example, the human resource manager considers whether the staff development programme is sufficient to enable employees to deliver the institution's products effectively. The MIS manager assesses the capacity of the information system to support those products, and explores how new technologies might create opportunities for delivering them more efficiently, or for developing entirely new products and markets.

Communicating to managers that they have a role to play in the ongoing product development process is potentially easy. Even a simple statement in each employee's job description could make it everyone's responsibility to gather product development ideas as part of their daily activities. Such a statement would create the expectation that even lower-level managers are supposed to contribute to ongoing product development and not just implement the decisions made by others.

In addition to this simple statement of responsibility, however, managers need to understand what they should do with the information they gather. Once systems are established to facilitate the flow of information, managers at all levels need guidance as to which systems they should use and when. Sometimes this can be included in the job description, for example if a manager's responsibilities include participation on the product management committee, or if an employee is to report to one person on administrative matters and another on technical matters. It may also be communicated through more informal conversations with a supervisor. The risk of using informal channels is that different supervisors may send different messages, or send some employees no message at all, which could easily lead to confusion and inconsistent implementation.

Motivating Contributions

Although a simple statement in the job description may communicate that managers have a role to play in product development, it will not necessarily convince them that they should spend time gathering and channelling information to fuel ongoing product development. Somehow MFIs must communicate that it is important for managers to spend time on these activities. There are several ways to do this. First, they can provide regular feedback to staff on

how the ideas and data that are coming from different parts of the institution are contributing to ongoing product development and, hopefully, to greater institutional outreach and competitiveness. Managers will be more willing to make an effort if they see that it is worth it.

Second, information users can encourage information collectors by letting them know that they are interested in receiving the information being collected, and by holding them accountable for making whatever contribution they have agreed to make. This can happen informally or by including contributions to ongoing product development as part of an employee's periodic performance appraisal.

Having a high-level product management committee that meets regularly and does not have its meetings cancelled when other "more important" issues arise can also motivate contributions. If members of the committee are knowledgeable and respected within the institution, and the committee is given the authority and budget to undertake ongoing product development, it will be more productive and more credible. Strong commitment to product development by top management and the board of directors will help as well. If the general manager expects to see minutes or progress notes on the work of the product management committee, and comments on them when they are received, that should motivate the committee to meet and to make progress.

Gain sharing, innovation awards or other financial and non-financial incentives for those who contribute successful product development ideas can motivate participation. CEP in Vietnam, for example, provides a financial bonus to employees who contribute successful new product ideas while, in Ethiopia, PEACE recognizes employees with innovative product development ideas at its annual staff meeting.

Last but not least, an MFI can communicate the importance of ongoing product development by making continuous improvement a key value of its institutional culture. All of the actions mentioned above can contribute to the creation of a culture of continuous improvement, but there is much more that an institution could do to shape its culture in that direction (see Chapter 23). One important initiative is to create and maintain an environment that encourages the sharing of information and respects dissenting opinion. When subordinates are seen to be lacking initiative or creativity, they may actually be full of ideas but be afraid to share them. Even when regular meetings, suggestion boxes, database reports, staff surveys and other communication channels are well established, employees need to believe that management is open to receiving their ideas and observations if information is to flow freely. Similar dynamics exist between an MFI's staff and clients.

Motivating staff to participate in ongoing product development is important for more than just information gathering. It is also critical to the successful implementation of product development decisions. If employees are part of the process, they will be more likely to support the changes that need to be made rather than resist them. They might even become enthusiastic about making the changes, instead of fearing the consequences, because they understand why change is necessary, and may have influenced the direction of the institution's response.

Facilitating Effective Communication

Perhaps the most challenging part about integrating product development into ongoing operational activities is creating the mechanisms that enable information to reach decision-makers in a timely and useful way. The more an institution embraces continuous improvement and welcomes the contributions of everyone in the institution, the more likely it is to become overwhelmed by the sheer volume of information flow. To avoid this, and encourage productive communication, MFIs can:

- Provide guidelines that help staff understand what kind of information is useful to collect, and where to send it for processing.
- Make sure managers have a mechanism for coordinating information needs and collection activities so they can avoid duplication of effort. If an MFI's finance manager and regional managers agree on a single set of reporting requirements, for example, branch managers can complete one report at the end of each month instead of two.
- Process information at different levels so that raw data is not all forwarded to top management for decision-making. Branch managers can process information received at the branch level, feedback received through hotline calls can be processed by the call centre manager, the results of customer satisfaction surveys can be processed by computer software, and so on. If horizontal communication channels exist, peers can quickly compare the information they gather, learn from each others' experiences and brainstorm solutions which can be channelled to decision-makers for consideration.
- Process information regularly. This will help prevent mailboxes, inboxes and other communication channels from becoming so full of data that they become blocked and information stops flowing. It will also help to make sure that good ideas are received by decision-makers quickly enough for timely action.
- Synthesize related information that has been processed in different places and put it in a format that facilitates analysis by decision-makers. For example, a customer service officer at the head office could collect feedback from branch managers, call centre managers and the computer database and circulate a monthly report on customer satisfaction that summarizes the findings from all sources, segmenting the data by product and by market segment.
- Analyze the synthesized information from a variety of perspectives before making a decision. Having representatives from different departments interpret the data allows an MFI to benefit from the knowledge and experience that different parts of the organization possess. These representatives can discuss the implications of the data and agree on priorities for action and resource allocation that benefit the organization as a whole and not just a part.

The more an institution can integrate managers from all areas into the product development process, the better informed the institution will be and the more opportunities will be created to increase outreach and competitiveness through product development. Once timely and relevant information is being channelled to decision-makers on a regular basis, those decision-makers will have regular opportunities to strengthen the product offering.

An efficient mechanism for facilitating synthesis and analysis, while providing regular opportunities for decision-making, is a **product management committee**. This committee of approximately five to eight people from different departments of the institution can meet monthly or quarterly to assess the signals emerging from various monitoring activities and to discuss the implications for product development (refer to Section 2.6 for a more detailed discussion of the committee's role and composition). In preparation for each meeting, committee members gather information from their respective teams and process it for distribution to others on the committee. When they meet, members share their information and perspective and bring different questions to the table. For example, a finance manager may be surprised by higher-than-expected deposit mobilization, the marketing manager may note a rise in dropouts among customers of the individual loan product, or the operations manager may highlight an increased number of complaints from individual borrowers about loan size limits.

Committee members can discuss the reasons for these trends, the implications, and possible courses of action. In the example described above, the sharing of information could result in the committee recommending that the ceiling for its individual loan product be increased. Rarely will the trends be sufficiently clear and connected to facilitate a single solution such as this, but coming together as a committee does allow managers from different departments to jointly synthesize and analyse information in a way that sheds light on solutions that may otherwise not have been seen or may not have been identified as quickly. It also builds consensus around decisions and generates buy-in from the participating departments, which is critical for effective implementation. Even when committee members bring unrelated issues to the table, and limited resources make it impossible for all to be addressed, the committee provides a mechanism for jointly prioritizing issues from an institutional perspective.

Many organizations, especially those that are young or small, may not have the resources for a product management committee, but can still carry out the above activities during regular senior management meetings. The advantage of having a body specifically focused on product management is that product issues are less likely to be overwhelmed by other management issues. It also enables operational staff who would not normally attend senior management meetings to contribute their expertise to the product management process.

2.3 To Diversify or Not to Diversify?

When ongoing management activities suggest the need to change an institution's product mix, the product management committee (or senior management team) will have to decide whether to recommend diversification, as well as what kind of diversification to recommend. Often, the available information will signal the need to do something, but additional data will be required to determine the most appropriate next step.

Sometimes the best place to get that additional information is from **clients** themselves. Although ongoing monitoring of customer satisfaction will gather complaints and suggestions, those complaints and suggestions will not necessarily be representative of the market. Such information will have to be supplemented with targeted market research to understand the root causes of problems identified and ensure that the voices of less vocal members of the market are heard. The research may also focus on opportunities rather than problems, such as how interested a particular market segment might be in a new product or service.

Another source of additional information is **staff** members in the field. If problems or opportunities are isolated in specific branches, then visits to discuss these issues with the relevant personnel would certainly be in order. If the issues are more widespread, perhaps a combination of meetings and staff surveys may be necessary (see Box 2.2). Staff surveys have the advantage of allowing respondents to be anonymous, and therefore increase the likelihood of honest responses, although they may not be an appropriate way of gathering additional information if a problem must be addressed urgently.

A third important place to seek out information is an **MFI's internal database.** Managers will have already analysed a lot of data as part of their ongoing activities, but this data could be explored in more detail or placed into context for decision-makers using the larger body of information that is gathered and stored by an MFI. Managers could, for example, examine a product's performance across all branches, compare growth rates and patterns for different market segments, or analyse the demographic characteristics of a particular customer group. Since information can usually be obtained more quickly and cheaply from an MFI's database than from primary research with clients or staff, this is often a good place to begin the search for additional insight.

Based on the signals generated during the course of managers' ongoing activities, and the additional information collected to interpret the signals properly, the product management committee (or senior management team) must decide whether it makes sense to pursue new product or market development. As discussed in Chapter 1, if an institution can respond to its problems and opportunities by adjusting the delivery of its existing product mix in markets that are already familiar, this is generally the preferred strategy, because new product or market development will generate additional costs and risk. Table 2.2 summarizes the wide range of risks that institutions are exposed to when they choose to diversify.

Box 2.2 Questionnaires Help Improve Service Delivery at KPOSB

In 2005–6, Kenya Post Office Savings Bank (KPOSB) organized three separate workshops to discuss problems with its service delivery and to generate ideas for follow-up action. The first two workshops were held for senior management and frontline staff, and a third workshop was subsequently organized for middle managers. Each participant in the workshops was given a copy of *MicroSave*'s Customer Service Diagnosis and Analysis Tool, which can be downloaded at: www.microsave.org. Participants completed the questionnaire anonymously; then the results were collated and discussed in the workshops. The process helped KPOSB to craft a Customer Service Strategy, which prioritized actions to increase staff members' product knowledge and decrease processing time, among other objectives. Implementation of this strategy resulted in measurable improvements in customer satisfaction by the end of the year.

Source: Authors.

Table 2.2 Diversification risks

Category	Risk	Description
MARKET	Product design risk	The possibility that a new product will not meet customer needs.
	New target market risk	The possibility that an MFI will not fully understand the needs of a new group of customers it wants to serve, owing to invalid assumptions based on experience with past customers.
	Demand risk	The possibility of over- or underestimating how many customers will want to use a new product, or how much they will want to use it.
	Competition risk	The possibility that a competitor's actions will affect the success of a new product or market development initiative.
	Positioning risk	The possibility that a new product will confuse, or change in an undesirable manner, the public's perception of what an MFI offers.
DELIVERY INFRASTRUCTURE	Delivery systems risk	The possibility that an MFI does not have adequate infrastructure to get a product to the customer as promised.
	Counterparty risk	The possibility that other organizations with which an MFI has joined forces might fail to perform in some way that harms the MFI.
	Information systems risk	The possibility that an MFI's data-gathering and processing technologies cannot handle the requirements or scale of a new product.
	Communication risk	The possibility that an MFI will not be able to market its new product effectively, internally or externally.
	Incentive systems risk	The possibility that a new product will distort existing staff incentive systems, or that the existing system will impede the success of a new product or market development initiative.
	Human resource risk	The possibility that sufficiently skilled staff are not available or are not assigned to work with a new product or market.
	Transaction risk	The possibility of human or computer error during daily processing of a product.
ENVIRON-MENT	Compliance risk	The possibility that a new product will not adequately meet the terms of the country's regulations and laws.
	External risks	The possibility that diversification will increase an institution's exposure to macroeconomic, demographic, physical environment or political risk.
STRATEGIC ALIGNMENT	Management / board commitment risk	The possibility that senior management or the board of directors will not fully support the development of a new product or market.
	Strategic risk	The possibility that poor decision-making or resource allocation will result in a new product not being compatible with the MFI's goals.
	Orphan product risk	The possibility that a new product will not be integrated into the institution's day-to-day operations.
	Culture risk	The possibility that weak institutional commitment to continuous improvement or client-centred product development could delay or impede a product.
	Product mix risk	The possibility that a new product will not complement the institution's existing portfolio of products, perhaps even cannibalizing one or more of those products.
	Reputation risk	The possibility that a new product will damage the institution's image or brand.
FINANCIAL	Credit risk	The possibility that borrowers will repay late or not at all.
	Financial management risk	The possibility that a new product or market development initiative will weaken the MFI's asset and liability balance, liquidity or earnings.
	Fraud risk	The possibility that a new product will create opportunities for staff to deceive or misrepresent the institution for the purpose of material gain.
	Security risk	The possibility that a product will increase the institution's vulnerability to theft or crime.

Source: Adapted from Pikholz et al., 2005.

Regardless of the additional risk and cost, if an MFI cannot respond adequately to its problems or opportunities through its existing product mix, it will want to consider the possibility of launching something new. By making an additional investment and being willing to manage a higher level of risk, the institution could generate strategic benefits for itself and its clients.

An MFI's decision to embark on new product development should be based on three key criteria:

- Is the development of a new product consistent with the MFI's strategic plans?
- Does the organization have sufficient capacity to develop a new product?
- Is this the right time to develop a new product?

Strategic consistency. MFIs have multidimensional strategies. Informed by senior management and guided by a mission and vision, the board of directors decides which outreach objectives an institution will pursue, and with what combination of priorities. Depending on the institution's stage of development, the board and senior management determine how much market expansion the organization can afford, and the degree of risk they are willing to take in product development. Guided by this strategic framework, the product management committee (or senior management team) then screens and prioritizes ideas for developing products and markets so that the projects that are pursued are the ones with the greatest potential to assist the organization in meeting its strategic objectives for a given period.

At Centenary Bank in Uganda, for example, the Board of Directors provided the general guideline that one new product could be developed each year. Ideas for new product development are then submitted by different parts of the institution and screened by the Business Development Department, which makes a recommendation to the Board for approval.

Sufficient capacity. Since the development of new products demands more from an institution than the development of existing products, MFIs should carefully consider whether they have sufficient internal capacity to diversify before spending too much time and energy trying to decide which new products should be developed. Box 2.3 summarizes some of the basic preconditions that should be met. If an MFI finds that its capacity in any of these areas is weak, it should strengthen its capabilities in the identified area of weakness before moving ahead with diversification. Otherwise, the capacity weakness could prevent diversification success.

Right timing. Even if diversification is broadly consistent with an MFI's strategy and capacity, the timing may not be right. Perhaps the MFI is already developing another product, and too many changes too close to each other might be confusing for staff or clients. Perhaps the organization is about to overhaul its MIS, or transform into a bank, and key staff do not have sufficient time or energy to devote to a simultaneous product diversification effort.

Preparing for Diversification

Once an MFI decides that it has sufficient capacity and a strategic, timely mandate for diversification, it can tackle the challenge of deciding which product or market it wants to diversify into. This decision is sometimes easy. Members of a product management committee may meet and quickly agree on the new product or market that they wish to develop because there is an obvious fit between what customers want and what the institution is well prepared to provide in an area with little or no competition. More often, however, managers bring several ideas to the table and are not sure which one to pursue, or which to pursue first. In such cases, there is a risk that ideas will be prioritized on the basis of one influential person's preferences, or the passion with which ideas are presented, rather than their potential for success. The following section provides tools to help MFIs screen their diversification ideas in a more thorough and objective manner.

Box 2.3 Capacity Prerequisites for Diversification

To ensure that new product or market development is appropriate, it is important for MFIs to determine whether they meet certain preconditions. For example:

- **Available resources.** Although product improvements can be made without major investments, new product development can be an expensive process. Are sufficient funds and appropriate human resources available for a diversification effort?
- **Financial viability.** Is the organization in sufficient financial health to accept the risks associated with diversification?
- **Customer service orientation.** Does the MFI already provide quality customer service and have a client orientation? Does it have systems in place to understand the changing needs, behaviours and preferences of its customers?
- **Marketing capacity.** Is the organization able to communicate the value of its existing products effectively in the markets where it currently operates?
- **Culture of innovation.** Is the MFI's culture geared towards innovation and continuous improvement? Do employees embrace change?
- **Effective MIS.** Does the organization have an information management system that can easily accommodate new products? Can it handle the increase in volume that might come from expansion to a new market?
- **Product profitability monitoring.** Does the organization already monitor the profitability of individual products by assigning both costs and revenues on a product basis?
- **Effective internal communication.** Does the MFI have effective internal communication channels, for both vertical and horizontal transmission?
- **Effective training function.** Does the MFI have the means to train its staff on the policies and procedures of a new product or the characteristics of a new market?
- **Low staff turnover.** Is the organization successful in retaining its key staff members?
- **Appropriate context.** Is the legal and macroeconomic environment suitable for new product or market development?

Source: Adapted from Churchill and Frankiewicz, 2006.

2.4 Prioritizing Diversification Ideas

There are three main techniques that MFIs can use to prioritize their options for new product and market development. Each one is described below.

Risk and Returns Analysis

This screening technique reviews the risks and returns that are associated with each diversification idea, and helps an MFI identify which ideas seem to offer the greatest potential returns with risks that can be managed. The technique is a useful tool for preliminary screening, because it can be applied by a product management committee in a couple of hours without preparation or research. Certainly, the accuracy of the results and analysis will be greater the more the committee knows and the more detail it analyses, but the tool can be used to facilitate immediate discussion, using existing knowledge as a starting point. More detailed analysis of risks and potential returns would be needed once the committee selects an idea or subset of ideas with which to move forward.

To assess risk, MFIs can consider all of the risks presented in Table 2.2, or they can select a few that are most important to the institution. In determining which risks are most important, MFIs may want to consider the following four dimensions:

1. **Likelihood.** What is the probability that a particular risk event will occur?
2. **Severity.** If the risk event occurs, how seriously would it impact on the organization?
3. **Trends.** Is the risk becoming more or less threatening?
4. **Manageability.** How prepared is the institution to avoid, transfer, control or accept the risk?

Risks that are becoming more likely and will have a serious impact on the organization if they occur should take priority over risks that will have little impact or could be managed well by the institution's staff.

To create a framework for analysing risks, an MFI should list the risks it wants to consider in the left-hand column of a table such as the one presented in Table 2.3 and then estimate the degree of risk exposure that each diversification idea is likely to create (H = high, M = medium and L = low).[1] The example provided in Table 2.3 compares six new product development ideas, but the same framework could be used to compare new market development ideas. Once the table is completed, an MFI can analyse the results by counting the number of low, medium and high risk ratings for each product. If certain risks are of particular concern to the MFI, they could be weighted more heavily in the analysis, perhaps by dividing the risks into different categories and analysing the results in each category separately, or by counting the rating of a "top priority" risk twice. Products with few high risk ratings will look immediately attractive, but the analysis cannot be completed without also looking at the potential returns.

1 This ranking of low, medium and high is preferred over 1, 2, 3 because it discourages analysis using averages, which would be inappropriate since these designations do not actually have values. For example, the impact of a risk rated as "high" would not necessarily be three times greater than a risk rated as "low", which is what the designations 1, 2, 3 would imply.

MFIs may want to consider three main types of return:

1. **Financial returns:** How profitable is the product or market likely to be? How large a contribution is it likely to make to the institution's return on equity or return on assets?
2. **Market returns.** What effect is the new product or market likely to have on the MFI's competitive position? Even if a product does not contribute directly or immediately to financial returns, it may dramatically increase an organization's outreach or market share, or have a powerful effect on customer loyalty.
3. **Social returns:** Will the development of this new product or market create jobs, alleviate poverty, or empower the disadvantaged? MFIs with a double- or triple-bottom line will be particularly interested in taking into consideration the broader impact of each diversification idea.

As with risks, the degree of return that each product or market idea is likely to generate (H = high, M = medium and L = low) can be estimated and recorded as in Table 2.3. Certainly, it is useful to estimate the relative magnitude of the financial returns that the MFI might be able to generate from each product, but it is not necessary (or possible) to quantify the financial returns at such an early stage of screening. This will come later, during the feasibility study or the development of the product concept.

To use risk and return analysis to draw some preliminary conclusions about which product diversification ideas an MFI should prioritize, it is necessary to consider the two sides of analysis together. In general, it would be good to identify low-risk products that will generate high returns, but a high-risk product might also be attractive if the expected financial, social and market returns are sufficiently high, and the organization can develop strategies for controlling the impact of the major risks. Pioneering MFIs that seek to differentiate themselves through innovation often take this kind of approach.

Table 2.3 Risk and return assessment framework (example)

	Contractual savings	Micro-pension	SME loans	Housing loan	Health insurance	Leasing
RISKS						
Demand	L	M	M	M	L	M
Product design	L	H	M	L	H	M
Financial	H	H	L	M	M	L
Product mix	L	L	L	H	L	M
Positioning	L	M	H	H	M	H
Competition	M	M	M	H	L	M
RETURNS						
Financial	M	H	M	L	M	L
Social	M	H	M	M	M	L
Market	L	H	L	M	M	H

Source: Authors.

In the example provided in Table 2.3, the micropension product seems likely to generate high financial, social and market returns for the MFI completing the assessment, but it also seems likely to generate significant risk exposure in five out of six of the risk areas assessed. If this MFI was particularly interested in protecting or expanding its market share, and possessed a competent marketing department, it might prioritize the leasing product, since it seems likely to generate high market returns, and the high positioning risk could probably be mitigated through proactive action on the part of the marketing department. If, however, this MFI was particularly interested in social returns, it might prioritize contractual savings, which has the lowest risk profile.

Rarely will the results of this broad analysis be sufficiently conclusive for an MFI to prioritize a single product for development, but the risk–return comparison can help managers reduce the number of ideas that they consider for further exploration. It can also raise their awareness of the information gaps they might need or want to fill before being willing to move forward with the development of a product.

Criteria-based

A second technique for screening diversification ideas involves the definition of criteria that an MFI thinks would make a new product or market successful. For example, if an institution was developing a new product to protect its market share and it believed it needed to introduce the product within the next six months, then it could screen its new product ideas on the basis of whether they could be developed within a six-month time frame.

Cooper and Edgett (1999) propose two main types of criterion, which they call "must-meet" and "should-meet" criteria. The criteria often take the form of yes/no questions, and they can be qualitative or quantitative in nature. **Must-meet criteria** typically assess strategic issues, feasibility questions, and resource availabilities: For example:

- Will this idea assist the MFI in achieving its mission and strategic plan for the period?
- Has the target market demonstrated some need for this product?
- Does it seem technically feasible for our institution to develop this product?
- Is the product likely to generate more return than risk?

A "no" response to any must-meet question would be enough to kill a diversification idea, or to warrant its being placed at the bottom of an MFI's list of priorities.

Should-meet criteria are highly desirable but not essential characteristics of a new product or market idea. A weak response to any one question would not kill an idea, nor automatically place it at the bottom of the priority list. Rather, each should-meet question is scored, and ideas earn points depending on the degree to which they meet each criterion.

Table 2.4 Sample should-meet prioritization criteria

Economic and financial potential	Corporate synergy	Production-design synergy	Product differential advantage
• How large is the market? • How fast is it growing? • Will it provide an entry point for new customers? • Would it make current customers more loyal? • How certain is it that the product will provide a return-on-investment of at least x%? • How many other institutions already offer this product? • How long will it take to get the product to the market?	• To what degree does the product align with the MFI's strategic direction? • How much would the product impact on the MFI's key objectives? • Does the product build on the MFI's strengths and competences? • How well does it complement the MFI's existing product menu?	• Will the product use existing delivery channels? • Could it be processed through the existing MIS? • Will the product resist cyclical or seasonal fluctuations? • Will current staff be able to deliver the product? • Is the MFI capable of managing the key risks associated with the development of this idea?	• To what extent does the product provide unique benefits to customers? • Does it fit customer needs and priorities better than competitors' products? • Can the product deliver better value than the competition (either more benefits or equal benefits at a lower cost)?

Source: Adapted from Cooper and Edgett, 1999, and Avlonitis and Papastathopoulou, 2006.

According to Cooper and de Brentani (1984), there are four main types of screening criterion for new product ideas: 1) economic and financial potential; 2) corporate synergy; 3) production-design synergy; and 4) product differential advantage. Table 2.4 provides a few examples of criteria in each of these categories that MFIs can use to screen their own ideas.

The selection of criteria is important, and can be extremely valuable in helping a product management committee to identify weak ideas while at the same time avoid screening out potentially good ideas too early in the process owing to entrenched institutional habits or the individual preferences of one person or department. Institutional SWOT (strengths, weaknesses, opportunities, threats) analysis (discussed in Chapter 24) can be very helpful in guiding the selection of appropriate criteria, because it identifies strengths and opportunities that the institution will want any new product to take advantage of, as well as threats or weaknesses it will want to avoid.

Once an MFI identifies which criteria it wants to use, it can create a rating tool such as the one shown in Table 2.5. In this sample grid, ten criteria were determined to be important in predicting new product success, and were listed down the first column. The criteria were weighted on a scale of 1 to 3 according to their importance to the institution. Three product ideas were then rated according to each criterion, also on a scale of 1 to 3. For example, the first criterion, "fit with strategy", was given a weight of 3 because the institution considers that criterion to be very important. Reviewing each of the product options, the first idea was considered to have a weak fit with the institution's current strategy, so it was given a rating of 1,

Table 2.5 Sample criteria-based screening tool

Criterion	Score			Weighted value	Weighted score		
	Idea 1	Idea 2	Idea 3		Idea 1	Idea 2	Idea 3
1. Fit with strategy	1	3	3	3	3	9	9
2. Fit with target market's priorities	3	2	1	3	9	6	3
3. Fit with current product mix	2	3	2	2	4	6	4
4. Size of potential market	3	2	1	2	6	4	2
5. Low risk of competition	1	2	3	1	1	2	3
6. Uses existing delivery channels	1	1	3	1	1	1	3
7. Resists seasonal fluctuations	1	3	2	3	3	9	6
8. Development and testing period (shorter is better)	2	2	1	2	4	4	2
9. Cost of development	1	3	2	1	1	3	2
10. Return on investment of 25% within 2 years	1	3	1	2	2	6	2
				TOTAL	**34**	**50**	**36**

Source: Adapted from Gorchels, 2003.

while each of the other ideas had a strong fit with the current strategy and were given a rating of 3. Since the "fit with strategy" criterion had been assigned a weight of 3, the first product idea received a weighted score of 3 (1 × 3) in that area, while the other two product ideas scored 9 (3 × 3).

Rating the three product ideas against all ten criteria, the tool pinpoints the second idea, which received a total score of 50, as the one that should be prioritized for development. Weights can also be assigned in terms of percentages so that the total value of all criteria (100 per cent) is divided unequally among different criteria on the basis of their importance to the institution (for example, the risk of competition might be relatively unimportant and receive a weight of 5 per cent, while the fit with institutional strategy might be highly important and receive a weight of 30 per cent). An example of a tool designed in this manner can be found in Table 20.2 in the chapter on rural microfinance.

The criteria-based screening tool can be used to prioritize completely different product or market development ideas as well as variations of a single product. For instance, an MFI may be unsure about whether it wants to introduce a new savings product that uses manual systems as its existing loan products do, or whether it wants to take advantage of the new product introduction to launch a smart-card-based service. It could use the tool to compare the attractiveness of the two product variations.

Criteria-based screening tools can also be used at various levels of detail. If the tool is being used to broadly screen a range of ideas, the criteria can be left broadly stated as in Table 2.5. However, if the tool is being used to choose between two "final candidates", the criterion can be made more specific, with measurable indicators. For example, instead of "fit with strategy"

the criterion could be "number of strategic objectives in the current five-year business plan that the idea will help to meet".

Feasibility Analysis

The third technique that MFIs can use to prioritize product diversification ideas is feasibility analysis. As suggested by its name, feasibility analysis is an assessment of the viability of a business idea. What distinguishes this technique from the two described above is the depth of the analysis, particularly with respect to quantitative data. An MFI will probably have gathered a great deal of information by the time it decides to pursue feasibility analysis, but it will almost certainly need to conduct additional research to obtain specific figures and/or to probe a more representative sample.

Barringer and Ireland (2005) recommend evaluating four types of feasibility:

- **Technical feasibility** evaluates whether the product being considered for development can operate in the manner desired. It investigates infrastructure constraints, legal limitations and technology reliability. It explores the local labour market and assesses the potential for accessing and attracting qualified personnel. If partnerships will be required, it examines whether appropriate partners are available and capable of delivering what will be required.
- **Market feasibility** evaluates whether there is sufficient demand for the new product or service. It assesses the size of the potential market, usage trends and the level of competition in the area that the MFI wishes to target. It estimates sales under various assumptions (for example, price or eligibility requirements). It can also assess the cost-effectiveness of different distribution and communication channels.
- **Organizational feasibility** evaluates whether the institution has the capabilities and resources not only to produce the product, but also to market and distribute it alongside its existing product menu. This part of the feasibility study would include an internal analysis of managerial skills, organizational structure, available employees and their skill sets, technology resources and regulatory status.
- **Financial feasibility** estimates the cost of developing and delivering the product, the amount and timing of capital requirements, the revenues that will be generated, the profit margin and break-even point. It assesses whether the product will generate adequate cash flow and profits.

Feasibility studies are more expensive and time consuming than the other two screening methods, and they will not necessarily indicate that one diversification idea is obviously more likely to succeed than another. The analysis will, however, help an MFI to challenge its assumptions and assess more accurately the risks and rewards associated with the idea(s) under consideration. Even if it is not used to prioritize diversification ideas, feasibility analysis is frequently used as a screen or gate through which any idea must pass before a product is actually developed and tested, or investments are made in building new infrastructure.

2.5 Using the Product Development Process to Manage Risk

Once an MFI decides to diversify, it will want to develop its new product or market idea in a way that maximizes the potential benefits while minimizing risk. Most institutions, regardless of whether they are introducing a new product or redeveloping old products to meet the needs of a new market, pass through the majority of the stages of the product development process described in Section 2.1 above. However, they do so with different degrees of formality, and spend different amounts of time and resources on each step (see, for example, the XacBank case at the end of this chapter). The first and second steps of the process are often given little time or attention, and the fourth is most frequently skipped. This is unfortunate, because all steps of the process offer valuable opportunities to identify and control risks, as Pikholz et al. (2005) explain:

> By breaking out the new product development process into discrete steps, there is a decision point, Go/No Go, before proceeding to the next step. Each step costs more than the preceding one. As the amount of money at stake increases, risk is managed by ensuring that the uncertainties of the project decrease: Do we have the capacity for this product? Do our clients want this product? Will our systems, pricing, and procedures work? The process is deliberately designed to drive uncertainties down at each successive step, so that by the time you have completed Step 2 you are much wiser than you were at the completion of Step 1.

Managers that rush the early steps of the product development process, or launch their adapted product in a new market without any testing, are taking on an unnecessary level of risk. Not only do they pass up opportunities to protect their institution from loss, but they also increase the cost of managing risk the longer they wait for a risk exposure to be identified. As illustrated in the Equity Bank case presented in Chapter 1, when problems are discovered during rollout, they are much more difficult to fix than they would have been had they been discovered earlier. More staff members are involved, more clients are affected, more money is at risk, more transactions have to be sorted out, and some solutions will no longer be feasible, given that the product has already been made public.

Of course, there is a trade-off between risk and return. Some MFIs deliberately skip steps in the product development process to respond more quickly to a competitive threat, or to gain first mover advantage in a new market. They make a calculated decision to accept higher risk in the hope of greater returns. This is a legitimate strategy, but institutions that adopt it should be prepared to cover their potential losses. They need to be ready to deal with the negative impact of product failure as discussed in Chapter 1, not only on the institution's profitability and reputation, but also on staff and the low-income clients the MFI is trying to serve.

In general, it is recommended that MFIs take a systematic approach to product development and look for ways to complete each step of the process efficiently in order to minimize the significant risks inherent in it. The higher the cost, the larger the change that needs to take place, and the greater the risk envisaged in pursuing a diversification idea, the more it makes sense to invest in a complete product development process.

MFIs that follow a systematic approach to product development will have opportunities to identify and control risk at each stage of the process. Table 2.6 lists examples of the risks that can be managed at each stage, along with a sample of strategies and tools that can be used to mitigate the risk exposure. For instance, one of the risks that institutions are exposed to in the first stage of the product development process is strategic risk. This risk can be partially mitigated through SWOT analysis, and there is a *MicroSave* toolkit on strategic business planning that can be freely downloaded from the Internet to guide MFIs through that analysis.

Table 2.6 Using the product development process to mitigate risk

Stage	Sample risks that can be managed	Mitigation strategies	Tools[2]
1. Evaluation and preparation	• Management/board commitment risk • Strategic risk • Staff risk • Product mix risk • External risks • Culture risk	• Be well informed about the MFI's capabilities, core competences, weaknesses, risks, environment • Have a business plan with clear objectives • Form a product management committee with high-level buy-in	• SWOT analysis (1) • Strategic business planning toolkit (1) • Institutional risk assessment and mitigation tool (2) • Cross product risk overview tool (2)
2. Market research	• Demand risk • New target market risk • Competition risk • Product design risk • Positioning risk	• Gather information to know the market's needs and context • Find out how potential customers perceive the institution and its competition	• Focus group discussions (3) • PRA tools such as financial landscape analysis or seasonality of income and expenditure (3) • Market segmentation (4)
3. Concept / prototype development	• Product design risk • Financial management risk • Compliance risk • Fraud risk • Product mix risk • Security risk	• Solicit feedback from clients and staff on initial design • Make projections • Verify compliance • Identify risks at each step in the delivery process and include controls in the product design	• Customer analysis matrix (5) • Product design matrix (5) • Costing and pricing (6) • Process mapping (7) • Product risk assessment tool (2) • Quantitative market research (8) • Modelling software such as Microfin (9)

2 The numbers in parenthesis throughout this column refer to resources where the specified tools can be found. Complete citations for each resource can be found in the bibliography at the end of this book: 1) Wright et al. (2007); 2) Pikholz et al. (2005); 3) *MicroSave* (2004); 4) Matul et al. (2006a); 5) Frankiewicz et al. (2004); 6) Cracknell et al. (2004); 7) Champagne et al. (2008); 8) Szubert et al. (2005); 9) Lunde et al. (2006); 10) McCord et al. (2003); 11) MicroSave (2005); 12) McCord et al. (2004).

Table 2.6 (continued)

Stage	Sample risks that can be managed	Mitigation strategies	Tools[2]
4. Pilot testing	• Demand risk • Financial management risk • Communication risk • Incentive systems risk • Information systems risk • Reputation risk	• Develop clear pilot test protocol • Define pilot test objectives • Include any new marketing materials or incentives in the test • Document procedures • Train staff before the pilot • Monitor and evaluate results	• Pilot testing toolkit (10) • Monitoring tools (10)(11) • Go/NoGo decision model (2) • Post pilot risk assessment (2)
5. Launch	• Delivery systems risk • Staff risk • Transaction risk • Orphan product risk • Positioning risk • Counterparty risk	• Adjust policies and systems in response to pilot test lessons before rollout begins • Document "should be" processes • Articulate a gradual rollout strategy • Develop a clear partnership agreement	• Pre rollout risk assessment tool (2) • Rollout protocol (12) • Rollout order worksheet (12) • Systems planning checklist (12) • Marketing plan (5) • Process mapping (7)

Source: Authors.

2.6 Product Development vs. Product Management

Whereas **product development** refers to actions that are taken to improve existing products and create new ones, **product management** refers to the ongoing process of planning, organizing, leading and controlling those product development activities so that they generate value for the MFI and its clients.

Many MFIs have a product development committee that takes responsibility for guiding a new product idea through its phases of development, hopefully culminating in a successful launch. This helps to ensure that the product development activities of different departments are coordinated along a common timeline and are focused on the same objectives. Once a product is ready for rollout, responsibility for the product is passed to operations, and the committee is disbanded or takes up another new product. The committee's composition is altered from one product to the next to ensure that appropriate technical and field expertise is represented, and to bring fresh energy and commitment to the new product's development, usually in the form of a new chairperson, who is often referred to as the **product champion.**

This kind of committee can play a vital role in managing the development of a particular product. It can keep the new product development process on track and take primary responsibility for managing the risks inherent in that process. It does not, however, take responsibility for

monitoring the ongoing performance and development of already existing products. This is usually carried out by the operations department.

Unfortunately, the operations department lacks the cross-departmental perspective of the product development committee. Its ability to interpret product performance and define future product portfolio strategy from a financial, marketing, technology and risk management perspective is limited, and for this reason it is not the ideal home for the product portfolio management function. MFIs that are currently managing product development through the operations department might want to consider other options, such as those described below.

Option 1: Convert the Product Development Committee into a Product Management Committee

A product management committee can be made responsible for the development of specific products as well as the definition and monitoring of product portfolio strategy. Its composition can vary depending on the nature of the product management activities taking place during a particular meeting, as summarized in Table 2.7. The committee might be led by the Director of Operations or the Head of Business Development, but this individual could delegate responsibility for leading a particular meeting to his or her deputy or to another member of the team. Heads of other departments could do the same. In general, idea generation and implementation meetings could be staffed by middle managers and technical specialists who are directly involved in the activities being discussed, while the institution's most senior managers would attend the meetings at which decisions are made and emergencies are addressed.

The exact composition of a product management committee will depend on an institution's size and structure, as well as the nature of the products being developed at a particular point in time. For example, inviting someone from the Credit Department to participate on the committee makes sense when a new loan product is being developed, but not for a new savings product. Subcommittees can also be organized, particularly to oversee intense periods of implementation activity, such as prototype development or a pilot test. If an MFI does not have internal expertise in all the areas required, it can invite Board members or external consultants to sit on the committee. MFIs often rely on the external advice of legal experts, for instance.

The frequency of product management committee meetings will also vary. It will depend primarily on the number and complexity of product development initiatives currently in process, as well as on the speed with which the institution is trying to complete those projects. The shorter the timeline and the more complex the activities, the more frequently the committee is likely to meet. Weekly meetings are not uncommon immediately before and during product testing, for example.

If an MFI is not developing or testing a new product, product management committee meetings might be held once per month or quarter, depending on how proactive the institution is about gathering and responding to information in order to strengthen the performance of its product portfolio. Special meetings can be called at any time if a member of the committee identifies a warning sign that requires urgent attention.

Table 2.7 Product management committee composition

Meeting purpose	Sample activities	Composition
Idea generation	• Monitor product performance • Identify trends and emerging risks • Gather, process, synthesize and analyse ideas for improving performance of the product portfolio • Recommend actions and next steps	• Departmental representatives – those gathering and processing information • Product managers
Screening	• Refine or prioritize product development ideas • Analyse potential risks and returns • Screen ideas against must-meet and should-meet criteria • Decide which ideas to explore further • Confirm whether product development has met established targets and can advance to next stage	• Departmental representatives – those with authority to approve spending or risk-taking at the level being discussed • Risk manager or head of internal audit • Legal advisor • Partnership manager • Product managers
Decision-making	• Approve budget and timeline for concept development • Decide whether the business case for a new product concept is strong enough to justify its risks • Approve product development plan, pilot testing protocol, or rollout plan • Decide whether the institution is ready to test or roll out a new product • Define product strategy	• Top management • Heads of each department • Risk manager or head of internal audit • Legal advisor • Partnership manager • Product manager(s)
Implementation	• Coordinate concept development, including costing and pricing, demand projections, sensitivity and break-even analysis • Coordinate preparation and implementation of product development plan, pilot testing protocol or rollout plan • Monitor performance against product development plan, pilot testing protocol or rollout plan • Monitor customer and competitor reactions • Monitor impact of new product development on other products • Process feedback from pilot test and coordinate changes in systems, marketing, infrastructure, training and other activities • Recommend adjustments to a plan	• Departmental representatives – those involved in doing the work • Product manager(s) • Middle management and/or frontline representatives • Partnership manager
Emergency response	• Brainstorm response to major competitive threat or other external event • Adjust plans because of implementation failure or complications	• Heads of each department • Risk manager or head of internal audit • Product manager(s)

Source: Authors.

Option 2: Assign Responsibility for Product Portfolio Management to an Existing Cross-functional Team

If an MFI already has a cross-functional team that is tasked with strategic decision-making, such as a business development team or senior management committee, it can assign responsibility for product portfolio management to this entity. As mentioned previously, this can be an appropriate option for small MFIs with limited resources. It can also avoid the creation of "yet another committee" in institutions that already have, for example, a research and development (R&D) committee and want to maintain a degree of separation between product development and product management activities.

There are two main challenges associated with this approach: 1) making sure that information flows effectively between those involved in product development and those involved in product management; and 2) making sure that product management activities are not overwhelmed by the existing management team's other responsibilities. Product management should be included in the team's terms of reference, regular meeting agenda and reporting, but this alone will not guarantee success. Top management must hold the team accountable for effective product management, and ensure that appropriate mechanisms are in place to facilitate communication.

Option 3: Create Product Managers

One of the ways to bridge the gap between product development and product management is through individual **product managers.** These managers focus on the health of one particular product or product line, and can either participate in senior management meetings or inform those meetings on an as-needed basis. The designation is rarely a full-time position, but rather a set of responsibilities that is assigned to specific staff members in addition to their basic job description.

Some MFIs award this designation to product champions who successfully manage a new product's development through to its launch. In this case, product managers are given responsibility for making sure that the product they championed is integrated into the institution's mainstream operations and remains successful over time. Other MFIs rotate the product manager responsibility among high-performing individuals as a job enrichment strategy or as part of a management trainee programme. This is because product managers gain exposure and visibility as they carry out their responsibilities. They have the opportunity to interact with different departments of the institution, develop their analysis skills, and demonstrate their ability to formulate recommendations that strengthen not only their own product's performance, but also the product portfolio as a whole.

This third option can be combined with either of the two described above. In fact, an MFI can integrate product managers into any structure it creates to manage product development. Doing so can help the institution maximize the value of its existing products and discern when product diversification is a strategic solution to a challenge or opportunity.

Main Messages

1. Make it every employee's responsibility to gather product development ideas as part of their daily activities.
2. Manage diversification risks through a systematic product development process.
3. Screen product development ideas to identify those with the greatest potential.
4. Assign responsibility for product management, not just new product development.

Case Study: New Product Development at XacBank, Mongolia

The XacBank (pronounced "haas bank") that exists today resulted from a 2002 merger between X.A.C. ("Golden Fund for Development"), a UNDP MicroStart project which financed microentrepreneurs, and Goviin Ekhlel (G.E.), a Mercy Corps project which provided SME loans to small businesses. As of December 2008, the Bank offered more than 30 different financial products and had approximately 63,000 borrowers and 230,000 depositors.

The first product development strategy followed by X.A.C. and later XacBank was to determine in general terms what clients wanted and to try to provide it. Market research consisted of talking to some potential or actual clients and brainstorming among staff. Start-up, growth and consumption loans were developed in this manner, and are still very popular products. However, as the range of products and services expanded, this strategy encountered constraints, which led XacBank to adopt a more deliberate approach to product development.

XacBank understands the importance of first mover advantage. Management knows that if they can get a new, innovative product to market first, they have a good chance to instil customer loyalty. According to XacBank, the products in which they were the first mover have proven successful. Examples include innovations such as the financial leasing product, children's savings ("Future Millionaire") and long-term savings ("Age Gracefully").

If one cannot be the first to market with a product, the sooner one develops a copycat product, the less of an advantage there will be for the first mover. Recently, XacBank has copied successful products of its competitors in order to maintain market share. At first glance, a strategy of copying other banks' products offers several advantages. The bank can save itself the expense of doing market research, and can save time by shortening the product development cycle, because the product is already designed and conditions are well established.

In developing a copycat remittance product, for example, XacBank conducted sales analysis instead of demand analysis, because it believed that other banks had already demonstrated the demand. Research included an analysis of the number of transactions, the size of transactions, and fee income earned by providers of both Money Gram and Western Union services. Bank staff acquired this data through market intelligence, and analysed it to estimate the level of profit to be earned from each service, which led to its decision to offer Money Gram remittance services.

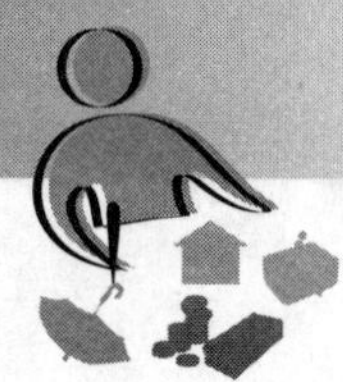

The diagram below shows the new product development process at XacBank as described by staff of the Strategic Planning and Marketing Department in 2005. Once a new product is designed, it is "tested" by being implemented in one branch for approximately two months. If no major problems occur, the product is rolled out.

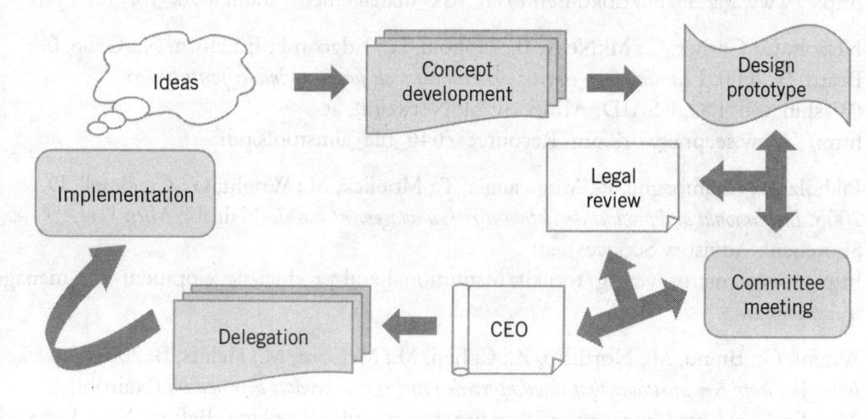

This case study was adapted from McGuiness (2005).

Recommended Reading

- Brand, M. 1998a. *New product development for microfinance: Evaluation and preparation*, Microenterprise Best Practices (MBP) Project, Technical Note Number 1 (Bethesda, MD, MBP Development Alternatives Inc., USAID), at: http://www.microlinks.org/ev02.php?ID=7478_201&ID2=DO_TOPIC
- Brand, M. 1998b. *New product development for microfinance: Design, testing and launch*, Microenterprise Best Practices (MBP) Project, Technical Note Number 2 (Bethesda, MD, MBP Development Alternatives Inc., USAID), at: http://www.microlinks.org/ev_en.php?ID=7477_201&ID2=DO_TOPIC
- Brand, M. 2001. *The MBP guide to new product development*, Microenterprise Best Practices (MBP) Project (Bethesda, MD, Development Alternatives Inc., ACCION, USAID), at: http://www.microlinks.org/ev_en.php?ID=7501_201&ID2=DO_TOPIC
- Brand, M. 2003. *Market intelligence: Making market research work for microfinance* (Boston, MA, ACCION), at: http://publications.accion.org/publications/InSight_7__162.asp
- Churchill, C.; Costner, D. 2001. *CARE's microfinance risk management handbook* (Atlanta, GA, CARE).
- Cooper, R.G.; Edgett, S.J. 1999. *Product development for the service sector: Lessons from market leaders* (Cambridge, MA, Perseus Books).

- Deutsche Gesellschaft für Technische Zusammenarbeit (GTZ). 2000. *A risk management framework for microfinance institutions* (Eschborn, GTZ, Division 41 Financial Systems Development and Banking Services), at: http://www.gtz.de/en/dokumente/en_risk_management_framework_for_MFI.pdf

- Nelson, C.; Garber, C.; MkNelly, B.; Lippold, K.; Edgcomb, E.; Horn, N.; Gaile, G.; Beard, B. 2000. *Learning from clients: Assessment tools for microfinance practitioners* (Washington, DC, USAID, AIMS, SEEP Network), at: http://www.seepnetwork.org/Resources/646_file_aimstools.pdf

- Pikholz, L.; Champagne, P.; Mugwang'a, T.; Moulick, M.; Wright, G.; Cracknell, D. 2005. *Institutional and product development risk management toolkit* (Nairobi, *MicroSave*, Shorebank Advisory Services), at: http://www.microsave.org/toolkit/institutional-and-product-development-risk-management-toolkit

- Wright, G.; Brand, M.; Northrip, Z.; Cohen, M.; McCord, M.; Helms, B. 2001. *Looking before you leap: Key questions that should precede starting new product development* (Nairobi, *MicroSave*), at: http://www.microsave.org/system/files/Looking_Before_You_Leap.pdf

3 Developing New Markets

Research has demonstrated that the range of clients currently using microfinance services is limited, concentrated in a population that ranges from 40% below to just above the poverty line. This leaves a large population, both above and below this band, that is largely unserved. At the same time, there are many within this band that do not access financial services. They include those that self-exclude, including those who previously used MFI services but now choose not to, and those who have been rejected by financial service providers. The "unbanked" present a significant opportunity for those MFIs who can discover how to market the MFI's services to this unserved population. ~ Matul et al. (2006a)

During the last three decades, MFIs have sought after similar market segments. They have focused, for the most part, on serving the needs of microentrepreneurs in urban and semi-urban areas. These markets are becoming increasingly competitive, however. Technology is creating new delivery channels, and stakeholders of various kinds are pushing the industry to fulfil more of its social and commercial potential. In response, MFIs are slowly but surely exploring and expanding into new markets.

This is an important trend, given that 50 to 80 per cent of the population in many countries still lacks access to formal financial services (World Bank, 2008). It is also a challenge for the majority of MFIs that have not yet diversified into new markets, or have done so with limited success. As Part III of this book demonstrates, there are many underserved markets that provide expansion opportunities for MFIs. The issue is how to develop those new markets effectively, particularly if it requires serving a different kind of customer than an MFI has served in the past.

This chapter will briefly discuss the process of new market development and then explore how MFIs can be more strategic about the way they use the process to select and develop their new market relationships. It is divided into six sections:

1. The process of new market development
2. Understanding market segmentation
3. Creating effective market segments
4. Profiling a market segment
5. Selecting a target market
6. Developing an outreach strategy

3.1 The Process of New Market Development

In many respects, the process of developing a new market is similar to that of developing a new product. An MFI evaluates whether new market development is a strategic choice, it conducts market research to determine which new market should be targeted, it designs a strategy for delivering a portfolio of products to that market, and then it costs and tests its strategy before full implementation. The major difference between the two is that in new market development the MFI is developing a relationship, not a particular product or service (see Table 3.1).

Table 3.1 Comparing new product and new market development

	New product development	New market development
Objective	Creating a new product or service	Serving a new group of customers
Product focus	Single product	Portfolio of products
Output for testing	Product prototype	Outreach strategy
Desired result	Successful product	Successful relationship

Source: Authors.

In developing a new market, MFIs will sometimes decide that it is necessary to develop one or more new products, but that is not always the case. Often they will be able to adapt their existing products, or the way they communicate and deliver those products, to make them useful to the new customer group. The key to successful new market development is first understanding the financial service needs of the new market, and then shaping a portfolio of financial (and perhaps non-financial) services to meet those needs as effectively as possible.

The arguments made in Chapter 2 for taking a systematic approach to product development apply equally to market development. A systematic process will help MFIs manage risk – not only new target market risk, but also strategic, communication, demand, financial management, delivery systems and many other risks. As shown in Figure 3.1, the process and the opportunities for managing risk begin with the decision to explore new market possibilities. If this decision is taken deliberately, and in line with an MFI's overall business strategy, the new market development process is much more likely to have the support and direction it needs to be successful.

Once a decision has been taken to explore the possibility of developing a new market, the MFI can analyse information about new market options that has already been gathered by staff, and screen those options using the tools discussed in Chapter 2 to identify a few ideas worth exploring in more detail. If information has not been gathered on an ongoing basis, or if promising opportunities are not obvious, market research and segmentation can help an MFI to identify options. The process of identifying attractive market segments will be discussed in Sections 3.3 and 3.5 below.

MFIs can explore several new market opportunities at once or one at a time. If a single market segment clearly stands out as having the most potential, or if an institution's resources are very limited, it will usually make sense to explore one segment first and to make a decision about whether or not to develop it before exploring other options. If an MFI has identified several options and is unsure which one to pursue, it can explore multiple segments simultaneously.

In either case, the next step in the new market development process is to define and profile the market segment(s) under consideration (see Section 3.4), and to analyse the opportunities that the MFI can take advantage of by reaching out to each market, the threats it could face if it attempts to serve that market, and the institutional strengths and weaknesses that would help or hinder the institution's ability to serve that market. In other words, the MFI should conduct a SWOT analysis. On the basis of that analysis, it can then make a strategic decision about whether it wants to move forward with the development of any of the market segments being considered.

If an MFI determines that it is not sufficiently strong or prepared to take advantage of opportunities in the market segment(s) it identified, it can put plans in place to strengthen its capacity in order to pursue those opportunities in the future, or it can use market research and segmentation to identify other opportunities that it might be able to take advantage of now using its existing capacity.

Figure 3.1 New market development process

Source: Authors.

Once an MFI has selected the market it wants to develop, it will need to design and implement an outreach strategy. There are four main issues that should be dealt with in that strategy:

1. What products will the institution offer to its new market?
2. How will the institution communicate the value that its products and services can offer to the new market?
3. What systems, processes or infrastructure will the institution have to adjust in order to deliver its products to the new market?
4. How will the institution build a relationship with its new market?

This last point is particularly important, and can make new market development more challenging than new product development. When a new product is being developed for an existing market, an MFI has established client relationships that it can leverage to develop an appropriate product and to survive failure if the product does not perform as expected. When developing a new market, an MFI may have existing products that it can try to use to meet the needs of the new market, but its products may not be appropriate, and the lack of pre-existing relationships can make it difficult to determine what would be appropriate. Furthermore, if an MFI takes its existing products to a new market and they fail to meet customer needs, the MFI will have no pre-existing relationships to fall back on as it tries to overcome the failure. New customers could easily lose interest and/or trust in the institution, particularly if competitors offer them other options.

MFIs tend to move rather quickly and informally through the new market development process, and it is precisely the speed and informality of their process that often leads to mediocre results. The skipping or very brief treatment of steps described above can end up wasting resources as institutions find new customers through trial and error rather than a systematic targeting of customers that they are in the best position to serve. Similar to new product development, the new market development process will benefit from pilot testing to check the assumptions made during previous steps in the process and to revise the outreach strategy before making large-scale investments in the new market. The rest of this chapter will explore how MFIs can use market segmentation to select new markets more strategically and to craft more cost-effective outreach plans.

3.2 Understanding Market Segmentation

Market segmentation is the process of dividing one's current or potential customers into smaller groups, or market segments, the members of which have at least one important characteristic in common which sets them apart from other customers. For example, customers with new businesses constitute a different market segment than those with established businesses; those who raise livestock fall into a different segment than those who sell goods in a market; customers who need to finance unexpected expenses can be grouped separately from those who seek to finance planned expenses, and so on. Indeed, there are dozens of ways to carve a market into segments. Table 3.2 lists some of the more common options.

Table 3.2 Market segmentation variables

Category	Examples
Demographic	Gender, ethnicity, age, household size, education, religion, level of income, source of income (salaried, self-employed, pensioner, remittances)
Geographic	Location, population density
Firmographic	Number of years in business, number of employees, sector, growth trends, business revenue or assets
Psychographic	Likes and dislikes, values, attitude towards risk, attitude towards saving and financial planning, reason for starting a business (survival, aspiration)
Behavioural	Usage frequency, usage intensity (average size of loan or deposit), user status (ex-client, potential client, first-time user, regular user, number of loan cycles completed, number of years as a client), use of other financial services (both formal and informal)
Benefit sought	Low price, high quality, excellent service

Source: Adapted from Frankiewicz et al., 2004.

Market segmentation is a critical tool for both product and market development. There are two main reasons for this. First, it can help MFIs to understand better the diversity and complexity of the market they are trying to serve. Most MFIs define their market in broad terms such as "economically active poor" or "low-income communities", but not all economically active poor want or need the same things. They are active in different economic sectors. They have varying levels of tolerance for risk. They have distinct priorities when it comes to minimizing financial, transaction and opportunity costs. By dividing a broad target market into smaller segments and researching the characteristics of these different groups, MFIs can identify opportunities for developing new products or adapting existing ones to better serve the needs of each group. For example:

- In Jordan, once Microfund for Women began analysing its service delivery to rural and urban customers separately, it was able to put in place a monthly repayment schedule for rural clients that increased credit officer productivity without increasing loan losses. The monthly repayment scheme was not attractive in urban markets where borrowers had weekly cash flows, and the competitive environment made more frequent follow-up necessary.
- In Pakistan, Kashf Foundation segmented its current customers on the basis of monthly disposable income to estimate what percentage would be eligible for larger loans using an individual lending methodology. When it launched its individual loan product, it targeted one segment in particular (McCarty, 2007).
- In Poland, Inicjatywa Mikro segmented the unbanked population within its area of operation using variables related to exclusion (were clients excluding themselves or was the MFI deeming them ineligible, and why?). It then developed outreach strategies for attracting two of the five segments it identified (Matul et al., 2006a).
- In the Dominican Republic, ADOPEM segmented its market into four income categories to determine what type of savings products to develop when it converted from an NGO to a bank. It ultimately developed three products: passbook savings, programmed savings and certificates of deposit, and marketed these products differently to different segments (McCarty, 2007).

The second reason why market segmentation is important is its ability to help MFIs make more efficient use of their resources. Once an institution divides its market into segments and understands the characteristics of those segments, it can focus its resources on meeting the priority needs of the segments it most wants to serve or is in the best position to serve. This can enable the MFI to increase its impact and/or decrease its risk. It can also help the MFI to increase its competitiveness by using its resources to provide more of what certain segments value than the competition.

- In South Africa, researchers used market segmentation to understand the characteristics of users of a category of basic bank accounts known as "Mzansi" accounts. After determining that young people (ages 16–25), those with a predictable income stream, and those with a positive attitude towards savings and money management were more likely to use an Mzansi account, they segmented all poor, unbanked households in South Africa using these three variables to identify and then profile the market segment that was most likely to adopt the product in the future (Porteous et al., 2008).
- In Bangladesh, BRAC segments its market to find the poorest areas and the poorest people living within those areas to participate in its Challenging the Frontiers of Poverty Reduction (CFPR) programme (see Chapter 14). Its targeting process helps ensure that its limited resources are channelled to the customer group it most wants to serve.
- In Morocco, when Al Amana segmented its customers on the basis of net profit and growth potential in preparation for the launch of an individual loan product, it identified vast differences in the gender balance of different segments. The segment least likely to qualify for an individual loan was predominantly female (70 per cent), whereas the segment most likely to qualify was predominantly male (84 per cent). The research results alerted Al Amana to the need for it to find ways to balance the growth of its individual loan product with its commitment to serving both low-income women and men (Dellien et al., 2005).

If an MFI wants to serve a broad market, such as "low-income communities", market segmentation can help it spend its limited resources more wisely to meet the priority needs of different groups of customers in those communities, rather than trying to meet all customers' needs in the same way. As shown in Figure 3.2, if an MFI divides its target market into segments and spends the same amount of money delivering its products to each segment, but uses its resources to deliver the product portfolio in a way that responds to each segment's priorities, then without increasing its budget it can give each market segment more of what it wants.

To provide a very simple example, if customers in urban areas want to receive product information in writing but 65 per cent of customers in rural areas are illiterate, an MFI could spend part of its marketing budget printing brochures for distribution in urban areas and part of its budget on local radio advertisements in rural areas. By communicating with its urban and rural market segments via different channels, the MFI's product delivery would be more cost-effective than if it tried to communicate with all customers using only brochures or only radio or both channels everywhere.

In general, an MFI's promotional campaigns will be more successful if they speak directly to one type of customer rather than trying to speak to all customers at the same time with the same message. Once an MFI segments its market, it can craft tailor-made messages for each segment that communicate the particular benefits that a product or service can bring to that segment.

Figure 3.2 Increasing value through market segmentation

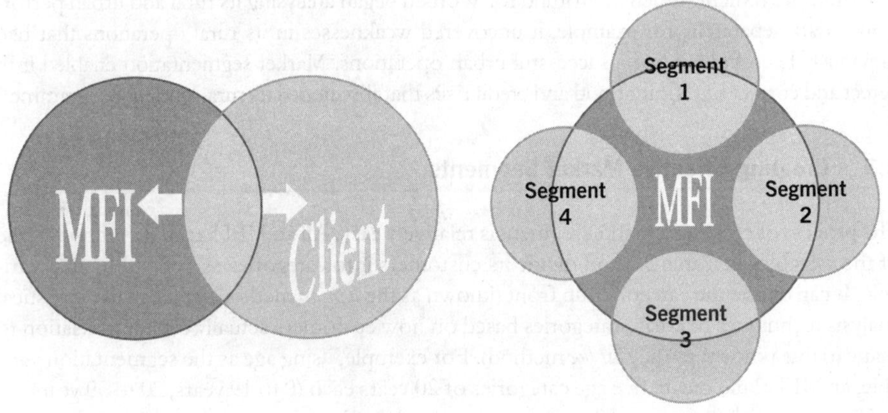

Source: Authors.

In Table 3.3, *MicroSave* demonstrates how the features of one product can be described succinctly yet differently to four market segments by focusing on the different reasons for which customers in those segments would want to use the new product. For clients that already have a savings account with the institution, the message highlights how much faster the new card-based savings product is than the current paper passbook product. For institutions, it focuses on the faster salary processing made possible by the product, while for petty traders it emphasizes how little time clients will have to be away from their businesses in order to use the product.

Through market segmentation, MFIs can make delicate trade-offs between price, quality and service for each segment in response to its priorities, thus increasing the value that the institution's products offer each segment. An MFI could, for example, offer the same basic savings product at two different interest rates: one for clients who come to the MFI to make deposits themselves, and one for clients who prefer to have the MFI come to them to collect the deposit.

Table 3.3 Different messages for different markets

Target market	Key message
Existing passbook account holders	"The Premium Fast Account is Faster, Safe, Easy and Earns Interest"
Institutions	"You can process salaries through this account and your staff will have fast, safe, easy access to their money"
Petty traders	"Why spend time away from your business? This account is fast, safe, easy and earns interest ... and has a minimum balance of only Tshs.5,000"
Savings groups	"Keep your money safe in this fast, easy access account that earns interest for your group"

Source: Frankiewicz et al., 2004.

One more way that market segmentation can help MFIs allocate resources more efficiently is by identifying areas of institutional strength and weakness, which can then be targeted for expansion or improvement. When Microfund for Women began analysing its rural and urban performance data separately, for example, it uncovered weaknesses in its rural operations that had previously been hidden by its successful urban operations. Market segmentation enabled it to detect and correct significant fraud and credit risks that threatened its rural lending programme.

3.3 Creating Effective Market Segments

The process of creating a market segment is relatively easy. All an MFI has to do is choose one of the variables in Table 3.1 and divide its customers into categories as defined by that variable. It can define the categories up front (known as the *a priori* method) or it can use statistical analysis techniques to create categories based on how customers actually cluster in relation to that variable (known as the *post hoc* method). For example, using age as the segmentation variable, an MFI could create five age categories of 20 years each (0 to 19 years, 20 to 39 years, 40 to 59 years, 60 to 79 years, and 80 years or more) and divide customers into segments based on their age. This would be an application of the *a priori* method.

Alternatively, an MFI could research the ages of its customers and organize them into segments based on the way they naturally cluster. For example, there may be no customers in the age category 0 to 15, relatively few customers above age 55, and several clusters between the ages of 15 and 55 divided roughly along generational lines. In this case, an MFI might define four age group segments using the *post hoc* method as follows: 15 to 24 years; 25 to 34 years; 35 to 49 years and 50 years or older. An example of *post hoc* segmentation at Kashf Foundation in Pakistan is provided in Table 3.4. In this case, customers were segmented on the basis of net business income, and three segments of approximately the same size were created, representing 30 per cent, 35 per cent and 35 per cent of Kashf's total client base respectively.

Table 3.4 Segmentation at Kashf Foundation, Pakistan

Net business income (rupees)	Segment 1 < 2,500	Segment 2 2,500–6,000	Segment 3 > 6,000
Average business net income	1,145	4,096	15,142
% of Cases	30.5%	35.2%	35.3%
Average total assets	30,347	60,802	69,667
Average "other family" income	6,651	5,230	6,425
% Net business income / total family income	19%	53%	71%
Average family expenses	5,794	5,971	9,963
Average family surplus	2,002	3,355	11,604
Average loan amount disbursed	11,574	12,306	13,432
Average monthly loan instalment	800	1,231	1,343
% Instalment / Family surplus	107%	43%	17%

Source: McCarty, 2007.

Although the creation of a market segment is relatively easy, the creation of an effective market segment is not. Of all the variables that an MFI could use to segment its market, which should it use? And how many segments should it create?

In general, an effective market segment will be:

- **Identifiable.** The customers in the segment will have at least one characteristic in common that makes them easy to identify. They will be similar enough to each other that they can be identified as a group.
- **Differentiable.** There will be something unique about the segment that distinguishes it from other segments.
- **Measurable.** It will be possible to measure the size and characteristics of the segment.
- **Substantial.** The segment will be large enough, profitable enough or important enough to make it worth paying special attention to.
- **Accessible.** It will be possible to reach the segment.
- **Actionable.** It will be possible to formulate a plan to attract and serve the segment.
- **Stable.** The segment is likely to exist in the foreseeable future.

If an MFI chooses a variable and defines segment categories in a way that divides customers into three groups which have 5, 50 and 5,000 members respectively, the segmentation will not be effective because two out of the three groups are too small to be substantial, and the third, with 99 per cent of all customers, is not actionable. There is little to be gained by focusing on that group separately from the total population of customers. There is also likely to be a high level of heterogeneity within the third group that will make it difficult for the MFI to identify common needs and priorities among its members.

In general, the more segments an MFI creates, the more similar it can make the members of each segment. However, the more segments it creates, the more difficult it becomes for the MFI to manage all the segments it has created. A general rule of thumb is that unless a market can be divided into at least three sizeable groups, the advantages of segmenting are not cost-effective over a general market approach, while targeting more than seven segments at the same time is not practical (MarketVision Research, 1998).

When it comes to the selection of appropriate segmentation variables, experts generally agree that the process is more an art than a science. There is no easy answer to the question of which variable is best. In fact, the same institution is likely to choose different variables at different points in time, depending on the reason for which it is segmenting its market.

In the context of new market development, there are two main reasons for which an MFI might want to segment its market: 1) to identify what options for expansion exist; and 2) to identify how to serve a potential new market most effectively. In both cases, MFIs can begin the search for appropriate segmentation variables by identifying ways in which their new market is likely to be different from their existing markets. For example, if an MFI wants to find a way to reach different types of customer in its existing areas of operation, an important point of difference is the fact that those customers are not currently using the MFI's services. To find opportunities for expansion, an MFI could research why non-customers in its catchment area do not use its services, and segment them according to the reason given. It could then explore which of the segments have needs that the institution might be able to do something about.

If an MFI wanted to reach customers outside its existing areas of operation, then one important point of difference would be the geographic location of the new market. It could divide the national market into geographic segments and then compare the attractiveness of the various segments on the basis of such factors as population density, level of competition, available infrastructure, exposure to weather-related risk, and so on.

Even when using market segmentation to determine *how* to serve a new market effectively, an MFI can start by identifying the likely points of difference between the markets it currently serves (and presumably already knows how to serve effectively) and the one it wants to serve. For example, is the new market more rural? Is it more conflict-affected? If it is more rural, the new market's economic activities are likely to be significantly different from the old, so dividing customers into segments based on economic activity would enable the MFI to identify segments with needs that are similar to markets it already serves, and to understand better the needs of segments with which it is unfamiliar (see Chapter 20). If the new market is more conflict-affected, potential clients' relationship to the conflict might be a useful segmentation variable. By exploring the needs of demobilized soldiers, refugees, inhabitants who remained in the community during the conflict and returnees separately, an MFI will understand better the range of financial needs that exist and how it might need to adapt its product offering to meet those needs (see Chapter 18).

Kotler and Keller (2006) recommend choosing the variable that is most critical to one's business. In other words, what is it that most influences customers' purchase decisions? For MFIs, the answer to this question might be customers' income level, the size of their business, or the type of benefit they seek. Benefit segmentation is often a good place to start because, after dividing potential customers into groups according to what they want most from a financial service provider, an MFI can choose to develop those segments that want what it is well positioned to provide.

Even with the above guidelines, MFIs will have many options when it comes to the selection of a segmentation variable, and it will not necessarily be obvious which to choose. Matul et al. (2006a) suggest that MFIs hold a brainstorming meeting with members of their outreach innovation team to create a list of different ways that customers could be divided into groups and then to jointly decide which would be best. This approach is attractive for at least two reasons. It would foster creativity and encourage new ways of looking at the market. It would also bring a variety of experiences and perspectives to bear on the selection decision.

When choosing a segmentation variable, it is important to make a choice that can be operationalized. For example, an MFI might determine that "attitude towards risk" is the variable that best explains customer purchase behaviour, followed by "age". Despite the explanatory power of the "attitude towards risk" variable, loan officers and branch managers might find it difficult to determine quickly whether they are talking to a client from Segment A or Segment B if the variable they are trying to analyse is "attitude towards risk". If they cannot place a client into a segment, then they cannot use their understanding of different segments' profiles to help them serve that customer effectively.

It might be more effective for the MFI to segment clients according to the next-best variable ("age"), because it is relatively easy for staff to determine into which age group a potential client belongs. Staff can then use their knowledge of that segment to quickly identify the portfolio of products they might recommend to the client, or the strategy they might use to communicate the value of a particular product. MFIs that are more experienced with segmen-

tation might want to use "attitude towards risk" as their segmentation variable, but the resulting segments must be defined and described clearly enough that staff can understand and use the segmentation to help them sell and support the MFIs' products.

3.4 Profiling a Market Segment

Once market segments have been created, an MFI needs to understand the characteristics of each one so that it can decide which segments it will target, and how it can best reach them. The process of recording and analysing the characteristics of a particular group of people in order to identify them as a group is called **profiling**.

MFIs can choose to include any characteristics they wish in their profile of a market segment. The same kinds of variables that were used to divide customers into segments can also be used to describe the characteristics of customers in a particular segment. For examples, see the partial profile in Table 3.5 and the ADOPEM case at the end of the chapter.

Since the amount of information that could be presented in a segment profile is significant, MFIs may want to create an initial profile for each of the market segments they are considering targeting and then construct a more detailed profile later for only those segments that they actually choose to develop. The initial profile should contain the kind of information that will help the MFI decide whether it wants to target that segment. It should provide some indication of the size of the market and how difficult or costly it will be for the MFI to reach it. One of the most important variables to include in an initial segment profile is a description of what the segment values – the benefits sought by its members, or the expectations that they have of financial institutions (see Table 3.6 for an example). This information will be critical to an MFI's decision about whether it is in a position to serve that segment effectively.

Table 3.5 Partial profile of Mzansi first-time users

Age	16–29 years (62%) 30–54 years (36%)
Rural	42%
Source of income	Formal employment (20%) Government grant (36%)
Attitudes	Believe savings accumulate (72%) Try to save regularly (55%) Sacrifice to save (46%) Work to a budget (55%) Don't trust informal groups (42%)

Source: Adapted from Porteous et al., 2008.

Table 3.6 Expectations in segments at Inicjatywa Mikro

Segment	Expectations about credit providers
Helpless starters	Opportunity to get credit (simple documentation, lack of credit history)
Active starters	Eligibility for credit (lack of credit history) Short processing time (they want their idea to come to life quickly)
Survivalists	Opportunity to get credit (lack of credit history) Processing time (otherwise they may go bankrupt) Close personal relations with loan officer (they want to discuss their problems)
Potential winners	Simple documentation required Processing time (otherwise they may go bankrupt) Close personal relations with loan officer (they want to discuss their problems)
VIPs	Bigger loan size (they make large investments) Low price (they have the chance to negotiate it) Flexible collateral (they have assets to pledge) Credible brand (they do not want to waste their time checking out an institution, and they care about prestige)

Source: Matul et al., 2006a.

Although there is no standard format for a segment profile, MFIs may want to consider the one presented in Table 3.7, because it guides institutions to gather the kind of information that they will need to assess each segment's attractiveness (see Section 3.5 below).

Table 3.7 Profiling market segments

	Segment A	Segment B	Segment C
Basic descriptive variables (demographic, geographic, firmographic)			
Current use of financial and non-financial services			
Attitude towards financial services			
Expectations or benefits sought			
Opportunities in the segment (What makes this segment attractive to our MFI?)			
Threats in the segment (What makes this segment unattractive or risky for our MFI?)			
Institutional strengths (What does this segment expect that our MFI can offer?)			
Institutional weaknesses (What does this segment expect that we cannot offer?)			

Source: Adapted from Matul et al., 2006a.

Box 3.1 FinScope

FinScope™ is a nationally representative study of consumers' perceptions on financial services and issues, which provides insight into how consumers source their income and manage their financial lives. It explores who is using what financial products, who is not using them, and why. One of the ways it does this is through the Financial Services Measure (FSM), a segmentation model that measures four components: 1) financial penetration (usage of formal and informal financial services); 2) physical access to banks (distance and time); 3) attitudes towards money (knowledge, control, discipline); and 4) connectedness and optimism (quality of life, future outlook, self-esteem).

The model classifies a person into one of eight "tiers" (or segments) for each of these components. The results are used to develop a profile for each tier and usage profiles for specific products, as well as to analyse changes in each of the model's component areas over time. A summary of the 2006 profile for FSM Tier 2 in South Africa is shown above. To see how the FSM calculator works, visit http://www.finscope.co.za/technicaloverview.html.

Market research will often be required to develop both the initial segment profile and the detailed segment profile that ultimately informs an MFI's outreach plan. Since this research will carry a price tag, institutions are advised to draw from the information they already possess, or can easily acquire from external sources, before developing a plan to gather additional information through primary research. An MFI's database is an excellent source of insight, particularly if its management information system has data mining capabilities.[3] National household surveys are another valuable source of information and can usually be accessed with ease even if an MFI does not yet have a copy in-house. One type of survey that is producing particularly useful data is FinScope, which focuses on financial needs and usage at a national level (see Box 3.1).

Once an MFI has analysed existing information about its target market, additional research will be very helpful for filling knowledge gaps, testing the institution's assumptions, and obtaining more accurate estimates about the size of the segment and its demand for specific products or features. This step of the process is critical to the effective management of new target market risk – the possibility that an MFI will not fully understand the needs of the new group of customers it wants to serve, owing to invalid assumptions based on experience with past customers.

3 Data mining is the process of identifying significant correlations, patterns and trends that are hidden among the wealth of information in the database, through a combination of statistics, mathematics, and recognition of patterns (Teskiewicz, 2007).

3.5 Selecting a Target Market

If an MFI segments its market using just two variables, it will easily identify between four and nine market segments. This does not necessarily mean that it should target each of these segments with a special marketing plan. Particularly in the case of new market development, which is risky and can be expensive, MFIs should focus their resources on the one or two segments in which they believe they can create the most value. Guided by the definition of successful product diversification presented in Chapter 1, this means that institutions need to seek out the segments that they are in the best position to serve, both from the customers' perspective and from their own perspective.

To accomplish this objective, McDonald and Dunbar (2004) recommend scoring each market segment on the basis of: 1) how well it meets the MFI's requirements; and 2) how well the MFI meets the segment's requirements. An MFI can make a list of its own priorities (for example, profitability, growth, low-risk outreach, or reaching those who have no access) and create a scoring model such as the one presented in Chapter 2 to rate the degree to which each segment can help it achieve those priorities. The score earned by each segment indicates how attractive that segment is to the MFI. A second scoring model can be created to rate the MFI's ability to meet the needs of customers in each segment. In this case, scores indicate the MFI's degree of competitiveness in each segment. Plotting the results in a chart like the one in Figure 3.3 can help an MFI identify which segment(s) it might want to target.

In this example, the institution is well positioned to meet the needs of Segment 1, but that segment will not generate many benefits for the institution, or it will do so at a relatively high cost compared with Segment 2. By contrast, Segment 2 is extremely attractive to the institution, but the institution is not well positioned to meet the segment's needs. Any benefits it obtains from developing that market are likely to be short-lived, if it is able to capture benefits at all, given the competitive environment. Of these two options, one might argue that Segment 1 is the better choice, as the segment is larger (indicated by the size of the circle) and customer loyalty is more attainable. As long as the segment can meet the MFI's minimum requirements, it may be worth developing. To understand how attractive a market must be in order for an MFI to be willing to purse it, a must-meet/should-meet screening test (see Chapter 2) can be helpful.

Figure 3.3 Comparing new market options

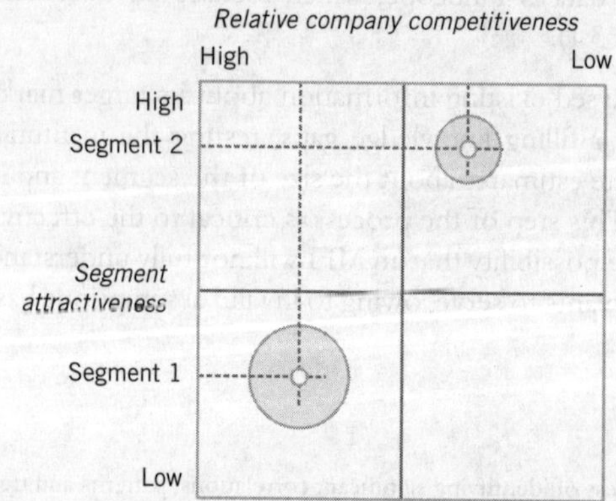

Source: McDonald and Dunbar, 2004.

Box 3.2 Scoring and Selection of Customer Segments at Inicjatywa Mikro

The scoring exercise used a 6-point scale: 0 was the minimum (i.e., there is no possibility to attract the group at all); 5 was the maximum (i.e., there is a very high possibility of attracting the group). To explore long-term business opportunities, demand and supply considerations were taken into account. The impact of the segment on the MFI's social objective (i.e., the possibility of realizing the MFI's mission) was scored using a binary scale.

Selection criterion	Helpless starters	Active starters	Survivalists	Potential winners	VIPs
Demand					
Segment size	3	1	4	3	1
Willingness to use and pay	1	2	4	2	2
Supply					
Potential to attract	2	3	3	3	1
Potential to retain	3	1	4	2	1
Total score	**9**	**7**	**15**	**10**	**5**
Opportunity to realize social mission	1	1	1	0	0

Source: Matul et al., 2006a.

Obviously, the segments most worth targeting will be the ones that are found in the upper left-hand corner of Figure 3.3, because it is in those segments that the MFI has the greatest potential to generate value for itself as well as for customers. Perhaps the most strategic choice for this institution is to not enter either segment until it can improve the value proposition for customers in Segment 2 or find ways to serve Segment 1 at a lower cost or risk.

Matul et al. (2006a) recommend a similar approach, but use a single scoring model and no chart (see Box 3.2). Like McDonald and Dunbar, they looked at both the customers' perspective (represented by the demand selection criteria) and the MFI's perspective (represented by the supply selection criteria) to calculate a total score. They analysed the opportunity to realize the institution's social mission separately. As a result of their analysis, Inicjatywa Mikro decided to target two segments. It targeted the Survivalists in an attempt to secure long-term growth and ensure that its social mission would be fulfilled, and it targeted the Potential Winners in order to mitigate short-term risks and ensure its financial viability.

Matul and his colleagues focus on the need to identify the segment in which an MFI has greatest advantage over its competitors. This emphasis is useful, particularly for MFIs operating in a competitive environment. Even in markets where there is little competition, MFIs will want to enter the segments where they have a core competence that is valued highly by that segment. Otherwise, they may invest in opening a market only to have a competitor enter six months later and easily attract their clients away by offering them something they value more.

To identify its competitive advantage in specific segments, an MFI can ask itself a series of questions:

1. What do customers in this segment care about?
2. What are their most important expectations?
3. Which of these expectations is the competition meeting well (or would it be able to meet well if it entered the segment)?
4. What are we good at?
5. Can we use these competences to meet any of this segment's top-priority expectations better than the competition? What can we offer customers in this segment that would make them want to enter into a relationship with us and stay in a relationship with us?

If an MFI has difficulty answering the last question for certain segments, it can remove those segments from consideration as opportunities for expansion. It can then compare responses to the last question across the remaining segments. Does the MFI have much more to offer one segment than others? Which of its competitive strengths would be most difficult for others to imitate? The segments that value what the MFI can offer most uniquely will be the segments in which the institution has the greatest competitive advantage.

An MFI's decision about which, if any, new market to target for development should be informed by its mission and business strategy, its institutional SWOT analysis (see Chapter 24), and the SWOT analyses conducted for each market segment. This should include an assessment of the risks the MFI is likely to face if it enters each new market segment (see Chapter 2). Would the institution be able to manage those risks effectively?

If an MFI does not find a viable market segment to develop as a result of its first segmentation attempt, it should not be discouraged. As noted previously, there are dozens of ways that MFIs can segment their current and potential customers. If the first attempt does not identify a new market development opportunity, an MFI can choose a different segmentation variable and try again.

3.6 Developing an Outreach Strategy

Once an MFI has identified a segment that it wants to target, it will have to come up with a plan for how it will reach and attract that market. As mentioned in Section 3.1 and summarized in Figure 3.4, an MFI's outreach strategy should have four main components: 1) a definition of the products and services that will be made available to the new market; 2) a plan for communicating the value that those products and services offer the new market; 3) a plan for adjusting systems, processes and/or infrastructure to deliver products and services to the new market; and 4) a plan for building a relationship with the new market.

Figure 3.4 Four components of an outreach strategy

Source: Authors.

The starting point for developing an outreach strategy for a new market is an understanding of why that market is not currently using the MFI's services. Is it because the MFI previously refused to serve that market, or is it because the members of that segment have chosen not to use the MFI's services? If the segment has access to the MFI's services but chooses not to use them, why does it not use them? Some of the possible answers include:

- lack of awareness (consumers do not know what the MFI has to offer);
- lack of understanding (consumers do not know how to use the MFI's services, or financial services in general);
- inappropriate design (product features do not match consumers' needs, for example the repayment schedules offered do not match their cash flow);
- access is unaffordable (product prices or the costs incurred to access the MFI's services are too high);
- access is unattractive (competitors offer better service, or the psychological costs of using the MFI's products outweigh the benefits).

This understanding is an important starting point, because the strategies for reaching out to customers who lack awareness are quite different from the strategies for reaching out to customers who know the MFI and understand its products and services, but choose not to use those services because they find access unaffordable. Once an MFI understands the source of the "problem" (in other words, why a relationship with that market has not developed in the past), it can look for ways to solve the problem.

If the market that an MFI decides to target has different reasons for not using the institution's services, the MFI could segment that market again to create smaller groups, each of which it could try to reach with a different outreach strategy. Alternatively, it could choose to target one or two groups at a time, starting with the largest group, or the ones that it can reach most quickly or cheaply.

In the Ukraine, for example, Matul et al. (2006b) used segmentation first to identify the potential market for microinsurance, and then to divide the largest segment into smaller segments using "attitude towards insurance", "willingness to buy", and "reasons for rejection of the product concept" as the segmentation variables. Once sub-segments had been defined, different strategies were designed to overcome the priority concerns of each (see Table 3.8). Since low-income households were located mostly in Segments B, E and F, the provision of insurance education was identified as the strategy most worth pursuing.

Although the Ukrainian example focuses on a single type of product, a similar approach could be used to identify priority initiatives for an outreach strategy that is designed to increase a market segment's willingness and/or ability to access an MFI's overall product portfolio. The initiatives may focus on one or more of an outreach strategy's four main components, each of which is briefly discussed below.

Table 3.8 Strategies for sub-segments in the market development zone

Segment	Description	Strategy for reaching this segment	
A	Seeing the value but hesitant	This group is interested in insurance but because of distrust is hesitant	Supply system reform
B	Not understanding insurance	This group rejects the idea of insurance because they do not get anything back when nothing happens	Insurance education provision
C	Excluded by product features	The product features are not adapted to this group	Product delivery innovation
D	Not seeing value for price	Interested in insurance but want a lower price	Product delivery innovation
E	Distrustful	Do not trust insurers and are sceptical about whether insurance can work in Ukraine	Supply system reform
F	Expressing no need	This group believes that they do not need insurance	Insurance education provision

Source: Matul et al., 2006b.

Product Strategy

As noted in Chapter 1, MFIs may choose to enter a new market with a core set of products or with their entire product offering. They may decide to develop a new product that specifically meets the needs of the new market, or may simply adapt the products that already exist. The decision about what products to offer a new market will be driven by the segment's profile. What are the priority needs of customers in this segment, and why have they not accessed the institution's products to date? If lack of awareness is the barrier, then the MFI may not need to make major changes to its product offering in order to enter the market. It can focus its outreach strategy on communication and promotion activities. If inappropriate product design is the reason for which the segment has not entered into a relationship with the MFI, then changes in the product offering will be mandatory.

Major issues about the relevance of the product portfolio to the new market segment should have been raised as part of the process of deciding whether to enter the market. The segment profile should have indicated whether a new product would need to be developed, and the degree to which an MFI is ready to develop that new product would have been factored into the decision about whether to invest in reaching the segment. By the time an institution gets to the stage of defining an outreach strategy, it is simply clarifying what new product will be developed, by what team, with what budget and according to what timeline.

Communications Strategy

This part of the outreach strategy is important no matter what the reason for the MFI's not having served this market in the past. Somehow the institution must communicate what it has to offer and why that offering is valuable to the particular market being targeted. The reasons

for past exclusion will help focus the promotional campaign. For example, if a target market has limited experience using formal financial services, then the MFI may want to include a financial literacy component in its promotional strategy. If a market is highly competitive, then the MFI's sales campaigns will have to explain clearly what makes its product or service better than that of major competitors. Strategies for adapting one's promotional strategy to the needs of a particular market are discussed in Chapter 23.

Delivery Strategy

The outreach strategy should describe how an MFI will deliver its product(s) to the new market. It should also define a plan for adjusting the institution's policies, procedures, partnerships, systems and infrastructure as necessary to implement that delivery. Even if an MFI is not going to launch a new product, when it tries to take existing products to a new market it may need to make changes in all major departments. For example:

- **Human resources.** Will new positions need to be created? Will new staff have to be hired, or can the responsibilities of existing staff be reorganized? Who will need training in the new market's characteristics, and how will they be trained? Should the staff incentive scheme be adjusted to reward outreach to the new market segment?
- **Operations.** Do additional service points need to be created? Is a new branch needed, or can people and/or technology be used to extend the reach of existing service points so that the new market can easily access the MFI's services?
- **Information.** What changes need to be made to the institution's management information system? Should these changes be made internally, or should they be outsourced?
- **Finance.** Does the MFI need to develop additional sources or types of capital to meet this market's cash flow and financing needs? Do systems need to be put in place to track the profitability of this new market?
- **Risk management.** In what ways could this new market make the MFI vulnerable, and what policies or procedures might the institution want to put in place to limit its risk exposure in these areas?

Regardless of whether an MFI is introducing new or existing products, it may find it helpful to map its processes prior to expansion. It could then use those process maps as a tool for analysing what might need to change, what risks those changes might create, and what new policies or procedures could be introduced to manage those risks. It could also use the maps as a tool for communicating to staff which steps of an old process they need to change, or how a new process should be carried out. The challenges of adjusting institutional infrastructure to accommodate a more diverse product portfolio are discussed in more detail in Chapter 23.

Relationship Strategy

There is nothing automatic about establishing a relationship with a new market segment, particularly if that segment consists of a different type of customer than the MFI has served in the past. Relationships are built over time, yet MFIs can reduce the amount of time that it takes to build new relationships, and strengthen the bonds that are built early on, by making sure their outreach strategy is designed to achieve the following:

1. **Get the new market's attention.** MFIs can design an initial marketing campaign that responds directly to the reasons for customers' lack of access in the past, and articulates a clear and compelling reason for them to enter into a relationship with the MFI in the future. The campaign should stand out in a way that is attractive to the market, perhaps through the use of colour, music, humorous characters, special language or even statistics. What makes the campaign attractive will depend on the market's characteristics. Since the first campaign makes the first impression, and it is impossible to know exactly how the market will receive it, it is very important that MFIs test the messages and the appropriateness of the delivery channels they want to use before launching their campaign, to help ensure that their communication will have the effect they desire.
2. **Make it easy for customers in the new market segment to enter into a relationship with the institution.** MFIs can make account-opening procedures as simple and clear as possible, provide a delivery environment that is comfortable and welcoming, and have mechanisms through which customers can quickly get their questions answered. In their initial marketing campaigns they can explain where and how customers can find more information. They might even include a promotional offer to entice new customers to follow up sooner rather than later, or they can plan ways to go to customers rather than wait for customers to come to them.
3. **Deliver on initial promises.** Actions always speak louder than words, so what an MFI actually delivers in its first months of operation in the new market will demonstrate much more than any marketing campaign. MFIs can design their outreach strategies so that they promise only what the institution is sure it can deliver early on. They can also put control mechanisms in place to ensure that those commitments are met, and find ways to highlight in the short term when those commitments have been met. This will help build trust, and give customers something to talk about with others.
4. **Provide excellent customer service.** If something goes wrong during the early months of the relationship with the new market, MFIs can make sure that customers have ways to let the institution know. As part of their outreach strategy, they can put systems in place that help ensure such problems are addressed; that action is taken to prevent them from reoccurring; and that customers are informed about the actions that have been taken to provide better service in the future. If the new market sees that the MFI is making a concerted and genuine effort to learn how to meet its needs, customers will be more willing to wait and see what happens, and may even be willing to help the institution identify what else it needs to do be successful in that market.

The difficulty of building a relationship with customers in a new market is one of the reasons for which MFIs should screen their new market development options according to the degree of competitive advantage that they bring to each. If an institution takes the time to get to know what a particular market segment's priorities are, and it chooses to serve a new segment because it knows it has the capacity to meet that segment's priority need(s), then it puts itself in a strong position to develop a successful relationship. The process of getting to know the new customer group, asking for information and feedback, and being able to respond to that

input in a productive way will build not only trust and a belief that the MFI will listen, but also confidence that the institution is capable of meeting the market's needs. By contrast, if an institution enters a market that it is not well prepared to serve, and it cannot respond productively to customer requests for better service or to competitive threats, then it risks losing those customers as well as damaging its reputation.

Putting the Strategy Together

The format of an outreach strategy is no different from that of any other strategy. It should include objectives, measurable indicators, activities, a budget, timeline and human as well as financial resource allocations. The segmentation process will generate data (for instance, on the size of the segment, its willingness and ability to pay for the MFI's services, and so on) that can inform an MFI's assumptions about the resources required and result in more accurate planning and cost/benefit analysis.

Once an MFI has defined its outreach strategy, it is always a good idea to pilot that strategy on a small scale before rolling it out. Following the same logic as that explored in Chapter 2 with respect to new product development, feedback received during the institution's initial attempts to reach the new market will suggest opportunities for improvement in other locations. Testing will help an MFI to refine its messages, adjust its management information system, adapt training curricula, refine cash flow projections, and so on. If these changes can be made while operations are still small in scale, they will cost less to implement and should make subsequent expansion more successful.

With new product development, there can be significant pressure to reduce the amount of time that it takes to get a product to market so that a competitor cannot copy an MFI's idea before it is fully launched. With new markets, however, the options are already there for competitors to see. They can develop an unbanked segment any time they like. What determines success is not so much which institution reaches the market first (although there can be a first mover advantage) but, rather, which institution is able to develop a sustainable relationship with that market. This means finding a way to meet the priority needs of customers in that segment while also meeting the institution's needs and establishing the expectation that the services provided will continue to exist and improve over time.

With new market development, the argument for caution is even stronger than with new product development. If an MFI gets a product wrong, it can always eliminate it and try again, but if it enters a new market and gets the relationship wrong, it must either uproot all its infrastructure and move to another market, or it will have to try to develop something new on the foundation of a weak relationship.

Thus it is worth taking a systematic approach. The chapters in Part III of this book provide numerous examples of outreach strategies that MFIs have developed to serve new markets effectively. MFIs can learn from and be inspired by their experiences, in terms both of the results that they achieved and of the processes through which they were able to manage the risks associated with new market development to achieve those results.

Main Messages

1. In new market development, focus on developing a relationship rather than a particular product or service.
2. Use market segmentation to develop a product portfolio that responds to the target market's priority needs and preferences.
3. Profile new market segments to understand their characteristics better and avoid making invalid assumptions based on experience with past customers.
4. Target those segments in which the MFI has the greatest advantage over its competitors.
5. The starting point for developing a new market outreach strategy is an understanding of why that market is not currently using the MFI's services.

Case Study: Market Segmentation at ADOPEM

ADOPEM in the Dominican Republic segmented its market on the basis of net household income to inform the design of its savings products. It then created a profile for each of the four segments it identified, one of which is summarized below:

Segment Description

Segment 1 is the lowest income segment, and therefore has the lowest savings capacity, but it represents 74 per cent of ADOPEM's current borrower base. It also represents a RD$256 million (US$10.8 million) market that is largely unserved by any formal savings institution.

This segment saves small amounts on a daily basis, and values liquidity and convenience much more than it does the interest earned. It finds the transaction costs associated with saving in a bank too high, and values many elements of ROSCAs, such as deposit collection, the commitment and the possibility of amassing a lump sum quickly. This segment is the most loyal to ADOPEM because it has the fewest alternatives.

Best Savings Products to Offer

The most effective savings products for this segment are passbook savings and programmed savings. The segment is unlikely to be attracted to Certificates of Deposit, given the relatively high minimum deposits required.

Key Products/Service Design Features

- Convenience
- Pricing that appeals to "mindset"
- Saver incentives such as raffles, programmed savings
- Privacy

Attitudes

Members of this market segment generally distrust banks, but also perceive MFIs as an unreliable place to save. They are optimistic, and believe they can improve their situation. They are also very entrepreneurial, and keen to find the highest return before investing their money. They have some loyalty to ADOPEM.

Marketing Strategies and Tactics

To appeal to Segment 1, ADOPEM needs to: 1) demonstrate that the institution is trustworthy; 2) appeal to customers' optimism and entrepreneurship; and 3) leverage existing customer loyalty. It can meet these objectives through the following activities:

- Design programmed savings products, for example "Save to build a house in three years", in order to appeal to customers' entrepreneurship and optimism.
- Develop customer loyalty programmes for clients who use ADOPEM for all their financial needs.
- Promote ADOPEM as a solution to clients' greatest challenges – in other words, health care and education – to create a sense of security and assurance that ADOPEM is part of the solution.
- Avoid gimmicky sales tactics such as coupons, lotteries, raffles, and so on to differentiate ADOPEM from dishonest bank gimmicks.

This case study was adapted from Murray (2005).

Recommended Reading

- Frankiewicz, C.; Wright, G.A.; Cracknell, D. 2004. *Product marketing toolkit* (Nairobi, *MicroSave*), at: http://www.microsave.org/toolkit/product-marketing-toolkit
- Kalanda, A.; Campbell, B. 2008. *Banking rollout approaches to rural markets: Opportunity International Bank of Malawi*, White Paper No. 8 (Oak Brook, IL, Opportunity International), at: http://www.opportunity.net/Publications/CaseStudies/
- Matul, M.; Szubert, D.; Cohen, M.; McGuinness, E. 2006. *Attracting the unbanked: Preliminary guidelines for maximizing existing infrastructure through serving untapped markets* (Washington, DC, Microfinance Opportunities and Microfinance Centre for Central and Eastern Europe and the New Independent States), at: http://www.microfinancegateway.org/gm/document-1.9.29432/36678_file_06.pdf
- Matul, M.; Szubert, D.; Vardanyan, G.; Lalayan, M.; Tomilova, O. 2006. *Entering new markets: How market research can inform new product development*, MFC Spotlight No. 13 (Warsaw, Microfinance Centre for Central and Eastern Europe and the New Independent States), at: http://www.mfc.org.pl/doc/Research/ImpAct/SN/SN13.pdf
- McCarty, M.Y. 2007. *Marketing for microfinance* (New York, NY, Women's World Banking), at: http://www.swwb.org/files/pubs/en/marketing_for_microfinance_e.pdf
- Porteous, D.; Collins, D.; Abrams, J.; Toniatti, D. 2008. *Segmenting the markets for savings among the poor across countries* (Somerville, MA, Bankable Frontier Associates), at: http://www.bankablefrontier.com/assets/pdfs/GF_SAVINGS_REPORT_v3_0-1.pdf

Product Options

Part II: Product Options

The next ten chapters of this book explore the different types of product that microfinance institutions might want to include in their product portfolio. Each chapter explores the characteristics and requirements of one type of product, using examples from MFIs around the world to illustrate variations in the way the product can be delivered. MFIs that have already defined their product development priorities will find some chapters to be more immediately interesting than others. Yet, reading all of the chapters in this section can be useful for several reasons.

First, it can increase awareness of the range of products that an MFI might consider offering in the future. Many of the assumptions about what is and is not possible in the world of microfinance have been challenged in the last five years, and product options that an MFI might have deemed unviable in the past may now be feasible. Reading about adaptations that others have made to products that an MFI already offers could inspire ideas for expanding an existing product line or taking the product to a new market.

Reviewing all the chapters in this section will also make it easier to understand the recommendations that are made in Part III of the book, which explores the combinations of products required by different market segments and the challenges that must be overcome to deliver an appropriate mix to each. Before considering these application scenarios, it is useful to understand the basic design of each product in the mix and the issues that must be managed to develop and deliver it successfully.

Finally, each of the product chapters discusses tools or delivery strategies that can be applied to the content of other chapters. Chapter 4, for example, discusses techniques for tackling the challenges associated with voluntary savings, which are relevant to Chapter 5 on long-term savings and micropensions. Chapter 6 compares the advantages and disadvantages of individual and group lending methodologies, which can be used to deliver the housing loans described in Chapter 7 as well as the emergency and consumption loans described in Chapter 8. Chapter 9 on insurance provides guidance on choosing between insurance, savings and credit products for helping clients manage risk, and so on. Even a quick glance at the content of each chapter in this section can help managers gain a broader and deeper perspective on their product options.

II Product Options

4 Savings[4]

When serving small depositors, the biggest product-related challenge is usually not to design a new product that is unique to a specific market but to find an overlap between what people want and what the microfinance institution can manage cost effectively. An MFI's challenge is to offer just a few products that meet as much of the target market's demand as possible – and are managerially feasible and financially viable. ~ Hirschland (2005a)

Often called the forgotten half of microfinance, savings services are absolutely important for a microfinance institution and its clients, not to mention for the greater community or economy. They can provide the basis for a long-term relationship between an MFI and its customers, one that facilitates better risk management and the building of assets. For MFIs, savings can provide a relatively stable means to finance the loan portfolio – a key to growth. They can dramatically increase an institution's client base and improve borrowers' capacity to repay.

Of course, MFIs incur operational, financial and administrative costs to mobilize savings. And when they use the deposits mobilized to finance loans, they put the savings of the poor at risk. As important a service as savings is, MFIs must prepare themselves carefully before diversifying into this area. This chapter provides an overview of the savings services that poor people need, the products MFIs might offer, and the challenges institutions must overcome if they are to offer viable and sustainable savings services. It addresses the following six topics:

1. Do poor people need savings?
2. What are the limitations of available savings options?
3. What are the characteristics of appropriate savings for the poor?
4. What are the product options?
5. Who should offer voluntary savings?
6. Meeting the challenges of voluntary savings for the poor

4.1 Do Poor People Need Savings?

Poor people save all the time. Savings are often the only way poor people can manage to pay for a major life event, survive a natural disaster, or take advantage of a business opportunity. In particular, poor people save for the following needs:

- **Life-cycle events.** Predictable events, such as childbirth, school fees, marriage and death, cause poor people to require larger amounts of cash than are usually available in the household. Some needs can be anticipated, but can cause great anxiety. In Bangladesh and India, the dowry system makes marrying daughters an expensive undertaking; in parts of Africa, funerals can be very costly; in many countries, recurrent festivals like Eid, Christmas, or Diwali can also be expensive.
- **Emergencies.** Unpredictable events create a sudden and unanticipated need for a larger sum of money than can normally be found at home. Personal emergencies include sick-

4 This chapter was adapted from Hirschland (ed.) (2005).

ness, the death of a breadwinner, the loss of employment, and theft; non-personal emergencies include war, floods, fires, and cyclones or hurricanes.

- **Opportunitie.** Besides *needs* for large sums of cash, there are also *opportunities* that create a demand for funds, such as investing in an existing or new business, or buying land or other productive assets.

4.2 What Are the Limitations of Available Savings Options?

Leaving microfinance institutions aside for the moment, there are two main options available to poor people who want to save. One is to save informally, and the other is to seek access to the savings services provided by regulated financial institutions that serve the general public. To understand better the challenges and opportunities facing MFIs in this area, it is necessary to consider the limitations of both informal and formal savings.

Limitations of Informal Savings

To save, poor people use a variety of informal savings mechanisms, such as:

- investing in kind (livestock, gold, jewellery);
- hiding cash at home (under a mattress, buried in backyard);
- keeping savings with neighbours;
- participating in informal savings groups.

However widely used, most informal mechanisms fail to meet the needs of poor people in a convenient, cost-effective and secure manner. In many cases, informal savings are high risk, illiquid, indivisible, or impose rigid or uniform terms. For example:

- **Savings in kind.** Livestock can die of disease and must be sold as a whole, not in parts, to obtain cash. The transaction imposes time and financial costs, and conversion into cash may be complicated if markets are not easily accessible or a buyer cannot be identified. The value of in-kind savings – be it gold, maize, land or livestock – will change over time as the market price for the good being saved fluctuates, which creates additional risk.
- **Saving at home.** Cash kept under the mattress runs the risk of theft and destruction. Because of its accessibility, saving at home is also at risk of trivial spending for less important purchases or demands of relatives. Although cash holdings offer a liquidity advantage, they do not provide a hedge against inflation.
- **Informal rotating savings groups** tend to be small, rotate limited amounts of money, and are not the best financial mechanism for coping with an emergency or building up a large sum of cash. They often require rigid amounts at set intervals and do not reflect changes in their members' ability to save.

Limitations of Formal Savings

Poor people lack access to safe, voluntary deposit services offered by formal institutions. Those deposit services that are offered by formal financial institutions often impose time, financial and other transaction costs:

- inconvenient location and opening hours;
- complicated procedures;
- inappropriate transaction sizes;
- minimum balance requirements;
- disrespectful or intimidating treatment by the institution.

4.3 What Are the Characteristics of Appropriate Savings for the Poor?

Typically, poor people want their savings to be secure, with low transaction costs, appropriate design, and, if possible, real returns. Their priorities in order of preference are (CGAP, 2002):

1. **Security.** Secure savings are not in jeopardy from fraud, theft, fire, or relatives' demands. Safety is paramount, even in the face of inflation.
2. **Low transaction costs.** Proximity is essential to reduce the high transaction costs of making deposits and withdrawals. Convenient opening times and minimal paperwork are also important.
3. **Appropriate design.** Individual voluntary deposit products that allow frequent deposits of small, variable amounts and quick access to funds are best. Contractual savings are also useful for planned expenditures such as weddings, home construction and education.
4. **Interest rates.** If transaction costs are low, rural saving takes place even with negative real returns, indicating that the poor can be relatively insensitive to interest rates compared with other savings characteristics. Nevertheless, demand for savings products does increase as real interest rates rise.

Since micro-savers represent different market segments with different saving needs, institutions should provide a mixture of deposit products that offer a range of liquidity, interest, convenience and flexibility options. As shown in Table 4.1, **highly liquid accounts** that allow flexible and perhaps frequent small deposits and withdrawals will best meet clients' unexpected savings needs. **Time-bound accounts** will be more appropriate for helping people to save for expected needs, such as school fees, weddings, etc. A single savings product will not be able to meet all the needs of all depositors. However, a few well-designed and complementary savings products will meet the needs of most depositors.

Table 4.1 What do poor people want most in a savings service?

For all savings needs	For unexpected savings needs
• Security • Convenience • Competitive returns • Confidentiality	• Voluntary deposits • Unrestricted access
	For expected needs
	• Restricted access • Fixed regular amounts

Source: Adapted from Churchill et al., 2002.

4.4 What Are the Product Options?[5]

MFIs mobilize savings in two different ways: 1) through compulsory deposits that are a condition of membership or access to credit; and 2) through voluntary deposits that are made entirely at the discretion of the saver.

Compulsory Savings

Also known as mandatory or forced savings, compulsory savings are funds that must be deposited by borrowers in order to be eligible for a loan, or sometimes by members of a cooperative to maintain their membership status. The amount may be a percentage of the loan being sought, or a nominal amount. Many MFIs mobilize compulsory savings because they believe these savings:

- provide clients with the discipline to save;
- protect clients' savings from less important uses;
- function as collateral for clients who otherwise have only social collateral (the group may use these savings to repay the loan if a member defaults); and
- serve as an important source of loan capital: for example, before offering voluntary savings services, the Association for Social Advancement (ASA) in Bangladesh funded 40 per cent of its portfolio with mandatory savings.

Since compulsory savings are a form of collateral, most countries do not treat such savings as deposits, provided that they are not financially intermediated (CGAP, 2010a). Thus even non-regulated MFIs can usually collect them.

For clients, however, compulsory savings have significant drawbacks:

- Customers have very limited access to their savings, so they cannot use the funds to manage their cash flows.
- They may have to borrow from other, more expensive sources to meet emergency needs.
- If circumstances force them to withdraw their savings, they lose access to credit.
- If members of their borrowing group default, they can lose some or all of their savings.

This risk and limited access result in clients perceiving compulsory savings as a cost of borrowing rather than as a service. For the very poor, tying savings to credit often makes the savings "service" inaccessible, as they are frequently not in a position to borrow.

These disadvantages can translate into undesirable consequences for the MFI. Compulsory savings can limit outreach, not only to the very poor, but also to any low-income person who wants to save but not borrow. If compulsory savings requirements are calculated as a percentage of the loan being sought they can limit growth as well, since clients are less willing to tie up (and risk, in the case of group lending) large amounts of savings. They may choose not to take larger loans to avoid the increase in savings required, and this creates loan plateaus that are unrelated to clients' debt capacity. Furthermore, the restrictions placed on clients' access to their savings can result in significant client dissatisfaction and desertion. For example, in 1995,

[5] This section is adapted from Churchill et al. (2002), Chapter 7.

Table 4.2 Advantages and disadvantages of compulsory savings

	Advantages	Disadvantages
Client	• Discipline to save • Protect savings from trivial uses	• Cannot access savings as needed • Cannot save unless willing to borrow • May exclude the very poor • To access savings, may have to forfeit access to credit
Institution	• Loan guarantee for clients without traditional collateral • Illiquid, reliable source of loan capital • Less costly than liquid savings services	• Clients desert to access savings • Clients do not take larger loans to avoid the increase in the effective interest rate • May limit outreach to the very poor

Source: Churchill et al., 2002.

Grameen Bank members in Tangail District went on strike to demand access to their locked-in savings. During that same year, a study found that nearly 57 per cent of the members of BRAC (Bangladesh Rural Advancement Committee) deserted because of their desire for access to savings during emergencies (Wright, 2000a). The advantages and disadvantages of compulsory savings are summarized in Table 4.2.

Voluntary Savings

Voluntary implies that savers determine the amount and the timing of their deposits and withdrawals. Voluntary savings services fall into three categories: demand deposits, contractual savings, and time deposits (see Table 4.3):

1. In a **demand deposit account** (also known as a **regular savings account** or **passbook savings**) the amount and timing of deposits and withdrawals are not set in advance. Two variations of passbook accounts are: 1) a completely **liquid** or **open access** account, which allows customers to deposit and withdraw funds as frequently as they please; and 2) a **semi-liquid** account, which restricts the number of transactions, such as two withdrawals per month. While, in aggregate, these accounts tend to be quite stable, they are costly for an institution to manage, with high administrative expenses overshadowing low financial costs. Yet if only one savings product can be offered, a demand deposit account is often the one that best meets the demands of most clients.
2. With **contractual savings** (also known as **commitment savings, targeted savings** or **accumulated fixed-term accounts**), the client agrees to deposit a set amount on a regular basis for a specified period of time. After the maturity date the client can withdraw the entire amount plus interest. Early withdrawal is either prohibited or penalized. On the surface, contractual savings and compulsory savings appear similar. However, to clients, the differences are important: contractual savings are not tied to a loan, and clients can set the amount and duration of the savings contract themselves, based on their ability and desire

to save. Often clients can define a specific goal for which they want to save, which helps to motivate regular deposits.

3. With a **time deposit**, such as a **certificate of deposit** (CD), a client deposits a lump sum and promises not to touch it for a specific period of time. The institution provides a range of possible terms from which the client can choose. Time deposits usually pay the highest interest of any savings product, since they involve the fewest transactions. They are seldom demanded by low-income households, since they require a large sum of money up front, but a three- or six-month time deposit could help farmers and other entrepreneurs with lumpy cash flows set aside a portion of their annual earnings for use during a season of the year when they have little income.

Table 4.3 Comparing voluntary savings product options

	Client perspective	Financial viability perspective	Management capacity perspective
Demand deposit accounts	• For emergencies and unexpected opportunities, for smoothing consumption, or for storing excess cash • Lowest interest rate	• Large amount overall, though small average balance • Less profitable: low financial cost, but high operating costs • Relatively stable	• Heavy demand for staff, MIS and internal controls because of large number of accounts with frequent and irregular transactions • Requires attention to liquidity management
Contractual savings	• For expected needs, such as school fees • Provides discipline • Higher interest rate	• Longer-term funds • Larger amount per account • More profitable: lower operating costs, somewhat higher financial costs • May be volatile	• Much more predicable than demand deposits • Fewer administrative requirements • Requires attention to liquidity management
Time deposit products	• For expected needs and for storing surplus • Requires large deposit • Highest interest rate	• Longer-term funds • Larger amount per account • Much lower operating costs; profitability depends on financial costs • May be volatile	• Very low management requirements: two transactions per account • Requires more attention to liquidity management

Source: Adapted from Wisniwski, 1999, and Hirschland, 2000, as published in Churchill et al., 2002.

Choosing a Savings Product Mix

As summarized in Table 4.1, clients need fundamentally different features in a savings product that will be used to meet expected needs compared with one that will be used to meet unexpected needs. For this reason, MFIs that offer savings services should aim to provide a mix of liquid and illiquid options. Many successful microfinance operations provide just two or three generic and flexible savings products that clients can use for a range of purposes. The well-known Bank Rakyat Indonesia (BRI) Unit system attracted 25.9 million deposit accounts with just three products: a liquid passbook account for the public, a similar account for institutions, and an illiquid time deposit product with terms of one to 24 months.

Other institutions, particularly credit unions, take a life-cycle approach to defining their savings mix in an effort to attract depositors of all ages. The World Council of Credit Unions (WOCCU) recommends a mix of six products: a regular savings account, a youth account, an institutional account (a liquid account with a high minimum balance and transaction fees), a pension account, time deposits, and contractual products named and designed to meet specific local demands.

Given the disadvantages of compulsory savings, MFIs may want to consider replacing their compulsory savings with a contractual savings product, or transforming compulsory savings into a compulsory-voluntary product that enables clients to save and withdraw savings in excess of the required minimum (see Box 4.1).

Box 4.1 Can an Institution Mobilize Both Compulsory and Voluntary Savings?

Many institutions, especially credit unions, mobilize large volumes of voluntary deposits as well as mandatory ones. For example, in Guinea, the Yete-Mali cooperative's required collateral savings represent just 5 per cent of total deposits. The rest are voluntary. In fact, many institutions allow clients to make a voluntary deposit along with – and into the same account as – their mandatory minimum. Depositors make good use of this service. For example, savings accounts at ASA and VYCCU, a cooperative in Nepal, allow members to save as much as they wish. In 2002, ASA's clients held, on average, 66 per cent more in the deposit account than the compulsory requirement – and had withdrawn about one-third of this excess over the course of the year. In a three-month period VYCCU members saved, on average, 78 per cent more than required. Furthermore, these mandatory-voluntary deposits represent just one-quarter of VYCCU's total deposits – the rest are completely voluntary.

Of course, customers will hardly deposit voluntarily if they believe that their savings might be taken to cover others' defaulted loans. Furthermore, credit officers who are accustomed to collecting required payments may be reluctant to promote voluntary savings. With appropriate policies, incentives and training, however, offering a mix of products that includes both compulsory and voluntary savings can be successful.

Source: Hirschland, 2005a.

4.5 Who Should Offer Voluntary Savings?

According to McKee (2005), institutions that want to intermediate deposits should meet four minimum conditions: client demand, institutional capacity, governance and sufficient external checks, represented by the four concentric circles shown in Figure 4.1.

1. The inner circle represents **client demand** – will the services that the institution can offer attract a sufficient volume of deposits? The answer to this question will depend, in part, on whether potential clients trust the institution enough to deposit their savings with it. An MFI should proceed only if effective demand is adequate.
2. The second circle represents the **supply side** – does the institution have the financial soundness, cost structure and capacity to successfully manage voluntary savings? For the security of both depositors and provider, an institution should offer voluntary savings services only if it is at or very close to profitability; otherwise the risks to the depositors are unjustifiable. It should also have stringent credit management, a realistic business plan for ongoing viability, strong liquidity, asset liability management and internal control systems, sufficient physical security, and management and staff that can manage the new product.
3. The third circle represents effective **governance**. Does the institution have a board of directors or other governance body that exercises reasonable oversight of the institution, ensures sufficient discipline, and serves as a check on management? At a minimum the institution should have a governance body that is sufficiently knowledgeable, engaged and powerful to be able and willing to step in if management is putting either savers' deposits or the institution's viability at risk.
4. Beyond the inner three circles are other **external checks** and environmental factors that can increase the likelihood of the institution operating as a disciplined provider of savings services. These include: well-informed creditors or donors that pay attention to the MFI's performance; external audits and ratings; industry performance standards and transparency initiatives; and accreditation, examination, and other self-regulatory mechanisms

Figure 4.1 Preconditions for intermediating savings

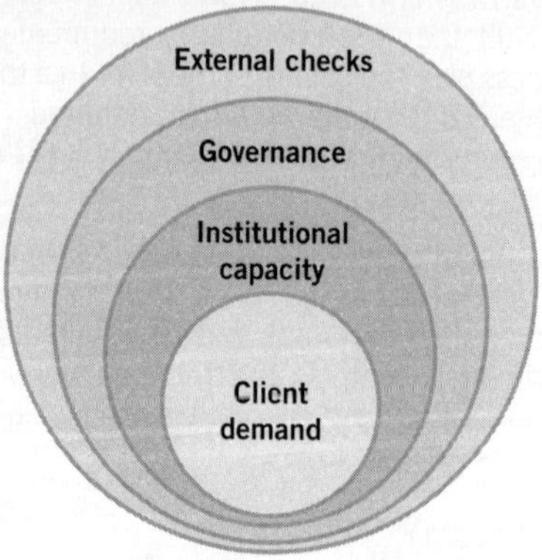

Source: McKee, 2005.

such as those provided by credit union federations. Ideally, any provider of savings services would be subject to capable external supervision or, at a minimum, a rigorous licensing process. However, although supervision and licensing are desirable, their absence should not necessarily prevent an MFI from offering savings services. The bottom line is that if an MFI is not supervised by the government, it should protect consumers through plain-language financial disclosures.

For an MFI, determining whether it has the capacity to manage savings operations and whether its governance is sufficiently strong will be easier and cost less than conducting market research to see whether there is sufficient effective demand. Therefore institutions generally consider the second and third circles before they consider the first.

With respect to the **external environment**, MFIs should be very cautious about trying to mobilize savings in countries plagued by high or highly erratic inflation, conflict, political instability, government restrictions on interest rates, or widely available subsidized credit, because these factors may make it difficult for a sustainable institution to provide clients with a positive real return on their savings. At the same time, not providing savings services in these difficult environments can deprive those most in need of savings of a vehicle for diversifying their risk. MFIs can determine whether they are capable of offering savings in an unfavourable environment by answering the same questions they would consider in a more favourable environment. Given the circumstances, is there still effective demand? Can the institution maintain its viability? A summary checklist of the prerequisites for intermediating deposits is provided in Box 4.2.

Organizations that do not have the capacity or legal ability to mobilize and on-lend deposits may provide access to services without actually intermediating deposits. For example:

- Rather than providing financial services directly, organizations might promote small cooperatives, village banks or self-help groups (SHGs) that can provide simple financial services to themselves. This strategy can be particularly useful in serving remote, sparsely populated areas, as demonstrated by the experiences of the Development Project Service Center (DEPROSC), which promotes autonomous cooperatives in hill regions of Nepal, and the Centre International de Développement et de Recherche (CIDR), which helped create autonomous village banks (CVECAs) in Mali.
- Organizations can also help link the groups described above to deposit-taking institutions so that they can have a safe place to store excess savings (and access other financial services). As of March 2008, the National Bank for Agriculture and Rural Development (NABARD) in India had linked 70 million rural poor to commercial, rural and cooperative banks through some five million SHGs. Collectively, the SHGs had outstanding savings of nearly US$760 million deposited in the banks (NABARD, 2008).
- Organizations could arrange for savings to be mobilized by collectors who are employed by a deposit-taking institution, for example at Atwima Kwanwoma Rural Bank in Ghana (see case at the end of this chapter) or Hatton National Bank in Sri Lanka (Christen et al., 2005).

Box 4.2 Summary Checklist of Prerequisites for Intermediating Deposits

- **Legality.** Is it legal? If this is unclear, are the authorities willing to waive or adjust legal or regulatory requirements? If the institution is not supervised, is it prepared to implement full disclosure on an ongoing basis?
- **Current profitability.** Has the institution reached sustainability?
- **Credit management.** Does it have a demonstrated history of stringent credit management and high portfolio quality?
- **Liquidity and asset liability management.** Does the institution have the skills, policies and systems needed for proper liquidity and asset liability management? Alternatively, do the proposed product terms nearly eliminate interest rate and liquidity risk?
- **Internal controls.** Are internal controls sufficient to protect savings from fraud and mismanagement, and to assure the physical security of funds? Are they reinforced by the MFI's culture, policies and procedures, information systems, and training and supervision of staff?
- **Human resources.** Does the MFI have (or can it add) adequate management and other staff to design and launch successful small savings operations? Does management have the skills to reorient existing staff or recruit and train new staff to interact with clients in new ways, inspire confidence, and, for credit-only institutions, handle the more complex management involved in mobilizing and intermediating deposits? Do managers have the trust of the target clients?
- **Facilities.** Will the physical facilities afford adequate protection, accommodate clients, and inspire their trust? Can the information system handle the expected number and type of transactions associated with the new service? Does the information system, whether manual or computerized, provide information that is sufficient, accurate, timely, and transparent?
- **Governance.** Does the institution have an effective board or other governance body that exercises reasonable oversight, ensures sufficient discipline, and serves as a check on management? Is it sufficiently knowledgeable, engaged and powerful to be able and willing to step in if management is putting either savers' deposits or the institution's viability at risk?
- **Demand.** Is there effective demand for the proposed product? Will it strike the balance among product features, security, convenience and price better than competing products?
- **Future profitability.** Does it have a realistic business plan that demonstrates its ongoing profitability? Is the plan explicit about what costs the new service is expected to cover by when? Are projections based on a cost of capital that includes the administrative and financial costs of savings? Does it include sufficient reserves, capital and operating funds to cover initial operating losses and losses due to catastrophic events without using client deposits? Does it have a profitable place to invest excess savings?

Source: McKee, 2005.

- Last, but not least, organizations could work as agents for deposit-taking institutions and use technologies such as point-of-sale devices or cellular phones to help clients conveniently access savings services. Although there are no examples of this kind of partnership to date, the opportunity is within reach, given the success of retail agent networks in Brazil and cellular phone payment services in Kenya and the Philippines.

4.6 Meeting the Challenges of Voluntary Savings for the Poor [6]

Institutions that wish to develop voluntary savings services for a low-income market face five major challenges: 1) preventing fraud; 2) covering costs; 3) managing liquidity; 4) inspiring trust; and 5) reorienting staff.

Preventing Fraud

Savings operations can be more vulnerable to fraud and errors than credit operations because of larger amounts of cash in the institution, and the unpredictability of the size and timing of deposits. **Dual control** is crucial. The person who handles the money should be different from the person who records the transaction.

In the absence of dual control, for example, when passbook savings are collected by field agents, **passbook verification** is necessary to check that the amounts written in passbooks are the same as in the field agents' records. Both to deter and to detect fraud, branch managers should periodically check all transactions in each passbook, and discrepancies should be systematically noted and immediately investigated. Pay should be tied to low error rates, and fraud should be immediately and severely penalized. Clients should also be trained to review their passbooks while the collector is present or, in the case of electronic technologies, to know what sounds or screens should appear to verify a properly processed transaction.

Covering Costs

Mobilizing frequent, small deposits is expensive, especially in the more difficult-to-reach areas where MFIs often work. According to Richardson and Hirschland (2005), there are two keys to making savings mobilization viable in the low-income market: 1) attracting an adequate volume of deposits; and 2) managing operating costs.

Volume is important, because it enables the fixed costs of savings mobilization to be distributed across a larger number of units, which lowers the unit cost of savings that must be covered by the MFI's revenue-generating activities. Some of the strategies that MFIs use to mobilize a larger volume of deposits include:

- searching for net savers (those who save larger amounts and typically do not hold a loan);
- developing a physical image and security systems that build confidence;
- offering savings services in safe and convenient locations (see Box 4.3);
- offering a mix of savings products that meet market demand;

6 This section is adapted from Hirschland, ed. (2005) and Churchill et al. (2002).

Box 4.3 Making It Easy to Make a Deposit

The easier it is for low-income savers to make small, frequent deposits, the more possible it becomes for them to accumulate large sums. The most convenient locations of all are the ones that clients already frequent daily, so MFIs must find creative ways to bring their savings services to these locations. Two channels that have proven effective for many MFIs are lockboxes and deposit collectors.

- In 1998, the agricultural bank of Thailand (BAAC) pilot-tested the use of vehicles to collect savings at village markets, temples and other frequented places, and found that the average balance in the vehicle accounts was four times the average balance in the branch accounts after just six months (Bankakademie, 2000a).
- Bank Dagang Bali, before it collapsed due to improper lending, employed three teams of collectors. The first served nearby areas by foot, the second served more distant clients by motorcycle, and the third served the most distant by car. The teams often collected many deposits at once by visiting government institutions or factories on payday (Hirschland, 2005b).
- Numerous commercial banks and not-for-profits in India, Ghana and Nepal use individual collectors to offer contractual savings products at clients' doorstep. *Safe*Save in Bangladesh uses them to provide voluntary deposit and withdrawal services on a daily basis in urban slums (Staehle, 2005).
- The Amhara Credit and Savings Institution (ACSI) is using lockboxes successfully in rural Ethiopia to give clients, particularly women, the opportunity to set aside small amounts of cash at home before it can be spent on other things. When clients want to access their savings, they bring the box to ACSI's office, where it is unlocked (Gobezie, 2010).
- At the Rural Bank of Talisayan in the Philippines, mobile agents open lockboxes biweekly or monthly and count and record the contents in the presence of the client. The introduction of lockboxes reduced its transactions per client dramatically – from 22 to 2 per month – while the savings per client increased (Hirschland, 2005b).

- building incentives into the savings product design to encourage higher account balances, for example bundling the savings product with life insurance that pays out a sum that is equal to (or a multiple of) the amount saved in the account (see Chapter 5);
- motivating and enabling all employees to market savings products effectively (see Box 4.5).

Of course, the more MFIs can lower the cost of providing savings services, the more likely they are to be able to cover those costs through their revenue-generating activities. To manage operating costs effectively, MFIs may consider the following strategies:

- **Serve groups** rather than individuals, or allow some clients to deposit for others.
- **Keep operations simple.** Simple products and policies allow for simpler and less costly accounting, monitoring, auditing and information dissemination, and can prevent fraud. ASA became famous for its ability to serve millions of depositors with a high level of efficiency using mostly manual systems. According to Md. Shafiqual Haque Choudhury, ASA's founder and President, "The keys to ASA's model are simple operational procedure, standardization and decentralization along with a simple written manual" (Choudhury, 2006).

- **Expect accuracy.** Following up on errors can consume large amounts of staff time. Strong internal controls, simple, standardized policies and procedures, a culture of intolerance for errors, and staff incentives that promote mistake-free work are important means to control staff costs.
- Do not pay interest for accounts under a **minimum amount.**
- Offer **"value added" features** in place of some interest. A ticket for a lottery with an attractive prize, valued household items, or a life-insurance policy such as the one mentioned earlier in this section may attract a higher volume of deposits than an interest rate increase of a similar value.
- Ensure an efficient **management information system** (to avoid recording transactions numerous times).
- When **hiring**, recruit employees with the minimum education level necessary, and consider using part-time staff and volunteers.
- Make use of **part-time satellite offices** with a minimalist structure that are supervised by a nearby branch. These offices can have limited hours or days of operation, so that one or two full-time employees might staff several offices. Opportunity International Bank of Malawi used 40-foot shipping containers to create modular branches that provided limited savings and lending services one-half-day per week and could be built for one-quarter the cost of a regular branch (Christen et al., 2005).
- **"Piggyback"** services onto other delivery systems, such as self-managed groups that collect deposits for the MFI to manage, post offices, or retail agents that facilitate electronic deposits and withdrawals (see Box 4.4).
- Share external **support services** such as training, auditing and the development of marketing materials with other small institutions. This can be done through outsourcing, networking or drawing on a central facility.
- **Manage liquidity** to have enough cash on hand to meet expenses and the demand for withdrawals while investing as many assets as possible to generate revenue.

Managing Liquidity

Demand deposits pose greater challenges for liquidity management than either credit or compulsory savings. After all, compulsory savings are deposited in expected amounts and times, and are rarely withdrawn. Matching loans to the inflow and outflow of voluntary savings requires more planning and management. The simplest approach involves precise matching of the terms of loans and savings, as practised by the CVECAs in Mali. Passbook deposits are not lent out, and time deposits are simply reprocessed as loans with a shorter maturity (Hirschland, 2005b).

MFIs with the capacity to manage a more complex approach will be able to offer a wider range and terms of services to clients, and may consider the following recommendations from Biety (2005) and Branch and Klaehn (2002):

- Expect many deposits and withdrawals, especially when demand deposits are first introduced, and plan for larger demand for withdrawals at particular seasons, such as before festivals and planting.

- Be aware that setting interest rates that are higher than those offered by the competition will attract savers that move with high returns. These savers are less stable, and are likely to move rapidly when market interest rates change.
- Set a higher liquidity reserve rate for larger accounts to compensate for the higher risk of the concentrated deposits in those large accounts.
- Use simple liquidity management tools such as daily cash forecasting, cash-flow budgeting, sources-and-uses analysis and ratio analysis to be more aggressive in ensuring adequate rather than excessive liquidity.
- Establish sources of backup liquidity, such as a line of credit/overdraft facility with a commercial bank, or a liquidity pool through a second-tier organization such as a credit union federation.
- Consider incentives or restrictions that reduce the number or volume of unpredictable withdrawals, for example by requiring advance notice for withdrawals over a certain amount, charging a fee to withdraw large amounts without advance notice, or paying a higher interest rate on accounts with limited withdrawals.
- Pay attention to cash management, so that the amount of cash held on-site earning no return is minimized. For example, coordinate loan disbursements with the receipt of savings deposits and deposit excess funds in short-term, interest-earning money market or demand deposit accounts, if only for the day.

Box 4.4 Piggybacking Savings Services on Retail Outlet Infrastructure

Financial access is fundamentally a problem of distribution. It needs systems that are accessible from every neighbourhood and every village, and which can efficiently handle a large volume of daily, low-value savings transactions. It is hard to reconcile these two requirements – ubiquity and low cost – if that requires building new infrastructure. Instead, the opportunity is to leverage existing retail outlets that already exist in every village and in every neighbourhood. These stores can be marshalled to the benefit of both banks and their customers.

Customers can be issued with bank cards (whether physical or embedded in their mobile phones) with appropriate security features, and the local store can be equipped with a point-of-sale device (a dedicated terminal or a mobile phone) controlled by and connected to the bank via a telecommunications network. If a customer wishes to make a deposit at a store, swiping his card puts him in direct communication with the bank. The bank automatically withdraws the equivalent amount from the store's bank account to fund the deposit, and issues a receipt to the customer through the point-of-sale device. The store keeps the cash in compensation for the amount taken out of its bank account.

This vision – of banking beyond bank branches – is now coming true. Brazil has seen 37,000 such retail "bank correspondents" (stores offering deposit and withdrawal services on behalf of banks) open up, most in the last five years, with the result that all municipalities are now covered by the formal banking system. In Kenya, the M-PESA mobile money service in its origins relied on a mobile operator's broad prepaid card distribution network to double up as cash in/cash out points. Although M-PESA was designed as a money transfer service, there is evidence that it is also being used for savings (Morawczynski, 2009).

Source: Adapted from Christen and Mas, 2009, and Mas, 2009.

Inspiring Trust[7]

People will deposit their savings with an institution only if they perceive it to be reliable, trustworthy and professional. Therefore institutions that seek to develop or strengthen their savings operations must carefully and methodically develop such an image. To start, managers can determine how their institution is currently perceived in the market versus how they would like it to be perceived. Then they can identify actions to change current perceptions in favour of the image they seek. To inspire trust, an MFI's actions will have to be deliberate and consistent across all aspects of its operations. For example:

- Deliver on promises, even if they seem insignificant or have no direct connection to a savings product. An MFI's failure to deliver will create the impression that it is unreliable.
- Serve customers in an efficient, friendly and responsive manner.
- Provide well-defined and transparent services.
- Create a secure, attractive and professional appearance.
- Hire and promote managers who demonstrate professionalism and are perceived by clients to be strong, risk-conscious and trustworthy.
- Make withdrawals simple and easy to access.
- Develop marketing campaigns and promotional materials that communicate safety, reliability, transparency and a long-term commitment to the community.
- Make public relations a more important component of the institution's marketing strategy (see Chapter 23).
- Provide financial counselling or financial education to increase potential clients' understanding of the benefits of saving and the measures the MFI is taking to ensure the safety of their funds.
- Invite supervision and inspection by outsiders.

The integration of savings products into an MFI's product portfolio can require a significant and important change in institutional culture, particularly for microcredit institutions. Strategies for managing this change are discussed below and in Chapter 23.

Reorienting Staff

New savings services will succeed only if staff members promote them. Yet getting the support of field staff can be difficult. Field officers who are accustomed to collecting uniform loan payments and compulsory savings may not easily accept more flexible savings products that are harder to "sell" and require more careful record keeping.

Managers must help their employees understand why savings mobilization is as important to their job and to their institution as credit. In addition, training, incentives and evaluation systems must be designed to ensure that field staff are both capable of explaining the benefits of flexible savings and motivated to prioritize savings (see Box 4.5). An MFI's leadership should be careful not to underestimate the scale of this challenge and to look for ways to prioritize not only savings, but also the values that support it.

7 This section is adapted from Hossain et al. (2005).

Box 4.5
Achieving Volume: Lessons from the BRI Unit System in Indonesia

One of the reasons for the BRI Unit system's successful mobilization of deposits was management's belief that staff members had to be motivated to mobilize deposits. To be motivated to mobilize deposits, they had to be responsible for, aware of, and affected by their performance in this area.

- So that branch staff could be held accountable for branch results, BRI began to account for its branches as profit centres.
- So that staff were aware of their performance, the MIS provided staff with key, timely, and transparent indicators of productivity and profitability.
- So that staff would benefit from the branch's good performance, BRI established a staff incentive system based on these indicators that rewarded profitability.
- So that mobilizing deposits was more profitable than borrowing funds, management set the cost for internal loans from within BRI – known as the internal transfer price – 0.5 per cent higher than the highest interest rate for deposits. For the incentive system to work, mobilizing deposits had to be more profitable than obtaining other funds for lending.

With these elements in place, the more deposits a branch mobilized, the greater its profitability and the higher the pay its staff received. These elements were reinforced by a new culture of service and productivity that emanated from the senior levels; comprehensive retraining of staff in the new products, systems, and service orientation; and intensive supervision – one supervisor for four units.

The final key to massive growth was to provide staff with a methodology and detailed training for how and where to mobilize deposits. BRI developed a book of case studies to use in training its staff – examples of how to mobilize savings from a wide range of individuals, groups, private institutions and government offices. Then, in 1987, it initiated its Systemic Approach to Savings Mobilization.

Staff were taught a system for identifying the 100 largest depositors in their service areas. First, staff were to visit government and village officials, heads of local institutions and government offices, better-off residents, and other local leaders and contacts. From talking to these people, staff compiled lists of potential large savers. After the unit noted their locations on a large map, each staff member was assigned names and dates for visiting these potential clients. Staff were taught how to talk to these people, including how to explain the uses and advantages of each savings product. They were also taught how to record the visits and the next steps needed for each potential client. Through talking with potential clients, managers and staff learned about their market in general as well as about individuals.

Source: Robinson, 2002, as published in Hirschland (ed.), 2005.

4.7 Conclusion

Poor people can and do save. However, most lack access to formal savings services that can meet their various needs appropriately with security and convenience. MFIs have the potential to meet many of these needs through the development and delivery of a strategic range of savings products, either on their own or in partnership with others. Doing so can assist low-income households to accumulate assets and to manage risk without becoming indebted. Yet this is true only if MFIs are capable of protecting the value of the deposits that low-income households entrust to them. An institution should take great care to ensure it is capable of managing the challenges inherent in deposit mobilization before asking clients to put their funds in its hands.

Main Messages

1. Poor people save for emergencies, for life-cycle events, and to be able to take advantage of opportunities.
2. What low-income savers typically value most in a savings product is security and accessibility.
3. Aim for a product mix that provides liquid and illiquid savings options.
4. MFIs should not intermediate savings unless they have adequate client demand, institutional capacity, governance and external checks.
5. Organizations that cannot mobilize deposits directly can work through self-managed groups or other financial institutions to make savings services accessible in the communities they serve.

Case Study: Mobile Collection at Atwima Kwanwoma Rural Bank

Established in 1983, Atwima Kwanwoma is the largest of Ghana's rural banks. A public bank with four branches and a head office, Atwima Kwanwoma serves the area within 20 miles of its central office. In 1999 the bank introduced two new products – a traditional *susu* product and a group-guaranteed savings-and-loan product – with which it hoped to increase its volume of deposits and improve its market position. In 2001 the bank also started deploying mobile units to bring services to villages in its service area. The results were dramatic. By 2002 the bank's deposits had grown from US$39,000 to US$3.7 million, and the number of accounts had doubled to 44,423. Half of the new depositors and over one-fifth of the new deposits were accounted for by the *susu* product.

The *susu* product was designed to attract savers such as traders and artisans who would deposit a fixed amount daily or weekly – if they could do so at their "doorstep". The product is familiar and convenient. Unlike deposits for the bank's other products, which require a visit to the branch, the *susu* deposits are made with mobile bankers during a daily or weekly visit to customers' workplaces. Withdrawals can be made at the bank, or literate customers can withdraw from the mobile banker by using a withdrawal cheque.

Clients must deposit a minimum of US$0.55 per day (or US$2.75 per week). The actual average deposit size is about US$2.20. The product is nearly identical to products offered by the informal *susu* collectors but promises more security, greater access to credit, and no service fee. Mobile bankers deposit customers' fixed daily or weekly deposits in the bank at the end of each day. The customer can withdraw these savings at the end of the month or, after three months, can use them as collateral for a loan or convert them into an interest-bearing account. The new product required many changes in operations:

Staffing: New staff included a product and service development manager responsible for all the new services, as *susu* coordinator, and 50 mobile bankers who have the esteem of the community and 12 years of schooling (three to five years less than the bank's regular tellers).

Promotion: The bank promoted the product over the radio, and met with local village leaders to ask them to promote it as well. Staff also visited churches, displayed posters, deposited handbills in all local post office boxes, and distributed free key holders to new clients.

Internal controls: Early on, a lack of proper internal controls resulted in fraud by mobile collectors. When these were fired, the bank found it difficult to locate all their customers. Therefore management created two new positions: stand-by mobile bankers, who periodically accompany the mobile bankers and take their place when they are ill or resign; and monitoring clerks, whose job is to check office records against client passbooks.

Incentive scheme: Because the mobile bankers needed a lot of motivation, the bank pays a commission in addition to salaries to mobile bankers who mobilize more than a target volume of deposits (and whose clients do not withdraw too frequently). Some of the mobile bankers are paid purely by commission.

The scheme was launched without pilot testing. As it grew, unanticipated issues arose. First, the MIS did not seem sufficient. Mobile bankers serve at least 500 depositors and must work overtime to post all transactions in the manual system. Second, the mobile bankers forward a lot of problems to management, possibly because some policies were not defined or communicated clearly.

Source: Godfried Odame-Asare, interview and email exchange with Madeline Hirschland, April 2003 and October 2004, published in Christen et al. (2005).

Recommended Reading

- Branch, B.; Klaehn, J. (eds.). 2002a. *Striking the balance in microfinance: A practical guide to mobilizing savings* (Washington, DC, Pact Publications and World Council of Credit Unions), at: http://www.woccu.org/publications/savings
- Consultative Group to Assist the Poorest (CGAP) Savings Information Resource Center. 2006. *Poor peoples' savings: Q&As with experts* (Washington, DC) at: http://www.microfinancegateway.org/p/site/m//template.rc/1.9.30272
- Hirschland, M. (ed.). 2005. *Savings services for the poor: An operational guide* (Sterling, VA, Kumarian Press, Stylus Publishing, LLC).

- Islam, S. 2006. *Introducing voluntary savings services: A how-to guide* (Washington, DC, Women's World Banking) at: http://www.microfinancegateway.org/p/site/m//template.rc/1.9.35040
- Microfinance Information Exchange. 2003. *The MicroBanking Bulletin,* Issue No. 9 "Focus on savings" (Washington, DC) at: http://www.themix.org/microbanking-bulletin/mbb-issue-no-9-2003-focus-savings
- QED Group LLC; International Resources Group. 2008. *Savings: The forgotten half of financial interventions? An online speaker's corner hosted by Madhurantika Moulik of MicroSave* (Washington, DC, USAID) at: http://www.microlinks.org/ev.php?ID=24986_201&ID2=DO_TOPIC
- Westley, G.; Palomas, X.M. 2010. *Is there a business case for small savers?* CGAP Occasional Paper No. 18 (Washington, DC, CGAP), at: http://www.cgap.org/gm/document-1.9.47356/OP_18_Rev.pdf

5 Long-term Savings and Micropensions[8]

Poor people well understand the purpose and value of saving. They sense that there may be a savings route to old-age security, and grab opportunities when they come their way. But they are beset by many difficulties, both in their own circumstances and in the financial services available to them, so that in practice success remains the exception rather than the rule.
~ Women's World Banking, quoted in Rutherford (2008)

This chapter describes the possibilities of providing long-term savings services – those with a duration of five years or more – to the poor. The first section explores why low-income households and MFIs might be interested in long-term savings, and considers some of the reasons why such products are not readily available. Next, the chapter reviews product design features that might meet the needs of microfinance institutions and their clients, including products that combine savings and insurance. The final section looks at some of the key issues in offering long-term savings products, and suggests ways in which potential risks can be managed.

This chapter covers the following topics:

1. Supply and demand perspectives on long-term savings
2. Long-term savings products for the poor
3. Key issues in offering long-term savings

5.1 Supply and Demand Perspectives on Long-term Savings

The limited availability of long-term savings products for the poor is due to a combination of both supply and demand challenges.

The Demand Perspective

Often policy-makers, practitioners, and even the poor themselves, believe that the poor cannot save, or are at least unable to save meaningful sums for the long term. In fact, a closer look at the savings behaviour of the poor shows that indeed they do save for long-term goals, or at least try to (see Box 5.1).

The poor often try to accumulate lump sums of money for some long-term goal. While the notion of retirement is quite different for workers in the informal economy than in the formal economy (see Box 5.2), security in old age is one of the many reasons for which poor people might save. Other long-term savings goals include children's education, purchasing land, buying or expanding a house, investing in businesses, and paying for children's weddings, as well as for religious ceremonies including funerals.

For the economically active poor the savings problem is not usually on the demand side, but rather on the supply side. Long-term savings products are often not available to this market segment, or if they are available, are not designed to meet their needs.

[8] This chapter was adapted from Roth et al. (2006).

Box 5.1 Long-term Savings and the Poor

Rahman, a low-paid transport worker living in a Bangladeshi slum, seemed pessimistic about his ability to save: "On the one hand there are my own parents, on the other my wife and children. I can't manage so many things. How can I save? Here is two taka: what shall I do with it, eh? Shall I take care of my family, or of my parents, or educate my kids, or marry off my daughter? Or you think I will save it for when I'm old? Which?" Yet researchers learned that Rahman does save. He had up-to-date passbooks for two ten-year term commitment savings accounts, and his wife paid US$1 each week into a savings account with a microfinance institution.

In South Africa, research into the market for voluntary long-term contractual savings (VLTCS) products aimed at low-income clients revealed that the poorer the household the higher their apparent propensity to purchase a VLTCS policy. The poorest policy-holders were saving just over 10 per cent of their household income. The purchase of such products by poor households was also found in work conducted by Daryl Collins and others in the Financial Diaries Project, despite the fact that the project did not specifically set out to find very poor households with VLTCS products.

In southern India, children may be enrolled soon after birth in "marriage funds" managed by institutions that are permanent but whose main function is not financial services – institutions such as churches, temples, and workers' clubs. Their parents (including many poor people) then pay in small regular deposits at convenient intervals – each Sunday as they come out of church, for example. The rules are simple and uniform: savers take out double what they put in, but only after a minimum of 15 years of regular deposits, and only if the child has reached the legal age for marriage and is betrothed or reaches age 25 unmarried.

Source: Adapted from Roth et al., 2007, and Rutherford, 2008.

The Supply Perspective

Many of the challenges associated with the supply of savings services that were described in Chapter 4 become magnified with long-term products. Regulators are especially concerned when institutions attempt to hold what are often the life savings of clients. A high level of trust is required to induce clients to part with their savings for five years or more, and trust in financial institutions is often not high in countries that have witnessed currency collapse, bank failure, inadequate capital markets, hyper-inflation and political instability. In such environments, it may not be feasible to offer long-term savings products.

Where the environment allows, microfinance institutions should be keen to be engaged in long-term savings products for several reasons. First, these products provide access to a long-term source of capital which could enable the MFI to then offer a corresponding long-term loan product, such as mortgages. Second, long-term savings products can be an important customer loyalty strategy. Since these products are typically illiquid for long periods of time, the depositor is unlikely to remove the funds, and therefore the MFI has an ongoing relationship with the customer that it can use for cross-selling purposes. Lastly, these products can be used as security for loans, so they serve as credit enablers as well.

Box 5.2 Micropensions?

Pensions are generally understood as a regular flow of receipts from retirement to death. They became common in the rich world as industrialization advanced and formal employment replaced casual or self-employment as the main source of income for most people. But in many developing countries formal employment is not the norm. Most poor villagers and slum dwellers patch their livelihoods together from a mix of self-employment, casual employment, or low-grade formal employment. To them, the idea of "retirement" is foreign. The question they raise about their old age is "what happens when I can no longer support myself?"

The ideal answer to this question would be some form of social pension, where the state raises revenue and redistributes it to the citizens. While there is some progress being made to expand the availability of social pensions in some developing countries, the coverage remains limited, leaving plenty of space for micropensions, or private savings accounts that allow the poor to manage their money for old age.

Micropension products will consist principally of medium- to long-term savings schemes that produce capital for reinvestment in real, human, social or financial assets that can create a flow of income to support the non-working elderly. In some cases the reinvestment will be property for rental, or in the businesses or education of family members in exchange for future income or subsistence support. But, crucially, micropension products will also offer the option of reinvestment in a financial asset that produces a flow of income.

In Bangladesh, wives are customarily younger than their husbands, and women tend to live longer than men. Women must anticipate a long widowhood, a cause of much anxiety. They hope that their children (especially their sons) will care for them, but are often not confident in such an outcome. If they could save up some money for old age, even sums as low as US$300, or accumulate assets such as land, their widowhood could be more dignified.

Source: Adapted from Rutherford, 2008.

When thinking about supply issues, it is useful to consider insurance and asset management companies as possible suppliers. Insurance companies have long provided long-term savings products combined with insurance. However, these products are often inefficient, as the insurance company's operating expenses are high and are hidden from consumers. Perhaps this result is not inevitable, but could be resolved through collaboration with an MFI that reduces the distribution costs and provides security and value to the client. A recent partnership between Unit Trust of India Asset Management Company (UTI–AMC), Invest India Micro Pension Services (IIMPS) and MFIs such as SEWA Bank and BASIX provides an innovative example of what might be possible (refer to the case study at the end of this chapter).

5.2 Long-term Savings Products for the Poor

Long-term savings products for the poor typically consist of small regular deposits over a period of time (usually five to 15 years) and a payout, which can come either in a lump sum or as an income stream. The product may be designed to help a depositor save up a particular sum by a specific date in the future or, alternatively, the depositor may identify how much she

can save each week or month and then the lump sum amount is what she has accumulated at the end of the period, plus interest.

Long-term savings products are typically ancillary products for existing customers, rather than entry-level products. According to Branch (2002), savings products exist along a continuum of trade-offs between liquidity (access) and return (compensation). Passbook accounts offer complete access, but limited or sometimes even negative returns. Long-term products are at the other end of the spectrum, offering higher returns, but very limited or no access. Consequently, many holders of long-term accounts also maintain a minimum amount in a liquid account for immediate needs.

To preserve savings against erosion by trivial withdrawals or against consumption by relatives, low-income people frequently have an illiquidity preference, at least for a portion of their savings. However, when low-income clients assess the value of a long-term savings product, they consider more than just liquidity. Research conducted on contractual savings schemes indicates that members often participate because they like the compulsion to save (Aliber, 2001). The idea of entering into a contract to save regularly has proven to be an important motivation for choosing these products over more flexible ones (Roth et al., 2007). Long-term savers also consider the transaction costs associated with making a deposit, along with the opportunity costs. Where else could they put their money, what is the likely return from those investment opportunities, and what is the associated risk?

There are several different ways of offering long-term savings products that can meet the needs of the low-income market, while being appropriate for microfinance institutions. This chapter covers the following: 1) long-term contractual savings, 2) savings completion insurance, 3) endowments, and 4) annuities. As summarized in Table 5.1, the first product type is pure savings; the other three combine savings and insurance.

Contractual Savings Accounts

Long-term contractual savings can, of course, be offered only by institutions licensed to accept deposits, with reputations that motivate their clients to trust them. The supply of such services is still limited, but there are some important examples of institutions offering these products successfully. Perhaps the best known is the Grameen Bank's deposit pension scheme (see Box 5.3). Although the product is used by some members to save for old age security goals, its use is not restricted to retirement needs. Collins et al. (2009) report that many younger families use the product to build resources for major expenses that loom in the medium term – such as the eventual need to pay for children's schooling or weddings.

The Centre for Agriculture and Rural Development Mutual Benefit Association (CARD MBA) in the Philippines also offers a long-term contractual savings plan, which is compulsory for members. The scheme, known as the "provident fund", involves members depositing 5 pesos per week (US$0.09). They receive an 8 per cent return per year on their savings, and are able to withdraw their deposits when they reach 65 (the local retirement age). Non-members who are clients of MFIs with whom CARD MBA has a relationship are also eligible to take part in the scheme (CGAP Savings Information Resource Center, 2006).

Table 5.1 Different types of long-term savings product

Product	Key design features	Advantages	Disadvantages
1. Long-term contractual savings (LTCS)	Small regular deposits toward a target amount or for a specific purpose Usually paid out in a lump sum upon completing the contract	Can be provided by most licensed deposit-taking institutions without involvement of an insurer Can serve as collateral for a loan	If the client dies or is disabled before completing the contract, the savings goal will not be achieved Should be offered only by licensed financial intermediaries
2. Savings completion insurance	Same as LTCS plus an insurance component to protect depositor	Able to achieve savings goal even if account holder dies or is disabled	Involves another party (insurer) Involves an additional cost Can be offered only by licensed financial intermediaries
3. Endowments	Similar to the savings completion product except that the insurer (not the MFI) typically keeps the savings, and the lump sum amount is unlikely to be guaranteed, as it depends on the return that the insurer receives on its investment of the deposits made	Can be offered by MFIs that are unable to offer savings accounts Can serve as collateral for a loan	Often does not provide good value to low-income customers
4. Annuities	Similar to an endowment product except that it pays an income stream, usually from retirement until death, instead of a lump sum benefit	Provides clients with regular source of income instead of lump sum	Very complicated product; may not even be available from insurance companies

Source: Authors.

Relative to other long-term savings products, the main advantage of contractual savings accounts for clients is that they can save without needing insurance. Yet that is also the disadvantage. If they die or are disabled during their savings-generating years, they (or their families) will have nothing to fall back on except the amount of savings that has accumulated thus far, and accessing that amount before the end of the savings contract could result in the payment of penalties, or the forfeiture of part of the interest accrued. If clients want insurance to complement this kind of savings scheme, they may be able to shop around. However, when seeking individual coverage, they are not likely to find a more affordable option than a term policy offered by the organization that takes their savings (ideally underwritten by an insurer).

Box 5.3 Grameen's Deposit Pension Scheme (GPS)

As part of "Grameen II" – the wholesale redesign of its products that Grameen Bank established in 2001 in a bid to recover from declining performance in the 1990s – Grameen began to offer one of the world's largest and fastest-growing long-term savings products for the poor. It is based very closely on an extremely popular product that has long been offered to wealthier Bangladeshis by the country's commercial banks, offering further evidence that it is shortcomings on the supply side, rather than on the demand side, that constrain the use of such services by poor people.

Terms are five or ten years, and equal monthly deposits are made in sums as little as US$1. Interest on the ten-year scheme is paid at 12 per cent per annum (about 8 per cent p.a. in real terms, and rather generous compared with rates offered by commercial banks for similar products, leading to a sudden new demand from non-poor households to obtain Grameen membership). The matured sum may be taken in cash, or as monthly income (not an annuity, merely the interest income on the sum at 12 per cent p.a.). Savers may also transfer the sum into one of Grameen's attractively priced fixed-deposit schemes. There is no insurance element, and no evident demand for it to be added.

Deposits are made during the weekly meeting that all Grameen members are obliged to attend. Grameen thus uses its own "agents", and does so extremely economically, since the agents are also responsible for servicing the loan portfolio.

When it was five years old, GPS had attracted more than 3 million accounts, and the total portfolio held by Grameen at the end of 2005 was approximately US$83 million. As of October 2009, the portfolio had grown to $430 million. The GPS has been one of the main elements in converting Grameen from a microcredit provider into a true financial intermediary; its total savings portfolio, from all savings products, is now US$1.2 billion and exceeds its outstanding loan portfolio by 52%.

Understanding precisely why the scheme is so popular is complicated by the fact that all borrowers with a loan of more than US$125 are required to hold a minimum-value GPS account. Nevertheless, many accounts have balances above this minimum, and many savers hold more than one account, suggesting that the scheme is valued for its own sake – a finding reinforced by testimonies taken from savers for a *MicroSave*-funded research project.

Source: Adapted from Roth et al., 2006, with updated statistics from www.grameen-info.org.

Where possible, MFIs should consider allowing depositors to use the accumulated value of their account as security for loans. According to Rutherford (2005), being able to tap savings – even if through relatively expensive borrowing – helps to foster confidence and to avoid conflicts between long-term savings goals and current liquidity needs. It also helps to finance the interest paid on the savings, of course.

Typically these products are accessible as a lump sum at maturity; or the depositor can roll over the accumulated sum into a time deposit and leave it in the bank. For persons who are using the product for retirement purposes, another option that MFIs could consider is to mimic the advantages of an annuity product by paying the interest as an income stream to the client as long as the principal is left on deposit with the MFI. This is one of the options offered by Grameen's deposit pension scheme. Clients can give up the income stream and withdraw their lump sum at any time.

Savings Completion Insurance

A second way of addressing the long-term savings needs of the low-income market is through savings completion insurance. This product is essentially the same as contractual savings except that it provides protection to the saver in case he or she dies or is disabled before achieving the target amount.

TUW SKOK, the primary provider of insurance to Polish credit unions, offers such a product to encourage credit union members to develop a regular savings programme. The member determines the savings goal and time period, up to a maximum of 10 years. The credit union has software that will then calculate the amount of the monthly deposit to achieve the savings target. The software also calculates the monthly premium for insurance coverage. In the event of accidental death of the member, TUW SKOK will pay the beneficiary the difference between the savings target and the savings balance at the time of death. There is also a disability component that supplements the member's salary if he or she is unable to work for more than 30 days (Churchill and Pepler, 2004).

This insurance product is of particular interest to the credit unions, because it is closely integrated into their core business, and helps them achieve their own goals by making the contractual savings product more attractive. It is also easier for credit union staff to sell than stand-alone insurance products, because they can ask when setting up the account whether the member wants the additional insurance coverage. First Microfinance Bank of Pakistan is currently testing a similar product, in collaboration with New Jubilee Insurance.

Endowment Policies

Endowment policies, commonly sold by insurers, combine life insurance and long-term contractual savings. They usually involve a regular payment paid over a term of five years or more. If clients survive the term, they receive a lump sum and perhaps a bonus. If a policyholder dies before the end of the term, and is up to date with premium payments, then his or her beneficiary receives a guaranteed payout, referred to as the **sum assured**. Endowments can be cashed in early (in other words, **surrendered**). In this case, the policyholder receives the surrender value, which will vary depending on how long the policy has been in effect and how much has been paid in to it.

A particularly interesting feature of endowment policies is that they can also facilitate access to credit, since clients can borrow against the surrender value of the policy. This combination of savings, credit and insurance could be an effective instrument to assist low-income households in managing a variety of risks if it were designed and delivered cost-effectively.

At present, endowment policies are controversial as vehicles for collecting the long-term savings of the poor. They are complex products to design and manage. They are relatively expensive, in part because they have traditionally been sold to individuals, and each policy must generate enough income to pay an acceptable commission fee to the sales agent. With small sums assured, insurance companies typically cover their costs by providing policyholders with comparatively little value. Payouts tend to be small, and penalties for late premium payment

can be large. The commission structure also tends to encourage sales practices that are not within the spirit of microinsurance (refer to Section 5.3 below). For endowment products to benefit the low-income market, these and other obstacles will have to be overcome.

A handful of insurers are testing innovative ways of overcoming some of the obstacles. Pioneer Life in the Philippines (see Box 5.4) and Max New York Life in India (see Table 5.2) are providing flexible long-term savings with insurance through partnerships and top-up cards that allow low-income users to decide when and how much they save. SBI Life's Grameen Shakti product offers much less flexibility and no investment returns (see Table 5.2), but the simplicity of its design has made it quite popular – one million lives were being covered as of March 2010 (Bhatt, 2010). The product is marketed as a group microinsurance product that refunds premiums at maturity. It is sold to MFIs, NGOs and self-help groups, not to individuals, which helps keep costs down.

A major difference between these long-term savings products and the savings completion insurance discussed above is that, with the latter, the insurer does not hold the savings – the credit union or MFI does. From the insurer's perspective, savings completion is a very simple product: just basic term life with a declining sum insured. It may be less attractive to insurers than an endowment product, because they would generally prefer to invest the funds and generate additional revenue. However, savings completion insurance may provide better value to clients than endowments, since the design is easier to understand, and clients' savings will not be used to pay an agent's commission.

Life Annuities

With life annuities, the policyholder or annuitant pays regular premiums until a specified date, usually their retirement date. In many countries, life annuities are referred to as retirement annuities. They do not, however, need to be linked to retirement; they can be linked to any date accepted by the insurer. From that date, the policyholder receives payments from the insurance company until he or she dies. Life annuities, like any other insurance product, work on a pooling principle. An annuity population can be expected to have a distribution of lifespans around the population average, so those dying earlier will support those living longer.

However, for annuities to work, the insurer needs accurate data for the population's age and mortality tables (along with other comprehensive demographic data), and must have actuarial expertise to predict future average lifespans. This is a difficult task even in developed countries with good data. In most developing countries the task is many times more difficult. In microinsurance schemes, even the age of the clients can be difficult to pin down. Predicting the future is also challenging, as small changes can have dramatic effects on long-term lifespans. For example, improvements in the provision of clean water and sanitation, or a successful vaccination or mosquito net campaign, can dramatically improve average lifespans. This makes pricing annuities very difficult.

Box 5.4 Using Top-up Cards to Mobilize Long-term Savings

Pamilyang Overseas Filipino Workers' (OFW) Savers and Wellness Club is a programme created by the Catholic Bishop Conference of the Philippines through its Episcopal Commission for the Pastoral Care of Migrants and Itinerant People (CBCP-ECMI) in partnership with Pioneer Life, Inc. It was founded to offer fun and exciting programmes that teach OFW families how to properly manage the hard-earned money of their loved ones abroad. The overall objective is to encourage the habit of saving, so much so that when enough savings is built, migrant workers can plan for their return home.

To join the club, prospective members get an application form from their parish or school coordinator, which they complete and submit together with the corresponding membership fee. Children between the ages of one and 16 can join the Saver's Club for a fee of P410 (approximately US$9.50) and gain access to financial literacy workshops, an insurance policy (P75,000 accidental death benefit, P25,000 burial cash assistance and P5,000 accident medical reimbursement), discounts from Pioneer Life's retail partners (for example, Generika Drug Store, Hi-Precision Diagnostics) and a P200 start-up savings fund, which they can grow and use to start a small business when they reach the age of 21.

Adults between the ages of 17 and 50 can pay P510 to become members of the Wellness Club. They also gain access to financial literacy workshop and discounts, but their insurance policy benefits are greater (P100,000 accidental death and P50,000 burial cash assistance), as well as a P300 start-up retirement fund, which they can access at the age of 65.

Members of both clubs can increase their savings fund by purchasing SPARX top-up cards from any Pioneer Life agent or partner, including financial institutions such as Union Bank, Banco De Oro and Chinatrust as well as 7-Eleven convenience stores. The cards can be loaded on site or by SMS in amounts as low as P100 for the Savers Club and P300 for the Wellness Club. Once activated, each card offers a guaranteed future savings value (for example, a P100 card purchased when a child is four years old will have a value of P144 at maturity ten years later). SPARX cards never lapse, and will earn interest over the years until maturity. They can be purchased by non-Club members also, in which case the life insurance component is equal to the guaranteed future savings value of the card.

Source: Adapted from Pioneer Life Inc., 2008, and Pamilyang OFW Savers and Wellness Club, 2010.

Life annuities for the poor were tried in the Philippines by CARD. However, as shown in Box 5.5 (page 104), CARD's "pension" scheme almost led the organization into bankruptcy. This case illustrates the potential disaster awaiting an institution that enters the risky world of insurance without the proper expertise.

Any saving facility with long-term guarantees should be reviewed by an actuary, and be managed to ensure viability. However, the lack of mortality risk expertise, investment management skills, and quality actuarial data in many countries makes this difficult. As a result, annuity products are generally not recommended for MFIs, although where quality data and expertise do exist, they are worth considering (refer, for example, to the case at the end of this chapter).

Table 5.2 Two long-term savings products available in India

Product name	Max Vijay	Grameen Shakti
Insurance company	Max New York Life Insurance Company, Ltd.	SBI Life Insurance Company, Ltd.
Term	10 years	5 or 10 years
Premium	First payment from Rs 1000 to 2500 (approximately US$22–55); subsequent premiums of Rs 10 (US$0.20) to Rs 2500 per day are voluntary	Annual payment of Rs 301 for a sum assured of Rs 25,000 (approximately US$6.50 for $532 of coverage); grace period of 30 days from the premium payment due date
Sum assured	5× premiums paid subject to a limit of Rs 50,000 to 100,000 (limit depends on amount of first premium payment)	Rs 5,000 to 50,000 (in multiples of 5,000); group decides the sum it wishes to insure
Maturity benefit	Account value at the time of maturity = (sum of premiums paid + investment return – account fees)	5-year term = 50% of premium paid net of service tax guaranteed; 10-year term = 100% of premium paid net of service tax guaranteed
Death benefit	Natural death = account value plus sum assured; accidental death = account value plus 2× sum assured	Sum assured
Withdrawal/surrender	Surrender and partial withdrawals possible after 3 years	Surrender possible after 3 years

Source: Adapted from Max New York Life, 2010, and SBI Life, 2010.

5.3 Key Issues in Offering Long-term Savings and Insurance

When offering long-term savings and insurance to the poor, several issues need to be carefully considered, including macroeconomic stability, financial sector infrastructure, mis-selling, premium collection mechanisms, lapses and surrender values. Some of these challenges affect endowments more significantly than the other savings products.

Macroeconomic Stability

For any financial instrument intended to retain value into the future, macroeconomic stability is a key concern. Many people from around the world, rich and poor, have awakened one day to realize the money they had saved was virtually worthless. The culprits: inflation and/or devaluation. These risks are not trivial. McCord and Buczkowski (2004) relate a story of a man who paid his premiums as required and waited until the endowment had reached full maturity. When he arrived at the insurance company office, his payout was less than the cost of the bus ticket he bought to come to town to collect the benefit.

In economies with high inflation, it is particularly difficult to offer long-term savings. There are, however, ways to manage inflationary risks. For example, the financial institution could offer foreign currency accounts and make international investments. Established insurance companies

Box 5.5 CARD's Foray into Annuities

In 1994, CARD began offering insurance through a Members Mutual Fund (MMF) designed to provide loan balance coverage plus burial assistance in the case of borrower death. This was a fairly straightforward insurance product. In December 1996, recognizing the need of its older members for pensions and feeling confident after the apparent initial success of the MMF, management decided to expand the product coverage. CARD members were offered a pension benefit for only US$0.05 more per week. The additional five cents meant that for both insurance and a pension, the new compulsory contribution was US$0.10 per week. This pension scheme was implemented across the membership without testing, and without actuarial input.

When the client reached 65, or became permanently disabled, the new product offered a lifetime monthly pension between US$5.45 and US$10.90, depending on how long the annuitant had been a CARD member. Under this arrangement, it took 14 months of monthly premiums of US$0.40 from a member to accumulate the lowest pension amount of US$5.45. There was no minimum participation period before the pension was available; members just had to turn 65 years old, although newer members would receive only the minimum pension.

During the 1998 audit, CARD's external auditors advised management that the pension situation was financially unsustainable. They had noted the liabilities building up under the MMF. Based on the auditors' insights, management realized that this liability was a very serious threat. Even though the average age of a CARD member was 43.6 (37.1 in 2004), the potential volume of soon-to-be pensioners would quickly deplete CARD's capital. The pension fund would destroy all the progress CARD had made, and indeed would destroy the institution itself.

CARD eventually managed to extricate itself from its liability and shut the pension scheme down in 1999. The premiums that had been paid into the scheme were used to capitalize a new and separate mutual benefit association (MBA) owned by CARD members and managed by an insurance professional.

Source: Adapted from McCord and Buczkowski, 2004

may be better placed than more recent financial intermediaries to carry out the complex transactions required to hedge effectively against inflation. Interest rates or investment returns are sometimes inflation linked, with deposits, premiums and benefits increasing based on inflation.

The financial security of low-income people is precarious. If policies with long-term investment components are to be sold to this market, the policies should be developed to provide protection from macroeconomic instability and real value to clients. All economies are subject to unforeseen inflation, so product design has to develop returns to policyholders to protect them from the ravages of inflation. If MFIs cannot achieve that objective, then clients should be encouraged to save in assets that retain their value, such as livestock or gold, and to explore short-term insurance coverage to manage risks.

Financial Sector Infrastructure

Another important requirement for long-term savings is the presence of an effective investment or capital market in the country. Long-term savings can be beneficial to all if the institu-

tion receiving the funds can invest them in a variety of instruments for varying lengths of time. Investments in bonds, treasury bills, equities and property would be possible forms of long-term savings to the extent that they match the desired investment time frame. It is also important that infrastructure exists to rate investments, so that MFIs and insurers can assess the risk profile of different investment options. In some countries these conditions do not exist, making it difficult to manage long-term savings properly.

A lack of financial sector infrastructure has a greater effect on endowment products than on savings completion or savings alone, because the insurer relies more on the investment market for returns. If there are limited investment opportunities, and it is difficult to assess the risk of the few opportunities that are available, it will be particularly difficult for endowment products to succeed.

Selling the Product

As the term of a savings product lengthens, the difficulties associated with selling the product grow. Long-term savings products are rarely sold passively – in other words, through a client coming to an MFI and requesting the product. More typically, a salesperson must develop a relationship with the client and use selling techniques similar to those of insurance, for instance asking questions such as "What will happen to you when you grow old?" or "How will you be able to pay your children's school fees?" The salesperson needs to reassure the potential client that the institution is stable and safe because, unlike with short-term savings products, the client has no immediate way to test the seller's claims (Roth et al., 2007).

Long-term savings products, particularly endowments and annuities, are complex and can be difficult to explain even when an institution wants to do so clearly. Sales staff must be capable not only of communicating product features, but also of helping clients understand the relationship between risk and return, the difference between lump sum and annuity payouts, and the effects of compounding interest rates. They have to be able to identify and overcome sources of client resistance to long-term saving (WWB, 2003). Staff members need to be well prepared and well supported to meet this challenge (see Box 5.6).

Since long-term savings products tend to be "sold, not bought" there is significant potential for those who are selling the products to mislead clients (see Box 5.7). They may do so deliberately in order to make a sale, or through the inadvertent withholding of information that makes it impossible for customers to fully understand what they are buying. Three-quarters of the long-term savings clients surveyed by Roth et al. (2007) in South Africa were unhappy with their savings product, and one of the main reasons for their unhappiness was a lack of awareness about key terms and conditions, particularly the early termination penalties. They believed that they would get back at least what they had put in, even if they stopped saving before their contract matured. This issue is much more problematic for endowment policies than savings schemes, because the latter are less complex and more transparent. In addition, the staff "selling" savings products are unlikely to earn an individual commission based on savings volumes, so they do not have the incentive to misrepresent the product or press persons who are not interested to buy it.

One needs to bear in mind that while it may be in the agent's interest to mis-sell policies (depending on the structure of the sales incentive), it may also be in the interest of the insurer, especially if the policy lapses. Some insurers rely on lapses in latter years to avoid paying benefits. Endowment plans designed to rely on lapses can be beneficial to the few clients who have the ability to maintain premiums, but they are of poor value for the majority of clients. Fortunately, with consumer pressure in some countries, a few insurance companies have been forced by regulators to pay out hundreds of millions of dollars to misled consumers. This has not only been costly, but has proved a public relations fiasco for insurers.

Savings and Premium Collection Methods

A key issue with all products is minimizing the costs of collecting deposits; otherwise the savings of the poor will merely be paying the operating costs of the provider. One way to reduce costs is to reduce the frequency of payments, but for the low-income market it is reasonable to assume that periodic payments (weekly, monthly or quarterly) are probably more appropriate for their cash flow than annual payments.

With long-term savings, there are three general models in use for premium collection: electronic deductions, micro-agents, and linking the product to another financial transaction.

Electronic deductions. In countries where low-income persons have bank accounts, the premium payment may take place electronically, with follow-up occurring only if the deduction fails. This is how endowment policies are sold to the poor in South Africa, where poor households often have one member with a formal sector job and bank account. Under present conditions this model would be inappropriate for many low-income countries, although as new technologies emerge, new opportunities may arise, for example premium deductions through mobile phone banking. In the Philippines, deposits can now be made via mobile phones for a charge of one peso (US$0.02) per transaction, which is considerably lower than the transportation cost to a financial institution (Chemonics, 2006).

Micro-agents. In India, Tata-AIG first began working with an MFI to sell its insurance policies. The relationship did not work, because the short-term nature of the MFI's loan conflicted with the long-term nature of the endowment policies. It was difficult to collect premiums from clients who took out an endowment policy but only a single loan. While it is relatively easy to deduct a premium from the disbursed loan, if the client stops borrowing,

Box 5.6 Selling Long-term Savings

To support its micropension product, SEWA Bank has undertaken a special financial education campaign that uses a variety of methods and tools to spread the message of micropension as an "Old-age Saviour". Classroom trainings, film shows followed by discussion, large group meetings for experience sharing, particularly between younger and older clients, question and answer sessions, essay-writing competitions, and financial camps where individual counselling is provided are some of the techniques used. SEWA believes the campaign is critical to its success, not just for communicating the importance of saving regularly and the power of compounding, or for increasing, clients' understanding about investment in the open market, but also for changing women's attitudes towards planning for old age.

Source: Adapted from Vyas, 2008.

Box 5.7 Mis-selling in South Africa

The Black Sash is a South African human rights organization that runs community advice bureaus that assist with a range of consumer protection issues. Many of the cases taken up by the Black Sash involve the agents of insurance companies who sell a plethora of insurance policies, including endowments, to rural consumers.

A fairly typical case involved a domestic worker in a local government agency. Until her retirement in March 1993, she earned US$162 each month. She paid US$37 per month for insurance policies from four major insurance companies. After her retirement, all she received from her numerous policies was US$58. She went to the Black Sash for assistance.

In this case, after a long struggle involving many months of correspondence with insurance companies, she eventually received US$169 in total (from surrendering policies). One policy was surrendered when she retired, four years before the policy became due. She was "assisted" by the personnel officer of the government agency she worked for, who failed to inform her that if she waited until the policy became due she would have received much more.

Source: Adapted from Roth, 1995.

then a new mechanism for premium collection is required. Tata-AIG therefore turned to individual agents, primarily low-income women living in the communities it wished to serve. These women form Community Rural Insurance Groups that operate like insurance agencies (Roth and Athreye, 2005). Delta Life, a Bangladeshi insurer, also relies primarily on poor housewives to be its army of agents collecting premiums door-to-door. Such an approach may work in the Indian subcontinent, where population densities are high and many people with sufficient levels of education are prepared to work for a low wage. It is unclear whether this model could apply to countries with lower population densities and low levels of formal education.

As mentioned previously, a few insurers are experimenting with scratch cards as a tool for facilitating savings account top-ups and premium payments. In theory, these cards can be sold by any type of retailer, and customers can buy them as gifts or for themselves, registering the purchase into their own account by SMS, Internet or telephone. In practice, identifying the right type of agent to sell the cards is proving difficult for insurers. Max Vijay is testing a wide variety of distribution partnerships, some of which have already been discontinued due to poor results (*Wall Street Journal*, 2010). More time is needed to explore what type of agents and what kind of terms might make this collection method viable.

Linked payments. In the examples from CARD, Grameen and TUW SKOK, the costs of savings collection are minimized by linking with another financial transaction. CARD and Grameen clients make their savings payments in the same weekly group meetings, generally located very close to their home, where they make loan repayments. At TUW SKOK, when the member makes her or his monthly deposit, a small amount is automatically deducted and at the end of the month accumulated with all the other premiums that the credit union needs to pay to the insurer.

Lapses and the Problem of Surrender Values

Another problem, which is very specific to endowment products, is lapsed policies. With savings products, if depositors miss a payment or stop depositing, they may earn a lower interest rate, but they will not lose their savings. If a policyholder stops paying the premium on an endowment policy, however, it will lapse and only the surrender value – often only a small part of the savings – is returned to the client. This leaves the client with fewer assets than he or she started with, and erodes trust in both long-term savings and the institution that provided the service. Given the irregular incomes of low-income households, lapsed policies are a very significant problem for products that combine savings and insurance.

The limited surrender value in the early years is related to the upfront remuneration of the agent along with other costs of initiating a policy, such as screening, data entry and contract preparation. Agents tend to receive their commission in the first few years of the sale. In a lapse situation, these costs are deducted from the savings component and the remainder is returned to the client. In the first few years of the policy, there is usually no surrender value at all.

There are various ways to deal with the issue of lapses. Delta Life allows a 30-day grace period for late payments, after which time the insurance component is suspended. Policyholders can refresh the policy within 12 months if they pay a late fee and undergo an underwriting review. Policies can even be revived after two years with a late fee plus medical report showing acceptable health. If Tata-AIG's policyholders are late with their premiums, the insurer deducts the premium from the amount accumulated in the surrender value. Policyholders can also request a loan from the insurer in order to be able to pay the premium within the grace period, as long as the policy is at least three years old and previous premiums have been paid. Max Vijay requires a larger initial premium payment, which helps to ensure that the cost of opening and maintaining the account will be covered and the account will not lapse if additional premium payments are not regularly made. Of course, potential customers may have difficulty accumulating sufficient funds to make the first payment, and they will not generate much return unless they make subsequent premium payments.

More innovation is required to deal with the problem of lapses. Perhaps an area to be explored would be the creation of incentives for regular payment, for example a bonus if all premiums are paid within five days of becoming due and a reduction in benefit if payments are not made, rather than a simple termination of cover. The crucial issue is that the surrender values must be fair, and clients must be aware of the policy conditions, including the surrender value. Fairness in this instance would mean that the savings and insurance portions of the premiums are understood by the policyholder, and that income or expense adjustments are clearly understood prior to the purchase of the policy.

5.4 Conclusions

The provision of long-term savings is an exciting new opportunity to expand the frontier of microfinance. The demand is there. The challenge is to find the right product design, delivery mechanism and institutional arrangement to address that demand in a cost-effective way that provides value.

To expand the availability of long-term savings and insurance products, insurers, bankers, asset management companies, donors and development agencies can play a significant role in improving the design of products for the poor, helping regulators to oversee them, and strengthening consumer protection mechanisms to ensure that the products are fairly designed and honestly sold.

None of the currently available products are flawless. Indeed, additional innovation is required to provide better long-term products to the low-income market. Such innovations would need to be evaluated on their own merits. Are they safe, protected from inflation and well regulated? Do they provide real value to clients?

Main Messages

1. The poor can and do save for long-term goals.
2. All long-term savings products are difficult to offer in unstable economic environments.
3. Long-term savings products tend to be sold, not bought.
4. Insurance companies could play a role in overcoming many of the difficulties associated with long-term savings, either on their own or in partnership with an MFI.
5. When bundling long-term savings with insurance, design the product to avoid lapses and to ensure that policy conditions are clearly understood prior to purchase.

Case Study: Micro Pension Services in India

Invest India Micro Pension Services (IIMPS) was established in 2006 by leading development and pension sector experts to enable low-income informal sector workers to build up savings for retirement in a competitive and well-regulated environment. IIMPS delivers pension and insurance products to low-income workers in collaboration with microfinance institutions, cooperatives, self-help groups, worker unions, multilateral and bilateral aid agencies, government departments and finance firms. It has developed a technology platform called Micro Pension™ that allows these organizations to channel retirement savings, short-term savings and insurance premiums of low-income individuals to regulated asset management and insurance companies.

IIMPS has as investors and board representatives two of the first big players in micropensions: UTI-AMC, one of the largest asset management companies in India, and SEWA Bank, a bank run by the Ahmedabad-based Self Employed Women's Association. SEWA Bank began working with UTI-AMC in April 2006 to offer its clients access to UTI's Retirement Benefit Pension Fund. Women between the ages of 18 and 55 who have a savings account with SEWA Bank can enrol in the scheme by authorizing the bank to deduct Rs. 50 to 500 (US$1 to US$10) per month from their savings account for a 10, 15 or 20-year period. SEWA Bank sends these contributions to UTI-AMC, which invests them in UTI Mutual Fund, a balanced fund consisting of 60 per cent debt (minimum) and 40 per cent equity (maximum). In exchange for acting as UTI's distributor, SEWA Bank receives 3 per cent of the amount collected as commission.

UTI-AMC opens an individual retirement account for each subscriber, who receives a quarterly report of her investment. There is no fee to enter the scheme, and no guaranteed return.[9] A member can withdraw at any time, but must pay an exit load, which varies from 1 per cent to 6.5 per cent, if she wants to leave the policy before it matures (see Table 5.3 below). SEWA Bank markets the product as one from which members should not withdraw until they reach 58 years of age, so that it can serve as a real pension scheme. At the age of 58, members can withdraw a lump sum amount or convert that sum into an annuity. Within one year SEWA Bank enrolled 40,000 women in this scheme, including vegetable vendors, domestic maids, handcart pullers, construction workers, bidi rollers, embroidery workers, rag and waste paper pickers, who contributed Rs.25,000,000 (US$625,000).

Table 5.3 Exit charges for UTI's retirement benefit pension fund

Period	Exit load
Less than 1 year	6.5%
1–2 years	4.5%
2–3 years	3%
More than 3 years up to the age of 58 years	1%
After 58 years of age	Nil

Source: UTI Bulletin, cited in Uthira and Manohar (2009).

9 UTI's Retirement Benefits Scheme, of which the micropension initiative is a part, has delivered 12.5 per cent returns over the years since it started in 1994. SEWA Bank used to offer a long-term savings product, Bhavi Suraksha Yojana, with a guaranteed return of 12 per cent, but had to re-launch that product in 2002 with a guaranteed return of 7 per cent owing to falling interest rates (Chaturvedi et al., 2005).

In April 2009 IIMPS and UTI-AMC formalized a new strategic alliance with the BASIX Group. Under this partnership, IIMPS will use its Micro-Pension Model to deliver the UTI-Retirement Benefit Pension Fund to BASIX customers, targeting 700,000 working poor in 2009–10. UTI-AMC and IIMPS are also trying to work with state governments to facilitate co-contributory social security schemes for low-income informal sector workers. MFIs and cooperatives are being recruited to help target such schemes through proxy means tests based on their local knowledge of members' actual incomes. They may also be able to provide financial education in support of the schemes, and collect members' social security contributions, which would be matched by the state government and then invested by UTI-AMC.

The IIMPS technology platform and implementation capacity are portable, and can be adopted in other countries that seek to offer contributory social security and pension schemes to low-income informal sector workers.

This case study was adapted from Vyas (2008), www.sewabank.org and http://www.iimp.in.

Recommended Reading

- Moulick, M.; Mutua, A.; Muwanguzi, M.; Ngurukie, C.; Onesimo, M.; Wright, G. 2008. "Cash, children or kind? Developing old age security for low-income people in Africa", in Matthaus-Maier, I.; von Pischke, J. D. (eds.): *New partnerships for innovation in microfinance*, pp. 265–278 (Berlin, Springer-Verlag).
- Roth, J., Rusconi, R.; Shand, N. 2007. *The poor and voluntary long term contractual savings: Lessons from South Africa*, Social Finance Working Paper No. 48 (Geneva: ILO), also available at: http://www.ilo.org/employment/Whatwedo/Publications/lang--en/docName--WCMS_106331/index.htm
- Rutherford, S. 2006a. "The Grameen pension savings scheme", in *Finance for the poor: Quarterly Newsletter of the focal point for microfinance,* Vol. 7, No. 3 (Asian Development Bank), at: www.adb.org/Documents/Periodicals/Microfinance/finance-200603.pdf.
- Rutherford, S. 2008. "Micropensions: Old age security for the poor?", in Matthaus-Maier, I.; von Pischke, J. D.: *New partnerships for innovation in microfinance*, pp. 241–264 (Berlin, Springer-Verlag).
- Women's World Banking. 2003. *Asset building for old age security: A case for hybrid long-term savings micropension products* (New York, Women's World Banking), at: http://www.microfinancegateway.org/gm/document-1.9.38456/33.pdf

6 Microenterprise Loans

Successfully designed credit products that meet the needs of microentrepreneurs are a necessity for any MFI. It is important that the people who provide and evaluate lending services understand the different elements of lending products and the way in which these elements affect both borrowers and the viability of the MFI. ~ Ledgerwood (1998)

Microenterprise loans are often the first product that MFIs offer when they open their doors. For most institutions, they also make up the vast majority of the loan portfolio. They can be offered by almost any institutional type: regulated and non-regulated financial intermediaries, public and private projects, individual and institutional moneylenders, and others. Microenterprise loan products facilitate income generation for clients as well as for MFIs, and thus play a critical role in enabling institutions to achieve both commercial and social objectives.

This chapter begins with a brief background on the history and general characteristics of microenterprise loans. It then discusses five primary methodologies for delivering them, and explores the conditions under which certain methodologies might be more appropriate for serving a particular market than others. The chapter concludes with a discussion of microenterprise loan product design and the trade-offs that must be managed for success. The outline of the chapter is as follows:

1. Background on microenterprise loans
2. Major microlending methodologies
3. Choosing a lending methodology
4. Designing a microenterprise loan product
5. Moving from one methodology to another

6.1 Background on Microenterprise Loans

The original purpose of microfinance was to help the poor to work their way out of poverty by providing small loans that could be used for microenterprises or for income-generating purposes. This development strategy assumed that credit was a missing link. Microentrepreneurs could put affordable investment capital to good use, creating or sustaining jobs for themselves and perhaps for others as well. This approach was possible because the high marginal returns on microenterprises could increase household income and still allow borrowers to repay their loan plus interest, as shown in Figure 6.1.

Microenterprise lending became a popular development approach in the 1980s and 1990s because it could be sustainable; in other words, the income earned on the loans could cover the costs of delivering those services, including the cost of capital. To do so, microlending methodologies had to overcome four significant design challenges:

- **Collateral.** One reason why poor households typically could not get a loan from the formal financial system was their lack of assets that could be pledged as security for the loan. Microlending methodologies therefore had to develop other techniques for controlling credit risk, such as non-traditional collateral, peer pressure, social capital, incremental lending and compulsory savings.

Figure 6.1 Logic of income-generating loans

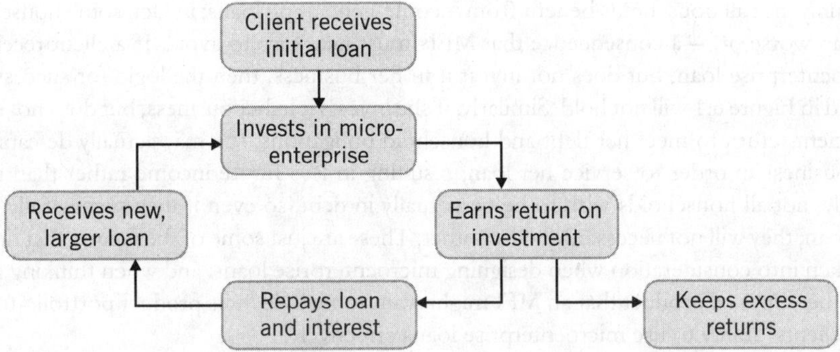

Source: Authors.

- **Information asymmetries.** To make good credit decisions, financial institutions also need to know about the borrower's character, and whether the intended purpose of the loan is likely to generate sufficient returns to service the debt. However, poor households often lack a credit history and business records, so it is difficult for financial institutions to get the information they need to make good decisions. Microcredit methodologies overcome this problem primarily by using: 1) borrower groups or guarantors to assess the character and capacity of applicants; and 2) **stepped lending**, to gradually increase the loan size over time, and learn about the borrower and the enterprise in the process.
- **Minimizing costs.** Since low-income households cannot usually make good use of particularly large loans, microlending methodologies had to develop efficient and streamlined means of delivering small loans. Some of the answers included simple procedures that could be implemented by low-cost staff members, the delegation of certain delivery activities to borrower groups, basic infrastructure in branch offices, high productivity through large client-to-staff ratios, immediate follow-up on delinquent loans, and credit scoring.
- **Reaching huge volumes.** The drive to reach large volumes of customers had a dual purpose. From a development perspective, there was a motivation to help as many people as possible; from a commercial perspective, volumes were necessary to achieve economies of scale that made sustainability possible. Innovations to reach large volumes of poor persons included group-lending methodologies, standardized policies and procedures, and more customer-responsive product design.

By finding effective ways to overcome these obstacles, microcredit programmes challenged conventional wisdom about financing the poor. They showed that poor people, especially women, could maintain excellent repayment rates, including portfolio quality that often exceeded that of the formal financial sector. Microfinance institutions demonstrated that microenterprises were a legitimate market niche.

The evidence regarding the effectiveness of microcredit in increasing incomes and creating jobs has been mixed. Thousands of client stories shared over the last four decades demonstrate that microcredit has helped many low-income households to increase or at least stabilize their incomes, but at present there is no conclusive evidence from a rigorous scientific perspective about the overall impact of microcredit (Rosenberg, 2010).

Certainly, not all households benefit from income-generating loans; in fact, some households end up worse off – a consequence that MFIs must take care to avoid. If a client receives a microenterprise loan, but does not invest it in her business, then the logic for success presented in Figure 6.1 will not hold. Similarly, if she invests it in her business, but does not earn a sufficient return to meet her debt and household obligations, she may actually de-capitalize her business in order to service her loan, resulting in less future income rather than more. Finally, not all households wish to be perpetually in debt, so even if they successfully repay one loan, they will not necessarily take another. These are just some of the factors that need to be taken into consideration when designing microenterprise loans, and when thinking about the other types of product that an MFI might want to include in its product portfolio to support clients' ability to use microenterprise loans effectively.

6.2 Major Microenterprise Lending Methodologies [10]

Microenterprise lending has taken different forms in different contexts. The differences often have a regional bias. For example, in South Asia, microloans are usually aimed at rural women who engage in agriculture, animal husbandry or other income-generating activities on a part-time basis, whereas in Latin America, microloans are largely for microenterprises in urban areas, including petty traders, small manufacturers and other informal businesses, which may employ up to five to ten people. Some microloans are intended to help people to start businesses, while others are only for existing enterprises. In certain places, microloans even target cooperative or community enterprises.

Microlending methodologies can be classified into five major schools or approaches: 1) solidarity group, 2) Grameen, 3) self-help group, 4) village banking and 5) individual microlending. Although there are numerous variations of each methodology, some of which incorporate elements of other methodologies, this section summarizes key aspects of the most common versions.

Solidarity Group Lending

This approach to microenterprise lending, popularized by ACCION International, began in the large urban markets and shanty towns of Latin American cities that were bustling with informal economic activities (see Figure 6.2). In solidarity group lending, a loan officer or promoter goes out into the markets to encourage microentrepreneurs to form borrower groups of three to ten people who already know each other, trust each other, and are willing to guarantee each other's loans. By lending to a small group of friends or business associates, solidarity group lenders overcome information asymmetry problems – group members implicitly assume some of the delivery costs, since they conduct due diligence assessments of each others' enterprises.

[10] This section was adapted from: Churchill (1999), Churchill et al. (2002) and Harper (2002).

Figure 6.2 Solidarity group lending

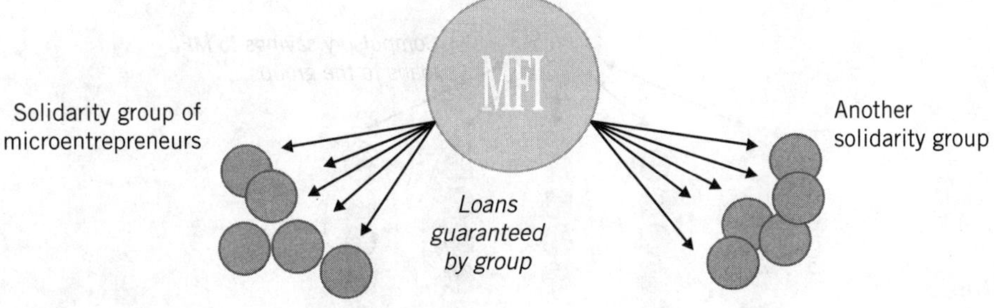

Source: Authors.

Solidarity group lenders use joint liability of the group, and the accompanying peer pressure, to control credit risk. They also usually target enterprises that have been in business for six to 12 months and have a regular cash flow; the microenterprise is often the household's primary source of income. Lenders typically employ a stepped loan approach, starting with very small loan sizes and then gradually increasing the amounts, presumably to mirror the growth of the business. This process allows borrowers to develop a credit history while minimizing the exposure of the lender. Initial loans are usually available within two to six weeks. Loan terms tend to be quite short, four to six months for initial loans and then lengthening somewhat with larger loans to repeat borrowers.

Loans are generally repaid at the MFI's branch office or into the MFI's account at a collaborating bank, with one member bringing the repayment for the whole group, although in some environments loan officers visit groups. Repayments are frequent – weekly for initial loans and monthly for more mature borrowers. Lenders may not allow groups to make partial payments, as a way of ensuring that members assist each other. There are usually no savings requirements in solidarity group lending.

The solidarity group approach appears to reach men and women in roughly equal proportions unless the lender has a particular bias or preference.

Grameen's Group of Groups

The Grameen methodology began in Bangladesh and has since been replicated, or adapted, in numerous countries around the world with varying degrees of success. Typically a self-selected group of five women – almost all Grameen borrowers are women – are linked with four or five other groups from their village to form a centre (see Figure 6.3). All meetings take place in the village, in someone's yard, or in a community centre. The centre structure enhances the efficiency of the field worker by allowing her or him to collect savings and repayments from 25 to 30 people during a one-hour meeting; and the MFI does not have to have physical infrastructure in the community.

Figure 6.3 Grameen centre

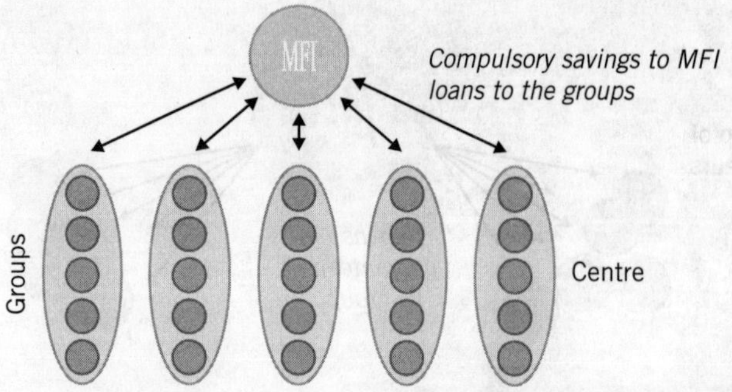

Source: Authors.

Before receiving a loan, groups undergo two to four months of weekly meetings for training and indoctrination, during which they also begin making small compulsory deposits. Income-generating loans are typically used to launch a new rural economic activity, such as cow fattening or paddy husking, which tends to be just one of the household's several income strategies. Although a profit from the investment might not be realized for six or nine months, borrowers are generally able to make the small weekly repayments during the 12-month loan term from other income, such as daily or occasional wage labour as agricultural workers.

Grameen lenders usually provide loans to individual group members on a staggered basis, initially to two of the five members. After two months of repayments, two other members are eligible for loans, and then the group leader two months later. While members are not legally liable for the debts of their fellow group members, members are not allowed to access a subsequent loan if anyone in the group is delinquent.

In the Grameen approach, the compulsory savings is kept by the MFI and serves three main purposes. First, it allows a prospective borrower group to demonstrate that it is disciplined – that the members can provide a prescribed amount of money each week. Groups that cannot manage the savings requirement do not receive loans. Second, compulsory savings serves as cash collateral for the loan. In some cases, borrowers are not allowed to access their savings unless they leave the programme. If a borrower defaults on her loan, the savings is liquidated and the balance is written off. Third, for some organizations, accumulated savings represents an important source of loan capital.

Self-help Group Approach

Originating in neighbouring India, the self-help group (SHG) approach is quite different from Grameen. The SHG approach is also known as the bank-linkage model, because it typically involves two institutions: an NGO promoter and a bank (see Figure 6.4). This relationship has been encouraged by the Indian government, through the National Bank of Agriculture and Rural Development (NABARD) and other government programmes, which pay NGOs a fee to form and train groups of rural women, and to assist them to qualify for a

Figure 6.4 Self-help group

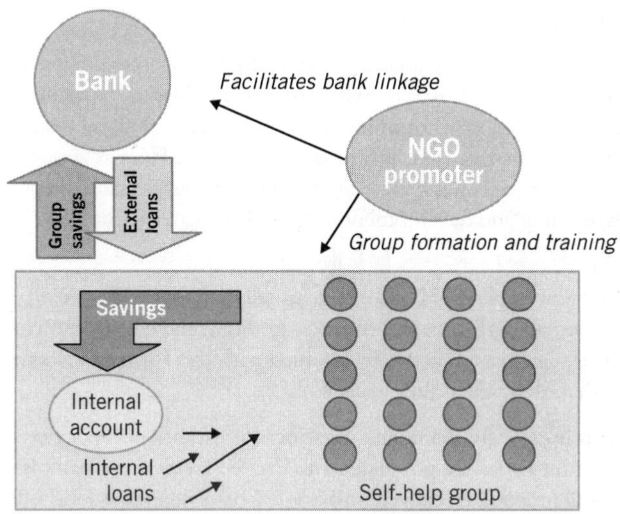

Source: Authors.

bank loan. After forging the link to the bank, if funding permits, the NGO may remain involved, assisting the members to manage their affairs, and possibly promoting federations of SHGs, or it may withdraw and work with other groups.

The members have their accounts with the SHG, not the bank; the bank does not have any direct dealings with individual members. To qualify for a bank loan, a self-help group of 20 or so members follows certain steps:

- The SHG members decide to make regular savings contributions, which are managed by the group.
- Members can then borrow individually from the SHG, for purposes, on terms and at interest rates decided by the group.
- The SHG opens a group savings account and deposits funds that are not loaned out to group members to qualify for a loan from the bank.
- The SHG maintains meticulous records of the group's attendance, savings and internal lending activities. The discipline shown in these records, and the corresponding balances in the group's savings account, can after six months make the SHG eligible for a bank loan, which it uses to supplement its own funds for on-lending to its members.

Internal loans are typically small, and used primarily for consumption purposes. Income-generating investments are more likely to occur after the SHG gets a loan from the bank. Loans are used for a wide range of farm and off-farm income-generating activities.

The SHG performs the same functions as those required by the Grameen system, but on their own behalf, since the SHG is effectively a micro-bank carrying out all the intermediation tasks associated with savings mobilization and lending. Banks may demand to know who the members are, and impose certain conditions as to the uses of the loans that they make to the SHG, but the SHG is an autonomous financial institution in its own right.

NABARD also encourages the banks to lend to SHGs by refinancing the loans at the subsidized rate of 6.5 per cent. Loans to SHGs are excluded from the maximum interest ceiling of 12 per cent that still applies to other loans under Rs 20,000, but banks have generally not taken advantage of this freedom, and most still lend to SHGs at about 12 per cent. The resulting 5.5 per cent spread is felt to be enough to cover the transaction costs so long as the SHG promotion, training and development task has been carried out by an NGO, at no cost to the bank.

The on-time repayment rates on SHG loans are usually well over 95 per cent. This is so much higher than the normal performance of loans granted under government "schemes" to poorer people that the banks are generally satisfied with this form of intermediation, even if the spread is less than that which they usually obtain.

Since India has a fairly extensive banking infrastructure, this methodology is reasonably effective in reaching out into sparsely populated rural areas. Even if the bank is not particularly close, groups can still function effectively and create a bank linkage as long as they do not have to keep their group funds in a bank account and can negotiate infrequent repayments to lower the transaction costs of interacting with the bank. Other groups do not link with a bank at all, but rather gradually build up their own capital.

Village Banking

Although similar to the SHG approach, the lending methodology commonly known as village banking was developed independently by FINCA in Latin America in the mid 1980s. In its original design, shown in Figure 6.5, village banks of 30 to 50 women had the same responsibilities for financial intermediation as Indian self-help groups – collecting regular savings from group members and lending it to each other (or investing it elsewhere). Well-performing village banks could then borrow money from an external organization (usually an international NGO), and on-lend to group members. To keep credit management simple for the village bank, loan conditions were highly standardized:

- four-month terms with 16 equal weekly repayments;
- US$50 initial loan with subsequent loans equalling the last loan plus accumulated savings;
- mandatory savings (20 per cent of the loan amount) per loan cycle paid in weekly installments; and
- full repayment by the entire group a prerequisite for additional funds.

Figure 6.5 Village banking model

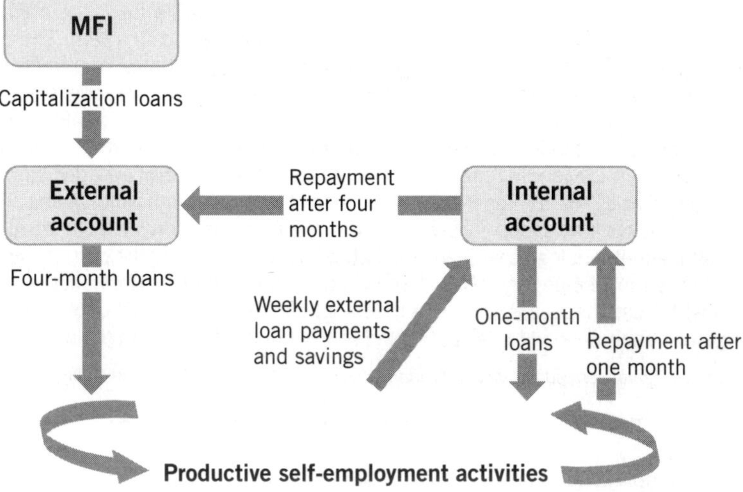

Source: Hatch and Hatch, 1989.

The initial expectation was that the village bank's internal account would grow over time and accumulate sufficient funds to capitalize its loan portfolio and become autonomous. This graduation objective was soon dropped, because it was not really in anyone's interest. Village banks generally preferred having access to external credit, rather than relying solely on their savings. For the international NGO, which played both the promoter and provider role – unlike in the Indian context, where the promotion was paid for by the government – graduation meant losing mature banks that generated the greatest revenues.

The village banking methodology has been adopted by MFIs around the world, and they have adapted it in different ways in an effort to make it more client responsive and sustainable. Some institutions have eliminated the internal account; others have accelerated the pace with which clients can access larger loans; many have relaxed restrictions on the loan term, repayment frequency or savings requirements. As a result, what now characterizes the village banking methodology is its delivery of services to relatively large groups of clients who have some level of control over decision-making (see Box 6.1). The methodology is often used to serve poorer and more rural market segments, and frequently includes the provision of non-financial services.

Individual Microlending

Individual microlending, the only methodology that does not rely on groups to overcome the challenges of designing microenterprise loans for the poor, adapts conventional banking to the unique characteristics of informal businesses. This approach gathers information to assess risk, not through documents, but through inspection of the business and household, and through recommendations of respected persons. Table 6.1 illustrates the combination of assessment tools used by four individual lending MFIs.

> **Box 6.1 Methodology Peer Groups at the MIX**
>
> The Microfinance Information eXchange (MIX) classifies MFIs into four methodology peer groups: 1) individual; 2) solidarity; 3) village banking; and 4) mixed. The principal criterion used to classify a methodology as village banking is control over decision-making. If there is group control over the lending out of internal funds or requests for external funds, then the methodology is classified as village banking. Thus MFIs that use a self-help group methodology are placed in this category. Other methodologies that involve groups in the lending process but do not give them control over decision-making are classified as solidarity, regardless of the size of group through which loans are made. Products that have no group involvement are classified as individual. Institutions that use multiple methodologies with no one methodology dominating the portfolio are classified into the mixed category. MFIs that wish to compare their performance with that of other institutions that use a similar methodology can refer to the methodology rows of the peer group benchmarking tables published semi-annually by the MIX (www.themix.org).
>
> *Source: Email correspondence with Blaine Stephens, COO and Director of Analysis, MIX, 2010.*

Like banking, individual microlending assesses character, collateral and capacity in making a credit decision, but places a different emphasis. The primary factor is the individual's character, followed by the capacity of the business and household to service the loan. The character of a prospective borrower is assessed through interviews with neighbours, customers, suppliers and community leaders. Loan assessments determine the cash flow of the entire family economic unit, based on the assumption that low-income households often have several sources of income as part of their survival and risk reduction strategy. The cash flow analysis does not usually take into consideration the impact of the borrowed funds on the earning potential of the household.

Individual microlenders will take collateral when possible, but the security options are more expansive than with conventional banking. Individual microlenders often request co-signers to guarantee the loans, and may accept jewellery, productive assets from the business, or even household furniture and appliances as collateral. These forms of **non-traditional collateral** serve primarily to demonstrate the borrower's commitment, and are rarely used as a secondary repayment source.

6.3 Choosing a Methodology

Whether an MFI is thinking about introducing a microenterprise loan product for the first time, or is thinking of introducing an additional microenterprise loan product to complement its existing product offering, the decision about which methodology to use will be determined by three main factors: 1) the MFI's outreach objectives; 2) the needs of its target market; and 3) the characteristics of the environment in which the product will be delivered.

Table 6.1 Tools used by individual microlenders to assess new borrowers

Credit assessment	ABA	ADEMI	BRI	CMACs
Credit officer visits business	Yes	Up to 3–4 visits, sometimes unannounced	Once	Usually once
Visit to client's home	No	Yes	Yes	Usually once
Analysis of business and household cash flow	Not detailed: assessment of productivity and age of business	Gradually refined with data accumulated over time	Important factor in determining loan size	Extremely detailed for first loan and updates with each additional loan
Check on outstanding debts from other sources	No	Yes, and review credit history based on utility bill payments	Yes	Yes
Calculate repayment capacity	Study potential profitability of activity	Include potential profits from use of loan	Instalment 75% of monthly net income of the business before the loan	Clients must be able to demonstrate repayment capacity before use of loan
Character references	Friends and neighbours	Neighbours, employees, local bar and shops, suppliers; recommenda-tions from current clients	At least two neighbours or influential community members	Neighbours, employees, local bar and shops, suppliers
Knowledge of community	Build inside information about existing clients and applicants	Build inside information about existing clients and applicants	Village head confirms that the applicant lives in the village and has a business	Not consciously, as occurs from other activities
Bank account information	When applicable	When applicable	When applicable	When applicable
Verification of collateral pledged	As psychological pressure	Deed or copy of ownership for client file	Copy of land/house title or tax receipts	Original proof of ownership held in client file during loan period
Verification of capacity and co-signer	N/A	Assess payment capacity including assets and income	N/A	Assess payment capacity including assets and income

Source: Churchill, 1999.

An institution that aims to serve remote areas that do not yet have access to formal financial services is unlikely to make the same methodology choices as an institution that wants to help existing customers in urban areas to grow. The poverty level, gender, and education level of potential borrowers will influence an MFI's decision, as will the cash flow of the income-generating activities to be financed. Population density, the cohesiveness of the communities where the MFI wishes to work and the infrastructure available in those areas will also have an impact.

Thus, to choose a methodology, an MFI must first be clear about who it is choosing the methodology for – who does it want to serve and where? Once it makes this decision, the next step is to determine whether a group or individual approach would be most appropriate.

Group vs. Individual Lending

The group approach enables an MFI to pursue social as well as economic objectives. Some MFIs use the group meeting to educate borrowers about such topics as nutrition, child immunization, family planning and HIV/AIDS. Others encourage the group to become a building block of a broader network that allows entrepreneurs to cooperate on business issues, such as bulk buying or hiring security guards for the marketplace, and on social issues such as digging wells or pit latrines. Group methodologies also have an implicit empowerment objective, as members develop leadership, facilitation and negotiation skills. For SHGs and the original village banking model, members also learn how to manage the group's accounts.

If given the choice, some low-income borrowers would prefer a group loan. They express concern about what would happen if they had an individual loan and could not make a repayment. Borrowers also appreciate and benefit from the social and economic support system inherent in group methodologies. Women in particular seem to appreciate the networking opportunity provided by the group approach.

But borrower groups are certainly not for everyone. People who are more entrepreneurial or who have larger businesses often feel constrained in a group, since the loan sizes or repayment conditions are frequently applicable to the group as a whole, and designed to meet the needs of the lowest common denominator (or the standardized system of the MFI). These individuals may also become victimized by free-riders in a group setting, which has caused some MFIs to lose their best borrowers.

The volatility of portfolio quality is a greater concern for group methodologies. Collateral, even non-traditional collateral, can have a stronger influence on repayment performance than group guarantees, particularly as loan sizes become larger and the cost of making a payment on another member's behalf may outweigh the benefits. Volatility also results from the connection between group members, which allows the repayment behaviour of one person to influence the behaviour of others more quickly than with individual borrowers. Delinquency problems within a group may not be visible to an MFI until they become serious enough to affect the group as a whole.

Group methodologies are more appropriate for new businesses or microenterprises that cannot predict their cash flow, and for persons who have no collateral. The group approach tends to be more effective in close-knit communities that have many fairly homogeneous businesses. In communities where persons do not trust each other, or where business persons do not know many others with similar-sized businesses, group lending is less likely to succeed.

The per-loan costs for individual lending are much higher than those for group lending. Rather than delegating responsibilities to a borrower group, the MFI assumes the expenses of assessing the character of the applicant and the cash flow of the business and household. Plus, field staff deal with one client at a time, during the loan application process as well as during disbursement and repayment transactions. Consequently, individual microlending approaches cannot profitably offer loan sizes that are as small as those offered by group lenders, and therefore cannot reach as poor a market. As summarized in Table 6.2, group and individual methodologies are complementary approaches to serving different markets.

Table 6.2 Pros and cons of group and individual methodologies

	Advantages of group lending	**Advantages of individual lending**
INSTITUTION	• Economies of scale – more clients served by a fixed operating investment • Economies of scope – ability to deliver multiple services through group mechanism • Achieve social and economic objectives • Reduce information asymmetry • Improve loan collection • Costs and risks transferred to clients • Reduce moral hazard risks through group monitoring	• Able to reach diverse markets • Effective to support growing businesses • Less volatile portfolio quality • Able to learn about individual clients' character and capacity
CLIENT	• Building block to broader social and business network • Collateral not required • Assistance with repayments • Social benefits including empowerment	• Product design can be more flexible and adapted to individual needs • Most clients would prefer not to guarantee the loans of others – no free-rider problem
	Disadvantages of group lending	**Disadvantages of individual lending**
INSTITUTION	• Less effective in heterogeneous markets • Difficult to enforce contracts • May contribute to desertion • Reduced learning of individual clients' credit histories • Dependence on group leadership • Covariant risk and contagion • Group formation and maintenance can be costly, time-consuming	• Not as effective in reaching women, very poor borrowers, start-ups • Costly delivery model – no efficiencies through bundling • Assume all of the credit risk • Purely an economic intervention • May not be cost-effective means for serving rural or remote communities
CLIENT	• Potential for corruption by group leadership • Limited flexibility of the loan product • Lack of privacy • Potential free-riders • Costs and risk are transferred to clients	• Requires collateral • No built-in support network to help during difficult times

Source: Adapted from Churchill, 1999.

Selecting a Group Lending Model

If an MFI is launching its first microenterprise loan product and it decides that it wants to use a group-based methodology, then the differences between group methodologies become important. Some of the factors that can help guide the selection of a model are listed below.

1. **Autonomy.** Is it a priority for the MFI to support the creation of autonomous or self-managing groups? If so, the SHG or village banking methodologies will be most appropriate.
2. **Group formation.** Does the MFI want to take responsibility for promoting the concept of group lending, and forming or finding groups through which to lend? If not, then the SHG model will be the one to consider. Identifying and developing a relationship with an appropriate local partner will be critical to success.
3. **Location.** Will borrower groups visit the MFI, or is the MFI going to bring its services to the borrower group? If the MFI will go to the groups, a large group methodology is likely to be more cost-effective, although technology or high population density could enable solidarity groups to work as well.
4. **Diversity.** How heterogeneous is the target market? The more diverse customers' needs are, the more difficult it will be to serve them effectively using a large group methodology.
5. **Business development.** The more enterprise experience clients have, and the larger their businesses are, the more likely it is that solidarity lending will be feasible. Larger groups spread both risk and the cost of providing financial services over a larger number of borrowers, which can make it possible to provide smaller loans to poorer borrowers or those just starting a business.
6. **Social cohesion.** How difficult will it be for clients to find or create a group? If there is a strong tradition of community organization or many existing groups through which to work, a large group methodology may be more convenient for clients and the MFI. If, however, there is little trust in a community, or population densities are low, institutions may find it easier to work through solidarity groups.

Diversification Options

Since group and individual methodologies complement each other so well, MFIs that already offer one are likely to find their greatest diversification opportunity in introducing the other. Many institutions that began by offering group loans have introduced individual loans in order to retain customers who have outgrown their group. Other MFIs, such as Equity Bank in Kenya and several of the BPRs in Indonesia, started with individual lending and have diversified into group lending in an effort to reach new market segments.

It is less common for MFIs that already offer a group-based microenterprise loan product to introduce another group-based microenterprise loan product using a different methodology, but institutions do occasionally find this strategic. CrediAmigo in Brazil offered solidarity group and individual microenterprise loans, but launched a village banking product in 2005 to serve rural clients. By September 2007, it had reached more than 33,000 customers in 11 states using the new methodology (Fonseca, 2008). In India, Bhartiya Samruddhi Finance Limited (BSFL), which is part of the BASIX Group, offers loans to individuals, SHGs, joint liability groups, mutually aided cooperative thrift and societies (MACTS) and revolving savings and credit associations (ROSCAs).

Of course, a third option is for an institution to introduce another microenterprise loan product using the same methodology already in use to target a particular market segment. XacBank in Mongolia, for example, offers household loans, salary loans, apartment loans, student loans, small business start-up loans, growth loans, development loans, harvest loans, herdsman loans, deposit-backed loans and overdraft loans, all through an individual lending methodology. Although this type of diversification is likely to be the easiest, it may not generate sufficient benefits to make the costs of doing so worthwhile. As discussed in Chapter 23, every product that an MFI adds to its portfolio increases the complexity of its operations. Thus institutions may find it more strategic to increase the flexibility of existing products to meet the needs of new market segments, rather than to introduce entirely new products (see, for example, the case of Prodem at the end of this chapter.)

6.4 Designing a Microenterprise Loan Product

No matter which methodology an MFI chooses, it will need to balance three competing objectives in its loan design: 1) minimizing credit risk; 2) maximizing accessibility and worth for clients; and 3) minimizing transaction costs. Each of these objectives is important, but there are trade-offs amongst them. Most microlending methodologies emphasize credit risk controls to compensate for the fact that their loans are unsecured. This tends to keep portfolio-at-risk low, but it also results in higher transaction costs and accessibility barriers that limit outreach.

Certainly MFIs need to minimize risk, but if they can find a better balance between their risk controls, their costs, and the value provided to clients, they can increase their volume and profitability. One way to find a better balance is to challenge assumptions about the contribution of each risk control. As MFIs define the features of their loan product, they should consider not only which controls they could put in place, but which controls would be most cost-effective. Some of the issues worth taking into account are described below.

- **Eligibility.** Who is eligible to access a loan? Anyone in the community? Only people with a certain amount of business experience? Only women? Persons with incomes below a certain level? The broader an organization's eligibility criteria, the larger its potential market within a specific geographic area. The narrower the criteria, the more control an MFI has over the risk it is exposing itself to.
- **Interest rate and fees.** Do all loans have the same interest rate, or does the MFI differentiate the rate for different segments of the market (for example, offering a discount for low-risk, repeat borrowers)? Will there be financial incentives or penalties for timely or late repayment? Will there be an application fee or any other additional charges associated with the loan? Will these charges be easily understood by clients?
- **Loan amount and duration.** Small loan amounts for short terms help keep the reins tight on credit risk, but they increase transaction costs for screening and disbursement, as loans come up for renewal more frequently. Ultimately, the loan term should be linked to the loan purpose and the household's or business's cash flow: for how long do they need to use the money?
- **Repayment frequency.** Similar to loan term, frequent repayments enhance credit risk control, but create higher transaction costs. In fact, most microlending costs are associated with repayments. What would be the effect on credit risk if instalments were paid

fortnightly or monthly instead of weekly? Can the slightly higher credit risk be justified by the dramatically lower transaction costs?

- **Payment schedule.** Most MFIs opt for equal instalment amounts to simplify record-keeping, but clients tend to have irregular incomes and expenses – some months they can afford to pay more, other months they cannot afford to pay anything. For organizations that have more advanced information systems, flexible repayment schedules will enhance the product's worth and probably lower credit risk. In addition, for low-risk customers, a line of credit would allow them to decide when and how much they repay.
- **Collateral and collateral substitutes.** The most common types of collateral and collateral substitutes in microlending are: 1) group guarantees; 2) co-signers or personal guarantors; and 3) non-traditional collateral such as business equipment, household appliances or livestock. Will one or more types of collateral be required? Certainly, the amount of collateral required will increase as the loan size increases, but will there be any flexibility in the type of collateral clients provide? For microloans, it is helpful to keep in mind that the market value of the collateral tends to be less important in leveraging timely repayment than its worth to the borrower. If group guarantees are used, how will the MFI ensure that members of a self-formed group have a strong bond?

Of course, these features are not the only elements of product design that need defining. MFIs must also decide how they will market their product, receive applications, screen those applications, disburse funds, collect repayments, and manage delinquency should it occur. As an institution defines each of these processes, it can look for ways to minimize risk, transaction costs and accessibility barriers.

Take, for example, the screening process. Assessing an applicant's creditworthiness can be quite expensive, but it is also quite important, especially if the lender's fallback repayment method is not particularly strong. An MFI could delegate part of the assessment process to a borrower group, but it would need to consider what kind of training borrowers might require to perform this function effectively. Would clients find the reduction in financial costs and increased access to loans more valuable than the increase in transaction costs (in other words, the time they would have to spend in group training and meetings)? Would the training cause long delays in accessing loans? Could it help borrowers understand better how to assess their own borrowing capacity and avoid over-indebtedness? What checks could the institution put in place to verify the quality of group assessments?

For individual loans, the MFI's assessment of each client is more rigorous and time consuming, and thus more expensive. How long will that assessment remain valid? Could one assessment be relevant for two or three consecutive loans? Could the client be offered access to a credit line for a particular period of time instead of one lump sum disbursement? Could subsequent assessments be made less onerous for the MFI and client on the basis of repayment performance or through improved record-keeping during the period of the initial loan? Credit committees are a critical part of the individual loan assessment process, but adjusting the number and seniority of participants sitting on the committee according to the size or riskiness of the loans being appraised can help manage the cost, risk and worth trade-offs.

Decisions about many of the other processes that an MFI needs to consider – such as the methods for disbursing and repaying loans – are usually made based on concerns regarding fraud and security risks, and are dictated partly by the financial sector infrastructure. For

example, do MFIs want field staff disbursing loans in cash, or can they issue cheques without creating significant disbursement delays and accessibility barriers? Does the group need to meet all together to make their loan repayments, or can a group representative collect individual repayments and remit them to the MFI?

Microlending methodologies are rapidly evolving as MFIs develop more experience and are willing to experiment in an effort to find a better balance between risk, cost and accessibility. Activity-based costing and process mapping are being used by more and more institutions to identify the steps in their lending process that are most expensive, and to gauge the impact that product design changes might have on transaction costs. Equity Bank's turnaround has been linked to market research that was done in 2001, which revealed access barriers created by its pricing policies. By revising its pricing strategy, increasing its transparency and responding to other issues raised by customers, Equity was able to vastly increase its outreach without sacrificing profitability. Within one year, it doubled the number of active borrowers to more than 18,000 (Coetzee et al., 2002). Today, it has more than 540,000 active borrowers.

A small but increasing number of MFIs are looking at ways to use the lending process to manage a much broader array of risks than just credit risk. This is tricky, as procedures that could be put in place to protect MFIs or clients from social and environmental risks could easily increase transaction costs and limit access to financial services. However, institutions such as FMO (the entrepreneurial development bank of the Netherlands), Triodos Facet and Triple Value Strategy Consulting are working together to create tools to make this more feasible (see Box 6.2).

Box 6.2 Designing a Loan Product for the Triple Bottom Line

In the view of FMO, the social and economic benefits for which microfinance is widely praised can decrease if environmental and social (E&S) risks are neglected. Thus it requires that all of its borrowers (including MFIs) implement an environmental and social management system (ESMS) that screens and monitors clients on E&S issues, and encourages action when necessary. Some of the main issues faced by MFIs include sanitation and safety in the work place, pollution, use of chemicals and pesticides, destruction of forest, child labour, and the financing of illegal activities.

To facilitate and support MFIs' implementation of a viable ESMS, FMO has developed a toolkit with practical guidelines for loan officers and other MFI staff to use when working with clients on environmental and social issues.

- The Office Guide explains how ESMS can be put in place in alignment with the MFI's regular credit evaluation, approval, monitoring and reporting processes.
- The Field Guide provides MFI loan officers with practical guidance for assessing and addressing E&S themes with clients. It includes fact sheets for 24 of the sectors that MFIs work in, which give practical examples of issues that might be raised, an explanation of the benefits to clients of doing so, and recommendations for possible prevention and mitigation measures that might be discussed with clients and possibly included in the loan contract.
- The Training Guide provides material to help MFIs build capacity among staff to establish and implement an ESMS system.

The Toolkit can be found at: http://www.fmo.nl/smartsite.dws?id=531

Source: Adapted from FMO, 2010.

Technology is also opening up tremendous opportunities to decrease risk and transaction costs while increasing client worth. SafeSave in Bangladesh, for example, has used handheld computers (PDAs) to provide dual controls without having two staff in the field at the same time. It also reduced its account error rate to less than 0.1 per cent, which was a tenfold improvement over its performance with paper-based systems (Staehle, 2005). In Peru, Mibanco used credit scoring to lower its weighted average response time from 8 days to 4.6 days for new clients and to 2.3 days for repeat clients without increasing portfolio-at-risk (Caire et al., 2006).

In Mexico, FINCA is using customized prepaid cards to give clients access to their loans on an as-needed basis 24 hours a day (Muñoz et al., 2009). And in Brazil, nearly 30,000 banking correspondent outlets use point-of-sale (POS) devices and bar code scanners to provide financial services in every municipality in the country, even though many are reachable only by boat or plane (Ivatury, 2005). As illustrated in Box 6.3, branchless banking is dramatically reducing the cost of delivering financial services to poor people.

Box 6.3 Using Branchless Banking to Overcome Transaction Costs

Branchless banking can offer basic banking services to customers at a cost of at least 50 per cent less than what it would cost to serve them through traditional channels. The biggest cost saving is on transactions that can be done completely electronically, through mobile banking. In the Philippines, a typical transaction through a bank branch costs the bank US$2.50; this would cost only US$0.50 if it were automated by using a mobile phone. The cost reduction from using agents rather than banks for remote cash transactions is equally dramatic. Banco de Credito in Peru estimates that a cash transaction at a branch costs about US$0.85, while the same transaction at an agent would cost US$0.32. Tameer Bank in Pakistan estimates that, in the Orangi slum of Karachi, the set-up cost of a bank branch would be 30 times more than the set-up cost per agent, which is about US$1,400. Monthly running costs average about US$28,000 for a branch, compared with US$300 for an agent, but also a much larger share of monthly running costs is variable for an agent than for a branch.

Source: Ivatury and Mas, 2008.

6.5 Moving from One Methodology to Another

For MFIs that decide to diversify by introducing a microenterprise loan product that uses a methodology that is different from the one(s) currently used, it is important to recognize that an effective product design will include more than a simple definition of the new product's features. The design needs to consider how the new product will integrate with existing products and systems.

As illustrated in Table 6.3, the lending processes for group and individual microenterprise loans differ substantially. Small and large group methodologies have more in common, but fundamental differences remain, particularly in the acquisition, appraisal and repayment processes. MFIs that wish to move from one methodology to another will need a plan for introducing and managing the changes that are required to transition staff and systems from an old way of doing things to the new. Some of the issues that will need to be dealt with include:

- How to ensure that employees are both able and motivated to make the changes required.
- Will clients access old and new products differently? Will they be able to access both at the same time? Under what conditions will existing customers be able to "graduate" from one product to another, and how will the MFI help them make this transition?
- Will existing infrastructure have to be adapted, or will new infrastructure be created? How will people, data and other assets be transferred from one system or location to another?
- Can the risks created by the new product be managed through existing staff and procedures?
- How will the MFI avoid the cannibalization of one microenterprise loan product by another?

These issues are discussed in Chapter 23, but they are raised here to caution MFIs against underestimating the level of effort and care that diversification will require, even within an existing product line.

Table 6.3 Comparing group and individual lending processes

	Individual	Group
Acquisition	• Variety of techniques used to market the product: personal sales, advertising, sales promotions, direct marketing and public relations • MFI decides who is eligible	• Members find new clients • NGO promoter may assist • MFI advertising through appropriate channels can also help • Group (mostly) decides who is eligible
Appraisal	• MFI decides who should borrow and how much • Credit committees enhance quality • Credit bureaus and collateral registries, if available, can support the process	• Members decide who should borrow and how much • MFI can request that groups follow a particular assessment process • MFI may provide training in assessment or mutual responsibility • MFI may look for group discipline before lending
Disbursement	• Clients usually come to MFI • Loan size and tenure are personalized • Timing of disbursement is personalized	• Occurs within weekly, bi-weekly or monthly meetings • Can be more frequent if internal account exists • Group may go to MFI, or loan officer may go to group • Loan sizes are often similar for all group members • Loan tenure is often fixed • Disbursements may be staggered

Table 6.3 (continuted)

	Individual	Group
Repayment	• Clients usually come to MFI • Repayment amount and frequency are personalized • MFI can track the individual's repayment	• Occurs within weekly, bi-weekly or monthly meetings • Group (or representative) may go to MFI or MFI go to group • Members of a group repay on same schedule • Schedule usually consists of equal payments • MFI usually tracks only the group's repayment
Renewal	• Clients usually come to MFI • Timing is driven by client • Dynamic efficiencies make repeat loans cheaper and faster	• Renewal takes place in regular group meetings • Stepped lending approach is common • Renewal typically is not allowed if anyone in group is delinquent • Instability can result if not everyone wants to renew
Delinquency Management	• Loan officer monitoring and follow-up • Escalation process is backed by collateral and/or personal guarantee	• Group monitors individual repayment; MFI monitors group • Members first pressure each other to pay, then pay for each other if necessary and seek reimbursement later • MFI exerts pressure on entire group • MFI is exposed to contagion risk

Source: Authors.

Main Messages

1. To choose a lending methodology, an MFI must first be clear about who it is choosing the methodology for – who does it want to serve and where?
2. Group and individual lending methodologies should be seen as complementary approaches to serving different market segments.
3. When designing a microenterprise loan product, strike a balance among three competing objectives: minimizing credit risk, minimizing transaction costs, and maximizing client worth.
4. Do not underestimate the changes that may be required to diversify within an existing product line.

Case Study: Adjusting Product Design for a New Market in Bolivia

When Prodem, a non-bank financial institution in Bolivia, moved into rural areas, it began lending with the same solidarity group methodology it had used in urban areas. It offered a joint-liability loan repayable in regular, equal instalments. It evaluated loan requests by examining the household cash flow of potential borrowers to ensure that they had the ability to repay the loan being requested. By focusing on household cash flow, Prodem introduced the first innovative element of its rural lending methodology. Rather than enter rural areas with a focus on agricultural lending, it entered with a focus on lending to microentrepreneurs, including farmers. It considered both farm and off-farm income sources when examining the cash flow of a potential borrower.

This was an interesting, but problematic, innovation. Since 90 per cent of Bolivia's rural population worked in the informal sector, and since much of their work was agriculture-based, monthly cash flows varied greatly with the timing and quality of harvests. Borrowers needed a loan product that was not only authorized on the basis of cash flow, but was also repaid on the basis of cash flow. The product Prodem initially marketed did not allow this flexibility.

After spending several months collecting information on its clients' activities and cash flows, getting to know local crop cycles and the experiences of neighbourhood moneylenders, staff at Prodem's Caranavi branch proposed to national management a loan product with repayment terms that would allow borrowers to service their loans in a manner that was appropriate for their cash flow. Instead of making equal monthly payments, groups could customize the size of each month's payment to concentrate payments of principal in those months when the group generated greater income. Payments would still be made monthly, but the amount and composition of each month's payment would vary. In some months interest only would be paid, and in others, capital with interest.

After a year of experimentation with the new product, Caranavi's active loan portfolio grew 36 per cent compared with the 29 per cent average portfolio growth of all other rural branches that were operating by the beginning of 1994. It achieved this level of growth while maintaining a 30-day portfolio-at-risk below 0.3 per cent.

Despite the successful implementation of the new product, Prodem's rural clients continued to press for more flexibility, and staff sought ways to accommodate that request. They recognized that the new payment plan had a fundamental weakness: it assumed that the members of each solidarity group were involved in the same productive activities. It did not allow for differences in cash flow needs. As such, it made it difficult to negotiate a payment plan that was equally sensible and convenient for all members of the group. Unless the group was extremely homogeneous, some members had difficulty making the large payments required in certain months, because their household's cash flow did not match the group's cash flow. At the same time, those groups that were highly homogeneous presented Prodem with a different kind of risk – that of total default. Should the common crop be destroyed by bad weather or disease, everyone in the group would suffer, and no one would remain in a strong enough position to help the others out.

Prodem saw room to improve the methodology and designed yet another, more personalized payment plan. As demonstrated in Table 6.4 below, this payment plan allowed each member of a group to design a personal repayment schedule that matched his or her household's cash flow. Members still made regular payments as a group, but the size of the payment varied from month to month, as did the size of each individual's portion of the payment. There were only two restrictions. Each payment had to include a portion of capital and interest, and no one payment could equal more than 40 per cent of the original loan amount.

The personalized payment plan was introduced in 1996, first at Prodem's most established rural agencies, and later nationwide. The product proved effective because it provided greater flexibility for clients while simultaneously lowering risk for the institution (see Table 6.4).

Table 6.4 Sample schedule for a three-person group using the personalized payment plan

Group member payments									
Group repayment date	Rafael coffee farmer / tyre sales Loan = US$474			Miguel coffee farmer / carpentry Loan = US$474			Jorge coffee farmer Loan = US$474		
	Payment	Interest	Total	Payment	Interest	Total	Payment	Interest	Total
Aug 21	9	18	27	19	18	37	19	18	37
July 18	9	17	26	19	17	36	19	17	36
Oct 16	19	17	36	95	16	111	19	16	35
Nov 13	9	16	25	19	13	32	19	16	35
Dec 12	95	16	111	19	12	31	19	15	34
Jan 8	95	12	107	9	11	20	19	14	33
Feb 5	95	9	104	9	11	16	19	13	32
March 5	95	5	100	66	11	77	19	13	32
April 3	19	2	21	66	8	74	95	12	107
May 3	19	1	20	76	6	82	95	8	103
May 28	10	1	11	76	4	80	132	6	138
TOTAL	**474**	**114**	**588**	**474**	**127**	**596**	**474**	**148**	**622**

Source: Lee, 2000.

This case study was adapted from Lee (2000) and Frankiewicz (2001).

Recommended Reading

- Berenbach, S.; Guzmán, D. 1992. *The solidarity group experience worldwide* (Washington, DC, ACCION International), at: http://resources.centerforfinancialinclusion.org/
- Churchill, C. 1999. *Client-focused lending: The art of individual microlending.* (Washington, DC, Calmeadow), available at: http://resources.centerforfinancialinclusion.org/
- Churchill, C., Hirschland, M.; Painter, J. 2002. *New directions in poverty finance: Village banking revisited*, Chapter 7 (Washington, DC, The SEEP Network), at: http://www.seepnetwork.org/Resources/637_file_New_Directions_in_Poverty_Finance.pdf
- Dellien, H.; Leland, O. 2006. *Introducing individual lending*, WWB how-to guide (New York, NY, Women's World Banking), at: http://www.microfinancegateway.org/gm/document-1.9.29474/33826_file_Individual_20Lending_20How_to_20Guide.pdf

- Harper, M. 2002. *Grameen bank groups and self-help groups: What are the differences?* (Filigrave, ITDG Publishing), at: http://www.microfinancegateway.org/gm/document-1.9.27267/3249.pdf
- Ledgerwood, J. 1998. *Microfinance handbook: An institutional and financial perspective*, Sustainable banking for the poor (Washington, DC, World Bank), at: http://issuu.com/world.bank.publications/docs/9780821343067
- Rosenberg, R. 2010. *Does microcredit really help poor people?*, CGAP Focus Note No. 59 (Washington, DC, CGAP), at: http://www.microfinancegateway.org/gm/document-1.1.4333/03.pdf
- Westley, G. 2004. *A tale of four village banking programs: Best practices in Latin America* (Washington, DC, IADB), at: http://www.microfinancegateway.org/gm/document-1.9.27393/22782_VB_BPP_FINAL.doc

7 Housing Loans

The problem with housing is not building it. We all know how to build houses. It's not demand. There are plenty of people who want houses. The problem is allowing the people who want the houses the financing capacity to buy them. ~ Miller, quoted in Phillips (2007)

Along with food and clothing, shelter is one of the most basic human needs. Seventy-five per cent of countries in the world consider adequate housing to be so important that they have ensured it in their national constitutions or legislation (Hokans, 2008). And yet UN-Habitat has reported that nearly 1 billion people currently live in slums. This represents one-third of the world's total urban population and 78 per cent of the urban population in the least developed countries. It predicts that an additional 3 billion people – approximately 40 per cent of the global population – will need housing by the year 2030 (UN-Habitat, 2003).

Given such trends in global demographics, financial products that can enable individuals and communities to improve existing housing or build new homes are likely to be in significant demand and represent an interesting opportunity for microfinance institutions. This chapter explores the nature of that opportunity, and the challenges that MFIs must confront if they wish to diversify into housing finance. It addresses five main themes:

1. Why offer housing loans?
2. What makes housing loans different from other loan products?
3. Key design decisions
4. Risks and challenges
5. Assessing potential demand

7.1 Why Offer Housing Loans?

Although savings products can be used to finance housing, these products can also be difficult for microfinance institutions to introduce (see Chapters 4 and 5). In addition, they can be relatively unattractive solutions for low-income households because of the time it takes to accumulate sufficient funds and, in many cases, the cost of accessing a savings service.

Housing loans, on the other hand, can be relatively easy for microfinance institutions to introduce using staff, structures and methodologies that they may already have in place for microenterprise lending. Cross-selling is possible without having to incur significant additional operating costs. The larger average size and longer term of housing loans lower administrative costs per unit lent, and repayment performance is often better than with other types of loan product.

Housing loans can make an MFI's overall portfolio more stable by moderating the seasonal fluctuations inherent in enterprise lending. They can improve client satisfaction by providing customers with another option for meeting their financial service needs. Housing loans can also give MFIs access to a huge new market. The potential demand for housing microfinance that was suggested in the introduction has been confirmed by MFI experience to date. In Peru, for example, Mibanco made 3,000 housing loans and was covering both the operational and capital costs of its new product within a year of its introduction (Brown and Garcia, 2002). Additional estimates of demand for housing loans are provided in Box 7.1.

Box 7.1 Estimating Potential Demand for Housing Loans

- In Morocco, two surveys found that 88 per cent of households have or are planning a productive activity in the home, and more than 83 per cent of households want to take a loan to finance home improvement – but 93 per cent of households did not have access to formal finance, and had to resort to other means (UN-Habitat, 2005).
- In Peru, 82 per cent of the 8 million people living in greater Lima are classified as poor. At least half of poor households and 60 per cent of the poorest households express a strong desire to expand or improve their home within the next 12 months (UN-Habitat, 2005).
- In Mexico, interviews with 1,000 households in three Mexican cities found that the effective demand for housing microfinance (US$122 million) exceeded that for microenterprise finance by six times (US$20 million) (Ferguson, 2004).
- In India, nearly half of SEWA Bank's total loans disbursed are housing and infrastructure loans (Biswas, 2003).
- Within ACCION's Latin America network, the total number of clients with outstanding housing microfinance loans grew from 15,000 to about 38,000 between December 2002 and December 2005, and the portfolio jumped from US$38 million to US$117 million in the same three-year period. By December 2005, ACCION affiliates that offer housing loans reported 18.7 per cent of their total loan portfolios in housing products (Mesarina and Stickney, 2007).

For low-income clients housing loans are attractive, because they speed up the building process. They can supplement the funds that clients are able to accumulate through other sources, making it possible to purchase at one time the necessary quantity of materials to complete a particular phase of construction. This is particularly important for materials that cannot be easily stored or are vulnerable to theft, such as cement or roofing material. Depending on their design, housing loans may also give clients access to electrical, plumbing or other expertise that they may not be able to find in their own social network.

In addition to these benefits, housing loans provide both MFIs and low-income households with an opportunity to invest in asset-building, which is important for several reasons:[11]

- **Housing is typically the greatest source of wealth creation available to the poor.** It usually appreciates in value over time. It can be rented out for extra income. It can be used as collateral for a loan to start or expand a small business, or to cope with an unexpected event, so that the need for cash does not result in the sale of productive assets.
- **An investment in the home can also be an investment in the business.** Microentrepreneurs often use their homes to generate income. The home might be a place to produce goods, store inventory, or conduct sales transactions. Thus improving the roof of a home could prevent inventory from getting wet; adding a room could allow the business to expand; and installing sewer or water infrastructure could improve sanitation and working conditions.

[11] This list was adapted from Brusky (2004) and Jamii Bora (2006).

- **Shelter helps ensure personal safety and health.** Poor housing condition is one of the major causes of disease and premature death among the poor. By contrast, improvements in housing can have a direct and positive impact on the health, security and self-esteem of homeowners and their families. Elderly parents who own a house can offer shelter to their income-earning children in return for food and other care. When housing is destroyed by a natural or man-made disaster, housing loans can help rebuild communities (see Chapter 18).
- **Housing is the biggest expense in the household budget.** Most urban poor are tenants, and even slum dwellers can pay considerable amounts in rent every month for their small shacks. If they could build their own house, they could pay the same amount of money per month in loan repayment and after a few years own their home. This will be a considerable saving in their household budget, and free up resources for investment in their businesses and their children's education.

Because of the potential for economic, social and environmental impact, housing loans will be a particularly interesting product for MFIs that are pursuing a triple bottom line. They can also be a valuable tool for encouraging customer retention, not only because of the progressive nature of housing microfinance, which is likely to keep customers coming back to finance various phases of construction, but also because of the psychological attachment that clients typically have to their homes. MFIs that are willing and able to support clients' efforts to improve their homes may find themselves rewarded with greater customer loyalty.

7.2 How Do Housing Loans Differ from Other Loan Products? [12]

Housing loans differ from microenterprise loans in that they finance customers' habitat needs rather than business needs. Such needs may include:

- repairs to walls, roofing or foundations;
- expansion (for example, adding rooms or floors);
- land purchase;
- property legalization;
- basic infrastructure, such as sewer, water or electricity hook-ups;
- new house construction; or
- the purchase of an entirely new home.

Traditionally, housing finance has focused on the last two needs listed above, and has consisted primarily of **mortgage lending**, in which loans are secured by a lien on the house or land that is being developed. This type of finance has not been very useful to low-income households because of their lack of credit history and legally documented land titles, as well as their inability to borrow enough money at real interest rates to finance a completed home, unless repayments are stretched over long periods of time. Even when institutions have found ways of providing such long-term financing through partnerships, poor borrowers have had difficulty sustaining repayments over such long periods.

[12] This section is adapted from Daphnis (2004a).

The financial services that are increasingly referred to as "housing microfinance" tend to focus on other habitat needs, specifically for home improvement and progressive construction. According to Ferguson (2004), studies show that low-income families highly prefer improving their existing home to purchasing a new home elsewhere, so that they can maintain relationships with friends, family and neighbours. If they build, they tend to build in small, incremental steps, so they need financing that fits the pace of that approach.

Institutions that provide housing microfinance use methodologies that are adapted from microenterprise lending:

- Loans are for relatively small amounts, and are based on clients' willingness and ability to repay.
- Repayment periods are relatively short (especially compared with mortgage lending), and are on par with mid- to high-end microfinance individual loans.
- Loan pricing is expected to cover the real, long-run costs (both operational and financial) of providing the service.
- Loans are not heavily collateralized, if at all, and collateral substitutes are often used.
- Loans tend to finance habitat needs incrementally.
- Loans can be linked to prior participation in savings or more traditional microenterprise loan services.

Table 7.1 summarizes these similarities, but it also highlights four important differences that distinguish housing loans from microenterprise loans. First, housing loans are designed to finance habitat needs, not business needs. Because of this focus, their evaluation procedures and auxiliary services can be quite distinct. Second, average loan sizes are typically larger and terms are generally longer than the average working capital loan. Third, because of the larger loan sizes and longer terms, interest rates tend to be slightly lower. For example, a 2005 survey of ACCION International's Latin American partners revealed that interest rates for housing loans ranged from 24 to 35 per cent, while the average microenterprise loan was priced at 48 per cent (Mesarina and Stickney, 2007). Finally, housing loans tend to be made to individuals, rather than groups. Holding a group collectively liable for all members' repayments of large sums of money over a long period of time creates higher risks that are less likely to be accepted by lenders or borrowers.

Since low-income households often conduct some portion of their entrepreneurial activities from their home, there can be overlap between microenterprise and housing loan products. Indeed, clients can and will seek to access microenterprise loans for housing and housing loans for microentrepreneurial activities, depending on which type of loan product offers them the best terms. In Mexico, for example, FinComun offers a successful housing microfinance loan product, yet it estimates that 10 to 15 per cent of its business loans are still used for housing improvements related to business operations (UN-Habitat, 2008).

Clients will also seek to use housing loans for purposes unrelated to business or housing, especially if housing loans are cheaper than other loan products. When construction assistance is not part of a housing loan's design, the product becomes, in effect, a consumer loan whose declared purpose is housing but whose actual purpose may never be known. MFIs need to take this into account when deciding whether and what kind of housing product to develop (see Box 7.2).

Table 7.1 Comparing microenterprise, mortgage and housing microfinance loans

Characteristics	Microenterprise loans	Housing microfinance loans	Mortgage-backed loans
Target market	Microentrepreneurs	Low-income microentrepreneurs and salaried workers	Middle- to high-income clients, salaried, formal sector workers with a stable income
Loan term	Usually 2–12 months	Usually 2–24 months for home improvements, and 2–5 years for land purchase or construction	Long-term (more than 5 years)
Loan amounts	Small, generally range from US$50 to US$1,000	Varies, but generally 2–4 times larger than average working capital loans (US$100–5,000)	Large
Interest rate	Between 25% and 90%	Same as working capital loans or slightly lower	Typically lower than business loans
Delivery method	Group or individual	Almost always provided to individuals	Individual
Loan use	Working capital	Home improvement Progressive building	New house construction House purchase
Type of guarantee	Mostly unsecured: co-signers, savings, pledged assets, psychological	Mostly unsecured: co-signers, savings, pledged assets (not necessarily land title), psychological	Formal mortgage (ownership of dwelling or land) collateralized by the property
Associated non-financial services	Possible access to business development services	Possible access to technical assistance for land acquisition, land registration and construction (including self-help building techniques)	Uncommon

Source: Adapted from Mesarina and Stickney, 2007, and Brusky, 2004.

7.3 Key Design Decisions

There are three main design decisions that must be made when developing a housing loan: 1) should the product be linked to other products or should it be delivered independently; 2) should the loan finance new home construction or only home improvement; and 3) should construction advice be provided as part of the loan product? Each of these issues is discussed below.

Box 7.2 How Many Loans Does an MFI Need?

The overlap between housing microfinance loans and other types of loan calls into question the value that will be added by introducing a housing loan product into a portfolio that already contains other loan products. Would it not be more efficient to offer one or two flexible loan products whose size and term can be adjusted to match the stated loan purpose and the borrower's household or business cash flow? BRI's Unit Desa system has successfully offered just one loan product for decades, and ADEMI in the Dominican Republic meets housing microfinance needs through a generic consumer loan product. Of course, the success of both institutions has been dependent on their having the staff and systems necessary to manage such flexibility.

Other institutions opt to launch a separate housing loan product despite the additional complexity that this brings (see Chapter 23), because they find multiple, standard products easier to manage than one flexible product. In highly competitive markets, it can be easier to market several slightly different products to different market segments than one general product. In addition, since housing is a basic need that provides security and health benefits, it is likely to be a more acceptable and less risky product than one that finances all types of consumption, but this is true only if it does, indeed, finance only housing, and if the assessment of a borrower's capacity to repay is accurate enough that the MFI can avoid over-indebting its clients.

A separate housing loan product will usually make sense for MFIs that want to lend beyond the zone of primary product overlap – in other words, to offer longer-term loans for relatively large amounts to individuals rather than groups. This kind of product will have features, eligibility requirements, assessment methods, delivery processes and risks that differ substantially from those of typical microenterprise loan products, and warrants being managed separately.

Source: Authors.

To Link or Not To Link?

There are two main types of housing microfinance loan: 1) linked products; and 2) stand-alone products. **Stand-alone housing loans** are delivered alongside but independently of any other products that an institution might offer. Thus a new client can apply for this kind of loan without ever having used the institution's services before. With **linked housing loans**, only clients that have an established relationship with the institution are eligible to apply. Access to the product is linked to previous usage of some other product.

Each type of loan has its advantages. Stand-alone products are better at helping MFIs to diversify their client base. They are generally seen to be more appropriate for institutions that already use an individual lending methodology and have the systems in place to evaluate borrower repayment capacity. Stand-alone products are fairly common in Latin America, but are also in use elsewhere, for example by the Kuyasa Fund in South Africa and by CHF International in the Middle East.

Linked products help institutions to manage their credit risk and costs by using the information provided through clients' previous performance to help determine willingness and ability to pay. They seem to be more appropriate for institutions that embrace group lending as their primary methodology. The Grameen Bank (Bangladesh) and SEWA Bank (India) are two of the best-known MFIs that link housing microfinance to other products. At SEWA Bank access is linked to a client's savings performance, while at Grameen access is linked to at least two years' membership as a borrower and saver. Linked housing loans can serve as a performance incentive and retention strategy, since clients usually value access to larger, longer-term term loans, and will pay on time and remain with the institution in order to gain (or retain) this access. Linked products can also be useful for MFIs that must limit the number of housing loans they make because of capital or other constraints.

New or Improved?

As discussed above, housing microfinance loans are typically designed to finance home improvement and progressive construction. The majority of the poor do not have clear title to the land they occupy, and would not be able to service a loan that would be large enough for new home purchase or construction. Even when the applicant and the property are able to qualify for mortgage financing, the high upfront lump sum costs associated with meeting down payments and title deed registration costs can present significant barriers to accessing a housing loan (Porteous, 2006).

Nevertheless, some MFIs are financing new home purchase and construction through mortgage loans. ACCION affiliates, for example, report that 38 per cent of their housing loan portfolio consists of new construction or mortgage loans (Mesarina and Stickney, 2007). Hokans (2008) reports on some of the creative strategies being used by MFIs to overcome the barriers to mortgage-backed lending. In Morocco, for instance, Al Amana and Zakoura offer short-term microloans to qualifying borrowers to finance down payments for the eventual purchase of subsidized housing units, with long-term finance being provided by Banque Marocaine du Commerce Exterieur (BMCE). In El Salvador, title processing and mortgage registration fees are being capitalized and rolled into the loan amounts approved. In India and Kenya, partnerships are making new home construction for slum dwellers possible (see Box 7.3).

The decision about whether to finance new home construction or purchase will largely be driven by the needs and resources of an MFI's target market. Market research can help inform an MFI's decision, but simply asking clients whether they would like to finance new or improved housing will not provide accurate enough information to inform product design. Clients will often express a preference for large, long-term loans but not be able to afford them (see Section 7.5 below).

Construction Assistance

One of the most substantial debates with respect to the design of housing loans revolves around the issue of technical assistance. Should construction advice or supervision be provided as part of the housing loan? Proponents argue that construction assistance can strengthen the quality of housing improvements, thus leading to greater client satisfaction and better repayment. At Grameen Bank, for example, homes built according to the Bank's standard specifications fared much better during the flood of 1987 than those that were not (Escobar and Merrill, 2004).

Construction assistance can also help borrowers determine how much of what kind of materials they need, where to find those materials at a reasonable cost, and how large a loan they

Box 7.3 Partnering for New Home Construction for Slum Dwellers

Two innovative examples of the potential of planning and participation for new home construction can be found in India and Kenya. The Society for the Promotion of Area Resource Centres (SPARC) is a large, membership-based NGO located in one of the largest slums in Mumbai, India. It launched a community mobilization and planning campaign that led to the resettlement of 50,000 slum dwellers in their own units, constructed by social developers. Although the whole project took over three years to complete, and involved significant efforts to bring the local government, banking sector and donors together, SPARC was able to fully finance new homes for displaced slum dwellers. By selling land rights in a hot real estate market, it was able to repay a commercial bank loan that was supported by a guarantee from USAID.

Jamii Bora Trust is an NGO that provides financial services to approximately 240,000 slum dwellers in Kenya. It procured 293 acres of land south of Nairobi and obtained planning permission to develop a community, known as Kaputei, which will eventually house 2,000 families. Jamii Bora collaborated with engineers from the University of Nairobi to develop systems for wastewater recycling and solar power that give the town a sustainable water and power supply. Building materials are being produced on site in a factory that provides employment to Jamii Bora members, and a commercial centre will eventually provide shops, a health centre, post office, primary school, and other facilities. Within Kaputei, neighbourhoods of 250 families each will have their own centre, planned and maintained by families themselves, with a park, playground for children and community hall. Jamii Bora clients who have been members for at least three years and have successfully managed three business loans are eligible to buy a home in Kaputei, which Jamii Bora will finance through a 10–15-year loan with instalments that are on par with rents paid in the slums (approximately US$20–35 per month). Capital is raised locally through a loan guarantee provided by social investor Unitus. As of May 2009, 300 families had moved into their new homes in Kaputei.

Source: Adpated from Hokans, 2008, Reavis, 2008, and www.jamiibora.org.

need to request in order to complete a particular housing improvement. It can assist borrowers with permits and other legal or safety requirements. Perhaps most importantly for MFIs, construction assistance may encourage repeat business (see Box 7.4). In an impact study on lenders in South Africa, for example, borrowers who received handouts that explained how to avoid common building problems reported that the information received was highly useful, and they were more likely to go back to that MFI for another housing loan (Hokans, 2008).

Those who do not support the integration of construction assistance into housing loan design argue that such assistance is costly, unnecessary, and outside an MFI's scope and expertise. Clients, they say, have their own trusted sources of advice within their community, and are more likely to live with their own decisions than someone else's. If clients do not like the outcome of a housing investment that involved construction assistance from an MFI, they may blame the poor results on the MFI and refuse to pay their loan.

Fundación Habitat y Vivienda (FUNHAVI) in Mexico and Asociación para el Desarrollo de Microempresas, Inc. (ADEMI) in the Dominican Republic demonstrate that both approaches to construction assistance can be successful. The two MFIs are similar in many ways, yet FUNHAVI sees the non-financial services that it provides to clients as a core component of its mission, while ADEMI has publicly stated that such assistance is contrary to its operating philosophy. Both MFIs report repayment rates approaching 100 per cent (Daphnis, 2004a). Analysis of these experiences and others (see Box 7.5) has led most in the microfinance industry to conclude that construction assistance may be useful, but it is not a necessary component of housing microfinance.

If neither approach is clearly better than the other, how can MFIs decide which one to take? Some of the factors that will influence the decision include:

1. **Attitude towards pre- and post-loan due diligence.** If an MFI already performs pre-loan due diligence on its microenterprise loans (for example, to assess whether a client's desired loan amount is appropriate to and can be used for the purpose declared on the loan application), it may want to extend this practice to housing microfinance. Similarly, if it follows up after a microenterprise loan is disbursed to ensure that it is used for the intended purpose, it may wish to provide construction oversight (Daphnis, 2004a).
2. **Mission.** If an MFI has a strong social mission to improve living conditions for the poor, it may find construction assistance helpful in ensuring that its social objectives are met. MFIs that work with the poorest often find that construction assistance is necessary to overcome deficiencies in human or social capital.
3. **Marketing strategy.** If an MFI operates in a competitive environment, construction assistance may help differentiate its housing loan product from others.
4. **Partnership potential.** If an MFI can identify other organizations that could provide construction assistance, it can offer clients these services as fee-based options that can be added onto a basic loan product without the MFI needing to have in-house expertise to deliver such services itself.

Box 7.4 Construction Assistance and Client Retention

Those in favour of construction assistance argue that it can affect client retention in several important ways. First, there is the connection between satisfaction and loyalty. If construction assistance can help a customer make her home improvements with higher quality or at a lower cost, she is more likely to value that assistance and her relationship with the MFI that provided it, and return for more in the future.

Second, construction assistance can help a client map out her desired home improvements over several incremental steps, creating a long-term goal with a clear plan of how to achieve it. Once a client has a plan that shows how a series of housing investments will achieve her long-term vision, she is likely to have greater incentive to repay her current loan and borrow again. With each step she takes towards her long-term vision, she is also likely to tell others about her positive experience, possibly generating new business for the MFI.

Finally, housing microfinance produces physical structures that people often identify with the financing institution. Thus the quality of the housing improvements financed by the MFI can have marketing and institutional image implications that microenterprise lending does not. Many MFIs believe that when a client's neighbours see her improved living conditions, they will be more likely to take loans to improve their own homes. Naturally, a highly visible, poorly constructed home would have the opposite effect. To the extent that construction assistance can ensure a minimum level of quality, it can also protect an MFI's brand.

Source: Adapted from Tilock, 2004.

Box 7.5 Mixed Results on Housing Loans and Construction Assistance

ACCION and Integral, an MFI in El Salvador, contracted an independent professor of architecture from the University of the Andes in Colombia to conduct a survey on housing quality in El Salvador. The survey's objective was to document the impact that housing loans had in improving client housing, in terms of quality of life, reduction of vulnerability (particularly to earthquakes), and client satisfaction. A nationwide sample of 56 recent home improvements covered three categories: improvements financed by Integral with construction assistance; improvements financed by Integral without construction assistance; and improvements not financed by Integral. A key conclusion from the survey was that there was no significant difference in construction quality among the three categories. In other words, construction assistance provided by Integral did not make houses more liveable, or reduce their vulnerability to natural disasters. Home improvements financed met minimum standards for earthquake resistance, whether or not clients had received construction advice from Integral. However, the budget portion of the technical evaluation did help clients by predicting the actual costs of home improvements, allowing borrowers to control their construction budgets and complete their projects with loan funds.

In housing loan pilot tests with Women's Union of Kien Giang (WU-KG) and Capital Fund for the Employment of the Poor (CEP), Habitat for Humanity Vietnam compared the satisfaction of clients who had not received a technical assistance package with those that did. Although additional study is needed, focus group discussions revealed that clients who did not receive technical assistance showed a clear willingness to pay for it in the future, having encountered problems that could have been foreseen and perhaps prevented by technical assistance, either before, during or after loan disbursement. Some of the problems mentioned include: 1) miscalculation of the cost or amount of materials needed, which resulted in under-borrowing (and subsequently, borrowing elsewhere at a high rate of interest or compromising the quality of construction to finish the project); 2) being overcharged for materials and labour; 3) damage to materials (for example, cement left in rain or damaged by flooding); and 4) cracks in foundations or tile work due to poor-quality materials or labour. Clients found that the loans cost them a lot more in the long run, both financially and emotionally, when they did not have sound advice.

Source: Adapted from Shumann, 2004, and Kruize, 2007.

Market research during the product development process can help MFIs determine the right approach. The key question to ask is whether borrowers would be willing to pay for construction assistance, and if so, how much they are willing to pay for what kind of assistance. As summarized in Box 7.6, there are many different types of construction assistance. The greatest challenge is finding an offering that clients will value sufficiently to be willing to pay for its cost.

7.4 Risks and Challenges

Institutions that want to offer a housing loan product should be prepared to meet a number of challenges. The first four, access to longer-term capital, insecure land ownership, eligibility criteria and collateral requirements, are faced by most providers. The last two challenges, lower life expectancy and subsidy management, may be faced depending on the environment within which an MFI is operating.

Box 7.6 Types of Construction Assistance

Construction assistance tends to fall within two main categories: pre-loan assistance and post-loan assistance. Pre-loan assistance is provided before a loan is made, and is part of the loan assessment process. Post-loan assistance is provided after a loan is approved, and tends to focus on compliance and construction quality.

Pre-loan assistance

- **Construction design.** This involves visiting the house to be improved, taking measurements, and sketching out the existing structure and proposed improvements. The design can be used as a basis for the construction budget, and should ensure that the proposed improvement is technically sound. It could involve working with clients to help determine and map out their needs and aspirations for their home.
- **Budget development.** This can range from assessing a budget provided by the client to ensure that the proposed cost estimates are reasonable, feasible, and in line with the client's repayment capacity, to developing the actual construction budget, including pricing the different inputs.
- **Client education.** This can include guidance on what materials to use and where to purchase them, how to negotiate with contractors and manage the construction process, as well as training in self-help construction.

Post-loan assistance

- **Construction follow-up.** This assistance is generally used to verify loan use, inspect work quality, and provide advice to the client or contractor. It can also be used to represent the client's interests with contractors and material providers. It is typically provided through site visits during construction, and may be tied to loan disbursements, so that the loan is disbursed in instalments on the basis of predetermined progress and quality criteria.
- **Construction materials.** Part or all of a loan may be disbursed in the form of building materials, or through vouchers or other pre-paid arrangements. By procuring construction materials itself or providing access to such materials through partnerships with suppliers, the MFI can help prevent loan diversion and provide access to lower-cost, quality materials through economies of scale.

Source: Adapted from Tilock, 2004.

Access to medium- and long-term capital. MFIs that want to offer medium- or long-term housing loans should fund them with liabilities of a similar duration in order to avoid interest rate and liquidity risks (see Box 10.6 in the chapter on leasing). Unfortunately, this kind of funding is usually difficult for MFIs to access. Some institutions solve the problem by capturing savings, but many MFIs are not legally allowed to mobilize savings, and those that are allowed are often unable to mobilize enough savings to be able to meet the demand for housing loans. Some MFIs, such as SPARC, Jamii Bora, Al Amana and Zakoura, have used credit guarantees and commercial bank lines of credit to access longer-term finance. Others have used their own equity, and have financed only as many housing loans as the available funds would allow them to finance.

Commercial banks have relatively easy access to medium- and long-term capital, and have thus been able to reach the greatest scale with their housing microfinance products. Mibanco, for example, had a housing loan portfolio of US$30 million (15 per cent of its total loan portfolio) at the end of 2007, and expects that to increase to 25 per cent by 2012 (Martin, 2008). Yet many commercial banks that are interested in the low-income market find it a challenging one to reach. They are entering housing microfinance by "outsourcing" a part of their portfolio to a service company or partner organization. In Ghana, HFC Bank and CHF International, with assistance from USAID and UN Habitat's Slum Upgrading Facility, created a non-financial service company, Boafo, that services housing loans which are kept on the balance sheet of the bank. HFC acts as a joint venture managing partner and minority shareholder. In India, ICICI Bank has partnered with CapStone Trust to deliver housing microfinance through a similar model (Hokans, 2008). Such partnership arrangements offer MFIs opportunities for access to longer-term capital while giving banks access to the low-income market.

Collateralized debt obligations like the ones being arranged by Housing Microfinance LLC, Microfinance Loan Obligations S.A., and Symbiotics have provided medium-term financing for a small but important number of MFIs providing housing microfinance (Hokans, 2008, and Symbiotics, 2007). These may be a more significant source of financing in the future, especially since they can include cross-currency swaps that allow the underlying term loans to be denominated in local currencies, which helps MFIs manage exchange rate risk.

Insecure land ownership. In most developing countries, poor families do not possess formal proof of land ownership. Thus, if regulations stipulate that housing loans may not be extended without formal property titles, MFIs may not be legally able to develop a housing loan. They could, however, develop a multipurpose consumer loan and tailor the loan amount and the repayment period as appropriate for housing, which is what ADEMI has done in the Dominican Republic (Daphnis, 2004b). If regulations do not require formal property titles, MFIs have more flexibility and can assess an applicant's land security status instead of ownership (see Box 7.7). Proof of land ownership is not critical for housing microfinance, as MFIs often use non-traditional collateral to secure housing loans, but land security is essential. Without evidence of a solid relationship between the borrower and the property being developed, housing microfinance becomes quite risky.

Eligibility requirements. Since housing loans finance habitat needs and not income-generating activities, the process and criteria used to evaluate whether a customer is eligible to receive a housing loan may be quite different from those used to assess eligibility for microenterprise loans. In housing microfinance, eligibility is based primarily on current income and debt levels, land security, and proposed loan use (CHF International, 2001). Thus MFIs must have the staff and systems in place to be able to measure business and household cash flows. Understanding the proposed loan use is particularly important so that the amount of funds required to complete the project can be reliably estimated. As discussed above, if an appropriately sized loan is not approved and the housing improvement cannot be completed, there will be disincentives for repayment. Loans will need to be secured, although not usually by a formal land title. A key finding from reviews of country experiences to date is that cost recovery rates on unsecured loans with flexible or multiple guarantees are as good as or even better than on mortgaged loans (Vance, 2004).

Box 7.7 Land Security

A client enjoys land security when the following conditions exist: 1) she has the use of a property at the time the loan application is made; 2) the MFI determines that the client will not be forced to vacate the property during the time it takes to repay the loan; and 3) that determination is supported by usual and customary local practices. In other words, in the absence of legal proof of ownership, the MFI should satisfy itself that potential clients would not be forcibly evicted while the loan is still active. The underlying assumption is that repayment performance will be enhanced if the client has a vested long-term interest in the property being financed.

Criteria for land security should vary from country to country – and perhaps, within a given country, from MFI to MFI, based on the MFI's attitude towards risk. These criteria include:

- a written agreement between the buyer and seller of the land;
- a long-term rental agreement between the home owner and government for use of public lands;
- the number of years during which a family has inhabited a property without paying rent and without due notice from the rightful owner; or
- payment by the home owner of taxes to the government.

Source: CHF International, 2001, and Daphnis, 2004b.

Large housing loans granted as parallel loans to clients who were already repaying working capital loans have been cited as the key causes of loan portfolio quality problems at both Finansol/Corposol in Colombia and Grameen Bank in Bangladesh (Christen, 2004). To avoid this outcome, MFIs that offer housing microfinance usually set a limit on the loan amount borrowed so that instalments are no more than 20 to 35 per cent of either net or gross monthly income (Daphnis, 2004b). CHF International, for example, recommends that monthly housing loan payments should not exceed 25 per cent of the household monthly income and that the total debt burden (including housing loan repayment) should not exceed 40 per cent of the monthly household income (CHF International, 2001).

Choosing the right combination of collateral and collateral substitutes.[13] There is a close relationship between loan size and the type and quality of collateral that should be requested to secure a housing loan. The main factors in determining the choice of collateral are:

- the transaction costs involved in verifying ownership of assets and valuating them;
- the ease of enforcement and foreclosure procedures; and
- the likely sale price.

The larger the loan, the more likely is the need for some form of collateral that retains its value over time. Current microfinance practice indicates that it makes sense to secure a mortgage for a loan of over US$5,000. However, owing to high transaction costs, there is a general preference for securing loans with a mix of guarantees. For the reasons discussed in Box 7.8, even

[13] This discussion of collateral and collateral substitutes is adapted from Vance (2004).

when a title is taken, it is used more to put psychological pressure on the borrower to honour her debt than as a means for recuperating capital in the event of default.

Co-signers provide the most common form of guarantee in housing microfinance, but compulsory savings is also popular as it demonstrates both an ability and a willingness to pay. The CEMEX case at the end of this chapter provides one well-known example of this strategy. Another common strategy is to put a lien on household assets. A few MFIs use pension fund contributions, life insurance policies or future wages as collateral. Along the US-Mexican border, for example, FUNHAVI has developed relationships with a number of manufacturing assembly plants (maquildoras) to lend to their employees, with loan payments being deducted directly from the borrowers' salary (Ferguson, 2004).

Life expectancy. In countries or communities with a relatively short life expectancy, it is more difficult to provide medium- to long-term housing loans. In Zambia, for example, one of the consequences of the AIDS epidemic is an average life expectancy of just 38 years. Housing lenders there require homeowners to purchase life insurance, which is included in the monthly mortgage payments (Phillips, 2007).

Managing subsidies. To reach poorer market segments, subsidies for construction assistance or infrastructure improvements may be necessary. Indeed, there are good reasons for governments to subsidize low-income housing. Housing microfinance can complement those subsidies (see Box 13.3 in the chapter on grants), but it is generally recommended that financial services be kept distinct from the subsidy element. In a slum improvement programme, for example, loans to individual slum-dwellers should be managed separately from state subsidies for infrastructure and sanitation (Brusky, 2004).

Box 7.8 Why Land Titles May Not Be Useful Collateral

For housing microfinance, the use of property as collateral can be problematic for several reasons. If land tenure is uncertain or foreclosure laws are not well developed, it may be difficult for the MFI to foreclose on the property should a client default on her loan. Even when local laws allow the MFI to take over the property of a delinquent client, other barriers may prevent the MFI from finding a new owner for that property. A formal real estate market may not exist, thus not allowing for accurate valuation of the property; potential buyers may not have the financial resources to purchase the property at the agreed-upon value. Assuming these barriers can be overcome, the MFI must decide whether it wants to be involved in the business of taking over and selling real estate – a new line of business for MFIs and a difficult one for socially oriented institutions that do not want to leave borrowers homeless, especially if the value of the loan outstanding is but a fraction of the value of property being seized.

Source: Adapted from Daphnis, 2004b.

7.5 Assessing Potential Demand [14]

It was argued at the beginning of this chapter that there is demand at a global level for housing microfinance. This is encouraging, but it is hardly sufficient information for MFIs to determine whether there is sufficient demand for housing microfinance within their particular target market to warrant development of a housing loan product. This final section provides MFIs with some guidance on the issues that should be considered when assessing demand for this product.

As shown in Figure 7.1, potential demand is a function of three factors: need, willingness to borrow, and affordability. Need refers to the range of housing improvements that potential clients might want to make. Willingness to borrow refers to the target market's interest in taking a loan to finance those needs. It is heavily influenced by the terms of the loan being offered, and is often expressed as a percentage (for example, 75 per cent of clients surveyed say that they would take on a three-year home improvement loan carrying a 35 per cent interest rate). Affordability is determined by the cost of the home improvement, the potential clients' repayment capacity, and the loan terms (for instance, repayment period, frequency and location, collateral requirements, fees and interest rate).

Once an MFI has selected its target market, it can use focus groups, surveys, site visits and case studies to collect the information it needs to assess these three factors. Some of the tools that may be useful in this process include:

- **Housing stock assessment.** This assessment determines, independently of borrowers' preferences, which habitat improvements appear to be needed and how often these "needs" occur. For example, 40 per cent of houses surveyed may need new roofs, 10 per cent may require improved or new latrines, and 75 per cent may need sanitary floors. The assessment requires a technically competent person to visit the targeted communities and systematically inspect the existing housing stock.
- **Potential client baseline survey.** The goal of this survey is to obtain baseline data on the targeted population. It should identify income and expenditure levels, current and past use of alternative formal and informal financial services, savings, debt obligation levels, and perceived housing needs.
- **Cost estimation.** A simple worksheet can be used to estimate the costs of completing the different home improvement activities identified in the housing stock assessment and target client baseline survey. It may be informative to interview individuals with local construction experience to determine the costs of materials and labour for the proposed improvement projects.

[14] This section is adapted from CHF International (2001) and Daphnis (2004b).

Figure 7.1 Estimating potential demand for housing microfinance services

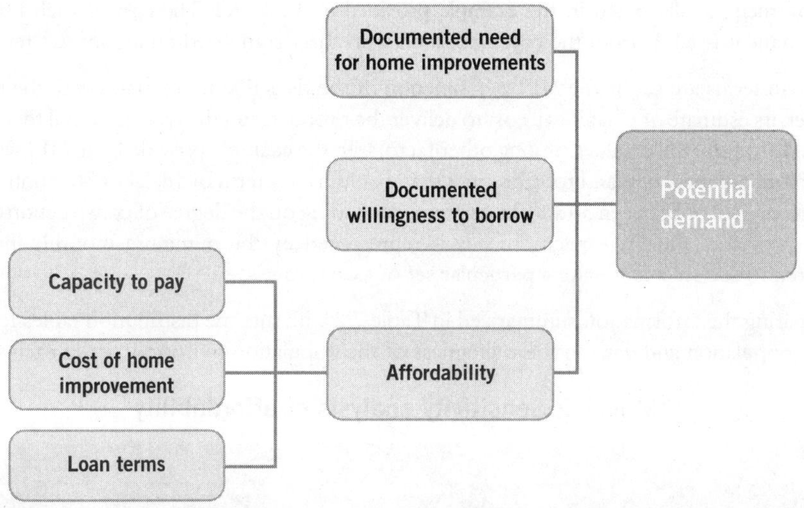

Source: CHF International, 2001.

Interpreting this data will not necessarily be a straightforward process. People do not always accurately disclose information on their income, expenses and savings, particularly if they are aware of the purpose of the survey. They may understate their income and overstate their expenses. In addition, their perceptions of how much they need to borrow may not correspond with how much they think they can afford for a monthly payment (see Box 7.9). Thus information should be verified by comparing data gathered from multiple sources. For example, disposable income could be estimated through a combination of direct client feedback, an assessment of expenses and savings, and interviews with people familiar with the population group surveyed, such as the MFI's loan officers, the promoter for a community-based organization, or a local builder.

Box 7.9 Estimating Demand at PLAN International

PLAN International's housing finance surveys showed that economically active but very poor PLAN families in nine countries around the world tended to consistently overstate housing needs and understate income. Only when PLAN asked clients about specific amounts for affordable monthly payments and narrowed the types of housing intervention to home improvements did it generate information that proved useful in the ultimate design of the housing loan. In those instances, PLAN had decided before conducting the surveys that it would offer some type of home improvement loans with a short repayment period, as opposed to the long-term, high-value loans its clients invariably wanted but could not realistically afford.

Source: Daphnis, 2004b.

Another useful process for analysing the data gathered is sensitivity analysis of affordability. This analysis examines the relationships between capacity to pay, loan terms and the cost of a housing improvement, as illustrated in the example provided in Table 7.2. The cost of each housing improvement is taken from the cost estimation worksheet completed during market research.

The loan terms are set by the MFI as a function of the risks that it associates with the target market, its estimate of what it will cost to deliver the product, and the type of capital that it has available to fund the product, among other factors. In the example provided, the MFI wanted to explore potential demand for a product that would have a term of 18, 24 or 36 months and an interest rate of between 30 and 38 per cent, depending on the degree of construction assistance provided. Finally, capacity to pay is represented by the minimum monthly income required to service a loan with a particular set of loan terms.

Comparing the information summarized in Table 7.2 with income distribution tables for the target population and data on the willingness of the population to borrow under each set of

Table 7.2 Sensitivity analysis of affordability

	Cost of improvement	Interest	Monthly payment in 18 months	Minimum income	Monthly payment in 24 months	Minimum income	Monthly payment in 36 months	Minimum income
With no construction assistance								
Roof	200	30%	$13.93	$63.34	$11.18	$50.83	$8.49	$38.59
Latrine	120	30%	$8.36	$38.00	$6.71	$30.50	$5.09	$23.16
Sanitary floor	150	30%	$10.45	$47.50	$8.39	$38.12	$6.37	$28.94
Room addition	400	30%	$27.87	$126.67	$22.37	$101.66	$16.98	$77.18
New core home	850	30%	$59.22	$269.18	$47.63	$216.03	#36.08	$164.02
With some construction assistance								
Roof	200	34%	$14.34	$65.17	$11.60	$52.72	$8.93	$40.61
Latrine	120	34%	$8.60	$39.10	$6.96	$31.63	$5.36	$24.37
Sanitary floor	150	34%	$10.75	$48.88	$8.70	$39.54	$6.70	$30.46
Room addition	400	34%	$28.68	$130.34	$23.20	$105.44	$17.87	$81.22
New core home	850	34%	$60.93	$276.98	$49.29	$224.06	$37.97	$172.60
With full construction assistance								
Roof	200	38%	$14.75	$67.03	$12.02	$54.65	$9.39	$42.68
Latrine	120	38%	$8.85	$40.22	$7.21	$32.79	$5.63	$25.61
Sanitary floor	150	38%	$11.06	$50.28	$9.02	$40.99	$7.04	$32.01
Room addition	400	38%	$29.49	$134.07	$24.05	$109.30	$18.78	$85.36
New core home	850	38%	$62.68	284.89	$51.10	$232.25	$39.91	$181.40

Source: Daphnis, 2004b.

loan terms, the MFI can estimate the potential demand for various loan sizes. It can also segment its targeted population by income and summarize the results from Table 7.2 in a separate chart that shows what improvements can affordably be carried out by each market segment. This information can inform the MFI's feasibility assessment as well as its marketing of the housing loan product, should the MFI decide to proceed with the product's development.

7.6 Conclusion

As discussed in Chapter 2, market demand is not the only factor that should be taken into account when deciding whether to develop a housing loan product. MFI managers will want to consider whether their institutions have the capacity to operate a housing loan product, and if not, whether they have the resources to build that capacity. They will also want to consider whether housing loans fit with their institution's mission and vision, and if so, what kind of loan design would fit best. Decisions about whether to link the loan product to other financial services, what kind of construction assistance to offer, if any, and whether to seek partnerships in delivering the product will have far-reaching implications for the level of demand, costs and competition. Most likely a market opportunity exists, but it will not look the same to all MFIs. Each institution must decide uniquely and carefully what it wants to achieve with the product, and through what strategy it will manage the risks inherent in it.

Main Messages

1. Housing is typically the greatest source of wealth creation available to the poor.
2. Low-income households tend to build in small, incremental steps, so they need financing that matches the pace of that approach.
3. Proof of land ownership is not critical for housing microfinance, but land security is essential.
4. The larger the loan, the more likely is the need for collateral that retains its value over time.
5. Clients will seek to access housing loans for non-habitat activities if the product offers them better terms than other loan products.

Case Study: Housing Loans at CEMEX in Mexico

CEMEX is the largest cement manufacturer in Mexico and the third largest in the world. The informal construction sector accounts for almost 40 per cent of cement consumption in Mexico, and represents a potential annual market of US$500–600 million. Moreover, the segment has shown stability even during the economic crisis of the mid 1990s. The goal of CEMEX's Patrimonio Hoy programme was to develop a delivery chain that would respond to low-income households. In order to tap this market, CEMEX had to adapt its existing business model, based primarily on selling its cement via large distributors, to a scheme that offers savings and credit combined with technical assistance, and engages directly with thousands of low-income customers.

The target communities are those with family incomes of US$10–15 a day. CEMEX's market studies showed that obtaining credit is one of the main barriers for the poor. They also found that women traditionally save in clubs called tandas. Hence Patrimonio Hoy is based on adaptations to the traditional saving clubs. Three-person savings groups are formed; housewives in the communities are enrolled as promoters of the programme, and are responsible for sales sessions and the collection of membership fees. The only requirement for membership is a commitment to save a fixed amount for a definite period, usually 70 weeks.

Upon enrolment each member saves for five weeks, whereupon CEMEX provides the first instalment of credit through the delivery of materials, equivalent to ten weeks' worth of collections. Savings and credit are at the core of the model. Prices of materials are at market rates, and remain fixed during the 70-week cycle. By making small regular payments, the poor benefit from the competitive pricing. For CEMEX and the distributors, this represents a continual revenue flow. Supplies are guaranteed and warehousing services are included, which adds significant value for low-income customers since it avoids deterioration of stored materials. Deliveries are made in stages, providing several cycles of extended credit for the duration of the building process. Each customer receives personalized technical advice from an architect in the planning of the incremental construction. All costs, including technical assistance, are covered by the weekly membership fee.

The package of services (credit, design layout, warehousing, and transportation of building materials) has resulted in benefits for the customer by reducing the time to add a room from 48 to 16 months, as well as a reduction in costs by more than two-thirds. For CEMEX, the programme operates at a profit, and additional revenue has come from sales to non-Patrimonio Hoy customers via exclusivity agreements with distributors that participate in the programme. Currently there are 86 service centres in 42 cities in Mexico. By early 2008 US$82 million had been loaned in credit, and 185,000 families reached. CEMEX's projections are to expand the services in the next five years via 1,600 offices and to 2 million families.

Despite the programme's success, Hokans (2008) reports that CEMEX may move in the future towards individual credit lines offered by consumer lenders in order to bring costs down. One model for possible replication is that of Lendcor, a South African company that offers cellphones equipped with WIZZIT, a mobile banking platform, to pensioners and microentrepreneurs that want to buy building materials and cement. Using a similar model, CEMEX customers could apply for a loan to purchase materials at one of CEMEX's building stores and then pay their loan instalments via their cellphone or ATM card.

This case study was adapted from Vance (2008).

Recommended Reading

- CHF International. 2001. *So, you want to do housing microfinance? A guide to incorporating a home improvement loan program into a microfinance institution* (Silver Spring, MD, CHF International), at: http://www.chfinternational.org/node/32902
- Daphnis, F.; Ferguson, B. (eds.). 2004. *Housing microfinance: A guide to practice* (Bloomfield, CT, Kumarian Press, Inc.).
- Hokans, J. 2008. *Maximizing choice: Diverse approaches to the challenge of housing microfinance*, USAID microREPORT #97 (Washington, DC, USAID), available at: http://www.microlinks.org/ev01.php?ID=23323_201&ID2=DO_TOPIC.
- Martin, C. 2008. *Going to scale with housing microfinance: The role of commercial banks*, USAID microREPORT #92 (Washington, DC, USAID), at: http://www.microlinks.org/ev_en.php?ID=22878_201&ID2=DO_TOPIC.
- UN-Habitat. 2008. *Housing for all: The challenges of affordability, accessibility and sustainability* (Nairobi, UN-Habitat), at: http://www.unhabitat.org/pmss/listItemDetails.aspx?publicationID=2547.

8 Emergency and Consumption Loans[15]

Economic poverty is not just a matter of low incomes, but also of irregular and uncertain incomes. ~ Rosenberg (2010)

Microcredit is known for its valuable contribution to poverty alleviation and – to a lesser extent – job creation. Small loans for income generation allow poor households to initiate economic activities or expand existing microenterprises. Yet enterprise loans fulfil only half of credit's poverty-alleviating potential. When considering the needs of the poorest households, equally if not more important are loans that allow them to smooth income and consumption.

This chapter attempts to answer the following questions:

1. What is an emergency loan?
2. Why do most MFIs not offer emergency loans?
3. Why should MFIs offer emergency loans?
4. When is credit the right choice?
5. How does one design an emergency loan?

8.1 What Is an Emergency Loan?

Low-income households are vulnerable to a range of risks and economic stresses, such as those highlighted in Table 8.1. The term "emergency loan" conjures up images of typhoons, earthquakes and post-war reconstruction. That is not the intended meaning of the term in this chapter. While MFIs should have contingency plans for dealing with disasters (see Chapter 18), this chapter focuses on loans that allow low-income persons to cope with **idiosyncratic risks**, risks that are associated with a specific individual, such as illness, a death in the family, and other urgent needs for cash. The primary purpose of these loans is to help households to smooth a temporary cash flow constraint so that consumption becomes less dependent on income during the short term.

Table 8.1 Economic vulnerabilities

Economic stresses	Idiosyncratic risks	Covariant risks
• Wedding	• Death	• Floods
• Ceremonies	• Illness	• Drought
• Childbirth	• Accidents	• Other disasters
• Education	• Loss of assets	
• Paying rent, utilities	• Business failure	
	• Unemployment	

Source: Authors.

[15] This chapter was adapted from Churchill (2003).

In that context, the main characteristics of an emergency loan are: a small amount of money, immediately available, and repaid in a relatively short period of time. In practice, such an emergency loan has the same characteristics as a **consumer loan** (see Box 8.1), and could in fact be used for a variety of purposes. Or, to put it another way, loans that are not specifically intended for emergencies could be used to address them.

Box 8.1 A Brief Look at Consumer Loans

Consumer credit has no defined financing purpose. Loans are approved based on the existence of collateral, typically the borrower's salary or in some cases an object purchased on credit. Loan analysis is simple, fast, and can be handled at low operational cost.

Consumer lending is a rapidly growing business, and consumer credit institutions are increasingly targeting low-income clients and the microfinance market. The results, at times, have been disastrous. In Bolivia, for example, consumer credit companies pushed into the country's microcredit market in the 1990s, which until then had been served by an established microfinance sector. To compensate for a lack of local market know-how, and in lieu of carrying out their own credit analysis or demanding collateral, the consumer credit companies settled for the knowledge that an applying borrower was already a client of an MFI. The lax credit handling and eventually excessive offering of loans resulted in the serious over-indebtedness of poor clients. When macroeconomic conditions deteriorated, the inflated system collapsed. Clients became insolvent, consumer credit institutions went out of business, and MFIs, although most could sustain their operations, had to accept substantial credit losses.

This has not been the consumer credit experience everywhere, however. What is called microcredit in South Africa is primarily consumer credit coming out of the formalization and expansion of informal consumer lending, rather than the development of income-generating activities through enterprise-based lending. It is widespread and is having an important, albeit incomplete, impact on low-income households' access to financial services. In Mexico, Banco Azteca, a wholly owned subsidiary of Latin America's largest specialty retailer (Grupo Elektra), took over the issuance of instalment loans tied to Elektra merchandise purchases in 2002, and then started offering US$500 consumer loans not tied to merchandise in 2003. By the end of 2007, it had 15 million customers and an average loan outstanding of US$257. Its growth and profits have been phenomenal. Clearly, it is providing a service that low-income households value, but the bank has been heavily criticized for annual percentage rates above 85 per cent and stories of client over-indebtedness (Epstein and Smith, 2007).

According to Mugwang'a and Cracknell (2005), a growing number of microfinance programmes are choosing to provide consumer loans to low-income salaried workers, who use their employment status to borrow on behalf of poor relatives, and to cover for family emergencies. The product is perceived to be a low-risk, high-return opportunity, but caution is warranted (refer, for example, to the case of Equity Bank that was presented in Box 1.2). Such loans usually represent a move to a new market segment and a shift away from direct relationships with clients to direct relationships with employers. The systems required to manage risk within this new kind of relationship are fundamentally different from those used to manage risk with a microenterprise loan product.

Source: Adapted from responsAbility, 2008.

8.2 Why Do Most MFIs Not Offer Emergency Loans?

Most MFIs consider loans that are not meant for income-generation purposes as non-productive. MFIs are often reticent about offering these loans, for a variety of reasons. The most common concern is the perceived credit risk associated with loans that do not generate income. This logic assumes that households cannot afford to repay a loan unless it is used to stimulate additional revenue. This belief is unfounded.

Many poor households borrow instead from friends, families and moneylenders – perhaps under disagreeable loan terms – and find some way to repay. In Indonesia, clients of BRI reported that about half of their loans were being used for non-entrepreneurial activities (Karlan and Morduch, 2010), while in India, a study of SEWA Bank clients reported that only 23 per cent of borrowings were used for business investment (Chen and Snodgrass, 2001). Yet repayment rates at BRI and SEWA were high at the time this research was conducted. Although some MFIs argue that their repayment problems are caused by clients using loans for non-productive purposes, an alternative explanation is that these problems stem from a mismatch between the design of a product and its use, and from the fact that credit decisions are typically based on repayment history rather than repayment capacity.

Some MFIs recognize that clients need emergency loans, but the organization's delivery systems are not structured to provide them. To offer quick, hassle-free loans, credit decisions must be made close to the clients, which requires loan approval authority in the field. Rural MFIs find it difficult and expensive to use their existing delivery channels to provide such a service. Typically emergency loans would also be for individuals, which may not synchronize well with all group methodologies. Furthermore, to control credit risk, some MFIs do not allow clients to have more than one loan outstanding at a time.

In some countries, policy-makers prevent MFIs from non-productive lending. There is a widely held perception that consumer loans are bad – that they contribute to over-indebtedness by encouraging people to spend beyond their means. Since consumer and emergency loans share some characteristics, the latter is victimized by the bias against the former. While over-indebtedness is a legitimate challenge, it should not prevent people from accessing an essential poverty-alleviating financial service.

8.3 Why Should MFIs Offer Emergency Loans?

The partiality for productive loans, and prejudice against consumption loans, suggests that some policy-makers and practitioners are seeing only half of the microcredit picture. Indeed, the provision of emergency loans could be extremely beneficial for clients and MFIs alike.

From the client's perspective, the vulnerability of low-income households is not eliminated by access to income-generating loans. While a microenterprise loan may help the poor reduce their vulnerability by boosting income and assets, it is not an effective means to manage risks. Loan sizes, terms and eligibility requirements (for example, group guarantees, weeks of pre-loan meetings, compulsory savings) make microenterprise loans unsuitable to address a household's short-term need for cash.

Figure 8.1 Microenterprise credit and emergency loans: two sides of the same coin

Source: Churchill, 2003.

Poor households that have access to microenterprise loans remain vulnerable to numerous economic stresses. Some risks contribute to unexpected increases in household expenses, such as rebuilding a damaged house, paying for burial costs, or travelling to visit a sick relative. Other risks, such as temporary unemployment, death of livestock or theft of productive assets, reduce a household's expected income. Some risks increase expenses *and* reduce income, such as the illness or death of a breadwinner. Emergency loans are therefore valuable complements to microenterprise loans, providing safety nets to low-income households to resist the downward pressures of economic stresses, as depicted in Figure 8.1.

From the MFI's perspective, varied loan products can enlarge an organization's market. Not all poor persons are self-employed or want income-generating loans, so the provision of non-productive loans can broaden an MFI's impact by allowing it to serve low-income communities as a whole. If the organization serves a broader market, then an emergency loan product also diversifies an MFI's credit risk. The cross-selling of emergency loans to existing clients allows the organization to increase the outstanding balance per client, which – assuming that risks are sufficiently controlled – increases per-client profitability, since there are no additional acquisition costs. By helping clients quickly during times of need, the MFI is also likely to strengthen customer loyalty.

Although many MFIs are interested in developing savings and insurance services to help clients to manage household and business risks, an emergency loan is probably an easier service to develop, particularly for non-governmental organizations (NGOs). Microcredit NGOs are typically prohibited from mobilizing deposits, and should offer insurance only as an agent for an insurance company. Also, the provision of emergency loans is similar to the core competency of microcredit NGOs – delivering microenterprise loans – and therefore will not require fundamental changes to their systems or human resource needs.

Microfinance institutions that develop delivery mechanisms for emergency loans may learn something about flexibility that could positively affect the design of their other loan products.

If such improvements were to occur, it would raise a pertinent question: is it necessary to have multiple loan products, or would it be better to have one flexible loan that could be used for many purposes?

8.4 When Is Credit the Right Choice?

Along with savings and insurance, emergency loans are one of three types of risk-managing financial services that enable low-income households to cope with economic stresses. Generally, savings is the most versatile and least expensive. Ideally, savings is the preferred option for expected expenses, such as school fees and religious ceremonies. Insurance is most relevant for larger expenses stemming from risks that are less likely to occur. An emergency loan may be appropriate to cover unexpected economic stresses in the event that someone has not built up sufficient savings reserves or prefers not to deplete them, and for risks that are not covered or not sufficiently covered by insurance.

As shown in Figure 8.2, low-income households operate at the margins. In some months income exceeds expenses, but in other months the household runs a deficit. In this particular example, even though during the 12-month period total income slightly exceeds total expenses, from December through to April the household is spending more money per month than it earns. If the household has not saved its surplus, or if that savings is not liquid (e.g., savings in livestock or jewellery), then an emergency loan can help the household to smooth consumption until May.

In this scenario, an emergency loan would reduce the need for **distress-selling** – the selling of assets to access quick cash, usually at a below-market rate – by allowing people to borrow against future earnings. Credit is a possible solution, however, only if prospective borrowers can convince lenders that they will have: 1) future earnings to repay the loan; and 2) sufficient security to guarantee the loan.

Figure 8.2 Income smoothing

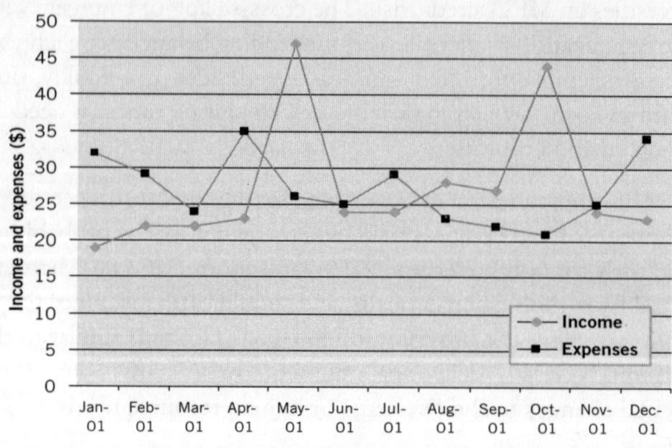

Source: Authors.

Figure 8.3 Coping with economic stresses

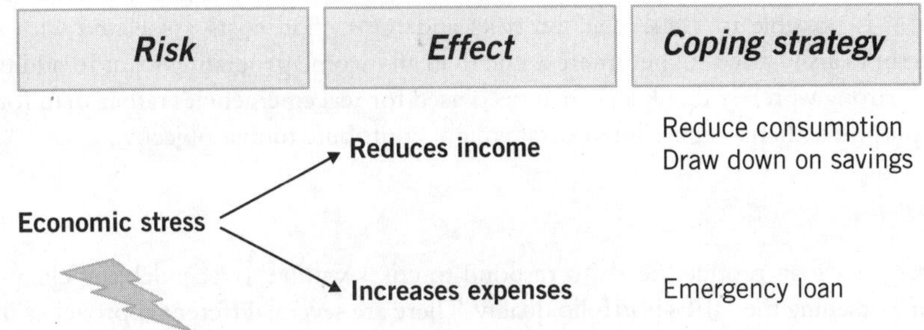

Source: Churchill, 2003.

The choice between relying on savings and borrowing depends partly on whether the economic stress decreases income or increases expenses in the medium term, as shown in Figure 8.4. Drought, for example, decreases income in the same way that a microentrepreneur would experience poor market conditions. In this situation, the preferred response would be to reduce consumption and/or draw down on savings. Credit is an undesirable coping strategy, because the expected reduction of income in the coming months means that it will be difficult to service the loan. An MFI should avoid extending a loan in these circumstances; it could worsen the borrower's situation, since inevitable late payments would damage the household's ability to borrow in the future.

When deciding between savings and credit, it is also important to consider whether the economic stress has created a temporary or permanent cash flow problem. A long-term problem, such as the death of a breadwinner, cannot easily be smoothed over by a small, short-term loan.

Alternatively, if the shock generates an expense, but does not adversely affect one's gross income, then an emergency loan could be a reasonable solution. For example, replacing a roof is an unexpected expense that does not affect income. So rather than draw down on savings, which should be reserved for a time when a peril suppresses household income, an emergency loan for the additional expense might be appropriate.

A slight twist to this logic emerges when accessing savings means cashing in on productive assets. If someone's primary savings strategy is to reinvest in his or her microenterprise, then drawing down on savings would decrease revenue generation. In this situation, a loan might serve the household better than de-capitalizing the business.

8.5 How to Design an Emergency Loan

Three issues of particular concern in designing emergency loans – interest rate, credit risk and delivery methods – are discussed below.

Interest Rate

Interest rate is the most straightforward of the three. There may be an inclination for organizations to offer emergency loans at a lower price than other credit products, since clients who request these loans are experiencing a financial hardship. That inclination should be avoided, because discounted loans will stimulate a huge demand for **ersatz**, or artificial, emergencies. In fact, it is possible to argue that the risks and transaction costs associated with small, short-term loans justify a higher interest rate than an income-generating loan. In addition, if the MFI strongly prefers that loans are indeed used for real emergencies rather than for consumer purposes, then a higher interest rate might contribute to that objective.

Controlling Credit Risk

An emergency loan product needs to respond to crises without over-indebting clients, and without worsening the MFI's portfolio quality. There are several different approaches that an MFI might take towards controlling the credit risk of an emergency loan.

The most common method for MFIs is to rely on the client's **credit history** as a collateral substitute. Borrowers who have repaid several loans without a late payment are eligible for a parallel loan, no questions asked, as long as the loan amount is below a pre-approved threshold. For example, Financiera Calpiá in El Salvador has a customer rating system based on repayment history (see Box 8.2). Clients with the best ratings are eligible for small, short-term loans that can be accessed concurrently with microenterprise loans. Along the same lines, in the Philippines, CARD Bank's multipurpose loan is a parallel loan available to existing clients with a good track record.

Box 8.2 Preferred Services at Calpiá, El Salvador

Financiera Calpiá, an MFI in El Salvador, has a customer rating system that enables its best customers to access preferred services. The rating system combines quantitative and qualitative indicators on a scale of 1 to 5. The quantitative measure is based on the average number of days late per repayment; customers who average less than three days late receive an excellent rating (1) and those between three and five receive a good rating (2). Using the same scale, the loan officer also gives the customer a rating based on his or her cooperativeness. Consequently, if a customer misses a payment for a good reason, such as a death in the family, the loan officer rating can make sure that she is not unduly penalized.

Customers who receive a 1 or 2 rating for several standard microenterprise loans become eligible to access a second tier of preferred loan products, including seasonal loans and automatic credit. **Seasonal loans** are short-term working capital loans intended for periods of peak business demand, although they could also be used for emergency purposes. These loans are accessed concurrently with microenterprise loans for customers whose previous loan was repaid with a 1 rating and who have never exceeded a 2 on any loan.

Calpiá's **automatic credit** is similar to a line of credit, except that each time customers draw down on their credit limit, they sign a separate loan contract. To access automatic credit, the customer must have repaid three standard loans with a 1 rating or maintained a 1 rating for 12 months. Once they are eligible for automatic credit, customers receive a "Preferred Customer" identification card, and the loan officer conducts a detailed analysis of the business to set the credit limit. The interest rate on the automatic credit is also lower than on the standard loan product to reward those customers and encourage their loyalty.

Adapted from Churchill, 1999.

The logic of this credit risk control is that the service is so valuable that clients would strive to maintain their good standing and retain eligibility for future emergency (and microenterprise) loans. The most important advantage of the credit history approach, besides the ease of administration, is that it creates a strong customer loyalty incentive: it rewards the MFI's best clients by providing them with access to a preferred service.

In using this approach, MFIs need to be careful to use credit history to determine eligibility, but not the loan amount. Automatically determining loan sizes based on the amounts repaid to date runs the risk of over-indebting households. The loan amount should be based on repayment capacity. Since a capacity assessment could delay the delivery of an emergency loan, some organizations conduct periodic assessments to determine how much clients would be eligible for, and then allow them to draw down amounts below that ceiling when and if they need it.

The primary downside of the credit history approach is that it has a limited scope. Because only persons with outstanding microenterprise loans are eligible, credit history "collateral" is not effective in serving the low-income community at large.

Guarantors or co-signers can also be used to control credit risk. Since vulnerable persons already rely heavily on the economic support of family and friends, a guarantor arrangement can formalize family or social obligations without upsetting the cash flow of the assistance provider. Guarantors could be provided within the context of a borrower group, whereby the group approves and guarantees a member's loan, or it could be organized on an individual basis outside the group system. An individual arrangement makes it possible for MFIs to address the broader community's need for emergency loans instead of just serving existing borrowers.

The main challenge to controlling credit risk through guarantors is whether the legal system can easily and cost-effectively enforce the contract. Another limitation is whether people who need emergency loans can find co-signers who would meet the MFI's criteria. In addition, the process of verifying that the guarantor indeed met the eligibility criteria might make it difficult to make credit decisions in a timely manner, unless prospective guarantors were pre-approved before a loan is actually needed.

Credit risk for an emergency loan can also be managed through non-traditional collateral, such as a **pawn lending** arrangement with jewellery or other small, valuable items (see Box 8.3). For this type of security to work, the MFI needs the expertise to assess the value of the collateral, and a safe means of storing it until the loan is repaid. A pawn-lending facility also requires a retail outlet or a method for selling unclaimed items. If these conditions could be met, then a pawn loan could be extremely versatile. Assuming that a pawnbroker is locally available, transaction costs are quite minimal for lender and borrower alike. Possible disadvantages are: do low-income households have assets to pawn, and is pawning a culturally acceptable means of accessing funds?

Box 8.3 A Fresh Look at Pawnshops

Pawnshops are an important source of microcredit in many developing countries. Nevertheless, many practitioners, policy-makers and funding agencies seem to be prejudiced against them. They consider pawning to be a "desperate measure", and an activity that needs to be curtailed. Persons interested in finance for low-income households should take a fresh look at pawning.

Where pawning is accessible, low-income persons use pawnshops to obtain cash for emergency cash needs, as well as to expand their businesses and finance consumption. In Thailand, for example, low-income households use pawnshops to obtain cash to pay school fees. Pawnshops in Shanghai receive frequent visits from a large number of small enterprise operators in need of relatively short-term and small-volume loans in the city.

Pawning has several attractive features for the pawnshop or the financial institution and the borrower:

- A pawning transaction is simple: the borrower pledges an asset for a specified sum of money (a percentage of the appraised value of the asset) and retains the right to redeem it within a specific time by returning the original sum plus interest. If the item is not redeemed by the agreed time, the borrower loses the asset. This is the end of the transaction, and hence there is no "ever-increasing debt" in pawning. For the pawning service provider, the main costs include labour, cost of capital, building, security, and insurance.
- Pawning substantially reduces the lender's risk compared with other types of microcredit. Also, the lender's transaction costs are minimal, because there is no need to collect and analyse information about the client's cash flow and creditworthiness, although the lender has to ascertain that the pledged asset has not been stolen. A pawn loan can be processed very quickly. Thus the lender can make a large number of small transactions in a short period. There is no need for frequent contact with clients, because each loan involves only two transactions (disbursement and recovery).
- Borrowers are not subjected to high transaction costs. A borrower makes only one trip to secure a loan and one to make the repayment. Disbursement is quick. Pawnshops, therefore, can be a reliable source of credit for emergencies. The need for distress selling of assets can also be minimized if pawning facilities are available. Clients can get a lower interest rate from pawnshops than from most informal commercial moneylenders. Another advantage is that clients are not involved in complex "social reciprocity arrangements" because the transaction is straightforward.

Adapted from Fernando, 2003.

Delivery Methods

Perhaps even more challenging than controlling credit risk is designing an effective delivery method. By definition, emergency loans need to be made immediately available at a location that is close to the client. Perhaps the ideal arrangement from the borrowers' perspective would be daily **door-to-door service**, such as that provided by *Safe*Save in Bangladesh, or a large **branch network** that would ensure facilities were close at hand. Unfortunately, these overhead costs can be justified only where there is a market concentration, in cities and towns.

To reach out to rural areas, one possibility is through **part-time branches** that are staffed only a couple of days a week – but what happens if someone desperately needs money during an off day? Another possibility is a system of **mobile outlets** that spend an hour in six or eight villages a day, although they may represent a security risk.

To overcome this delivery challenge, the original design of the village banking methodology called for groups to maintain an **internal account**, which would be capitalized through mandatory savings. Village banks could then lend out that money as they saw fit. These funds were often used for emergency loans, to help members who had urgent needs for small amounts of money. A similar arrangement occurs in the self-help group methodology common in India.

Another approach worth exploring is to establish mutually beneficial **partnerships with local shopkeepers**. They already have financial transactions with poor people, and may already be acting as moneylenders. Shopkeepers may be experiencing some difficulties in getting repaid and they may not have sufficient cash to keep up with demand. An MFI, on the other hand, wants to help low-income persons manage their irregular cash flows better, but doing so creates credit risks and transaction costs. If they work together, the MFI might be able to develop systems to improve the shopkeepers' lending efforts, such as pricing, screening and monitoring, which would also improve the shopkeepers' business by reducing loan losses and increasing sales. Shopkeepers would effectively work as agents for the MFI. The microfinance institution would provide loan capital, training, documentation, and assistance in delinquency management, but the two partners would share the risk. This arrangement might be a boon to the MFI as well, because the shopkeepers' familiarity with their customers could reduce information asymmetries, and their proximity to the clients would improve customer value and minimize transaction costs, all with hardly any additional overhead expenses.

Main Messages

1. Emergency loans are a valuable complement to microenterprise loans because they provide a safety net that reduces the impact of risk events.
2. Consumption loans are not bad as long as the household can repay them.
3. If an economic shock simultaneously increases a client's expenses and reduces income, emergency loans will rarely be appropriate.
4. Resist the temptation to offer emergency loans at a lower price than other credit products.
5. Access to emergency loans can provide a strong customer loyalty incentive.

Recommended Reading

- Churchill, C. 2003. "Emergency loans: The other side of microcredit", in *ADB Finance for the Poor*, Vol. 4, No. 3 (Asian Development Bank), available at: www.adb.org/documents/periodicals/microfinance/finance_200343.pdf
- Fernando, N. 2003. "Pawnshops and microlending: A fresh look is needed", in *ADB Finance for the Poor*, Vol. 4, No. 1 (Asian Development Bank), available at: www.adb.org/documents/periodicals/microfinance/finance_200341.pdf
- Gonzalez, A. 2009. *Consumption, commercial or mortgage loans: Does it matter for MFIs in Latin America?* MIX Data Brief No. 3 (Washington, DC, Microfinance Information eXchange, Inc.), at: http://www.themix.org/publications/consumption-commercial-or-mortgage-loans-does-it-matter-mfis-latin-america
- Mugwang'a, T.; Cracknell, D. 2005. *Microfinance institutions and salary-based consumer lending*, *MicroSave* Briefing Note No. 45 (Nairobi, *MicroSave*), at: http://india.microsave.org/briefing_notes/briefing-note-45-microfinance-institutions-and-salary-based-consumer-lending
- Rosenberg, R. 2010. *Does microcredit really help poor people?*, CGAP Focus Note No. 59 (Washington, DC, CGAP), at: http://www.microfinancegateway.org/p/site/m//template.rc/1.1.4333

9 Microinsurance[16]

Risk and vulnerability to risk are fundamental causes of underdevelopment.
~ Mosley (2009)

Insurance is a financial service that helps people manage risks, but it is not the only financial service that can do this. After defining insurance, this chapter describes risk-managing financial services, and explains the conditions under which insurance is preferred over savings and credit. In addition, this chapter provides some examples of microinsurance products offered by MFIs, describes different structures for delivering insurance, and offers practical recommendations to MFIs that are interested in providing insurance. The structure of this chapter is as follows:

1. What is insurance?
2. Savings, credit or insurance?
3. MFIs and their motivation
4. Institutional arrangements
5. Microinsurance products
6. Where to begin?
7. Conclusions and recommendations

9.1 What Is Insurance?

Insurance is commonly a misused term. People often say *insurance* when they are referring to savings or credit products that fulfil a risk-managing function. For insurance to be insurance, it needs to involve a **risk-pooling mechanism**. This mechanism combines the resources of the many to compensate for the losses of the few. In effect, policyholders pay premiums for the average loss suffered by the group rather than for the actual cost incurred when a risk event occurs. Risk-pooling benefits the *few* who suffered the loss, while the *many* basically receive "peace of mind" in exchange for their premium payments.

Because of this risk pooling, the value of an insurance benefit is related to the cost of the loss, not to the value of the premium payments that have been made. If the payout amount is directly related to the value of the "pay-in", then the client is receiving a savings service, not insurance.

Insurance is a new business for microfinance institutions and not merely another product. The insurance business has a more complicated risk structure that requires different management skills than those commonly found in MFIs. Therefore they should tread carefully, recognizing that insurance is significantly outside their area of expertise.

[16] This chapter is adapted from Churchill and Roth (2006) and Churchill et al. (2002). The specific experiences of microfinance institutions are drawn primarily from ten case studies that are part of the "Good and Bad Practices in Microinsurance" case study series: ASA and Shepherd (Roth et al., 2005); BRAC (Ahmed et al., 2005); CARD (McCord and Buczkowski, 2004); Columna (Herrera and Miranda, 2004); Opportunity International (Leftley, 2005); TATA-AIG (Roth and Athreye, 2005); TUW-SKOK (Churchill and Pepler, 2004); TYM (Tran and Yun, 2004); Vimo SEWA (Garand, 2005); and Yeshasvini (Radermacher et al., 2005). Complete citations for these case studies are provided in the bibliography.

9.2 Savings, Credit or Insurance?

Risk management has always been an objective of microcredit customers. Most MFIs admit that clients occasionally use business loans to pay for medical expenses or funerals, or to smooth household cash flow. Even if they do not have an immediate emergency, some customers invest only a portion of the loan in their businesses, and they save the rest so that they will have a cushion to fall back on if they experience repayment problems. In these examples, clients use a product designed for one purpose to fulfil a different objective because that is the only financial service that is available.

As MFIs begin providing products that more accurately fit the purpose for which clients use them, they need to think more about risk management. Three classes of risk-managing financial product are: 1) liquid savings accounts; 2) emergency loans; and 3) microinsurance, which includes coverage for death, illness, disability, and property loss.

Although all three can help reduce vulnerability, when is insurance a more appropriate response than savings or credit? Figure 9.1 depicts areas that insurance products can best address, based on the following two variables:

1. the degree of uncertainty about whether, when, and how often a loss will occur; and
2. the cost of the potential loss.

Insurance is not an effective response in three areas. First, for losses that are very certain to occur, the risk-pooling mechanism cannot work.[17] Second, insurance is also not appropriate for small losses, because administrative and transaction costs would make the product too expensive. Third, insurance is not always effective in addressing **covariant risk,** when many people in the risk pool are affected at the same time.

Figure 9.1 Credit, savings, or insurance?

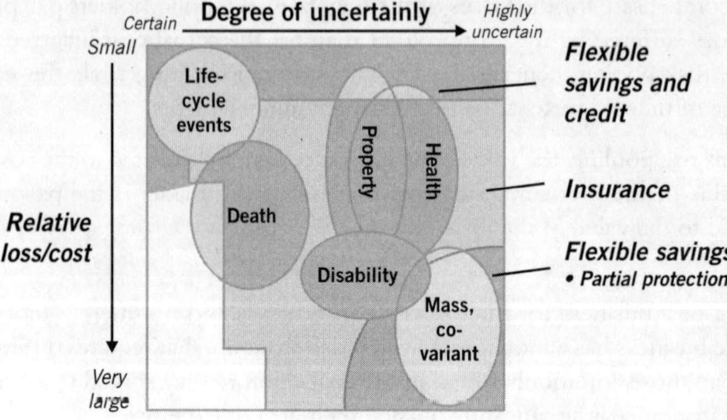

Source: Brown and Churchill, 1999.

17 Although it is certain we all will die, uncertainty arises because we do not know when.

On the basis of this assessment, normal life-cycle events (births, weddings, education) are better addressed through various savings products. Even unplanned but relatively inexpensive losses can be served through liquid savings accounts. But the poor cannot always save for a rainy day. For them, emergency loans could address sudden and unforeseen needs.

Savings and credit are much more flexible than insurance. A life insurance policy, for example, will not help someone who is robbed, or whose house burns down. Most losses experienced by low-income households are small. To help reduce their vulnerability, liquid savings and emergency loans are the most appropriate responses to deal with the bulk of their risks. Before venturing into the confusing world of insurance, a MFI would provide its customers with greater value if it first developed these other risk-managing financial services. Once an organization helps its clients to reduce their exposure to most of their risks, then it can consider how to reduce vulnerability to the fewer, but more expensive, risks that can be covered by insurance.

It is important to note that the poor are often unfamiliar with insurance, or uncomfortable with it. Indeed, insurance may not be their preferred means of managing risks for personal or cultural reasons. Low-income households may see insurance as a luxury that only people with excess income can afford. If a low-income household must choose between putting food on the table and paying for protection against a future calamity that they do not know will occur, they are likely to spend their money on food. Furthermore, if the risk does not occur, they will believe that they have spent their limited resources unnecessarily, and all they have to show for it is peace of mind. One cannot eat peace of mind.

The relationship between a financial institution and its customers is quite different for savings, credit and insurance. With credit, the MFI puts its money at risk. Despite intentions to reach large volumes of people, microfinance institutions need to select creditworthy applicants carefully. Credit should not be oversold, because if the supplier aggressively drives outreach, it will invariably reach an increasingly risky market. For savings, the risk roles are reversed. Depositors need to trust that the institution will be financially solvent and safeguard their assets. Savers can fairly easily test whether their money is accessible and secure by withdrawing their funds.

The risk relationship with insurance is more complex. As with credit, there is a screening element to ensure that the client pool does not include an over-representation of high-risk individuals. But, like savings, there is a critical need for prospective policyholders to trust the institution. Unlike depositors, however, policyholders cannot easily test whether the insurer will fulfil its obligations – with life insurance, the policyholder has to die before the insurer has to respond.

9.3 MFIs and Their Microinsurance Motivation

Microfinance institutions are indeed a major delivery channel for microinsurance, but before getting into detailed recommendations, it is important to start with a basic question: should an MFI get involved in offering insurance? When microfinance institutions are interested in insurance, their main motivation is often to reduce their credit risk in the event that borrowers or their family members experience death, illness or other losses. If insurance can help protect the households in such circumstances, it will indirectly safeguard the MFI's portfolio.

Another motivation behind the interest in insurance is to improve the welfare of their clients. MFIs typically have dual missions to alleviate poverty or promote economic development while generating a profit (or covering their costs). The social mission of improving the welfare of poor households can be enhanced through the protection provided by insurance.

There are also a number of legitimately commercial reasons why MFIs might be interested in providing insurance, such as:

- **Customer loyalty.** Many MFIs realize that they need to offer a variety of products to enhance retention, so that even when clients do not want a loan, they may still appreciate a savings account, a wire transfer service, or… insurance protection.
- **Product profitability.** A diverse product menu allows cross-selling opportunities and spreads the acquisition costs for a client across multiple products, enhancing product profitability.
- **Diversifying income streams.** Microinsurance provides an additional source of income, either from profit if the scheme is provided in-house (and well managed), or from fees if done in partnership with an insurer. The latter situation is particularly interesting to MFIs, which welcome opportunities to earn income without taking risks.

Of course, there are also disadvantages to offering insurance. It is a different business from savings or credit, requiring different expertise. Even offering insurance products in partnership with an insurer can be time-consuming and demanding. A number of organizations, like ProCredit banks in Eastern Europe, have no interest in offering insurance, directly or indirectly, so they are not distracted from their core services. Other MFIs may be willing to purchase credit life coverage to protect their loan portfolios, but are less interested in providing additional benefits to their customers because of the additional work required.

If an MFI believes that there are more pros than cons, and decides that it wants to branch out into the brave new world of insurance, there are two key questions it needs to consider when offering microinsurance:

1. Through what institutional arrangement should it offer insurance?
2. What types of cover should it offer?

9.4 Institutional Arrangements

If an MFI wants to offer insurance to its clients, there are four main ways to do so: 1) in partnership with an insurance company; 2) by creating its own insurance brokerage; 3) by self-insuring; or 4) by creating its own insurance company.

Partner-agent Model

Under what circumstances is one option preferable to the others? Certainly, if no insurance company is available or willing to offer protection through the MFI, then it could go on its own. However, the possibility of not being able to find an interested insurance partner is becoming increasingly less likely as more insurers seek opportunities to reach new markets.

MFIs are also becoming more convincing, arming themselves with arguments and experiences to persuade insurers that this is indeed a valuable market opportunity for them.

In general, if an MFI cannot entice an insurer into a partnership, it is probably not effectively communicating what it has to offer. Many insurers are attracted to the prospect of accessing a large number of new clients through a cheap distribution network. MFIs should recognize that insurers and bankers may have very different attitudes towards the masses of low-income people. For bankers, whose money is at risk when they lend, the poor are a risky market. Insurers, however, tend to be interested in ways of reaching an expansive market cost-effectively. For insurers, volumes speak volumes.

To make the partner-agent model work effectively for MFIs, the following recommendations emerge from the experiences of MFIs around the world:

- **Tell them what you want.** To get good products and processes from insurers at a decent price, MFIs need to know what they want, and they have to sit in the driver's seat in the negotiations. The larger they are, the more demanding they can be. ASA, an MFI in Bangladesh, and Opportunity International affiliates in the Philippines have designed their own product specifications and then sent requests to insurers to bid on their proposed product.
- **Know your stuff.** MFIs need to speak with authority, using language that insurers understand, backed up with compelling data. One advantage of an MFI is that it can often create useful actuarial data from its own experience of working with clients, to which the insurer otherwise would not have access.
- **Choose a trustworthy insurer.** It is often preferable to partner with a well-known insurance company, because it helps create trust and confidence in insurance. Without trust, clients may be unwilling to pay premiums today against the promise of a possible future benefit. In India, Tata-AIG has a significant advantage in the low-income market because of the high name recognition of the Tata brand.
- **Do not be afraid to switch partners.** MFIs do not have to be wedded to one insurance partner for ever. If the insurer is not performing, the MFI can look for a new partner. This should not be taken to an extreme though; changing insurance partners frequently can cause confusion among clients and staff.
- **Involve the insurer.** The alternative to changing partners is to get existing partners to improve. Shepherd (India) found that it was useful to invite insurers into the field so they could understand the target market better and recognize the differences between insurance and microinsurance.
- **Ask for training.** A major challenge in introducing insurance is training the MFI's employees, particularly the frontline staff who are responsible for sales and service. Several MFIs have persuaded their insurance partners to train their employees in insurance in general and the products in particular.
- **Manage claims.** An efficient claims-processing system is one of the most important points for negotiation. MFIs should insist that they pay the claims (at least for life insurance), and then be reimbursed by the insurer, on the basis of documentation that is appropriate for their clients.

- **Create a review committee.** Since claims processing tends to be one of the most contentious issues, Shepherd formed a review committee, with representatives from the MFI, insurer and clients, which meets quarterly (or more often if necessary) to improve claims processes.
- **Eliminate exclusions.** Strive to persuade insurers to drop as many exclusions as possible, even if the MFI has to pay a higher price, because that simplifies the product and makes it easier to explain to customers. It also reduces claims rejections that could cause significant public relations problems for the MFI.
- **Maintain and analyse data.** MFIs should maintain good information about insurance performance, enabling them to develop expertise over time and to push insurance partners for better deals. An appropriate and "actuarially approved" management information system (MIS) is crucial.
- **Determine the costs.** MFIs need to conduct a costing analysis to determine how much they need to earn in commission (or through a premium mark-up) to cover their administrative expenses. Even seamlessly integrated insurance, like compulsory coverage, creates some additional administrative costs for the MFI.
- **Own the clients.** Some entrepreneurial insurance companies might be interested in stealing the clients in the future. The MFI should always "own" the client. This can be done if the MFI is always the institution that sees the client.

Insurance Brokerage or Agency

The creation of an MFI-owned insurance brokerage is essentially a more sophisticated version of the partner-agent model. This approach, often used by credit union networks, facilitates access to formal insurance for MFIs and members alike. As with the partner-agent model, this arrangement has the advantage of outsourcing the risk to formal insurers.

The advantage of the brokerage arrangement over the basic partner-agent model is that an organization affiliated to an MFI (or a group of MFIs) develops insurance expertise to negotiate the best deals. The brokerage is not tied to any one insurance company, so it can explore various options on behalf of its two main customers: the MFIs and their clients. In addition, the brokerage is not limited to using MFIs as the distribution channels. Once it understands the needs of the low-income market, it can explore other strategies for extending insurance to the poor, such as through cooperatives, community organizations, and even retailers. Opportunity International has recently launched such an initiative (the Micro Insurance Agency). The insurance brokerage could also be seen as a first step towards creating an insurance company, although that does not necessarily have to be the objective.

Going Solo

A third option is for MFIs to self-insure – in other words, to carry the risk themselves. There are compelling reasons why some microfinance institutions would want to self-insure, as well as some strong arguments against it.

One argument for self-insurance is a belief that the MFIs (or their customers) will have to pay extra for the insurer's overhead. For the most basic products, like credit life, that logic might

be valid. However, basic credit life insurance largely benefits the lender, since it means the MFI does not have to solicit loan repayments from the deceased's survivors.[18] If the MFI really wants to reduce the vulnerability of its customers, more complicated products are required – products that an MFI probably cannot offer on its own.

Both TYM (Viet Nam) and CARD (Philippines) had negative experiences trying to enhance customer value on their own. They provided credit life on a self-insurance basis and generated significant surpluses. Consequently, they thought it would be a good idea to offer additional benefits, by including other family members or by covering additional risks. They added these benefits, however, without assessing the impact that they might have on claims. As a result, CARD's pension plan nearly bankrupted the company (see Box 5.5 in Chapter 5), and TYM's hospitalization benefit threatens to do the same, even though the benefit is extremely modest.

Another concern surrounding self-insurance is the extent to which an MFI will cope if it experiences catastrophic losses. The primary reason why MFIs should not self-insure – besides not having the expertise to price and design products appropriately – is that they will have difficulty meeting claims if many clients are affected by a peril at the same time. Since they are not formal insurers, they do not have access to reinsurance, which is how insurers cope with covariant risks.

Vimo SEWA (India) learned this lesson the hard way. After several years of negative experiences with insurance partners, it began offering in-house health insurance in 1996, and then added asset insurance in 1998. Initially, Vimo SEWA's transition to self-insurance had positive financial and service benefits – claims were paid faster and not rejected, and Vimo SEWA began building up some reserves. However, when the January 2001 earthquake struck Gujarat, over Rs 3.4 million (US$75,000) was required to satisfy claims, causing a severe financial strain. Prior to the earthquake, annual payouts for asset protection were below Rs 30,000 (US$662). This experience helped Vimo SEWA appreciate the need for reinsurance, and led the organization back to the partner-agent approach.

The main point is that a self-insuring MFI must think carefully about how it will control covariant risks. It could exclude such risks to limit its exposure, which is what the Indian MFI Spandana does. This approach, however, abandons clients when they need the help most. Moreover, excluding cover does not help the MFI manage its credit risk in a disaster situation. Alternatively, a self-insuring MFI could solve this problem by buying catastrophe cover with an insurance company, so the MFI covers idiosyncratic risks in-house while outsourcing covariant risks to an insurer.

A further argument against going solo is that it may be illegal to offer insurance without a licence. Regulators generally do not bother with small schemes. Some organizations manage to disguise their schemes by calling it a member benefit instead of insurance. Insurance regulators may be willing to look the other way, or may not even realize that the scheme exists. However, once it achieves significant scale, it is bound to attract attention. In addition, regu-

[18] There is some debate about the usefulness of credit life insurance. Some MFIs feel that it is a complicated means of dealing with loan losses due to death, and they prefer to write off the loan and provision accordingly. This argument might be valid for predictable loan losses due to death, but would not be appropriate if an MFI experiences a natural disaster or other covariant risks. The provisioning approach is also not relevant if an MFI is small and cannot afford to write off loans; if an MFI starts issuing larger loans, creating a concentration risk; or if the mortality rates are volatile or changing, as in an area with high incidence of HIV/AIDS.

lated MFIs are probably not allowed to keep insurance liabilities on their balance sheets, so for them (or MFIs planning to transform) self-insurance may not be an option.

Some MFIs self-insure because they do not want to share the insurance profits with another organization. Similarly, if going solo means lower overhead costs, the coverage could be cheaper for the clients. Consequently, some MFIs contend that they can provide greater customer value without involving an insurer.

Another aspect of customer value is the service standard for claims payments. For MFIs that have tried working with insurers and given up, problems with claims – including delays and rejections – are probably the number one reason for the divorce. If the MFI self-insures, it can pay claims quickly and impose less onerous documentation requirements on the beneficiaries. For example, when Spandana was collaborating with the Life Insurance Corporation of India, claims often took two to three months or more to be paid. After the MFI moved the scheme in-house, it was able to settle 73 per cent of claims within seven days.

Experts have mixed opinions on the topic of self-insurance. Leftley (2005) feels strongly that there are no good reasons why MFIs should take on insurance risk as long as there is existing underwriting capacity in the country. Other experts are more open-minded about the issue, willing to concede that self-insurance might even be preferable to the partner-agent approach if certain conditions are met:

1. The MFI is large enough to pool risks (at least 10,000 members), and those risks are reasonably homogeneous.
2. The product is kept simple.
3. The MFI obtains catastrophe coverage from an insurance company.
4. The MFI accesses appropriate technical assistance to help with product design, pricing, data management and performance monitoring.
5. Regulators will allow it.

Creating an Insurance Company

The fourth option is for an MFI or an association of MFIs to create their own insurance company. In many countries, credit unions and cooperatives have satisfied their insurance needs through insurers owned by the association and its members. The typical approach has been for the credit unions to create a brokerage company that facilitates access to insurance for the credit unions and members alike. Over time, the brokerage builds up sufficient expertise in underwriting, settling claims and managing data, and amasses sufficient funds to form a credit-union-owned insurance company.

In some jurisdictions it might be appropriate for other types of MFI or MFI association to create their own insurance company. In the Philippines, CARD has created a mutual benefit association (MBA) that is "owned" by the members, but structured to meet the insurance needs of the MFI. Some advantages of creating an insurance company over self-insurance are:

- It separates the credit and insurance risks into different organizations.
- It ensures that expertise is engaged in the management of the insurance business.

- It can collaborate with multiple distribution channels to extend insurance to the poor, and hence it can reach many more people.
- It enables the microinsurer to access reinsurance.

Compared with the partner-agent approach, an MFI-owned insurance company allows the MFI greater influence on product design and service standards. Furthermore, it enables any profits to be redistributed to the policyholders. However, the management of the insurance company should be kept at arm's length from the MFI so as not to jeopardize the soundness of its insurance decisions. In particular, careful consideration should be given to the investment strategy, since it is unwise to mix the credit and insurance risks by investing too great a proportion of premiums in the MFI's loan portfolio.

The transformation of an informal scheme into an insurance company is not without its challenges. In some jurisdictions there may be significant start-up and reporting requirements that do not justify the effort. For years, Self-Employed Women's Association (SEWA) in India has had its sights set on creating an insurance company. However, it has not been able to raise the minimum capital requirement, and the Indian insurance regulators are not interested in making an exception for microinsurance.

9.5 Microinsurance Products[19]

There are three basic types of insurance product: life insurance, property insurance and health insurance. Each of these is discussed briefly below.

Life Insurance

Of the three types of insurance, life insurance can be the most simple, and is the one most commonly offered by microfinance institutions. The insured event – death – is easy to verify, it is difficult to fake, it occurs only once per person, and the risk of moral hazard is low because most policyholders do not purposely increase the chances that the event will occur by engaging in risky behaviour. There are many different kinds of life insurance, with varying levels of complexity:

- **Credit life insurance** pays the outstanding balance of a loan in the event of the death of the borrower. Thus the insurance term corresponds with the loan term.
- **Term life insurance** provides coverage against the death of an insured person for a specified period of time, such as one, five or ten years. The amount paid out in the event of death is predetermined in the insurance contract. The savings completion insurance discussed in Chapter 5 is a type of term life policy.
- **Whole (or permanent) life insurance** differs from term insurance in two ways. First, it offers protection for a lifetime rather than just a fixed term. Second, it has a cash value that can be drawn down or borrowed against like a savings account. The cash value equals the premiums paid, less the cost of providing the insurance, plus interest earned on the premiums.

[19] This section was adapted from Brown and Churchill (1999) and Churchill et al. (2002).

- **Endowment life insurance** combines features of both term and permanent insurance. Like permanent life, endowment policies have a cash value. However, endowment policies provide protection for a fixed term, rather than for a lifetime. If an endowment policy reaches the end of its term and the policyholder has not died, he or she receives a fixed pay out representing the cash value of accumulated premiums plus interest. Endowment policies are discussed in more detail in Chapter 5.
- **Life savings insurance** provides a death benefit that is linked to the amount of savings that the insured person has in his or her account. Popularized by credit unions as a way to promote savings, premiums are paid by the financial institution to an insurer based on a multiple of the total value of its savings accounts. Depositors implicitly assume a lower interest rate on their savings in exchange for this member benefit. In the event of death, beneficiaries receive a payout equal to a multiple (usually double) of the savings in the account of the deceased (usually up to a maximum amount).
- **Annuities** are among the most complex life insurance products. As discussed in Chapter 5, they are basically retirement savings plans that pay policyholders a regular payment until they die. If a policyholder dies before a certain age, then the beneficiary earns either a lump sum or a series of payments. There are two periods associated with annuities: the accumulation period when the policyholder pays premiums, and the payout period when the insurer makes payments to the policyholder.

Property Insurance

Property insurance can protect against the cost of damage or loss of just about any type of asset. The assets that low-income households might need to protect include livestock, homes, business stands, inventory, equipment, modes of transport (for example, rickshaws or boats, in the case of fishing communities), tools and personal valuables. Property insurance is similar to term life insurance in that it offers coverage of a fixed amount for a limited period of time. It differs from life insurance in that it covers damage to, as well as loss of, the insured asset. As a result, the provision of property insurance tends to be riskier and more administratively complex than many types of life insurance. There are four main reasons for this:

1. **Greater complexity in asset valuation.** Property insurers need to have a reliable method for determining the value of the asset to be insured. For example, should the compensation for a poor family that has their insured pig stolen be determined based on the original purchase price of the pig, or on the cost of replacing the pig today, or should a fixed value be placed on all insured pigs? Conducting asset valuations increases the administration required to issue a property insurance policy.
2. **Possibility of repeat damage.** Unlike life insurance, a single property insurance policy may experience multiple claims – people can die only once, but an insured asset can be damaged many times.
3. **Higher risk of moral hazard.** A policyholder with insurance protection may be less likely to take proper care of whatever is insured.
4. **Higher likelihood of fraudulent claims.** Households can more easily make false claims about damage to an asset than about death of a family member. Property insurers need greater controls to protect against such abuses, and these controls increase the administration required to verify claims.

Property insurance is usually offered by microinsurers to insure the property that is collateral for an MFI loan or a lease. For instance, Grameen Bank requires insurance coverage on all loans used to purchase livestock, and the NLC of Pakistan has mandatory insurance on leased assets (Havers, 1999). To reduce the risk and complexity of the property insurance policies, benefits are often limited to the outstanding balance of the related credit rather than the replacement value of the asset. A few MFIs do provide other types of property insurance. SEWA offers a multiple risk policy that covers the loss or damage of household and business assets due to natural calamities, human-made disasters and fire up to a predetermined amount. Columna in Guatemala offers similar coverage as a single risk policy.

Disaster insurance and crop insurance are two products that could be extremely valuable for low-income communities, yet there has been little success with these products to date. Threats from natural disasters, such as earthquakes, hurricanes or floods, are difficult to insure against for three main reasons. First, disasters are usually difficult to predict. Historical occurrences of such risk events are not strong predictors of future disasters. Second, when a disaster does occur, the total financial losses can be very high. And third, a natural disaster is a covariant risk that will affect many of an insurer's policyholders at once. The only way to provide disaster insurance is through a reinsurance arrangement that broadens the risk pool across countries and regions, and protects insurers against catastrophic losses.

Agricultural insurance schemes in developing countries have produced poor results for decades, partly because they were operated by para-statal organizations that were not subject to rigorous financial discipline, and partly because they were not able to overcome the risk of moral hazard. They typically offered "area yield guarantees" which provided loan repayment and occasionally income supplements to farmers suffering crop yields below an established minimum, but no incentive for farmers to put maximum effort into producing the best yield possible (Mosley, 2009).

An important innovation has been the recent pilot-testing of weather insurance schemes that are based on rainfall instead of crop yield. If the rainfall index falls below a certain percentage of its average value, payouts are made in proportion to likely crop losses. By linking benefits to rainfall, weather insurance resolves several of the challenges that earlier crop insurance schemes failed to overcome: 1) moral hazard is eliminated, since nobody can influence rainfall; 2) administrative expenses are dramatically reduced, since claim verification is unnecessary; 3) benefits can be paid out as soon as the size of the local rainfall deficiency is known; and 4) low-income individuals who are affected indirectly can also benefit from the scheme (for example, landless labourers, who will have little work if a harvest is poor). Additional details about these schemes can be found in Chapter 20 on rural microfinance.

Health Insurance

Health insurance helps households cover the costs of hospital and surgical expenses, medications, and doctor's fees. Health insurance policies usually pay for some or all of the costs incurred as a result of specified accidents or illnesses. These costs are generally reimbursed to the household after verification of a claim, or paid directly to the care provider. The range of health problems covered and the expected cost of treating these problems determine the premiums and the degree of risk for the insurer.

The provision of health insurance is more risky and more complex than either life or property insurance. There are multiple reasons for this:

- The range of causes of health risks is varied, and it is difficult to estimate the probability that each illness will occur for each subset of the population.
- Health insurance usually includes preventive care, such as annual check-ups, that cannot be risk-pooled.
- Detailed information is required to identify and classify the relative risk level associated with a potential policyholder.
- Multiple claims are likely, and there is potential for over-usage.
- There is significant risk of adverse selection and moral hazard. Those in poorer health will be more likely to buy health insurance policies, and once policies have been bought, policyholders may not be as careful with their health, since they know they have access to affordable treatment.
- The involvement of the health care provider as a third party naturally increases the complexity of each transaction, but it also increases the potential for inefficiency and abuse. A doctor may over-prescribe or add additional procedures to a client's bill if he knows that the bill will be paid by an insurance plan rather than by the client. Policyholders and health-care providers can also collude to defraud the insurer.

Although health insurance is a difficult product for MFIs to offer, two compelling arguments may entice an institution to diversify in this direction. First, MFIs with a strong social agenda may see themselves as much more than just a microfinance institution. Second, the health expenses of borrowers and their family members could adversely affect an MFI's loan portfolio. Without protection from the financial risk associated with illness, members often use their income-generating loans to pay for health expenses, and then have difficulty repaying their loan. Their other options for covering health costs – withdrawing from their savings account, borrowing from moneylenders, or selling productive equipment – can all have negative effects on the microenterprise, and consequently on the MFI's loan portfolio.

Most health microinsurance products that exist today restrict coverage to low-frequency, high-cost events such as hospitalization. India's Yeshasvini Cooperative Farmers Health Scheme takes this approach, covering more than 1,600 different surgeries but no expenditures that are unrelated to hospitalization with surgery. In situations where health-care costs are low compared with opportunity costs in the event of a hospitalization, benefits sometimes take the form of a per diem payment which the policyholder can use as he or she pleases. In Jordan, for example, Microfund for Women's CareGiver product pays out a lump sum benefit for each night a borrower spends in the hospital, and clients can use the funds to cover costs such as transportation, childcare and medical fees, as well as lost income. Borrowers are automatically covered when they take a new loan; they do not need to have a medical exam, and there are no exclusions for pre-existing conditions (Microfund for Women, 2010).

Minor health shocks are a more pressing concern for most low-income households than hospitalization, however, and there are few schemes in operation that cover outpatient services. This is unfortunate, since such schemes could encourage regular check-ups, early diagnosis and timely care for minor illnesses, reducing overall treatment costs and lowering claims for inpatient insurance products. They might also increase the take up of microinsurance and sta-

bilize the risk pool (Leatherman et al., 2010). A handful of more comprehensive health insurance schemes are being tested using technology to help manage costs and risk, which may provide insights and lessons for other MFIs in the near future. In Nigeria, for instance, Clearline International has partnered with four major banks to introduce a health insurance scheme specifically targeted at the informal sector using electronic "Magicards" and recharge scratch cards to facilitate transactions and monitoring (Clearline International, 2010). In India, the CARE Foundation is planning to use hand-held devices to enable the delivery of basic health care, data collection, biometric identification, insurance and financial transactions in rural areas (CARE Foundation, 2010).

Since the link between an MFI's core services and health insurance is not particularly strong, and health insurance is both a complex and an expensive product, most MFIs tend to steer clear of it. As an alternative, some have developed savings and loan products specifically to meet clients' health-care financing needs. At Réseau des Caisses Populaires du Burkina (RCPB), for instance, clients who open a health savings account agree to set aside a minimum monthly amount and must show medical receipts or a doctor's order to be able to withdraw funds. The account is blocked during an initial six-month "capitalization period", after which clients who continue saving become eligible for a health loan in the case of a major medical expense that their health savings cannot cover (Reinsch and Ramirez, 2010).

MFIs interested in offering health insurance would be wise to keep the scheme at arm's length from their microfinance activities. Unlike life insurance, where it is advantageous for the MFI to manage claims, with health insurance the MFI should avoid the administrative burden of claims processing. In addition, it is difficult for health microinsurance to be self-sustaining. Consequently, MFIs need to ensure that any insurance losses do not adversely affect their microfinance operations.

9.6 Where to Begin?

One of the key factors in deciding what type of insurance to offer is the MFI's motivation for doing so. MFIs' motivations generally fall into two categories: 1) to reduce credit risks by being able to recover loans if borrowers die or are too ill to repay; and 2) to assist their clients in managing risks and to cope with crises and economic stress. Of course, many organizations may be motivated by both objectives, but their primary motivation will probably influence their choice of insurance services and the means of offering them.

In general, it is easier for MFIs in the first category to meet their objectives than for MFIs in the second category. Owing to its relative simplicity, basic credit-linked insurance is more likely to be available to MFIs and more affordable to clients, and it is more likely that MFIs can self-insure. Comprehensive coverage – to protect the poor from the many risks that they really worry about – is very difficult for MFIs to offer on their own, and may not be available from other sources.

If MFIs are motivated to offer insurance primarily because they want to help their clients manage risks, and if they are not already offering savings, then that should be their first priority (where the law allows). The poor are vulnerable to a range of risks and economic stresses, many of which represent relatively small but nagging expenses for which insurance is not an appropriate solution. Insurance covers larger losses and is very risk-specific: for example, a life insurance policy cannot help someone whose valuables are stolen. Savings (and emergency loans) are more flexible and responsive than insurance in coping with risks.

MFIs with a broader development objective should also consider helping their clients to prevent or mitigate their risks, like Shepherd, which offers health workshops and cattle-care camps. While an MFI might undertake prevention strategies to fulfil its social mission, such measures could have the additional advantage of reducing claims, and therefore have a positive impact on the viability of the insurance product.

In selecting insurance products, it is important for MFIs to recognize that they cannot cover all risks, and clients cannot afford to buy numerous insurance products. Indeed, this might be a reason to avoid insurance altogether, since MFIs do not want clients to pay insurance premiums at the expense of loan repayments or savings deposits. If an MFI does decide to go ahead with insurance, the challenge is to figure out the most cost-effective solutions to its clients' primary problems.

Credit Life or Credit Life Plus?

In general, it makes sense for MFIs to start with a simple policy to learn about insurance. Simple products work best because they are easier to administer and easier for clients to understand. Once MFIs know how to manage insurance risks (either on their own or in partnership with an insurer), then they can move on and provide coverage that meets clients' needs better. Similarly, once the market understands better what insurance is, and begins to develop an insurance culture, clients will be more willing to pay for broader benefits.

The simplest insurance product is a basic credit life policy. However, on its own, such a policy will not meet the objectives laid out above. It will not create a firm foundation on which to build other insurance products, because it does not require the necessary infrastructure. Since the benefit is paid to the MFI, no mechanism needs to be developed to pay claims to clients. And since the product is usually mandatory, staff do not have to explain it to customers. Thus no opportunity is created for staff or customers to learn about insurance, and no contribution is made towards creating an insurance culture among the poor. The premiums will be integrated into another financial transaction, so no mechanism needs to be developed to pay premiums. The only additional operational infrastructure required is to collect the necessary claims documents, but that is not a firm foundation on which to build other insurance products.

To begin to create a culture of insurance among the poor, it would be preferable to start with a credit life plus product that requires some training of staff, client education, and tangible benefits that the clients (or at least their beneficiaries) actually see. For that to happen, clients should have some choice of benefits so they have to make an educated decision about what coverage they want. The additional benefits that could be offered with a credit life insurance policy include:

- **Credit disability.** This covers the outstanding balance of the loan in the event of permanent disability and not just death.

- **Additional benefit.** If the borrower dies during the loan term, beneficiaries would receive a fixed payout to cover funeral and other immediate expenses, in addition to having the outstanding balance of the loan paid.
- **Additional lives.** The policy would cover not only the borrower, but also a certain number of additional household members.
- **Continuation.** A one-month renewable term policy could be purchased at the end of a loan term if a client wanted to continue his or her insurance coverage without taking another loan.

An MFI could make basic credit life mandatory, but then give clients the option of purchasing one or more of the above benefits. At minimum, it would be good to extend some coverage to other family members so that clients can actually benefit from insurance without dying. This would also increase the likelihood that people in a community will have a chance to see that the MFI is fulfilling its insurance obligation.

Integrated or Stand-alone?

To offer insurance cost-effectively to the poor, one of the main strategies is to combine it with another financial service, in other words with savings or loans, so that the transaction costs can be minimized. Since credit is the core business of many MFIs, the insurance and loan terms can coincide so clients can renew their loan and their insurance at the same time. By linking cover to the loan, an MFI can also make the premium easier to pay by deducting it from the loan amount. However, not everyone wants a loan, and even people who want loans do not want them all the time, so credit-linked insurance provides incomplete coverage.

Consequently, a link between savings and insurance provides more continuous coverage than the credit–insurance link. For savings-linked insurance products, premiums can be also be paid by automatically deducting the amount from the savings, although there is a public relations risk that depositors may not be aware that the money is being deducted.

From an MFI's perspective, the insurance products that make the most sense are integrated into or linked to the organization's core services of credit and possibly savings. Not only do integrated products enhance efficiency, they also bolster the MFI's core products.

Still, there may be justification for considering stand-alone insurance. The strongest argument is to retain policyholders who want to stop borrowing. MFIs that offer loan-linked insurance should seriously consider a continuation policy that enables clients to retain insurance cover between loans. As long as the MFI has a premium collection method that is independent from a loan, this is a fairly low-risk product, because it does not require additional screening.

A second reason to offer stand-alone insurance is to expand the MFI's market, reaching people it cannot serve through savings and loans. If the MFI does adopt that approach, and it sells microinsurance to non-members, the organization (or its insurance partners) is vulnerable to adverse selection risks. To control this risk, insurance should be offered only to persons who have joined a group for purposes other than accessing insurance, or benefits should be increased gradually over time, or both.

Table 9.1 Advantages of voluntary vs. mandatory loan coverage

Voluntary	Mandatory
1. Voluntary insurance requires that the **client and staff understand the product**. This ensures a sufficient investment in developing the product in clear, communicable terms for marketing purposes. 2. It enables the institution to **assess the demand** for the product. 3. A voluntary service provides better **value to clients** because it does not force them to purchase products they do not want.	1. Mandatory insurance requires a **simple tracking and management** system. It is easier to track insurance for all clients than to distinguish those who are insured and those who are not. 2. It **reduces the risk of adverse selection**. Because all clients are required to join, there is not a high percentage of high-risk policyholders. 3. It enables the insurance provider to **reach large numbers** of policyholders, which allows for both economies of scale and a higher likelihood that actual losses will track closely to the expected losses. 4. It is much **less expensive** for customers.

Source: Churchill et al., 2002.

Mandatory or Voluntary?

Another key decision is whether insurance should be mandatory or voluntary, as summarized in Table 9.1. Either approach can be taken; however, for group methodologies the coverage must be consistent within each group. If a group decides to have insurance, then all members must carry it. Because of joint liability, it would be unfair for some members to pay premiums and therefore relieve the group from the burden of paying for them in the event of default caused by an insured risk, while others continue to depend on the group as the fallback.

Long-term or Short-term?

Short-term insurance is easier for MFIs to offer than longer-term coverage. It is easier to predict whether an insured event will occur in the next year than over the next five or ten years. If an insurer makes errors in the pricing, it is committed to those mistakes for only a short period of time, after which it can make adjustments. It is strongly recommended that microfinance institutions do not get involved in long-term insurance on their own.

Furthermore, many MFIs are not in a position to offer long-term insurance in partnership with an insurance company, because their delivery systems typically revolve around short-term loans. For example, Tata-AIG (an insurer) and the Bridge Foundation (an MFI) linked up to sell a long-term life insurance product that required premiums to be collected over many years. The pilot proved unsuccessful, because the loan term and the insurance term did not coincide. When clients decided to stop borrowing, the MFI did not have a mechanism for them to continue to pay their premiums, resulting in many lapsed policies.

An MFI that uses a savings account as a delivery mechanism could theoretically offer long-term insurance. Yet microfinance institutions may see long-term insurance offered on behalf of an insurance company as competition for the MFI's own savings products.

How to Sell It?

Although studies consistently find that the hypothetical demand for insurance is high, the uptake of a new insurance product is often slow and renewal rates low (Dercon, 2009). In the mainstream insurance market this phenomenon is well known, and has resulted in the saying "insurance is sold, not bought." Many of the reasons for which the marketing of insurance products is difficult have already been mentioned: a lack of understanding about what insurance is, the upfront cost of the insurance premium, the lack of trust in insurance companies to provide compensation when a crisis strikes, and the lack of opportunities for potential clients to test an insurance provider's solvency and credibility.

When an MFI decides to offer an insurance product for the first time, it must think seriously about these barriers, and include strategies for addressing them in its product design. Some of the features that have helped MFIs get their microinsurance products off the ground are:[20]

- **Simplicity.** A simple product design, with as few exclusions as possible, is easier for staff to explain and for clients to understand. La Equidad in Colombia, for example, has two microinsurance products, but has had more success with the one that is simpler.
- **Ease.** In Nicaragua, one MFI gave away tickets for six free months of insurance. All the winners had to do was go to the MFI with their documents, ID, photo, and copies of children's birth certificates to register. Yet only 27 per cent of the winners signed up; the rest said it was too inconvenient. When surveyors were sent to fill out forms and take pictures so that potential clients could do everything at their shops, enrolment went up to 68 per cent (Leatherman et al., 2010).
- **Clarity.** Insurance products are burdened with more jargon than most other financial products, so microinsurers must make a special effort to ensure that terms and conditions are explained in a way that staff and potential clients can understand. Many microinsurers have used consumer education campaigns to help communicate the concept and appropriate use of insurance. Typically, these campaigns rely on pictures, games and theatre, rather than simply words, to communicate effectively.
- **Piggybacking.** MFIs often link their insurance product to something potential clients already trust, perhaps a well-known insurance company, a well-respected public figure, or well-functioning community groups. These entities can help communicate with prospective clients about the product, deliver the product, or strengthen the product's brand. In Poland, for instance, the logo of TUW SKOK resembles the logos of the credit unions with which it works, to draw a connection between the trust that the members have in their credit unions and the credit union's insurance company.
- **Public relations.** As discussed in Chapters 4 and 23, MFIs that want to encourage potential clients to trust them tend to spend more time building relationships that demonstrate a long-term commitment to the community that goes beyond making a profit.
- **After-sales service.** One way that microinsurance distinguishes itself from conventional insurance is by de-emphasizing sales and emphasizing service. In the world of insurance, service is linked largely to claims: making sure clients know how to make claims, assisting them in meeting the documentation requirements, and ensuring that claims are paid quickly with a bare minimum of rejections. Excellent service creates a demonstration

[20] This list is adapted from Churchill and Cohen (2006).

effect whereby the non-insured begin to see that the MFI is fulfilling its obligations and is trustworthy.

- **Publicity around claims.** Positive word-of-mouth experiences early on are key to a product's growth. One of the most common public relations activities for life insurers is to hold claims award ceremonies, where a beneficiary receives an insurance payout at a public event. Testimonials from beneficiaries can be used to communicate the importance of receiving an insurance settlement when a family needs it most.
- **Fairness.** MFIs can promote the solidarity nature of insurance so that people do not feel they have wasted their money if they do not make a claim. If a claim is denied, they must do their best to demonstrate that the denial is fair. An appeals process that is well advertised, simple, friendly and free from political and social manipulation can help facilitate this.

As highlighted in Chapter 23, it is important for an MFI to consider the different market segments that may find its insurance product useful, and to design multiple communication and sales strategies that respond to the different segments' needs and attitudes towards insurance.

Insurance for MFIs?

Besides considering what insurance products to offer their clients, microfinance institutions also need to consider their own insurance needs. MFIs working in partnership with an insurance company should consider packaging their entire insurance needs – those of the MFI and its clients – into the discussions to achieve a better deal. In addition, if staff members are covered by the policies that they also sell to the MFI's clients, it helps ensure that staff understand the policy. If they do not like the product, there is a strong likelihood that the MFI's clients will not like it either.

In general, MFIs should assess whether they need the following types of corporate coverage:

- **Life and health insurance for employees.** MFIs should be concerned with protecting their most valuable assets, their employees. Modest investments in life and health cover for employees and their families can reap significant returns in the form of staff retention, higher productivity and fewer working days lost to illness.
- **Fidelity insurance.** Bonds guarantee a payment or a reimbursement of financial losses resulting from dishonesty, failure to perform and other acts. One type of bond is fidelity insurance, which protects the MFI from losses incurred due to fraudulent acts perpetrated by specified staff members.
- **Money storage and handling.** Any MFI that stores or transports cash is vulnerable to theft. As the amount of cash in the safes or in transit increases, MFIs would be wise to supplement their internal control and security policies with insurance coverage.
- **Property loss or damage.** Many MFIs have a lot of money invested in their office infrastructure, and these offices are often located in high-risk communities. Certainly, protection against fire, vandalism and other property loss is worth considering.
- **Deposit insurance.** In many countries, deposit insurance is a public service provided by or in association with the central bank for regulated deposit taking institutions. However,

such an arrangement could be delegated to an insurance company that has better information about the health of certain financial institutions than the central bank.

9.7 Conclusions and Recommendations

There are no reasons why an MFI has to offer insurance. Indeed, most MFIs should focus on improving the effectiveness of their lending activities and introducing savings facilities before they distract themselves with insurance.

If an MFI decides to offer insurance, it needs to recognize that it cannot address all risks for everyone; it needs to determine the most cost-effective way to help clients solve their primary problems without undermining the organization's core business. It also should consider whether it has sufficient skills to provide insurance, either on its own or with an insurance company. Insurance training for microfinance managers will strengthen their ability to negotiate appropriate products on behalf of their clients.

Microfinance institutions that are keen to offer insurance to protect themselves, their clients, or both, should explore the potential for partnerships with insurance companies. Where such partnerships are possible, they should adapt the products and systems to accommodate the characteristics and preferences of the low-income market. Where the regulatory environment allows, MFIs or associations of MFIs could also consider creating brokerage firms or even their own insurance companies, although these need to be managed at arm's length to ensure that credit policies do not influence insurance policies, and vice versa.

When determining what products to offer, and through which channels, an important consideration is how an MFI can best create an insurance culture in its target market. For example, what can the MFI do in terms of product design, service standards and customer education to create conditions in which low-income households appreciate insurance and are willing to pay for additional benefits?

There remains a gap between the risks that the poor really worry about – such as affordable health care and protection from natural disasters – and the insurance products that MFIs can realistically offer, even in partnership with an insurer. Microfinance institutions have to be realistic about what they can and cannot provide, and at what cost. Indeed, some types of insurance for the poor, such as health insurance, may need to be subsidized, which might not make sense for an MFI with a commercial business model.

Main Messages

1. Insurance is one way for MFIs to help their clients to manage risk, not the only way.
2. Microinsurance requires a different skill set than savings and credit.
3. In most circumstances, MFIs should partner with regulated insurance companies to provide microinsurance.
4. In the partner-agent model, the MFI needs to manage the relationship with the insurer to ensure that it is able to provide valuable services to its clients.

Recommended Reading

- Banthia, A.; Johnson, S.; McCord, M.; Mathews, B. 2009. *Microinsurance that works for women: Making gender-sensitive microinsurance programs* (Geneva, ILO), at: http://www.ilo.org/public/english/employment/mifacility/download/mpaper3_gender.pdf
- Brown, W.; Churchill, C. 1999. "Providing insurance to low-income households. Part I: A primer on insurance principles and products", in *New Products for Microfinance,* Review Paper 1 (Bethesda, MD, USAID MBP Project), at: http://www.microfinancegateway.org/gm/document-1.9.26877/2459_file_02459.pdf
- Brown, W.; Churchill, C. 2000. "Insurance provision in low-income communities. Part II: Initial lessons from micro-insurance experiments for the poor", *New Products for Microfinance,* Review Paper 2 (Bethesda, MD, USAID MBP Project), at: http://www.microfinancegateway.org/gm/document-1.9.28683/2460_file_02460.pdf
- Churchill, C. (ed.). 2006. *Protecting the poor: A microinsurance compendium* (Geneva, ILO), also available at: http://www.munichre-foundation.org/StiftungsWebsite/Projects/Microinsurance/2006 Microinsurance/Microinsurance_Compendium.htm
- Churchill, C., Liber, D., McCord, M., Roth, J. 2003. *Making insurance work for microfinance institutions: A technical guide to developing and delivering microinsurance* (Geneva, ILO)
- Good and Bad Practices in Microinsurance Case Study Series, available at: http://www.ilo.org/employment/Whatwedo/Publications/lang--en/WCMS_123376/index.htm
- Leatherman, S.; Christensen, L.; Holtz, J. 2010. *Innovations and barriers in health microinsurance,* Microinsurance Paper No. 6 (Geneva, ILO), at: http://www.ilo.org/public/english/employment/mifacility/download/mpaper6_health_en.pdf
- Mosley, P. 2009. *Assessing the success of microinsurance programmes in meeting the insurance needs of the poor,* DESA Working Paper No. 84 (New York, United Nations Department of Economic and Social Affairs), at: http://www.un.org/esa/desa/papers/2009/wp84_2009.pdf
- Roth, J., McCord, M.; Liber, D. 2007. *The landscape of microinsurance in the world's 100 poorest countries* (Appleton, WI, MicroInsurance Centre), at: http://www.microinsurancecentre.org/UI/DocAbstractDetails.aspx?DocID=634
- Wipf, J.; Garand, D. 2008. *Performance indicators for microinsurance: A handbook for microinsurance practitioners* (Luxembourg, ADA), at: http://www.microfinancegateway.org/p/site/m//template.rc/1.9.29234

Useful Websites

- Microinsurance Centre: www.microinsurancecentre.org
- Microinsurance Innovation Facility: http://www.ilo.org/public/english/employment/mifacility/
- Microinsurance Network: www.microinsurancenetwork.org

10 Leasing[21]

It is now widely recognized that the acquisition of equipment is often a key channel through which microentrepreneurs expand their businesses, improve their products, and raise their incomes – underscoring the importance of equipment finance. ~ Westley (2003)

Equipment finance is a significant part of microfinance. Based on a July 2002 survey of 25 MFIs in Latin America, many of which are considered to be industry leaders, equipment loans and leases account for an average of 21 per cent of MFIs' overall portfolios. Of these 25 MFIs, 23 offer equipment loan or lease products with at least two-year terms (Westley, 2003). Most of this equipment finance consists of loans, but there is a small and growing movement towards leasing, which reflects the advantages of leasing over lending in certain circumstances (ILO, 2007a; Westley 2003).

This chapter seeks to clarify the major differences between leasing and lending, and to explore the conditions under which MFIs might consider adding leasing to their existing product portfolio. It covers the following five topics:

1. What is leasing?
2. What can be leased?
3. Leasing vs. lending
4. Under what conditions is leasing viable?
5. Can partnerships make it work?

10.1 What Is Leasing?

Leasing is a contract in which someone uses equipment owned by somebody else. The user, the **lessee**, pays specific regular amounts to the **lessor**, the equipment owner. The important feature of leasing is that the use of the equipment is separated from its ownership. The leasing arrangement benefits both parties: the lessee generates extra income from the use of the equipment, and the owner receives income while retaining the security of ownership.

Enterprises throughout the world use leasing to finance vehicles, machinery and equipment. In developed countries, up to one-third of equipment investment is financed this way. Leasing in developing countries started slowly, but during the 1990s the leasing industry saw spectacular growth, mostly through leases to large and medium enterprises.

In a standard lease operation, summarized in Figure 10.1, the lessee goes to an equipment supplier, chooses the needed equipment, and negotiates the price and terms of delivery. Then, rather than approaching a bank for a loan, the lessee approaches a lessor. The lessor evaluates the lease application, and if it is approved, the two parties sign a lease contract. The lessor purchases the equipment from the supplier and leases it to the lessee for a period that is usually close to the estimated economic life of the asset. During this **lease term**, the lessee uses the equipment and makes regular payments to the lessor. In many cases, the lessee has the option

21 This module was adapted from Deelen et al. (2003).

Figure 10.1 The standard lease operation

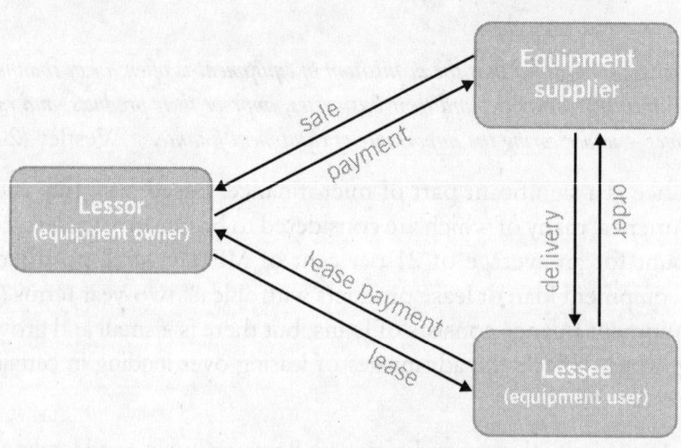

Source: Deelen et al., 2003.

to buy the equipment at the end of the lease term. Typically, the lessee is responsible for any insurance or repairs that are not covered by the supplier's warranty.

The word "lease" has a number of slightly different meanings, depending on the type of contractual arrangement. The meaning also can differ from country to country.[22] Broadly, there are four different types of leasing:

- A **financial lease** is a way of financing the purchase of equipment. In a financial lease, the lease term is set close to (although less than) the expected economic life of the equipment. The lease payments are set so that their total over the lease term will cover the cost of the asset plus interest and profit. At the end of the lease term, the lessee usually has the right to purchase the equipment. The residual value of the equipment at the end of the lease term is of little or no significance to the lessor.
- In an **operating lease** a lessee signs a contract for the short-term use of the equipment – a common example is car rentals. The lessor purchases the equipment and makes profits by renting it out to different users. The lessor bears the risk related to the residual value of the equipment, as well as the risk of obsolescence.
- **Hire-purchase**, which is similar to a financial lease, is a way to finance the purchase of equipment. It is normally used for small items such as sewing machines and refrigerators. In hire-purchase, part of the ownership is transferred with each payment. Upon payment of the last instalment, the lessee becomes the full owner.
- **Sale and leaseback** is much like a financial lease, except that the client is the initial owner of the equipment. The client sells the equipment to the lessor, and signs a contract to lease back the equipment through regular payments. The lessor in turn provides funds for working capital.

For microfinance, a financial lease or hire-purchase scheme would generally be the most relevant approaches, since they allow the lessee to own the asset at the end of the lease term (unlike

22 For example, in India, a financial lease cannot have a buy option; leases with an option to buy are called hire-purchase schemes. In Ghana, however, leases with purchase options are called financial leases.

an operating lease) and they do not require the lessee to own equipment upfront (as with sale and leaseback). The rest of this chapter focuses on issues related to financial leases.

10.2 What Can Be Leased?

Leasing is often associated with the financing of such major assets as tractors, vehicles and heavy-duty machinery. However, leases can be used to finance any asset that is durable, identifiable, movable and sellable. This can include livestock, land, and many types of small equipment, as shown in Table 10.1.

Table 10.1 Sample of assets with leasing potential

Retail trade	Refrigerators, freezers, weighing scales
Food processing	Juicing machines, honey-harvesting gear, oil presses, pasteurizers, milk separators, canning and bottling equipment
Information technology	Computers, printers, fax machines, photocopiers, UPS units
Transport	Bicycles, pushcarts, rickshaws, motorcycles, taxis
Small-scale manufacturing	Hand tools, electrical or carpentry equipment, welding machines, grinders, cutters, generators
Entertainment and hospitality	Chairs, cooking pans, utensils, stoves, tents, music systems
Health clinics	Admission beds, blood pressure machine, stethoscopes, sterilizers, simple microscopes, refrigerators for vaccination, filing cabinets
Agriculture	Small-scale spraying equipment, hand tools, wheelbarrows, land
Small mining	Picks, shovels, wheel barrows, portable compressors, crushers

Source: Adapted from Mutesasira et al., 2001.

One of the issues that generates significant debate among those who design leasing products is whether or not lessors should finance second-hand (or used) assets. Used assets are more affordable for clients, and lessors can finance them over shorter terms. Most MFIs will appreciate these advantages, given the markets they serve and the lower credit risk and asset and liability management risk associated with shorter terms. At Development Finance Company Uganda (DFCU), which serves primarily small and medium enterprises, more than 60 per cent of the leases written are for used equipment (Kisaame, 2003). Caisses d'Epargne et de Crédit Agricole Mutuel (CECAM) in Madagascar and Network Leasing Corporation Limited (NLCL) in Pakistan serve the microenterprise market and also offer leases on used equipment.

Of course, second-hand assets have a higher risk of breakdowns than newly purchased assets, and if a leased asset breaks down, the lessor is much less likely to be paid. To compensate for this risk, CECAM requires a higher down-payment on its used equipment leases (40 per cent) than its new equipment leases (20 per cent) (Fraslin, 2003). Other lessors request additional collateral. Some MFIs, such as Asociación Nacional Ecuménica de Desarrollo (ANED) in Bolivia and Grameen Bank in Bangladesh, simply do not finance used equipment. This can be a wise decision if maintenance facilities are not available nearby, as is often the case in rural areas such as those served by ANED and Grameen.

10.3 Leasing vs. Lending

If an MFI wants to provide asset financing and it already has the capacity to make equipment loans, or if it is debating between the introduction of such a loan product and a leasing product, leasing may be an attractive option, as explored below.

The Advantages of Leasing

Leasing offers several advantages over loans for organizations that want to provide asset financing. As Nair and Kloeppinger-Todd (2006) explain, these advantages stem from the way the two types of financing are structured as well as the regulatory framework that governs them. In a lease the lessor owns the asset, while in a loan the creditor has only a **lien**, or a legal claim, on the asset. This fundamental difference in the two products results in the following:

- **Stronger security position.** In case of default, legal ownership of the leased asset makes it easier for the lessor to seize and sell the asset if this becomes necessary due to a lessee's default on payments. This is an important advantage in many developing countries, where unclear property rights, weak court systems and poorly functioning asset registries can make it difficult to enforce liens.
- **Lower collateral requirements**. Since ownership strengthens the lessor's ability to recover its funds in the event of default, the leased asset itself is often all that is required to secure a leasing transaction. Thus leasing can enable MFIs to finance the acquisition of assets by clients with limited collateral without a group guarantee. This makes leasing a particularly valuable product for replacing assets that may be lost due to natural disasters or man-made crises (see Chapter 18). It can also be valuable in rural areas where land titles may not exist, and movable assets such as livestock and warehouse receipts may not be legally permissible as collateral.
- **Simpler evaluation.** A lease can be concluded more quickly and simply than a loan. Rather than looking into the credit history and asset structure of the client, the lessor has only to make sure that the client has the ability to generate sufficient cash through the leased equipment. Less detailed documentation is necessary, and the appraisal can be processed relatively quickly.
- **Smaller down payments.** An upfront payment of a certain percentage of the asset value demonstrates clients' commitment to the lease and minimizes potential loss to the lessor. Leasing down payments tend to be lower than what would be required for a similarly sized loan, although they can approach similar levels when the leased asset is expected to deteriorate rapidly, or when the regulatory environment makes it difficult to seize and sell leased assets. Down payments tend to be higher for rural leases to compensate for the higher cost of recovering assets and the higher risk associated with financing rural assets. CECAM, for example, requires 20 per cent down payment for equipment, but requires 25 per cent for farm animals because of the higher risk of losing this asset. John Deere, Mexico, demands 30 per cent down payment for agricultural equipment, but only 15 per cent for construction equipment. Although upfront payments may be less for leases than for loans, they can still represent a significant access barrier for low-income clients. CECAM has dealt with this problem by offering clients a savings plan through which they can accumulate the funds for the leasing down payment (Nair et al., 2004).

- **No risk of fund diversion.** In leasing, the funding provided goes directly to the purchase of equipment without even passing through the hands of the lessee. This averts the risk that the lessee might use the funds for purposes not agreed upon. It also avoids the risk that the lessee might use the loan to repay a debt to another financial institution.
- **Longer terms, larger amounts.** Loan terms for microcredit rarely exceed one year, and the amounts tend to be restricted by the type and availability of collateral. Leasing allows for longer terms, generally two to five years, as well as a larger amount of financing.
- **Less aggressive approach to delinquency.** Because a lease is secured and the leasing contract is relatively easy to enforce (at least compared with a loan contract), the lessor can adopt a less vigilant approach to delinquency management than one commonly finds in microfinance.
- **Fewer legal restrictions.** Many countries impose ceilings on loan interest rates, particularly for small or rural loans, but they do not regulate lease rates. Leasing companies also face less stringent requirements on capitalization, debt-equity ratios and credit allocations, which gives leasing operations more leverage in raising funds and more flexibility to charge market interest rates that let them extend their reach to client segments that lenders might consider too high risk (Rozner, 2006)
- **Lower costs.** Simpler evaluation, the avoidance of foreclosure and asset registry expenses, less aggressive delinquency management, and less stringent regulatory requirements typically make it less expensive to contract a lease than to issue a loan. In addition, MFÌs that receive numerous requests to finance the same type of equipment may have sufficient bargaining power to negotiate better prices than individuals who finance an asset purchase through borrowing would be able to obtain on their own (see Box 10.1). ACBA Leasing in Armenia, for example, gets a 5 per cent discount on the purchase of both Kamaz Trucks (imported from Russia) and Heidelberg printing equipment (imported from Germany). This discount is passed on to lessees (Hakobyan, 2006).
- **Tax benefits.** Leasing can offer both lessees and lessors tax advantages that borrowing/lending cannot. In many countries, the lessee can offset lease payments against tax-

Box 10.1 Dealer Discount Programmes

MFIs that contract numerous leases for the same type of equipment each year may have sufficient bargaining power to negotiate discounted prices, extended warranties or additional service benefits with one or more dealers. Such MFIs should select reputable equipment dealers with good products, service, and availability of spare parts, and then try to negotiate discounts and other benefits from these dealers. The MFI should then make the dealer discount programmes known to their lease clients, but should not require that clients choose equipment only from these dealers. Leading Latin American MFIs as well as Mutesasira et al. (2001) argue that clients should be allowed to choose which model of equipment they buy and from which dealer they buy it, although the MFI should reserve the right to veto the choice by denying financing. Some lessors that have not followed this strategy in the past have found that if something goes wrong with the equipment the client may blame them and possibly use this as a pretext for withholding payments.

Source: Adapted from Westley, 2003.

able income, while borrowers can only deduct the interest paid on loans. Furthermore, the lessor as owner of the asset can claim depreciation benefits, which the lessor may or may not pass on to the lessee through reduced financing costs. The net impact of taxes on leasing depends on many factors, however, including a variety of other taxes (for example, value-added tax, capital gains tax and property tax), whether the lessor and lessee are tax-paying entities, and the length of lease terms (Westley, 2003).

The Challenges of Leasing

In a leasing contract, the fact that the leased asset is owned by the lessor but will be operated by the lessee creates two main challenges. First, the lessor must ensure that the asset remains in working order throughout the life of the lease. Otherwise, the lessee may not earn enough income from the leased asset to make payments on the lease (see Box 10.2), and it will be difficult for the lessor to sell the asset to recover its investment. This challenge becomes more acute when leasing used equipment because of the technical expertise that is required to accurately determine the condition of the asset to be leased, and therefore the life over which the asset can realistically be financed. The challenge is also greater in rural areas, where maintenance facilities are not easily accessible and monitoring costs can be high.

Rozner (2006) notes that monitoring costs can be reduced by engaging local partners to help monitor the leases, but fostering such relationships can require considerable time and effort. An alternative is suggested by CECAM, which successfully monitors its leases through solidarity groups (see Box 10.3). Lessors may be able to encourage equipment maintenance through incentives such as a purchase option at the end of the lease, or by requiring equipment maintenance capabilities as a precondition for applying for a lease. They can also facilitate contracts with equipment suppliers that include technical training for new lessees (see, for example, the case of ANED at the end of this chapter). Some lessors, such as United Leasing Company (ULC) in Tanzania, try to facilitate maintenance by

Box 10.2 GIE Hari Goumo in Timbuktu, Mali

GIE Hari Goumo leased irrigation motor pumps valued at US$6,700 each with the help of the Belgian NGO "Îles de Paix". The pumps were rented to farmers at US$670 per season. The leasing scheme failed because:

- The European-manufactured motor pumps were not designed for the African environment, and were too expensive to be viable.
- Farmers overused their pumps and used cheap, dirty oil, which caused them to break down quickly.
- Lessees were expected to pay half the season's rent in advance, and half at harvest, but most failed to pay the final instalment.
- When pumps broke down, backup pumps were not available for farmers to use during repair.
- The lessor had no system to monitor the proper use of rented equipment.

Source: Sempangi and Messan, 2005.

Box 10.3 Rural Leasing at CECAM, Madagascar

Caisses d'Epargne et de Crédit Agricole Mutuels Madagascar (CECAM), a network of savings and agricultural credit cooperatives, was created in 1991 by the farmer organization FIFATA with the financial and technical assistance of a French NGO, FERT. It is the largest financial institution in rural Madagascar, with 170 local offices and eight regional credit unions. It provides working capital loans, grain storage loans, term loans and microleases. Leases account for 27 per cent of its portfolio.

CECAM uses leases to finance a variety of assets including capital equipment for agriculture (ploughs, harrows) and animals, equipment for rural artisan implements (wielding units, vans) and domestic equipment (bicycles, sewing machines, solar lights, televisions). To qualify for a lease, the lessee needs to be a network member. Secondary income sources are not required. Leases are secured through the equipment and by the verbal promise of solidarity group members, who monitor that the equipment is well maintained and not sold or destroyed. Lease applications are appraised by local credit committees, and payment schedules are flexible to fit clients' production cycle.

Source: Adapted from Fraslin, 2003, and Nair et al., 2004.

scheduling lower lease payments during periods when maintenance is more likely to be required, thus increasing the likelihood that lessees will have cash on hand to pay for the maintenance (Mutesasira et al., 2001).

The second challenge posed by the separation between asset ownership and usage is an increase in liability and litigation risks. As the owner of the leased asset, an MFI could be liable for third-party losses arising out of its client's operation of the asset. This risk is particularly important in the case of vehicle leases, where there is a risk of accidents that could harm others. The risk can be mitigated through liability insurance, as NLCL has done in Pakistan (see Box 10.4). The potential for legal disputes is greater for leases than loans because the difference in ownership and usage rights makes leases more complex, especially in the case of sale and lease-back arrangements (see Box 10.5), but researchers have found this risk to be relatively minor for MFIs (Nair et al., 2004).

Box 10.4 Insurance and Leasing at NLCL, Pakistan

Network Leasing Corporation Limited (NLCL) pioneered microleasing in Pakistan in the mid-1990s and currently is one of the leading providers in the country. Its lease portfolio in 2004 was US$11.6 million. Twenty-one per cent of its portfolio and 43 per cent of its leases were in rural areas. All NLCL leases are covered by insurance on the life of the client, so that NLCL does not have to repossess the asset when the client dies. This is both prudent for NLCL and humane for the client's family. NLCL also takes out insurance to cover all risks (fire, theft, etc.) on each leased asset, as well as a residual value insurance in case a repossessed asset is worth less than the outstanding amount of the lease. All the costs of this insurance are included in the lease payments made by the client.

Source: Adapted from Havers, 1999, and Nair and Kloeppinger-Todd, 2006.

Box 10.5 Litigation Risk

Consider, for example, a leased machine that requires repairs during the equipment warranty period. If the dealer baulks at making the repairs, claiming that the lessee abused the machine, the MFI, as owner, could find itself in the middle of an unwanted, and perhaps unexpected, legal battle. Leasing operations may give rise to legal problems not experienced with loans in cases where leasing is new to the country and many courts still do not understand it fully. This may occur even with an adequate leasing law or other legal framework for undertaking leasing operations. As an example, the head of ANED's microleasing operations tells of a legal problem involving a disputed sale and leaseback transaction in rural Bolivia. The judge who was hearing the case kept asking ANED whether they were buying the good or leasing the good, unable to understand that they were doing both.

Source: Nair et al., 2004.

In addition to the challenges that result from the separation of ownership and usage, leasing may be less attractive than lending for a few other reasons:

Set-up and operating costs. It is likely to cost more to set up and operate a leasing product than a loan product designed to finance similar assets. The main reasons for this are summarized below:

- MFI staff must familiarize themselves with leasing.
- Marketing campaigns must be designed to explain leasing to clients.
- An insurance strategy will have to be developed.
- If value-added tax (VAT) is charged on lease payments, the MFI's information system may have to be modified so that it can track and pay VAT on its leasing operations.
- For each lease transaction, the MFI will have to incur the cost of purchasing the equipment desired by the client.
- If the MFI wishes to negotiate dealer discount programmes, this will create some set-up and operating costs, although it will also help steer clients to reputable dealers, which can benefit both the MFI and the client in the long run.

Working capital constraints. A financial lease can only finance the purchase of fixed assets. It cannot fulfil a client's need for working capital directly. Lessors need to be aware that a lack of working capital could jeopardize their clients' capacity to generate extra cash flows through the leased equipment, and this in turn could jeopardize their ability to keep up with lease payments.

Cannibalization. If an MFI already offers an equipment loan, or a working capital loan with a sufficiently long term and sufficiently large amount that it can be used to purchase assets, the introduction of a leasing product may decrease demand for the MFI's existing product. If the leasing product attracts new customers, the cannibalization will not be a major concern, because the costs of developing the new product can be covered by the additional revenue generated through growth in the total number of clients served. If, however, the leasing product attracts only the same types of customer that have already been using the MFI's existing loan product, the leasing product may not increase the total number of clients served, and the

costs of introducing the new product will be covered only if the leasing product is delivered more efficiently than the loan product. In any case, institutions should take into account the potential decrease in the size of their loan portfolio that could result from the introduction of a leasing product as they make their projections.

The characteristics of loan and lease products designed to finance assets are summarized in Table 10.2.

Table 10.2 Comparing loan and lease products

Characteristics	Loan	Lease
Ownership	Borrower	Lessor
Equity/down payment	Usually 30–40%	Usually 15–25%
Collateral	Usually seek land and/or collateral in addition to equipment being financed	Usually only equipment being leased, may require additional collateral
Security position	Lien on equipment, other collateral	Title to equipment gives stronger legal position for equipment seizure and sale in the event of client default
Transaction costs	High: costs include creating, perfecting and enforcing lien position; many countries do not have efficient asset registries	Lower: repossession easier because lessor owns equipment
Regulation	Banks subject to prudential regulation	Leasing companies not as regulated (unless deposit-taking, which is unusual); fewer restrictions re interest rates, credit allocations, collateral requirements
Tax benefits	Borrower recognizes depreciation, borrower records interest on loans as expenditure, lender records interest on loans as taxable income	Depending on the tax regulation: 1) the treatment of a financial lease is the same as for loans, or 2) the lessor recognizes the depreciation of the asset, the lessor records the entire lease payment as taxable income, the borrower records the entire lease instalment (capital plus interest) as expenditure
Portfolio risk	Similar analysis procedure; lessor has less risk because of stronger ownership position	
Liability and litigation risk	Little/none	Lessor may have liability for third-party losses from operation of asset (especially vehicles); ownership/use rights more complex

Source: Adapted from USAID, undated.

10.4 Under What Conditions Is Leasing Viable?

Leasing is more challenging for MFIs that currently provide short-term, group-based working capital loans and want to introduce medium-term individual leases that finance asset purchases. As mentioned previously, it is also more challenging for MFIs that work in rural areas. How can an institution know if it is up for the challenge? This section discusses the minimum internal and external conditions that must exist in order for a leasing scheme to succeed.

External Conditions

Enabling regulatory environment. Lessors will survive only if an enabling regulatory framework for leasing is in place. This means that:

- There should be a clear definition of what constitutes a financial lease transaction, and what the responsibilities and rights of the lessor and lessee are.
- Procedures for obtaining a leasing license must be transparent.
- Requirements regarding the capitalization of a leasing scheme should be less stringent than for deposit-taking financial intermediaries.
- Procedures for lessors to repossess equipment in case of default have to be straightforward. The easier and faster it is to reclaim an asset and claim payments and damages due, the more feasible it will be for lessors to take on riskier clients and offer leases with lower risk premiums.
- Liability for third-party losses arising from the use of a leased asset should also be clear.
- The tax treatment of lessors and lessees has to be consistent and favourable to leasing.
- Under conditions of bankruptcy the lessor's claim to the asset should be superior to any claim creditors may have on the lessee.

In countries where no specific regulation for leasing exists, the regulatory framework should at least not pose impediments.

Sufficient demand for leasing. A critical mass of entrepreneurs must be in need of medium-term investment finance for similar types of equipment. What constitutes a critical mass will vary depending on an MFI's cost structure, but several hundred potential customers within a serviceable geographic area will usually be necessary.

Existence of equipment markets. Leasing needs reliable equipment suppliers who value their relationship with the MFI as part of their own marketing strategy. In distorted or uncompetitive equipment markets, MFIs will have difficulty negotiating favourable prices and conditions with suppliers. If the leased equipment will serve as its own collateral, the existence of a second-hand market will also be important, because MFIs will need a way to sell repossessed equipment. Institutions that extend leases for equipment without a second-hand market usually take household goods that can be easily resold as the primary or only collateral. However, this strategy works only as long as the leased asset is not very expensive, so that its financing can be fully collateralized by a collection of household goods.

Technical support and after-sales service. As mentioned previously, one of the major challenges for lessors is the maintenance of equipment. Because lessees do not own the equipment, and may not opt to own it at the end of the lease, there is a moral hazard risk that they will not keep the leased assets in good repair. Unless lessees have access to efficient workshops and spare parts, even those who want to keep their equipment in good condition will not be able to do so. Access to technical analysis expertise is also important, particularly when used equipment serves as collateral for the leae, so that MFIs and clients can make appropriate decisions about what technology and equipment to finance. Most financial institutions do not have this capacity in-house, so they have to establish links with institutions that can provide technical assistance and recommendations. One of the reasons why NLCL has been able to lease used equipment successfully is that it has a number of reputable independent machinery valuers that it can rely upon to determine resale values and consequent lease amounts (Havers, 1999).

Internal Conditions

Matching of financial resources. The larger amounts and longer terms of leases (generally two to five years) require that MFIs have sufficient equity and/or access to medium-term debt to meet demand for the product. If an institution attempts to finance medium-term leases with short-term loans or a volatile deposit base, it exposes itself to interest rate and liquidity risks, which could result in financial loss or even bankruptcy if one day it does not have enough cash on hand to meet its short-term obligations (see Box 10.6). MFIs with substantial capital (in other words, paid-in shares, retained earnings or grants, none of which has a fixed maturity) can finance medium- or even long-term leases without interest rate or liquidity risk. However, MFIs that do not have sufficient capital to finance a leasing portfolio will have to attract these funds, which can be difficult in many developing countries.

Human resources. Lease officers need to be able to assess the value of the equipment to be leased, the business and household cash flow of the lease applicant, the extra cash flow the leased asset can be expected to yield, and the environment in which the leased asset will be used. These skills may be quite different from those required by an MFI's existing product(s). If so, the institution will need to either develop such skills among existing staff or hire new staff with a different profile. When Africa Village Financial Services, S.C. (AVFS) launched its leasing product in Ethiopia, it found it necessary to hire a full-time staff person to explore possible suppliers and maintenance persons, to obtain insurance, and to negotiate with suppliers to train clients on how to use the leased equipment (Dawit, 2010). In Armenia, ACBA Leasing created an asset manager position to analyse the equipment being leased and to maintain good relations with distributors, since much of the equipment it leases must be imported (Hakobyan, 2006).

Operating systems. Besides an information system for financial monitoring, lessors need to be able to keep track of the status and value of all leased assets. If an MFI's leasing operations are subject to VAT, it will also have to be able to track how much tax is owed. Standard banking software is unlikely to meet these requirements.

Box 10.6 Interest Rate and Liquidity Risks

Interest rate and liquidity risks arise when an MFI's assets and liabilities have different maturities. Suppose, for simplicity, that an MFI makes a substantial amount of four-year equipment leases in a short period of time at an interest rate of 35 per cent, and funds all of these leases with a two-year bank loan at 12 per cent. Also suppose that the MFI requires a margin of 18 per cent to cover its operating costs and expected loan losses. Under these circumstances, the MFI looks to make a healthy profit of 5 per cent on these loans (= 35% – 12% – 18%). But what happens if, in two years' time, the country has entered into a period of tight money or inflation that has pushed bank loan rates up by 10 percentage points, from 12 per cent to 22 per cent? When the MFI goes to renew its two-year bank loan, its 5 per cent profit turns into a 5 per cent loss. This is an example of interest rate risk, which is the risk that changes in market interest rates will affect the financial institution's profitability.

Even worse is the possibility that after two years the bank might not renew its loan to the MFI at all. This could provoke a serious liquidity crisis for the MFI, because its four-year equipment loans would then be unfunded for their last two years. Such non-renewals can happen in periods of tight money or recession, for example, because during such periods banks often pull back and fund only their larger and more profitable clients. Or after the initial two years, the bank simply might not deem the MFI creditworthy any longer, and so may decline to continue funding it. Both interest rate and liquidity risks could have been avoided in this example had the MFI matched the maturity of its assets (the equipment leases to clients) with that of its liabilities (the bank loan). That is, had both maturities been four years (or two years), the MFI would not have been exposed to these risks.

Source: Westley, 2003.

10.5 Can Partnership Make It Work?

If an MFI wants to make a leasing product available to its clients but cannot meet one or more of the conditions described above, it may be able to partner with leasing companies, equipment suppliers, investors or NGOs to achieve this objective. The most straightforward partnership would likely be a **broker–lessor relationship** in which an MFI takes on the role of broker in partnership with a leasing company. The MFI would provide some of the services in the lease transaction in exchange for a fee, but it would not hold the lease in its own portfolio.

An MFI's role as broker would depend on the arrangement between it and the leasing company. It could be involved in marketing the lease product, screening potential clients, arranging for the equipment with the manufacturer and/or collecting and monitoring lease payments. All of these services could be provided for a fee, or an MFI could share the risk of the leasing contract with the leasing company and also share the profit. DFCU Leasing, which operates primarily in urban areas, and the Gatsby Trust, a local NGO in Uganda, partnered to increase leasing outreach in rural areas, and their agreement is based on equal risk-sharing whereby each partner supplies 50 per cent of the cost of financing (Nair et al., 2004).

Figure 10.2 Supply chain leasing

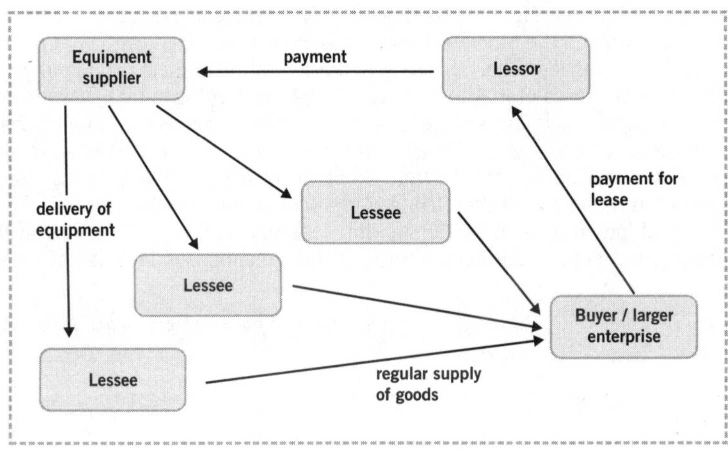

Source: Deelen et al., 2003.

Beyond the relative simplicity of a broker–lessor relationship, there is another type of leasing partnership that might be useful to MFIs. **Supply chain leasing** targets industries where many micro- or small enterprises produce inputs on a regular and predictable basis for larger companies further down the supply chain. This model assumes that both the enterprises and their buyer have a strong interest in increasing production and maintaining their commercial relationship. A lessor can take advantage of this relationship between supplier and buyer by leasing equipment to the enterprises, which will produce a minimum quantity of goods/services for the buyer, and the buyer's payment for those goods/services covers the lease payments. The buyer monitors the enterprises, deducts lease instalments from its payments to the enterprises (the lessees), and transfers the amount owed to the lessor. In the event of default, the lessor has a claim not only on the leased asset itself, but also on any outstanding payment (typically 60 or 90 days' supply) that the buyer owes the lessee (see Figure 10.2).

This model has several advantages. First, since the buyer will incur extra administrative costs to participate in the scheme, its willingness to participate confirms a market for the lessees' products/services, and hence the viability of lessees' businesses. Second, the buyer significantly reduces the lessor's costs by collecting lease payments through its own financial systems. Third, the buyer is in a privileged position to monitor the performance of lessees' businesses, since it should become aware of problems in output long before default occurs. Finally, the lessees' incentives against default are increased by the prospective penalty of losing payments owed by the buyer.

Supply chain leasing has not been used much in microfinance. Available examples (see Box 10.7 for one) tend to be "lease-like" contractual arrangements rather than pure leases. It is a more complex type of partnership to negotiate and manage, but it could be a relevant option for MFIs operating in rural areas.

Box 10.7 Innovative Partnership for Microleasing

In the Jordan Valley, the USAID-funded PAPA project partnered with Alrafah Microfinance Bank and the Sinokrot Food Company to experiment with greenhouses for smallholder farmers as lease-based collateral. Participating farmers had to put up 20 per cent of the investment capital. An additional 50 per cent of the capital was provided by the project as a grant, and farmers could access financing from the MFI for the balance, pledging their greenhouse as collateral. The farmers received input supply, marketing, certification and packaging services from Sinokrot, which effectively owned the greenhouses until the farmers paid their loans to the MFI in full. Sinokrot, as a buyer of the farmers' output, could deduct any outstanding loan balances from the sales revenue of their produce, but could also reclaim and sell the greenhouses in cases of default by farmers.

Source: Adapted from Hishigsuren and Husseini, 2007.

Main Messages

1. Leasing facilitates the acquisition of equipment, which can enable entrepreneurs to start, improve or expand their businesses.
2. Leases can be used to finance any asset that is durable, identifiable, movable and sellable.
3. In a lease, the lessor owns the asset, whereas in a loan the creditor has only a lien on the asset.
4. The fact that a leased asset is owned by the lessor yet will be operated by the lessee creates advantages and disadvantages that are distinct from asset-based lending.
5. When the conditions do not exist for an MFI to develop its own leasing product, partnerships can make leasing viable.

Case Study: ANED's Leasing Programme, Bolivia

In 1997, Asociación Nacional Ecuménica de Desarrollo (ANED) in Bolivia developed a microleasing programme to complement its existing microloan programme. It was designed to respond to the need for medium-term investment finance, especially among peasant farmers.

ANED started by offering financial leases with lease terms varying between two and seven years. Potential clients had to have experience operating the equipment to be leased, and the ability to make a 15 to 25 per cent down payment. In addition, no more than 30 per cent of total net household income could be allocated to lease payments. The most common types of assets leased were tractors and motorized water pumps. Within three years the leasing portfolio reached US$890,000, with arrears over one day not exceeding 8 per cent of the portfolio. No case of repossession was necessary during this time. As of April 2003, ANED had 877 leasing contracts outstanding with a median lease value of US$596.

To run its leasing programme, ANED had to make considerable investments in staff training and systems development. Many loan officers lacked the necessary experience to evaluate the contribution of equipment to the cash flow of the enterprise. Software programs were developed both for the design of lease payment schemes adapted to cash flow projections and for the monitoring of the leased equipment. ANED also established close links with suppliers, most notably for tractors and pumps, which often led to discounts for bulk purchases and contracts that included guarantees against breakdown, technical training, and other after-sales services.

ANED now offers a virtual catalogue at its web site (www.aned.org) where anyone with an Internet connection can find information about the suppliers with which ANED works and the products they offer. Potential lessees can search the catalogue by type of equipment. Thirty-three different equipment categories are now financed, including solar panels, sewing machines, beekeeping and construction equipment. Users will find a variety of brands and models of equipment with photographs, technical specifications, information about pricing, availability, the useful working life of the asset, warranties, pre- and post-sales service, and other characteristics of the asset. They can calculate a payment plan by specifying their desired lease term and number of instalments. They can also search for consultants and consulting companies that offer technical assistance in 23 areas of specialization (for example, law, marketing, hydrology and construction) and 21 different product categories (for instance, livestock, coffee, potatoes, leather, ceramics) in different regions of the country.

This case study was adapted from Dupleich (2000 and 2003), Nair et al. (2004) and www.aned.org.

Recommended Reading

- Deelen, L.; Dupleich, M.; Othieno, L.; Wakelin, O. 2003. *Leasing for small and micro enterprises: A guide for designing and managing leasing schemes in developing countries* (Geneva, ILO), at: http://www.microfinancegateway.org/gm/document-1.9.29539/13819_13819.pdf
- Mutesasira, L.; Osinde, S.; Mule, N. 2001. *Potential for leasing products: Asset financing for micro- and small businesses in Tanzania and Uganda* (Nairobi, *MicroSave* Africa), at: http://www.microsave.org/research_paper/potential-for-leasing-productsasset-financing-for-micro-small-businesses-in-tanzania-
- Nair, A.; Kloeppinger-Todd, R.; Mulder, A. 2004. *Leasing: An underutilized tool in rural finance*, Agriculture and Rural Development Discussion Paper 7 (Washington, DC, World Bank), at: http://www.microfinancegateway.org/gm/document-1.9.29537/23470_file_23470.pdf
- Westley, G. 2003. *Equipment leasing and lending: A guide for microfinance*, Sustainable Development Department Best Practice Series (Washington, DC, Inter-American Development Bank), at: http://www.microfinancegateway.org/gm/document-1.9.26285/3772_file_03772.pdf

11 Money Transfers[23]

I tried the remittance services of courier companies; they were charging a processing fee of 130 pesos which was 13% of the amount I was sending. Now, I only have to shell out 10 pesos! Imagine how much I get to save using Text-A-Deposit! ~ Evelyn, a G-Cash user in the Philippines (Owens, 2006)

People of all economic backgrounds engage in money transfers with other individuals, households, and businesses. They transfer money to meet everyday financial obligations, such as bill payments. They also transfer money for less common reasons, such as providing money to children away at school, sending money to family members living elsewhere, or transferring partial earnings to other parties.

The volume of money being transferred is astonishing. Remittances, the money sent home by migrants, are estimated to have reached US$325 billion in 2010, and are expected to increase by 6.2 per cent in 2011 (World Bank, 2010). In many countries, remittances account for a very significant portion of the gross domestic product (GDP): for example, in Tajikistan (35 per cent), Lebanon (22 per cent), Honduras (19 per cent). In Kenya, the mobile money service M-PESA is processing US$320 million per month in person-to-person money transfers, which is roughly equivalent to 10 per cent of Kenya's GDP on an annualized basis. M-PESA processes another US$650 million per month in cash deposit and withdrawal transactions (Mas and Radcliffe, 2010).

Because of the size and growth of the money transfer market, a wide range of actors have taken an interest in providing the service. This includes not only formal banking institutions, but also mobile network operators, software and hardware companies, and governments that recognize the need for regulation as well as an opportunity to extend public services. International money transfer companies have long dominated the global market, but smaller regional and national providers are beginning to explore the market potential.

This chapter briefly examines why money transfers might be an interesting product for MFIs to consider. It then explores the various options through which MFIs could offer the product, and the major considerations that should be taken into account before embarking on product development. The outline of the chapter is as follows:

1. Money transfers and MFIs
2. How money transfers work
3. Money transfer business models for MFIs
4. Developing a money transfer strategy

11.1 Money Transfers and MFIs

MFIs have been drawn to the money transfer market because it offers them the opportunity to fulfil their financial goals as well as their social objectives. From a financial perspective, money transfers can be a lucrative business. Western Union's dominance in this market has

[23] This chapter was adapted from Isern et al. (2005, 2008).

earned the company hefty profit margins, estimated to be 150 per cent higher than those of the average US commercial bank (Bezard, 2003). M-PESA earned Safaricom US$94.4 million in 2009, and has become the single biggest driver of new profits for the company (McKay and Pickens, 2010). MFIs are unlikely to earn such high profits, but money transfers can provide them with an additional source of revenue and an opportunity to diversify their income. The additional product offering might also help MFIs to retain clients, and to attract new clients who might approach the institution for the purpose of making a payment, but later purchase other products as well.

From a social perspective, MFIs can channel remittances and government transfer payments to low-income households living in isolated areas that are not served by other providers (see for example, Boxes 13.10 and 13.11 in the chapter on grants). If made regularly, these payments can provide a steady injection of cash into poorer communities, which could be used to meet basic needs, manage risk or support income-generating activities. As discussed later in this chapter, MFIs can design special savings, credit and insurance products that encourage the use of remittances for productive purposes. Of course, remittances can also be sent "on demand" to assist households in coping with a crisis.

Even in communities where other payment providers already exist, MFIs might be able to provide a valuable service if they can meet the needs of their particular market better than the competition. Perhaps they can make their system more user-friendly to illiterate clients, or offer domestic transfers through their own branch network at a lower price. One of the best ways for an MFI to differentiate itself in the market is to link its money transfer service to other products already being used by clients to make their overall financial management easier and safer.

Money transfer products have not always been successful for MFIs, however. Many institutions have struggled to be profitable with the product. One MFI that started its own money transfer service offered the product for seven years before it became profitable. Other MFIs have been profitable in as little as two to three months when working as an agent for a money transfer company in a region with a high volume of transfers. While many MFIs have reported significant and rapid growth in the number and volume of transfers they process, that increase has not necessarily resulted in greater profits for the MFI. One of the lessons that has been learned by the microfinance industry to date is that a careful understanding of the mechanics of transfers, as well as the environment in which an MFI wishes to offer them, is critical to successful product development.

11.2 How Money Transfers Work

Money transfer systems can be thought of as having three main elements:

1. the entity (or entities) that provide the transfer;
2. the mechanism that carries a transfer from point A to point B; and
3. the customer interface through which cash is collected from senders and/or disbursed to recipients.

These elements are summarized in Figure 11.1 and briefly discussed below.

Figure 11.1 Building blocks of a money transfer system

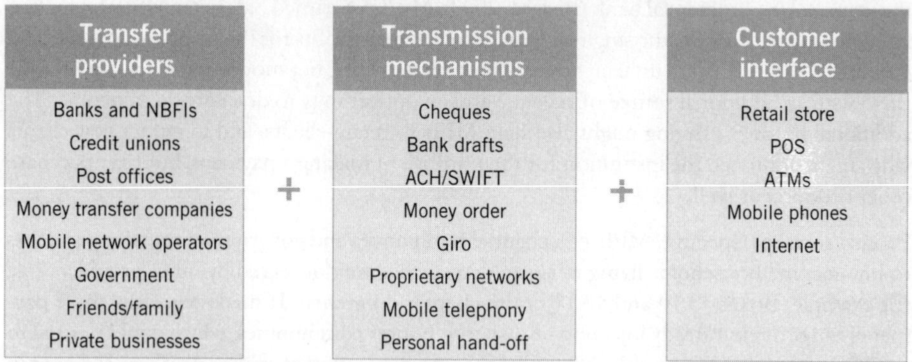

Source: Adapted from Isern et al., 2005.

Transfer Providers

Money transfers can be sent through formal or informal channels. Formal money transfer services are provided by banks, credit unions, MFIs, post offices, money transfer companies and other licensed entities that report in some way to government authorities. Informal transfers are provided by family members, friends, or businesses that are not formally licensed to provide such services (see Box 11.1).

MFIs may decide to provide money transfer services directly, or to work through alliances with other providers who can supply certain aspects of the service while the MFIs acts primarily as the customer interface. The choice of an appropriate partner will depend on whether the MFI wishes to provide domestic transfers, international transfers, or both, and whether it expects clients will want to send and/or receive transfers.

Transfer Mechanisms

With informal transfers, money is either hand-carried from one point to another, or it is moved in a virtual way through personal networks, as described in Box 11.1. Formal money transfers require some kind of paper or electronic mechanism to facilitate the transaction. The major options include:

- **Cheques and bank drafts.** These are some of the oldest mechanisms, but they are losing popularity for several reasons. First, they must be physically delivered to the recipient, which makes them vulnerable to theft, delays, and the reliability of the postal service. Second, the law typically allows only banks and other regulated financial institutions to use them. Customers must wait for their cheque to arrive and clear, and the physical processing of the paper-based instrument is expensive for providers.
- **Money orders.** Since these are paper-based instruments, they have some of the same disadvantages as cheques, but they can be issued by and redeemed at a variety of financial service providers, including money transfer companies. They do not require a bank account; the recipient receives cash simply upon presenting the money order to an authorized agent (such as a post office).

Box 11.1 Informal Money Transfer Systems

Informal funds transfer systems vary tremendously in structure and complexity. Hand-carrying cash, usually by migrants themselves or by family and friends, is the most basic system, and is especially common in situations of seasonal or circular migration, where migrants frequently return to their place of origin. In some countries, the physical transfer of cash is also done by couriers (internationally) or bus companies and taxi drivers (domestically).

Other systems involve only the virtual movement of funds. A basic two-way system is common between West Africa and France, where two people (one in the home country and one overseas) collect and distribute money transfers in their respective communities, settling periodically through their respective individual bank accounts. These transfer providers can move sums significant enough to meet the needs of travelling business people, who often do not hold credit cards and prefer to transfer cash via informal channels rather than face the safety, customs and foreign exchange issues involved in carrying large amounts of cash.

More sophisticated informal systems exist under different names around the world, including *hundi* (South Asia), *fei-chen* (China), *hui kwan* (Hong Kong), *padala* (Philippines), *phei kwan* (Thailand), and *hawala* (Middle East). Many of these systems, such as those common in African mineral-exporting countries like Angola, evolved as mechanisms for trade financing and net funds transfers against the movement of goods.

The hawala system used in the greater Middle East is representative of how such systems work. Typically, a migrant makes a payment to an agent (*hawaladar*) in the country where he works and lives, and the hawaladar gives him a code to authenticate the transaction. The hawaladar requests his counterpart at the receiving end to make the payment to a beneficiary upon submission of the code.

After the transfer, hawaladars settle accounts through payment in cash or in goods and services. They are remunerated by senders through a fee or an exchange rate spread. Hawaladars often exploit fluctuations in demand for different currencies, which enables them to offer customers better rates than those offered by banks (most of which will only conduct transactions at authorized rates of exchange). Since many hawaladars are also involved in businesses where money transfers are necessary, such as commodity trading, remittance services fit well into their existing activities. Remittances and business transfers are processed through the same bank accounts, and few, if any, additional operational costs are incurred.

Source: Isern et al., 2005.

- **Electronic funds transfer (EFT).** At the domestic level, the most common types of EFT systems are the automated clearinghouse (ACH), which settles transactions in batches, and the real-time gross settlement system, which settles transactions immediately but is more expensive. ACHs can accept payment instructions from a financial institution or directly from clients, who can link into these systems using their bank-issued debit or credit cards. These networks are often owned and operated by central banks, although private players such as Visa also operate ACH systems in certain countries. At the international level, the most commonly used system is operated by the Society for Worldwide Interbank Financial Telecommunication (SWIFT), an industry-owned cooperative that provides real-time payment messaging services to member institutions. Transfers over such electronic networks are quite reliable, but non-bank MFIs may not have access to them. Even if the law allows it, cost, information technology and staff capacity requirements can make access impractical.

- **Giro.** "Giro" is the term used for the electronic cross-border payments offered by post offices in more than 40 countries. This system enables holders of a postal bank account to send money (domestically or overseas) to another postal account, to a bank account, or to a post office for cash payment. Postal giros tend to be cheaper than bank transfers for small amounts, but it usually takes two to four days for the transfer to be received.
- **Proprietary networks.** This type of payment system is restricted to agents of the company or association that owns the network, such as Western Union or MoneyGram, but many types of institution can become agents, including banks, non-bank financial institutions, post offices and retail businesses. The service is usually very reliable, neither the sender nor the receiver has to hold an account or complete extensive paperwork, and recipients can collect transferred funds almost instantaneously. Proprietary networks are the most expensive of all transfer mechanisms, however.
- **Mobile telephony.** In a mobile banking (m-banking) money transfer model, customers go to a retail agent to exchange cash for an electronic record of value, which is stored on the server of a mobile network operator. Customers can then use a mobile phone to order the transfer of funds to others using a wireless communications channel such as SMS (short messaging service) or USSD (unstructured supplementary service data). They can receive payments in the same manner and convert stored value into cash by visiting an agent. This method of transferring funds can be very convenient and affordable for clients, especially when taking transaction costs into account, but it is usually not regulated and there are no paper receipts to help resolve disputes. Regulated financial institutions can develop their own mobile money transfer service, but they need the cooperation of at least one mobile network operator to channel the wireless communications.

The strengths and weaknesses of these main mechanisms are summarized in Table 11.1.

Customer Interface

The third main building block of a money transfer system is the customer interface. Those who wish to send money need to be able to hand their cash over to the transfer provider, and recipients need to be able to collect cash as close as possible to their home or business. If there are problems with a transfer, senders and receivers need a place to go to resolve the situation.

In informal money transfers the customer interface is usually a specific human being, although it may also be a retail store where a hawala agent works, or the bus terminal where drivers can be found to carry money to a recipient for a fee. In formal money transfers the customer interface has traditionally been a fixed location (for example, a bank branch or post office), which customers must visit during regular business hours to access the transfer service. More recently, new technologies are enabling clients to send and receive transfers at a much wider range of locations, even from their own mobile phone, 24 hours a day (see Box 11.2). ICICI Bank's "Money2India" remittance service delivers money transfers to remote Indian villages through Internet kiosks (see Box 11.3).

Table 11.1 Comparing money transfer mechanisms

	For customers	For MFIs
Cheques	• Commonly available from regulated financial institutions • Slow • Subject to loss/theft • Must be physically delivered • Require bank accounts to send (not necessarily to receive)	• Well-known, traditional product • Access often limited to regulated financial institutions only • Generates relatively high processing costs
Money orders	• Do not require bank accounts to send or receive • Slow • Subject to loss/theft • Must be physically delivered	• Postal money orders for postal financial service providers only; others can be issued/paid by a variety of financial service providers • Generates relatively high processing costs
Electronic funds transfer (EFT)	• Faster than paper-based instruments • Requires bank account to send and receive • Cheaper than proprietary network transfers	• Lower labour costs than cheques, but requires link to network and infrastructure • Fees lower than for proprietary network transfers • Can be accessed by many MFIs through the financial institutions with which they conduct business
Giro	• Requires a postal account for sending, but generally cheaper and more accessible than bank-based EFTs	• Lower labour costs than cheques, but requires link to network and infrastructure • Only postal financial service providers can originate transactions; both postal and other MFIs can receive
Proprietary networks	• Real-time delivery possible • No bank accounts required • Numerous access points • Higher price	• Infrastructure requirements and costs can vary, depending on agency relationship • Generally more lucrative than other transfer mechanisms • Agents sometimes restricted to banks, with fewer restrictions on subagents
Mobile telephony	• Convenient; can send an SMS from almost anywhere anytime • Low-cost • Sending stored value is fast, but must visit an agent or ATM to convert value into cash and vice versa	• Requires some degree of cooperation with a mobile network operator • May require significant investment in system upgrades and interface design • No paper receipt to facilitate dispute resolution

Source: Isern et al., 2005.

Card-based technologies have been used by a variety of MFIs. At Banco Solidario in Ecuador, for example, remittance recipients receive a stored value card, which they can use to withdraw money from automatic teller machines (ATMs) or point-of-sale (POS) devices whenever and in whatever amount they choose. In Tanzania, CRDB Bank installed POS terminals in savings

Box 11.2 M-PESA in Kenya

M-PESA was developed by mobile phone operator Vodafone and launched commercially by its Kenyan affiliate Safaricom in March 2007. M-PESA ("M" for mobile and "PESA" for money in Swahili) is an electronic payment and store of value system that is accessible through mobile phones. To access the service, customers must first register at an authorized M-PESA retail outlet. They are then assigned an individual electronic money account that is linked to their phone number and accessible through a SIM card-resident application on their mobile phone. Customers can deposit and withdraw cash to/from their accounts by exchanging cash for electronic value at a network of retail outlets. Once they have money in their accounts, they can use their phones to transfer funds to other M-PESA users and even to non-registered users, pay bills, and purchase mobile airtime credit. All transactions are authorized and recorded in real time using secure SMS, and are capped at US$500. As of January 2010, M-PESA had 9 million registered customers, equivalent to 23 per cent of Kenya's population, and approximately 16,900 retail outlets, which is more than seven times the number of ATMs and bank branches in the country. Registration and cash deposits are free, but person-to-person transfers and bill payments cost 30 Kenyan shillings, or approximately US$0.40.

Source: Adapted from Mas and Radcliffe, 2010.

Box 11.3 Money Transfers through Internet Kiosks at ICICI Bank in India

The computer kiosk system work as follows: a sender remits a money transfer to the recipient's ICICI account, either through an ICICI branch office or a Money2India agent. As soon as the transaction has taken place, the Money2India agent informs the kiosk operator, who in turn informs the recipient. The recipient can then collect the remittance either at ICICI or at the kiosk, which is equipped with a low-cost ATM. ICICI estimates that kiosks can be profitably placed in villages as small as 2,000 residents. This option is very attractive for rural recipients, because it eliminates transaction costs involved in travelling to a larger town to visit a bank branch.

Kiosks used by ICICI Bank offer a combination of telephone, financial, educational and other services. Kiosk operators are independent business people, remunerated through commissions paid by service providers and user fees paid by customers. They pay for set-up costs themselves, for which they typically obtain a partial loan from ICICI Bank. Since ICICI Bank does not incur any fixed costs, the system has proven a cost-effective way for the bank to extend its outreach to rural areas. By June 2005, more than 2,000 kiosk operators offered ICICI services. From an operator's perspective, the business model is viable only if multiple services are routed through a single kiosk. However, experience indicates that the kiosks can become profitable even without the money transfer service, which can easily be added at a later date.

Source: Isern et al., 2005, and Finextra Research, 2005.

and credit cooperatives (SACCOs) in remote areas of the country so that rural clients can load their debit cards in the capital and then withdraw cash at their hometown SACCO and avoid the risk of travelling with large sums of money.

The Money Transfer Value Chain

To develop a successful money transfer service, an MFI will need to decide which aspects of the service it wishes to provide, and which it can outsource more effectively to others. To make this decision, it is important to have a clear understanding of the different activities that are involved in making a money transfer, and how they come together to provide customers with a valuable service. As shown in Figure 11.2, there are seven primary activities involved in the money transfer value chain:

- **Marketing and selling.** The marketing of money transfer products differs somewhat from that of other financial products, because both the sending and receiving clients need to be considered. MFIs may be able to market cost-effectively to one but not the other.
- **Originating and funding.** The customer must provide information, either manually or electronically, to request the transfer. The amount to be transferred must then be collected (either in cash or through a transfer of funds from the customer's card or account), and payment must be made for the transfer service itself.
- **Sending.** The paper or electronic request for funds transfer must be transmitted.
- **Clearing.** The sending and receiving financial institutions must exchange information about the payment, and the amount of funds to be settled by those institutions has to be calculated. Once the sending institution receives a valid financial claim from the receiving institution, it can settle the claim by making a payment to the receiving institution, and the final settlement is recorded and communicated.
- **Receiving.** Payment instructions must be received at a location where the recipient can access them. MFIs play an important role here, particularly in remittance transactions, because of their presence in the less developed areas where recipients live and work.
- **Payment.** Funds must be disbursed in local or, if regulations permit, foreign currency in the form of cash, cheque or credit to the receiver's account. MFIs that perform this activity must ensure they have sufficient liquidity to make the payouts, even at short notice and during peaks in demand.
- **Customer service.** Questions about the product, requests for information about specific transactions, complaints and suggestions must all be addressed. The ability to provide both senders and recipients with effective customer service is what generates customer confidence, trust, and repeat business.

Figure 11.2 Primary activities of the money transfer value chain

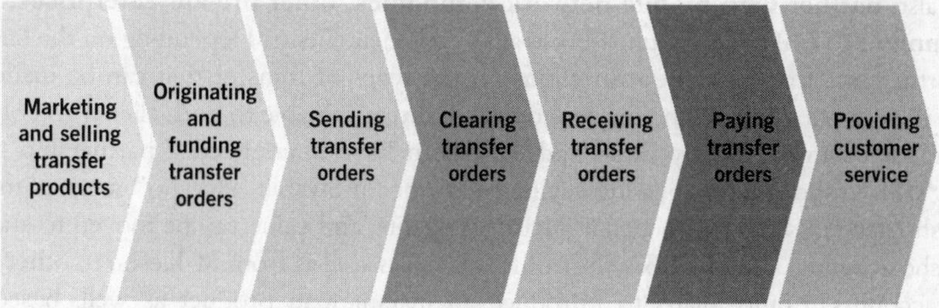

Source: Isern et al., 2008.

Of course, the seven primary activities described above must be supported by appropriate financial, technology, risk management and human resource infrastructure. If an MFI feels it is not capable of delivering one or more of the primary activities with quality, then it needs to either strengthen its own capacity or enter into one or more partnerships with entities that already have the infrastructure and can assist the MFI in delivering a quality service.

11.3 Money Transfer Business Models for MFIs

MFIs offer money transfer services through a variety of business models. The one that is most common is that of **partnership with a money transfer company** such as Western Union or MoneyGram. It is an attractive option, because it provides a simple and fast way to enter the market. Many companies offer agents a preset package of well-tested products, a technology platform, marketing materials and sometimes training or call centre support to help launch operations. Their established brand, foreign exchange access, risk management expertise and international payment networks can reduce both the cost and the risk of an MFI's entry into the market. In exchange for all this, MFIs must pay the money transfer company a fee.

Another popular option has been to **partner with banks**, either as a subagent to a bank that is already operating as a money transfer company agent, or to gain access to the bank's payment networks or card systems (for example, SWIFT or Visa). The postal network Posta Moldova established such a partnership with ING and Deutsche Bank, for example. Through partnership, MFIs can avoid bearing the full burden of licensing, investment, fees, and other requirements of joining a payment network or card system. However, access is usually limited to licensed financial institutions, and may have membership requirements beyond the means and capacity of most MFIs.

Financial institutions with bank licences can provide money transfer services via an electronic payment network by setting up **correspondence relationships with banks** in other countries or regions. The relationships between FONKOZE in Haiti and City National Bank of New Jersey in the United States, and between Spanish savings banks and Banco Solidario in Ecuador, are two such examples. In both cases, money transfers are bundled by the sending institution and transmitted to an account at the recipient institution, which unbundles the payments for distribution to receiving clients. Non-governmental organizations (NGOs) like the one described in Box 11.4 may also set up partnerships with banks to provide their clients with money transfers.

As described in Boxes 11.2 and 11.3 above and Box 13.11 in the chapter on grants, MFIs could also **partner with mobile network companies, other private enterprises, or the government** to make money transfers available to their clients. Depending on the nature of the partnership, there may be restrictions on the types of transfer that can be made or to whom they can be sent, yet the service could still prove valuable to both clients and MFIs. In Kenya, for example, Equity Bank and Safaricom have announced a partnership around Equity's M-Kesho interest-bearing savings account (in Swahili, "Kesho" means "future"). M-Kesho accounts can be opened at M-PESA agents, and value can be moved to and from M-Kesho accounts and M-PESA electronic wallets, as well as from M-Kesho to other Equity Bank accounts. Equity plans to introduce an instant loan product as well, based on a credit-scoring model, once six months of transaction data are available. Carrier services like

Box 11.4 Partnering with a Commercial Bank to Provide Domestic Remittances

In India, the NGO Adhikar is piloting a domestic money transfer service for the large number of migrants who travel from the eastern state of Orissa to work in the western state of Gujarat. Adhikar's comparative advantage in money transfer services is knowledge of customer needs and preferences, as well as the ability to service clients in remote locations. When designing its transfer system, Adhikar decided to leave the actual transmission of funds to Corporation Bank, which has branches in both Orissa and Gujarat and the infrastructure to make timely, secure transfers. Although bank transfers take place regularly between Orissa and Gujarat, most migrants do not have bank accounts and find it costly to visit a bank branch. Adhikar centralizes the collection and dissemination of these small transfers and routes them through one account at the bank. This process spreads transaction costs over a larger number of transfers, bringing down the per-transaction fee. Adhikar is now looking to leverage the system by involving NGOs that serve other districts in Orissa as distribution agents, lowering per-transaction fees even further while enabling the NGOs to earn a new source of revenue to support their work.

Source: Isern et al., 2005.

the ones being offered by M-PESA and by SMART in the Philippines can make it possible for even small MFIs to use mobile phones to facilitate loan repayments and deposits, lowering risk and costs for themselves and their customers (Ketley, 2010, and Kumar et al., 2010).

Smaller MFIs that do not have the leverage to negotiate favourable terms with larger partners sometimes **form a consortium** to become the primary agent of a money transfer company. This approach has been used by a number of MFI federations, including the Jamaica Cooperative Credit Union League (JCCUL), which has partnered with a local money transfer company to bundle four foreign money transfer companies into a service under its own proprietary brand. IR*net*, a money transfer service created by the World Council of Credit Unions (WOCCU), bundles transactions from credit unions in Africa, Asia, Latin America, Europe and Australia in order to obtain discounted service from mainstream money transfer companies. Senders have the option of making a transfer from a credit union to a credit union, from a credit union to a non-credit union (typically, a retail outlet serving as a money transfer outlet), or from a non-credit union to a credit union. In Ghana, 125 rural banks use "Apex Link" to transfer funds between themselves as well as to receive payments from abroad (see Box 11.5).

Partnerships offer MFIs many advantages, but they can be complex and expensive. An alternative chosen by numerous MFIs is to offer money transfer services **directly, using in-house systems** that range from basic solutions built around their core accounting package to more sophisticated solutions based on EFT systems or m-banking platforms. In-house systems can work well for domestic money transfers, particularly for MFIs with large national networks, although some MFIs have creatively extended their in-house outreach internationally by **opening up branches in other countries**, primarily to provide remittance services to migrant workers. FIE Private Financial Fund, for example, provides such services to Bolivian migrants in Argentina (see Box 11.6).

Box 11.5 Apex Link: Going the Last Mile in Ghana

Apex Bank is a central treasury for the rural banks of Ghana, a network that represents over 400 points of service, some in villages as small as 500 people. Market studies in the rural areas served by these banks revealed that clients were having difficulty accessing transfers from urban areas in Ghana. Crime made it especially difficult for traders, who carried large sums of cash on their person for business. At the same time, the rural banks were looking for new revenue sources and ways to attract more customers.

In response to this dual need, Apex Bank developed the "Apex Link" domestic money transfer system. The service uses proprietary software to manage money transfers between rural banks using coded messages sent by phone, fax, or express mail. Turnaround time is between 15 minutes and 24 hours, and transfers can be made from an account or in cash, making the service accessible to customers and non-customers alike. If recipients lack the government-issued identification card or passport normally required for identification purposes, they may come to the bank accompanied by a "locally known person" to act as a witness to the transfer. Transfer fees are paid by the senders on a sliding scale, depending on the amount transferred (usually 0.5 per cent of the transfer amount for customers, and 0.75 per cent for non-customers). These fees are shared between Apex Bank and the sending and receiving rural banks.

Apex Link can also be used as the "last mile" in an international funds transfer, because Apex Bank has a partnership with a local commercial bank that is licensed to handle foreign exchange. The local bank deposits funds from abroad into Apex Bank's central account in local currency. Apex Link then transfers the funds to a rural bank for final payment to the receiving client. In its first year of operation, the system made 24,000 transfers totalling over US$27 million.

Source: Isern et al., 2005.

Box 11.6 Opening Branches Abroad to Facilitate Remittances at FIE

FIE Private Financial Fund in Bolivia, a formal, regulated non-bank microfinance institution, works with its branch FIE Gran Poder in Buenos Aires, Argentina, to offer remittance services and microcredit to Bolivian migrants in Argentina. Remittances serve as collateral for loans, which are typically used for commercial activities. These migrants generally have no access to loans in Argentina, owing to their national origin and their informal, undocumented status. FIE requires little documentation from its loan applicants. Bolivian identification papers suffice, and hence FIE is easily accessible to its customers.

The direct provision of money transfer services offers MFIs several advantages, namely the ability to control product and service quality, the client relationship, and the total revenue generated. In-house systems can be relatively quick and inexpensive to pilot and launch. However, they typically have high maintenance costs, so MFIs need to generate a high volume of transfers to make the per-transaction cost viable. This can be problematic, since both senders and receivers must access the service through the MFI's service points. Also, the MFI must take full responsibility for marketing and regulatory compliance. The advantages and disadvantages of the main money transfer business models for MFIs are summarized in Table 11.2.

Table 11.2 Comparing money transfer business models for MFIs

	Advantages	Disadvantages
Direct approach	• Retain 100% of revenue • Can protect client relationships • Control over product design and delivery • May be able to offer a lower-cost product in niche markets • Can be quick and inexpensive to pilot	• Low transaction volumes if small network of service points • High maintenance costs • Responsibility for marketing • Responsibility for compliance • Some technology solutions, such as m-banking, are time-consuming and expensive to implement
Single partnership	• Simple start • Access to networks and systems • Marketing and compliance support • Potential for greater transfer volume	• Exclusivity may limit outreach • Must share revenue • Must compete with the partner's other agents • Dependent on partner's strength
Multiple partnership	• Chance to diversify operations • Better access to the market in sending countries • Can establish strong positions in countries that best fit MFI needs • Potential for much greater transfer volume	• More complex • Requires strong staff training • May need to develop IT platform to manage multiple relationships • Must share revenue
Consortium	• Can negotiate better terms with larger partners • Can share costs	• Dependent on consortium's strength • May benefit members unequally • Must share revenue

Source: Adapted from Isern et al., 2008.

The options described above are not mutually exclusive. An MFI could offer paper-based money orders for use in occasional domestic money transfers or bill payment; operate as an agency of a money transfer company for simple, low-value domestic or international transfers; and establish a correspondent relationship with a bank for higher-value, higher-reliability international transfers. The Association of Cambodian Local Economic Development Agencies (ACLEDA) in Cambodia, the National Microfinance Bank (NMB) in Tanzania, ProCredit Bank Bulgaria, XacBank Mongolia and Apex Bank Ghana all entered the money transfer market by offering domestic transfers only, using either their own branch network or member bank networks. Later, they took up international transfer services, typically becoming part of a brand name network (Sander, 2008).

11.4 Developing a Money Transfer Strategy

Developing a money transfer product is somewhat complicated. Not only are there a range of providers with which to potentially collaborate or compete, but there are many types of transfer mechanism to choose from, and a rapidly expanding range of options for creating a customer interface. How can an MFI decide which strategy is best?

As mentioned above, MFIs can start by assessing their own internal capacity and the business models that others have used successfully. Issues related to management information systems and liquidity are particularly important. Opportunity Bank in Malawi had to do an entire systems upgrade – a process that took a year and cost more than US$100,000 to complete – before it could implement its m-banking solution (Kumar et al., 2010). Even for less technologically demanding strategies, MFIs need to have systems that can handle large volumes of data flow and ensure transaction security. They need be able to anticipate the quantity of cash they must have on hand to meet customer demands, and to manage the increased operational risk that comes with greater cash handling, including employee error and fraud.

MFIs should also give careful consideration to three external factors that heavily influence money transfer product design: the regulatory framework, client preferences, and competition. Finally, strategy development should combine the internal and external analyses, and look carefully at the opportunities for linking a money transfer service with other services being offered by the MFI.

Regulation

An MFI's choice of strategy will often be limited by its regulatory environment. National laws may prohibit certain types of institution from accessing specific transfer mechanisms (for example, non-bank financial institutions may not be allowed to conduct foreign exchange transactions, issue cheques, or link into payment networks). In Brazil, for example, all international transfers must be channelled through the central bank. In many countries, MFIs without a banking licence can act only as agents or subagents of a money transfer company, or establish a correspondent relationship with a licensed financial institution.

MFIs need to understand not only the direct implications of the regulatory framework for their ability to offer money transfer services, but also the indirect impact that regulations might have on their ability to partner and compete with other service providers. MFIs may find it difficult to comply with rules for anti-money laundering and combating the financing of terrorism (AML/CFT) as well as customer due diligence. Their low-income clients may not possess the documents required for identity verification, and the cost of keeping detailed records for very small transactions can make money transfers unviable (Lyman et al., 2008). In Viet Nam, migrants are required to pay 30 per cent of their remittances to the government, which makes it difficult for MFIs to compete with informal money transfer systems, whereas in Pakistan, formal remittances can be sent free of charge and free of taxes, banks are eligible for a rebate on each transaction processed, and international money transfer companies are given performance-based incentives for mobilizing higher volumes of remittances (Pakistan Remittance Initiative, 2010). Such policies obviously make it easier for financial institutions to compete with more informal mechanisms.

Client Preferences

The identification of client preferences is more complicated with money transfer products than with other financial services, because there are two types of client to consider: the senders and the receivers. These two types of client are likely to have fundamentally different profiles. In the case of remittances, MFIs are likely to have first-hand information about receivers, but not about senders.

Certainly, market research will be necessary to identify the characteristics that different market segments value in a money transfer product. The main characteristics to consider are summarized below.

- **Safety and trust.** All remittance users want their funds to be transferred safely, but perceptions of safety have a lot to do with clients' trust in the provider. Although robbery is a common concern with informal transfer systems, low-income clients may still use them, because they distrust formal financial service providers. Other clients seek out institutions that have a track record in handling transfers, and those that belong to large, well-known international networks.
- **Speed.** The speed of a money transfer varies, usually between one hour and two weeks (in the case of a bank draft) although mobile phone transfer mechanisms are now reducing this to minutes. Since there is usually a trade-off between speed and cost, senders will often choose a service on the basis of the urgency of a particular transaction. However, many people prefer "real-time" transfers, regardless of their cost or urgency.
- **Cost.** Most people seek transfer services that offer low fees, attractive exchange rates, and transparency on fees and rates at both the sending and receiving ends.
- **Ease of use.** Senders and receivers prefer limited paperwork, especially if they are not literate. Some prefer interacting with a sales agent for reasons of ease and personal service. Others prefer the convenience and anonymity of ATMs or POS devices.
- **Proximity.** Senders and receivers usually want to access money transfer services at nearby locations so that they can minimize transaction costs such as travel time and transportation expenses. However, this is not always the case. In Moldova, for example, remittance recipients preferred to use a payout point away from their village or neighbourhood, for fear that others would learn about the arrival of the cash (Sander, 2008).
- **Accessibility.** Requirements such as opening an account, maintaining a minimum balance, or presenting specific identity documents can limit poor people's access to money transfer services. Many migrants, especially undocumented workers, prefer services with few or no identity requirements, and this makes them a difficult market for formal financial institutions to serve.

Other client characteristics that are worth researching in preparation for the development of a money transfer product include: the socioeconomic profile of both senders and receivers, geographic patterns and seasonality of the transfer flows, and the size and characteristics of money transfers from both international and domestic sources. Segmenting senders and receivers into smaller subgroups can also be helpful, not only in understanding the demand for money transfers, but also for assessing demand for other financial products that might be linked to the money transfer. An interesting example of segmentation for money transfer product development is provided in the case study at the end of this chapter.

Competition

Experts estimate that the total value of global money transfers made through informal channels is somewhere between 40 and 100 per cent of the volume of formal transfers. Bezard (2003) estimates that informal money transfer systems in Asia and the Middle East may manage two and a half times the value of transfers processed by formal systems. Given these estimates, MFIs would be wise to include both formal and informal service providers in their competition analysis. They can learn from the strengths of each, and they need to find some competitive advantage over both if they are to bring a money transfer product successfully to their market.

Formal systems are generally quite safe, and can be fast. They are also often expensive, in terms of both the fee paid for the service and the transaction costs incurred. Prices are falling, however, as competition increases. In Latin America, for example, the cost of sending US$200 internationally is estimated to have dropped from over 15 per cent to less than 5.6 per cent from 2001 to 2005 (Orozco, 2006).

Informal systems are often faster and cheaper than formal systems. Hand-carriage is the least expensive, but comes with the greatest risk; hawala systems typically charge between 0.25 and 1.25 per cent of the remitted amount, and offer a premium exchange rate. Informal systems also have certain client-friendly features, such as confidentiality and minimal paperwork, which make them popular, and they are often available in areas where no formal sector providers exist.

MFIs that manage to compete against both formal and informal systems do so by meeting clients' needs in a way that competitors do not. They may provide service in areas where formal financial institutions do not operate, or offer greater security than informal service providers can. They may focus on delivering a very tailored and convenient service for a particular diaspora community, such as Prodem with its office in Argentina, and Banco Solidario through its partnership with commercial banks in Spain (see Box 11.7). The Banco Solidario example highlights another important strategy, that of linking money transfer services to other products and services offered by the MFI. Perhaps more than any other strategy, creative cross-selling can help an MFI distinguish its product in a competitive market.

Box 11.7 Tailoring a Remittance Service for Ecuadorians in Spain

Banco Solidario, an Ecuadorian MFI, entered into an agreement with two major savings banks in Spain (Caja de Ahorro de Madrid and Caja de Ahorro de Murcia) to create the programme *Mi Familia, Mi País, Mi Regreso* [My Family, My Country, My Return]. Through this partnership, Banco Solidario and the Spanish banks provide remittance services to Ecuadorian migrants in Spain. They expanded their distribution network in Ecuador by linking up with cooperatives and a courier company.

Banco Solidario bundles its remittance service with a variety of other products, starting with a travel loan for Ecuadorians who are moving abroad, and later an opportunity to make regular deposits into a savings account for the purpose of saving up money for building or buying a house, or starting an enterprise. In fact, Banco Solidario describes its programme not as a remittance service, but rather as an offering of tools to migrants to be able to fulfil their goals of having a house and business upon their return to Ecuador.

Migrants can also transfer money to family members in Ecuador, who can use the remittances as collateral for a loan, to pay an insurance premium, or to fund everyday purchases using *la chauchera*, the electronic debit card that migrants' families receive to access their remitted funds.

Source: Adapted from Inter-American Development Bank, 2007, and Banco Solidario, 2002.

Cross-selling and Bundling

The linking of an MFI's money transfer service to other financial services can not only differentiate an MFI from its competition, but also encourage customer loyalty and generate additional revenue. It can deepen the developmental impact of money transfers if, for example, senders are able to transfer funds directly into an education or pension savings account, or make payments on a housing loan or insurance policy. By giving customers options other than a full cash payout, MFIs can make money transfer transactions more profitable for the institution and more productive for their clients. Some of the options for linking money transfers are (Comstock et al., 2009):

- **Demand deposits.** Clients of WOCCU credit unions can receive remittances directly into a savings account using the IR*net* money transfer service. They can then withdraw funds whenever and in whatever amount they please.
- **Commitment savings accounts.** The Infant/Youth Savings Plan at Salcajá in Guatemala is one example of a savings account into which remittances can be regularly deposited to accumulate assets for education, housing, or starting a business.
- **Health or life insurance.** At Banco ADOPEM (Asociación Dominicana para el Desarrollo de la Mujer) in the Dominican Republic, remittances can be used to pay the premium on insurance coverage for remittance recipients. Other institutions have considered **remittance insurance**, a life insurance policy that would guarantee a stream of income equal to the migrant's regular remittances for a set time period in the event that he or she should pass away.
- **Payment services.** Clients of rural banks in the Philippines can pay their loans, school fees, electricity and hospital bills using mobile phone-based money transfers (see Box 11.8).
- **Microenterprise loans.** At Banco Salvadoreño in El Salvador, clients can borrow up to 80 per cent of the value of their last six months' remittance flows.
- **Home purchase or construction.** Cemex's Construmex programme channels remittances from migrants in the United States towards the purchase of construction materials for building a home in Mexico. Banco de Crédito in Peru gives loans for home purchase and construction, backed by the regular reception of remittances. Remittances can also be used to fund the down payment on a home, either as a lump sum or gradually.

Box 11.8 Linking Money Transfers and Financial Service Provision in the Philippines

Since 2004, the Microenterprise Access to Banking Services (MABS) programme has partnered with G-XChange, Inc. (GXI), a wholly owned subsidiary of Globe Telecom, in the development and implementation of mobile phone banking applications and mobile commerce services for rural banks and their clients. Approved by the Bangko Sentral ng Pilipinas (BSP), rural banks can now offer electronically driven financial services in the comfort of their homes, business or offices. These services include:

- **Text-A-Payment** to make microloan payments
- **Text-A-Remittance** to transfer money locally and abroad
- **Text-A-Deposit** to make remote deposits into a client's savings account
- **Text-A-Withdrawal** to transfer money from a client's savings account to their mobile wallet
- **Text-A-BillPay** to facilitate payments to local utility companies, enterprises, hospitals and schools
- **Text-A-Sweldo** to pay staff salaries and support payroll services for local companies
- **Text-A-Credit** to disburse loans and pre-approved credit lines through clients' mobile wallets

The banks and their clients are finding that mobile phone banking offers significant benefits in terms of reduced costs, security, convenience, and expanding business opportunities.

Source: RBAP-MABS, 2010a and 2010b.

Main Messages

1. Segment the market to understand better how clients might use money transfer services.
2. Senders and receivers may require distinct marketing strategies.
3. Analyse competition from both formal and informal money transfer systems.
4. Consortia can provide smaller MFIs with the leverage to negotiate favourable terms with larger partners.
5. MFIs should look for ways to link their money transfer service to other financial services on offer.

Case Study: Segmenting the Market for Remittances at ACCION

Segmenting the market by stages in the immigration life cycle can help an MFI determine how remittances are being used, and the potential that exists for providing recipients with access to other financial services. It can also assist MFIs in developing communication and marketing strategies that can reach potential clients effectively. The following analysis by ACCION International provides an example of how segmentation can support an MFI's

Figure 11.3 Evolution of financial service needs after migration to the United States

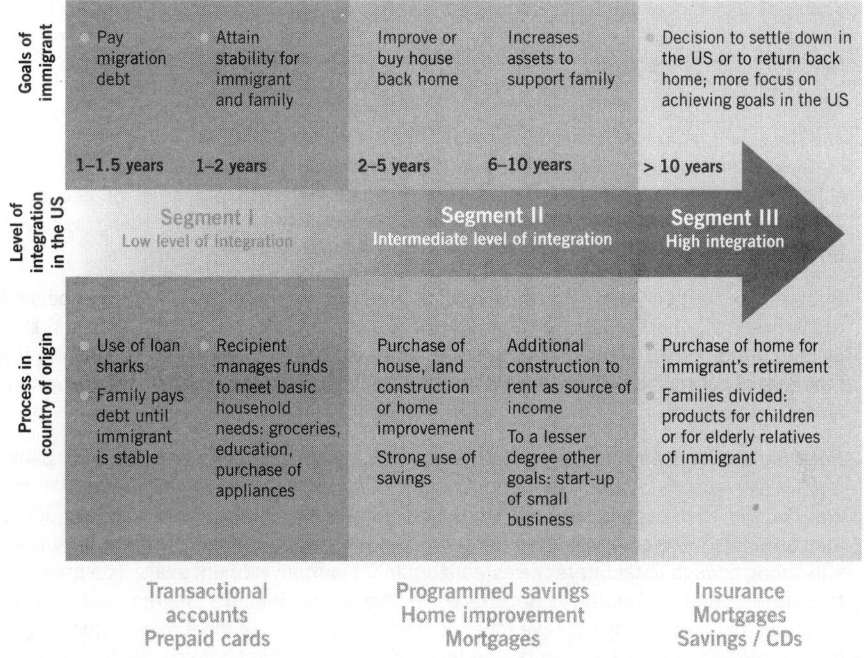

Source: Jaramillo, 2008.

product and relationship development (see Figure 11.3 for an overview).

Segment I corresponds to the initial years after an immigrant has arrived in the host country. During this time remittances are sent mainly to pay for the debt that was incurred back home to finance the migration travel to the host country. It is estimated that once this debt is paid – approximately one to one and a half years into the migration cycle – remittances begin to be used mainly to improve the economic situation and the living conditions of the family back home.

Potential products for this segment. Since most of the remittance funds will be spent to repay debt or meet basic household needs, the savings capacity or potential to access other financial services is lower in this phase. A low-cost transactional account or a prepaid remittance card, to which funds may be directly deposited, is most appropriate. These products make it unnecessary for recipients to visit a bank branch and wait in line for extended periods of time to receive their money. They also provide greater security, as people do not need to walk out of the bank with all their remittances in cash. Prepaid cards or debit cards linked to transactional accounts can also give convenience as payment mechanisms that can facilitate the use of remittances to pay for daily household needs.

Segment II corresponds to the following years in the migration life cycle, approximately two to five years from the time the immigrant arrived in the host country. In this phase, debts incurred back home have generally been paid, the immigrant and his or her family back home are more financially stable, and the emotional bonds that unite them are still strong. It is in this phase that remittances begin to be sent for savings or investments in the country of origin and, consequently, where there is greater potential for linking these funds to financial services.

After achieving economic stabilization, one of the main investment goals of immigrants and their recipient families revolves around their housing situation back home. Carrying out home improvement projects, the purchase of land for construction, or the building of a home are the key goals in this phase. A house becomes a symbol of economic well-being and a representation of the financial improvement that is being achieved through the migration.

Between six and ten years into the migration life cycle, remittances continue to be sent to increase the assets of recipient families or to carry out joint investment projects. Projects to build houses are consolidated, and other investments are pursued, such as the purchase of cars or trucks as business options, the building of a second floor to be rented as an additional source of income, or the start of a business.

Potential products for this segment. This segment presents greater opportunity for banking, for two reasons. As the immigrant becomes more stable and more integrated in the host country, their capacity to send funds for savings or investments with more frequency increases. Also, the emotional ties between the immigrant and their recipient family are still strong enough to facilitate the establishment of joint investment goals. The products that have greater potential to be offered in this phase include programmed savings accounts that help recipients save for education or the down payment of a mortgage, and home improvement loans or remittance-insurance products that help secure the continuation of income. Mortgages adapted to the needs of immigrants also have potential in this phase; however, it is important to take into account that immigrants carrying out home investments back home have mentioned savings as their primary means of purchasing or constructing homes. Incorporating savings as a key component in the design of these loan products could be important in order to respond to the needs and ways in which immigrant families are currently implementing their home-construction goals.

Segment III. In this phase, which for most immigrant communities can take approximately ten years, a very difficult process takes place for the transnational family. Immigrants confront the decision of either returning to their country of origin or staying to live in their host country. Often these decisions are made in an indirect way or by default. Immigrants postpone their decision to return home, or they want to return but do not concretize their plans, turning them into more hopes or wishes for the future. This often results in families breaking up or immigrants supporting two households, one in the host country and the other left back home.

Even though ties with the family back home tend to change after a period of ten years, this does not necessarily mean that remittances decrease or stop. However, there is a shift in the recipient of the remittances and in how the funds are used. In Ecuador, for example, it was observed that after ten years into the migration period the flow of remittances continued to be the same, but rather than the spouse being the recipient, immigrants sent funds directly to their children. In this segment remittances tend also to be sent to provide support for elderly relatives, or to take care of children that were left behind and that will need to continue to be supported until they are adults.

Potential products for this segment. In all three segments described above, there is potential to offer insurance products that can help immigrants address one of their main concerns – caring for the well-being of their families back home. However, in Segment III there is greater potential for insurance products that can guarantee the continuation of income from remittances in case the immigrant dies, insurance products that can support the education of children back home, or health-insurance products to help take care of elderly relatives and close family members. In this phase – because the number of years that have passed in the migration life cycle have weakened the bond between the immigrant and their immediate family – there is less potential to offer financial services to help families implement joint investment goals. There is, however, potential to develop products to meet the specific needs of immigrants interested in savings, mortgage products that help them prepare for their retirement back home, or products that can help recipient families achieve their own goals.

This case study was adapted from Jaramillo (2008).

Recommended Reading

- Isern, J.; Deshpande, R.; van Doorn, J. 2005. *Crafting a money transfers strategy: Guidance for pro-poor financial service providers*, CGAP Occasional Paper No. 10 (Washington, DC, CGAP), at: http://www.cgap.org/gm/document-1.9.2704/OP10.pdf
- Isern, J.; Donges, W.; Smith, J. 2008. *Making money transfers work for microfinance institutions: A technical guide to developing and delivering money transfers* (Washington, DC, CGAP), at: http://www.cgap.org/p/site/c/template.rc/1.9.3003/
- Kumar, K.; McKay, C.; Rotman, S. 2010. *Microfinance and mobile banking: The story so far*, Focus Note No. 62 (Washington, DC, CGAP), at: http://www.microfinancegateway.org/p/site/m/template.rc/1.9.45556/
- Mas, I.; Radcliffe, D. 2010. *Mobile payments go viral: M-PESA in Kenya* (Seattle, Bill and Melinda Gates Foundation), at: http://www.microfinancegateway.org/p/site/m/template.rc/1.9.43376/
- Orozco, M.; Hamilton, E. 2008. "Remittances and MFIs: Issues and lessons from Latin America", in Matthaus-Maier, I.; von Pischke, J.D. (eds.): *New partnerships for innovation in microfinance* (Berlin, Springer-Verlag), pp. 129–146.
- Sander, C. 2008. "Remittance money transfers, microfinance and financial integration: Of credo, cruxes, and convictions", in Matthaus-Maier, I.; von Pischke, J.D (eds.): *New partnerships for innovation in microfinance* (Berlin, Springer-Verlag), pp. 113–128.

12 Non-financial Services

Access to financial services is powerful because it offers people opportunity – a greater range of options to change their lives. But credit, even combined with other financial services, addresses only one factor of many constraining the poor – lack of liquidity. Just as they have been bypassed by formal banking and other financial institutions, the poor have little or no access to education, health and other services to build their human capacity. ~ Dunford (2001)

The factors that keep disadvantaged people in poverty are multiple and interrelated, and cannot be overcome solely by financial services. In recognition of this reality, some MFIs complement their financial services with education, health, business development and other non-financial services to broaden the impact of their work. By facilitating access to certain non-financial products, they strive to increase their clients' ability to use their financial products. It is important to note, however, that this approach is not universally embraced. Critics do not deny the importance of non-financial services, but they do question the appropriateness and the viability of non-financial service delivery by microfinance institutions.

This module explores the decision about whether or not to provide non-financial services, and offers some insight into the design of an appropriate linkage. Specifically, it addresses the following questions:

1. What are non-financial services?
2. How can non-financial services be provided together with financial services?
3. When is it appropriate for MFIs to provide non-financial services?
4. How should the integration process proceed?

12.1 What Are Non-financial Services?

The area of non-financial services is vast, and hard to specify precisely. By definition, non-financial services are services that do not involve brokering, banking, or the creation of money through the use of capital (Farlex Financial Dictionary, 2009). Non-financial services may be offered, however, for a fee. In the context of microfinance, non-financial services are sometimes linked to financial ones because the effect that they produce is complementary. Like financial services, they have an impact on clients' productivity and economic development.

In general, non-financial services can be divided into three categories: 1) social intermediation, which focuses on group capacity building and empowerment; 2) business development; and 3) social services.

Social intermediation prepares marginalized groups or individuals to enter into solid business relationships with MFIs, for example by forming borrower groups, or explaining the roles and responsibilities of being an MFI member. Evidence has shown that it is easier to establish such relationships in societies that already encourage cooperative efforts through local clubs, religious associations, or work groups – in other words, communities with high levels of social capital. Perhaps more than other economic transactions, microfinance depends on social capital, because it requires trust between the borrower and the lender, and perhaps between the borrower and his or her guarantors. Where neither traditional systems nor modern institutions provide a basis for trust, financial relationships are difficult to establish.

Business development services are intended to improve the performance of a client's business. They can do this by strengthening management of the business, improving investment decisions, reducing operational constraints or costs, increasing workplace safety, or expanding opportunities for growth. Generally, business development services involve the transfer of knowledge to micro and small business owners in the form of "how to" advice, training, market information, or linkages to knowledgeable organizations or networks. They can also connect business owners to market infrastructure, such as storage facilities, technology or certification systems, and to other actors in a value chain.

Social services such as those in the areas of health, education or nutrition, strengthen human capital, and create conditions for the poor to make better use of microfinance services. In this way they improve the impact of microfinance on income generation and poverty reduction.

Table 12.1 provides examples of services that fall into each of these categories. One type of non-financial service that could arguably be placed in all three categories is financial education. Financial education is the transfer of knowledge, skills and attitudes required to adopt good money management practices for earning, spending, saving, borrowing and investing (Cohen et al., 2003). It is a valuable non-financial service, because it builds confidence as well as the capacity to make better financial choices, and this affects not only the relationship between an MFI and its clients, but also the development of clients' businesses and the well-being of their families. Many MFIs incorporate some kind of financial education into their initial orientation session with borrowers, but there is a wide range of topics that could be addressed by MFIs, particularly those that are diversifying and want their clients to be able to make effective use of the new products and technologies being introduced (see Box 12.1).

Table 12.1 Examples of non-financial services

Social intermediation	Business development services	Social services
• Mobilizing groups • Developing group cohesion • Training group members in participatory management, accounting, or basic financial management • Helping groups establish a good record-keeping system • Raising awareness of available financial services • Helping individuals increase their self-confidence when dealing with a financial institution	• Technology transfer • Business management training • Production training • Management consulting or advisory services • Legal advice and advocacy • Value chain analysis and interventions • Linking enterprises with markets or buyers • Export and trade services • Improving access to inputs • Building business networks • Providing market information through agents, databases, publications • Certification and quality standards	• Provision of basic education in areas of health, hygiene or nutrition • Provision of basic health, hygiene or nutrition services • Literacy training • Mentoring or advisory services in basic human rights, personal development, family planning, children's education, or housing construction

Source: Authors.

Box 12.1 Examples of Financial Education Topics

Basic principles of money management
- Assessing your financial situation
- Setting financial goals
- Distinguishing between needs and wants

Managing cash flow
- Making a financial plan
- Developing a budget
- Following a budget
- Spending wisely – stretching your money

Building assets
- Housing, land, property and other physical assets
- Investing in a business
- Protecting assets

Dealing with life-cycle events
- Marriage
- Household formation
- Birth and education of children
- Retirement/old age
- Death

Earning money
- Moneymaking ideas
- Looking for a job (paid employment)
- Starting and managing your own business
- Career planning

Dealing with special challenges
- Illness or death of family members
- Own illness
- Extending help to other families
- Divorce or family breakdown
- Job loss
- Natural disasters / calamities

"Interfacing" with formal and informal financial institutions
- Saving – opening a savings account; setting savings goals; participating in ROSCAs
- Borrowing – when to (and not to) borrow; risks associated with borrowing; comparing loan terms and conditions; calculating interest; how to manage debt
- Insurance – understanding what it is and what it can do
- Technology – why and how to use it; privacy of personal information

Financial decision-making processes
- Joint decisions
- Independent decisions

Planning ahead for the future
- Investments
- Old age/retirement
- Death

Source: Cohen and Sebstad, 2003.

12.2 How Can Non-financial Services Be Provided Together with Financial Services?

If an MFI wants to provide non-financial services to its clients, it can do so in one of three ways: 1) by partnering with a non-financial service provider; 2) by establishing a parallel department or programme inside the institution to deliver non-financial services; or 3) by delivering integrated financial and non-financial services through a unified infrastructure. These options, as well as whether they should be offered on a voluntary or compulsory basis, are discussed below.

The Partnership Approach

Financial and non-financial services can be provided to the same client by two independent organizations. In this model, the MFI does not provide non-financial services directly; it partners with a non-financial service provider. For example, it might ally with a local clinic and allow health-care professionals to give presentations at borrower group meetings and/or attend to the health needs of clients and their families. Under this arrangement, each organization focuses on what it does best. A partnership approach is particularly appropriate when the expertise or infrastructure required to deliver the non-financial service is quite different from the expertise or infrastructure possessed by the MFI.

A potential disadvantage of the partnership approach is that the MFI cannot control the quality of a partner's services. Tension may also arise as the two organizations compete for clients' time and attention. Thus, for the approach to be successful, MFIs must invest time and effort in building and managing the partnership (see Chapter 22). This is made easier if the two organizations have some common roots or history. When the non-financial service provider is established by one or more microfinance stakeholders, it is more likely to have both a compatible culture and an interest in maintaining a successful relationship over time.

The Parallel Approach

An organization committed to providing multiple services could create distinct programmes or departments within the same institution to deliver financial and non-financial services in parallel, but with separate, specialized personnel. Staff would work for one organization, and perhaps share the same physical and administrative infrastructure, but they would deliver different services and be managed separately. This arrangement is similar to a private-sector holding company, and has a clear division of functions. Quality control is in the hands of the single overarching organization, which is an advantage of this model over the partnership model.

The parallel approach places a larger financial and management burden on MFIs, however. Fundraising and accounting for each programme must be distinguished to assure donors and other sources of capital that their funds are allocated to the programme of their choice, and to enable the performance of each programme to be assessed separately. One of the most famous examples of the parallel approach is BRAC in Bangladesh, which is discussed in Box 12.2.

The Unified Approach

Using this strategy, the provision of financial and non-financial services is fully integrated. The same staff members provide multiple services to each client. Direct costs are lower than with the other two approaches, because the delivery channel is the same for both types of services, but employees may need to be paid more because of the multiple skills their jobs require. If staff members are to remain productive, the scope of the non-financial services must be limited to activities that can fit into regular financial service delivery, and incentive schemes must balance the need for quality financial and non-financial service provision with the need for efficiency and productivity. Described in Box 12.3, the Credit with Education model is an example of the unified approach that has been adopted by MFIs across the globe.

Box 12.2 Parallel Service Provision at BRAC in Bangladesh

The Bangladesh Rural Advancement Committee (BRAC) provides multiple services to some 8.5 million members throughout Bangladesh. It works through village organizations, which are composed of seven to eight BRAC groups of five individuals each. Microfinance, education, health and social services are offered to the village organizations by functionally independent, sector-specific service programmes, each with its own administration and staff and revenue stream. In the past, the same BRAC staff were responsible for all services to their assigned groups. However, the rigours of running an efficient credit programme meant that other sectors and tasks tended to be neglected. Moreover, BRAC realized that a field agent who is good at managing credit may not necessarily be suitable for carrying out social awareness-raising programmes, and vice versa.

BRAC acknowledges that coordination between different programmes is sometimes difficult, and that the total cost for separate management and staff for each programme is higher than if there were a single set of managers and staff for all services. However, the microfinance programme is financially self-sufficient. There is some cross-subsidy of the education and training programmes from BRAC's microfinance and subsector development (poultry, silk culture, social forestry and others) programmes. But education and training programmes are also funded by external grants, and partial dependence on external funding is expected for the foreseeable future.

Source: Adapted from Dunford, 2001.

Box 12.3 The Unified Delivery of *Credit with Education*

Freedom from Hunger launched *Credit with Education* in 1989 with 50 women in Mali and 50 women in Thailand. In 2009, the model was being used by 30 different MFIs in 15 countries. All MFIs use a group lending methodology to distribute the product, although not all institutions use *Credit with Education* or the group lending methodology as their only product. At Faitière des Unités Coopératives d'Epargne et de Crédit du Togo (FUCEC-Togo), for example, *Credit with Education* is just one of the products offered by member credit unions, and is specifically designed to reach rural women who would not have been reached otherwise by the credit unions.

In the *Credit with Education* model, a portion of each group's regular meeting (preferably 20 to 30 minutes) is set aside for a "learning session", which is led by a *Credit with Education* field agent (usually a moderately educated person from the local area). Field agents are responsible for both financial and non-financial service delivery at the meeting. Their role in education is to introduce a topic, help participants understand its relevance to issues in their lives, offer basic information about practical changes they can make, identify obstacles to such change, encourage any participants who have mastered these obstacles to share their successful experiences, and promote solidarity to help each other persist in their efforts to change. The field agents are not experts in the education topics. Their training focuses on techniques for presenting simple information messages, and on facilitation skills for drawing the participants into learning from each other as much as from the field agent.

The topics addressed in learning sessions range from group management, through the basics of microenterprise management, to the improvement of health and nutrition of women and children. Each *Credit with Education* practitioner organization promotes a different mix of topics depending on its organizational objectives, local needs and demand, availability of training and support for delivering different topics, and availability of good-quality local services (for example, immunization or primary health clinics) which can be promoted by the education. Typically, during a loan period of four to six months, one or two topics are explored in depth in a series of learning sessions, each building on the last. Some practitioners alternate between two topics, a learning session on a health topic, the next on microenterprise and group management, then back to health, from one meeting to the next over the loan period. Visit http://www.ffhtechnical.org for more information.

Source: Adapted from Dunford, 2001.

Compulsory vs. Voluntary

The partnership, parallel and unified approaches can all be implemented via a compulsory or voluntary linkage. If the linkage is compulsory, clients must receive both financial and non-financial services as part of a single package. If the linkage is voluntary, clients can decide which service or services they want to receive. While voluntary linkages are generally the most attractive, some organizations have found that a compulsory linkage is actually more effective in helping them achieve their outreach objectives (see Box 12.4).

While in no way comprehensive, Table 12.2 illustrates the fact that MFIs use all of the approaches described above to make non-financial services available to their clients. Each option has advantages and disadvantages. The unified approach offers an MFI greatest control and the ability to offer services that may not be available in the communities where it operates, but the range of services that can be offered is quite limited. The parallel approach gives an MFI some control and expands the potential range of services that can be offered, but presents greater financial and coordination challenges. With the partnership approach, an MFI can potentially offer the greatest variety of services, but with the least control over the quality of service delivery.

The best choice depends on local options for providing diverse services, as well as an MFI's will and capacity to provide more than microfinance. In general, institutions that use large-group delivery channels have had more success integrating non-financial services into their product portfolio, while those that work through small groups or individuals have relied

Box 12.4 Can Compulsory Linkages Be Worthwhile?

Non-financial services tend to provide benefits over time. Unlike credit, which appears immediately as cash in hand, the benefits of non-financial services are not immediately tangible. For that reason, low-income clients may not initially be willing to pay for them. Studies by Freedom from Hunger reveal, however, that participants come to value non-financial services, such as health education, over time. Once in the programme, clients indicate a willingness to pay more for these services, and cite the education component as a principal reason for continuing to borrow from the organization, even if other credit facilities are available.

In 2006, Innovations for Poverty Action and FINCA-Peru evaluated the effectiveness of integrating entrepreneurship education with microfinance services using a randomized control trial which assigned over 4,000 FINCA clients from pre-existing lending groups to treatment groups (which were given access to training) and control groups (which were not). The study found that repayment among treatment groups was three percentage points higher and client retention was five percentage points higher than among control groups, which generated significantly more net revenue for FINCA than the marginal cost of providing the training. Nevertheless, treatment clients often cited the extended length of weekly meetings as a factor in dropping out of the programme. FINCA could have solved this problem by making the training voluntary, but it was precisely those clients who expressed the *least* interest in business training prior to the programme whose repayment and retention rates improved the most as a result of the training. Following this study, FINCA decided to make entrepreneurship training compulsory.

Source: Adapted from Dunford, 2001, and Karlan and Valdivia, 2006.

more on partnerships to make such services available to their clients. As MFIs evolve, their approach may change, as illustrated by BRAC (Box 12.2), Financiera Solución (Box 12.5) and the Grameen Bank (refer to the case at the end of the chapter).

Table 12.2 Typology of linkages

Type of linkage	Voluntary (client decides)	Compulsory (institution decides)
Unified	ADEMCOL (growth clients) (Colombia) Al Amana Tkwin Jdid (Morocco) Financiera Solución (Peru) MiBanco (Peru)	ADEMCOL (micro clients) (Colombia) Bank of Khyder (Pakistan) Freedom from Hunger-supported institutions GDREP/PRIDE (Guinea) Papir (Mocambique) ProMujer (Bolivia)
Parallel	BRAC (Bangladesh) IDEPRO (Bolivia) PRIDE (Guinea) SEEDS (Sri Lanka) Fundación Mario Santo Domingo (Colombia)	ISSIA (Uganda) SEEDS (Sri Lanka)
Partner	ADA-CEREM/LUX Youth project–MFIs (Mali) BASIX (India) Care Bosnia Credit and Market Access components (Bosnia-Herzegovina) EDA Banja Luka – Microfins (Bosnia-Herzegovina) MEDF Banks – Business Centres (Macedonia) Bank Niaga – Swiss contact supported Business Centres (Indonesia) SIYB – Barclays bank/MFIs (Zimbabwe) Fundación Carvajal (Colombia)	Primero Emprego youth employment programme (Brazil) VanCity Credit Union (Canada) LEDA (Croatia)

Source: Sievers and Vanderberg, 2007.

12.3 When Is it Appropriate for MFIs to Provide Non-financial Services?

The debate about whether or not to integrate financial and non-financial services reflects the tension between different aspects of outreach at the heart of microfinance. Proponents of integration argue, above all, that non-financial services are essential to overcoming poverty (and thus are in the interest of the client), and can be provided without detracting from the quality and ultimate sustainability of an MFI (see Box 12.6). When compared with minimalist credit models, integrated programmes can achieve a greater impact, potentially leading not only to higher incomes and asset accumulation, but also to more tangible social improvements.

Box 12.5 Non-financial Services as a Retention Strategy at Financiera Solución

Due to increasing competition for micro- and small enterprise clients, Financiera Solución decided to introduce a variety of incentive schemes to retain its clients. This included offering the International Labour Organization (ILO)'s Improve Your Business (IYB) management training as a marketing instrument and a reward for client loyalty. Of the clients it contacted, 10–15 per cent completed the training. During the sessions, each client developed an investment plan that was passed on to a credit committee for evaluation.

Training began in 2001, and 2,609 clients were trained in IYB by mid-2003. Financiera Solución received advice from the ILO but self-financed the linkage programme. It invested a total of US$78,000 between 2001 and 2003, of which US$50,000 was spent on advertising costs that also served to promote Financiera Solución's other products. In 2003, the ILO commissioned a study that found that the 2,609 trained clients had leveraged additional credit totalling US$462,000, which in turn generated additional income of US$42,000 for Financiera Solución. The study also found that out of 114 entrepreneurs interviewed, those taking the non-financial service expressed stronger loyalty to Financiera Solución, achieved better business performance, and employed significantly more people than those who did not take the service.

Between March 2003 and February 2004, Financiera Solución was acquired by Banco de Crédito del Perú (BCP), the largest bank in Peru. After having integrated the core financial operations of Financiera Solución, BCP decided to continue offering management training to its best clients in a strategic partnership with the Centro de Promoción de la Pequeña Empresa – Propyme, backed by the Universidad del Pacífico.

Source: Sievers and Vanderberg, 2007.

From the MFI's perspective, integration is attractive because of its potential to increase client loyalty, improve portfolio quality, and differentiate the MFI in the market. In Bolivia, for example, when microcredit borrowers were politically organized to default purposely *en masse* to protest at the high interest rates and repayment requirements of local microfinance institutions in 1999, CRECER clients remained loyal and continued their on-time repayment. When asked why, many clients responded, "CRECER cares about us. They are not just here to collect our loans. They talk with us and give us education" (Dunford, 2001). The FINCA and Financiera Solución examples in Boxes 12.3 and 12.5 also highlight the potential utility of non-financial services as a client retention strategy.

An additional reason to consider non-financial services, and perhaps the most important one in the context of this text, is to reach new market segments. As described in Chapters 14–21, non-financial services have a potentially powerful role to play in making financial services more accessible and more useful to youth, women, refugees, small and medium enterprises, disabled persons, people living with HIV/AIDS, and other underserved groups.

Critics of integration contend that financial service providers should focus on their core business, rather than expanding into areas in which they are less knowledgeable and less capable of delivering a quality service. Unless provided by a partner, non-financial services increase operating costs and the complexity of managing, accounting and controlling these costs. They can

Box 12.6 Evidence that It Can Be Done

Although it does not stand up to the rigours of academic research, there is some preliminary evidence to suggest that the benefits of providing non-financial services can outweigh the costs:

Case 1: In a study of 543 borrowers, Halder (2003) reports that BRAC clients who received credit, vocational training and access to inputs where markets were missing or weak (for instance, newborn chicks) generated twice the gross annual income of those who received credit alone (US$217 compared with US$107). The fees clients paid for the non-financial services covered 47 per cent of BRAC's cost of providing the services, yet the additional income gained by clients who received them was 8 to 66 times higher than the fees paid, suggesting that clients could cover the full cost of the service delivery.

Case 2: Of the 30 institutions currently using the *Credit with Education* methodology, 23 report to the Microfinance Information eXchange (MIX), and 78 per cent of these were profitable in 2008. Scientific research studies in Bolivia, Ghana, Mali, Peru and Thailand have documented that women participating in *Credit with Education*, when compared with similar women not participating, have more income and assets, a greater sense of personal empowerment to make decisions, and better-nourished and healthier children. The women manage their businesses better and earn more money (especially during slow seasons) as compared with non-participants.

Source: Adapted from Sievers and Vanderberg, 2007; http://www.ffhtechnical.org and http://www.themix.org.

also undermine competitiveness if clients are obliged to invest additional time or pay higher prices to receive services they did not request. The high cost of providing microfinance services already leads to tight profit margins, and adding non-financial services makes the challenging task of achieving sustainability even more difficult.

Both sides of this debate are compelling, as summarized in Table 12.3. Thus the useful conclusion to draw is not whether one side or the other is correct, but rather under what conditions would the integration of financial and non-financial services make sense.

An MFI's decision about whether or not to develop a non-financial product will depend on the institution's goals, its vision, and the depth of its desire to provide clients with more than financial services. It will also depend on the local options available for the provision of non-financial services and, at least initially, on the MFI's ability to attract funds to subsidize costs. MFIs should consider the integration of non-financial services only if they can fulfil the conditions outlined in Chapter 2 of this manual, and if:

1. **They have a strong commitment to providing the complementary services.** Successful integration depends on a clear commitment from all levels of the organization – from the board of directors to loan officers – to the provision of both financial *and* non-financial services. Half-hearted attempts at forging the delicate balance that integration requires cannot succeed. It is difficult to create a corporate culture that simultaneously provides basic human services while not tolerating late loan repayments.
2. **The strategy to provide these services matches the MFI's timeline for sustainability.** Clients may need a particular service, and the MFI may have a strong social

Table 12.3 Pros and cons of integrating financial and non-financial services

Potential benefits	Potential risks
• Has broader impact in more areas of a client's life and on her community • Provides much-needed basic services that might not otherwise exist • Can be financially sustainable because, after seeing the benefits, clients are often willing to bear higher costs to pay for non-financial services • Increases customer loyalty from clients who appreciate the MFI's concern • Heightens incentive for timely repayment • Facilitates steady repayment by increasing profit (due to newly acquired business skills, or better health conditions, which increase client productivity) • Strengthens institutional and staff commitment to the social mission • Differentiates the MFI from competitors, and increases its marketability to clients and donors • Can facilitate outreach to underserved market segments	• Has lower impact, because the MFI takes on too many services that lie outside its core competence *or* has no additional impact because not enough time and resources are invested in the non-financial service for it to be effective • Provides redundant services if similar services and resources are already available in the region • Increases costs, compromises operational efficiency, and takes longer to reach sustainability • Increases client desertion among clients who dislike the increase in transaction costs associated with non-financial services • Is harder to control costs because of complex accounting, which can make the MFI less marketable to funders • Requires a stronger institutional structure because management is more complex • Creates confusion over corporate culture (financial programmes project a tough, serious image while non-financial services present a softer quality)

Source: Adapted from Churchill et al., 2002.

commitment, but if the MFI intends to become sustainable within a specific period of time, it may have to compromise on how the non-financial service is provided. Options include linking with an existing NGO or private service provider, or selecting only services that can be fully integrated into existing operations without overburdening clients or staff.

3. **The supply of services in the area is not matching demand or cannot be adapted to the needs of MFI clients.** MFIs should conduct a market study to determine the non-financial needs of clients and the supply of services available to meet those needs. MFIs often are among the few agencies operating in remote areas with vulnerable populations. In such environments, it may make sense for them to use their infrastructure and staff to provide additional business, health and education services that would not otherwise be accessible. It would not make sense to launch a non-financial product that competes with an already existing, quality service.

12.4 How Should the Integration Process Proceed?

While there are no certain rules for success, the following principles can help MFIs move effectively down the path of integrating one or more non-financial services into their financial service portfolio:

- Seek potential partners that are already providing high-quality non-financial services in a relevant area and could benefit from the MFI's outreach.
- Use market research to identify which services will respond to real wants and needs of the population.
- Select services that complement the MFI's core competences, or which fit easily into its lending process.
- Decrease product development time by taking advantage of training curricula and other tools that have already been developed by others (see, for example, Box 12.7)
- Decide whether the non-financial service will be voluntary or mandatory, or should become voluntary over time. Recognize that if the service is mandatory and clients do not value it, integration may become a liability for the MFI.
- Depending on the type of service being provided, consider targeting particular sets of clients (for example, women, parents, rural clients, new clients or young clients), so that participation requirements and content can be tailored to them.
- Train managers who oversee financial and non-financial services at the same time, so as to develop sensitivity for each other's work.
- Promote a tough-love culture in which non-financial services can be provided with sensitivity without financial services losing their seriousness.
- Modify incentive schemes and performance evaluations to value both financial and non-financial services.
- Reconsider the current profile used to hire field staff. (Is it easier to train a health educator to be a good loan officer or vice versa?)
- Use clear accounting policies and separate cost centres to monitor efficiency and productivity of the delivery of financial and non-financial services, both separately and jointly.
- Monitor the quality and consistency of financial and non-financial service provision, as well as client satisfaction with the services being delivered. If the costs of the linkage come to outweigh the benefits for either an MFI or its clients, the delivery strategy must change.

Chapter 22 provides additional guidance for MFIs that choose to deliver non-financial services through a partnership approach.

Box 12.7 Sample Training Tools

The **Global Financial Education Programme** develops curricula targeted to low-income households, and trains a broad range of service organizations to use it. The core curriculum is available in English Spanish, Russian, Portuguese, Arabic, Chinese and French and includes the following five topics: budgeting, debt management, savings, bank services, financial negotiations. Four additional modules focus on a specific population or product: young people, remittances, risk management and insurance, and consumer protection. Each module contains a content note that provides a basic overview of the topic, a trainer's guide and a training-of-trainers manual to prepare financial education trainers. Visit
http://www.globalfinancialed.org/curriculum.html for more information.

The International Labour Organization (ILO) offers four training packages to support microenterprise development: 1) **Generate Your Business Idea** (GYBI) is for men and women who want to start a business but do not yet have a concrete business idea; 2) **Start Your Business** (SYB) introduces potential entrepreneurs to practical examples of business start-ups, concepts and procedures and guides them through the process of creating a business plan; 3) **Improve Your Business** (IYB) introduces existing entrepreneurs to the principles of efficient small business management, namely marketing, buying, stock control, costing, record-keeping, business planning and people and productivity; 4) **GET Ahead for Women in Enterprise** promotes enterprise development among women in poverty who want to start or are already engaged in small-scale business. All four training packages include written materials for participants as well as trainer's guides and reference resources. More information is available at:
http://www.ilosiyb.co.zw/training_materials.html and
http://www.ilo.org/public/libdoc/ilo/2004/104B09_356_engl.pdf

Developed by the International Finance Corporation (IFC), **Business Edge** is a management training programme for small and medium enterprises that includes 36 courses on five different topics: marketing, human resources, production and operations, finance and accounting, and productivity skills. It is delivered through certified trainers and local franchisees in Viet Nam, China, the Middle East and Africa. See
http://www.ifc.org/ifcext/africa.nsf/Content/SMED_BusinessEdge for details.

Source: Adapted from the Global Financial Education, ILO and IFC web sites noted above.

Main Messages

1. The factors that keep disadvantaged people in poverty are multiple and interrelated, and cannot be overcome solely by financial services.
2. By facilitating access to certain non-financial products, MFIs can increase their clients' ability to use their financial products.
3. MFIs can integrate non-financial services into their product portfolio and still be profitable.
4. Successful integration of financial and non-financial services requires a clear commitment from all levels of the organization; it will not be strategic for all MFIs.
5. If a non-financial service is mandatory and clients do not value it, integration may become a liability for the MFI.

Case Study: The Evolution of Non-financial Services at Grameen

Established as a pilot project in 1976, the Grameen Bank transformed into the world's first microfinance bank in 1983. Some say it invented the unified delivery model of non-financial service provision with the introduction of its Sixteen Decisions (see Box 12.8). The decisions are resolutions that were made by centre leaders when they gathered together at a national level in 1980, 1982 and 1984 to review their problems and achievements, identify areas of concern, and look for solutions to their social and economic challenges. Ever since, the decisions have been recited at the beginning of each centre meeting, and provide a focus for the diversified products and services that Grameen offers today.

In its first 15 years, the bank experimented with everything from organizing client-run preschools to partnering with local government agencies to organize immunization days, to distributing vegetable seeds and saplings at cost. By the early 1990s it decided to turn most of its non-financial initiatives into separate companies. That way, individual CEOs could have more control over their operations, and the bank could reduce the effect of failed enterprises on other Grameen initiatives.

Most of these companies use bank resources, such as staff, knowledge, relationships and facilities, to take on poverty reduction opportunities that microfinance alone could not adequately address. For example, GrameenPhone, Bangladesh's largest and most profitable telecommunications company, has helped 300,000 Grameen Bank clients establish profitable mobile payphone businesses. Grameen Kalyan has set up more than 30 health clinics located alongside Grameen Bank branches. The non-profit organization uses a health insurance model in which Grameen clients and other poor families pay a yearly insurance premium and receive preventive and curative services for a small co-payment. They can also buy medicine at a discounted rate. Because health crises are the primary reason why microfinance clients default on their loans, the clinics' successes help facilitate the success of Grameen Bank.

Box 12.8 The Sixteen Decisions

1. We shall follow and advance the four principles of Grameen Bank – discipline, unity, courage and hard work – in all walks of our lives.
2. Prosperity we shall bring to our families.
3. We shall not live in a dilapidated house. We shall repair our houses and work towards constructing new houses at the earliest opportunity.
4. We shall grow vegetables all the year round. We shall eat plenty of them and sell the surplus.
5. During the plantation seasons, we shall plant as many seedlings as possible.
6. We shall plan to keep our families small. We shall minimize our expenditures. We shall look after our health.
7. We shall educate our children and ensure that they can earn to pay for their education.
8. We shall always keep our children and the environment clean.
9. We shall build and use pit latrines.
10. We shall drink water from tube wells. If they are not available, we shall boil water or use alum to purify it.
11. We shall not take any dowry at our sons' weddings; neither shall we give any dowry at our daughter's wedding. We shall keep the centre free from the curse of dowry. We shall not practise child marriage.
12. We shall not commit any injustice, and we will oppose anyone who tries to do so.
13. We shall collectively undertake larger investments for higher incomes.
14. We shall always be ready to help each other. If anyone is in difficulty, we shall all help him or her.
15. If we come to know of any breach of discipline in any centre, we shall all go there and help restore discipline.
16. We shall introduce physical exercises in all our centres. We shall take part in all social activities collectively.

Another thriving initiative is Grameen Shakti, a profitable yet non-profit renewable energy company that sells, finances and services solar power systems for families and businesses, thus providing clean power without subsidy. It had installed more than 320,000 solar power systems by December 2009. In total, the Grameen family consists of 25 different companies, all with the common goal of alleviating poverty. The companies are independent entities, but members of the bank's Board of Directors and senior management sit on other companies' boards, which helps facilitate collaboration.

This case study was adapted from Yunus and Jolis (1999) and http://www.grameen-info.org.

Recommended Reading

- Cohen, M.; Stack, K.; McGuinness, E. 2003. *Financial education: A win-win for clients and MFIs* (Washington, DC, Microfinance Opportunities), at: http://www.microfinanceopportunities.org/docs/Financial_Education_A_Win_Win_for_Clients_and_MFIs.pdf

- Dunford, C. 2001. *Building better lives: Sustainable integration of microfinance and education in child survival, reproductive health, and HIV/AIDS prevention for the poorest entrepreneurs* (Washington, DC, Microcredit Summit Campaign), at: http://www.microcreditsummit.org/papers/BBLcomplete.pdf

- Miehlbradt, A.; McVay, M. 2002. "Developing commercial markets for business development services: Are 'how-to-do-it' recipes possible?", Seminar Reader (Turin, ITCILO), at: http://www.bds-forum.net/bds-reader/theory/2-bds-reader-turin-2002.pdf

- Sievers, M.; Vanderberg, P. 2007. "Synergies through linkages: Who benefits from linking micro-finance and business development services?", in *World Development*, Vol. 35, No 8, pp. 1341–1398 (Oxford, Elsevier), at: http://p31.itcilo.org/entdev/synergies/en/category-2

13 Grants

Grants are a financial product that can reach the most vulnerable groups.... [They are] a risk-free opportunity for the poor to start a business, build assets, expand an already existing business, or re-establish assets that have been lost. ~ Palaniswamy (2005)

A grant is a sum of money or an in-kind benefit, such as food or business equipment, provided to members of specific target groups to help them with a particular situation. There may be conditions attached to the grant, but there is no requirement for it to be repaid.

A few years ago, no one could have imagined that a microfinance book would include a chapter on grants. In an effort to promote a credit culture, and avoid creating any possible excuse for not repaying loans, most microfinance institutions would not even consider providing their clients with grants. But times are changing.

The anti-grant bias of the microfinance community has been confronted by the provision of financial services in challenging environments and to difficult market segments. In post-conflict and post-crisis environments, for example, it is often inappropriate to consider giving microenterprise loans since most people have neither microenterprises nor a way of repaying the loan. So instead, to bridge the gap between relief and development, agencies have been experimenting with grants to address basic needs, to help people initiate income-generating activities, and then once they have a revenue stream, to link to microcredit (see Chapter 18). The same concept is applicable in serving the "poorest of the poor", for whom credit could be a detrimental burden, but who might be able to graduate into mainstream microfinance through a combination of grants and other interventions (see Chapter 15).

Although the provision of grants is not a core element of microfinance, and is certainly not a product as such, it can present opportunities for MFIs. This chapter explores those opportunities, and provides some guidelines for managing grants effectively. It covers the following topics:

1. When and how can grants be useful?
2. General characteristics of effective grant design
3. Leveraging public cash transfer schemes
4. Financing micro-grants

13.1 When and How Can Grants Be Useful?

Grants can be provided in cash, in kind or as a voucher – a piece of paper that can be exchanged for goods or services. A cash grant gives the most flexibility to the person receiving the funds, but it also creates a greater risk that the funds will be misused. In-kind grants can be targeted for more specific purposes, but involve additional administrative efforts to purchase and deliver the supplies. Vouchers combine some of the flexibility of cash (for instance, the receiver can decide when and where to access the goods or services) while still restricting the use of funds to a specific purpose. The decision about which type of grant is more useful depends partly on what the grant will be used for.

There are three main ways that micro-grants can be used: 1) as a tool for deepening outreach; 2) as a strategy for rebuilding livelihoods; and 3) as a temporary safety net in the event of an emergency.

Deepening Outreach

A growing body of evidence shows that financial services enable poor people to reduce their vulnerability, build assets, and link into the wider economy. Yet millions of poor people lack access to financial services, and hooking them up with services that are affordable, close by, and appropriately designed is often not easy. Technology, partnerships and more market-driven product development have the potential to create access for the majority of people, but for the most vulnerable and disadvantaged market segments, micro-grants can help the "unbanked" get connected.

One example of a market segment that microfinance institutions are not serving well is start-up enterprises. Most MFIs do not lend to start-ups because they find them too risky, but some organizations have used grants to help entrepreneurs finance their initial operations and build up a track record that can make MFI access possible.

Perhaps the most prevalent example of this approach is Trickle Up, which has been providing start-up and expansion grants to the very poor since 1979. Trickle Up identifies potential entrepreneurs with help from local organizations in eight countries in Asia, Africa and Central America. Its local partners then provide these entrepreneurs with business training, assistance in preparing a business plan, and seed capital of about US$50 to start a business. After three months, entrepreneurs who are working hard and have a business with some potential become eligible for a second US$50 grant. This combination of cash and in-kind grants has enabled Trickle Up and its partners to reach customers who would otherwise not have been served. This includes youth, refugees, immigrants, people living with disabilities, and people living with HIV/AIDS (see, for example, Box 13.1).

As discussed in Chapter 15, in-kind and cash grants can also be packaged to reach the poorest of the poor. In this case, cash grants may be provided early in the process, not as seed capital, but as consumption support to stabilize a poor person's situation and help ensure that his or her basic needs are being met. Vouchers in the form of food stamps or ration cards can also serve this purpose. The early grant "frees up" time and energy that the person would have otherwise spent trying to survive, and enables the poorest to make more effective use of training, health care and other support services, which are often provided as in-kind grants. These

Box 13.1 Using Grants to Finance Start-Ups

Harriet Mukuba, a young widow living in the suburbs of Kampala, Uganda, tested positive for HIV after her husband died 12 years ago. She received counselling and medical care from AIDS Widows and Orphans Family Support (AWOFS). With no proven business experience, Harriet did not qualify for their loan programme, so AWOFS selected her to receive a Trickle Up grant to start a clothes-embroidering business. Her success at managing her business and savings later gave her access to AWOFS' loan programme, allowing her to expand her business further.

Source: Palaniswamy, 2005.

Box 13.2 Micro-grants on a Graduation Pathway

Since 2006, the Consultative Group to Assist the Poorest (CGAP) and the Ford Foundation have been exploring how a "graduation model" can create pathways out of extreme poverty, adapting a methodology developed by the Bangladesh Rehabilitation Assistance Committee (BRAC) (refer to the case study at the end of Chapter 15). The term "graduation" refers to participants moving out of safety net programmes and graduating into income-earning activities that let them sustain themselves without external subsidies.

The graduation model includes the transfer of an asset, which is selected by each participant from a menu of five to eight different options, based on their preferences and past experience. The options are identified through value chain and subsector analysis, with careful attention being paid to available support services and market infrastructure. In Ethiopia, for example, market analysis identified four livelihood options: sheep and goats, cattle fattening, honey production and petty trade, plus a fifth "open" option for those with past experience in another area. These options were identified through a scoring exercise that prioritized sectors with potential for growth and outreach (in other words, the sector's ability to incorporate target beneficiaries as core actors of the value chain).

Before the asset transfer takes place, participants receive skills training on caring for their selected asset, and where to go for assistance and services. After the transfer takes place, weekly household visits by staff allow for monitoring and "coaching" over the 18 to 24 months of the programme. During these meetings, staff help participants with business planning and money management, along with social support and health and disease prevention services.

Source: Adapted from El-Zoghbi and de Montesquiou with Hashemi, 2009.

grants can enable the poorest to manage their existing resources and income-generating activities more effectively, and to enter into a relationship with a financial service provider to build their assets through savings over time. Alternatively, an in-kind grant or voucher can provide an asset transfer that enables the poorest to launch a new income-generating activity.

In reaching out to the poorest, the transfer of an asset rather than cash can be strategic for several reasons. First, it ensures that 100 per cent of the grant will be used to finance a new income-generating activity. Second, steps can be taken to ensure that the asset that is acquired will be part of a value chain that can absorb new entrants. If individuals are given a cash transfer and they all choose to start the same kind of business – selling vegetables in the local market, for example – they may create an oversupply of vegetables that weakens all market vendors' ability to succeed. Third, by incorporating a specific type of asset transfer into the design of an outreach strategy, training and other non-financial services can be planned to support the care and optimal use of the asset, as described in Box 13.2.

When members of a vulnerable market segment already have income-generating activities, an alternative approach for deepening outreach is to use grants as an entry point for building a savings-led relationship with a financial service provider. Although vulnerable market segments may not be in a position to borrow, they can build assets over time with the help of an MFI that provides the right mix of security and access. A grant can serve as an incentive for members of a vulnerable market segment to take the initiative, accept the costs, and overcome the fear of entering into a relationship with a financial institution.

One way to use grants as a financial service entry point is to encourage public cash transfers that are made into individual savings accounts rather than in cash (see Section 13.3 below). Another option is matched savings. Edge Finance S.A. has been experimenting with Personal Capitalization Accounts (PCAs) in Peru since 2003. It offers very poor peasant women small monetary incentives for opening and using individual savings accounts in a banking institution of their choice. The PCA concept is promoted in financial education workshops, during which participating women receive training in personal financial management and information on investment projects that could be made possible by savings. Approximately 25,000 PCAs had been opened as of April 2009 (Zimmerman and Moury, 2009), but data is not yet available on the percentage of women that continue to use their account after the incentives are removed.

Experience with matched savings programmes has been mixed in the past, as participants sometimes saved only to access the grant, and no behavioural change or long-term relationship with a financial service provider was observed. However, results from Individual Development Accounts for low-income earners in the United States suggest that such programmes have the potential to bring the unbanked into the financial system, and to facilitate asset building (see Box 13.3).

Box 13.3 Individual Development Accounts Facilitate Outreach and Asset Building

Individual Development Accounts (IDAs) are matched savings accounts for low-income people in the United States. For every dollar saved, depositors receive a corresponding match which serves as both a reward and an incentive to further the saving habit. Savers agree to complete financial education classes and use their savings for an asset-building purpose – typically for post-secondary education or job training, home purchase, or to capitalize a small business. They may receive additional training based on their asset choice, for example, guidance on choosing and enrolling in post-secondary education or job training.

IDAs are offered through partnerships between financial institutions and local non-profit organizations. Match dollars come from many different sources, including government agencies, private companies, churches, and local charities. An IDA programme can be as short as six months or as long as five years.

A review of the effectiveness of 14 IDA programmes conducted from 1997 to 2001 revealed that one in five participants was unbanked when joining the programme. Eighty-five per cent of participants said that IDA classes had helped them to save. Opportunity Fund, one of the largest IDA Savings Programmes, released a study in 2007 that tracked its IDA clients two years after they graduated and found that 77 per cent of programme graduates continue to save – saving an average of 10 per cent of their annual income. In addition, 70 per cent of graduates had opened savings accounts for their children.

In 2008, a five-year evaluation of the Assets for Independence (AFI) programme, which funds IDA programmes nationally, found that those who participated in the programme were 35 per cent more likely to become homeowners, 84 per cent more likely to become business owners, and nearly twice as likely to pursue post-secondary education or training than their non-AFI counterparts.

Source: Adapted from CFED, 2010, Mills et al., 2008, Schreiner et al., 2002, and Silicon Valley Community Foundation, 2007.

Box 13.4 Combining Grants and Leasing to Get Restarted in Indonesia

In Banda Aceh, Indonesia, the World Vision Livelihood Team developed a leasing product to assist motorized becak (a three-wheel rickshaw) drivers who lost their livelihood as a result of the tsunami. The programme involved the drivers, a motorcyle dealer and World Vision. World Vision provided 50 per cent of the purchase price of the becak to the dealer, on the condition that the dealer financed the second 50 per cent of the purchase price with the driver under a lease agreement. The monthly payments at prevailing market rates (18 per cent per year) were structured over 18 months to make the payments manageable for the driver. In this scheme, the drivers had to set aside Rp17,000 (US$1.80) a day from their daily income to repay the lease and own the becak. World Vision community facilitators undertook a background check at the becak registry in Banda Aceh to ensure the beneficiaries were becak operators prior to the tsunami.

Source: Adapted from Banking with the Poor Network, 2006a.

Getting Restarted

A second way that grants can be used is to help persons displaced by a conflict or affected by a natural disaster to rebuild their livelihoods and replace lost assets. Of course, in the absence of adequate savings or insurance, recipients of cash grants could use the funds for immediate consumption needs, or to repay outstanding debts, rather than to restart livelihood activities. Thus MFIs that use micro-grants to help clients replace productive assets tend to look for ways to provide at least part of their support through in-kind grants.

World Vision developed a leasing product that provided a unique combination of asset financing and an in-kind grant to victims of the 2004 tsunami in Indonesia (see Box 13.4). In Mozambique, CARE's cash grants to the clients of two MFIs after the floods in 2000 made refinancing and asset replacement possible, while other organizations' in-kind provision of building materials, food and clothing supported clients' basic needs (refer to the case study at the end of this chapter).

In a disaster recovery situation, micro-grants often do not need to be accompanied by additional training, since presumably many of the affected persons already have skills that could be reapplied. In a post-conflict situation, however, complementary skill training may be required, especially if the conflict lasted a long time and resulted in the loss of the previously skilled workforce.

Providing Social Protection

A third way that grants can be useful is as a temporary safety net in the event of an emergency. Small grants at the right time can keep vulnerable clients from falling back into poverty just as they are beginning to make progress climbing out. Increasingly, MFIs are using a combination of savings, insurance and emergency loan products to provide social protection to their clients. However, there are a few examples of MFIs that have added grants to the mix in a sustainable way.

Where formal insurance products are not accessible, for example, community-based organizations sometimes use a combination of savings and micro-grants to provide social protection

Box 13.5 A Rainbow of Boxes

Efficiently formed by local NGOs and church organizations, *mutuelles* in Haiti are self-help groups of 8–60 members each. Members save, borrow, and keep careful track of their transactions using a simple method to separate accounts. Every *mutuelle* has three boxes, each of a different colour – blue, green and red. The blue box tracks money from outside the *mutuelle*, such as loans from a bank or an MFI. The green box represents a group's internal savings and loan activities. The funds inside the red box are for emergency, humanitarian purposes only, such as medicine for a sick child, a sudden trip to the doctor, or a funeral. Red box disbursals are in the form of grants. Members who receive the emergency amounts need not repay them. Red boxes are funded in a variety of ways, depending on how each *mutuelle* sees fit. Some *mutuelles* set aside a portion of the interest earned from their green boxes, or allocate 10 or 15 per cent of their regular green box contributions, automatically channelling a steady sum to the red box. Some periodically pass the hat in a separate red box collection. Each box has a special committee that decides how to disburse and collect funds for that box.

Source: Adapted from Wilson and Burpee, 2008.

to their members (see Box 13.5). Such mechanisms offer less reliable protection than formal insurance products, since the benefit received depends upon the amount of funds available, the number of other claims being made on those funds, and the discretion of a committee. Nevertheless, they can be low-cost, easy to access, and simple to understand and manage.

Other MFIs, such as Fundo de Credito Comunitario (FCC) in Mozambique and Fundación León 2000 in Nicaragua, have partnered with non-governmental agencies to provide in-kind grants to clients in the wake of a natural disaster. By offering their client networks and delivery infrastructure to relief agencies, MFIs can provide social protection to both clients and employees without making grants themselves. To the extent that MFIs can develop these partnerships before disaster strikes, as part of their contingency planning, they may be able to play a pivotal role in helping to coordinate the distribution of emergency relief in the areas where they operate.

Last but not least, MFIs such as Opportunity International Bank Malawi (OIBM) and Equity Bank in Kenya are partnering with government agencies to facilitate the distribution of public assistance in remote areas, generating new clients and cross-selling other financial services in the process (see Section 13.3 below).

In summary, micro-grants can be useful as stepping stones and as safety nets. As stepping stones, they can help specific groups enter into a long-term relationship with a microfinance institution that supports their future development. As safety nets, they can help prevent vulnerable groups from falling back into poverty just as they are making progress climbing out.

13.2 General Characteristics of Effective Grant Design

Although micro-grants can serve as stepping stones and as safety nets, they can also create dependence, discourage savings, or distort the market for sustainable microfinance in the process. To avoid these outcomes, micro-grants need to be targeted, complementary, participatory, temporary, transparent, supported, and delivered separately. This section briefly explains these seven design characteristics.

Targeted. As described in Chapter 14, targeting can be a contentious issue in microfinance, but for micro-grants it is crucial. Because the supply of grants is finite, it is important to ensure that the limited resources that are available reach those who could not otherwise be served by a conventional microfinance institution.

The Trickle Up programme, for example, employs a poverty assessment tool in the form of a five-question survey, which scores the poverty level of potential programme participants according to locally determined criteria (Maes et al., 2006). BRAC's Income Generation for Vulnerable Group Development (IGVGD) programme first used a rather passive targeting method, extending services to food-insecure women who were selected by local elected representatives to participate in the programme. However, an analysis of the effectiveness of this screening mechanism revealed that it was missing some of the intended target group while including some persons who were not ultra poor. This is one the factors that led BRAC to develop a new programme, Challenging the Frontiers of Poverty Reduction – Targeting the Ultra Poor (CFPR/TUP), which is described in the case study at the end of Chapter 15. Details of the more active targeting approach used by CFPR/TUP can be found in Box 14.1 in the chapter on targeting marginalized markets.

Complementary. Micro-grants should not be given in isolation. They should complement an MFI's other products and services and, indeed, complement the financial services infrastructure that already exists (or is being built) within the communities being served. If the needs of a target market can be met through the provision of sustainable savings, loans, payment services and/or insurance, they should not be met by grants. In Haiti, for example, Fonkoze was able to meet many of clients' immediate needs in the aftermath of the 2010 earthquake by getting them cash, not through grants, but through access to their own savings and remittances. Where grants are used by an MFI, they should serve a longer-term purpose, either enabling a sustainable relationship to be built between a disadvantaged target group and the institution, or by protecting relationships with existing clients through the provision of a temporary safety net.

Delivered separately. Wherever possible, grants and loans should not be provided through the same organization. If there is no alternative, however, the MFI should at least separate staff and offices providing grants from those providing loans (see Box 13.6). This will help the MFI to avoid sending mixed signals that could confuse both clients and staff members. It is difficult, for example, for loan officers to develop a disciplined approach to collecting loan repayments if they are also involved in giving away money that they do not intend to collect.

Box 13.6 A Case of Separation

The American Refugee Committee (ARC) operates in many conflict- and disaster affected areas, including drought-affected regions of Africa and parts of northern Sri Lanka affected by conflicts and the tsunami. It provides small initial grants to refugees and internally displaced persons in camps, and then later inducts recipients into regular microfinance programmes. ARC operates grants separate from microfinance programmes by using staff dedicated solely to either relief or microfinance activities, separate office spaces, and individual names for the programmes. It also operates in a two-step manner where loans "follow" grants. ARC monitors grantees to determine whether they have asset growth at the end of the grant period, whether a viable on-going business has been created or restarted, and whether the business is able to tap into sustainable financial services such as savings and loans after the grant period ends. ARC learned that sequencing grants and loans encourages investment in productive assets.

Source: Banking with the Poor Network, 2006b.

Conditional. Grants should not be perceived as free, but rather as a contribution to a joint investment in the recipient's economic and human development. They can be linked to specific conditions, such as participation in training or the achievement of certain results. In the case of Trickle Up, for example, the two-phased grant with subsequent links to microcredit or savings is designed to encourage microentrepreneurs to invest sufficient time and effort in their businesses to access the next benefit. If they do not make that investment, they lose access to the next instalment.

Some MFIs in tsunami-affected areas insisted that those who received grants for rebuilding their livelihoods make a cash contribution of at least 5–10 per cent of the grant value to ensure that they were committed to the proposed economic activity, and had not simply dreamt it up in response to grant availability. In highly affected areas, where funds were not available owing to total loss of assets and incomes, organizations required clients to contribute their labour to rebuild community assets (Banking with the Poor Network, 2006b).

Temporary. Micro-grants should support the target group for a limited time period, and include a mechanism for transitioning recipients to sustainable microfinance services, as discussed above. If the grant lasts too long, it can create dependence and discourage recipients from building the skills and asset base required to manage their own risks and resources effectively. If, however, field staff explain to beneficiaries how their successful use of the grant can enable their access to other financial services, the grant can actually encourage the building of capacity and assets, as noted in Box 13.6.

Transparent. To avoid distorting the market for other microfinance services, micro-grant providers need to communicate clearly with recipients to make sure they understand the purpose of the grant, the conditions that are attached to it, the limited duration of support, and the benefits that effective use of the grant can bring. The criteria for selecting grant recipients should also be made clear. If grants are well targeted to reach those who cannot make effective use of other financial services, it can help reduce conflicts within a community over access to the grants. Some MFIs involve local communities in identifying who will receive a grant, not only to facilitate effective targeting, but also to increase transparency and understanding about who will receive the grants and why.

Supported by non-financial services. Particularly when they serve as stepping stones, micro-grants should be accompanied by other interventions that address the basic needs and critical capital deficits (human, social and financial) of the target group. These financial and non-financial services can help to ensure that the factors that make a target group vulnerable are sufficiently addressed to enable members of the group to climb out of poverty. For example, the combination of temporary employment, training and savings services provided in the Rural Maintenance Programme of CARE Bangladesh (see Box 13.7) enables thousands of destitute rural women to create their own enterprises each year.

13.3 Leveraging Public Cash Transfer Schemes[24]

Cash transfers are a form of social assistance to the poor or those who face a probable risk of falling into poverty. They typically take the form of small cash grants or vouchers that are provided on a regular basis (for example, monthly) to disadvantaged groups, such as women-headed households, or in exchange for certain conditions being met, such as immunizing children or sending girls to school (which is why they are often called conditional cash transfers).

Box 13.7 From Workfare to Entrepreneurship

The Rural Maintenance Programme (RMP) of CARE Bangladesh began in 1982 as a public works programme that provides employment for destitute rural women – women who are heads of households or married to disabled men and who have no other income source. Women are recruited to the RMP for a fixed four-year period. They receive cash wages for maintaining earthen village roads. Women who are selected for the programme must be 18–35 years old and physically able to do the job. Every woman in the programme is required to participate in a compulsory savings plan that captures a fifth of her earnings. The participants are trained in numeracy, human rights, gender equity, and health and nutrition, as well as income-generating skills and microenterprise management. CARE continues to provide business management advice for a year after the end of the programme cycle.

RMP is active in 90 per cent of rural districts in Bangladesh. Programme crews maintain 84,000 kilometres of roads. More than 40,000 women participate in the programme at any one time, with 10,000 completing the programme each year. RMP aims to move its participants beyond needing continuous external assistance. The strategy is to create new microentrepreneurs with adequate skills training and seed capital from the forced savings.

Although not all women succeed as microentrepreneurs, RMP has an impressive track record. Seventy-nine per cent of graduates continue to be self-employed in microenterprise activities three years after the end of the programme cycle. Women in the programme receive information on local MFIs, and are encouraged to approach the MFIs for working capital and expansion needs after they graduate.

[24] This section was adapted from Pickens et al. (2009).

Box 13.8 Oportunidades Cash Transfer Scheme in Mexico

Initiated in 1997 as PROGRESA, Mexico's Oportunidades is a flagship programme for targeted human development. The scheme aims to eradicate extreme rural poverty by promoting investment in human capital by the poor, strengthening their demand for education and health services, and providing some support to schools and health service providers. Women in beneficiary households receive cash transfers, school supplies and nutrition supplements, conditional on their children's school attendance and regular preventive health care visits.

Oportunidades targets beneficiaries in three steps. First, localities are identified using a marginality index that is constructed using socioeconomic variables associated with unsatisfied basic needs. The second step selects beneficiary households in those locales using a proxy means-testing methodology. Finally, the community reviews the beneficiary list to ensure that it has identified the most needy and has excluded others.

The programme is run by a federal agency that gathers all relevant data, applies the scoring system to determine eligibility, issues payments to households, contracts for external evaluations, and coordinates service delivery with other federal agencies. Voluntary "mother leaders" are selected and trained to help provide participants with information about programme rules, when and where payments will be made, which clinic to attend, what to do in case of problems, and so on.

Source: Adapted from Grosh et al., 2008.

Public cash transfer schemes have a long history, but they have received increased attention in recent years because of significantly improved standards for targeting, payment systems, management and impact evaluation. More than 30 countries now have active programmes or pilots, and many more are considering whether to add a scheme to their social protection programmes. According to Grosh et al. (2008), the largest relative coverage is in Ecuador, where the Human Development Grant (Bono de Desarrollo Humano) covers 5 million beneficiaries, or 40 per cent of the total population. Brazil's Family Grant (Bolsa Familia) covers 46 million beneficiaries, making it the largest in absolute terms, followed by Mexico's Oportunidades with 25 million, or 23 per cent of the total population (see Box 13.8).

The impact of public cash transfer schemes is increasingly well documented, and some programmes report dramatic results. For example, Lindert et al. (2007) found that Brazil's Bolsa Familia programme accounts for 20 per cent of the reduction in inequality in recent years, and has led to a marked jump in school enrolment. Mexico's Oportunidades programme has not only reduced poverty, but has also encouraged behaviour change – health visits increased by 18 per cent in areas with programme recipients, compared with other areas (Barrientos and Scott, 2008).

What Is the Opportunity for MFIs?

Governments make regular payments to at least 170 million poor people worldwide – far more than the 99 million or so who have active microloans. This includes social transfers as well as wage and pension payments. These payments could become a vehicle for extending microfinance services to millions of poor people who currently do not have access. Evidence

Box 13.9 From Cash Transfer Recipient to Microfinance Client?

- In Mexico, Oportunidades recipients are offered a full savings account in Bansefi, a state-owned bank, and more than 1.5 million people have elected to use it (or 30 per cent of the 5 million total recipients). A randomized control experiment shows these households saved an average of 12 per cent of their government grant, with subsequent investments leading to a 35 per cent increase in consumption after five years in the programme.
- In South Africa, banks have managed to sell at least one additional product to 11 per cent of clients with Mzansi accounts (an entry-level account with savings and transactional functionality), many of whom are G2P recipients. Net1, a private company supplying electronic payment services to the unbanked, has been offering loans to social grant recipients since 1999, with the total portfolio reaching a high of US$13.5 million.
- In Brazil, Caixa Economica reports strong uptake of conta facile (easy accounts) by 2 million Bolsa Familia recipients, who can access it via one of more than 20,000 touch points in the country, including POS-equipped merchants who handle deposits and withdrawals, ATMs, and branches. Caixa has also experimented with offering insurance to conta facile holders, and has developed a financial literacy programme for new account holders. It is considering offering microloans. Research conducted by Brazil's Ministry of Social Development indicates that there is demand for microloans from 1 million households annually (out of the 12.4 million households participating in Bolsa Familia).
- In Malawi, OIBM reports that 45 per cent of recipients enrolled in the Dowa Emergency Cash Transfer (DECT) scheme, which ended in 2007, are still using their bank account more than two years later.

Source: Pickens et al., 2009.

indicates that poor recipients of government-to-person (G2P) payments will use financial services if these are offered to them, provided the services meet their needs (see Box 13.9).

In most countries, unfortunately, fewer than one-quarter of G2P payments to the poor land in a financially inclusive account – in other words, one that enables recipients to store G2P payments and other funds until they wish to access them and make or receive payments from other people in the financial system, while also being accessible in terms of cost and distance. Most low-income public sector employees as well as pension and social transfer recipients receive their payments in person, in cash, so the recipient has to be at a specific location on a specific date, which is inconvenient and risky.

This is changing, however. An increasing number of governments are switching to electronic delivery of G2P payments because of the security concerns and transaction costs generated by cash payments for governments and recipients alike. The mode of electronic delivery varies, and can include direct deposit into an entry-level savings account, a simplified or basic account that the government mandates financial institutions to offer, or even a pooled mechanism where the financial institution holds all recipients' funds in a single account. In all cases, the common element is that funds are electronically transferred from the government into a financial institution, where they are stored until recipients collect them. Typically, recipients collect their funds using an electronic card that carries information about the recipient and the benefit that should be received.

For such electronic payment systems to work, governments must build an electronic infrastructure that can reach recipients, including those in remote areas. Microfinance institutions could both benefit from and be a part of that infrastructure. They could provide and maintain the access points that enable governments to reach remote areas, and they could use the electronic infrastructure, once built, to provide a range of financial services to both G2P recipients and non-recipient households in the same communities. This kind of arrangement could make it feasible to cover the costs of serving remote areas.

To date, the electronic benefit cards issued by social transfer programmes have been designed with limited functionality for the recipient. Governments wanted to promote immediate consumption of grant funds to bolster living standards and also enable recovery of unclaimed funds. For example, Brazil's Bolsa Familia programme began with an electronic benefit card from which recipients could make a free withdrawal of grant funds, but to which they could not deposit money. Funds left on the card after three months were returned to the government. This kind of design misses out on opportunities to facilitate linkages to financial services.

Box 13.10 The Dowa Emergency Cash Transfer (DECT) Scheme

A woman living in a rural part of Malawi took out her bank card and swiped it. A teller checked her identity with a thumbprint scan and then she went to the back of a pick-up truck. Here, under the shade of a tree, a cashier from Banki Yanga handed over her cash entitlement for the month to meet her basic needs.

Smart card technology and mobile banks/ATMs were used to provide cash to about 10,000 households in 259 villages in the remote area of the Dowa region facing severe food shortages during 2006/2007. This was the first time electronic cards had been used to provide cash to people facing severe hunger. Opportunity International Bank of Malawi (OIBM) deployed staff into the field and invested in a mobile bank, a modified Toyota pick-up truck or *bakkie*. The Toyota *bakkie* catered for two OIBM tellers to be locked safely into two kiosks built and added to the loading bay of the *bakkie*. OIBM issued smart cards to beneficiaries, who would then present themselves over a period of five months to receive an emergency cash transfer. At the end of a registration day, the OIBM mobile banking team would return to the Kasungu branch and "up-load" the day's transactions via a network link to the OIBM head office in Lilongwe.

During the evaluation of the project, it became clear that the demand for access to savings facilities in rural Malawi, even among the very poor, is great and not being met. This was most evident at the DECT pay-points, when many beneficiaries (all women receiving their final DECT payments) approached OIBM staff, asking if they could use their smart cards after DECT ended, for the specific purpose of making deposits and withdrawals. As a result of the success of this model, the UK's Department for International Development (DFID) and Concern Worldwide agreed to continue to support the operational expenses in reaching this area for an initial two-year period to enable OIBM to offer financial services, rather than just facilitating cash payments to the rural poor in the Dowa district.

Source: Adapted from Pearson and Kilfoil, 2007, and Opoku and Foy, 2008.

Innovative experiments like the ones being carried out by OIBM in Malawi and Equity Bank in Kenya (see Boxes 13.10 and 13.11) illustrate the potential for collaboration among microfinance institutions and governments to provide poor people with more valuable access

Box 13.11 Building a More Inclusive Financial System in Remote Kenya

Halaku Mohamed is a widow who cares for three school-age children. She was recently identified by her community to be enrolled in the pilot phase of Kenya's Hunger and Safety Net Programme (HSNP), which began in April 2009. As one of 60,000 HSNP beneficiaries, Halaku will receive a regular cash benefit disbursed every other month for at least three years. If the pilot is successful, it will be scaled up to reach more than 1 million food insecure families.

Haluku lives in the arid north, a sparsely populated region the size of the United Kingdom that is beset by bandits, and contains just seven bank branches. To reach her and other micro-grant recipients in the region, HSNP contracted the non-governmental Financial Sector Deepening Trust (FSD Kenya), together with Equity Bank (Kenya's largest microfinance institution) to come up with an alternative way of making payments.

A network of ordinary shopkeepers with adequate cash flow was selected to make the payments on behalf of HSNP using point-of-sale (POS) payment machines. Where there is no electricity, Equity Bank installs solar panels that produce AC electricity when put through an inverter. This power gives the shopkeeper light, and charges the batteries of the payment machine. At the base of each machine are two mobile phone SIM cards that automatically transmit data back to Equity Bank, as well as record it on the shopkeeper's bank card (which is also a smart card and is stored at the base of the POS device).

To avoid crowding at participating shops, beneficiaries line up on different dates according to the colour of their Equity Bank-issued smart cards. Upon arrival, they insert their smart card into the POS device and verify their identity by placing their thumb on the machine. The smart card starts off with no credit, so the first step is to transfer credit, in this case Ksh.2,150 (approximately US$25) from the shopkeeper's bank card account to the beneficiary's smart card. Two receipts are produced by the machine, one confirming that the beneficiary's smart card has received a credit, and another confirming that the shopkeeper's bank card has been debited. A second thumbprint is taken, and on verification, the beneficiary can enter the amount of cash that she would like to receive at that time. Two additional receipts are then printed off, one for the beneficiary and one for the shopkeeper. The beneficiary is given her money, her card, and two printed receipts.

Shopkeepers pay out cash using money they receive from normal trading, but any cash paid out is immediately recorded on their bank card as credit, and transmitted via the SIM card to the shopkeeper's account with Equity Bank. Money left on the beneficiary's smart card is secure, since no one can use the card, even if it is stolen, without a matching thumbprint, and all transactions result in a paper confirmation for the beneficiary as well as the shopkeeper, backed up by an electronic record transmitted via the SIM card to Equity Bank.

When shopkeepers visit their local Equity Bank branch, they hand over their bank card and draw down however much cash they require to purchase new supplies. This lowers their risk of keeping too much money at their shops, and carrying large sums of cash from their shops to the main towns to buy goods.

Source: Adapted from Pickens et al., 2009, and http://www.hungersafetynet.org.

to financial services. The public cash transfer could provide an initial safety net or stream of income that could facilitate investments in productive assets, the accumulation of savings and, later, access to other financial services that could help the poor to manage their resources and risks in the longer term.

13.4 Financing Micro-grants

Micro-grants can be financed through a variety of sources, as illustrated by the case studies presented in this chapter. IDAs, for example, are funded through contributions from federal and state governments, religious organizations, charities and private companies. Nearly 80 per cent of World Vision's funding comes from private sources, including individuals, corporations and foundations, and includes both cash and gifts in kind, typically in the form of food commodities, medicine and clothing. The remaining 20 per cent comes from governments and multilateral agencies (World Vision, 2010). Trickle Up, CARE, ARC and Concern Worldwide are funded through similar sources, although the percentage of support received from public and private sources varies. Sixty-two per cent of Trickle Up's funding comes from private individuals, some of whom give as little as US$20 (Trickle Up, 2010, and Wagner, 2010).

In Haiti, the *mutuelles* self-finance their grants. BRAC also self-finances 73 per cent of its services, largely through the success of its social enterprises. The remaining 27 per cent is funded through donations (BRAC, 2010). For-profit MFIs which operate as part of a holding company that includes a non-profit organization could work together with that organization to finance micro-grants. Commercial microfinance institutions could also finance their own grants as part of their corporate social responsibility, or as a tool for deepening their outreach. This option is likely to become more attractive as pilot projects such as the ones being implemented through the CGAP-Ford Foundation Graduation Program gather more information on the cost and effective design of a graduation initiative.

For most MFIs, the solution to micro-grant financing will be found in partnerships, either with governments that have made a commitment to provide social protection to their citizens, or with organizations that have built the infrastructure to mobilize funds from private individuals, corporations and foundations for the purpose of supporting economic development in the area where an MFI is operating. One innovative new idea for connecting private individuals, companies and governments at an international level is the Global Social Trust currently being piloted in Ghana (see Box 13.12).

13.5 Conclusion

The notion of giving away money and not expecting it back runs counter to standard microfinance logic, and is certainly not a sustainable operation, since money that is given away needs to be replaced. However, as a temporary intervention that complements market-based financial services, micro-grants can provide opportunities for MFIs to strengthen client capacity to make effective use of their financial services, and to increase the depth of the market they are able to serve sustainably.

Box 13.12 The Global Social Trust

The mission of the Global Social Trust is to systematically reduce poverty in developing countries through a partnership that invests in and sponsors the development of sustainable national social protection schemes. The basic idea is to request people in richer countries to voluntarily contribute a modest monthly amount to a Global Social Trust, which will then invest those resources to build up basic social protection schemes in developing countries and sponsor concrete benefits for a defined initial period until the schemes become self-supporting.

The Confédération Syndicale Indépendante du Luxembourg OGB-L through its NGO Solidarité Syndicale, the Ministry of Health in Ghana, and the International Labour Organization (ILO) have entered into an agreement to implement the Global Social Trust pilot project in Ghana. The Luxembourg partner (in collaboration with the Social Insurance System) will mount a fundraising campaign among persons covered by the Luxembourg social insurance, asking them to contribute 5 euros per month on a voluntary basis. The Luxembourg partner will collect the voluntary contributions from individuals in Luxembourg, manage the funds thus collected, transfer the funds to Ghana as they are needed, and audit the use of the funds.

The project will provide a cash benefit of approximately US$10 per month to Ghanaian indigent pregnant women and mothers with children under the age of five who meet conditions of pre-natal, post-natal and regular health check-ups. Contributions from workers in Luxembourg would constantly refuel the funds available to the project. Since the size of the project will be determined by the number of actual contributors in Luxembourg, the pilot will follow a gradual implementation procedure, starting with one district and then integrating others as funds become available.

Source: Adapted from International Labour Office, 2010a.

Main Messages

1. Micro-grants can be useful as stepping stones and as safety nets.
2. Grant providers and recipients should each contribute resources as part of a joint investment in the future.
3. Design micro-grants to be targeted, temporary and transparent. They should complement rather than compete with microfinance.
4. Separate the delivery of grants from that of market-based financial services.
5. MFIs can both benefit from and be a part of G2P payment infrastructure.

Case Study: Coping with Disaster in Mozambique

After the floods of February 2000, CARE provided one-off cash grants averaging US$100 each to around 2,000 families, including clients of two MFIs – Fundo de Crédito Comunitário (FCC) and Caixa Comunitária de Crédito e Poupanca (CCCP). The MFIs approached their clients and informed them of the grants, but the grants were actually disbursed by CARE staff.

To those grant recipients that had active loans, the MFIs offered the option of applying the grant to repay their outstanding loan balance, so they could maintain their credit line and immediately qualify for a new loan. The MFIs then provided new loans to those that had repaid their old debts. Alternatively, clients could receive the entire cash grant and reschedule the repayment of their existing loans over a period of time decided by the MFIs. New loans, however, were not made available until the restructured loans were repaid. Repayment effected through the grants helped the MFIs to avoid cash-flow problems, service their clients immediately, and protect their credibility. Resumption of the loan cycle quickly helped to revive the MFI's business and, as a result, the incomes at the end of the year were not significantly different from the previous year.

This approach was effective due to several factors:

Coordination among agencies. CARE, FCC and CCCP worked well together, enabling effective design and delivery of the product, and helping to avoid duplication of grants to the same recipients.

Small grant size. There were many small grants rather than a few large grants, thus spreading their positive impact and minimizing the potential for inequitable distribution.

Implicit link between grant and loans. Although implicit, the cash grant was tied to the repayment of loans. Therefore it was perceived less as a handout and more as a mechanism to help them continue as clients of the MFI.

Good timing. The grants were made after the emergency stage, when markets began to emerge. Therefore people could resume their economic activities using either the grants or new loans received after repaying previous loans.

Other assistance. Other forms of assistance, such as building materials, food and clothing, were provided by other relief organizations. This meant that the cash grant was available to restart economic activities. In the absence of this other assistance, the cash grants could have been diverted for consumption purposes, and the MFIs could have experienced repayment problems.

Good communication. Frequent contact with clients and clear communication by MFI staff before grants were disbursed was effective. The staff informed returning clients of the possibility of a grant from an external agency that could be used to repay outstanding debt, making them immediately eligible for a larger loan to restart their business.

Immediate resumption of regular loan cycles. The MFI avoided a liquidity squeeze, because clients kept up loan repayments and helped FCC and CCCP to disburse regular loans. Client desertion was low.

This case study was adapted from Nagarajan (2001).

Recommended Reading

- Barrientos, A.; Scott, J. 2008. *Social transfers and growth: A review*, Brooks World Poverty Institute Working Paper No. 52 (Manchester, University of Manchester), available at: http://www.bwpi.manchester.ac.uk/resources/Working-Papers/bwpi-wp-5208.pdf
- Grosh, M.; del Ninno, C.; Tesliuc, E.; Ouerghi, A. 2008. *For protection and promotion: The design and implementation of effective safety nets* (Washington, DC, World Bank), available at: http://siteresources.worldbank.org/SAFETYNETSANDTRANSFERS/Resources/ProtectionandPromotion-Overview.pdf
- Nagarajan, G. 2001. *Looking into the gift horse's mouth: Implications of cash grants for disaster response by microfinance institutions in Mozambique*, MBP Project (Washington, DC, USAID), at: www.microlinks.org/ev_en.php?ID=8082_201&ID2=DO_TOPIC
- Parker, J.; Pearce, D. 2002. *Microfinance, grants, and non-financial responses to poverty reduction: Where does microcredit fit?*, CGAP Focus Note No. 20 (Washington, DC, CGAP), at: http://www.cgap.org/gm/document-1.9.2565/FN20.pdf
- Pickens, M.; Porteous, D.; Rotman, S. 2009. *Banking the poor via G2P payments*, CGAP Focus Note No. 58 (Washington, DC, CGAP), at: http://www.cgap.org/gm/document-1.9.41174/FN58.pdf
- Zimmerman, J.; Moury, Y. 2009. *Savings-linked conditional cash transfers: A new policy approach to global poverty reduction*, A Global Assets Project Policy Brief (Washington, DC, New America Foundation), at: http://www.newamerica.net/files/nafmigration/NAF_CCT_Savings_April09_Final.pdf

Market Segments

Part III: Market Segments

As discussed in Part I, two of the primary reasons for which MFIs diversify their product portfolio are to meet the needs of their current customers better and to expand into new markets. The next eight chapters are designed to help managers explore the characteristics of new market segments, the nature of the product mix that can meet the needs of each, and the strategies that MFIs are using to overcome key challenges associated with each segment. This section is designed primarily to increase familiarity with market segments that are underserved, but it also hopes to provide perspective and examples that can assist MFIs already working in these markets to serve them more effectively in the future.

Chapters 14 and 15 open the section with a look at some of the most difficult-to-serve market segments – those that are isolated, small, dispersed, very poor, or for some other reason relegated to the lowest positions or outer edges of society. They illustrate that such groups can benefit from access to microfinance, and that MFIs are learning how to identify, recruit and serve them effectively. All other chapters in this section focus on market segments that tend to be larger and easier to identify and recruit, but can still be quite challenging to serve effectively: youth, women, crisis-affected communities, Islamic communities, rural areas and small and medium enterprises. By exploring the methods that have been used to overcome these challenges, Chapters 16 to 21 aim to inspire more MFIs to enter these markets, albeit with a realistic perspective on the requirements for success. Although they encourage a broader understanding of what is possible, they also caution MFIs against rushing into new market segments without an outreach strategy that can generate value for both clients and the institution.

III Market Segments

14 Targeting Marginalized Markets

MFIs tend to target clients. It is part and parcel of their anti-poverty mission, to correct market failure and build bridges to those excluded by conventional financial institutions.
~ International Labour Office (2007a)

Some market segments are difficult to identify and serve, because they are small, isolated, or face particular vulnerabilities. These groups, such as bonded labourers, the poorest of the poor, or persons living with HIV/AIDS[25] (PLWHA) often do not meet an MFI's standard eligibility criteria or make use of its standard infrastructure, and yet there may be an interest from MFIs and/or from donors in serving them.

This chapter focuses on active approaches to finding, recruiting and serving such marginalized market segments. After a brief discussion of targeting and the reasons for which MFIs might want to serve more vulnerable groups, it explores how institutions can identify and recruit such segments. It then discusses whether these segments can be served through an MFI's mainstream services, or whether separate products, staff or infrastructure are needed to reach them effectively. The final sections of the chapter illustrate strategies that MFIs are using to serve two marginalized groups with some success: disabled persons and PLWHA. Chapter 15 focuses on serving the poorest of the poor. The outline of this chapter is as follows:

1. Motivations for targeting
2. Targeting techniques
3. To integrate or not to integrate?
4. Serving disabled persons
5. Serving persons living with HIV/AIDS
6. Subsidies and sustainability

14.1 Motivations for Targeting

Financial systems are not inherently accessible to all. They are accessible to those with money, those who know how to use the system and trust its operations, those who can meet the eligibility requirements of service providers, and those who live or work within a reasonable distance of a service point and can afford the cost of the service provided.

For decades, MFIs have been working to provide low-income households with access to better-quality and lower-cost financial services than those provided by the informal sector. In general, their target market has been broadly defined to include anyone who does not have access to appropriate products and services through the formal financial system. Defined in this way, the potential market is vast, and with the exception of urban markets in a handful of countries, demand is far from being met.

[25] Human immunodeficiency virus (HIV) and acquired immunodeficiency syndrome (AIDS).

Under these circumstances, most MFIs have rationally prioritized breadth of outreach over depth of outreach. Serving as many poor clients as possible has been more important than serving the most disadvantaged or vulnerable segments of society. As the microfinance industry develops, however, two factors are driving institutions to target groups that are more difficult to reach. First, in markets where the easy-to-reach clients are now being served, competition is forcing MFIs to look for new sources of growth. This is the principal factor driving institutions to explore relatively large market segments, such as rural areas and SMEs. Serving one or more niche markets in addition to the mainstream poor can also be a way for MFIs to differentiate themselves in a competitive marketplace.

The second factor driving MFIs to target more difficult market segments is their social mission. Institutions with a developmental mandate are recognizing that a special effort needs to be made to link marginalized segments with the financial system, or the system will only perpetuate, and perhaps exacerbate, the inequality and discrimination that already exist within society. For example, MFIs commonly reject loan applications from individuals who do not have an established business or cannot supply guarantors. Insurance providers may exclude the elderly, or persons with pre-existing medical conditions. Although less restrictive criteria are used to determine who can open a savings account, the poor may find official identity documents difficult to obtain, and minimum balance requirements impossible to meet. In general, the more vulnerable people are, the less likely they are to approach a financial institution, so MFIs that want to reach these customer groups have to be proactive about their recruitment.

In some cases, it is donor organizations that provide the motivation for targeting. With a mandate to ensure that the most vulnerable are not left behind, they provide incentives or subsidies to increase MFIs' willingness and/or ability to serve riskier clients. One example of this is American legislation that requires 50 per cent of all USAID microenterprise resources to benefit the very poor, defined as those households living in the bottom (poorest) 50 per cent below the nationally defined poverty line, or those living on the equivalent of less than US$1.25/day (in purchasing power parity, or PPP). As a result of this legislation, MFIs that receive support from USAID must document the extent to which they are reaching the poor.[26]

Donor-motivated targeting can fuel innovation, but it can also be risky if MFIs blindly experiment with whatever donors are willing to finance. Before designing interventions for vulnerable market segments, it is important to answer one critical question: How will access to financial services improve the lives of the targeted persons? Too often, donors and policy-makers assume that microcredit is a special ingredient that will magically help the poor and all sorts of other needy groups, but in practice badly designed or inappropriate products can actually make the poor worse off. For example, giving enterprise loans to persons who are not particularly entrepreneurial may help them to put food on the table for a few weeks, but if their business fails, how will they repay the loans? Borrowers may choose to sell off assets, send children to work or reduce food consumption in order to make their payments. Furthermore, the experience of failure could have a negative and lasting impact on their self-confidence and hope for the future.

[26] For more information, refer to: http://www.povertytools.org/index.html

14.2 Targeting Techniques

Targeting is a relatively straightforward process when a market segment is large and is identified by a characteristic that is easy to measure, such as gender, age or geographic location. As described in Chapter 3, MFIs can use market research to define a segment's characteristics, and to design products and delivery channels that meet its needs. They can then set outreach goals and monitor performance to make sure they achieve their objectives. There may be arguments about how exactly to define what is "rural" or "small enterprise" or "youth", but once this has been settled, finding clients in these segments is not particularly difficult. Recruiting and serving them cost-effectively can be challenging, however, and that is why separate chapters of this book explore how to reach those markets.

Targeting is more difficult for market segments that are identified by a characteristic that is hard to measure, such as HIV status, vulnerability to debt bondage, or being among the poorest of the poor. Described below are some of the techniques that have been used to identify and recruit clients in these segments.

Targeting the Poorest

Historically, most MFIs relied on indirect targeting approaches to identify and reach their intended market. For example, by using group lending methodologies and offering only small loans, institutions assumed that they would reach poor clients. These indirect approaches have enabled MFIs to reach low-income households in general, but they have caused some institutions to reach a better-off market than they envisaged. Research conducted on the poverty levels of clients often finds that they are just above or just below the poverty line, but few are among the extreme poor. One of the tools that MFIs are using to measure their clients' poverty status is the Progress out of Poverty Index, which is discussed in the case study at the end of this chapter.

In recognition of the fact that the poorest will not necessarily be reached by indirect targeting, an increasing number of MFIs are being more direct and more proactive about their client recruitment. Some are taking a very different approach to determining who is eligible to be their customer. Prospective clients have to demonstrate that they are sufficiently poor to gain access to their services. This approach has generated some debate within the industry, particularly when targeting techniques are used to completely exclude those who are less poor, rather than restrict access to a particular product or service (see Section 14.3).

On the surface, it may seem like a straightforward process to identify the poorest. In practice, however, the concept of poverty is complex; it is strongly influenced by local cultural and socioeconomic conditions; there is no clear consensus on how it should be defined; and measurement is difficult. Standard international methodologies for assessing poverty, such as the Living Standards Measurement Surveys (LSMS), define poverty in monetary terms, but they are costly, and obtaining reliable income estimates in a timely manner can be difficult.

MFIs have recognized that poverty is multidimensional, and encompasses not only income but also other types of capital (mainly human and physical, but sometimes also environmental, social and even political). They use poverty assessment tools with indicators that are related to these forms of capital rather than direct measures of income. Some of the tools that MFIs use to target the poor are described below.

- **Landownership.** The most common technique for assessing whether applicants are poor enough to be microfinance customers is based on how much land they own. For example, many Bangladeshi MFIs target persons who own half an acre of land or less, although, as Rutherford (1995) points out, this can be a misleading indicator, since landholding can easily be disguised or concealed.
- Freedom from Hunger has developed several **food security scales** to assess household and individual caloric and nutrient intakes, and economic measures such as household food expenditures. This method assesses experiences and behaviours that consistently characterize food insecurity and hunger, such as anxiety that food may be insufficient, the experience of running out of food, and having to reduce food intake.
- CASHPOR's **Housing Index** is an observational methodology that produces an indicator that characterizes the quality and the status of an applicant's house. Three dimensions are considered: 1) size of the house, 2) physical condition of building materials, and 3) material of the roof. The ranking of the poor and less poor is done within the geographic and social context. People living in houses constructed from mud bricks, with poor-quality thatch roofing, small windows and in a general state of disrepair, tend to be selected as the poorest.
- **Participatory wealth ranking** (PWR) allows communities to rank themselves according to their own perceptions of poverty. Detailed discussions are held with a large number of people in each community to define poverty, and to rank the community according to their criteria. These methods are based on participatory rural appraisal and wealth-ranking techniques. The Small Enterprise Foundation (SEF) in South Africa uses this approach to identify and target the very poor, helping to draw characteristics of poor and very poor people in each village and determine a cut-off line for the very poor, therefore identifying those eligible for its programme, which is especially designed for the poorest. Bangladesh Rehabilitation Assistance Committee (BRAC) also uses PWR in its CFPR/TUP programme, but combines it with other targeting techniques, as described in Box 14.1.

These poverty-targeting tools are a first step towards identifying and motivating very poor people to join a microfinance programme. Organizations use these tools to segment their market and understand the differing poverty of their clients. This is especially important in terms of identifying the most marginalized people so that interventions can be designed to meet their particular needs, and great care can be taken to ensure that they do not become more vulnerable because of an MFI's interventions (see Chapter 15).

Box 14.1 Combining Targeting Techniques

In 2002, BRAC's Challenging the Frontiers of Poverty Reduction / Targeting the Ultra Poor (CFPR/TUP) programme started its operations in three northern districts of Bangladesh, where BRAC has an extensive network of offices and programmes. Local-level knowledge of the programme staff is used to draw up a list of clusters within their working area where NGO operations are relatively low and poorer households are concentrated. A team of three TUP agents then visits these clusters and surrounding areas to verify, build rapport, and arrive at a final list of clusters called "spots".

The next step is to conduct a participatory wealth ranking (PWR) exercise in these selected spots. Because the maximum size of such a PWR exercise was deemed not to exceed 150 households, this set a natural limit to the size of each spot. Once the PWR exercise is done, a survey is administered on the "poorest" households identified through the PWR exercise. These are the households in the bottom-most two wealth categories. The information from the survey is then tallied with programme-set eligibility criteria (see table below) to draw up a list of preliminary potential beneficiaries. This preliminary list is fully cross-checked by a team of managers at the BRAC field offices and senior programme managers from the head office by visiting the preliminarily selected beneficiary households to arrive at a final list of programme members.

Programme set criteria

Exclusion conditions (all selected households will have to satisfy these conditions)	The household should not be borrowing from a microcredit-providing NGO
	The household should not be receiving benefits from government programmes
	There should be at least one adult woman in the household who is physically able to put in labour towards the asset transferred
Inclusion conditions (at least two of these conditions will have to be satisfied)	Total land owned less than 10 decimals (1000 acres)
	Adult women in the household selling labour
	Households where main male income earner is disabled or not able to work
	Households where school-aged children have to sell labour
	Households having no productive assets

Combining various targeting approaches and drawing from different streams of knowledge has been the main innovation in the targeting methodology. BRAC did not have money-metric poverty measures of the households. However, using various poverty sensitive attributes of households and comparing them with those who were ranked the poorest in the PWR exercises was extremely effective.

Source: Adapted from Matin and Halder, 2004.

The process of delivering financial services to low-income households is already quite expensive, and in cost-covering or sustainable programmes customers have to pay for those costs through higher interest rates. Consequently, for targeting tools to be justifiable, it is important that they be as simple and easy to administer as possible to avoid adding even more administrative costs.

Targeting Other Segments

When trying to target segments based on characteristics other than poverty, alternative approaches need to be considered. For example:

Persons living with HIV and AIDS. Because of the importance of confidentiality associated with one's HIV status, this is a particularly difficult market to target. The two main approaches to targeting PLWHA are through support groups and through clinics. In this environment, the financial service provider makes information available to persons working in clinics or leading support groups, who pass it on to patients or members, and then they decide whether or not to access the financial services.

Persons with disabilities. In some ways this is among the easier segments to target, at least for persons with physical disabilities. Yet in some cultures persons with disabilities are hidden away so they do not bring shame on their family. The primary means of targeting microfinance to disabled persons is through collaboration with advocacy groups and social service organizations that work on issues for the disabled. Where they exist, rehabilitation centres that provide training to handicapped workers are also a good referral source.

Bonded labourers. The International Labour Organization (ILO) estimates that at least 12.6 million persons are victims of forced labour, including 7.8 million that are economically exploited, for example through debt bondage (ILO, 2005).[27,28] Although there are many varieties of debt bondage, typically a worker in need of money will borrow from an employer and then repay it through salary deductions. But the design of the repayment schedule could mean that the worker is never able to repay the loan, and sometimes the debt is even passed down to the next generation.

Of the millions of people in debt bondage in South Asia, where the problem is acute, most work in the agriculture sector, although bonded labourers can also be found in mining and gem polishing, brick-kilns, carpets and textiles, as well as domestic service. To address this critical issue, the ILO has tested different approaches to microfinance-led interventions, either to help rehabilitate former bonded labourers who have been released, or to target persons who are vulnerable to bondage.[29] Box 14.2 describes a tool used to identify persons in the latter category.

Child labourers. Like bonded labour, child labour is also illegal in most jurisdictions, yet it is still all too common. In 2008, there were 215 million children trapped in child labour, including 115 million in hazardous work (IPEC, 2008). One of the key targeting strategies is to focus on those in the worst forms of child labour, which includes work that exposes children to physical, psychological or sexual abuse, and work in hazardous environments or which may expose children to hazardous substances. The focus on the worst forms is not just morally justified, but is also an effective way to mobilize society to address the problem of child labour

[27] Besides economic exploitation, forced labour can also be imposed by the state or military (2.5 million persons) and through commercial sexual exploitation (1.4 million persons). These first global estimates of forced labour are probably conservative.

[28] The UN 1956 Supplementary Convention Against Slavery defines debt bondage as the combination of a credit and a labour contract in which the value of labour services as reasonably assessed is not applied towards the liquidation of the debt (for example, only interest is repaid by the labour; principal is never repaid) or if activities are neither defined nor limited (for instance, the labourer can be required to work at any time, day or night).

[29] Bonded labour is illegal in Nepal, Pakistan and India. If persons are in bondage, then the ILO recommends using the legal system to enable them to be released and have their debts written off.

Box 14.2 Vulnerability to Debt Bondage Index (VDBI)

Certain regions, social groups and occupations are known to be more prone to bondedness, although there is no single social, cultural or occupational indicator of vulnerability. Consequently, the ILO developed the VDBI, a set of indicators that could be used for identifying and targeting households vulnerable to debt bondage in South Asia.

The development of indices that identify vulnerability to bondage revolves around certain research questions relating to the problem of identifying poor households with certain sets of characteristics, some of which may reveal their bondedness, while others may show their degree of vulnerability, and yet other characteristics may show the capability of the households being prevented from debt bondage. In particular, the VDBI considers indicators in four categories:

1. characteristics of debt bondage, such as outstanding debts to an employer;
2. trigger factors, including borrowing from moneylenders or working as a migrant labourer;
3. socioeconomic factors, such as caste and literacy level;
4. preventive factors, including access to safe drinking water and sanitation systems.

The VDBI is a tool that comes to the aid of public agencies and microfinance institutions in their efforts to help vulnerable households. An appropriate basis for identification of vulnerable households is expected to minimize leakage of resources to non-priority users and help channel the same properly to vulnerable sections of the population. It is also important to note that the methodology should be situation specific. There cannot be one set of indicators that can be prescribed to articulate bondedness in all regions, irrespective of their local specificity.

Source: Adapted from Reddy et al., undated.

in general. Successful measures against the worst forms often have a multiplier effect that benefits other working children.

To identify the worst forms in a particular country, the ILO recommends involving multiple stakeholders – including academics, workers' and employers' associations, NGOs and community groups – to determine which industries have the most severe abuses, and then to focus efforts on those particular sectors. For example, in Pakistan, the ILO and its social partners focus on child labour in deep sea fishing, coalmining, rag picking, tanneries, bangle processing and the assembly of surgical instruments, which are considered the worst forms of child labour.

Another key element is to establish community watch groups and strengthen their capacity by involving them in the identification and monitoring of target children. Child labour monitoring (CLM) involves the identification, referral, protection and prevention of child labourers through the development of a coordinated multi-sector monitoring and referral process that aims to cover all children living in a given geographical area. When children are taken out of work, or if the parents or guardians voluntarily remove them, usually the households need to replace the lost income somehow. Therefore CLM processes can be used to identify families for whom microfinance might be relevant, although as Box 14.3 indicates, adaptations are required.

Box 14.3 Child Labour and Microfinance

Blume (2005) identifies the main **causes of child labour** as income poverty, vulnerability to income and expenditure shocks, and the high cost and low returns of education due to poor school quality or malfunctioning labour markets that do not allow accumulated human capital to generate sufficient returns. If returns to education are high, child labour can also be explained through failures in the capital markets, as households are unable to borrow against the children's future income. Finally, parents may not be aware of the harms of child labour and the benefits of education if they have not attended school themselves.

When designing financial services for the families of child labourers, it is important not to assume that they are extremely poor or vulnerable. They may have income and asset levels similar to mainstream microfinance clients, and choose to send children to work not out of desperation but rather based on a rational economic decision. Consequently, interventions need to first consider the parents' motivations and economic situation before determining the appropriate package of interventions.

In addition, microfinance institutions must recognize that they could be unintentionally creating a demand for child labour. When family businesses have access to credit, they may choose to take children out of school to work in the growing enterprise rather than hire unrelated workers who are expensive and risky. This is an impact that MFIs should seek to minimize by explicitly mentioning this issue in the loan contract and monitoring school attendance.

Source: Authors.

14.3 To Integrate or Not to Integrate?

Once an MFI has found a way to identify and recruit a targeted market segment, the next step is to determine the general approach it will take to serving that segment. If a target group makes up a large percentage of the community being served, such as in the case of women, it makes sense for an MFI to develop a diverse mix of products that can be delivered to that group through the MFI's mainstream operations.

If, however, a segment is small or marginalized, the following two questions require careful consideration:

1. Should the MFI attempt to offer a diverse mix of products and services?
2. Should the segment be served through a separate delivery channel, or should members be integrated into the MFI's mainstream microfinance activities?

An Integrated Package of Services

By itself, microcredit can only do so much. Even a diverse mix of financial services, including savings, insurance and money transfers, will not be able to solve complex problems such as child labour or HIV/AIDS. Consequently, when designing interventions to assist persons and households inflicted with or vulnerable to these hardships, microfinance is typically just a small piece of a broader package of services that are needed to promote social and economic empowerment.

Despite the fact that microfinance is just one of several interventions, it can be the lead activity because of the convening power of finance. Often projects to assist vulnerable households begin by forming savings and credit groups, and then use that forum for other interventions, such as vocational and entrepreneurial training, adult literacy classes, or collective action to address community needs such as sanitation infrastructure. Since there are significant challenges in coordinating the activities in an integrated programme, savings and credit groups can serve as the focal point or wheel hub to which all interventions are linked.

MFIs that use an individual lending methodology will find it more difficult to use microfinance as the lead activity in an integrated package of financial and non-financial services. The provision of non-financial services on an individual basis is prohibitively expensive, and services designed to build social and human capital often require interaction among a group of people. MFIs without a group-based infrastructure are more likely to partner with non-financial service providers that can bring members of the targeted group together and connect them to the MFI on an "as needed" basis.

Multi-purpose NGOs that provide both financial and non-financial services may be able to deliver an integrated package of services more easily than two independent organizations that partner. Coordination within an organization can be easier than between agencies, but there can also be strong obstacles within organizations that prevent different departments from working together effectively. In addition, an NGO's regulatory status will likely limit the flexibility and range of financial services that can be offered. Partnerships between a regulated microfinance institution and its "sister" organizations, such as in the case of the Grameen family of companies described in Chapter 12, or a "mother" NGO from which a regulated MFI transformed, can be even more effective.

Integrated Delivery Channels

When designing interventions for smaller or more vulnerable market segments, one of the most difficult questions to answer is whether they should be served exclusively, or whether they should be served in the process of serving the community at large. From a development perspective, an exclusive approach is reasonably sound. Poverty-oriented MFIs use targeting to ensure that their services are not leaking to the non-poor, for several reasons:

- **Capture by elites.** When poor and non-poor persons are accessing the services, the not-so-poor often find ways of working the system to their advantage, and to the disadvantage of the poor.
- **Finite resources.** Assuming that the financial and human resources of the MFI are limited, then it is understandable that poverty-focused MFIs want to channel those limited resources to benefit the neediest.
- **Narrowing the inequality gap.** If the poor and not-so-poor are benefiting equally from the same programme, the gap between the haves and the have-nots is unlikely to decrease.

Of course, not all MFIs are concerned about benefits leaking to the non-poor. From a microfinance perspective, exclusively serving a small minority of persons in a community, while purposely excluding others, creates challenges. By supporting only selected individuals, microfinance institutions are not able to exploit service delivery efficiency (see Box 14.4). Field staff can manage only a small number of persons, because their clients are usually dispersed over a wide geographic area. Scattered pockets of clients discourage service providers from creating a branch infrastructure that can be more responsive to client needs than group meetings every week or two. In addition, small numbers of relatively homogeneous clients make it difficult to intermediate between net savers and net borrowers. The more homogeneous the group, the more an institution exposes itself to concentration risk.

Some MFIs believe that by serving a heterogeneous market, they will be more viable institutions with a larger outreach, and therefore be able to benefit more vulnerable people than if they exclusively served the vulnerable. By serving as many people as possible within a particular geographic area, they can spread the fixed costs of a branch office over more customers, and keep their prices down.

An increasing number of MFIs are experimenting with a two-tiered approach that provides special services to vulnerable segments of the market while being a financial intermediary for the community at large. Some of these experiments offer special products to the vulnerable market segment; others simply adapt the delivery of their existing product portfolio to make it more accessible and more useful to the vulnerable market segment. The last two sections of this chapter explore some of these experiments in the context of two specific market segments that MFIs are trying to serve: disabled persons and PLWHA. Chapter 15 also provides examples of how the two-tiered approach is being used successfully to serve the poorest of the poor.

In general, the decision about whether or not to integrate a vulnerable market segment into an MFI's mainstream product delivery seems to depend on four factors:

1. **How large is the market segment?** If the segment constitutes a substantial percentage of the total market an institution is trying to serve, then it could be financially feasible to design special products or delivery mechanisms for that market. If the vulnerable market segment is small, the likelihood of that market generating enough revenue to cover the cost of developing and maintaining a specialized product is low.
2. **Is the market segment relatively homogeneous?** If not, MFIs will find it difficult to create specialized products and services that can meet members' needs in a cost-effective manner.
3. **Could members of the vulnerable segment eventually move out of that segment and into another that is less vulnerable?** The poorest, youth and bonded labourers, for example, have the potential to move out of their vulnerability and become more profitable clients for an MFI. Under these conditions, an institution might be willing to subsidize specialized products or services for a vulnerable segment in order to help its members become part of mainstream society with a strong attachment to the MFI for helping them get there.
4. **Is a donor or government willing to subsidize the cost of non-integrated services for this segment?** If so, then an MFI could pursue a strategy of exclusivity. This is often what happens in the case of pilot projects that seek to understand a segment's needs, and experiment with different approaches to meeting those needs, before attempting to integrate one or more successful approaches into an institution's mainstream operations.

Box 14.4 Financial Services to the Families of Child Labourers in Pakistan

Pakistan's First Women's Bank Ltd (FWBL) collaborated with the ILO's International Programme on the Elimination of Child Labour (IPEC) in the provision of financial services to the families of former child labourers in the carpet industry. This project showed that efforts to stimulate alternative income-generating activities in households, through training and credit, had a positive effect on children's enrolment in non-formal education centres. It furthermore showed that microfinance can have a strong impact on the empowerment of women, in addition to increased income.

FWBL is a government-controlled commercial bank, although it is more appropriately labelled as a development finance institution. In 2005, the bank served 133,000 clients, primarily SMEs, of which 60 per cent were female. The bank had a limited microfinance outreach, and saw its cooperation with the ILO as an opportunity to pilot services for smaller borrowers. After completing the pilot, the bank planned to establish microfinance units in each of its 38 branches.

FWBL's microfinance component included loans for start-ups and working capital, as well as medium-term loans for equipment purchases. The loans range from PKR 5,000 (US$80) to PKR 25,000 (US$400) with about PKR 10,000 (US$160) being the average. The bank charges 17 per cent interest on a declining balance, with biweekly repayments. There is a small savings component, PKR 10 to 50 (US$0.15 to 0.80) per month.

While FWBL has, in its cooperation with ILO-IPEC, provided a generic loan product, along with a minor savings component, the bank is currently developing other products for the low-income market, such as loans for agricultural purposes (including for the purchase of livestock), education and consumption. The advantage of the bank's approach is that once a vulnerable customer graduates, the bank is capable of providing commercial bank services to those with good track records.

Since FWBL has its own loan capital, the ILO can move away from the rotating credit funds previously utilized by IPEC projects, and use its limited resources to support needed complementary activities, such as BDS and agricultural extension services, to help strengthen the reliability of the household's new income-generating activity.

From the perspective of the First Women's Bank, the major drawback to its cooperation with ILO-IPEC was the restriction of serving only the IPEC target group. While FMBL understands why the ILO would want to ensure that subsidies are used to benefit the relevant families, it is an inefficient approach that could undermine the long-term provision of services to those clients. Instead, FMBL would prefer to expand the coverage to other households in the same communities to make the programme sustainable.

Adapted from Kring, 2005.

14.4 Serving Disabled Persons[30]

There are approximately 650 million persons with disabilities in the world, or 10 per cent of the global population. Eighty per cent of these persons live in developing countries, and evidence suggests that they tend to be poorer than their counterparts without disabilities. One out of every five persons who live on less than US$1 a day has a disability. In developing countries, 80 to 90 per cent of persons with disabilities do not have a formal job, so most turn to self-employment (United Nations, 2007).

Unfortunately, people with disabilities are usually under-represented among the clients of formal and informal financial institutions. In a global study by Handicap International (2006), microfinance organizations reported that less than half of one per cent of their clients had a disability, although most of them do not monitor this indicator. There are many reasons for the under-representation, including:

- **Self-exclusion.** Disabled people often lack the knowledge and/or self-confidence to join an MFI. Their repeated experience with exclusion and rejection can result in low self-esteem, and a belief that they are more appropriate recipients of charity than of financial services.
- **Institutional exclusion.** Negative attitudes, preconceptions and misconceptions about disability, as well as issues of physical access, result in MFIs deliberately or unconsciously excluding disabled people from their programmes. Steps, stand-up cash counters, uneven paths, distant branches and the lack of devices that can assist the blind or deaf to communicate with the MFI all create barriers to access.
- **Exclusion by group members.** Persons with disabilities are often perceived by community members to be risky, either because of stereotypes about their capacity or because of cultural norms that make it unacceptable to exert pressure on them if they borrow and do not repay. As a result, disabled persons are often excluded from group-based microfinance mechanisms.
- **Exclusion by design.** The products offered by microfinance institutions can hinder persons with disabilities from participating. For example, weekly instalments are a greater obstacle than monthly instalments for people with mobility challenges. High compulsory upfront savings requirements and an unwillingness to lend to start-up businesses also exclude the participation of many disabled persons, as they do others who live among the bottom poor.

People with disabilities are not a homogeneous group. They have different types of impairment with various degrees of severity. They also have diverse combinations of education, skills and access to networks. People who have had a disability since birth or early childhood have often been denied formal education, or have lived in social isolation. As a result, they may have poorly developed social skills, and may suffer from lack of self-esteem. They may need more time and training prior to starting economic activities.

[30] This section is adapted from Handicap International (2006).

In contrast, persons who were injured or developed impairments at a later age face a different set of problems. They may require trauma counselling and special training in new occupational skills suited to their situation. However, they are often less stigmatized, and may have had the opportunity to go to school or to gain prior work experience. Usually, people with physical impairments face fewer problems for social and economic inclusion than people with visual or hearing impairments. Persons with intellectual impairments tend to be the most disadvantaged.

Approach to Integration

Since disabled persons face multifaceted exclusion and are often, but certainly not always, amongst the poorest of the poor, they will usually require an integrated package of services that enables their basic needs to be met, and their financial, social and human capital deficits to be addressed (see Chapter 15). The nature of that package will vary, depending on the type and severity of disability, as well as on the nature of the deficits that need to be addressed. As shown in Figure 14.1, there could be a need for rehabilitation, assistive devices, psychological support, public education, vocational training, start-up capital, transport, advocacy, and other services.

Disabled persons who are not amongst the poorest may not need such an array of services, but they will almost inevitably require a variety of financial services, just like those who are not disabled. They may benefit from access to savings, credit, insurance, leasing and payment services.

Figure 14.1 Integrated services for people with disabilities

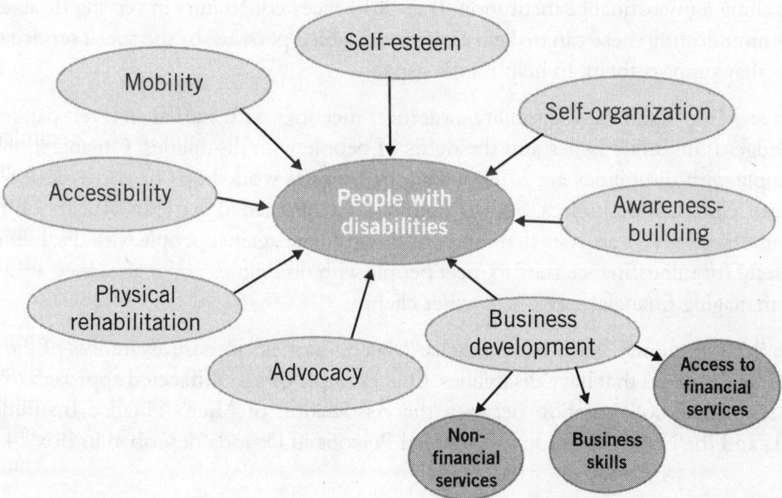

Source: Handicap International, 2006.

Although disabled persons constitute a significant percentage of the low-income market, the development and maintenance of special products for this market segment is usually not cost-effective for MFIs. There are several reasons for this. First, the heterogeneity of the segment makes it difficult to create products that can meet everyone's needs. Second, introducing special arrangements for people with disabilities can reinforce the idea that people with disabilities are not capable of managing their risks and resources in the same way as the rest of the population, and this can perpetuate discrimination. Third, since people with disabilities usually live far from each other and belong to different social networks, regular loan monitoring and debt collection can become expensive if MFIs take a non-integrated approach.

Institutions that are serving disabled persons successfully are doing so by mainstreaming the segment into their regular operations. This does not mean that they attempt to provide all of the services that disabled persons require on their own. Usually, they partner with other organizations that work in different domains, particularly when it comes to the provision of non-financial services. The efforts MFIs themselves take to make their services more accessible to persons with disabilities generally fall into one of two categories: 1) awareness raising; and 2) the adaptation of products and delivery mechanisms. These are discussed in more detail below.

Awareness Raising

There is usually a need to raise awareness among disabled persons, among MFI staff, and within the communities where MFIs operate. Disabled people are often not aware of the financial services that are available, the requirements for accessing those services, or the benefits that access can bring. Individual coaching, workshops or seminars can remove misconceptions about the criteria an MFI uses to select clients, and reduce disabled persons' fear of approaching a microfinance institution. If an MFI faces constraints in serving disabled people, communicating these can make it easier for disabled persons, or the social service organizations that support them, to help fill the gaps.

Within an MFI, seminars or disability-awareness meetings with staff at all levels can improve knowledge of disability issues and the rights of people with disabilities. Organizations of or for people with disabilities are often willing to conduct workshops or conferences to help reduce or eliminate prejudices. Special training may be needed for loan officers on how to make an objective risk analysis that does not discriminate against people with disabilities. It is also useful for microfinance staff to meet people with disabilities and realize they are as capable of managing financial services as other clients.

Within the community, MFIs can publicize "success stories" to raise awareness of the potential of entrepreneurs that have disabilities. One example of a multifaceted approach to raising awareness is the collaboration between the Association of Micro Finance Institutions of Uganda and the National Union of Disabled Persons in Uganda described in Box 14.5.

Box 14.5 Raising Awareness in Uganda

In 2005, the Association of Micro Finance Institutions of Uganda (AMFIU) and the National Union of Disabled Persons in Uganda (NUDIPU) launched the Microfinance and Disability Project, with support from the Norwegian Association of Disabled (NAD). The project aims to raise awareness among MFIs about the largely untapped market for financial services among people with disabilities, and to raise awareness among organizations for people with disabilities to eliminate fear and misconceptions regarding MFIs. To achieve this goal, activities included:

- Organizing a two-day workshop for organizations of/for people with disabilities and microfinance institutions in the Tororo district, which created a positive attitude among participants and showcased successful examples of entrepreneurs with disabilities.
- Training of MFI staff at the branch level. The 90-minute sessions usually took place early in the morning, and covered four areas: 1) the definition of disability and its causes, and the mechanisms hindering the inclusion of persons with disabilities; 2) the market opportunities that the MFIs are missing, and the role that MFIs can play in being more proactive in their inclusion efforts; 3) how to look beyond a disability to analyse the person and their willingness and capacity to repay a loan; and 4) a list of "do's" and "don'ts".
- Creating an award for the most disability-friendly microfinance institution.
- Implementing a survey among AMFIU members to find out the proportion of people with disabilities among their clients, and to analyse their knowledge and experience on equalisation of opportunities for people with disabilities.

AMFIU actively disseminates the project and the idea of inclusion in its regular contact with its member institutions. Articles have been printed in the local *Microbanking Journal*, and inclusion has been promoted in industry-level trainings and member meetings. Both AMFIU and NUDIPU have employed a special officer to manage the project. The AMFIU disability officer raises awareness among microfinance institutions on disability issues, and the NUDIPU microfinance officer meets people with disabilities, advises them, trains them in business skills, and tries to raise confidence in their business capacities.

Source: Adapted from Bwire et al., 2008.

Adaptation of Products and Delivery Channels

MFI delivery models that already provide integrated services, such as ProMujer's village banking methodology (see Box 14.6) and the Leprosy Mission Trust's self-help groups (see Box 14.7), have been able to reach disabled persons through their core methodology, without making major adaptations. Some MFIs have used individual lending methodologies to reduce exclusion by borrower groups, whereas others have stuck to a group delivery model, but made the model more flexible to accommodate disabled persons' needs.

Oportunidad Latinoamérica (OLC) in Colombia, for example, decided to specifically target people with disabilities when it realized they were over-represented among the poorest. It allowed smaller solidarity groups if they included people with disabilities (five to ten persons instead of the usual 15), gave smaller loans than usual if requested, and agreed to provide loans for start-ups, which it does not do for the rest of its clients. Persons with disabilities now represent 6 per cent of Oportunidad's client base.

Box 14.6 Serving Disabled Persons through a Village Bank Model

ProMujer provides loans through the village-banking methodology. Village banks are called "communal associations" in Nicaragua. The members of these associations receive training on loan management, business skills, and health and personal development services.

The experience of ProMujer with women with disabilities has been two-fold. On the one hand, there are instances in which they have been included in mainstream communal associations. On the other hand, there is a communal association of only women with disabilities in Chinandega. The latter was created by a group of 30 women who were already organized as an association to produce traditional piñatas. This group has been as successful as any other communal association; women with disabilities are even more committed with the programme to overcome discrimination. The methodology is exactly the same as with other groups.

Source: Adapted from Handicap International, 2006.

Box 14.7 Serving Disabled Persons through a Self-Help Group Model

The Leprosy Mission Trust India (TLM) carries out community-based rehabilitation in 11 states. The goal of these programmes is to establish partnerships with health, education, social and government services as well as private sector institutions to facilitate access to mainstream services for people affected by leprosy and other disabilities. Members of TLM organized themselves into self-help groups that, with the support of volunteers, have developed a successful microfinance system providing savings and loans to its members. The average group size is 15 to 20 members; both male and female participants are accepted. Members themselves decide on the size of the savings, which are deposited in a bank to create an internal capital fund. Loans from the internal capital fund can be lent to members, and the group decides its own lending terms (most charge 2 per cent monthly). Loans may be used for investment, but also for current spending such as medicines or school costs. Once a group has been saving for six months, it may apply for external loans from TLM or banks.

Source: Adapted from Handicap International, 2006.

The main strategies that MFIs have used to adapt their products and delivery methodologies to better meet the needs of disabled persons are:

- conducting market research to identify the specific needs and capacities of disabled persons in their target market;
- seeking out disabled persons who already use the MFI's services and working with them to reach out to new clients or to improve product design and customer service;
- joining efforts with disabled people's organizations to understand disability issues better, to improve communication with disabled persons, and to seek practical and locally relevant solutions to access issues (see, for example, Box 14.8);

- being open to hiring qualified people with disabilities among MFI staff. This can help make people with disabilities feel welcome and accepted, while also providing the MFI with a resource person who understands the strengths and weaknesses of people with disabilities.

Box 14.8 Productive Partnerships between MFIs and Disabled People's Organizations

In 2002, Mobility International USA (MIUSA) entered into a partnership with five members of the InterAction consortium of development organizations. One of these organizations was the Trickle Up Programme, which implements microenterprise development projects in Asia, Africa, and the Americas. Through a grant from the United States Agency for International Development (USAID), MIUSA provided these organizations with three years of technical assistance and training on creating and sustaining inclusive development programmes.

MIUSA and Trickle Up began their partnership with an initial training that helped Trickle Up staff realize that serving people with disabilities would help them to achieve their mission of working with the poorest, and that this target population could benefit even more than others from the economic independence that microenterprise can offer. Later, MIUSA visited Trickle Up's project in northern Mali to provide technical support and to meet with Trickle Up's 15 partner agencies there. Trickle Up staff had already outlined their organization's commitment to including people with disabilities in its programmes, and the partner agencies were enthusiastic about inclusion, but they were having some very practical difficulties with being inclusive. For example, because of mobility issues, people with disabilities were struggling, not always successfully, to attend entrepreneur meetings. Non-disabled entrepreneurs were frustrated when disabled participants did not show up.

MIUSA invited local disabled persons' organizations (DPOs) to a networking meeting with Trickle Up partner agencies, and encouraged them to work together to find solutions to access issues that were preventing the full inclusion of people with disabilities. MIUSA also established links with the local office of Handicap International, which joined the network meeting as a resource. During the workshop, Trickle Up partner agency staff became so enthusiastic about inclusion that they started talking about advocating for the rights of people with disabilities in their community.

Today, 10 per cent of Trickle Up grant recipients have some kind of disability. Trickle Up credits its partnership with MIUSA for enabling it to become a more inclusive organization, and believes that bringing DPOs into its existing network was key to success. DPOs can help MFIs to understand the particular challenges that people with disabilities are facing in their area of operation, develop strategies for inclusion, and identify local governmental, international and local NGO resources available to MFIs and to people with disabilities within their communities.

Source: Adapted from Heisey, undated.

Table 14.1 provides a summary of specific strategies that MFIs are using to address the different types of exclusion described earlier, and to increase their outreach to disabled persons.

Table 14.1 Strategies for increasing MFI outreach to disabled persons

Type of Exclusion	Activities that address this type of exclusion
Self-exclusion	• Training of entrepreneurial persons with disabilities on the aspects of business, microfinance and savings • Bridge-building between disability and microfinance "communities" • Active use of role models and peer support; inviting those who have been successful to talk and share their experiences with potential entrepreneurs • Supporting people with disabilities (or finding a partner organization that can do so) to complete their loan applications and/or to create a business plan, which reduces the possibility of rejection and business failure • Using recruitment methods that seek out disabled persons rather than waiting for them to come to the MFI
Exclusion by group members	• Building partnerships with local media to spread "success stories" • Advocating for social acceptance and inclusion through the MFI's own marketing (for example, including a photo of successful disabled and non-disabled clients on the cover of a brochure) • Organizing seminars for groups that raise awareness on disability issues and the rights of people with disabilities
Exclusion by staff	• Organizing seminars for staff that raise awareness on disability issues and the connection between an MFI's mission and its mandate to serve this segment • Discussing stigmatization and prejudice with loan officers, managers, owners • Providing training for loan officers on how to make an objective risk analysis that does not discriminate against people with disabilities • Publicizing "success stories" to raise awareness of the potential of entrepreneurs with disabilities within microfinance institutions, and the society as a whole • Introducing incentives that can encourage outreach among the disabled population, for example, prizes or certificates to groups that include disabled members, bonuses to staff who reach out to disabled clients
Exclusion by design	• Meeting with disabled persons to understand their needs, and what makes it difficult for them to access financial services • Making existing products more accessible to all, rather than developing special products for disabled clients (for example, introducing methodologies or technologies that require fewer visits to the MFI's office, or that bring the MFI's services closer to clients) • Checking that insurance policies do not exclude those with disabilities • Accepting that a relative represents the person with disability in group meetings • Ensuring that service points are accessible (for instance, that branches have low counters for people in wheelchairs, and group meeting spaces can be reached by those with mobility challenges) • Using more than one type of communication channel to disseminate information (for example, one that can be seen and one that can be heard)

Source: Adapted from Handicap International, 2006, and Bwire et al., 2008.

14.5 Serving Persons Living with HIV/AIDS [31]

According to UNAIDS (2009), approximately 33 million people worldwide are living with HIV/AIDS. There were 2.7 million new HIV infections in 2008 alone, 430,000 of which were children born with HIV, and 2 million AIDS-related deaths. The AIDS virus is the leading cause of death and disease among women between the ages of 15 and 44 (World Health Organization, 2009).

The HIV/AIDS pandemic has been recognized as more than a health crisis. It poses serious socioeconomic challenges at the national, community and household levels. Poor households are the hardest hit, facing increased vulnerability to HIV/AIDS due to limited access to health care and education, and few means of coping with the medical and economic impact of the disease. The onset of AIDS can quickly pull moderately poor families into destitution, and can create poverty among working class people as income and assets are depleted by the cost of health care, the burden of caring for the sick, funeral expenses, and the adoption of orphans by the extended family unit. If people cannot afford the necessary food required during treatment, or transportation to health centres, even the availability of life-saving anti-retroviral drugs will not help them.

The extent to which households and communities are able to cope with the consequences of HIV/AIDS depends on the type and amount of resources at their disposal. Financial services, including loans, savings and insurance, can help poor households mitigate the economic impact of the disease. They can help clients to maintain a consistent income stream, build a savings base that may be liquidated to cover emergency expenses, and avoid selling productive assets, such as land and equipment, which may have a devastating effect on their future earning potential and ability to recover from the crisis.

Specific Challenges

HIV/AIDS poses several critical challenges for MFIs and the communities they serve. Understanding these challenges can help institutions to design programmes to overcome them.

- **Rapidly changing circumstances**. People affected by HIV/AIDS can shift rapidly from economic security to destitution. Yet, with increasing access to anti-retroviral therapies, many can also recover from debilitating circumstances and once again participate actively in income generation.
- **Loss of skilled income earners**. When AIDS claims the lives of trained and experienced adults, their families, local communities and youth lose knowledge and skills.
- **Labour shortages and unemployment**. Some families experience labour shortages due to loss or reduction in adult energy levels and/or the burden of caring for the sick or for orphans. At the same time, large numbers of young people have missed the opportunity for education and are now above school age, unskilled, and often responsible for caring for siblings or grandparents.
- **Stigma**. Stigma can present barriers for HIV-positive people or their affected families. They can be excluded from group-based financial services and business or farming associ-

[31] This section is adapted from SEEP Network (2008) and USAID (2008).

ations. People known to be HIV-positive may face difficulties in running a business in communities where stigma is high and there is reticence to buy goods or services from people who are HIV-positive.

- **Health challenges**. People living with HIV/AIDS can lead productive lives with drug treatment. However, their HIV status may require extra attention and resources to ensure a balanced diet, adequate sleep, access to regular health care, and support for psychological and emotional well-being.
- **Gender discrimination**. Women in many cultures are more heavily affected by HIV/AIDS. For example, in most parts of Africa, widows can be blamed for their husbands' death from AIDS, are not able to inherit their husband's land or business, and may be cast out from the family and made homeless.
- **Pressure on community safety nets**. In most developing countries, where government social services are not able to care for the most vulnerable, extended family and community members provide a "community safety net". However, in areas of high HIV prevalence, this system is often strained to breaking point.

Approach to Integration

The provision of financial services generally does not (and should not) require knowing the HIV status of clients. Thus it is virtually impossible to serve PLWHA through specialized products and delivery channels. Even if clients voluntarily identify themselves as HIV-positive, serving them separately would be unattractive for several reasons: it would exacerbate rather than alleviate the isolation and exclusion that PLWHA already experience; the frequent drop-outs caused by illness and death would destabilize and perhaps even destroy groups; and MFIs would lose opportunities to work together with the communities where they work to support PLWHA. Family members, friends and caregivers of PLWHA will also be MFI clients, and an integrated approach would not only assist the MFI in identifying and meeting their needs, but also enable it to encourage awareness and mitigation activities that help prevent further spread of the disease.

When serving PLWHA, MFIs approach integration in one of two ways. Those that take a **minimalist approach** monitor the changing needs of their clients and adapt their products and services in response, but they stay focused on financial services and tend to pay close attention to their bottom line. They link clients and staff to AIDS support organizations (ASOs) rather than provide health or prevention services themselves. Institutions that take an **integrated approach** tend to see HIV/AIDS prevention as their social responsibility. They either directly organize or engage ASOs to organize workshops on prevention for clients and staff. They may also have links to other ASOs that provide voluntary counselling and testing, or anti-retroviral therapies, or which work with orphans and vulnerable children. Examples of the types of partnership and product adaptation being made by MFIs serving PLWHA are discussed briefly below.

Product Adaptations

While financial institutions are not designed to provide support services to PLWHA, they can design flexible products that allow their clients to weather changes in their financial situations. It is important to talk to communities affected by the disease to understand their vulnerabilities and financial service needs. Research by *MicroSave* shows that households experience different financial pressure points as HIV evolves (Donahue et al., 2001):

- early stages when the family is first called on for assistance, or the first signs of AIDS appear;
- frequent hospital visits, when the person living with HIV/AIDS is in and out of hospital;
- bedridden patient, either at home or in the hospital;
- death and burial; and
- care for orphaned children or grandparents, including payment for children's education.

The proportion of the target market in each of these segments, and their ability to use financial services, can inform an MFI's design and delivery of products.

Savings product considerations. In the face of HIV/AIDS, savings products can be designed to help build both productive assets (those that generate additional income, such as machines, livestock and land) and cash reserves. Looking at flexible savings products that allow clients to access their money when it is needed may be important for HIV/AIDS-affected communities that have greater expenses for health care, nutrition or support of orphans. Likewise, providing products that help children who have lost their parents to AIDS is also useful. Ensuring that savings account holders indicate beneficiaries on account-opening forms can also protect assets for children or other family members in case of death. Savings-led microfinance models, such as accumulating savings and credit associations (ASCAs) and village savings and loan associations (VSLAs), are also proving to be a strategy that enables HIV/AIDS-affected individuals to build a protective safety net (see, for example, Box 14.9).

Box 14.9 Flexible Savings Services Support PLWHA in Mozambique

In northern Mozambique, the NGO Ophavela promotes the establishment of rotating credit and savings groups (Poupança e Credito Rotativo, or PCR) that consist of 10 to 30 members in rural and peri-urban areas. The groups save regularly and then use their pooled savings to make loans to members of the group. Groups usually have two savings pools: one called a social fund that is lent to group members without interest for emergencies, and a general fund that is lent with interest for other purposes. One of the ways that Ophavela responded to the threat of HIV/AIDS was through a review of the internal rules of the PCR groups. The objective was to determine whether the groups' policies were flexible enough to accommodate local circumstances while keeping in line with the original PCR methodology. The NGO found that groups were able to modify the rules according to their needs. In groups that had been directly affected by HIV/AIDS, contributions to the social fund were more important, and there was more focus on catering for emergencies. In less affected groups, there was more emphasis on using savings and credit to develop small enterprises or test new business ideas, build household assets, and contribute to education and community events.

Source: Adpated from Bundred et al., 2007.

Loan product considerations. Some HIV-positive people may need to change their livelihoods if they become sick and try new opportunities, such as home-based businesses or less physically demanding activities, or leave formal employment for the flexibility of self-employment. Helping clients transition to different activities during periods of illness or liquidate their business can be a way to protect the client and the institution against default.

Considering loan products that help clients "restart" or "bounce back" from illness and rebuild their business can also be a means to address HIV/AIDS. If a client was able to run a business activity successfully, but had to close because of illness, financing to restart this activity (an already known and proven livelihood) might be appropriate.

Some institutions have offered *Credit with Education*, (see Box 12.3 in the chapter on non-financial services), through which health information, such as messages on prevention, stigma, and caring for people with HIV, is delivered in short, facilitated sessions during group meetings. The additional cost of this service might be acceptable for programmes that are mission-driven and want to face the HIV/AIDS crisis proactively, and in areas with a high prevalence of HIV/AIDS.

Microfinance service providers need to be sensitive to the needs of HIV/AIDS-affected households when collecting on loans that have fallen delinquent. Using the right terminology when discussing illness and death, and making careful decisions on whether or not to force households to repay an outstanding loan contracted by someone who has died, are important for the institution's reputation in the community. Although an institution cannot absorb all losses resulting from HIV/AIDS, it can create flexible mechanisms or accommodating repayment schedules (and consider loan insurance, as explained below).

Existing or potential clients should not be discriminated against on the basis of their HIV status. Although MFIs are often advised not to lend directly to people with advanced stages of AIDS, in those communities where treatment can be readily accessed and HIV-positive clients can lead healthy lives, there is no need for discrimination in services.

Insurance product considerations. One of the best ways financial service providers can assist clients through crisis is to provide loan insurance in case of death, sometimes called credit life insurance. For a small fee, this coverage can be added to loans so that, were the borrower to die, their loan would be repaid. Clients seem to appreciate the extra protection this offers, so their family does not have to shoulder their debt. Some institutions have extended this further to pay benefits to a named beneficiary and/or to include the lives of other family members. The design of insurance services should be done carefully to ensure there will be adequate coverage (based on the percentage of clients who could die and their average outstanding loan balances), and is usually best done in collaboration with an insurance company. The microfinance institution can collect the premiums from clients and pay the insurance company for the coverage (see Chapter 9).

Beyond credit life, extending insurance services in general through private firms can also help with health-care needs and disability due to HIV/AIDS. Because of the complicated nature of insurance risk pooling, it is best to work with specialized companies when offering these sorts of services. Health insurance in particular can be challenging to manage, and requires good-quality health care in the community. Helping clients access these products by linking with private providers, however, can be a role for microfinance institutions.

Delivery systems considerations. The way financial services are delivered to clients can be as important as the products themselves. Since most products are still driven by human delivery channels (for example, credit officers, bank tellers or group facilitators), microfinance institutions can ensure the language used by staff is supportive, and avoids stigma in the community. Helping to reduce barriers to entry and eliminating stigma for people living with HIV/AIDS in a group-based delivery system are important functions staff can fulfil. Discussing with group-based loan clients before they borrow money what their strategies for collecting loans will be if someone is unable to repay or dies is also important as a risk mitigation strategy for other clients and the institution.

Partnerships[32]

Regardless of whether MFIs take a minimalist approach or an integrated approach, institutions that serve PLWHA almost inevitably use partnerships to help them confront the challenges posed by HIV/AIDS. As discussed in Chapter 22, there are a wide range of partnership types, and different MFIs make use of different models depending on their mission, the availability of potential partners, the prevalence of HIV/AIDS in the communities where they work, and the needs and resources of PLWHA in those communities. The financial and non-financial services that MFIs have provided through partnerships include:

- **Prevention and nutrition information.** MFIs may simply distribute information provided by an ASO, invite ASO representatives to help deliver content during a group training session, or pay an ASO to provide certain services to the MFI for a specific period of time (see Box 14.10). MFIs may also participate in local working groups that bring government representatives, donors, ASOs and other relevant service providers together to share experiences and coordinate their efforts to address HIV/AIDS within a particular community.
- **Peer educator training.** In some instances, partnerships between MFIs and ASOs have relied on borrower groups to identify strong leaders who are trained to become peer educators. The leaders then teach others in the community about HIV/AIDS, motivating community members to practise healthy behaviours and reduce stigma. Peer educator training was a component of both the NMB partnership described above and the Intervention with Microfinance for AIDS and Gender Equity (IMAGE) project described below.

Box 14.10 A Targeted Partnership at NMB

In 2002, the National Microfinance Bank of Tanzania contracted the African Medical Research and Education Foundation to conduct a knowledge survey of the bank's staff, provide HIV/AIDS prevention education to staff members and families, train peer educators who would provide ongoing education to staff, family and the community following the completion of the internal training programme, and assist the bank in developing its own workplace policy. This contract was done on a one-time basis, with the option of adding additional services at the end of the contract period.

Source: Green, 2008.

32 This section is adapted from Green (2008).

- **Gender equity training.** Partnerships between MFIs and organizations that support women's empowerment can build awareness, confidence and communications skills among women that make it possible for them to influence positively behaviour that contributes to the spread of HIV/AIDS. In South Africa, the IMAGE project brought together the MFI Small Enterprise Foundation and the Rural AIDS and Development Action Research Programme of the University of Witwatersrand to provide microfinance services in conjunction with 12 to 15 months of gender and HIV training. Women in the project experienced a 55 per cent decrease in physical and sexual abuse, a 24 per cent increase in the use of condoms, and a 60 per cent increase in voluntary HIV testing (Simanowitz, 2008b).
- **Voluntary counselling and testing.** In this partnership, an MFI sets up an agreement with an ASO, clinic or medical facility to provide services for staff and/or clients. The most successful partnerships provide these services confidentially at no cost. In Ghana, for example, Sinapi Aba Trust (an MFI) formed an alliance with Planned Parenthood to raise awareness about HIV/AIDS, and to offer confidential voluntary testing, health referrals and support to its clients. In Uganda, one local MFI pays a one-time membership fee to the AIDS Support Organization as a way of encouraging clients and their families to obtain the support and care that they need outside the MFI's infrastructure.
- **Health care.** An increasing number of MFIs are experimenting with using their infrastructure to give clients access to affordable health care. In Bolivia, for example, CRECER (Crédito con Educación Rural) has linked with mobile doctors that provide health education as well as preventive and diagnostic services to clients in rural areas. In the Philippines, CARD (Centre for Agricultural Research and Development) is creating linkages with health-care providers to increase affordable access to primary care, and is exploring a franchise network for the distribution of affordable essential drugs.
- **Savings.** Unregulated MFIs often partner with commercial banks or other regulated MFIs to offer voluntary savings services when the law prohibits them from offering these services themselves.
- **Insurance.** MFIs partner with insurance companies to offer health, life, credit life and funeral insurance to all clients, not only those with HIV/AIDS. Major international insurance companies such as AIG, Allianz and Zurich, as well as national insurers such as State Insurance Company of Ghana and Madison Insurance Zambia Limited, have been successful in accessing the low-income market through partnerships with MFIs, even in high HIV-prevalence countries. Particularly interesting is the fact that, over time, a number of life insurance providers have changed their approach with respect to HIV/AIDS (see, for example, Box 14.11).
- **Business development services.** PLWHA are not unique in their need for business development services, but the types of services they prioritize may differ from those demanded by mainstream clients. For example, they may appreciate counselling services that highlight labour-saving technologies, or business opportunities with low labour demands. Value chain partnerships might consider devising products that serve HIV-positive customers, such as nutritional flour mixes, or soaps and creams for the skin. Youth apprenticeship programmes could facilitate the transfer of skills from one generation to another before a breadwinner becomes incapacitated by AIDS, and entrepreneurship and

> **Box 14.11 Insurance Providers Choose to Cover Deaths Due to HIV/AIDS**
>
> Both AIG Uganda and Madison Insurance in Zambia began providing life insurance with an explicit exclusion clause for HIV/AIDS in their policy documents. However, due to the negative publicity generated by this clause and the fact that AIDS is rarely if ever listed as the cause of death, both insurers decided to drop the clause, which ultimately had no significant impact on their bottom line.
>
> *Source: Adapted from Green, 2008.*

savings programmes could help youth build the enterprise and financial management skills required to start a business when they finish school.

Of course, partnerships bring their own challenges. Miscommunication, conflicting objectives, logistical complications and competition for clients' time and attention can create tensions between even the best-intentioned partners. Chapter 22 can help MFIs think through the steps they can take to build and maintain successful partnerships over time.

14.6 Subsidies and Sustainability

Although integrated service delivery is usually what marginalized market segments need, MFIs are unlikely to generate sufficient income through interest and fees to cover the cost of delivering multiple, flexible, supportive services to these segments. This reality requires the microfinance industry to re-evaluate its attitude towards subsidies, and to assess under what circumstances, and in what fashion, subsidies might be appropriate (see Chapter 13).

During the "start-up" phase, when a target group is vulnerable to or engaged in bonded or child labour, subsidies will be necessary to pay for both the non-financial services and the extra effort required to establish a productive relationship between the target group and a microfinance institution. These subsidies are not intended to be ongoing. Just as an MFI is expected to achieve financial self-sufficiency, target group families are expected to become less vulnerable and more independent over time, eventually graduating to the MFI's standard financial services that are designed to achieve full cost recovery.

This is true even for disabled persons and PLWHA. Although members of these target groups are unlikely to leave their disabled or HIV status behind, they can become less vulnerable and more independent over time. If HIV-infected clients eventually die from AIDS, an appropriate package of financial and non-financial services can make it possible for their families to carry on with healthy, productive lives.

Since vulnerable families are expected to eventually be mainstreamed, it is important to design the "intensive care" services in such a way as to best facilitate the transition. Therefore the services should generally mirror the footprint of the MFI's regular service. Interest rates, for example, should be the same for marginalized and mainstreamed groups, so that there is no incentive for inappropriate persons to pretend that they are vulnerable. If institutions want to lower the cost of borrowing for marginalized target groups, they can do so more effectively by lowering opportunity and transaction costs. Additional research is required to determine what services are needed, for how long and in what sequence, and to ascertain the average subsidy needed to move someone out of vulnerability and into mainstream society.

To the extent that MFIs can partner with other institutions that bring both expertise and funding, MFIs will be in a better position to tackle the challenges that face marginalized groups, and to do so at significant scale. However, if financial partners cannot be found, MFIs may have good reason to temporarily subsidize service delivery to marginalized groups with revenue generated by serving better-off clients. This can be justified, in part, by an institution's social mission, if clients support that mission as much as the institution's founders.

Cross-subsidies can also be justified, in part, by improvements in mainstream service delivery that can result from an MFI's efforts to reach these marginalized market segments. For example, if an MFI redesigns its products so that they require fewer visits to the branch office, or can be accessed through agents that operate in the communities where clients live and work, all clients will benefit, not just those with disabilities. Similarly, providing ASO referrals will not only help clients living with HIV/AIDS, but also assist other clients to avoid the disease and to support those they know who are living with it to mitigate its effects. In this way, targeting marginalized markets can be a valuable strategy for enabling an MFI to meet its mainstream objectives.

Main Messages

1. Microfinance can play a lead role in promoting social and economic empowerment.
2. Before designing interventions for vulnerable market segments, define how access to financial services will improve the lives of the targeted persons.
3. Targeting tools should be simple and easy to administer, to minimize costs.
4. Consider a two-tiered approach that pays special attention to vulnerable market segments while being a financial intermediary for the community at large.
5. Design subsidies to facilitate the transition to mainstream financial services.

Case Study: Using the Progress out of Poverty Index™ (PPI™)

The Progress out of Poverty Index (PPI) was introduced in 2005 by Grameen Foundation, the Consultative Group to Assist the Poor (CGAP) and the Ford Foundation, based on an approach developed by Mark Schreiner of Microfinance Risk Management, LLC. The PPI comprises ten easily observable indicators to measure a person's poverty status relative to national or international poverty lines. A given country's PPI is created by taking the most statistically relevant indicators from a nationally representative income and expenditure survey for that country. The indicators are then tested and vetted by local practitioners and other experts to ensure that staff find them easy to use, understand and trust. As of April 2011, PPIs had been developed for 38 countries in five regions.

Once a PPI has been developed for a particular country, interested parties can download it free of charge and use an online trainer's guide to test it with their organization. Generally, field staff implement the tool by interviewing clients, observing their households, and collecting responses to the PPI questions (see Figure 14.2 for an example).

Figure 14.2 Philippines PPI: sample PPI scoring

	Indicator	Value	Points	Total
1	How many people in the family are aged 0 to 14?	A. Five or more	0	**4**
		B. Four	4	
		C. Three	9	
		D. Two	15	
		E. One	20	
		F. None	26	
2	Do all the children in the family of ages 6 to 14 go to school?	A. No	0	**0**
		B. Yes	2	
		C. No children aged 6 to 14	4	
3	What is the education level of the female head/spouse?	A. Graduate primary or less	0	**3**
		B. First- to fourth-year secondary	3	
		C. Graduate secondary	6	
		D. First-year college or higher, or no female head/spouse	11	
4	Do any family members have salaried employment?	A. No	0	**0**
		B. Yes	5	
5	What are the house's outer walls made of?	A. Light materials (cogon, nipa, or sawali, bamboo, anahaw)	0	**4**
		B. Strong materials (iron, aluminium, tile, concrete, brick, stone, wood, asbestos)	4	
6	What is the house's roof made of?	A. Light materials (salvaged, makeshift, cogon, nipa, or anahaw)	0	**2**
		B. Strong materials (galvanized iron, aluminium, tile, concrete, brick, stone, or asbestos)	2	
7	What kind of toilet facility does the family have?	A. None, open pit, closed pit, or other	0	**7**
		B. Water sealed	7	
8	Does the family own a refrigerator?	A. No	0	**0**
		B. Yes	10	
9	How many television sets does the family own?	A. None	0	**6**
		B. One	6	
		C. Two or more	21	
10	Does the family own a washing machine?	A. No	0	**0**
		B. Yes	10	
Microfinance Risk Management, L.L.C.			**Total score**	**26**

Source: Grameen Foundation, 2010.

Figure 14.3 Calculating the percentage of clients who fall below the poverty line

For example, a PPI user has 3,000 clients

- 1,000 clients with scores of 10
- 1,000 clients with scores of 22
- 1,000 clients with scores of 33

PPI score	Total below national poverty line	Total above national poverty line
0–4	96.60%	3.40%
5–9	93.70%	6.30%
10–14	91.50%	8.50%
15–19	87.80%	12.20%
20–24	80.90%	19.10%
25–29	68.50%	31.50%
30–34	59.60%	40.40%
35–39	48.90%	51.10%
40–44	36.80%	63.20%
45–49	21.10%	78.90%
50–54	14.80%	85.20%
55–59	7.20%	92.80%
60–64	5.00%	95.00%
65–69	3.20%	96.80%
70–74	1.40%	98.60%
75–79	1.40%	98.60%
80–84	0.00%	100.00%
85–89	0.00%	100.00%
90–94	1.50%	98.50%
95–100	0.00%	100.00%

The poverty distribution for the 3,000 clients is:

$$\frac{1{,}000 \times \underline{91.5\%+80.9\%+59.6\%}}{3{,}000}$$

This is the average of all the poverty likelihood percentages

= 77.3% of the 3,000 clients are below the national poverty line *(2,472 clients)*

Source: Grameen Foundation, 2008a and 2010.

Based on their responses, the PPI gives each household a score that can then be associated with the likelihood of falling into certain poverty categories, such as living on less than US$1.25/PPP per day, or living below the national poverty line (an example is provided in Figure 14.3).

Organizations can use the information generated by the PPI in a number of ways. First, they can calculate the percentage of their clientele that falls below a particular poverty line. Figure 14.3 shows a simplified PPI data summary exercise in which a fictitious organization applied the PPI and found that one-third of its clients received a score of 10, one-third scored 22, and one-third scored 33. The example shows how to use the lookup table to find the likelihood of poverty associated with each client's score, and then average those probabilities to find the likelihood of poverty within the overall portfo-

lio. In this case, the average of the poverty likelihood percentages associated with scores of 10, 22 and 33 was 82.4 per cent, which means that 82.4 per cent of the organization's 3,000 clients were estimated to fall below the national poverty line. The example is used to simplify the analysis. In normal practice the portfolio poverty rate would be determined by averaging each respondent's poverty likelihood. This is easily accomplished through MS Excel or any database program.

A second way in which organizations can use the PPI is to track the progress of a group of clients over time by monitoring the change in its estimated poverty rate. If, for example, the same group of households that was interviewed in Figure 14.3 was interviewed again one year later, and it was estimated that 70 per cent fell below the national poverty line at that time, then the overall poverty rate would have improved by 12.4 percentage points (82.4% – 70.0% = 12.4%). In other words, 372 of the 3,000 clients would have moved out of poverty (12.4% × 3,000). Dividing this number by the number of clients that were estimated to be poor one year ago (82.4% of the total 3,000), the PPI user can report that 15 per cent of its poor clients crossed the national poverty line from one year to the next [(372 / 2,472) × 100 = 15%].

Negros Women for Tomorrow Foundation (NWTF) in the Philippines uses the PPI in this way. It also analyses the movement out of poverty for each branch, so that it can compare results, investigate what a branch with higher movement out of poverty is doing to achieve such results, and then replicate successful strategies in other branches. An important caveat is that PPI results simply show what took place, not why. A rigorous assessment of impact generally requires the ability to draw a causal link between what took place and why, and the PPI by itself does not provide that. Another caveat is that results will be skewed by clients that drop out of the programme between PPI data collection points. This is of course true of any data analysed over time, and not just the PPI.

A third way in which organizations can use the PPI is to facilitate market segmentation and more effective product development. An organization can divide clients into groups on the basis of their PPI scores, profile each group, and then design different products, product mix strategies, recruitment mechanisms, or other aspects of delivery to meet the needs of each group better. If an organization collects information regarding clients' age, marital status, type of business, number of loan cycles, or other characteristics, the PPI data can also be segmented within these categories to examine differences between groups. For instance, if an organization wants to know the poverty status of young clients (ages 17–30) as compared to older clients (ages 31–50), it can pull up the PPI data for these two groups from its management information system (MIS). If one group appears to be consistently poorer than the other at all cycles, follow-up studies through focus groups can be used to find out why, and to identify products, training or services that can help the disadvantaged group bridge the gap.

NWTF has done this with a variety of indicators, including a number of entrepreneurial activities, as shown in Table 14.2. It uses this information to understand whether and how poverty varies with the number of businesses a client operates. It compares this data with that of other indicators, looks at how they relate to each other, and picks out the ones that tell it the most. NWTF intends to use this information to target eligible populations better, and to provide the kinds of products and services that enable them to move out of poverty faster.

Table 14.2 NWTF: Analysing the relationship between number of businesses and poverty

Number of businesses	Bottom half below poverty line	Top half below poverty line	Above the poverty line	Sample size
1	33%	25%	42%	844
2	29%	23%	48%	384
3	23%	20%	58%	104
4 to 7	19%	17%	64%	21

Source: Grameen Foundation, 2008a.

Some organizations, including NWTF, have also used the PPI to determine whether a potential client is eligible to access its services. After its first application of the PPI indicated that 41 per cent of its entering clients were estimated to be above the poverty line (a number that it considered unacceptably high), NWTF designed a system for screening new applicants on the basis of their PPI score. Potential clients with scores in a certain range were served with the highest priority; those with scores in another range were given second priority; and those with scores outside both ranges were deemed ineligible to access the MFI's services. Six months after implementing this system, only 25 per cent of NWTF's entering clients were above the poverty line. However, because of the margin of error associated with individual scorecard assessments (Boucher et al., 2010), organizations should be wary of applying the PPI in this manner, and consider establishing an appeals system or using other targeting tools in parallel with the PPI to avoid dependence on this or any other single methodology.

This case study was adapted from Grameen Foundation (2010, 2008a, 2008b) and http://www.progressoutofpoverty.org

Recommended Reading

- Daniels, A.; Jeans, A. 2009. "Integrated approaches to enabling the most vulnerable to participate in markets", in *Enterprise Development and Microfinance,* Vol. 20, No. 2, pp. 139–157 (Rugby, Practical Action Publishing), at http://www.ingentaconnect.com/content/itpub/edm/2009/00000020/00000002/art00006
- Daru, P.; Churchill, C.; Beemsterboer, E. 2005. "The prevention of debt bondage with microfinance-led services", in *The European Journal of Development Research,* Vol. 17, No. 1, pp. 132–154 (Basingstoke, Palgrave Macmillan).
- Handicap International. 2006. *Good practices for the economic inclusion of people with disabilities in developing countries* (Lyon, Handicap International), at: http://www.handicap-international.org/uploads/media/goodpractices-GB-2coul.pdf

- ImpAct. 2003. *Microfinance and poverty: Developing systems for monitoring depth of poverty outreach and impact* (Brighton, ImpAct), at: http://www.microfinancegateway.org/gm/document-1.9.26659/17.pdf
- Liber, D.; Gommans, C. 2007. *Partners and action: Financial institutions and health, HIV and AIDS risk management*, Guidebook (Dakar, AfriCap Microfinance Fund), at: http://www.microfinancegateway.org/gm/document-1.9.25583/40058_file_49.pdf
- Mersland, R. 2005. *Microcredit for self-employed disabled persons in developing countries* (Oslo, Atlas Alliance), available at: http://mpra.ub.uni-muenchen.de/2068/1/MPRA_paper_2068.pdf
- SEEP Network. 2008. *SEEP Network guidelines for microenterprise development in HIV and AIDS-impacted communities: Supporting economic security and health, Book 2 – For microenterprise development practitioners* (Washington, DC, SEEP Network), at: http://communities.seepnetwork.org/hamed/node/764
- Van Doorn, J.; Churchill, C. 2004. *Microfinance against child labour*, ILO Technical Guidelines (Geneva, ILO, Social Finance Programme), at: http://www.ilo.org/ipecinfo/product/viewProduct.do?/productId=1019
- Zeller, M. 2004. *Review of poverty assessment tools*, Report submitted to IRIS and USAID as part of the Developing Poverty Assessment Tools Project (Washington, DC, IRS/USAID), at: http://www.microfinancegateway.org/p/site/m//template.rc/1.9.33305

15 Pre-microfinance for the Poorest

Extreme poverty is not just a more severe form of moderate poverty… it's a structural break… a trap… a complex knot… For the extreme poor, initial endowments in several spaces (nutrition, assets, demographic resources, social capital, voice and representation) are below critical thresholds…The extreme poor desperately "need a break"… "a cushion"… "a window of opportunity" that provides security over some critical dimensions that trap them…. ~ Matin (2005)

In general, microfinance products are targeted at persons right around the poverty line, perhaps a little bit above or a little bit below. Some call this market segment the upper poor or the economically active poor. Typical microfinance customers are either self-employed, running microenterprises in the informal economy, or have paid labour opportunities with other enterprises, such as tea plantations or middlemen who buy their handicraft piecework. Microfinance institutions target these customers because experience has shown that, with the proper lending methodology, they are reasonably low-risk borrowers, often more reliable than the market segment traditionally targeted by commercial banks.

However, some MFIs have a very strong social mission, and they are aggressively committed to poverty alleviation. These organizations are not satisfied serving the "low hanging fruit", the clients that are easy to reach and serve. To really alleviate poverty, these MFIs strive to find ways of helping the poorest of the poor through a combination of financial and non-financial services designed to address the root causes of poverty. This approach requires a fundamentally different paradigm and concept of sustainability.

Just as microfinance has created innovations to serve the unbanked, **pre-microfinance** is now a relevant discussion to develop ways of serving those persons that mainstream microfinance does not reach. Toward that end, this chapter introduces the topic by exploring the following questions:

1. Who are the poorest of the poor?
2. Why do most MFIs not serve this market?
3. What products and services are required to serve this market?
4. How should services be adapted to accommodate this market?

Although the chapter uses the term "microfinance institution" to refer to the organization that is providing services to this vulnerable market, the actual service provider might not consider itself an MFI. Often interventions to serve the poorest of the poor are provided by non-governmental organizations (NGOs) that provide integrated services that include microfinance.

15.1 Who are the Poorest of the Poor?[33]

The definition of the "poorest of the poor" certainly varies by country and region. Even the term varies around the world; this market is also called the bottom poor, extreme poor,

[33] This section is adapted from Maes et al. (2006).

Figure 15.1 Degrees of poverty

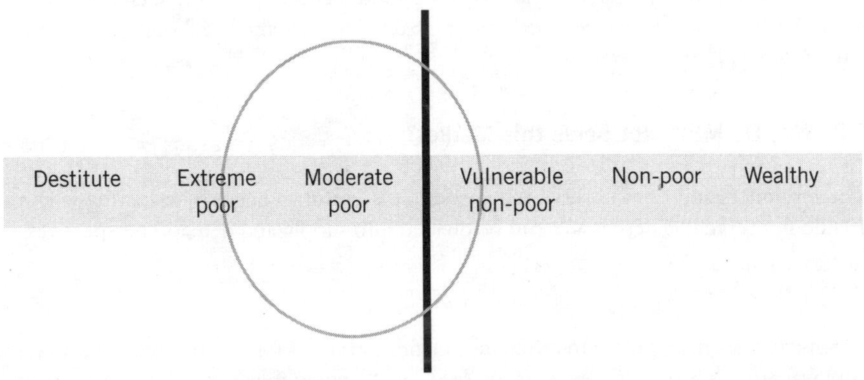

Source: Cohen, 2003.

chronic poor, hardcore poor, ultra poor and destitute. Sometimes the poorest of the poor are beggars, widows, divorced or abandoned women, bonded labourers or the parents of child labourers.

Traditionally, poverty has been conceptualized in terms of income, with the poor defined as those living below a given income level (see Figure 15.1). But poverty has been increasingly recognized as a multidimensional phenomenon that encompasses not simply low income but also lack of assets, skills, resources, opportunities, services, and the power to influence decisions that affect an individual's daily life. Poverty also frequently overlaps and reinforces other types of social exclusion, such as those based on race, gender, or ethnicity. This more comprehensive understanding of poverty better captures how the poor themselves define their situation.

The complex and multidimensional nature of poverty makes it a challenge to measure. For the sake of simplicity, an income-based measure of poverty is used most widely, as it permits comparisons between regions and countries. The World Bank, for example, defines extreme poverty as an income of less than US$1.25/day. This measure can be converted to local currency using the purchasing power parity (PPP) exchange rate, which is based on relative prices of goods and services in different countries. The Consultative Group to Assist the Poorest (CGAP) defines the extreme poor as those households in the bottom 10 to 50 per cent below the poverty line, and the destitute as those households making up the poorest 10 per cent (Helms, 2006).

An important feature to keep in mind is that one's poverty classification is not necessarily fixed; for many people it is likely to change over time, for better or for worse. With the exception of the chronic poor, low-income people may move in and out of extreme poverty depending on their opportunities, and their crises. Poor households can easily become poorer if they experience a crisis or economic shock, especially if they experience more than one at a time. For example, people may become bonded labourers or put their children in work because they need money to pay for a health crisis, or even to pay for a wedding or religious ceremony.

As discussed below, in addition to assisting the poorest to break the structural bonds that keep them in extreme poverty, it is necessary to understand the local factors that create poverty so that the MFI can develop a safety net of sorts that will reduce the likelihood that people will fall back into extreme poverty.

15.2 Why Do MFIs Not Serve this Market?

To better understand how to serve this market, it is useful to begin by clarifying why most MFIs do not serve it. These issues can be divided into supply and demand perspectives.

Supply Perspective

The primary reason why most microfinance institutions do not serve this market is that they do not want to. They see the market as too risky, or it is not in their mission to serve the poorest. If they tried to serve this market, their sustainability or profitability would be threatened.

It is more interesting to look at MFIs that are committed to poverty alleviation and are trying to serve the poorest, yet are not reaching their intended market. Research using the Poverty Assessment Tool developed by the International Food Policy Research Institute (IFPRI) shows that even MFIs with a poverty focus do not necessarily reach the market that they think they are reaching unless they are engaged in actively targeting and recruiting the poorest (see Box 15.1).

Understanding why organizations that want to serve the poorest are not doing so, or at least are not doing so as well as they would like, can help illustrate strategies that are needed to reach this market effectively. The main reasons are:

- **Not providing appropriate products.** Many MFIs do not offer voluntary savings and hardly provide basic needs services, such as food security. Many MFIs have a credit-driven bias, focusing on income-generating or microenterprise loans, which may not meet the needs of this clientele.
- **Inappropriate product design.** The loan products offered by MFIs typically do not have product features that are suited to the target market (for example, loan amount, term, repayment schedule).
- **Staff prejudice or preference.** The poorer the client, the harder the job for field staff. Consequently, even if they do not do it intentionally, many frontline staff members gravitate toward easier-to-serve, less-poor clients.
- **Institutional culture and incentives.** Incentive schemes for loan officers typically reward large volumes of clients and excellent repayment rates. Where such rewards are in place, loan officers are unlikely to reach their targets if they serve more vulnerable clients.
- **Pressure to achieve sustainability.** One of the big selling points of microfinance is that it is a sustainable development tool, but that may not be the case if MFIs are targeting and actively recruiting the poorest of the poor.
- **Performance management.** Without a clear definition of "the poorest" and systems that measure clients' poverty level, MFIs may think they are serving the poorest when in reality they are not. Only by monitoring performance against poverty-related targets can an MFI ensure that it actually reaches the poorest.

Box 15.1 Poverty Assessment Results and Active Targeting

Evidence from poverty assessments conducted by the Consultative Group to Assist the Poorest (CGAP) on a number of MFIs indicates that although all those surveyed were reaching some very poor clients (defined as those in the bottom third of the population), few were reaching large numbers from this group. Most MFIs were biased towards less-poor clients, or at best reflected the general population distribution.

These findings show that MFIs do not automatically reach large numbers of very poor clients by using conventional design features, such as small loan sizes. It is striking that, of the organizations assessed, the four that have analysed and designed their programmes to focus on the needs of the very poor are the only ones with significant depth of poverty outreach: Small Enterprise Foundation (SEF) in South Africa, SHARE in India, Crédito con Educación Rural (CRECER) in Bolivia, and OTIV's Caisses Feminines in Madagascar. Those that use active poverty targeting are especially effective in biasing their outreach towards the poor and very poor.

The SEF and OTIV examples are particularly interesting, because both organizations have two programmes: the first is designed along the lines of conventional microfinance, and the second is designed with the needs of the very poor explicitly in mind, and with active poverty targeting. As illustrated in the charts below, there is a remarkable contrast between the poverty profiles of the two programmes in both MFIs. The clients in the poverty-targeted programmes are overwhelmingly situated in the poorest and poor categories, while the majority of clients in the non-targeted schemes are found in the least poor category.

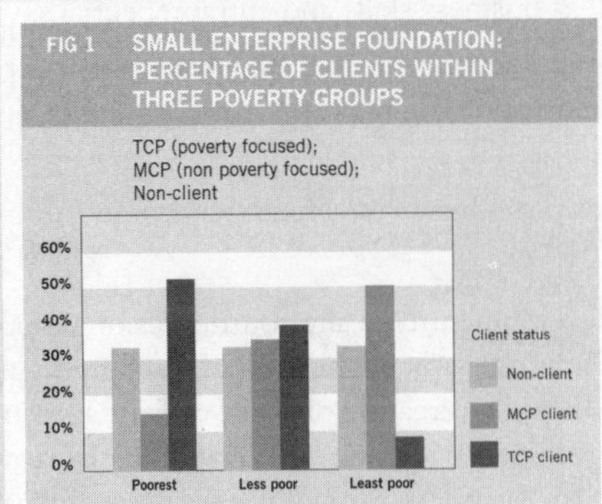

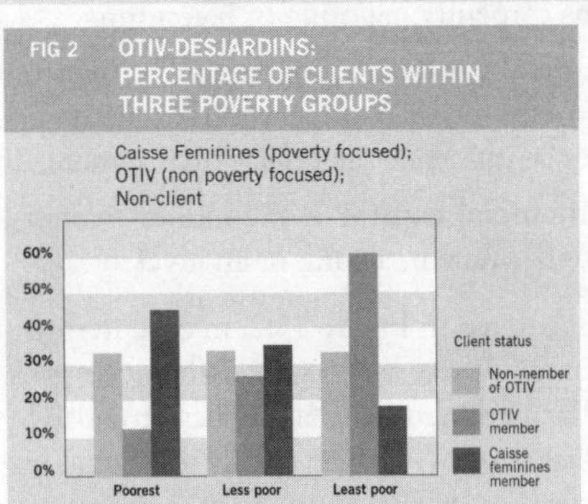

Source: Adapted from Simanowitz with Walter, 2002, and Simanowitz, 2003.

Demand Perspective

While MFIs may not be actively recruiting the poorest of the poor, there are also issues on the client side that make the idea of approaching a microfinance institution unattractive:

- **Fear of borrowing.** Often the bottom poor are afraid to borrow because they have heard about the rigid products and stern repayment pressure from MFIs. With few assets, little or no income and irregular cash flows, they recognize that they might have trouble making regular, on-time loan repayments, and are not willing to risk their reputation and the assets in their possession to access a loan.

- **Lack of confidence.** This target market is often characterized by disempowerment or a lack of confidence that might prevent them from joining a borrower group or starting a new income-generating activity. If MFIs rely on passive targeting and do not actively encourage the poorest of the poor to participate, the organizations are unlikely to attract this market.
- **Excluded (or kicked out) from the group.** Even when the poorest of the poor are interested in accessing services from an MFI, borrower groups might exclude them because they represent a risk that the groups do not want to incur.
- **Unable to meet savings requirements.** Often MFIs have savings requirements that must be met before clients can access a loan, and these may be too onerous for the most vulnerable.

15.3 What Products and Services Are Required?

The best way to understand how to serve this difficult market is to see it in contrast to the mainstream microfinance market. Many MFIs are involved in this business because they want to support the growth of microenterprises. Generally speaking, entrepreneurs or would-be business persons need three types of capital:

- **human capital**, including technical skills required for a particular type of business, such as carpentry, tailoring or haircutting, as well as business skills and entrepreneurial savvy;
- **social capital** such as personal connections and networking that allows the business person to secure contracts, attract customers, learn about market opportunities and perhaps even influence the policy environment; and
- **financial capital** or the money to start and run a business, which may come from the entrepreneur, a bank or an investor.

As illustrated in Figure 15.2, microenterprise development typically contributes or supports all three of these aspects, in different degrees. Financial capital is addressed through savings, credit and other financial services provided by MFIs. The creation of social capital can also be facilitated by MFIs, particularly those that engage in group lending (see Chapter 6). Borrower groups often become important social resources for members, providing each other with support and encouragement, business suggestions, and perhaps even joint initiatives such as bulk buying of inputs. As discussed in Chapter 12, some MFIs provide training and business development services to build the human capital of their clients, or partner with organizations that provide those services.

For the poorest of the poor, however, such a development framework is not sufficient. It assumes some existing foundation of social, human and financial capital on which the interventions can build. More importantly, it assumes that targeted clients are meeting their basic needs already, which is usually not the case with the bottom poor. If a family cannot meet its basic consumption needs and is given an income-generating loan, chances are fairly good that the loan proceeds will be eaten rather than invested.

Figure 15.2 Microenterprise development and the three types of capital

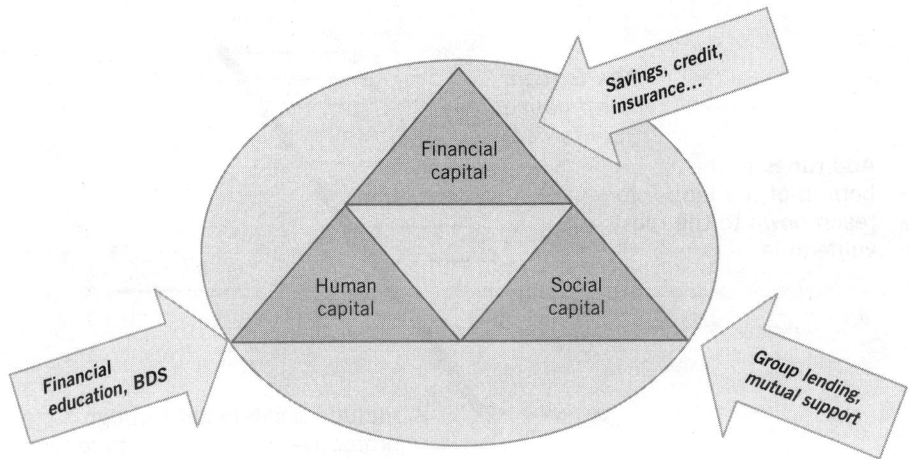

Source: Authors.

Consequently, another dimension must be added to the enterprise development effort when targeting the poorest to first take care of clients' basic needs, including food, shelter, clothing and health. Typical methods of dealing with these basic needs issues are food transfers, ration cards and conditional cash transfers, for example, to households if their children stay in school, to released bonded labourers to help them start over, or to very poor people who are willing to start a business (see Chapter 13). In an emergency situation like an earthquake or tsunami, meeting basic needs may involve the direct provision of housing, water, clothing or health care.

Generally, relief efforts address only the symptoms of poverty, and under some conditions can even foster dependence. What is needed is to develop a more systematic, integrated approach that addresses all four of the components described above, beginning with basic needs, but also including social, human and financial capital.

When designing such a strategy, it is necessary to consider two elements. First, what is the objective: employment or self-employment? Not everyone is an entrepreneur, and not everyone wants to be self-employed. Efforts to help the poorest become employable will require different types of intervention, and a different balance between the three types of capital, than microenterprise development.

Second, what are the deficits that need to be addressed in all four components to help the target market achieve the objective of employment or self-employment? These deficits will vary depending on the circumstance. In a post-crisis situation, for example, perhaps the target market has human and social capital, but they lack basic needs and financial capital. With abandoned women or formerly bonded labourers, perhaps a greater emphasis must be placed on building social capital.

Once the deficits are identified, a service provider can design a set of interventions that will add rungs to the bottom of the opportunity ladder to make it possible for the bottom poor to climb up (see Figure 15.3). If mainstream microfinance starts only on the fifth rung, the poorest of the poor

Figure 15.3 Microfinance for the poorest of the poor

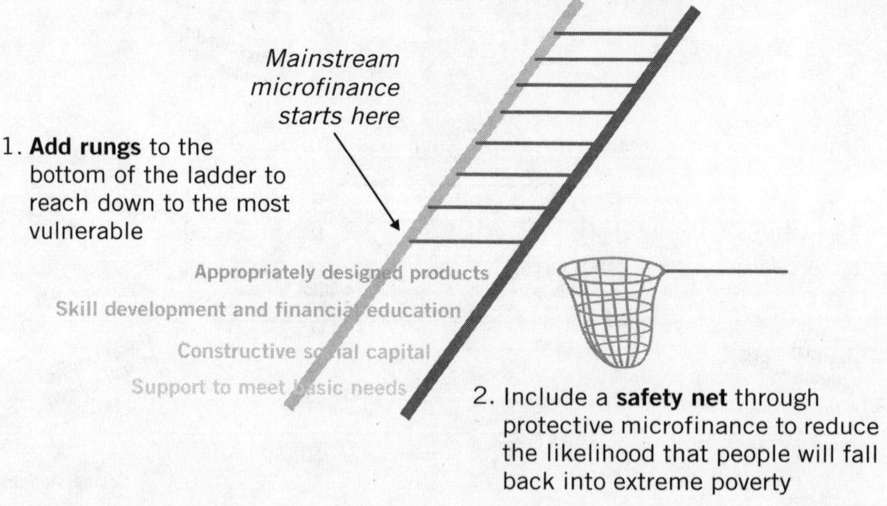

Source: Authors.

need additional rungs below that to assist them with their basic needs and the development of the three capitals. Ideally, once the identified deficits are addressed, clients can then be mainstreamed into an MFI's regular services (see Box 15.2 and the case study at the end of this chapter).

Given the dynamic nature of poverty, a pro-poor strategy needs to complement pre-microfinance services with a second element to reduce the likelihood that clients will become ultra poor. Microfinance institutions should have a safety net scheme through protective financial products – such as savings, insurance and emergency loans – that will reduce the likelihood that people will fall (back) into extreme poverty. This set of services should be for all microfinance customers, however, and not just the poorest of the poor.

15.4 Product Adaptations[34]

When designing financial and non-financial services for the poorest of the poor, considerable adaptations are required to make them appropriate for this market.

Non-financial Services

In addition to appropriate business skills, the bottom poor generally require significant attention on empowerment. Social empowerment initiatives can be provided to groups of vulnerable persons based on the premise that the process of functioning within a group will raise members' confidence, contribute to the empowerment of target families, and facilitate collective action. Without a certain level of bargaining power, discrimination and exploitation will prevail. Without social awareness and financial education, unproductive expenditures (for

[34] This section is adapted from Churchill and Guerin (2004).

Box 15.2 Testing the Graduation Model at Fonkoze

With the technical assistance of Concern Worldwide, and as part of the nine-site CGAP-Ford Foundation Graduation Program, Fonkoze initiated Chemin Levi Miyo (CLM) in 2007. CLM (which translates as "A Path to a Better Life" in Creole) is a multi-pronged livelihoods protection and promotion scheme that is modelled after the Bangladesh Rehabilitation Assistance Committee (BRAC)'s "Challenging the Frontiers of Poverty Reduction: Targeting the Ultra Poor" (CFPR/TUP) programme. It provides extremely poor women in rural Haiti with assets for entrepreneurial use, enterprise training, health services, housing support, a consumption stipend and social links with village élites, facilitated by the close support of a CLM case manager.

Intensive support in CLM gives way to an intermediate six-month microfinance programme, Ti Kredi ("Little Credit" in Creole), which combines a very small loan with savings and close supervision. This in turn provides a gateway to the mainstream solidarity programme, which still includes individual attention and support by a loan officer. The aim, therefore, is not to move CLM members out of poverty in 18 months, but to bring them to the stage where they can successfully graduate to the next level.

One of the most striking results of the 18-month evaluation of the CLM pilot is the shift in participants' poverty status as measured by Fonkoze's poverty scorecard. Every single CLM member improved her score over the 18-month period, with the average score almost doubling from a baseline of 13 to an end score of 25. This is reflected in a movement of 20 per cent of clients above the US$1.25/day extreme poverty line. The assessment also indicated that 93 per cent (140 out of 150 initial participants) had strengthened their livelihoods to the extent that they could graduate into Ti Kredi. Fonkoze obtained these results during a dramatically negative year for Haiti, when the price of basic staples such as rice doubled and a third of the country was hit by a series of four hurricanes that swept through the country in August 2008.

Although the number of individuals involved is relatively small, Fonkoze's pilot test demonstrates that the CFPR/TUP model can work outside Bangladesh; it can be adapted to the most difficult states and local contexts; and organizations without the varied expertise and capacities of BRAC can implement the model through strong partnerships, linkages and staff development.

Source: Adapted from Huda and Simanowitz, 2009.

example, ceremonies, dowry and alcohol) will continue to offset any increase in income (see Box 15.3).

Savings

It may not be appropriate to give the poorest of the poor a loan and hence increase their vulnerability. Consequently, MFIs serving this market often prioritize savings and asset building to create a buffer to fall back on if the household experiences an economic shock. The most appropriate product is contractual savings, which is offered along with financial education and counselling. By assisting the household to identify expected income and expenses, it is possible to highlight the need to curtail some expenses while saving up money for future lump sum needs, such as home improvement, school fees, or religious ceremonies.

Box 15.3 Social Empowerment and the Prevention of Bonded Labour

To contribute to the social empowerment of persons who are bonded or vulnerable to bondage, the International Labour Organization (ILO)'s PEBLISA (Preventing and Eliminating Bonded Labour in South Asia) project relies on two main approaches: learning conversations, and participatory rural appraisal (PRA) tools.

Learning conversations are based on real stories that illustrate the daily problems faced by the participants, such as the cost of marriage, the risks of over-indebtedness, the consequences of illiteracy, and the conflicts among communities. Sometimes, participants themselves tell their own stories. Discussions about the story serve several purposes:

- to help participants to become aware of a specific problem;
- to collectively solve a specific problem faced by one of the members;
- to reinforce cohesion among group members;
- to take collective action, thus increasing their bargaining power.

The PRA tools are used to help participants understand household budgeting and planning, to prepare for seasonal fluctuations by setting aside more savings during periods with net income, and to identify "leakages" where funds are not spent wisely. In Tamil Nadu, the ILO's partners have involved men in the PRA activities. As a consequence, the women have reported substantial shifts in the men's behaviour, including greater participation in housework and income-generating activities, and less time and money spent on gambling and alcohol.

Source: Adapted from Churchill and Guerin, 2004.

A typical argument against a savings-led strategy for the poorest is that, if the poorest do not have sufficient funds to pay for food, how they can possibly save money? In fact, the majority of the target population does save in some way, whether it is cash kept at home or given to a trusted person, or purchasing assets such as small livestock, jewellery and crockery. These savings practices lack security, and are vulnerable to temptation as well as to requests from family and friends. They may not be sufficiently liquid, in the case of assets, or if liquidated in haste they may not fetch their true value.

To overcome these challenges, organizations need to find a way to encourage regular and frequent savings without significant transaction costs. They need to create savings opportunities that make it possible for clients to put money aside on any day that income exceeds expenditures. They also need to find ways of balancing liquidity and security.

One approach, used by National Rural Support Programme (NRSP) in Pakistan and others, is to use locked boxes or piggybanks to promote daily savings without the cost of daily transactions. For the *Haris*, or former bonded labourers supported by NRSP, this approach represented an adaptation of an existing informal system in which people saved in a clay pot. In contrast to the pot, which needs to be broken to access funds, the metal box balances liquidity and security. The locked box is kept at home, and every two weeks NRSP staff open the boxes and allow savers to choose between withdrawing their savings or transferring them to a bank account. At the same time, staff provide financial advice to promote two objectives: to convince clients of the usefulness of saving, even if it amounts to only one rupee a day; and to

help them to analyse their income and their expenses, and to budget for future needs. This arrangement provides a secure and convenient saving place, and encourages people to save regularly.

Locked boxes are also used by Malankara Social Service Society (MSSS) and Integrated Rural Community Development Society (IRCDS), two NGOs operating in Tamil Nadu, India. They were introduced as an experiment to see what effect they might have on people's savings practices. The results were quite dramatic, with households increasing their savings by an average of 250 per cent over the fixed savings amount previously required by the groups. Several factors account for this increase. First, previously members were bringing only savings that they had set aside from the previous days to the group meeting, but the box enables them to easily set aside a little bit every day. Second, the boxes were placed in positions of honour in the household, for example near the portraits of gods and goddesses in Hindu households (which also reduces the risk of theft). To promote savings, the boxes were decorated with slogans, such as "drop by drop, we fill the ocean." Finally, all members of the household were encouraged to contribute to the savings, which persuaded some husbands to cut back on drinking and increase savings.

Income-generating Loans

To serve high-risk clients with irregular and unpredictable income flows, the basic microenterprise or income-generating loan requires a fresh look to ensure that it does not put clients in a situation that could actually make them worse off, yet finds a way to balance repayment discipline with a concern for the clients' vulnerability.

With typical microfinance customers, MFIs are very strict, following up immediately when clients miss a repayment. Persons with less-than-perfect repayment records may lose access to future loans. This approach is considered necessary because the loans are unsecured; tight delinquency management is effectively a collateral substitute. Furthermore, in some group lending methodologies, groups impose their own sanctions on struggling members, perhaps seizing assets from them and removing them from the group at the end of the loan term.

With the poorest of the poor, a hard-line commitment to repayments would invariably cause more damage than good. But would a soft approach be more effective? Regardless of the client's poverty level, if the MFI does not take repayments seriously, borrowers certainly will not either. Consequently, it is necessary to cultivate a "tough-love" approach to repayments in which carrots greatly outweigh sticks (although sticks are still there), with lots of chances for redemption as long as the problem clearly stems from an inability, rather than an unwillingness, to repay. Important elements of this approach include:

1. **Financial education.** A trusting relationship between lender and borrower is critical so that the latter is willing to fully disclose information about the household's cash flow, including other outstanding debts and repayment requirements. Accurate information is important to engage in an effective discussion about how much the household can afford to borrow, but it also helps to illustrate borrowing and expenditure patterns that are not sustainable.

2. **Cautious beginnings.** With this target market, lenders need to take great care that they are not setting up their borrowers to fail. Loan sizes need to start smaller and increase gradually. A loan analysis should ensure that the household will have the capacity to repay even if the business venture fails (or if the household chooses to use the loan for other purposes).
3. **Tailored repayment schedules.** The lender and borrower could jointly establish a customized repayment schedule that mirrors the household's expected cash flow. Customized repayments are particularly needed for the poorest households, because they have fewer sources of income and smaller cash buffers, so they are less able to patch together the regular, equal instalment amounts required by most MFIs (see Box 15.4).
4. **Repayment holidays.** If the MFI's management information system cannot accommodate tailored repayment schedules, loan products for the poorest could accommodate irregular cash flows by including a certain number of repayment holidays. For example, a 40-week loan could be repaid over a 50-week period, with the borrower deciding which 10 weeks she does not have to pay.
5. **Open discussion about rescheduling loans.** Another consideration is whether the MFI should initiate discussions about its rescheduling and refinancing policies even before clients receive a loan. The intention is for lenders to emphasize the huge upside of establishing a positive credit history while communicating that the organization will assist clients who experience unforeseen problems during the loan term.
6. **Establishing benchmarks for vulnerable clients.** Given the vulnerability of this market, it is expected that a portolio-at-risk (30 days past due) target of less than 5 per cent, which is commonly used by MFIs, may not be appropriate for this market. Consequently, lenders serving the poorest of the poor should consider sharing data to create appropriate benchmarks.

Emergency Loans

One of the more important services for vulnerable clients is an emergency loan, perhaps in parallel with an income-generating loan, which can be accessed if clients experience a severe cash flow problem. While income-generating loans are intended to help the poor work their way out of poverty and reduce families' dependence on a single source of income, emergency loans are designed to reduce the likelihood that poor clients will have to seek out the assistance of moneylenders or sell their productive assets in order to meet their basic needs when they face a temporary shortage of cash.

In village bank or self-help group approaches, this service is often provided through the group's internal account, from which members can borrow in times of need. While this approach is reasonably effective in controlling credit risk and screening out inappropriate loan usage, there are two important constraints. First, loan amounts are limited by the quantity of group savings, so only very small loans are available to one or two people at a time during the group's early days. The second constraint is that loans are usually available only during group meetings, which is not sufficiently responsive for some emergencies. To address this problem, some organizations encourage their self-help groups (SHGs) to keep a balance in the group's trunk box, which can be lent out in emergency situations with approval from three of the group's officers (or 50 per cent of the members).

Box 15.4 Grameen Bank Lends to Beggars

Begging is a survival strategy employed by many poor people in Bangladesh, especially when their household experiences a shock, such as river erosion, divorce, death of the earning member in the family, unemployment or disability. For many, it becomes a lifetime occupation. Beggars in Bangladesh are not reached by most poverty alleviation programmes and subsist on the margins of society.

To reach out to the beggars, Grameen Bank created a special programme, called the Struggling Members Programme, which began in July 2002. The objective of the programme is to provide financial services to beggars to help them find a dignified livelihood, send their children to school, and graduate into becoming regular Grameen Bank members. Grameen wants to make sure that no one in the villages has to beg for survival.

The basic features of the programme are:

- Existing rules of Grameen Bank do not apply to beggar members; they make up their own rules.
- The struggling members are not required to form any microcredit group. While they may be affiliated with a regular group, they are not obliged to attend the weekly meetings.
- The bank treats its struggling members with the same respect and attention as regular members, and refrains from using the term "beggar", which is demeaning.
- Once struggling members start a business activity, Grameen encourages its other members to be customers of the struggling member's business.
- All loans are collateral-free, and there is no interest charged.
- The repayment schedule is flexible; the instalments are paid according to convenience and earning capability as determined by the struggling member. Loans can be for a very long term to make repayment instalments very small. For example, for a loan to buy a quilt or a mosquito net, many borrowers are paying Tk 2.00 (US$0.03 cents) per week.
- Instalments must not be paid from money earned from begging, but from money earned from their new businesses.
- The struggling members are welcome to save with Grameen Bank if they wish.
- Beggar members are covered under life insurance and loan insurance programmes without paying any premium.
- Each member receives an identity badge with his/her picture and name, and Grameen Bank logo. Members can display this as they go about their daily life, to let everybody know that they are Grameen Bank members and this national institution stands behind them.
- Members are not required to give up begging, but are encouraged to take up an additional income-generating activity such as selling popular consumer items door to door, or at the place of begging.

Source: Adapted from Barua, 2006.

What constitutes an emergency need depends on local expectations. For the poorest, the repayment of old debts can relieve them of a significant financial burden (for example, interest as high as 10 per cent per day) as well as alleviate a moral weight, including verbal, physical and sexual violence. Consequently, a few MFIs are experimenting with a debt consolidation loan specifically intended to help households manage their debt better and more cost-effectively.

15.5 Conclusion

When serving the poorest of the poor, there are several important challenges that need to be addressed. These include the following:

1. **Motivating the poorest to participate.** MFIs need to take a proactive approach to encouraging the poorest to participate in the programme. Consequently, activities need to take place in a location and at a time that is appropriate for this market, and they need to be provided with incentives to join.
2. **Developing an appropriate package of products and services.** Pre-microfinance requires a set of financial and non-financial services – the new rungs at the bottom of the ladder – for both productive and protective purposes. It is important to define these interventions to address the deficits of the target market regarding basic needs as well as social, human and financial capital.
3. **Determining the right sequencing of services.** Should interventions start with food aid or savings, social empowerment or financial literacy? The poorest of the poor generally have a range of critical deficits, and it is unrealistic to address these all at once, so the support organization has to determine an appropriate sequencing that addresses the most critical areas first and then gradually builds the capacity of the clients toward mainstream microfinance.
4. **Creating a safety net for all clients.** A focus exclusively on the poorest of the poor overlooks the dynamic nature of poverty. The pre-microfinance services for the most vulnerable should be complemented by a safety net of risk-managing financial services for all low-income clients to reduce the likelihood that they will fall deeper into poverty when struck by a crisis.
5. **Time frame.** How long should the pre-microfinance services last? There is no consensus around this issue, perhaps because it depends on the severity of the deficits of the target market and how long it takes to address them.
6. **Finding appropriate partners.** Whenever possible, services to the poorest of the poor should be provided in collaboration with other organizations that have access to specific expertise and resources that MFIs typically do not have, such as health-care providers and food aid programmes.
7. **Clarifying the relationship between mainstream services and those for the poorest.** Creating a package of services for the poorest can have considerable impact on an MFI. For example, will the poorest be served through a separate delivery channel or will they be integrated into existing delivery channels? If they are served in separate groups, will they be served by existing staff members? How will such a programme affect an MFI's institutional culture? What type of incentives should be used for staff working with the bottom

poor, and how can the bottom poor be encouraged to graduate to mainstream services instead of becoming dependent? These are questions that must be answered as part of the process of reaching out to the poorest.

8. **Availability of smart subsidies.** Finally, the critical question: who will pay for these services? Certainly subsidies are required if an organization is to meet basic needs and build human or social capital in addition to financial capital. As discussed in Chapter 13, partnerships with public and non-governmental organizations that have a mission to provide social services can make it possible for MFIs to provide a package of support that reaches the poorest. However, for this approach to be effective, the subsidies must be carefully designed. Refer to Box 15.5 and Section 13.2 of the chapter on grants for guidelines on how to make subsidies smart.

Box 15.5 Is There Such a Thing as a "Smart Subsidy"?

"Smart subsidy" might seem like a contradiction in terms to many microfinance experts. Worries about the dangers of excessive subsidization have driven microfinance conversations since the movement first gained steam in the 1980s. From then on, the goal of serving the poor has been twinned with the goal of long-term financial self-sufficiency on the part of MFIs: aiming for profitability became part of what it means to practise good microfinance.

Much of the excitement around microfinance stems from the possibility of achieving massive scale through highly efficient operations. And one of the fears of relying on subsidies is that it can undercut both scale and efficiency. So, a beginning point in considering smart subsidies is recognizing that the same forces driving efficient outcomes in free markets (hard budget constraints, clear bottom lines, and competitive pressure) can also be deployed in contexts with subsidies. If deployed well, there are circumstances in which subsidies can increase the scale of microfinance outreach, access to commercial finance, and depth of outreach to the poor. By the same token, over-reliance on subsidies and poorly designed subsidies can limit scale and undermine incentives critical to building strong institutions.

The idea of "smart subsidy" springs from the premise that subsidies are neither inherently useful nor inherently flawed. Rather, their effectiveness depends on design and implementation. Smart subsidies maximize social benefits while minimizing distortions and mistargeting. They "crowd in" other funding rather than crowd it out. Subsidies can be powerful for clients and MFIs alike by reducing the risk of entering into a relationship that, once established, is sustainable.

Source: Adapted from Morduch, 2005.

Main Messages

1. Low-income people may move in and out of extreme poverty, depending on their opportunities and their crises.
2. Pre-microfinance can play a critical role in building opportunity ladders for the extreme poor.
3. A package of interventions must be adapted to the particular deficits of the targeted clientele, beginning with their basic needs.
4. Serving the poorest requires significant innovation, commitment and smart subsidies.

Case Study: BRAC's Poverty-focused Programmes

During the mid-1980s, as BRAC was scaling up its microfinance activities and making them more structured and standardized, it realized that these changes might be excluding the extreme poor. It began to look for some other route to be inclusive with a poverty focus.

The Government of Bangladesh and the World Food Programme (WFP) had a country-wide food safety net programme, called Vulnerable Group Feeding Programme (VGF), in which very poor women were provided with a monthly food ration for two years. However, studies found that few improvements were sustained after the food aid period was over. Therefore BRAC decided to run a pilot during the two-year food aid period through which it provided some simple income generation skills training, mobilized savings, formed groups, and provided small amounts of credit to women participating in the programme. The initial results suggested that these women managed to build assets at least up to the value of the food aid transfer after the food aid period was over.

The pilot transformed the food aid programme. In the early 1990s, this experiment evolved into a nationwide programme and changed its name from Vulnerable Group Feeding Programme to Income Generation for Vulnerable Group Development Programme (IGVGP). Today, every two years, almost a quarter of a million extreme poor women graduate to BRAC's regular microfinance programme, and over 70 per cent of them maintain an active membership for at least three years.

Despite this impressive performance, BRAC recognized that about 30 per cent of participating women did not manage to stay in the programme, and not all extreme poor households managed to get the food aid cover. So in 2002 it started a new experimental programme, "Challenging the Frontiers of Poverty Reduction: Targeting the Ultra Poor" (CFPR/TUP), which uses transfers and microfinance cleverly to kick-start a new beginning for the extreme poor.

In CFPR/TUP, a one-time asset transfer (for example, high yielding variety chicks, livestock, or inputs for vegetable cultivation) and a few months of cash stipends to cover the asset return gestation are provided to a carefully targeted group of the extreme poor. Skills transfer, regular follow-up, and health support are also provided. Savings mobilization begins soon after the enterprises yield a return, to build up resources for subsequent non-subsidized cycle investments. Village elites are mobilized to provide social support and create an enabling environment for the extreme poor.

After two years of intensive grant-based support, the members of the CFPR/TUP programme form their own microfinance groups and are offered access to credit. As of December 2006, over 15,000 CFPR/TUP members had formed their own groups. BRAC had disbursed over US$500,000 to these members, and they had saved close to US$366,000.

Because of the intensive nature of the programme, BRAC's investment is relatively high, although the cost per beneficiary fell from US$434 for those who entered the programme in 2002 to US$256 for those who entered in 2005. BRAC hopes that the initial subsidy in this approach will reap benefits by allowing the extreme poor to build a more solid and comprehensive base from which to move ahead.

Recent impact assessments suggest positive results thus far. According to Rabbani et al. (2006), CFPR/TUP members have been able to diversify and accumulate assets beyond those transferred by BRAC. Compared with their position in 2002, they have greater access to land, reduced morbidity, improved participation in the financial market, improved social and legal awareness, and reduced vulnerability to crises such as chronic illness. Despite being worse off than their neighbours in 2002, they were found to be better off than them in 2005. The percentage of households living under the $US1/day threshold reduced from 89 per cent to 59 per cent. The net decline in extreme poverty was 30 per cent for the beneficiaries, while it was only 13 per cent for the non-selected ultra poor. The beneficiaries of the programme were able to diversify food items and increase their per capita energy intake, which was sustained well after the graduation period (Hassen and Sulaiman, 2007).

Several key research findings have refined BRAC's understanding of extreme poverty to effectively retune its intervention. The most important finding was that the ultra poor are not a homogeneous group. Differences in financial market participation as well as the comparatively slow progress of the non-selected ultra poor households have led BRAC to design different packages for different groups of ultra poor, with varying levels of transfer and intensity of supervision in the second phase of the programme.

This case study was adapted from Matin (2005) Abed and Matin (2007) and Matin et al. (2008).

Recommended Reading

- CGAP – Ford Foundation Graduation Program at: www.cgap.org/graduation
- Collins, D., Morduch, J., Rutherford, S.; Rothven, O. 2009. *Portfolios of the poor: How the world's poor live on $2 a day* (Princeton, NJ, Princeton University Press).
- Hashemi, S; Rosenberg, R. 2006. *Graduating the poorest into microfinance: Linking safety nets and financial services*, Focus Note No. 34 (Washington, DC, CGAP), at: http://www.cgap.org/gm/document-1.9.2586/FN34.pdf
- Hickson, R. 1999. *Reaching extreme poverty: Financial services for very poor people*, Office for Development Studies, UN Development Programme (New York, NY, UNDP), at: http://www.microfinancegateway.org/gm/document-1.9.26895/2853_file_02853.pdf

- Huda, K.; Simanowitz, A. 2009. "A graduation pathway for Haiti's poorest: Lessons learnt from Fonkoze", in *Enterprise Development and Microfinance*, Vol. 20, No. 2, pp. 86–106 (Rugby, Practical Action Publishing), at: http://www.ingentaconnect.com/content/itpub/edm/2009/00000020/00000002/art00003

- Maes, J.; Foose, L.; Hishigsuren, G. 2006. *Microfinance and non-financial services for very poor people: Digging deeper to find keys to success*, SEEP Technical Note (New York, NY, SEEP, Poverty Outreach Working Group), at: http://communities.seepnetwork.org/edexchange/system/files/POWG+Microfinance+and+Non-Financial+Services.pdf

- Matin, I.; Sulaiman, M.; Rabbani, M. 2008. *Crafting a graduation pathway for the ultra poor: Lessons and evidence from a BRAC programme*, CPRC Working Paper No. 109, BRAC Research and Evaluation Division (Manchester, The Chronic Poverty Research Centre (CPRC)), at: http://www.microfinancegateway.org/gm/document-1.9.29364/16.pdf

- Narayan, D; Petesch, P. (eds.). 2007. *Moving out of poverty, Volume 1, Cross-disciplinary perspectives on mobility* (Basingstoke, Palgrave Macmillan and Washington, DC, World Bank), at: http://siteresources.worldbank.org/INTMOVOUTPOV/Resources/9780821369913.pdf

- Simanowitz, A. with Walter, A., 2002. "Ensuring impact: Reaching the poorest while building financially self-sufficient institutions, and showing improvements in the lives of poor women and their families", in Daley-Harris, S. (ed.): *Pathways out of poverty: Innovations in microfinance for the poorest families* (West Hartford, CT, Kumarian Press).

16 Microfinance for Youth[35]

Scepticism exists regarding the viability of youth-related microfinance programs. However, evidence is now emerging to show that youth clients are bankable and that creativity of approach, differing only slightly from adult-focused microfinance, is required.
~ Nagarajan (2005)

Almost 90 per cent of the world's youth live in developing economies.[36] Compared with adults, they are almost three times as likely to be unemployed. In fact, youth between the ages of 15 and 24 make up 40.2 per cent of the world's unemployed, even though they constitute just 24.7 per cent of the total working-age population. Many of the youth that are employed are employed in the informal sector, working long hours in substandard conditions and earning low wages. It is estimated that one in four youth are working but living in extreme poverty at the US$1.25/day level (International Labour Office, 2010b).

Access to financial services could help youth become economically active, start their own enterprises, finance education, and manage risks. Nevertheless, few microfinance programmes actively target youth. More often, they actually avoid having youth in their loan portfolio. This chapter briefly explores why MFIs are not reaching out to youth, and then shares the experiences of those institutions that have found ways to serve youth effectively. The outline of the chapter is as follows:

1. Should MFIs target youth?
2. Characteristics of youth
3. How can microfinance meet the needs of youth?
4. Designing a portfolio of products for youth
5. Overcoming the challenges of serving youth

16.1 Should MFIs Target Youth?

Although MFIs may state that young people are eligible to access their services, their coverage of youth is generally quite low. There are several reasons for this:

- **Risk.** Youth are considered to be high risk-takers. They usually cannot provide collateral, have limited business and life experience, might have unrealistic expectations about markets and profits, and lack a track record or credit history. Also, young people tend to be more mobile than adults, which makes them harder for MFIs to monitor.
- **Costs.** As entry-level clients, youth are likely to make very small deposits and borrow small amounts for short terms. The full cost of providing these services is unlikely to be covered by the immediate revenue generated. Furthermore, youth are likely to need

35 This chapter was adapted from Nagarajan (2005) and Making Cents International (2009).

36 Youth are defined by a range of age groups. While the United Nations (UN) and the World Bank consider the population between 15 and 24 years as youth, the Commonwealth Secretariat uses the range 15 to 29. Some national governments consider those up to age 35 years as youth. For the purposes of this chapter, youth can be generally defined as potential microfinance clients who are underserved because of their young age.

non-financial services to support their use of financial services, and this could add cost and complexity to an MFI's operations.

- **Staff resistance.** According to Making Cents International's Global Youth-inclusive Financial Services Survey of September 2009, the most common challenge to providing youth-inclusive financial services is staff members' negative perception of youth. Forty-five per cent of financial service providers indicated that their staff consider youth to be irresponsible, unable to manage money, and risky due to a lack of collateral (Making Cents International, 2010a).
- **Public opposition.** The idea of microfinance for youth is sometimes opposed on the grounds that it may facilitate child labour; that working may divert young people's attention from schooling; that it may curtail their physical and psychological development; or that young, lower-paid workers may "steal" jobs from adults.
- **Legal issues.** In many countries, youth under the age of 18 cannot legally hold a bank account or enter into a legally binding contract.

Despite these challenges, there are two important reasons why MFIs may want to serve youth. First, young people may become profitable clients over time, and may be very loyal to the institution that supported them when they were first starting out. Youth with entrepreneurial spirit, who are willing to take risks and experiment with new ideas, have great potential for growth. They may also draw others from their social networks into a relationship with the MFI. This has been the experience of Proyecto FCF-WOCCU, a technical assistance project to support credit unions in Ecuador, which has noted that young accountholders have brought family members as well as other youth into participating credit unions as new customers (Meyer et al., 2008).

Microfinance institutions might also want to target youth to fulfil their social mission. Most youth have limited educational opportunities, and even those who do have access to education are often not taught skills that the labour market needs. Some find work in unskilled, low-end jobs and become trapped there because the job offers them no opportunity to gain new skills. Those who cannot find work may become a burden to families and fall at risk of being sold or traded to human traffickers. Unemployed youth are also more susceptible to recruitment by gangs, drug dealers, rebels, warlords and militia. By providing youth with access to financial services, MFIs can create additional opportunities for youth to gain skills, accumulate assets, become economically active, and engage productively within their communities. This benefits youth as well as society at large.

16.2 Characteristics of Youth

As a target group, young people have a number of characteristics that set them apart from other customer groups an MFI might serve (see Box 16.1). Within this group, however, members are not homogeneous. Life-cycle changes occur rapidly during youth, so the needs of 15–17 year olds can differ significantly from those of 22–24 year olds. Young women have different needs than young men due to the different roles and responsibilities that society tries to prepare them for, and the differing constraints that society imposes upon them. Even

Box 16.1 General Characteristics of the Youth Target Market

- Eager to learn
- Open-minded; willing to try new things
- Energetic
- Optimistic
- High potential for growth
- Limited work experience; limited or no track record of running a business
- Limited life experience, perhaps resulting in unrealistic expectations about the future
- Limited social and professional network
- Little or no opportunity to accumulate capital or assets to date
- Unstable or mobile living conditions
- Potentially unable to enter into a legal contract with an MFI because of their age

Source: Authors.

youth of the same age and gender can have varying needs and priorities depending on where they live, how much education and work experience they have had, and whether they have a family of their own.

Although youth are often stereotyped as a risky market segment, this is not necessarily the case. Certainly, some of the characteristics listed in Box 16.1 present risks, but many of these risks were also attributed to poor people and women some 30 years ago and have since been overcome by MFIs using a variety of delivery methodologies. The experiences of MFIs such as Hatton National Bank in Sri Lanka, Fundación Paraguaya in Paraguay and Al Amal Microfinance Bank (AMB) in Yemen illustrate that young people will not necessarily engage in risky behaviour simply because they are youth. AMB obtained 100 per cent prepayment on its first round of loans to youth, including the loans it made to start-ups (Hamed, 2010). In Indonesia, a study of 21 MFIs serving youth in five different regions of the country found that youth borrowers have higher repayment rates than average in 85 per cent of the institutions surveyed, and generally receive loans that are equal to or larger than the average loan size for all borrowers (Shrader et al., 2006).

Nevertheless, the fact that youth have limited life, work and business experience does mean that they will have to make decisions without a deep foundation of lessons learned to guide them. They will also have to try new things, and any new initiative runs a higher risk of failure than investments made within a zone of competence. Thus MFIs that want to work with youth need to find ways of helping youth manage these risks.

16.3 How Can Microfinance Meet the Needs of Youth?

Microfinance can support youth in four main ways: 1) by helping to finance education; 2) by facilitating self-employment; 3) by encouraging asset accumulation; and 4) by providing tools for managing risk.

Financing for Education and Training

In decisions related to the education and training of youth, costs usually play a major role – both direct costs in the form of fees, books and living expenses and opportunity costs in the form of forgone earnings. Youth from poorer and more disadvantaged segments of society often find it difficult to complete their basic education or pursue apprenticeship, technical training or university opportunities, because they lack the necessary financial support from their families or guardians. Financial services, tailored to the needs of this target group, can enable young people to access education and training opportunities that improve their chances of finding decent wage employment or succeeding at self-employment. The products MFIs might offer to facilitate education and training include savings, loans for school or apprenticeship fees, and financial literacy training.

Facilitating Self-employment

Self-employment is an important employment alternative for youth with entrepreneurial spirit. In an ILO study on apprenticeship financing in Ghana, for example, 77 per cent of apprentices had ambitions to start their own enterprise, either immediately or shortly after the training (Breyer, 2006a). One of their main concerns, however, was the lack of capital. Access to enterprise start-up loans, leases for productive assets, and innovative savings products such as the one described in Box 16.2 can facilitate youth's transition into self-employment. Youth that already operate their own business may have a need for microfinance products as well, including savings, insurance, payment services and working capital loans.

Box 16.2 Targeted Youth Accounts: "Youth with Opportunities" in Mexico

In 2003, Jóvenes con Oportunidades (Youth with Opportunities) was added to Mexico's Oportunidades conditional cash transfer programme (see Box 13.8 in the chapter on grants) as an additional benefit for participating families. The programme consists of savings accounts for Oportunidades youth to incentivize continued education. An account is opened in a child's last year of Secondaria (which is typically completed at the age of 14), and "points" are deposited in the account for each year of Educación Media Superior (EMS) the student successfully completes. Upon graduation from EMS, typically at age 18, the points are converted into approximately US$336 cash, which youth can then withdraw or leave in their savings account at BANSEFI, the programme's affiliated financial institution. Students are able to use their savings account as soon as it is opened to make or withdraw deposits, but the cash payout associated with accumulating points is not available until the account holder graduates. Since its inception, more than 330,000 youth have opened savings accounts with the Jóvenes programme. Although the programme was designed to incentivize continued education, the payout upon graduation could be used for any number of purposes, including start-up of a microenterprise.

Source: Zimmerman and Moury, 2009.

Encouraging Asset Accumulation

Youth learn by doing. If MFIs can provide saving, leasing or credit opportunities that enable young people to acquire assets, the experience can generate a number of benefits. The simple act of setting a financial goal and achieving it can build self-confidence among youth, and increase the likelihood of future goal-setting. Youth can use their asset base to generate income, and their status in their household and/or society may improve as a result. With improved status and confidence, youth may engage more in their community. They may also become more self-reliant, future oriented (since assets open up opportunities) and risk averse (since they now have something to lose) (Youth Save Consortium, 2010). Even if youth choose to consume the first lump sum they accumulate, early success with asset-building can convince them of the power of proactive financial management, and develop habits and attitudes that they can apply more productively in the future.

Managing Risk

MFIs can offer youth products and services that help them manage risk regardless of whether they are employed. Savings and emergency loans can help young people cope with unexpected events that temporarily decrease income or increase expenses. Networks, mentors, training and technical assistance can support self-employed youth during the start-up phase of their business when the risk of failure is greatest. Insurance can protect the health of youth as well as the assets that can give them an early start at climbing out of poverty. Indirectly, clauses in adult clients' loan and commitment savings contracts that name youth as the beneficiaries of an insurance policy can provide youth with a safety net in the event of a guardian's death.

16.4 Designing a Portfolio of Products for Youth

Although youth may need a very similar set of financial products as adults, those products may need to be adapted to the special characteristics and needs of this target group. The nature of an appropriate product mix for youth is discussed below.

Savings Services

Experience to date has shown that savings products are important for youth, often more important than credit. They help young people accumulate assets for the future, and create a cushion that they can fall back on in the event of an emergency or crisis. Savings are also the preferred mechanism for financing expected expenses such as education and training.

MFIs can design savings products to support youth both directly and indirectly. Indirectly, they can provide their adult clients with products that enable them to save up resources to cover school fees, apprenticeship costs and living expenses for the education and training of their children. If parents have a specific target in mind (for example, the start of an apprenticeship in three years), a contractual savings product can help them accumulate a specific amount of money in a specific period of time (see Chapter 4). As mentioned above, contractual saving accounts can also include an insurance component to make sure that the child for whom the parent is saving gets the target amount even if the parent dies or is prevented from work through illness or disability.

Alternatively, MFIs can offer savings services to youth directly. Institutions such as XacBank in Mongolia offer special demand and time deposit accounts to girls between the ages of 14 and 18 that allow them to manage their savings independently. The Children's Development Bank in India and *SafeSave* in Bangladesh provide daily deposit services to youth living on the street and in slums, which enables them to safely set aside very small amounts of money that can eventually become usefully large sums.

MFIs that cannot legally mobilize deposits can seek partnerships with a regulated institution to make savings services available to youth. Zakoura Foundation in Morocco entered into this type of partnership with La Poste Bank, and found that more youth opened savings accounts than applied for credit. In Bangladesh, Population Council is now linking with local commercial banks to experiment with mobile banking to collect daily deposits from young migrant girls employed in garment factories.

The success of such partnerships depends on many factors (see Chapter 22), but in particular, the terms of the saving product being offered to youth must match their needs and resources. Opening balance or minimum deposit requirements that are too high will prevent most youth from being able to use the product. Since commercial banks may be quite interested in partnering with MFIs to recruit youth, MFIs can leverage that interest to negotiate more favourable terms for youth. Partnering with multiple banks might yield more benefits than partnering with one, since competition between institutions can result in a more attractive product offering for youth over time.

In areas where regulated financial institutions do not operate, youth have been able to access deposit services through informal savings groups, such as those being promoted by Save the Children US and PLAN International in Sub-Saharan Africa (see Box 16.3).

As with other market segments, MFIs that want to provide savings services to youth must build a relationship with young people that motivates them to save with their institution. They must build confidence in their ability to protect the savings they receive, but also, since most youth are first-time customers, MFIs have to make a special effort to communicate the benefits of saving and build youth's confidence in their own ability to save. Some MFIs, such as K-Rep Bank and Faulu Kenya, provide incentives to encourage regular savings habits, such as bi-annual awards for the most frequent depositor in each group of youth, and interest payments to motivate higher account balances (Austrian and Ngurukie, 2009). The recruitment of young savers is not necessarily easy, and is discussed further in Section 16.5.

Loan and Leasing Products

Youth can benefit from loans for education, enterprise start-up and working capital. For MFIs, educational loans can be among the most difficult, since investments in education usually take a long time to produce real financial returns and, as a result, they typically require very long grace and repayment periods. Most commercial banks that offer education loans extend the repayment period beyond graduation. In Bolivia, educational loans from EDUCA-PRO, a programme financed by the second-tier lender FUNDA-PRO, have terms as long as ten years (EDUCA-PRO, 2010). Such extensive loan periods increase the risk as well as the cost of lending. Most MFIs find it difficult to make these loans, since the bulk of their own financing is of a shorter-term nature.

Box 16.3 Village Savings and Loan Groups for Youth

Save the Children US, with support from the Nike Foundation, is creating Village Savings and Loan (VS&L) groups for young people in Malawi. In the VS&L model, groups begin with savings, and members are responsible for bringing a small amount of savings each time they meet. Members purchase passbooks from Save the Children staff and learn how to record transactions in their passbooks. Between meetings, a treasurer keeps the savings in a locked box, with three keys held by the three VS&L administrators. After a specified number of weeks, usually at the fifth or sixth meeting, members begin lending to each other from their savings. Prior to lending, they establish loan criteria, including the term (usually one month), the interest rate, late payment penalties, and so on. The interest collected on loans is distributed periodically to members as dividends on their savings, proportional to the amount saved.

When a Save the Children US baseline survey in Malawi identified high demand for VS&L groups among youth, particularly adolescent girls, Save decided to try this model with young people already engaged in livelihood activities. These girls were at risk from early marriage, pregnancy, and sexual and physical abuse, and Save felt that a VS&L programme might help mitigate some of these risks. Although one option was to integrate youth into the adult programme, market research with youth showed they preferred their own groups, and Save agreed to help them start youth groups.

The programme involving rural youth, both boys and girls ages 15 to 20, began in 2007. The methodology is the same as the adult model. Save the Children US provides technical assistance in bookkeeping, business management, leadership and group dynamics, with an initial intense period of training that gradually decreases. At the end of one year, groups are supposed to be able to function independently. By September 2008, some 236 girls and boys were saving approximately US$0.20 per week in VS&L groups, making decisions about lending their money, following up on loans made, and distributing their earnings. A year later, a similar pilot by PLAN International had mobilized nearly 4,000 youth in Senegal, Sierra Leone and Niger.

In areas without access to financial institutions, VS&L groups make an interesting model for providing youth with financial skills, savings, and small loans. In areas with financial institutions, the VS&L model can help give youth financial skills and provide them with collateral in the form of savings as well as a credit history with which to approach financial institutions in the future.

Source: Making Cents International, 2009, and Schiller, 2009.

Microfinance institutions have successfully offered school fee and apprenticeship loans, however, that provide parents or students with the liquidity necessary to make a lump sum payment at the beginning of a school year or apprenticeship period, which is then financed over some period of time. These loan products can be scheduled over shorter periods without a grace period, because they are repaid from existing sources of household income. They are much less risky than a multi-year education loan, but they may not be accessible to disadvantaged youth without the intervention of a programme such as the one being offered by Sinapi Aba Trust in Ghana (see Box 16.4).

Box 16.4 Apprenticeship Financing in Ghana

A survey by the International Labour Organization (ILO) on the financing of informal apprenticeships in Accra, Ghana, showed that the average amount of fees charged for a training of two to six years is US$160, a large part of which must be paid up front. During the training, apprentices receive allowances (in cash and in kind), which support them in financing meals and other daily needs. Nevertheless, the majority of apprentices depend on their family to pay the apprenticeship fees and to offset their living expenses. Vulnerable youth, such as street children or former child labourers, and those whose families do not generate enough income to pay these fees, do not have access to apprenticeship opportunities and find it difficult to get started on the climb out of poverty.

Sinapi Aba Trust, a microfinance NGO operating in Ghana since 1994, recognized the financial challenge of access to apprenticeships. It therefore developed a Youth Apprenticeship Programme (YAP) which links vulnerable youth with master craftsmen, provides them with basic equipment and pays the apprenticeship fees, which may include an examination fee for nationally accredited qualification. Newly qualified apprentices become eligible for start-up loans from Sinapi Aba Trust to finance their own enterprise. The aim is to provide disadvantaged youth with relevant employment skills and eventually graduate them into Sinapi Aba's microfinance client base. More than 1,000 young people have taken part in the programme since it started in 2004. Going forward, the goal is to train 400–450 youth each year.

Source: Adapted from Breyer, 2006, and Opportunity International, 2010.

Business loans to youth are fairly straightforward, and MFIs have been able to reach young entrepreneurs with this kind of product using a variety of methodologies, and with very few modifications to their standard terms and conditions (see Table 16.1). What institutions have adapted, however, is the package of support services they offer young clients alongside credit (refer to the discussion on non-financial services below).

Experience suggests that both group and individual loan products can be appropriate for youth. For example, the Tap and Reposition Youth (TRY) project, supported by K-Rep in Kenya, successfully uses Grameen-type group lending to serve youth aged 16–24 years in Nairobi slums, while Umsobomvu Youth Fund in South Africa is partnering with the Savings and Credit Cooperative League to provide financial services to young entrepreneurs participating in youth cooperatives. *SafeSave* in Bangladesh and Children's Development Bank in India offer individual loans to youth over the age of 16 with good repayment records.

Group loans have the advantage of supplying an alternative to physical collateral. In addition, the group lending approach creates a forum for discussion, peer exchange and the delivery of non-financial services. Individual loans, on the other hand, provide greater flexibility and make it easier for an MFI to adjust to the frequent life-cycle changes and specific demands of youth. Educational loans, for example, tend to be individual loan products.

In the absence of a group guarantee, MFIs have found personal guarantors and guarantee funds to provide effective alternatives to physical collateral. Some MFIs, such as Partner Microcredit in Bosnia and Herzegovina, require a personal, non-family guarantor, whereas other MFIs, such as Fundación Paraguaya and Zakoura, allow parents to be the guarantor. Youth Charitable Organization (YCO) in India was able to secure financing from domestic

Table 16.1 How MFIs have adapted their loan products for youth

Organization	Adaptation of support services	Adaptation of financial products
BRAC	Provides youth with a clubhouse, life-skills training, livelihoods training, financial education	No group collateral for the adolescent group; all other conditions are the same
Fùndación Paraguaya	Adaptation of training package to youth	Parents are co-debtors; all other conditions are the same
Pro Mujer Bolivia	Had to adapt business development services to be youth-oriented and added health and self-esteem programmes	Same terms and conditions as adult financial products except that the guarantee falls strictly within the youth solidarity group rather than the entire adult communal bank
Zakoura	Created a six-week training programme for youth covering entrepreneurial skills, financial education and business development services	For youth, the group may be as small as three members (the usual group size is five). Parents may be the guarantors (these are the only loans where family members are allowed to guarantee another family member's loan)

Source: Making Cents International, 2009.

commercial banks with the help of a credit guarantee provided by Homeless International Guarantee Fund in the UK. In Central America, the Katalysis Network is launching its own loan guarantee fund for members (see Box 16.5).

MFIs have also found other ways to manage risk when lending to youth. XacBank, for example, reserves its education loans for students in their second year of higher education who already have some record of attendance. Vittana in India lends only to children of existing cli-

Box 16.5 Loan Guarantees Facilitate Lending to Youth

The Katalysis Network in Central America is launching a loan guarantee fund to stimulate its member institutions to lend to youth under 30 years of age. Instead of using a bank partner, the Network, which provides technical assistance to its MFI members, will manage the fund itself. The Youth Guarantee Fund was established with US$75,000 of loan capital from three foundations (Peery Foundation, Cordes Foundation, and Fundacion Covelho of Honduras), with each foundation providing a third in long-term, zero-interest loans. To participate in the Fund, an MFI network member must meet the Network's certified training standards. Once certified, the terms of the guarantee are that 50 per cent of defaulted loans will be reimbursed by the Network if the appropriate loan recovery steps have been followed.

Source: Making Cents International, 2009.

ents (Economist, 2010). Al Amal in Yemen will lend to start-ups, but requires a business plan and looks at entrepreneurship training as a collateral substitute (Hamed, 2010).

Asset-backed loans and leases could help youth acquire a productive asset without initial collateral. Barbados Youth Business Trust, for example, allows youth to use the equipment purchased with a loan as collateral. Although MFIs have experimented with leasing products (see Chapter 10), few if any have done so to meet the particular needs of youth.

With respect to loan size, term and price, loans to youth should be designed according to the same good practice principles that MFIs follow for adults (see Chapter 6). Although MFIs are often tempted to charge below-market rates on their loans to youth, despite the higher expenses that these loans can generate, doing so can create two serious problems. First, the sustainability of the services offered to youth will be called into question if they cannot cover their costs. Second, young clients may come under pressure from adult family members who want youth to borrow on their behalf so that they can access lower-priced financing. If this happens, youth will be left responsible for servicing an adult's debt without having control over how the loan is spent. Pricing loans to youth at or above the level charged to adults will discourage this kind of behaviour.

MFIs often give very small initial loans to first-time clients, including youth, to minimize the risk inherent in lending to someone with no documented credit history. This approach can be effective with working capital loans, but not with enterprise start-up loans. Start-up loans to youth need to be large enough to cover the financial needs of the enterprise as outlined in the business plan, or underfunding can lead to business failure. Since returns on investment in enterprise start-ups usually do not accrue immediately, start-up loans might also require an initial grace period and an extended repayment term.

Insurance and Money Transfers

Although savings and credit appear to be the financial products most demanded by youth, insurance and money transfer services could have their palace in a portfolio of products for youth as well. Young entrepreneurs are likely to be confronted with higher risks compared with more experienced entrepreneurs. For example, young construction workers may be more likely to injure themselves or damage the property they are working on due to lack of experience. Youth may want to purchase enterprise risk insurance to protect themselves against accidents, asset damage and liability. As mentioned previously, they may also wish to safeguard their health through the purchase of health insurance. Since many youth are part of the migrant work force, and since youth in general are a more mobile segment, money transfer services can be important.

Non-financial Services

What most distinguishes the product portfolio offered to youth is not the selection of financial services, but rather the non-financial support services that accompany whatever financial services an MFI might choose to offer. There are four types of non-financial services that have been particularly important in meeting the needs of youth to date: financial education, business development services, mentoring, and the creation of safe spaces.

Financial education. Adolescence is a time when young people shift from economic dependence to economic independence, and learning how to manage money is a critical part of that transition. In the words of the Global Financial Education Program (2009), "The more young people know about money – good ways to earn it, how to spend it wisely, and how to save it – the more power and control they will have over their lives."

Financial education helps youth develop the skills to manage day-to-day expenses, set financial goals and design strategies for achieving them. It can also help youth to become more aware of their personal financial choices, introduce them to the various financial services that are available to them, and help them understand how they might be able to benefit from using them. As Women's World Banking (WWB) and XacBank learned during the piloting of XacBank's "Aspire" product, youth need to understand the "why" and "how" of saving before they will open accounts (Banthia and Shell, 2009). In this respect, financial education is a key factor in the success of any financial product for youth.

Business development services. Although the potential scope of business development services is wide (see Chapter 12), MFIs serving youth have used primarily training and technical assistance to help youth:

- understand where gaps exist in the market (so they avoid simple replication of what they have seen others already doing);
- transfer knowledge and skills associated with a particular trade;
- test the viability of a business idea;
- develop a business plan;
- strengthen their ability to run a business (follow-up support after the start-up phase has proved crucial);
- develop non-technical skills such as time management, professionalism, communication, and punctuality.

Box 16.6 provides a few examples of business development services that have supported access to finance for youth.

Mentoring. Mentors give youth access to experience and perspective that they have not yet had an opportunity to acquire. As role models, mentors can help youth learn business and financial skills, navigate legal and bureaucratic procedures such as licensing, taxes and permits, and gain greater self-confidence for taking on more responsibility. They can also assist youth in troubleshooting as they encounter challenges along the way. In general, mentorship opportunities are highly appreciated by youth. In a 2003 survey conducted by the Barbados Youth Business Trust, for example, 100 per cent of the young entrepreneurs interviewed thought they would not have done so well in business without the input of their mentors (Barbados Youth Business Trust, 2007).

"Natural" mentors from the immediate community (for example, family members or teachers) may be most effective, but mentors can also be recruited from the "outside" as long as there are rigorous reference and community checks. At K-Rep Bank and Faulu Kenya, groups of 10–15 girls between the ages of 10 and 18 select their own mentor, who must be a young woman above the age of 18 from the community (Austrian and Ngurukie, 2009). Motivated and committed mentors will often volunteer their time, but institutions may want to provide

Box 16.6 Business Development Services Improve Access to Finance

In Mongolia, Mercy Corps provided training and technical assistance in business plan preparation to rural youth between the ages of 20 and 30 who had limited collateral for a loan. This assisted youth in understanding how large a loan they could and should ask for. Fifty-four per cent of those who received training were able use their plans to obtain a bank loan (Making Cents International, 2009).

In Egypt and Morocco, MEDA's YouthInvest Programme brings financial and non-financial service providers together to supply youth between the ages of 15 and 24 with an integrated package of support that includes savings services, training in life skills, financial skills and entrepreneurship, access to start-up loans and internships. A survey of participants after the Programme's first year indicated that 96 per cent now have savings accounts (vs. 19 per cent before entering the programme) and 11 per cent have accessed loans (MEDA, 2010).

At Pro Mujer Bolivia, adult clients receive no more than two hours of pre-credit training in order to fill out their loan application, while youth receive a one-week pre-credit training that begins by helping young clients to develop a business concept, followed by an in-depth cost analysis with cash flow projections. Youth are also required to participate in a one-day business practicum where they work in teams to operate a business applying sales and marketing techniques (Storm-Swire, 2009).

In India, BASIX Academy for Building Lifelong Employability Ltd (B-ABLE) is establishing vocational training centres that support youth with education, real-time connections between job providers and job seekers and, in collaboration with its parent company BASICS Limited, student and enterprise loans. It collaborates with government and employers in targeted industries to identify relevant training courses that build technical, commercial and life skills (B-ABLE, 2010).

them with stipends to cover their travel costs. Occasionally, MFIs find it a challenge to motivate appropriate persons to become mentors. Partner Microcredit in Bosnia and Herzegovina solved this problem by identifying employees who fit its desired profile and then training them to be mentors.

Safe spaces and supportive social networks. Safe spaces that are enclosed, private, and out of public sight can be critical for empowering youth, especially girls, since young people feel more comfortable expressing their thoughts, concerns and hopes within them. The spaces can facilitate the sharing of ideas, mutual support, and the development of social skills and confidence. They can provide leadership opportunities for older youth to mentor younger youth, and can be used by MFIs to deliver both financial and non-financial services. Ideally, adults are not found in the safe spaces most of the time, except for those who are associated with the organization that is offering the safe spaces. Safe spaces are an integral part of the youth financial services programmes being promoted by the Population Council in Kenya and at BRAC in Bangladesh (refer to the case study at the end of this chapter for more details).

As discussed in Chapter 12, MFIs do not have to offer non-financial services themselves, as doing so requires additional expertise and generates additional costs. Instead, they can partner with other organizations to make these services available to young clients. If an MFI believes that the delivery of non-financial services is an integral part of its mission, or if it cannot find

service providers within its area of operations with which to partner, it may prefer to offer both financial and non-financial services itself. This approach has the advantage of enabling the MFI to build a close relationship with its young clients, which can facilitate credit screening and monitoring later on. It does, however, require personnel with expertise in both microfinance and business development or education, and such staff can be difficult to find and retain. One possible solution to this challenge is to have different units or departments of a single institution provide the financial and non-financial services using a parallel approach.

Grants

Grants have been used to facilitate youth's access to financial services in two main ways. First, organizations such as Camfed Zambia use grants as seed money to help young women gain experience and skills in running a business before being burdened by debt. Those who manage their initial grant successfully and can demonstrate the capacity of their business to grow can apply for loans to expand their businesses. As described in Box 16.4, Sinapi Aba Trust takes a similar approach, providing in-kind grants that enable youth to gain experience and skills as apprentices before accessing financial services.

Grants have also been used to assist disadvantaged youth in meeting basic needs that might otherwise consume funds provided through a working capital loan. The Youth Development Foundation (YDF) in Ghana actually experimented with two different types of youth enterprise loan, those with and without a grant component, and it found that loan repayment increased considerably once a grant component was added. According to Nelson Agyemang, founder of YDF, the grant enabled youth to invest their loan fully in productive activities, thus generating more income and making it more feasible to make loan payments (Breyer, 2006b).

16.5 Overcoming the Challenges of Serving Youth

At the beginning of this chapter, it was mentioned that legal constraints, public opposition, higher costs and higher risk make the delivery of youth financial services difficult. The strategies MFIs are using to overcome these challenges are discussed in this section. There is a fifth challenge that MFIs have had to meet in order to serve youth, which is also discussed below, and that is marketing. Although this last challenge is not unique to the youth market segment, the strategies that MFIs have found effective thus far in reaching youth are somewhat unique, and merit a brief exploration.

Legal Constraints

In Paraguay, where the law prohibits youth below the age of 18 from entering into legally binding contracts, Fundación Paraguaya has asked parents to co-sign their child's loan. This not only guarantees the loan but also indicates parental support for the young person's use of the loan. In Kenya, which does not allow youth under the age of 18 to make withdrawals, K-Rep Bank is piloting a product that allows girls to make deposits on their own and to make withdrawals when accompanied by the group's mentor, who serves as a proxy for the guardian figure. Even an NGO might serve as a joint signatory with youth (Hirschland, 2009).

Some MFIs have chosen to offer only youth savings accounts that restrict withdrawals until the age of 18. Such accounts can satisfy legal requirements while also preventing caretakers from misusing the savings of a young person for whom they co-sign. However, to ensure that these accounts generate real value for youth over the long term, MFIs may need to partner with an insurance or asset management company in the design of their product (see Chapter 5). Depending on the nature of legislation in a particular country, community-based microfinance organizations may be able to provide both savings and credit to youth, since they do not extend services on the basis of a legal contract.

Public Opposition

MFIs that want to work with youth may face opposition not only from politicians and child advocates, but also from community leaders, parents and even their own staff. Before attempting to deliver financial services to youth, it is important to work with community members, parents, staff and youth themselves to develop an understanding of the benefits of financial service access for youth, and to generate support for the MFI's outreach to young people. When BRAC first started working with adolescent girls in Bangladesh, it took several years to convince community members, parents and girls themselves of the power of financial independence and the positive effects it can have on a girl's life. In Malawi, Save the Children US has faced less resistance, but it still begins its outreach to youth by speaking with local tribal leaders, district authorities and community members during a three-week preparatory phase that precedes the establishment of any youth village savings and loan groups.

Most MFIs serving youth have had to overcome some degree of internal and/or external opposition to the idea of reaching out to this market segment. Some of the strategies they have identified for minimizing or neutralizing this opposition are described below.

1. **Involve the community in the development and implementation of financial services for youth.** This informs the quality of product design while helping to ensure the community's support for the services that are ultimately delivered. It can also help engage members of the community as leaders or mentors to youth. Such is the case with Camfed Zambia, which involves local and regional authorities, tribal leaders, head teachers and local businesswomen in the initial screening of applicants. These people then provide mentoring for the young women who enter the programme.
2. **Invest in establishing and maintaining a positive image in the community.** Community perceptions, whether true or untrue, will directly impact on the success or rejection of an MFI's outreach to youth. The community must trust that an MFI will influence its youth's development positively and not contribute to their exploitation or disempowerment. To build this trust, an MFI must proactively address the way it is perceived at the community level, which is likely to mean that public relations and direct marketing will need to become more important components of its overall marketing communications mix (see Chapter 23).
3. **Start with a small pilot to test the effectiveness and feasibility of any product or program for youth**. As discussed in Chapters 2 and 3, this is an important strategy for managing the risks inherent in new product and market development. It is also a useful strategy for encouraging MFI staff and members of the public to change their attitude about the provision of financial services to youth (see Box 16.7)

Box 16.7 Using Market Research and Pilot Testing to Challenge Assumptions

Before designing their financial products for youth, Zakoura Foundation staff doubted that youth had any money of their own. During the project design phase, however, market research conducted with Save the Children dispelled this stereotype, because it showed that youth did have money. The research simultaneously dispelled a second stereotype, or assumption, which was that youth wanted loans. An evaluation of the pilot held in mid-2008 found that youth could save and indeed wanted to save, but only 3 per cent of the 90 youth who completed the training phase of the programme took loans.

Staff at Pro Mujer Bolivia were also sceptical about young people's ability to manage money. In initial meetings to discuss the development of a youth-specific loan product, staff felt that youth were irresponsible and showed little interest in developing such a product. To move forward, the product development team had to identify new and existing staff with the proper profile to work with youth. It also had to provide training and incentives to all staff before rolling out the product. According to Pro Mujer, it was important to generate buy-in at all levels of the institution, not only by explaining the processes and procedures but also by taking the time to show staff concrete results from the pilot that proved the youth loan to be a viable product. The results of the pilot showed that youth clients were actually very punctual and organized, and loan officers who integrated youth clients into existing adult communal associations began to see their incentives increase as the youth clients promised higher client/loan officer ratios as well as a larger portfolio.

Source: Making Cents International, 2009.

4. **Find staff who have interest and experience with youth to pilot products for this market segment**; then provide training and sensitization for other staff based on results of the pilot before roll-out. As illustrated by the case of Pro Mujer in Box 16.7, staff that feel youth are irresponsible will show little interest in developing services for youth. One or more champions are needed who believe in youth and can lead the institution through the process of product development to demonstrate results that can be used to change staff stereotypes.
5. **Take preventive measures to avoid doing harm.** Often market research is conducted on the basis of the question "What will help?", but ignores the opposite question, "What might hurt?" Both questions are important in the context of youth financial services because of the physical, psychological and financial vulnerability of youth, particularly those who are very poor, marginalized or orphaned. MFIs must take care that their products and services do not increase that vulnerability.

   If young people lack business skills or have no long-term prospects to pay back a loan, if they do not clearly understand loan obligations or do not have the coping mechanisms to handle the pressure to repay, then giving them a loan can do more harm than good. Organizations should be especially careful when considering whether to offer credit products to younger girls because it may increase the girls' vulnerability to pressure, theft and/or false accusations about where or how they got the money. With savings products, MFIs can protect youth's deposits by restricting access to the funds, either for a specific purpose such as education or health care, or until youth accountholders are old enough to legally withdraw the funds without a co-signer's signature. One Ugandan programme experimented with a triple security number or pin, one each being held by the guardian, youth and youth service organization (Hirschland, 2009).

6. **Develop a clear code of conduct** that guides staff in their delivery of services to youth, and in the resolution of problems or conflicts (see Box 16.8). If youth or other community members believe processes are unfair, confusing or mismanaged, an MFI's credibility and ability to continue to work with youth and in the community could be severely damaged. A code of conduct can help avoid this if it is widely disseminated, clearly explained and carefully enforced. Clear procedures should outline how concerns regarding improper behaviour should be raised, and what staff should do if they are concerned that their actions or words may have been misunderstood.
7. **Work with youth to fill market gaps** rather than displace or replicate existing enterprises with youth-run enterprises. This is an area where business development services can play a critical role. At Zakoura, young entrepreneurs attended financial and market literacy training during which they mapped their market, identified gaps in product and service availability, and talked to business owners and clients to determine whether their business idea was viable before being eligible for a loan (Conklin et al., 2008).

Managing Risk

Although many of the risks inherent in serving youth are risks that MFIs are already experienced at managing (for example, the lack of collateral, business experience and credit history), the limited life experience possessed by youth and the tender state of their personal development does add additional layers of risk that must be managed if MFIs are to serve youth effectively. The strategies that have proven most effective in managing this risk are those that involve non-financial services, market research and youth-sensitive personnel. These and other strategies are briefly discussed below.

1. **Non-financial services.** MFIs serving youth typically integrate non-financial services into the delivery of their financial services, and sometimes incorporate a grant element as well, to help ensure that youth have sufficient knowledge, experience and support to make effective use of financial services the first time they access them. Often the integrated services are sequenced so that riskier financial services are not delivered until youth have demonstrated a certain degree of money and business management skill. At Camfed Zambia, for instance, young women receive a modest grant and access to mentors to help them start their business, and will progress to a loan only if their business idea succeeds and they demonstrate the ability to generate revenue to service a loan. This approach protects both the MFI and youth.
2. **Market research with segmentation.** MFIs should not assume that youth are the same as adults, or that all young people will have the same needs or priorities. Youth of varying ages and backgrounds will have varying levels of education and societal support, access to information, degrees of independence and aspirations for the future. As illustrated by the case presented in Box 16.9, market research can help an MFI understand better which youth need what kind of services, which group(s) of youth it is in the best position to serve, and how it might need to adapt its marketing and delivery strategy to the specific characteristics of the youth it decides to serve. MFIs that already serve some youth as part of their mainstream operations can begin by profiling the segment(s) they already serve.

Box 16.8 Developing a Code of Conduct

Codes of conduct help prevent abuse of trust, where one party is in a position of power or influence over the other by virtue of their work or the nature of their activity. By setting a clear benchmark for acceptable standards of conduct and care, a code of conduct can promote safe, positive and encouraging environments. It can minimize opportunities for abuse, and help to prevent unfounded allegations. In this way, codes of conduct help protect young people as well as employees and volunteers.

Listed below are a few examples of guidelines that could be included in a code of conduct:

- Treat everyone with respect, honesty and fairness (this includes staff, volunteers, young people and parents).
- Remember to be a positive role model to youth in all your conduct with them.
- Set clear boundaries about appropriate behaviour between yourself and the youth in your organization – boundaries help everyone to carry out their roles well.
- Always have another adult present or in sight when conducting one-to-one coaching.
- Raise any concerns about behaviour that may be harmful to youth as soon as possible.
- Record and act on serious complaints of abuse.
- Do not develop any "special" relationships with youth that could be seen as favouritism, such as the offering of gifts or special treatment.

Source: Adapted from Department for Families and Communities, 2007, and Child Wise, 2004.

3. **Clear communication with parents.** MFIs need to inform family members and guardians about the terms, processes and procedures associated with the financial service a young person is obtaining. In the case of loans, it is particularly important that parents understand that the loans are not for the parents' business, but rather for the young person's business, unless these are one and the same. When youth take out loans that go directly to their parents rather than to an independent activity, both arrears and desertion tend to increase.
4. **Youth-sensitive personnel.** MFIs entering the youth market have had to retrain their staff, acquire new staff with special expertise in working with youth, or both. An emerging consensus among those who have started youth-inclusive financial services programmes is that it is better to develop a new core of staff with different profiles for working with youth clients than to utilize existing staff who have experience only of working with adults. This may have the effect of raising costs, but it can also lower risk, since specialized staff are able to screen youth applicants more effectively, and establish stronger relationships with youth once they become clients (see Box 16.10). Specialized staff can also increase demand for the institution's services, both by helping to ensure that product design meets the needs of youth and by communicating more effectively what the MFI has to offer youth.
5. **Leasing.** By introducing a micro-leasing or asset-backed loan product, MFIs address the problem of youth's lack of collateral while simultaneously supporting youth in acquiring productive assets.

Box 16.9 Market Segmentation and Risk at Pro Mujer in Bolivia

Although Pro Mujer's market research analysed the potential for offering financial services to a new youth market, one key mistake was to disregard the young clients who were already being served by Pro Mujer through its traditional product offering. When initially considering the youth segment, staff distinguished these clients as young people who were living the lives of adults, namely women who had already married and started a family and therefore carried greater responsibilities in providing for their growing families. These young clients function seemingly well within Pro Mujer's regular product offering, but studying the differences between them and the new youth segment might have helped Pro Mujer to differentiate its product offering and improve its retention of new youth clients.

Since most young people are first-timers to the world of microenterprise, Pro Mujer decided to invest time and resources in providing its new youth clients with specialized training, including a business practicum, prior to disbursing loans. In addition, specially trained loan officers dedicated extra time to meet with young people, listen to them, and provide advice on any problems they might confront during the loan cycle.

While these efforts did pay off in some cases, arrears still rose higher than expected. Research showed the majority of youth clients to be transitory in nature, prone to experiment with different options, testing out Pro Mujer and then deciding to pursue further education or join the military. This was a more volatile group than what Pro Mujer was accustomed to working with, since the new youth clients were often looking for a loan to fill a gap rather than to invest in an ongoing, more long-term business. This made it very difficult for Pro Mujer to retain youth clients, and as a result, staff spent most of their time in search of new clients to replace the increasing number of deserting youth.

Research conducted after the pilot showed that the most successful youth entrepreneurs were those who did not have the opportunity to further their studies, but rather their situation required them to work full-time. This segment was identified within Pro Mujer's initial market study, but was overshadowed by young people coming from higher socioeconomic backgrounds whose greater opportunities made them less likely to stay with Pro Mujer longer than one or two loan cycles.

Source: Storm-Swire, 2009.

6. **Guarantee funds.** As mentioned previously, MFIs can access guarantee funds to secure loans that are made to young entrepreneurs, thereby reducing the degree of risk associated with the youth portfolio. The examples provided in Section 16.3 referred to non-governmental examples, but governments occasionally provide access to guarantee funds as well. The Government of Algeria has set up the Fond de Garantie Credits-Jeunes Promoteurs (FNSEJ), for example, which guarantees loans to young entrepreneurs at a 0.35 per cent fee on the outstanding loan amount.
7. **Partnerships.** Although partnerships can increase risk by decreasing an MFI's control over the quality of service delivered by a third party, they can also be designed to help reduce risk. In Uganda, for example, Equity Bank, with the assistance of Banyan Global, has negotiated with Mayanja Memorial Training Institute to offer education loans to its nursing students aged 17–24. In exchange, the Institute has agreed to hold the certificate of any student being financed by the bank until his or her loan is repaid. This reduces the potential for students to migrate without completing their payments. The Institute is also

> **Box 16.10 Hiring Staff that Understand Youth**
>
> An important reason for the success of the Seed Money Programme at Camfed Zambia is that it is implemented by young rural women who share a common background with the beneficiaries of the programme; they are all acutely aware of the problems facing the young rural women who apply for grants and loans, and have the empathy, experience and commitment needed to support them. Young women entering the programme identify with them, and look up to them as mentors and positive role models.
>
> *Source: Camfed International, 2008.*

talking with district health authorities to arrange job placements for graduating students at rural health centres. This is a valuable service for students to begin their professional career, and a security measure for the bank, since students will be able to complete their loan payments upon earning a salary (Chandani and Twamuhabwa, 2009).

Covering Costs

Since youth tend to make small deposits and borrow small amounts for short terms, it will be difficult for MFIs to cover the full cost of serving youth in the short term. This does not mean, however, that financial services cannot be provided to youth in a sustainable manner. At Hatton National Bank in Sri Lanka, nearly 65 per cent of the total microfinance portfolio consists of youth between the ages of 18 and 26, and the portfolio maintains a 97 per cent recovery rate. The bank has also mobilized US$20 million in savings deposits from rural youth (Abeywickrema, 2009). The integrated financial and non-financial service programmes implemented by the Commonwealth Secretariat in India and by Streetkids International in Zambia became operationally sustainable in three years (Nagarajan, 2004).

MFIs that are serving youth are attempting to cover their costs in eight main ways:

1. **Partnering with non-financial service providers.** MFIs often avoid the cost of providing necessary non-financial services by collaborating instead with social service NGOs, business development service providers, youth organizations or government-sponsored youth employment programmes to provide these services. An MFI may contract these services for all its clients, or simply refer clients who are in need of a service to an organization that provides it. In either case, partnership enables the MFI to concentrate on its core business of financial service provision, while facilitating access to complementary services for youth, probably at a higher quality and lower cost than the MFI could have delivered if it had developed the capability in house. Partnerships can also reduce an MFI's operating expenses, since the partner organization can recommend youth and even monitor and support their performance.
2. **Cross-subsidizing services to youth.** If an MFI's fixed costs can be covered by a sustainable basc of adult customers, then the marginal cost of serving a new young customer might be small enough to be affordable. Some MFIs use profits gained in other markets to subsidize the services provided to youth, in the hope that young clients will become profitable over time. For this strategy to be successful, however, MFIs need to identify subsegments of the youth population that are likely to remain with them over the years, as suggested in Box 16.9.

3. **Cross-selling.** A recent CGAP study by Westley and Palomas (2010) found that small savers can produce several times their savings balance in profits, owing to the revenue generated by the other financial services they use. Although similar research focused on youth is not yet available, experiences such as those of Proyecto FCF-WOCCU suggest that by recruiting and servicing youth clients MFIs may create opportunities to cross-sell products to their parents, relatives and teachers. These additional sales could generate enough revenue to cover the costs of serving the youth who introduced these customers to the MFI.
4. **Integrating youth into the MFI's mainstream delivery channels.** As noted in Section 16.3 above, most institutions working with youth are offering financial products through delivery channels that are very similar if not identical to those being offered to adults. This avoids the cost of setting up special infrastructure for youth, but it brings its own challenges, as illustrated by the experience of Pro Mujer Bolivia, which tried to incorporate youth solidarity groups into existing communal banks to minimize costs, but achieved disappointing results (see Box 16.11).
5. **Linking youth to volunteer mentors**, such as established businesspeople, teachers or community leaders. Mentors not only help an MFI to manage risk, but can also help reduce its monitoring costs by providing youth with a regular point of contact, encouragement for on-time repayment, and troubleshooting assistance in the event that something goes wrong. By fulfilling these functions, mentors decrease the workload of an MFI's field staff.
6. **Accessing subsidized funds from donors or governments.** This is a popular strategy at present, as institutions are still testing what products and delivery models will be most effective at reaching youth, and donors are willing to finance this experimentation, but it is not a sustainable strategy. Dependence on subsidies limits the number of youth that an MFI is able to reach, and donor or government involvement poses reputation as well as credit risks that could affect an institution's overall performance.
7. **Working through community-based models of microfinance.** The VS&L groups described in Box 16.3, self-help groups, or even informal rotating savings and credit associations (ROSCAs) can give youth initial access to and experience with financial services. Since youth are often familiar with these models, it can be relatively easy for them to develop money management skills working through that methodology and then graduate to an MFI once they have accumulated some savings and/or a credit history.
8. **Leveraging technology.** The cost of servicing small youth accounts could be dramatically reduced through electronic deposit services. In the Philippines, some rural banks are already testing a delivery model through which youth over the age of 12 frequently transact by ATM and mobile phone (Hirschland, 2009).

Marketing to Youth

MFIs that set out to overcome the four challenges discussed above have found themselves almost invariably confronted by a fifth challenge – how to market their products and services effectively to youth. Initially, Panabo Multi-Purpose Cooperative (PMPC) offered its youth products only in credit union offices. It delivered marketing messages through parents as they came into the office and then waited for youth to sign up, but the results were minimal. In Bosnia and Herzegovina, Partner Microcredit found it extremely difficult to motivate youth to attend its business training, even after they had signed up. In Mongolia, girls between the

> **Box 16.11 Mainstreaming Youth Brings Challenges at Pro Mujer**
>
> Initially, the idea of combining youth with experienced clients in an existing communal bank seemed to make sense from a cost standpoint and also from a social standpoint, in that older clients were expected to serve as mentors for younger clients. While this did happen occasionally, the majority of experiences were less than positive, from the perspective both of adults as well as youth. Young people with higher levels of education were more adept at finishing paperwork, and often became impatient waiting for the older clients to finish repayment documentation. In addition, many of the adult clients felt the young people were disrespectful of group rules such as arriving on time and staying for the entire meeting. The adult-themed trainings, such as menopause, that occur during the repayment meetings also did not resonate with young people. Finally, young people found group meeting times conflicted with their class schedules. Pro Mujer examined the possibility of adding after-hours and weekend staff to accommodate class schedules better, but cost restrictions prohibited such additions.
>
> *Source: Storm-Swire, 2009.*

ages of 14 and 18 expressed interest in XacBank's product prototype, but when the product was piloted, only 31 per cent of the girls who participated in the financial education programme actually opened a savings account.

Experiences like these have taught MFIs that they need to be more proactive and more creative about developing marketing strategies that will encourage youth to enter into a relationship with a financial institution. Some of the strategies used by MFIs mentioned in this chapter include:

- partnering with experienced professionals and institutions already interacting with youth (see, for example, Box 16.12);
- visiting classrooms, setting up kiosks or establishing student banking units in schools to collect savings deposits;
- sponsoring a classroom in partner schools that is partially dedicated to financial education;
- involving teachers in promoting the value of savings and financial preparedness on an ongoing basis;
- customizing a youth-friendly brand, complete with a name, tagline, logo, promotional materials and information boards that are attractive to youth;
- involving all MFI staff in creating a more youth-friendly environment, making service points convenient, safe, welcoming and comfortable for youth;
- providing toolkits and training in direct marketing for front-line staff;
- marketing youth products together with other products;
- adding financial education messages to all marketing, not just the marketing designed for youth;
- hiring young people to serve young people; recruiting university students as trainers to deliver financial education sessions for youth;
- making presentations on specific financial products being offered by an MFI during the financial education programme;

Box 16.12 Partnerships Bring Savings and Financial Education to Youth in Mongolia

Women's World Banking (WWB), a global network of MFIs that offer financial products and services to adult women, has partnered with the Nike Foundation to find ways of reaching girls and young women as a new market segment. The project's first site was Mongolia, where it worked on a combined financial education and savings programme with XacBank.

To deliver financial education and provide face-to-face direct marketing in a cost-effective manner, more partnerships were formed. Microfinance Opportunities, an international NGO with experience in financial education, and the Mongolian Education Alliance (MEA), a leading local NGO, were brought in to help design the content. When it came to delivery, the project drew upon MEA's extensive experience with the public school sector while also partnering with another local NGO, Equal Step Centre, to reach working girls. These relationships represented some of the first local public–private partnerships in the history of Mongolia's education sector.

Through eight learner-centred sessions, the financial education curriculum teaches new skills and behaviours around saving, using banks, and personal budgeting. To reach schoolchildren, XacBank and MEA are partnering with schools to organize groups of girls to meet weekly as an extracurricular activity, with facilitation from trained female university students. For working girls, professional trainers from Equal Step gather girls in training centres near large markets.

Source: Adapted from Banthia and Shell, 2009.

- giving youth who attend financial education classes a tour of the nearest MFI branch;
- supplying working youth with handouts that explain how to obtain official IDs;
- providing youth-oriented gifts and/or recognition as incentives for opening accounts, saving regularly and saving larger amounts;
- sponsoring funfairs, inter-school competitions, and artistic contests;
- introducing an academic scholarship programme for youth members.

16.6 Conclusion

One of the main conclusions of Making Cents International's Global Youth Enterprise Conference in 2009 was that "youth can benefit from appropriate financial services. Not all youth. Not all products. What is important is to ensure that youth have access, and can make informed choices" (Making Cents International, 2010b). By providing access to financial services, MFIs can create opportunities for youth to acquire new skills, accumulate assets, start and expand their own businesses, and manage risk. Yet to do so effectively, they must under stand this segment's unique needs and find ways to overcome the challenges that are created by youth's limited life, work and business experience. A small but growing number of institutions are demonstrating that this can be done, but services are required at a much larger scale to reach the millions of youth that would like to make use of them.

Main Messages

1. The youth market segment is not homogeneous.
2. For youth, savings services are often more important than credit.
3. What distinguishes the product portfolio offered to youth is the non-financial services that accompany the financial ones.
4. Mentors can give youth access to experience and perspective that they have not yet had an opportunity to acquire..
5. Proactive and creative marketing strategies are needed to encourage youth to enter into a relationship with a financial institution.

Case Study: Safe Spaces for Youth at BRAC in Bangladesh

BRAC started its adolescent initiatives in 1993 under its education programme. After observing that many female graduates of primary school in Bangladesh did not continue in school, nor did they maintain their educational level after they left school, BRAC established reading centres for adolescent girls of all backgrounds. Eventually, the reading centres became places where BRAC taught adolescent girls about reproductive health and life skills. Once it realized that many of the girls also needed financial services, it tried to offer them loan products as well.

In the lending programme's pilot phase, which began in 2000, BRAC faced great difficulties. The first challenge came from local community members, especially parents who refused to let their girls get involved in monetary matters. BRAC realized that it had to increase the emphasis it placed on community sensitization in order to stress the importance of financially empowering girls and gain buy-in from adolescent girls' family members.

To do this, BRAC started working with adolescent girls through a savings service, which seemed less intimidating to both the girls and their parents. After a year and a half of the girls only saving through this programme, and the parents having many dialogues with other community members and BRAC, the community started to recognize the positive impact the programme was having on the girls. The success of the pilot led BRAC to launch the Employment and Livelihood for Adolescents (ELA) programme, which offers financial services to young women between 14 and 25 years who live in rural Bangladesh. ELA offers its group members different kinds of training to help them earn an income and develop a savings habit, and it provides access to small loans. Through these services, it hopes to help girls begin to become economically self-reliant and unleash a process of overall empowerment.

As of December 2006, over 272,000 adolescent girls had become members of ELA and formed over 9,000 ELA groups, each consisting of 15 to 20 members. They had saved a total of nearly US$3 million, and over 87 per cent of the girls had taken on a loan averaging US$70 (Abed and Matin, 2007). An evaluation of the programme found that an average cumulative borrowing of US$188 over five years produced an increase in the annual per-capita household expenditure of US$9, which is equivalent to 7 per cent of the moderate poverty line and 11 per cent of the extreme poverty line.

In response to lessons learned as well as suggestions gathered during focus group discussions with youth, parents, communities and staff, BRAC decided to integrate its safe space centres and its youth-inclusive financial services programme in 2008. This integrated approach became the Social and Financial Empowerment of Adolescents (SOFEA) programme. The SOFEA program has six components: 1) a clubhouse, which provides a safe place for girls to socialize and share their stories; 2) training in life skills to help the girls make informed decisions; 3) livelihood training for girls to learn a skill they could utilize for earning a good living; 4) a financial literacy course to enhance the girls' capacities to manage money; 5) savings and credit facilities to provide the youth with access to finance and a safe place to keep their money; and 6) community sensitization to raise awareness within the community on the contributions that adolescent girls could make to socioeconomic development in Bangladesh. While it is too early to know the full impact of this new programme, results to date show the important role that safe spaces have played in enabling adolescent girls to participate and thrive in a youth-inclusive financial services programme in Bangladesh.

This case study was adapted from Kashfi (2009) and Making Cents International (2009).

Recommended Reading

- Global Financial Education Program. 2009. *Young people: Your future your money*, Content Note (Washington, DC, Microfinance Opportunities, Citi Foundation, Freedom from Hunger), at: http://www.globalfinancialeducation.org/documents/Youth%20Module%20Content%20Note.pdf
- Hirschland, M. 2009. *Youth savings accounts: A financial service perspective*, USAID microREPORT #163 (Washington, DC, USAID), at: http://www.microlinks.org/ev02.php?ID=43511_201&ID2=DO_TOPIC
- Making Cents International. 2010b. *State of the field in youth enterprise, employment and livelihoods development: Programming and policymaking in youth enterprise, employment, and livelihoods development; and youth-inclusive financial services* (Washington, DC, Making Cents International), at: http://www.makingcents.com/products_services/resources.php
- Nagarajan, G. 2005. *Microfinance, youth and conflict: Emerging lessons and issues*, microNOTE # 4 (Washington, DC, USAID), at: http://www.microlinks.org/ev_en.php?ID=7123_201&ID2=DO_TOPIC
- Nulty, M.; Nagarajan, G. (eds.) 2005. *Serving youth with microfinance: Perspectives of microfinance institutions and youth serving organizations* (Washington, DC, USAID), at: http://pdf.dec.org/pdf_docs/Pnadf315.pdf
- Youth-Inclusive Financial Services Case Studies Series 2009, at: http://www.makingcents.com/products_services/resources.php
- Youth-Inclusive Financial Services Portal, at: http://www.yfslink.org/
- Youth Save Consortium. 2010. *Youth savings in developing countries: Trends in practice, gaps in knowledge* (Westport, CT, Youth Save Initiative), at: http://www.microfinancegateway.org/gm/document-1.9.45704/youth%20savings.pdf

17 Microfinance for Women

Targeting women continues to be important in the design of products and services, both because women by default have less access to credit and because they face constraints unique to their gender. Product design and program planning should take women's needs and assets into account. By building an awareness of the potential impacts of their programs, MFIs can design products, services and service delivery mechanisms that mitigate negative impacts and enhance positive ones. ~ Cheston and Kuhn (2002)

Many microfinance programmes focus on women. A review of the *MicroBanking Bulletin*'s benchmark reports shows that three-fifths of microcredit borrowers around the world are women, although there are significant variations depending on the type of institution, the lending methodology and the region, as illustrated in Table 17.1.

This does not mean, however, that microfinance products and services are always gender sensitive, or that women are the ultimate beneficiaries of the services. Are MFIs deliberately targeting women? Should they be? Are their services benefitting women as much as they could be? How might MFIs benefit from changing the nature of the products and services they offer to women? These are some of the questions that will be considered in this chapter, which is organized into four parts:

1. Characteristics of the female market segment
2. Targeting women
3. Product design
4. Outreach strategy

Table 17.1 Percentage of borrowers who are women

	2005	2006	2007	2008
All MFIs	**62.6**	**64.4**	**63.4**	**60.0**
Bank	47.6	50.2	48.5	43.5
Credit union	44.8	51.3	45.7	45.1
NBFI	54.5	53.5	53.9	54.2
NGO	78.1	80.6	75.5	79.1
Individual	51.5	51.3	49.7	46.2
Individual/solidarity	65.0	67.4	66.4	64.9
Solidarity	100.0	99.3	99.3	98.7
Village banking	95.0	96.4	94.0	86.3
Africa	60.0	64.0	62.9	57.2
Asia	99.4	99.0	99.4	93.8
ECA	46.8	46.5	45.1	43.1
LAC	60.0	61.8	61.4	59.6
MENA	71.8	69.5	67.9	65.4

Source: Microfinance Information eXchange, 2006, 2007, 2008, 2009.

17.1 Characteristics of the Female Market Segment

Women are the child-bearers and the caretakers in most societies, as set out by their traditional gender roles (see Box 17.1). These are not the only roles that women play, and not all women are child-bearers or caretakers, but these are the roles that most define the female market segment. Differences in the way men and women spend their time, set their priorities, and define their expectations of each other are heavily influenced by these and other gender roles.

Unfortunately, the distinct responsibilities that have been assumed by men and women, and the value that society has placed on each, have led to significant inequality in men's and women's access to resources, economic opportunities and power. This observation is extremely important for MFIs, even those that aim to serve women and men equally, because women and men will not be able to make equal use of an MFI's services as long as they have unequal resources with which to access those services. Consider the following:

- **Although women make up 50 per cent of the global population, they own just 1 per cent of the world's property** (United Nations, 2009a, and UNICEF, 2007). Land titles and household assets are usually not in a woman's name, but rather in the name of a father, brother or spouse. Without assets of their own, women cannot access loans that require hard collateral, and they have little to fall back on in the event of a spouse's death.
- **Women earn less income.** According to UNICEF (2007), women account for more than 60 per cent of the world's labour force, but earn only 10 per cent of the world's income. They make up 70 per cent of the population living on less than one dollar per day (OECD, 2008). Women engage in much more unpaid work than men, and when they do work outside the home, they are often paid less than men in similar positions (United Nations, 2009a). As a result, it can take them longer to accumulate assets.
- **Women have had less access to education** and, as a result, represent a disproportionate percentage of the world's illiterate population. According to UNESCO (2010), two-thirds of all illiterate adults in the world are female. Those who lack the ability to read and write will find it more difficult to access information about financial services and to enter into written agreements with MFIs.

Box 17.1 What Is Gender?

Gender refers to the socially constructed roles and responsibilities of women and men. The concept of gender also includes the expectations held about the characteristics, aptitudes and likely behaviours of both women and men. These roles and expectations are learned, changeable over time, and variable within and between cultures. They are influenced by many factors including class, age, ethnicity and religion. Taking the example of household finances, in some cultures women control money for small household items while men control the money for larger items. In others, women's and men's assets are completely separate, and when money is required to purchase an item, bargaining takes place within the household. In some Buddhist cultures it is considered "lowly" to handle money, and handling money is often women's responsibility because their status is lower. In some Islamic cultures, men may control household finances and purchase all items for household use.

Source: Adapted from Canadian International Development Agency, 2010, and Murray and Boros, 2001.

- **In many countries, cultural or religious norms restrict women's mobility.** This can limit their access to markets, business networks, technology, information, and even MFI offices. It can also affect their ability to negotiate with buyers and suppliers.
- **Women have less time to devote to enterprise activities.** The time and energy they dedicate to household maintenance, cooking and caring for their children, spouse, parents and/or in-laws severely restricts the amount of time and energy they can dedicate to income-generating activities. Simultaneously, their willingness to assume these responsibilities gives men more time to invest in their businesses. When women do engage in microenterprise activities, they tend to enter areas with low barriers to entry, which generate lower returns (Banthia et al., 2009).
- **In some environments, women do not have the same rights as men** to sign legally binding contracts or to inherit land. In Lesotho and Botswana, for example, women married under customary law are considered minors, and must have their husband's consent to borrow money (Mutangadura, 2004).
- **Women have less control over decisions that affect their lives.** An analysis of ILO data for 70 countries, for instance, found that women held only 27 per cent of positions that were classified as having "status, influence, power and decision-making authority", such as legislators and senior government officials, corporate managers and general managers (Anker, 2005). In a sample of 198 MFIs in 65 countries, McCarter (2006) found a somewhat higher, but still unequal, percentage of women in senior governance or management positions (30 to 40 per cent in most institutions). According to the World Bank (2009a), "Women are [also] generally subject to higher levels of 'social control' within communities and are less likely to have their interests represented by local power hierarchies." Even at the household level, women often lack the bargaining power to resist male family members' demands.
- **Women face a disproportionate level of physiological vulnerability.** This makes their property more susceptible to theft and crime. It also exposes them to greater harassment, abuse and exploitation. According to the United Nations Population Fund (2010), "Around the world, as many as one in every three women has been beaten, coerced into sex or abused in some other way – most often by someone she knows, including by her husband or another male family member."

Women are frequently praised for being peacemakers and protectors of family welfare. They are often recognized as resourceful, determined and loyal. Individually, they are capable of excellence in any discipline, yet overall they are disadvantaged. The inequalities and vulnerabilities described above expose the female market segment to a unique set of challenges that make it more difficult for them to access financial services, and more difficult for MFIs to serve them effectively. Table 17.2 summarizes these challenges.

17.2 Targeting Women

As explained in Chapter 14, targeting in the context of microfinance refers to active approaches to finding, recruiting and serving a particular group of people. MFIs target women for both social and commercial reasons.

Table 17.2 Gender-based obstacles in microfinance and microenterprise

	Individual	Household	Wider community/ national context
Financial	• Women's lack of assets, skills, knowledge, experience and/or confidence to engage with formal financial sector	• Men's control over cash income • Men's expenditure patterns	• Perception of men as controllers of money
Economic	• Women often undertake activities that produce low returns • Women have a heavy domestic workload	• Gender division of labour • Unequal access to and control of land, labour and inputs • Unequal control of joint household produce and income stream from this	• Stereotypes of appropriate roles for women in the economy • Women underpaid for equal work • Lack of access to markets for inputs and outputs if women's mobility is constrained
Social/ cultural	• Lower levels of literacy among women; girls' education not prioritized • Women's lack of self-worth • Health risks associated with pregnancy and childbirth	• Limited role for women in household decision-making • Polygamy can result in conflict or competition between wives • Violence towards women	• Banks often do not view women as a potential market • Women's mobility and market access may be constrained by social norms • Women face disproportionate levels of physical vulnerability
Political/ legal	• Women not knowing their legal rights • Lack of confidence among women to claim political and legal rights	• Women's lack of legal rights to jointly owned household assets • Under customary law, women may be considered minors dependent on their spouse	• Inheritance laws that discriminate against women • Women's lack of legal rights to land and/or other assets; rights that are insufficiently defined to be useful for collateral purposes • Few women in policy-making or legislative positions to influence appropriate laws

Source: Adapted from Johnson, 2000.

On the commercial side, many institutions experience better repayment performance from their women borrowers, and therefore target women to control credit risk. Since women typically have less access to credit than men, they often make a special effort to create and maintain an excellent credit history. They also tend to be less mobile than men and are therefore less likely to disappear with an outstanding debt. The fact that women make up more than 50 per cent of the world's population gives commercially driven MFIs another reason for targeting them. They adapt their product design, delivery channels and communication strategies in

the hope of attracting and retaining more female clients. By helping women make better use of their financial services, they aim to create more profitable clients.

Few if any MFIs target women for purely commercial reasons, however. In fact, it is the social agenda and the potential for developmental impact that have primarily motivated MFIs to target women in the past. A wide range of institutions are using microfinance as a tool for empowering women and increasing their well-being and that of their family. Figure 17.1 illustrates what Mayoux and Hartl (2009) refer to as the three "virtuous spirals" that can be created by increasing women's access to microfinance services:

- **Virtuous spiral 1: Economic empowerment.** Women's roles in household financial management may improve, in some cases making it possible for them to access significant amounts of money in their own right for the first time. This might enable women to start their own economic activities, invest more in existing activities, acquire assets, or raise their status in household economic activities through their visible capital contribution. Increased participation in economic activities may raise women's incomes or their control of their own and household income. This, in turn, may enable them to increase longer-term investment in and the productivity of their economic activities, as well as their engagement in the market.
- **Virtuous spiral 2: Household well-being.** According to the United Nations (2009b), "Studies over an extended period have built up a robust body of evidence to show that women's access to resources... has a far stronger impact on child survival, welfare and education than similar resources in men's hands." Even if women use microfinance services to support the activities of other household members, channelling credit or savings options to households through women can enable them to play a more active role in household decision-making, decrease their own and household vulnerability, and increase investment in family welfare.
- **Virtuous spiral 3: Social and political empowerment.** Women often value the opportunity to make a greater contribution to household well-being, which gives them greater confidence and sense of self-worth. The positive effects on women's confidence and skills, their expanded knowledge, and the formation of support networks through group activity and market access can enhance the status of all women in a community. Individual women who gain respect in their households and communities may become role models for others, which can lead to a wider process of change in community perceptions.

By combining financial and non-financial services, MFIs have been able to help women build financial, human and social capital which enables them to make more strategic choices and enhances their ability to meet their goals. The catalytic role that women can play in economic and social development is what has inspired the MFIs best known for targeting women (see Box 17.2 for a few examples).

Although access to microfinance can be empowering for women, it is important to recognize that it can also cause harm. For example, women may be pressured by male members of the household to borrow on their behalf (this is a particular risk for institutions that serve exclusively women). If this happens, women will be held responsible for repaying the loan but may not have control over how the money is spent. If women borrow for their own activities but take on more debt than they can handle, they may increase the time spent trying to generate income to repay the debt at the expense of fulfilling family or household obligations. If women become over-indebted, access to credit can leave them in a worse situation than before.

Figure 17.1 Microfinance and women's empowerment: virtuous spirals

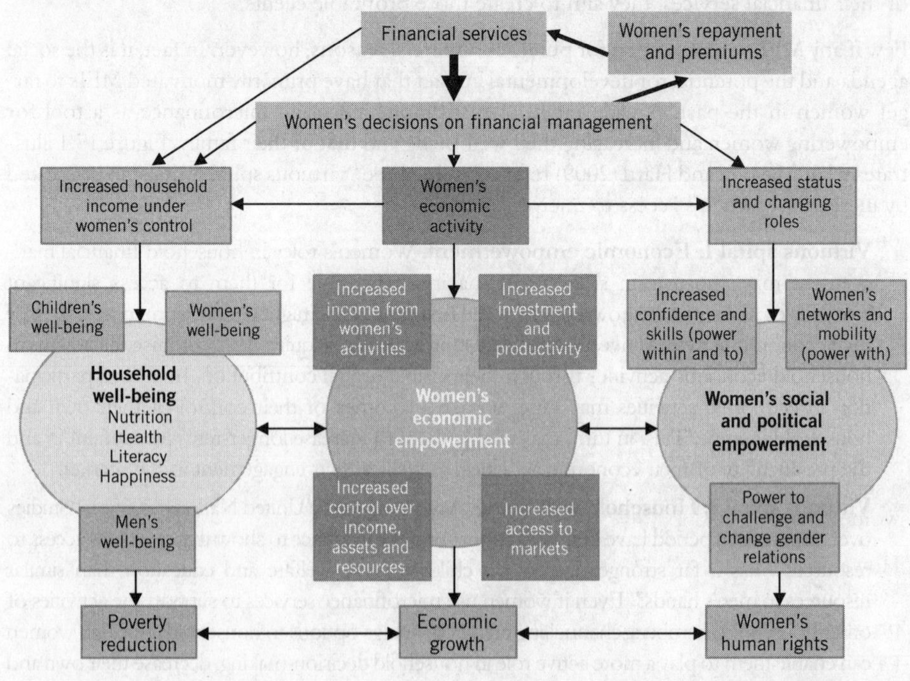

Source: Mayoux and Hartl, 2009.

Box 17.2 Vision and Mission Excerpts from MFIs Targeting Women

Women's World Banking: "Our vision is to improve the economic status of poor families in developing countries by unleashing the power inherent in women. We believe that when a woman is given the tools to develop a small business, build assets, and protect against catastrophic loss, she is empowered to change her life and that of her family... Our goal is to continue to build a network of strong financial institutions around the world and ensure that the rapidly changing field of microfinance focuses on women as clients, innovators and leaders."

Pro Mujer: "Pro Mujer is an international women's development and microfinance organization whose mission is to provide Latin America's poor women with the means to build livelihoods for themselves and futures for their families through microfinance, business training, and health-care support."

SEWA (Self-Employed Women's Association) Bank: "SEWA Bank exists to reach the maximum number of poor women workers engaged in the unorganized sector and provide them with suitable financial services for their socioeconomic empowerment and self-development, through their own management and ownership."

Source: www.swwb.org, www.promujer.org, www.sewabank.com.

Even if access to financial services helps women succeed, children may be taken out of school to help with the growing business. Male members of the household may decide to decrease their contribution to family expenses and take less responsibility for household well-being. To the extent that an increase in women's empowerment threatens men's power, status or self-confidence, it can also lead to domestic violence and abuse. As early as 1999, household surveys from Bangladesh recorded that microfinance was increasing frictions between husbands and wives (Armendáriz and Roome, 2008).

MFIs that wish to serve women effectively must do more than aim to have women be the ones who buy their products and services. They must make a special effort to ensure that they are providing women with access to the kinds of products and services that will enable them to improve their lives and the lives of their families. Some MFIs pursue this objective by serving women only, which can be an effective strategy for addressing the structural causes of gender inequality. Particularly in countries where women have little access to financial services, MFIs that focus exclusively on women can concentrate their resources on breaking down the barriers that have limited women's access to date. They can design products and services to leverage women's strengths and address their weaknesses. They can deliver those products in a supportive environment, and combine financial and non-financial interventions to increase women's confidence and ability to make productive use of financial services.

However, a women-only approach will not necessarily succeed in empowering women. To avoid the negative impacts described above, Johnson (2004) argues that a gender approach to programme design is what is needed, an approach that works with men as well as women "to pave the way for changed attitudes towards women's contribution to the household economy". A gender approach examines the social roles of women and men, the dynamics of relations between them, and the ways in which a microfinance initiative might alter those roles and/or be affected by them (Murray and Boros, 2001).

As the MFIs that target women strive for greater impact, more and more are choosing to involve men in some way. Their strategies vary depending on their mission, their methodology, the cultural context in which they operate, and other factors. At the Centre for Agricultural Research and Development (CARD) in the Philippines, for example, loans are made only to female clients, but savings are mobilized from the general public, both men and women (Frank, 2008). The Microfinance Agency for Development and Rehabilitation of Afghan Communities (MADRAC) serves women and men in separate groups of five to 20 members each, while Grameen Trust Chiapas (GTC) in Mexico has evolved over time from serving entirely women-only groups to serving a majority of mixed groups of women and men. Its rationale for making the transition is described in Box 17.3. Some MFIs, such as TYM in Vietnam, serve women only but include men in their communication strategy so as to increase their understanding and support for the MFI's activities (see Section 17.4 below).

In sum, targeting women does not necessarily mean excluding men. It does, however, require an active effort to find, recruit and serve women, so as to overcome the obstacles that women face in making productive use of financial services. Can women access an MFI's products as easily as men? Are the MFI's products meeting women's needs strategically? Are they empowering women to remove obstacles rather than working around the obstacles? Will they contribute to greater gender equality? The remaining two sections of this chapter explore how MFIs are designing products and institutional strategies to answer these questions affirmatively.

Box 17.3 A Case for Integrated Groups

Grameen Trust Chiapas, A.C. (GTC) in Mexico is one of the first replications of the Grameen model of microfinance in Latin America. It began in 1997 by lending to women-only groups, but in 2003 it took the risk of lending to men in some previously women-only groups. Since then, the organization has grown rapidly, and now has over 12,000 borrowers, with a large majority of mixed groups of women and men.

When branch managers in different locations were asked why they accepted men into women-only groups, they offered several explanations. The first relates to informational asymmetries between men and women. One loan officer argued that even if loan disbursements and repayments are publicly known in women-only groups, men tend to overestimate the amount of money that women are handling. They therefore decide to contribute less to overall household expenditure, which often creates frictions within the household and results in women diverting some of their loan to make up for the shortfall. Inviting some men to join the group allows them to have a more accurate estimate of women's real investments and their realized returns. With this information they are less likely to reduce their contributions to household expenditures. In those groups that became mixed, the improvements in information symmetry were accompanied by women borrowers investing more, and increased repayment rates by both men and women.

A second explanation relates to the potential workload externalities of having women as the only recipients of loans within the household. Staff argued that when women contract a loan from GTC, they become busier and the quality of the services that women provide to the household, such as meals and household chores, decreases in quantity or quality or both. This irritates men and creates a "tense" atmosphere within the household. The tension causes women to default more often or prevents them from making their repayments on time. In contrast, when men are invited to join groups, they seem to internalize the negative workload externalities created by GTC microloans to women. In one loan officer's words: "Invited men help their spouses more in their businesses and in household chores, which in turn reduces tensions, and enables women to repay on time, as men become de-facto business partners of women."

A third explanation relates to the absence of secure places for women to hide money while they save for two consecutive weeks or more in order to make their loan repayments. Women borrowers try to hide money from their husbands in different places, generally in the house, but they are not always successful. When men are invited to join a GTC group, the situation changes because the man becomes responsible for the debt of the other men and women members of the group. "Women become happier. They no longer complain about their husbands or men in general. The household heads work harmoniously together", the loan officer explains.

Source: Armendáriz and Roome, 2008.

17.3 Product Design

In this section, features specific to the design of loan, leasing, savings, money transfer, insurance and non-financial products are discussed. Section 17.4 explores ways that MFIs can adjust their overall product portfolio, communication and delivery strategies to serve women more effectively.

Loans

The characteristics of the female market segment discussed in Section 17.1 present significant barriers to successful loan product design: lack of assets, investment in low-return economic activities, a heavy domestic workload, lower levels of education and literacy, mobility constraints, and a lack of confidence to interact with financial institutions. Eight recommendations for designing loans that can meet the needs of women in the face of these challenges are described below.

1. **Find appropriate collateral substitutes.** Given that women own just 1 per cent of the world's property, it is generally difficult for them to access loans that require hard collateral. Thus MFIs that want to serve women must find other ways to guarantee their loans. Group lending methodologies have been the most popular alternative to date, since women often belong to groups already, or value the opportunity to join one that provides support during the repayment process, and MFIs find peer pressure and joint liability mechanisms to be cost-effective means of obtaining high repayment rates.

   Compulsory savings is another popular collateral substitute, as it provides an MFI with cash collateral while providing women with a means to accumulate assets. MFIs that offer individual loans use cash flow analysis to help ensure that women will be able to generate the income stream necessary to make repayment. They also accept personal guarantors and non-traditional assets, such as jewellery or household utensils, that woman would be more likely to possess.

2. **Have an equitable policy on spousal signatures.** MFIs take different approaches with respect to a spouse's co-signing or consenting to a borrower's loan application. Some programmes (especially those that target women only) do not require a spousal signature, because they want to empower women to access credit independently of their husbands. Others, such as Spandana in India, lend only to women but require the husband's signature on the demand promissory note. Both approaches have merit, but if an MFI is lending to both men and women, then the same policy should apply to equally to men and women. If an MFI is going to require a husband's signature on a wife's loan application, it can require the wife's signature on a husband's loan application.

3. **Design product terms to match the cash flow of women's economic activities.** Women are unlikely to be engaged in the same types of activity as men, and the cash flow of those activities will vary. By matching repayment plans to cash flows, MFIs make on-time repayment easier, and decrease the risk of women sacrificing household welfare in order to service their loan. When analysing cash flows, it is important to look at the aggregated revenues from the multiple businesses that women operate, and not simply at the revenues of a single business, since investment across multiple businesses is common among women microentrepreneurs (Frank, 2008).

   The South Indian Federation of Fishermen Societies (SIFFS) developed a new loan product for women who travel in groups to distant markets, buy large quantities of fish for drying, and then sell the fish locally during the lean season. Since this enterprise requires a large initial investment and returns come only after four months, SIFFS offered a loan of 10,000–20,000 rupees (approximately US$200–400) on which the interest is paid monthly and the principal is repaid at the end of five months (Mayoux and Hartl, 2009).

4. **Offer loans that facilitate women's asset ownership, including land.** By accumulating assets, women can simultaneously decrease their vulnerability and increase their options for generating income. Loans that enable women to acquire land or build a home can be particularly valuable, as highlighted in Box 17.4. An increasing number of MFIs are offering housing loans, although most offer home improvement loans that women could use to build a home in instalments over time (see Chapter 7). A few MFIs, such as Grameen Bank in Bangladesh and SEWA Bank in India, offer large, longer-term loans to facilitate the purchase of housing or land. A condition of the loan is that land must be registered in a woman's name, both as security for the loan and to increase women's control over assets (Mayoux and Hartl, 2009, and SEWA, 2009). Whether loans are given to men or women, making it a condition for spouses to jointly own the property on which a home will be built can also facilitate women's asset ownership.

   The Council for Economic Empowerment for Women of Africa (CEEWA-U) collaborated with Uganda Microfinance Union (now Equity Bank Uganda) to introduce a capital asset loan that offered a larger amount, longer repayment period and more flexible disbursement schedule than other loans available at the time. After just 18 months, the pilot product had attracted new clients, improved client retention, and was contributing to 14 per cent of UMU's total income, illustrating the value of such a product both for clients and for the MFI (Agnes, 2002).

   An innovative loan product for adolescent girls was developed as part of the Credit and Savings Household Enterprise (CASHE) project in India. The loan, available for both parents, enables the girls to purchase a productive asset to help them earn an income, delay marriage, have an asset to bring to their in-laws' house when they do marry, and reduce demands for dowry (Mayoux and Hartl, 2009).

5. **Provide a loan package that enables women to enter non-traditional and more lucrative activities.** The skills and resources women possess have steered them into activities such as food preparation, sewing and vegetable selling that have low barriers to entry, but also generate relatively low returns. The more women gain access to credit and enter these activities, the more saturated local markets become, decreasing income-generating potential for everyone. Women who want to diversify out of traditionally "female" activi-

Box 17.4 The Importance of Property Investments

Many poor women view owning property as a critical strategy for managing the risks of divorce, widowhood or old age. With their name on a land title, women can avoid complicated and costly legal battles over property if divorced or widowed, thereby securing their place to live after such circumstances. Owning a home allows women to pass the house on to their children, creating security for their old age, as most women would then live with the adult children to whom they passed the property. It also guarantees a place to live if other options, such as living with their children, are not available or not desirable. A home is also a productive asset, because many women work from home. Lastly, owning a home gives many women an option to rent either all or part of the house, which is particularly vital for elderly women who need a source of income but are not physically able to work.

Source: Banthia et al., 2009.

ties may need a larger loan amount than is available through a standard microenterprise product, or may need non-financial services to help them acquire the knowledge and skills to succeed in activities with higher entry barriers.

6. **Provide clear avenues for upward mobility.** Whether it be a new delivery channel or clear graduation procedures for accessing additional products through existing delivery channels, MFIs can find ways to enable and encourage women who succeed in their businesses to continue growing. ADEMCOL in Colombia, for example, has a Senior Trust bank for women with growing businesses and larger loan demands who do not want to leave the group lending programme (Cheston and Kuhn, 2002). When Sinapi Aba Trust in Ghana found that women were not taking up its larger individual loan products, it introduced support services to help women overcome the confidence and skill barriers they faced in making the next step in business growth (Johnson, 2004).
7. **Take care with stepped lending.** Since women's businesses often do not grow, the stepped lending methodology used by many MFIs needs careful consideration. While women may be able to repay small loans without too much difficulty, they should not automatically receive larger loans unless they have the capacity to repay them. Otherwise, the MFI will burden women with loans they may have difficulty repaying and expose itself to unnecessary credit risk. Instead of automatically increasing loan size, loan officers can assist their borrowers to keep track of basic business records so that repayment capacity can be assessed. MFIs might also link access to larger loans with business development training, as KASHF is exploring in Pakistan.
8. **Offer some form of emergency or consumption loan.** Many women will be more concerned with managing risk within their household or stabilizing their economic situation than with expanding their economic opportunities. Providing a combination of savings, insurance and emergency loans can reduce women's vulnerability and also protect assets from being sold off in a desperate situation. If MFIs offer loans for microenterprise purposes only, women will use those loans for emergency and consumption purposes, which will increase the risk that the design of the loan will not fit the borrower's needs and will generate repayment problems.

Leasing

Leasing products provide an attractive alternative to loans for helping women acquire assets, finance larger asset acquisition, and move into new economic activities. In Ethiopia, African Village Financial Services (AVFS) developed its leasing product explicitly to support the growth of small and medium enterprises owned and operated by women. In Bangladesh, leases associated with the Grameen Bank's Village Phone programme enable women to enter into entirely new lines of business (see Box 17.5).

Through leasing, MFIs can provide women with larger amounts of financing over a longer term at an affordable price, because their risk is mitigated by the fact that they own the asset being financed until the lease contract is fulfilled, there is no opportunity for fund diversion, and the leased asset can often be insured (refer to Chapter 10 for more information on leasing product design). Typically, the asset itself is all that is required to secure a leasing transaction. A down payment is usually required to demonstrate a client's commitment to the lease, but this payment tends to be smaller than that which would be required for a similarly sized loan.

Box 17.5 Leases Facilitate Village Phone Start-ups at Grameen Bank

The Grameen Bank's Village Phone Programme in Bangladesh allows members with good repayment records to purchase mobile phones under a lease-financing programme and receive training from Grameen Telecom to sell incoming and outgoing telephone services at the village level. The price of the phone and the connection fee are paid by Grameen Bank to Grameen Telecom, and the member pays these costs back to Grameen Bank within a two- or three-year period. This has allowed the transfer of both a new form of business and new business skills.

The women phone operators are generally poorer than the average villager, but the income they earn is significant, generally accounting for 30 to 40 per cent of household income. Interestingly, where women are operators (approximately 75 per cent of the total), 82 per cent of their clients are women. Where men are the operators, women constitute only 6.3 per cent of users. Since 2006, the Grameen Foundation has promoted similar village phone businesses in Cameroon, the Philippines, Uganda and Rwanda.

Source: Adapted from United Nations, 2009b.

In the case of Grameen Bank's phone leases, no down payment is required (Dowla, 2004). MFIs that want to include a down payment in the design of their leasing product could offer women a contractual savings product that would assist them in accumulating the funds necessary to make that down payment.

If women are leasing equipment they have never used before, special attention to training will be required to ensure that women are able to operate and maintain the equipment properly. As with loans, if MFIs allow variable repayment schedules, they can increase the likelihood that women will be able to cover their lease payments with their cash flow. At Grameen, for example, leasing clients can arrange lease payments as low as 100 taka (approximately US$1.50) during an off-peak period of up to three months by agreeing to make larger payments during peak periods (Dowla, 2004). If MFIs allow prepayments, they can enable women to achieve ownership of their asset faster.

Savings

> *Women are keen savers, although their saving is generally driven by a need to be able to deal with shocks when they occur. By contrast, men usually manage larger businesses and larger absolute amounts of income, with which they often favour more aggressive investment strategies to make sure their businesses survive and expand. Women typically utilize their earnings to improve the care and standard of living in their households by either spending business profits immediately for these purposes or saving them for the future.* ~ Banthia et al. (2009)

Women are more likely to engage in precautionary savings behaviour. They put money aside during good times so that they can maintain the health, welfare and stability of their home even in bad times. They find ways to accumulate the lump sums required by life-cycle events such as childbirth, school fees, deaths in the family, and so on. Even if they do not own or control household assets, women are often expected to manage the food, health and education requirements of the household, and this makes them attentive resource managers.

Women's active savings behaviour and their need to save for a variety of purposes create demand for a diverse portfolio of savings products. Most women will desire, at minimum, a liquid product that gives them easy access to their savings when they need it, and a restricted access product that helps them accumulate larger amounts and achieve specific savings goals. **Demand deposit** and **contractual savings** products are best designed to meet these needs (see Chapter 4). Long-term contractual savings products can be particularly valuable, because they offer women a means to accumulate larger-sum assets and security for their old age (see Chapter 5). The amount of money saved through regular deposits over a ten-year period, for example, could be enough to purchase a small plot of land.

Time deposits will be relatively less useful, since women must already have a large sum of cash before they can make use of the product. Time deposits could be useful, however, for long-term savings purposes when combined with a contractual savings product that helps women accumulate the lump sum for deposit. Relatively short-term time deposits, such as those for three- or six-month periods, might also be helpful to women in households whose income is concentrated in just one or two months of the year, perhaps generated by an annual harvest of a single cash crop. Part of the income could be set aside for household expenses three or six months from the time of the harvest.

Compulsory savings can enable a woman to access credit without having other assets in her name to pledge as collateral. It can also provide a means for women to protect their income against the demands of husbands and other family members. For very poor women, compulsory savings products can be linked to asset transfers or public works programmes to help women build a lump sum for investing in an income-generating activity and/or a safety net to protect themselves against future shocks. In Bangladesh, for example, very poor women were given temporary employment in road maintenance as part of GTZ's Tangail Infrastructure Development Project. Compulsory savings were deducted from their earnings and deposited in the bank. The women were given training in income generation and subsequently used their savings to set up successful income-generating activities (Adam, 2003, as summarized in Mayoux and Hartl, 2009).

As discussed in Chapter 4, however, compulsory savings schemes have many disadvantages. Often women cannot access them unless they leave the programme or institution where the savings are being held. The savings may be used as a guarantee for other group members' loans, and thus be at risk. Regular deposit requirements may divert women's resources from more flexible savings mechanisms, such as indigenous savings and credit associations or demand deposits, leaving women with fewer options to manage their daily cash flow needs. Compulsory savings can also divert resources from women's businesses, where an investment in working capital could generate much better returns than the capital locked into a compulsory savings account. Requiring that funds be set aside as a condition for borrowing increases the effective interest rate of a loan.

Given the fact that women's assets often take the form of jewellery, a **safe deposit box** outside the home where a woman could protect a certain quantity of her in-kind savings might be greatly valued. Here, too, she could keep a copy of any legal papers documenting her ownership of land or other major assets.

Regardless of the particular type of savings product being offered, three additional design features are important to consider when targeting women:

- **Low minimum deposit requirements.** Since women earn less income, have fewer assets and tend to invest more of their earnings in the household, deposit requirements will exclude them more than men.
- **Security.** Public knowledge of savings may in some circumstances increase social status, but in others it can expose women to unwanted pressure from family, friends and neighbours. In many parts of Africa, for example, where in-laws are likely to take the wife's as well as the husband's property when he dies, women's ability to have confidential and protected savings accounts can be a crucial means of security for the future. This combination of benefits was the primary reason for the early popularity of OIBM's smart card product in Malawi (see Box 17.6). Unlike a passbook account, the card-based savings product keeps both depositors' funds and their information secure.
- **Sufficient returns.** Although security is likely to be more important to women than financial returns, MFIs that wish to empower women will want to make sure that they pay a sufficiently high interest rate on women's deposits that the value of their savings increases over time and is not eroded by inflation.

Box 17.6 Red Light: No Match

Opportunity International's bank in Malawi, OIBM, offers a biometric smart card that enables illiterate customers with no official government identification (the vast majority of the population) to open and manage a savings account using fingerprints for identification. The minimum opening deposit is US$4.50. One early savings customer was a domestic servant whose employers had granted her severance pay when they moved away. She deposited the full amount at OIBM using her smart card. A few weeks later, when her husband died of AIDS, the husband's relatives came to seize the property of his widow. They found her smart card and took it to the bank, but the biometric reader showed "red light: no match". Although the relatives argued with the teller that this was their due, he held firm that the account belonged to the woman. Her savings were protected and became her only asset as she began her life again.

Source: Quisumbing and Pandolfelli, 2008.

Money Transfers

The amount of money sent by women and men, how it is sent, and how it is used are determined not only by individual decisions or markets, but also by the gendered power relations within households and economies (Mayoux and Hartl, 2009). MFIs that want to serve women effectively should not assume that women will want to access money in the same places, make payments through the same channels, or value the same product features as men.

If women's mobility is restricted, for example, the location of the money transfer service will be important. Women will need to access the service in an area they frequent. Cellular-phone-based money transfer services, such as those offered by G-Cash in the Philippines and M-Pesa in Kenya, are ideal for women because they can be used even in their own home.

Women do not have to take time away from their business or family to make a transaction. Money received can be stored electronically until a time when women can safely and confidentially go to retrieve it. Those who are illiterate can learn how to use numbers and symbols to complete a transaction without having to complete any forms.

Market research will be particularly useful when it comes to linking a money transfer service to other financial products that an MFI might offer (see Chapter 11). For instance, women migrants might find a remittance product attractive if they were able to deposit money directly into a school fees savings account, out of which their children's school fees would be automatically deducted when they come due, thus ensuring that the funds would not be diverted for other purposes. If women are the ones receiving remittances, they might find it helpful to have access to an emergency or microenterprise loan product that is linked to some percentage of their last six months of remittance flows.

Women are an increasing proportion of migrants, and in most destination countries their numbers are growing faster than those of males. A study by the United Nations International Research and Training Institute for the Advancement of Women (INSTRAW) found that women represented almost half of the international migrant population (Ramírez et al., 2005). In some countries, such as the Philippines and Indonesia, women constitute 70 to 80 per cent of all migrants (World Bank, 2009a, and Micra Indonesia, 2010). MFIs can help women make the most of the economic opportunities that migration can bring by channeling some of their remittances into a contractual savings account that enables women to safely accumulate assets with which they can make a living upon their return.

Insurance[37]

To design effective microinsurance products for women, MFIs must understand both the risks that poor women face, and the way household dynamics influence how women manage risk. In terms of exposure, women face several health risks that men do not, principally those related to pregnancy and childbirth. Their physiological vulnerability exposes them to greater physical abuse and risk of sexually transmitted disease. It also makes their property more vulnerable to theft and crime. Women dominate the labour force in certain industries, such as textiles and electronics, and are more exposed to risks associated with those industries, for example hazardous chemicals, eye-strain and poor ventilation. Gender differences in crops grown make women's crop and weather insurance needs different from those of men as well (Mayoux and Hartl, 2009).

As household caregivers, women assume responsibility for coping with many risks, such as the health-care needs of children, losses to family income due to a spouse's ill-health or death, and ensuring the future of their children in the event of their own death. This responsibility for household risk management, combined with their own vulnerability, tends to result in women being more risk averse than men. Albeit a rational response, this attitude adversely influences the effectiveness of their risk-management strategies, since risk-averse approaches tend to result in low returns, which make it harder to break the cycle of poverty. As mentioned previously, women often save more than men, but the savings they set aside earn little or no income, and leave fewer resources available for investment in higher-return business activities.

[37] This section is adapted from Banthia et al. (2009).

By enhancing the stability and security of cash flows, microinsurance can free up resources and make women more confident about investing in riskier enterprise strategies. It can spread the costs of expensive health treatments or death-related expenses over many years and enable poor women to tackle expensive health-related costs for themselves and their family members without taking high-cost loans or cutting food expenses. Well-designed life microinsurance can help poor women cope with both the short-term expenses (funeral costs) and long-term adjustments (loss of a breadwinner's income) associated with the death of a husband, without having to sell productive assets or depend exclusively on children or social relationships for support. It can also help poor women ensure that their children, especially their daughters, are cared for in case of their own death. Property insurance policies can encourage the formal registration of assets in a woman's name.

Although microinsurance can be very useful to poor women, often it is not (World Bank, 2009a):

- Insurance products are often bundled with loans, so women cannot access them unless they go into debt.
- Insurance policies frequently exclude health concerns that apply to large numbers of women (pregnancy is one example), because they present too great a risk for insurers.
- Since the majority of MFI borrowers are women, and loan-linked coverage typically protects the life of the borrower only, women are left unprotected if their husbands die, which is often when they are in greatest need.
- Women's lower incomes make them less able to afford insurance payments. The instability of their income also puts them at greater risk of having their policy cancelled due to a missed payment.
- A lump sum premium payment is often required, and many women find it difficult to accumulate this sum.
- Given illiteracy levels and mobility restrictions, women may be less able to understand policy conditions and pursue claims. They may be deceived into taking up schemes that are not to their advantage, and may be less able to take advantage even of good insurance schemes without considerable follow-up by insurance providers.

Microinsurance programmes that are successfully serving women have found ways to avoid these problems. Institutions such as CARD in the Philippines and FINCA in Uganda have modified their credit life insurance policies to cover spouses. In Sudan, Learning for Empowerment against Poverty (LEAP) offers loans, and in India, SEWA offers savings products that help women pay their annual insurance premium (see Boxes 17.7 and 17.8). Larger MFIs, such as BancoSol in Bolivia, have been able to cover maternity-related risks at a reasonable cost by negotiating with insurers. Others have used market research to hone in on the product attributes women most desire. The Micro Insurance Academy presents clients with a "menu" of benefits, allowing women to pick and choose attributes depending on their needs and ability to pay.

Regardless of the approach taken, microinsurance programmes that want to target women will need to strike a balance between providing coverage that meets their needs, minimizing operating costs for MFIs and insurers, and keeping premiums low to foster affordability and accessibility. Insurance policies and claims processing will need to be simple and easy to understand. Exclusions and complex provisions should be kept to a minimum, payouts should be straightforward,

Box 17.7 Facilitating Payment of a Lump Sum Insurance Premium

The Sudan Ministry of Health runs a heavily subsidized health insurance programme that salaried people access through their employers. Poor people could not access the programme, because of difficulties in arranging it, and because a large yearly payment is required. Learning for Empowerment Against Poverty (LEAP), with representatives from its Women's Centres, established an agreement with the Health Insurance Department whereby Women's Centres provide the institutional channel for the yearly payment, and individuals repay the Centres in smaller monthly instalments.

Source: Mayoux and Hartl, 2009.

and the MFI should offer sufficient information during the application process that potential policyholders can be clear about the terms and conditions of the product they are buying.

Because of their roles as childbearers and caregivers, women typically value insurance schemes that protect their family as well as themselves. However, high incremental costs for adding family members often make family coverage unaffordable, or force women to pick and choose who to insure. The latter response raises serious issues for women and girls, because they are often the ones left out. SEWA in India has attempted to mitigate this problem by offering its clients packaged family health microinsurance plans, which automatically include all family members with no need to pick and choose. While the packages are more expensive than insuring one individual, SEWA found that it was able to keep incremental costs low by insuring a larger population (see Box 17.8).

Box 17.8 India's SEWA Bank: A Pioneer in Gender-sensitive Microinsurance

With a tagline of "Our lives are full of risks, Vimo SEWA makes our life secure!", India's SEWA Bank offers its clients – all self-employed poor women – a choice of three microinsurance schemes that have been designed to provide unique "cradle to grave" coverage for many of the key financial pressures faced by poor women. Available at various price points to ensure affordability, the schemes cover the death, health and assets of women, with options to also cover husbands and children for a low incremental fee. The children's coverage provides protection for all the children in the family in one premium, to avoid families having to choose which of their children to insure. Starting with 7,000 clients in 1992, Vimo SEWA now covers nearly 200,000 women, men and children. The programmes are uniquely integrated with SEWA's fixed deposit savings accounts, giving clients the option to pay insurance premiums with the interest accrued from their savings account.

SEWA uses a variety of communication strategies to promote these products and educate clients about microinsurance. They have found that regular face-to-face interactions with clients are highly valued by women, who appreciate the feeling of involvement and the opportunity to ask questions about their policies, and to discuss broader family issues relating to risk. SEWA also provides comfortable women-only forums to discuss issues such as what can happen when a woman or a poor family confronts a major risk, and how they can protect their families from those risks by using microinsurance.

Source: Banthia et al., 2009.

In the case of life insurance, women often appreciate being given a choice over who the beneficiary of their policy will be. Many women nominate their daughters or a guardian whom they trust to ensure the benefit is spent on their children's education. A few insurance companies have designed life microinsurance plans to support surviving dependants over a period of time. At All Lanka Mutual Assurance Organization (ALMAO) in Sri Lanka, for instance, the "Senehesa" policy pays out 20 per cent of the sum insured upon the death of a parent and 20 per cent of the sum insured on each subsequent anniversary of death for four years. In Colombia, where one of the key mechanisms for coping with the death of a breadwinner is to take children out of school, La Equidad's "Amparar" product pays a lump sum for funeral support, a monthly payout for food for one year, and a monthly education benefit for up to 24 months.

Non-financial Services

As summarized in Table 17.2, the barriers preventing women from making productive use of financial services are many, and they cannot be eliminated through better access to financial services alone. For this reason, MFIs that target women typically integrate one or more non-financial services into their product portfolio, either through direct service provision or in partnership with a non-financial service provider (see Chapter 12).

The non-financial services that MFIs have found helpful in enabling women to use their financial services more effectively include:

- **Business management training.** This category of non-financial service has been popular among both commercially and socially oriented MFIs, because it not only helps women manage their businesses better; it also makes them better clients of financial institutions. The training can take many forms, from short educational sessions integrated into the loan application process to independent curricula such as the ILO's Generate Your Business Idea, Start Your Business, Improve Your Business, and GET Ahead for Women in Enterprise programmes (see Box 12.7 in the chapter on non-financial services) or the online resource centre recently launched by Standard Chartered Bank (see Box 17.9). As mentioned in the section above on loans, business management training is often key to enabling women to take the next step in expanding their business.

Box 17.9 Women in Business Resource Centre

In March 2010, Standard Chartered launched the Women in Business Resource Centre, an online tool designed to help women entrepreneurs start and grow their own businesses. It contains training modules and exercises on topics such as analysing balance sheets, controlling cash flow and penetrating new markets, as well as tools that have been specifically designed for women entrepreneurs on leadership practices, management styles, negotiation skills, and marketing to women. The site also showcases success stories from women entrepreneurs. The Resource Centre is currently available in eight languages: traditional Chinese, simplified Chinese, Korean, Thai, Bahasa Indonesia, Hindi, Bengali and English. It is hosted online at: http://www.standardchartered.com/sme-banking/resourcecentre/

Source: Standard Chartered, 2010.

- **Other business development services.** As discussed in Chapter 12, MFIs across the globe are providing advisory services, production training, market linkages and other types of support to their clients. These services can be useful to both men and women, but they are particularly important in helping women enter non-traditional, more lucrative economic activities about which they have limited knowledge. They can also help mitigate the risks of business expansion.
- **Financial education.** To counter women's lower levels of education and market exposure, and to assist them in making more strategic financial management choices, a growing number of MFIs are formally incorporating financial education programmes into their product offering. A variety of courses and methodologies have been developed by SEWA in India, SIEMBRA in Mexico, Microfinance Opportunities and Freedom from Hunger, among others. An innovative approach to financial education that can be used with illiterate women is described in Box 17.10.
- **Literacy.** Helping women learn how to read and write has obvious benefits for MFIs that wish to develop long-term, productive relationships with those who are currently illiterate. Combining literacy training with access to financial services also has the potential to generate significant economic benefits for clients, as illustrated by the WORTH Nepalese case study presented at the end of this chapter.
- **Childcare.** Opportunidad Latinoamerica in Colombia and the Bullock-Cart Workers Development Association (BWDA) in India found that childcare was a key constraint to women's business growth, and sought out ways to overcome that barrier. BWDA not only runs a childcare centre for children of low-income working women, but also holds summer camps for rural children during the school summer holidays, which are attended by 25,000 to 30,000 children annually (Shahnaz and Shankar, 2010). BancoSol in Bolivia provides childcare while clients attend its business management training.
- **Advocacy.** Some MFIs have developed strategies aimed at changing social norms and legal frameworks. In the case of WORTH, a Rights, Responsibilities and Advocacy (RRA) curriculum helped women's village banks to develop action plans for achieving goals that they set to bring about change in their communities. SEWA organizes and promotes the rights of low-income women workers in India. In 2007, it won a series of historic legal cases to the Supreme Court to support and protect vendors in Delhi. It also negotiated with the Municipal Corporation of Delhi to verify the identity of female construction workers, which enabled them to receive a pension and benefits (One World Action, 2010). MFIs in Bangladesh disseminated voter education material to women through their organization before the last elections, and CARE-Niger has been very effective in developing women's leadership to compete in local elections (Mayoux and Hartl, 2009).
- **Referrals.** Instead of offering non-financial services on their own, MFIs often publicize the availability of these services (for example, legal aid, reproductive health, counselling, etc.) from third parties. They may distribute marketing materials in their branches, provide staff with a list of referral organizations or, in the case of institutions that use a "credit with education" model, provide a list of speakers that could be made available to groups. In Bolivia, Banco FIE has partnered with Iniciativa de Microjusticia and International Legal Alliances to implement a pilot programme known as Microjusticia Bolivia that provides legal support to clients and non-clients from information desks in FIE branches (Banco FIE, 2010).

Box 17.10 Livelihood Road Journeys and Trees

Oxfam Novib, in partnership with LEAP in Sudan and GreenHome and Bukonzo Joint Savings in Uganda, is developing a combined market research and financial literacy methodology. Based on experience with the Gender Action Learning System for working with people who cannot read or write, the underlying idea is that these tools can be used either as part of any organization's market research process or on an ongoing basis by microfinance groups, themselves, as a continual process of participatory product development. The tools are designed to increase participants' understanding of their situation and financial literacy, and hence using them is an empowering process in itself.

There are two main types of tool: livelihood road journeys (see Figure 17.2) and trees. Livelihood road journeys either: 1) identify people's future livelihood ambitions compared with where they are currently and establish time-bound targets for achieving their goals, based on an analysis of risks and opportunities; or 2) look at experiences in the past, such as opportunities seized, how livelihoods have been built up from multiple strategies and opportunities, crises that have occurred, and how they were dealt with. Road journeys help identify how client strategies can best be supported, and which products are likely to give maximum benefit.

Figure 17.2 Livelihood road journey

Source: Mayoux, 2005.

Livelihood trees facilitate more detailed analysis of the sources of household income, the labour contribution of various household members, and differences in expenditure and benefit. Income and expenditure can be analysed by gender on separate sides of the tree, and used to identify "how far the tree leans and towards whom" in patterns of inequality in contributions and in access to or control of income within the household. Trees also include analysis of potential or actual loan use, savings and reinvestment. They can be used to identify particular areas of consumption in which loans or savings products might be useful, sources of repayment, and how women's control can be increased.

The livelihood road journeys and trees can be used as business plans and loan contracts with MFIs. In India, Sudan and Uganda, groups now use some of these tools, with very little external supervision, to increase the poverty inclusion of their groups and to develop their own livelihood plans. Individuals are also teaching the individual planning tools to others in their households and communities. Thus the methodology has the potential to be self-replicating and, once established, instead of being a cost to the organization, could be an effective means of recruiting reliable new clients who are able to credibly communicate their own financial needs.

Source: Mayoux and Hartl, 2009.

- **Health-care support and training.** With affordable health care being a high priority for women, yet difficult to find, a few MFIs have integrated the provision of health care and financial services, as in the case of Pro Mujer. In Nicaragua, Peru, Bolivia, Argentina and Mexico, Pro Mujer offers both health care and financial services, often from neighbourhood centres, which clients visit regularly to make loan payments, attend workshops, and get advice from their peers. Its physicians, nurses and trainers provide basic health education during times set aside before and after repayment meetings to discuss nutrition, hygiene, pre-and post-natal care, family planning and other reproductive health topics. To provide health-care support, Pro Mujer operates clinics on-site or partners with other health-care providers, depending on local needs and health infrastructure (Pro Mujer, 2010.)
- **Empowerment.** While all of the non-financial services listed above can increase women's self-confidence, their access to resources and/or their ability to set and achieve strategic goals, some MFIs design a multifaceted package of non-financial services with a broader empowerment objective. The IMAGE and WORTH initiatives are two examples of such approaches (see Box 17.11 and the case at the end of this chapter).

The advantages and disadvantages of making non-financial services voluntary versus compulsory are discussed in Chapter 12, and do not need to be debated again here. When targeting women, however, it is important for MFIs that offer non-financial services to make sure those services are available at a time and in a location that is convenient for women, given their enterprise and household responsibilities and their potential mobility limitations.

17.4 Outreach Strategy

As introduced in Chapter 3, a market outreach strategy consists of four main components: 1) a definition of the products and services that will be offered to a targeted market; 2) a plan for communicating the value of those products and services; 3) a plan for delivering the product offering to that market; and 4) a plan for building a relationship with the targeted market. This section explores each of these components for an outreach strategy focused on women.

Product Strategy

Since the design characteristics of specific products that MFIs might offer women were discussed in the previous section, here it is worth commenting on the overall product portfolio strategy only. MFIs that target women often begin their relationship with new clients by offering a savings product. Early on, they also typically rely on group-based lending methodologies and non-traditional forms of collateral, to give women opportunities for building assets, skills, and confidence. Later, they provide access to other products that facilitate growth, such as individual loans or leasing products.

Most MFIs that specifically target women also integrate some kind of non-financial service into their product portfolio, often in partnership with a non-financial institution that has a mission and financing to support the provision of such services. The WORTH and IMAGE initiatives provide excellent examples of how partnerships can bring results for financial as well as non-financial actors that they could not have achieved on their own. As articulated above, non-financial services are an important ingredient enabling women to overcome the obstacles they face in making productive use of an MFI's financial services.

Box 17.11 Combining Microfinance with Gender and HIV Training

The Intervention with Microfinance for AIDS & Gender Equity (IMAGE) project is an example of how a well-designed microfinance programme can provide a platform for addressing a range of broader developmental issues. Developed by the Small Enterprise Foundation (SEF) and the Rural AIDS and Development Action Research (RADAR) programme, the IMAGE project was designed to be integrated into SEF's existing microfinance programme.

The training component, Sisters for Life (SfL), consists of ten one-hour participatory sessions delivered by RADAR staff at the beginning of SEF centre meetings, which take place every two weeks and are compulsory for clients. The training is structured to give participants an opportunity to strengthen their confidence and skills relating to communication, critical thinking and leadership. Training topics include: gender (roles, inequality and culture); the body, sexuality and gender-based violence; communication and relationships; and HIV transmission and prevention. The training is followed by a six-month community mobilization phase.

Overall, the microfinance component of IMAGE performed as well as other SEF operations, if not better. During the pilot phase (2001–2004), exit rates were consistently 50 per cent lower than the average for SEF, portfolio growth rates were above average, meeting attendance was high, and the repayment rate was over 99 per cent. The project also achieved impressive changes in terms of women's self-confidence, relationships with their partners, and engagement in their communities. The most remarkable achievement was a 55 per cent decrease in violence (physical and sexual abuse) experienced by women within the family, and a significant change in risky sexual behaviour that might lead to HIV infection, evidenced by a 24 per cent increase in the use of condoms and a 60 per cent increase in those accessing voluntary testing for HIV.

Combining two specialist projects created synergies resulting in impacts beyond those that have been achieved by either organization independently. Financial services enabled women to increase their economic contribution to the household, which strengthened women's bargaining power, while training provided the awareness, self-confidence and support necessary for women to challenge violent behaviour within the household. As one client commented, "Now that we have money we are able to say how we feel without fearing that your husband will stop supporting you… Now we know how to talk to our husbands about sexual matters, but before they would beat you when talking about those things."

Source: Adapted from Simanowitz, 2008a and 2008b.

Regardless of the products developed, MFIs should resist the temptation to simply replicate models that have been used elsewhere. They should design services based on a sound understanding of women's financial needs and the gender constraints being faced in the local environment. To identify which products and design features can best contribute to women's empowerment under a particular set of circumstances, MFIs will have to conduct market research. The most widely disseminated toolkit for market research in microfinance was developed by *MicroSave*, and can be adapted to explore gender dimensions of product design (see Box 17.12).

It is important to stress that neither women nor men are a homogeneous group, and should not be treated as such. Women, for example, can be widowed, single, newly married, pregnant, young girls, unemployed, employed, rural or urban. MFIs can usefully segment the female market segment by age, marital status, income level, health status, degree of control over assets, and so on. Such segmentation will enable an MFI to tailor its product portfolio, as well as the communication, delivery and relationship strategies discussed below, to the needs

Box 17.12 Market Research Tools for Gender-sensitive Products

- **Wealth ranking or poverty diamond tools** provide rapid ways of segregating a community into three or four basic poverty categories according to local criteria. Participants then rank themselves or people in their community according to the levels or the indicators. They can also compare their current positions with their situations before they joined a programme, or their target positions after one year or a specified period of time. Microfinance providers and groups can use diamonds to identify gender-specific dimensions of poverty; to examine the socioeconomic characteristics of women who choose to join (or not join), those who leave or whose accounts become dormant; and to develop more inclusive products in collaboration with clients or potential clients.
- **Seasonality analysis of household income, expenditure, savings and credit** provides insights into some of the risks and pressures faced by female and male clients, how they use MFIs' financial services to respond to these, and what product improvements or innovations MFIs can design in response.
- **Seasonality analysis of migration, casual employment and goods/services** looks at the availability of cash, and examines how far women and men might have to migrate to find work. This has important implications for the ability to make regular savings and loan repayments, and also for women's control over household incomes earned by men.
- **Cash mobility mapping** provides an understanding of where women and men go to acquire or spend cash (for example, markets, waged labour, cooperatives, informal financial organizations) and leads into discussions of which financial service institutions they trust or value and why.
- **Relationship mapping** analyses intra- and inter-household support networks and power relationships in order to increase understanding of the dynamics of households and communities. For MFIs, they can be quantified to estimate, for example, the incidence of polygamy or of households headed by women. They can also be used to understand which relationships are important to women, and to examine how groups can be used to strengthen rather than undermine social networks.
- **Life-cycle analysis** identifies events that require lump sums of cash. In addition to births, marriages and deaths and the gender differences in needs related to these, a gender-sensitive analysis would also look at pregnancy, divorce and widowhood and other times of particular vulnerability.
- **Time series of asset ownership** (this year, last year, five and ten years before) is useful in determining what "productive" and "protective" assets are valued the most, and thus the potential for designing or refining corresponding financial products for housing, education, health insurance and so on. A gender-sensitive analysis would include consideration of gender differences in control and ownership.
- **Financial service Venn/Chapati diagram or matrix** identifies financial service providers within the community and their roles, which providers are used by whom, the rates they charge, etc. This can provide important insights into how poor women's and men's perceptions of financial services sometimes vary substantially from the actual terms and conditions being offered. It also leads to discussion of how different services can be improved.
- **Ranking of products and/or service providers** helps an MFI understand the relative importance/desirability of different product features (for example, interest rate, opening balance, grace period etc.) for different groups of women and men. It could also help identify product features that would facilitate women's control over incomes and resources.

Source: Mayoux, 2006, adapted from MicroSave tools.

of specific subsegments. Given the size of the female market segment, this is a particularly useful product development strategy.

Communication Strategy

To communicate with women, MFIs can build on relationships or networks that women already use to access and disseminate information, such as women's associations, religious organizations, or informal credit and savings groups. They can distribute information in places where women already congregate, such as markets, water sources or health clinics. They can also be creative with mass-marketing techniques, such as the social soap opera being developed by Women's World Banking and the live theatre performances being used by Kashf (see Box 17.13). Regardless of the channels chosen, MFIs should analyse the cost–benefit ratio of the various strategies with which they experiment, and focus their resources on those that best reach the women they are trying to serve. What works for one institution or market will not necessarily be cost-effective for another.

Attention also needs to be paid to the content of the messages sent to women. In marketing materials, as well as application and transaction forms, institutions should ensure that their language is client focused and easy to understand, so that clients will be clear about product benefits as well as the institution's requirements and procedures. With illiterate clients, this will require verbal as well as visual communication channels. Messaging for women should take into consideration the tendency, in many cultural contexts, for women to require more information than men before they are willing to make a financial decision (Banthia et al., 2009). Financial literacy campaigns can be very helpful in increasing women's awareness and understanding of the various financial services that might be available to them.

Box 17.13 Creative Communication

To educate the public about saving, Women's World Banking (WWB) will support the creation of a "social soap opera" in the Dominican Republic. Because low-income women often believe that saving small amounts of money in formal financial institutions is not worth the effort, the soap opera will feature stories highlighting responsible management of money. WWB will work on the project with Puntos de Encuentro, a Nicaraguan NGO with experience in using television serial dramas to change cultural attitudes. Through the soap opera, WWB will not only illustrate both positive and negative money management practices – and the consequences of these actions – but will also follow up with a communications campaign that will use the buzz created by the soap opera to encourage people to save more money through formal bank accounts.

In Pakistan, Kashf's Gender Empowerment and Social Advocacy (GESA) team uses theatre to educate clients on themes of gender empowerment, violence and other critical threats to low-income women and their families. It has been a particularly effective tool for Kashf as it expands into rural areas where the institution is less well known. The live performances are used to educate the local community about the institution, its values and objectives, and what it can offer. It is also a useful tool to inform families of potential women loan officers who would be hired to staff the local branches.

Source: Iskenderian, 2010, and Lynch, 2009.

Besides being clear, MFI messages must be attractive to women. Images and photographs are powerful – not only for those who are illiterate. Visuals can connect readers with the institution through the use of familiar scenes and activities while also challenging stereotypes, for example by depicting women in non-traditional activities. An MFI's marketing can encourage women's aspirations, for instance to be successful businesswomen, to be recognized as financial contributors to the household, or to be independent and capable of making financial decisions (Frank, 2008). This can help motivate women to approach an MFI, and to tackle the challenges that may be involved in accessing or utilizing the MFI's services.

One element that successful gender-sensitive communication strategies often have in common is a means to ensure frequent contact with women clients, not just to sell a product, but to support usage and answer queries about the product over time. Regular contact was specifically mentioned as a success factor by the IMAGE project, for instance, and by both SEWA and BRAC (Bangladesh Rehabilitation Assistance Committee) in their livelihood interventions with girls.

Who communicates with women can also be important. In Pakistan, for example, the success of NRSP's maternity health loan was hindered by a lack of female staff who could market the loans and appraise applications. People in the community had reservations about discussing maternity matters with male credit officers (Chen, 2009). Hiring and training women sales agents from local communities has been a critical success factor for Tata-AIG in India as well. Female sales agents have been more approachable and accessible to local women (Churchill, 2006).

Although an MFI may target women, its communication strategy may need to address messages to both women and men, as illustrated by the case of TYM in Box 17.14. If men do not understand an MFI's objectives, product offering, benefits or requirements, they will be less likely to support female members of their family who wish to be involved with it. Financial literacy campaigns that address both sexes and incorporate examples of men and women jointly discussing household financial plans can help change attitudes and behaviour. Clear communication with men can also help avoid the potentially negative impacts of extending financial services to women, and ensure that an MFI's interventions ultimately create a strong household, not empowered women and disempowered men.

Box 17.14 Enhancing Communication with Men to Reach More Women

After recognizing that some women were not able to access its services because of a lack of support from their husbands, TYM (the first licensed microfinance institution in Viet Nam) began investing more in communication to reach a larger public. Events such as its annual anniversary and Women's Day celebrations are now open to the entire community and not just women members. TYM also started to include men in training activities that were initially intended for members only. For example, when the ILO's GET Ahead for Women in Enterprise training package was introduced to clients in 11 of TYM's branches, it was modified to include a half-day session with husbands. These and other communication efforts have helped TYM to increase understanding and endorsement of the MFI's activities among men. TYM is now considering opening its services to men, possibly by the end of 2011.

Source: Nguyen and Duong, 2010.

Delivery Strategy

There are three main issues to consider in this section: 1) where should services be delivered; 2) by whom should they be delivered; and 3) through what processes should they be delivered?

Where should services be delivered? Given their heavy domestic workload and, in some cases, mobility restrictions, women generally prefer MFIs that can bring financial services as close to their homes and/or businesses as possible. They tend to value delivery strategies that minimize transaction costs more than they value a low-priced service, 24-hour access, or a product design that perfectly meets their needs. One of the reasons why large group delivery models have been so popular in rural areas is that they bring financial and non-financial services to women instead of women having to go to an MFI or its partners. The other transaction costs created by large group methodologies, such as the time spent in meetings or training, are outweighed by the time and money saved by not travelling to the MFI.

Groups also provide a power platform: a forum for sharing information and developing new skills; a source of peer support and encouragement that can motivate savings and build confidence; a space for identifying common issues and organizing for change (Murray and Boros, 2001). In some cultures, groups must consist entirely of women in order for this power platform to benefit women. In other cultures, the gender divide is less severe. An MFI's approach to group organization will depend on the degree of gender segregation within a community, on women's and men's interests, and on the mission of the MFI itself.

Safety is also a concern for women, and is another reason why group-based delivery channels have worked well for them historically. Women group together with other women whom they trust, and they meet in a known, safe place. MFIs that want to introduce women to other delivery channels, such as branch offices, ATMs or POS devices, will need to make sure that these access points are located in areas that are accessible to women – areas that are safe, where it is culturally acceptable to be seen, and where they feel comfortable.

Technologies such as cellular phone banking and smart cards are making it possible for MFIs to bring their services ever closer to women, often through individual channels. This can bring greater confidentiality, much greater convenience and lower transaction costs, for example if physical meetings between the MFI and clients are no longer required, or can be held less frequently or for a shorter duration. Different approaches will be valued by different segments of the female population, so MFIs need to match their delivery strategy with the preferences of the sub-segments they wish to serve.

Who should deliver the services? As discussed above, it can often be advantageous to employ women staff to serve women more effectively. While male loan officers treating women clients with respect and dignity is empowering in and of itself, many women clients indicate that they can relate more easily to female loan officers, and that female loan officers provide a role model of achievement. In some cultures, MFIs and their partners must have female staff to serve female clients, be it with financial or non-financial services. In Pakistan, Mennonite Economic Development Associates (MEDA) and the Entrepreneurship and Career Development Institute (ECDI) created an entire "woman-to woman" network that enabled isolated rural embroiderers to access quality inputs, more sophisticated designs and high-value urban markets through knowledgeable women sales agents (Jones and Snelgrove, 2006).

Table 17.3 Good practices in staff gender policy

Practice	Example
Recruitment and promotion	• Include gender awareness in job descriptions and as a key criterion for recruitment and promotion. • Advertise employment opportunities through channels likely to reach more women. • Create an in-house mentoring programme. • Adopt proactive hiring and promotion strategies to recruit high-potential women into senior management positions until gender balance is reached.
Rights at work	• Review all norms and job descriptions from a gender perspective. • Give equal pay for equal work. • Guarantee freedom from sexual harassment (women and men). • Establish rights and responsibilities. • Establish structures for all staff to participate in decision-making.
Family-friendly work practices	• Provide flexible working arrangements: flexi-time, flexi-place, part-time work, and job sharing at all levels, including senior managers. • Develop maternity and paternity leave policies. • Provide childcare and dependant care leave and support.
Training	• Provide ongoing training for all men and women staff in participatory gender awareness, sensitization, planning and analysis. • Provide follow-up training with specific tools and methodologies. • Provide training for women to move from mid-level to senior positions.
Implementation structure and incentives	• Adequately resource a gender focal point to coordinate the implementation of gender policies throughout the organization. • Integrate gender equality and empowerment indicators into ongoing monitoring and evaluation. • Establish staff targets and incentives for achieving gender equality and empowerment.

Source: World Bank, 2009a.

Through what processes should services be delivered? Given women's lower levels of literacy, education and free time, processes need to be kept as simple and streamlined as possible. This applies not only to the delivery of financial products, but also to the delivery of whatever non-financial services or empowerment initiatives an MFI might decide to facilitate. Often, empowerment initiatives can be mainstreamed into an MFI's core activities, thus avoiding extra costs for the client and the MFI. This may be easier for institutions that use a large-group credit-with-education model, but it can also be implemented by for-profit MFIs that deliver only financial services directly to individuals.

In the latter case, for example, MFIs might adjust the questions asked during the application process to promote a vision of empowerment, to encourage applicants to think through their financial planning, or to help them challenge inequalities in power and control within the household (Mayoux and Hartl, 2009). Group processes could actively promote women's participation and leadership. Advertising campaigns could include financial education messages.

Loyalty rewards and sales promotions could be designed to empower the recipient or the women and girls in her family.

Another important process that has not yet been discussed is the management of information. Information systems need to segment data by gender, and managers need to analyse that information regularly to monitor the status of their relationships with women and men, to increase their understanding of the female and male market segments over time, and to identify opportunities for improving service delivery to specific sub-segments in the future. With segmented data, an MFI can compare, for example, the marketing channels that successfully recruit women in different income brackets, or the clusters of products that women purchase in different stages of their life cycle.

If an MFI does not have a sufficiently robust information system to segment all of its data, it can track a handful of specific indicators as part of its ongoing performance management. The indicators it might consider include:

- percentage of women clients;
- percentage of women accessing larger loans or higher-level services;
- percentage of female staff;
- percentage of decision-making positions within the MFI held by women;
- volume of product usage by women and men;
- frequency of product usage by women and men;
- repayment, arrears or default rates among women and men;
- exit or retention rates among women and men;
- customer satisfaction among women and men.

Relationship Strategy

The final component of an MFI's outreach strategy considers how the product, communication and delivery strategies will come together to build a strong relationship with the female market segment over time. It will not necessarily require a separate action plan, but thinking about how the MFI wants to build a relationship with women and what kind of relationship it wants to build will influence how its product, communication and delivery strategies ultimately take shape.

For example, regular interaction was noted above to be an important contributor to effective communication, but it can also be a critical component of a strategy for building long-term relationships with women. As part of its relationship strategy, an MFI might want to consider how it can create regular communication opportunities with women clients, and how its communication with clients might evolve as the relationship strengthens. How might the MFI leverage communication opportunities to develop a relationship? In the WORTH and IMAGE projects, women's regular participation in some kind of joint activity was necessary for empowerment. This suggests that communication strategies that facilitate interaction will be more powerful than the simple dissemination of information.

Advocacy and empowerment investments are not necessarily required for an MFI to serve women, but can significantly strengthen an MFI's relationship with its female clients. These

investments can differentiate the MFI from its competition, put women in a better position to use the MFI's services, communicate that the MFI cares about the well-being of its clients and not just profit, and generate customer loyalty.

For an MFI's relationship with women to grow and strengthen over time, the institution may want to make a special effort to protect that relationship, and to protect women from the potentially negative effects of financial service access, by developing and implementing gender-sensitive consumer protection guidelines or a customer care charter.[38] By emphasizing privacy, ethical behaviour, and treating each customer with respect, these guidelines can offer substantial protection to women as well as men, particularly if guidelines are combined with gender training for staff and/or financial literacy training for clients.

MFIs can also develop a brand and an institutional culture that is women-friendly and empowering. They can honour women both as contributors to household economies and as business owners and operators. They can tailor their sales promotions and loyalty programmes to provide incentives that female clients find attractive. Rewards that showcase women's success, increase their confidence, or confront obstacles that prevent women from making productive use of financial services can strengthen the MFI's relationship with these clients in addition to recognizing their loyalty to date.

If an MFI wants to serve women more effectively and does not know where to start, a good first step might be a gender audit.[39] A gender audit has two main objectives: 1) to ensure that an MFI's services are equally attractive for men and women, taking into account their different needs, priorities and characteristics; and 2) to recommend adaptations that could create a better working environment for both sexes (Athmer, 2004). A gender audit helped the Christian Enterprise Trust of Zambia (CETZAM) realize that its collateral requirement was disadvantageous to women and its loan processes were too complex (Mutalima, 2006). In Bangladesh, ASA used the Organizational Gender Assessment tool developed by Women's World Banking to uncover institutional policies that negatively affected employees who were mothers, such as regular field staff rotation and a requirement that staff members at all branch offices work late into the night managing loan recovery and overdue payments (Iskenderian, 2010). Once these MFIs identified their weaknesses, they were able to do something about them.

An ongoing process of understanding women's challenges and opportunities, and developing products and services that can support them in tackling those challenges and opportunities, is perhaps the strongest foundation that an MFI can build for building and sustaining a long-term relationship with the female market segment.

[38] For more information on client protection, go to www.smartcampaign.org/tools-a-resources. An example of a customer care charter can be found in Chapter 23.

[39] See, for example, International Labour Organization, 2007, *A manual for gender audit facilitators* (Geneva, ILO), available at: http://www.ilo.org/dyn/gender/docs/RES/536/F932374742/web%20gender%20manual.pdf

Main Messages

1. Men and women will not be able to make equal use of an MFI's services if they have unequal resources with which to access those services.
2. Aim to create strong households, not empowered women and disempowered men.
3. Segment and analyse performance data by gender.
4. Look for ways to mainstream empowerment initiatives into an MFI's core activities.
5. Make sure women's voices are heard at the tables where decisions are made.
6. A staff gender policy can help an MFI to promote gender equity internally and externally.

Case Study: The WORTH Programme in Nepal

Background. In response to extremely low literacy rates among virtually all groups of Nepali women, the US Agency for International Development (USAID) awarded Pact, a non-profit international development organization, a grant to provide literacy training to 500,000 rural Nepali women through a project known as Women Reading for Development (WORD). Through this programme, which was conducted in 71 of Nepal's 75 districts, Pact asked women what had motivated them to become literate. They answered consistently that being able to read and write would help them increase their family income.

In response to this feedback, Pact began to explore ways to bring income-generating programmes to poor women in Nepal. It designed a programme rooted in the informal groups that had proved so successful in the implementation of WORD. It believed that this strategy would not only reach large numbers of women in the shortest possible time and at the lowest possible cost, but also make it possible to reach groups in rural, even remote, areas where MFIs could not readily work. Pact believed that women would appreciate their inherent strengths if they became literate and generated and controlled their own wealth, particularly by helping themselves and each other. If they created their own village banks with their own savings, if they read self-help books together and mastered literacy, banking and business skills, they could be entirely self-reliant.

The Women's Empowerment Programme (WEP), as it was known in Nepal, began in 1998, but later, when Pact took the programme to other countries, it was renamed WORTH. In Nepal, Pact chose to work through 240 local grassroots entities rather than try to work directly with women, and as a result was able to engage over 100,000 women in just a few months.

WORTH was an empowerment programme for all rural women, not only the very poor. Pact did not expect that the better-off would be greatly attracted to a self-help programme dealing, at least initially, with very small sums. It believed, however, that those better-off women who were interested in WORTH could be an important asset, contributing their skills and savings. It also recognized that even better-off women in Nepal's Terai region were still relatively poor, often illiterate, marginalized, and disadvantaged. As it turned out, according to a survey of WORTH's impact in 2001, bank members earned considerably less than Nepal's annual per capita income of just over US$200. Forty-five per cent of the members were deeply poor, subsisting on less than US$75 per year. Another 35 per cent were only a little better off, earning at most US$160 a year.

How WORTH works. Every woman contributes to her group's savings fund every week. At the same time, women who know how to read and write use WORTH materials focused on

business and banking to help others learn. Women then practise their literacy skills by reading together materials that guide them in turning their savings fund into a loan fund. The group lends to individual members, charging interest on the loans. Periodically the group distributes the interest back to the members as a dividend. At the same time, the members who receive loans are encouraged to invest the money in their own small businesses. WORTH women thus develop two streams of income – one from their individual businesses and one from their collective business, the village bank.

The WORTH curriculum consists of a series of self-instruction handbooks that deal sequentially with literacy, banking and business. The books make it possible for women to learn sounds, letters and numbers in Nepali through a simple keyword method and the ample use of cartoon drawings. Women build their skills in both reading and arithmetic as they read together about how to develop their group, master WORTH village banking, and create vibrant businesses. The messages are highly targeted, and presented through stories and pictures that encourage discussion and facilitate informed decision-making by group members. Women are expected to pay small joining and book fees, which are deposited into their group fund. They must seek their own literacy volunteer and purchase a cash box and calculator for their banking activities.

Appreciative Planning and Action. An innovative group process methodology, Appreciative Planning and Action (APA), was one of the most important elements of WORTH. First developed in Nepal from the principles of Participatory Rural Appraisal (PRA) and Appreciative Inquiry, APA encouraged women to focus on their successes rather than their problems. It invited women to share stories as a foundation for learning, and helped them make their own story a driving force in the programme. Women who have been immersed in problems all their lives usually have given little thought to their strengths and opportunities, and the APA process enabled women, perhaps for the first time, to listen to the success stories of their peers, and to gain both a sense of their own potential and the confidence to try new things.

Women shared their stories, achievements, aspirations, and plans for the future through regularly organized Family Days to which their families and communities were invited. Successes that started with one member ended up empowering the whole group, women's families, and the larger community. The groups also participated in "Monthly Mobile Workshops" in which two members of each of ten groups came together to share success stories, ask questions of one another, and receive additional training. These workshops were enormously popular among women, and helped create networks of Village Banks throughout the programme area.

Rights, Responsibilities, and Advocacy training. Interspersed among the various WORTH activities was a six-month-long Rights, Responsibilities, and Advocacy (RRA) curriculum delivered by The Asia Foundation. This module, which complemented WORTH's empowerment agenda and the APA process, made use of trained facilitators, focused on a rights-based framework for learning, and promoted the notion that women have both the opportunity and the responsibility to be active members of civil society. Groups commonly developed action plans to achieve goals that they set to bring about change in their communities. Thousands of activities took place in all 21 districts as a result of this training and planning, including campaigns dealing with such issues as alcoholism, gender-based violence, marriage registration, polygamy, child marriage, and girls' education.

Results. Prior to the programme's start, the 125,000 women in WORTH had already accumulated about US$720,000 in savings. During the two years of WORTH they nearly tripled that amount, almost all of which was parcelled out in loans to over 52,000 women at the end of the programme in 2001. Women were earning 18 to 24 per cent annual returns on their savings. Twelve per cent of the groups reported one or more late payments, but only four per cent had ever made a loan on which a woman actually defaulted. Over the course of the programme the number of women in business grew from 19,000 to 87,000. Microenterprise sales in the final six months of the programme were close to US$5,500,000, up from US$600,000 for a similar six-month period two years earlier. Eighty-five per cent of members were reading and writing at some level (although some only to write their names) compared with approximately 40 per cent prior to WORTH.

In 2006, Pact conducted research to determine whether any of the village banks still existed despite the civil war and the collapse of national governance, and, if so, how they were faring as community banks and as vehicles of change. It found that 64 per cent of the original 1,536 village banks were still active eight and a half years after the programme began, and five to six years after all WORTH-related support ended. The average village bank holds total assets of over Rs 211,000 (US$3,100), more than three times its holdings in 2001. Forty-three per cent of women said that their degree of freedom from domestic violence had changed because of their membership in a WORTH group. One in ten reported that WORTH helped "change her life" because of its impact on domestic violence. Eighty-three per cent of women reported that because of WORTH they were able to send more of their children to school. A quarter of the existing WORTH groups have helped start an estimated 425 new groups involving another 11,000 women with neither external assistance nor prompting from WORTH itself.

This case study was adapted from Mayoux (2008).

Recommended Reading

- Banthia, A.; Johnson, S.; McCord, M.; Mathews, B. 2009. *Microinsurance that works for women: Making gender-sensitive microinsurance programs* (Geneva, ILO), at: http://www.ilo.org/public/english/employment/mifacility/download/mpaper3_gender.pdf
- Bauer, S.; Finnegan, G.; Haspels, N.; Deelen, L.; Seltik, H.; Majurin, E. 2008. *GET ahead for women in enterprise: Training package and resource kit*, 2nd edition (Geneva, International Labour Organization), available at: http://www.ilo.org/wcmsp5/groups/public/---ed_emp/---emp_ent/documents/publication/wcms_116100.pdf
- Cheston, S.; Kuhn, L. 2002. *Empowering women through microfinance* (New York, NY, UNIFEM), at: http://www.microcreditsummit.org/papers/empowerintro.htm
- International Labour Organization. 2007b. *A manual for gender audit facilitators* (Geneva, ILO), available at: http://www.ilo.org/dyn/gender/docs/RES/536/F932374742/web%20gender%20manual.pdf
- Lynch, E. 2009. *Transforming the landscape of leadership in microfinance: Maintaining the focus on women* (New York, NY, Women's World Banking), at: http://www.swwb.org/files/pubs/en/transforming_the_landscape_of_leadership_in_microfinance_e.pdf
- Mayoux, L.; Hartl, M. 2009. *Gender and rural microfinance: Reaching and empowering women*, Guide for practitioners (Rome, IFAD), at: www.ifad.org/gender/pub/gender_finance.pdf.

- Murray, U.; Boros, R. 2002. *A guide to gender sensitive microfinance, Socio-Economic and Gender Analysis Programme – SEAGA* (Rome, FAO, Gender and Population Division), at: http://www.fao.org/sd/seaga/downloads/en/microfinanceen.pdf
- World Bank. 2009a. *Gender in agriculture: Sourcebook* (Washington, DC, World Bank), at: http://siteresources.worldbank.org/INTGENAGRLIVSOUBOOK/Resources/CompleteBook.pdf

Useful Websites

- Sustainable Microfinance for Women's Empowerment, http://www.genfinance.info/
- United Nations Entity for Gender Equality and the Empowerment of Women, http://www.unwomen.org/
- Women and Development Resources on the Internet, http://www.gdrc.org/gender/link-resources.html

18 Post-crisis Microfinance[40]

From Bangladesh to Central America, and from Haiti to Rwanda, it [microfinance] has been an especially powerful tool in helping the poor get back on their feet after natural and man-made disasters.... Our team's findings suggest that tens of thousands of survivors are being held back in their efforts to recover because they lack investment capital, even as little as US$50. ~ Counts et al. (2005)

Armed conflicts, economic crises, coups, earthquakes, floods and other natural and man-made disasters are unfortunately too common to ignore their existence and their impact on development, including on microfinance. A crisis poses serious challenges for microfinance programmes.

At the same time, microfinance programmes can have positive social and economic impacts on post-crisis settings by integrating different groups of clients (for example, residents and returnees), building trust and social capital (through group lending), facilitating reconstruction, and expanding economic opportunities.

This module introduces basic concepts and considerations for MFIs that are interested in serving crisis-affected communities. It addresses the following six topics:

1. When is microfinance an appropriate intervention?
2. Characteristics of a post-crisis environment
3. Characteristics of post-crisis clients
4. Designing a post-crisis product portfolio
5. Delivering a post-crisis product portfolio
6. Preparing clients and institutions for crisis

18.1 When Is Microfinance an Appropriate Intervention?

If an MFI is present in a community when crisis strikes, then the question it must answer is not whether to intervene, but rather which services it can and should offer during and immediately after the crisis (see Section 18.4). For an MFI that seeks to enter a crisis-affected area for the first time, or to re-enter an area from which it previously had to exit, the question of when to enter that area is critical.

Unfortunately, there is no easy answer to this question. There are many types of crisis, some of which last for decades and others that stabilize more rapidly. The timing for entering a crisis-affected area and introducing or reintroducing financial services depends less on the amount of time that has passed since the outbreak or resolution of the crisis and more on the nature of destruction caused. Somewhat surprisingly, microfinance can be an appropriate intervention as soon as three basic conditions are met (Larson et al., 2004):

[40] This chapter is adapted from Magill, J. 2003. *The first 30 days: A practical guide to managing natural disasters for microfinance institutions* (Bethesda: Development Alternatives, Inc.); Miamidian, E.; Arnold, M.; Burritt, K.; Jacquand, M. 2005. *Surviving disasters and supporting recovery: A guidebook for microfinance institutions*, Disaster Risk Management Working Paper Series No. 10 (Washington, DC, World Bank), and Doyle, K. 1998. *Microfinance in the Wake of Conflict: Challenges and Opportunities* (New York, SEEP Network).

1. **Political stability.** The operating environment must offer a reasonable degree of security and safety to an MFI and its clients. Put negatively, there must be an absence of chaos. This does not mean that there must be a total absence of conflict, or of the possibility that conflict might flare up again. MFIs such as LEAP in Liberia and URWEGO in Rwanda have demonstrated that microfinance can be done successfully in one area of a country while conflict rages in others (see Box 18.1).
2. **Economic activity.** According to Doyle (1998), "If there is a single, determining factor across organizations and contexts that signals the possibility of initiating microfinance activities, it is the reappearance of open-air markets." The resumption of basic economic activity seems to indicate that clients' lives are returning to normal, and that potential demand for income-generating financial services exists. MFIs that survive a crisis may be able to offer clients risk-managing financial services (such as access to savings and remittances) before economic activity resumes, but those that wish to launch new microcredit activities will want to wait until they see opportunities for productive investment.
3. **Population stability.** To operate successfully in a post-crisis environment, an MFI must be reasonably sure that the people it wants to serve will remain in its area of operations long enough to repay their loans.

Of course, just because microfinance can be an appropriate intervention does not mean that it will be an appropriate intervention. MFIs that choose to operate in a post-crisis environment must be willing and able to experiment and be sufficiently flexible to manage changing circumstances. It will help if they have a long-term interest in serving the area and are prepared to face higher costs and risks in the short-term. It will also help if there is some degree of macroeconomic stability and a functioning commercial banking system. If none of this is present, an organization should seriously consider whether the timing is right for it to launch microfinance activities. Emergency relief and humanitarian assistance might be more appropriate interventions at that point in time.

In general, if an organization was not active in an area prior to a crisis, launching a full-scale microfinance programme immediately after the crisis is not recommended. Start-ups are inherently risky, and the pressures and challenges of a post-crisis environment elevate that risk substantially. Information will be difficult to gather, and local resources will already be strained by relief efforts. It may be useful, however, to initiate some pre-credit activities such as group formation, internal savings mobilization or training that could prepare the way for microfinance activities during the recovery phase (Seller, 2008).

Box 18.1 What Is Sufficient Stability?

World Relief Rwanda started Urwego, a microfinance institution, in 1996, nearly two years after the genocide of 1994. Even then, many observers questioned whether Rwanda was sufficiently stable for microfinance, given the existence of insurrections in certain parts of the country. Urwego's response was simply to stay away from those areas, focusing on the more stable areas of the country.

Source: Larson et al., 2004.

Table 18.1 Essential and favourable conditions for post-crisis microfinance

	External	Internal
Essential conditions	• Political stability • Sufficient economic activity and demand for financial services • Relative population stability	• Capacity and will to experiment • Flexibility in product and programme design
Favourable conditions	• Macroeconomic stability • Functioning commercial bank • Support institutions developing • Social capital, trust (among population as well as in institutions)	• Availability of long-term funding • Interest in long-term engagement in the area • Willingness to face higher costs and risks

Source: Authors' summary of USAID, 2004.

18.2 Characteristics of a Post-crisis Environment

According to Nourse et al. (2006), crises are typically classified into one of three categories: 1) rapid-onset disasters, which are caused by events such as earthquakes and floods; 2) disasters, such as drought or desertification; and 3) conflict, either high-intensity or low-intensity. Although these three types of crisis impact on communities in different ways, there are certain characteristics that all post-crisis environments tend to have in common.

Persisting insecurity. When a crisis ends, fear, uncertainty, violence and lawlessness do not immediately disappear. Especially after a prolonged armed conflict, demobilized soldiers who possess weapons but not jobs may survive by stealing from others, including MFI staff and clients. A lack of respect for the rule of law will affect the way people deal with disagreements long after the shooting has ended. Unresolved problems may persist in new forms, and conflict can return after a short period of peace. Even in the case of natural disasters, the lack of capacity for general law enforcement can create an environment that is ripe for looting and crime.

Human resource limitations. Crises deplete a community's human resource base in several ways: people may be killed or injured, they may flee, or if the crisis lasts a long time, they may spend years without access to education or training. As a result, MFIs may find it considerably more difficult and more expensive to recruit and train staff in a post-conflict environment. Clients are also likely to be less educated and may require more training and support than in other environments. Both staff and clients may require counselling to overcome the trauma they experienced during the crisis.

Population mobility. A large percentage of the population may be forced to leave their home or even their country as a result of a crisis. The long-lasting conflict in Mozambique between 1964 and 1992, for example, caused 10 per cent of the total population to flee the country and 23 per cent to displace internally (Wilson, 2001). In Bosnia, during five years of conflict, 51 per cent of the population was displaced (Doyle, 1998), and the 2010 earthquake in Haiti left approximately 15 per cent of the population homeless (Associated Press, 2010).

Once a crisis ends, these populations will often try to return home, with varying consequences for MFIs that may try to serve them.

Temporary increase in self-employment. Crises destroy both formal and informal employment opportunities, but the informal sector re-establishes itself much faster than the formal sector. As a result, many people turn to self-employment and to the informal sector in an effort to make a living, some for the first time and some only until the formal sector is rebuilt.

Destruction of physical capital. Damage to infrastructure such as roads, markets, electricity and telecommunication systems affects economic and financial activity as well as the delivery of basic services, such as health, education and sanitation. The loss of shelter and other productive and non-productive assets increases the poverty and vulnerability of households in post-crisis environments.

Destruction of social capital. Crises damage and often destroy social capital – the networks, norms, values and understandings that facilitate cooperation within or among groups. The damage is worst in prolonged conflicts, when certain segments of society cause harm to others, which creates resentment and often leads to a lack of trust in local institutions, in people and in the future. This is especially problematic for community-based financial institutions, and for supplier credit and other forms of value chain finance. Natural disasters can disperse populations and cause emotional distress, but their effect on social capital is usually temporary. Even though social infrastructure may be destroyed, the ties that bind the community together are usually not, and as soon as people can find a way to come together, those ties help them cope with the crisis. Social capital is often strengthened by the experience of having survived the crisis together.

Instability. Persisting insecurity, population mobility, and the destruction of physical and social capital all contribute to ongoing economic instability. At both at the macroeconomic and microeconomic levels, this unstable and unpredictable environment makes it difficult and risky to make plans for the future.

Influx of donor funds and grants. In the early stages of crisis response, relief and humanitarian assistance has an important role to play. Nevertheless, the introduction of grants and subsidies can create dependence and distort the market for sustainable microfinance if they last too long, or if the rationale for and short-term nature of the grants is not clearly communicated. MFIs operating in a post-crisis environment will need to invest time in advocacy to encourage the appropriate use of grants (see Chapter 13), to raise donor agency awareness of how microfinance can help transition communities from relief to development, and to communicate messages that avoid confusion between loans and grants.

Table 18.2 summarizes the impact of the three main types of crisis on various levels of an economy. The exact impact of a crisis will depend on its duration, scale and intensity, as well as on the strength of the affected community's social and physical infrastructure prior to the crisis, and its degree of crisis preparedness. In general, conflicts have greater impact than disasters, especially long-lasting conflicts, because they destroy the relationships and community structures that are needed to cope with the consequences of a crisis.

Table 18.2 Levels of impact by type of crisis

Crisis type		Micro-level (businesses, households)	Meso-level (institutions)	Macro-level
CRISIS TYPE	**Slow-onset disasters**	• Loss of assets • Loss of skills due to migration • Declines in productivity	• Weak marketing networks due to migration • Damage to or loss of natural resources	Localized reduction in capacity to enforce laws and provide basic services
	Rapid-onset disasters	• Loss of assets • Disrupted markets • Trauma	Infrastructure damaged or devastated	
	Conflict	• Loss of assets • Loss of skills due to migration or ineffective education • Instability or loss of networks and increased operating costs limiting market scope • Trauma	• Infrastructure damaged or devastated • Licit networks disrupted; illicit networks strengthened	Reduced national capacity to enforce laws and provide basic services

Source: Nourse et al., 2006.

18.3 Characteristics of Post-crisis Clients

People behave differently in response to a crisis. Some remain in their home community throughout the entire crisis (inhabitants). Others may be forced to flee, either to other areas within their home country (internally displaced persons) or to other countries (refugees). When the crisis ends, some might return to their original community or to a new area within their home country (returnees). While all of these can be found both after disasters and after armed conflicts, another group (demobilized soldiers) is specific to armed conflicts.

Experience with microfinance in post-crisis settings has led practitioners to conclude that it is more effective and less risky to offer microfinance services to a mixed clientele rather than to target any particular subgroup. An inclusive approach helps to avoid tensions between subgroups and is more supportive of reintegration, stabilization and peace. It also facilitates greater scale and efficiency. Nevertheless, it is useful to think about the different characteristics, demands and risk factors of each population group to be able to design and market products that meet their needs.

Inhabitants, the individuals who stay in their home community during a crisis, are probably the closest to clients in normal settings. They are settled, might still possess some productive assets and/or land, and are usually eager to restart their economic activities and take on economic opportunities as soon as the crisis ends. They are therefore among the prime candi-

dates for microfinance in post-crisis settings. The products they typically demand include reconstruction and emergency loans as well as savings.

Returnees are former refugees or internally displaced persons who have returned to their country of origin. Having returned to settle permanently and rebuild their homes and economic activities, they are also highly favourable microfinance candidates. Together with inhabitants, they provide the engine for development of the local economy. Returnees often receive cash or grants as incentives to return, and they may bring along some money earned or have access to remittances. Besides start-up and working capital loans, savings and money transfer services might therefore be in great demand.

Refugees are people who fled from a crisis and live outside their country of origin. They can be among the poorest and most vulnerable, although in some contexts those who flee are the ones who can afford to flee. They have usually left behind their productive assets, have lost their social capital, might have legal, cultural and skill-related (for example, language) difficulties in engaging in economic activities abroad, often lack access to markets, are usually dependent on humanitarian assistance, and by definition are not permanently settled. They are more challenging microfinance clients, but if they reside in a camp for a longer period, microfinance might be a feasible intervention. As the example of IRC (International Rescue Committee) in Côte d'Ivoire illustrates, small, short-term loans as well as savings-first approaches can work well for this market segment (see Box 18.2). Refugees might also have a demand for money transfer services to send and receive remittances.

Box 18.2 Microfinance for Refugees – Experience from IRC in Côte d'Ivoire

Recognizing the benefits of savings and credit for the establishment of economic activities and the reduction of vulnerability among Liberian refugees in Côte d'Ivoire, IRC started the SEAD (Small Economic Activities Development) programme in March 1998. The methodology of the SEAD programme was based on the formation of "clubs" among refugees who trusted each other, were interested in improving their economic status by engaging in small economic activities, and planned to live in the same area in the future. IRC encouraged the clubs to save money with the prospect of receiving matching loans after eight weeks of successful club formation and saving. The savings were deposited in the closest commercial banks or in the club's cash boxes. The maximum loan size was three times the amount deposited, and the loan term ranged from 4 to 12 weeks.

By December 1998, IRC had facilitated the formation of 146 clubs and had given matching loans with a value of US$89,708 to 1,822 families. One major benefit of the SEAD methodology was the built-in sustainability of the clubs beyond the resettlement period. First, clubs were formed among refugees who intended to settle in the same area once they returned to their home country. This enabled club members to continue their savings and credit activities after returning home. Second, to facilitate the return of refugees even if they had not fully reimbursed their loans, IRC accepted the club's deposits as cash guarantees until the outstanding loans were repaid. Upon full loan repayment, IRC handed back the cash guarantees. This mechanism provided returnees with a safe place to store their savings during the resettlement phase, and ensured access to their resources once installed. Finally, by economically empowering refugees, IRC facilitated the economic recovery and reintegration of former refugees in their home country.

Source: Alles, 1999.

Internally displaced persons (IDPs) are individuals who are displaced within their country of origin, and resemble refugees in many ways. They are usually not permanently settled, are eager to return to their home communities, and have left their productive assets behind. Their advantage over refugees is that they remain in their home country and thus may be familiar with the language, culture and legal framework, and might have the opportunity to earn income during displacement. IDPs, similar to refugees, can be successfully integrated in microfinance programmes, especially if they remain in their displacement area for a longer period, or if the microfinance programme can follow them to their areas of origin.

Demobilized soldiers are former military forces that have been disarmed and demobilized. They are usually in greater need of non-financial assistance including education and training, mentoring and counselling as well as psychological support. In some countries, ex-combatants are still teenagers, having been recruited as junior soldiers during childhood. In general, microcredit programmes for demobilized soldiers have experienced low recovery rates. Demobilized soldiers tend to regard loans as gifts – compensation for the burdens experienced during the conflict. Also, they typically lack the skills and entrepreneurial spirit to become self-employed and invest loans effectively. They are often supported best by services other than microfinance (see, for example, Box 18.3), although savings services can also be useful, especially if ex-combatants have pensions or entitlement payments they want to protect.

Box 18.3 Ex-Combatant Reintegration in Congo/Brazzaville

In 2000, the International Organization for Migration (IOM) and the United Nations Development Programme (UNDP) launched a pilot effort to reintegrate ex-combatants into self-employment and simultaneously collect small arms in Congo/Brazzaville. The programme intended to use microcredit to launch enterprises for the ex-combatants. Priority access to loans would be given to former soldiers who turned in their weapons, and to group projects in order to lower administrative and supervisory overhead costs. Through a two-month pilot phase, this concept was carefully tested by the technical team. The majority of ex-combatants had little experience in business, and the business plans they developed lacked viability. The technical team recommended significant revisions to the programme before proceeding.

The team therefore modified the strategy to focus on training. The training would be followed with one of two options. Those with the experience or capability to run a business could still be supported through microloans to open a new venture. The team recommended that microcredit be provided through a strategic partnership with a local microcredit institution rather than by creating a new microcredit window. For the majority of ex-combatants, however, self-employment remained highly risky. The project therefore aimed to create jobs within existing businesses or as subcontractors of services to local governments, through a range of incentives to stimulate the supply of jobs.

By becoming more realistic about clients' abilities, the team removed much of the pressure on microcredit institutions to give loans when they could not guarantee client or institutional discipline. Within the first ten weeks of launching the revised approach, the project reached over 4,000 ex-combatants with reintegration support. Initial funding ran out, and based on strong early results, the programme was able to raise significant follow-on funding.

Source: Parker and Pearce, 2001.

18.4 Designing a Post-crisis Product Portfolio

The demand for microfinance in a post-crisis environment evolves with the passage of time. Immediately after a crisis, customers are trying to cope with the most urgent consequences of the crisis, and their financial service requirements are focused primarily on meeting basic needs. Once they stabilize their situation and markets begin to function, their focus shifts to rebuilding what was lost during the conflict or disaster. Some clients take longer to make the transition than others. Refugees, demobilized soldiers and those who have lost all their assets to an earthquake or flood need more time to get their bearings than inhabitants who survived the crisis with minimal losses, for example. This section explores the nature of the product portfolio that tends to be useful in the period immediately following a crisis, referred to as the emergency response phase, versus the subsequent period of reconstruction and development, referred to as the recovery phase.

Emergency Response Phase

MFIs that were operating in an affected area before crisis hit can be in the best position to support that area immediately after the crisis. They are already on the ground, they have infrastructure in place, they know the environment, and they have many established relationships upon which to build. However, institutions that are present during a crisis can also be victims of the crisis. Branch infrastructure, communication channels, vehicles and other assets can be damaged or destroyed; staff can be injured or killed. The first thing an on-site MFI must do after a crisis is assess its situation and determine the extent to which it can operate in the post-crisis environment.

Donors, non-governmental organizations (NGOs) and other stakeholders that were not operating in the affected area before the crisis will not be able to build infrastructure fast enough to provide microfinance services during the emergency response stage. They can, however, support MFIs that are already established in the area and assist them in recovering from the crisis. This kind of partnership is something that can be negotiated in advance as part of a contingency plan (refer to Section 18.6), and will increase the speed with which action can be taken after a crisis.

MFIs that survive a crisis might usefully provide the following products and services:

- **Access to savings.** One of the main reasons why clients save is to set aside funds for use in the event of an emergency (see Chapter 4). If they have savings with an MFI, they are likely to want to access at least some of that savings to pay for the additional expenses that a crisis can bring. An MFI might allow access not only to voluntary savings, but also, on an exceptional basis, to compulsory savings. Institutions should be aware, however, that compulsory savings withdrawal patterns tend to be more radical than those of voluntary savings, as clients take advantage of the rare opportunity to access the funds in their compulsory savings account. If an MFI is perceived to be a safe place to store funds, it may see an increase in voluntary savings deposits immediately after a crisis, particularly if there has been large-scale destruction of housing. Usually, increased expenses, persisting insecurity and a general lack of trust in institutions limit savings deposits during this phase.

- **Safe deposit boxes.** Due to the destruction of physical infrastructure and the increase in insecurity, households may need a safe place to store their valuables. If they have cash, a savings account can be useful, but more often, especially in the case of refugees, access to a safe deposit box would be more helpful.
- **Money transfer services.** After both conflicts and natural disasters, a money transfer service (see Chapter 11) can enable households to receive cash from relatives and friends to help them recover from the crisis. If an MFI has the liquidity, providing these services to the general population and not just to pre-crisis clients could attract new clients to the institution that might stay and use other services once their lives have stabilized.
- **Emergency loans.** Especially after natural disasters, emergency loans (see Chapter 8) can be a valuable product for clients who have not lost their productive capacity, but face a temporary increase in expenses due to the crisis, which they cannot finance from their savings. For example, they may need to repair their roof, or restock supplies damaged by water. The purpose of the loan is usually consumption, but it can help borrowers keep their business going and avoid the sale of productive assets. Emergency loans are made available as quickly as possible to clients in good standing for small amounts and with a short repayment period, often one month or less. Many MFIs have reported a 100 per cent repayment rate on emergency loans disbursed under these terms (Miamidian et al., 2005).
- **Non-financial services.** For those households hit hardest, non-financial services may be more appropriate than any of the financial services mentioned above. Depending on the availability of aid from government, NGO or corporate sources, MFIs may need or want to provide services that help clients meet their basic needs (for example, food, water, blankets, temporary shelter) or volunteer their branch and client network as a distribution channel for other organizations to make these services available. In post-conflict situations, MFIs might also provide referrals to trauma counsellors and begin rebuilding social capital through group formation and training activities. Organizations that want to offer microfinance services during the recovery phase can begin developing relationships and credibility in crisis-affected communities by providing non-financial services during this phase.
- **Emergency relief grants.** MFIs may offer one-time emergency relief grants to their most vulnerable or most severely affected clients to mitigate the immediate impact of the crisis. It is important that the short-term and extraordinary nature of these grants be well communicated, that the conditions for eligibility be transparent, and that the grants be designed to support a long-term and productive relationship between recipients and the MFI. As explained in Chapter 13, grants are usually best delivered through a partner organization or, in the case of multi-service NGOs, through a separate operational window.

The immediate period after a crisis is usually not a good time to make new microenterprise loans. Insecurity, instability and the influence of grants make it a riskier time to lend, and borrowers are more likely to consume at least part of their loan instead of investing it in their business. Typically, an MFI's own human and financial resources will be stretched by emergency demands, leaving little capacity for non-emergency loans. If a crisis affects only some areas or members of a community, an MFI might be able to make new microenterprise loans to others, but it must also ensure that it allocates sufficient resources to safeguard its crisis-affected portfolio.

Clients who are in the process of repaying an existing loan may face temporary or permanent disruptions in income as a result of the crisis that affect their ability to repay. MFIs must assess whether the design of their existing loan products can meet customer and MFI needs in the post-crisis environment, or whether product policies and procedures need adjustment. There are five types of adjustment that MFIs often make during the emergency response phase of a crisis. The first two might be made for all clients, but the remaining three should be made only if a specific client's situation warrants it.

- **Grace period.** By granting a grace period on payments of principal, interest or compulsory savings, MFIs leave resources in clients' hands to help cope with the immediate impact of the crisis. It is a gesture of goodwill that avoids a clash with clients who are suffering and may not have the capacity to repay.
- **Late payments and penalties.** MFIs may want to allow clients to make late payments for reasons directly related to the crisis. For example, there may be days when a branch is closed, a loan officer is unable to make scheduled visits to clients, or clients are unable to reach their branch because of police barricades. MFIs that have late payment fees or penalties may want to relax these requirements during the period immediately following the crisis.
- **Rescheduling.** If good clients are unable to make loan payments according to their pre-crisis repayment schedule, MFIs can provide a new repayment schedule that gives them time to recover from the effects of the crisis and become re-established in their businesses. The new schedule typically extends the loan term, decreasing the size of each instalment payment or postponing the payment of interest and/or loan principal for a specified period, after which clients are expected to make regular payments for the remaining contract period. Loan rescheduling in the wake of natural disasters has become a common practice among MFIs. Institutions recognize that if they push too much for on-time repayment, they may force otherwise outstanding clients to default or to sell productive assets, which harms clients' livelihood and their relationship with the MFI. Overall, rapid and well-targeted (see Box 18.4) restructuring appears to save an MFI from significant write-offs, at a short-term cost of delayed interest and principal payments.
- **Refinancing.** If good clients' productive assets are destroyed in the crisis, time alone will not be enough to stabilize their situation. They will need a cash injection to re-establish

Box 18.4 Rescheduling Loans after a Rapid-onset Disaster

Rather than the previously endorsed "blanket approach" to rescheduling all loans in hard-hit areas, current "sound practice" advocates rescheduling on an individual or borrowing-group basis. Although the customized approach requires tracking down and meeting with all affected clients as well as greater administrative and monitoring complexity, most MFIs agree that the customized approach makes better use of the MFI's limited supply of funds after a disaster hits, and ensures that MFI staff are in the field meeting with clients throughout the emergency period. Individually rescheduling thousands of loans will require a lot of work on the part of the MFI's accountants, branch managers, and staff. To make the system moderately manageable, a specific policy should be established to give loan officers parameters for rescheduling, as well as some standardized choices among payment schedules.

Source: Chua and Miehlbradt, 1999a.

> **Box 18.5 To Write Off or Not to Write Off?**
>
> When Hurricane Mitch hit Nicaragua, ProMujer did not condone anyone's debt, even when portfolio at risk reached 40 per cent. By reminding women of their commitment to pay their loans, they were pushed to start working quickly and effectively. This was a success, most loans were repaid, and this is why ProMujer survived.
>
> *Source: Handicap International, 2006.*

their businesses. After the 1998 floods in Bangladesh, for example, the Bangladesh Rehabilitation Assistance Committee (BRAC) permitted clients to take up to 50 per cent of their current loan as a new loan and to extend repayment by six months. Refinanced loans need to be structured so that the business being financed can generate enough cash to service both loans, while still allowing borrowers to care for their family. This requires greater focus by the loan officer on clients' cash flow, collateral, and character.

- **Loan cancellations and write-offs.** Loan cancellations (in which clients are no longer held liable for repayment) are not generally recommended, because they negatively affect the MFI's income and capital as well as the credit culture that an institution has worked to develop. Most clients will be able to repay their loans if given the chance to do so through rescheduling or refinancing (see Box 18.5). Institutions may consider changing their normal policy for write-offs, however, extending the amount of time that can pass before writing off loans in the event of a crisis. For clients that are deceased, MFIs often have no choice but to write off, unless a loan is covered by an appropriate insurance product.

The objective of any revision in credit policy immediately after a crisis should be to enable clients to maintain a productive relationship with the MFI. Institutions need to show their clients that they understand their predicament and will do their best to help. At the same time, they must send a clear message that they expect clients to honour their obligations to the MFI as soon as they are able to do so.

Recovery Phase

As markets start to reopen, business activities re-emerge, and infrastructure begins to be reconstructed, a different microfinance product portfolio will be demanded. As communities recover from the crisis, they will eventually need access to the full range of products and services laid out in Chapter 1, but the products that are most likely to be demanded are summarized in Figure 18.1: microenterprise loans, housing loans, leasing, non-financial services and savings.

In the recovery phase, demand for credit to finance reconstruction and working capital needs is sure to be high. Some clients will want to take advantage of opportunities to rebuild or perhaps expand their businesses (see Box 18.6). Others will want to start a business for the first time. Still others will seek a loan to repair or rebuild a home. Given the variety of credit needs, organizations that entered a crisis-affected area during the emergency response phase in order to begin lending during the recovery phase might want to start by offering one flexible, multipurpose loan product with a wide range of sizes and maturities to meet as many of these different needs as possible. It will simplify service delivery for an institution that is just getting started.

Figure 18.1 Post-crisis product mix

Emergency response phase	Recovery phase
Access to savings Safe deposit boxes Money transfers Emergency loans Non-financial services (counselling, referrals, conduit for in-kind grants) Grants	Microenterprise loans Housing loans Leasing Non-financial services (business development, literacy training, value chain intervention) Savings

Source: Authors.

MFIs that existed before the crisis may already offer several different products that can meet these needs in a more specialized fashion, and they can adapt these products as necessary to accommodate the post-crisis environment. For example, an MFI that survives a major earthquake might add a construction assistance component to its existing **housing loan** product (see Chapter 7) to help clients invest in more durable housing. If many clients were killed or had to flee during the crisis, an MFI using a group lending methodology might allow a **smaller group size** than normal so that it can continue its relationship with the well-performing clients who remain in each group rather than destabilize groups with the injection of a large number of new members (see Box 18.7).

Microleases and asset replacement loans can assist clients who lost assets during a crisis and wish to replace them (see Chapter 10). Both types of product generally bear terms of at least one year, and are for larger amounts than the typical working capital loan. Because of this, only MFIs with significant liquidity are able to provide them in a post-crisis situation.

In-kind loans might be appropriate if inflation or theft is a serious problem, or if there is widespread dependence on cash grants. In Angola, Jesuit Refugee Service found that its in-kind loans, such as chicken and goats for reproduction, achieved far better recovery rates than its cash credits.

Box 18.6 Disasters Also Create Opportunities

Disasters can create opportunities for both microentrepreneurs and MFIs. Many microenterprises are engaged in small-scale construction activities and manufacturing that lends itself to reconstruction efforts. A disaster creates a sudden increase in the demand for their goods and services. Surviving microenterprises engaged in food service or petty commerce may find an increase in demand for their products as traditional distribution channels and food preparation facilities are destroyed. Small commercial vendors are well positioned to change their product line to meet the demand for goods such as water, plastic and other items needed to cope with the disaster. The earthquakes in El Salvador demonstrated the resilience and adaptability of the microenterprise sector, as microentrepreneurs were back in business the day following the earthquakes selling entirely new lines of products suited to client needs, including water, gloves, masks and quick-food items. As in the case of individual clients, disasters create opportunities for financial institutions that are in a position to capitalize on them. Opportunities may come from the ability to attract new clients, generate new business, or offer new products.

Source: Magill, 2003.

Box 18.7 Group Lending in a Post-conflict Environment

Since community structures and social capital are often destroyed or badly damaged during a conflict, large group lending methodologies that require 20 or 30 people to guarantee each others' loans are more difficult to implement successfully than other methodologies. Even if groups are willing to come together for the purpose of borrowing, extensive counselling and trust building are often required before they become cohesive and stable enough to record full and on-time repayment. MFIs that are accustomed to using group lending methodologies must decide whether they want to invest in helping members of a community build social capital or to switch methodologies. In the Balkans, for example, many microfinance programmes decided to offer individual loans, requiring guarantors or collateral, rather than group loans (see Chapter 6 for a discussion of different lending methodologies). This can be a particularly attractive option for MFIs that offered an individual loan product prior to the crisis.

MFIs that choose to stick with a group lending methodology often reduce the size of the groups that they work with or modify the village bank methodology, as World Relief did in Cambodia, so that members form solidarity groups of five or six that serve as the first level of guarantee. Some programmes choose to target rural communities where trust levels are almost always higher, although rural operations often face higher transaction costs due to lower population density and weaker infrastructure.

Source: Adapted from Doyle, 1998.

Value-chain finance, which supports and relies upon relationships between producers, buyers and suppliers, is limited after a crisis because key actors are inevitably missing from the chain, trust may have deteriorated between those who remain, and market opportunities may be poor. MFIs are sometimes able to speed the reconstruction of value chains by seeking out actors whose capacity is weak, and finding ways to meet their financial service needs. As in the case of Fonkoze and Concern International in Haiti (see Box 18.8), this effort can bring the MFI new clients in addition to benefitting existing clients who are already part of the chain.

Box 18.8 Value-Chain Interventions Aid Recovery in Haiti

After violent political conflicts on the Central Plateau between 2003 and 2004, the Haitian MFI Fonkoze and its NGO partner, Concern International, went quickly to the field to determine the current standing of clients, employees, physical assets and portfolio quality, and whether the situation should be viewed as a humanitarian crisis. Concern quickly determined that it should not – that the situation was rather a simple disruption of the economic value chain that could be resolved by using Fonkoze's Business Development programme to make special loans to key suppliers of Fonkoze solidarity group clients. A combined Concern/Fonkoze team then followed up with market research to identify the key suppliers of Fonkoze clients, and also to learn what those suppliers would need to get their businesses up and running again. The response this research led to turned out to be much more effective than treating the situation as a humanitarian crisis would have been. Food aid or other handouts would only have deepened problems for the small businesswomen Fonkoze exists to help. Instead, working with their suppliers helped them and their communities as well.

Source: Werlin and Hastings, 2006.

Non-financial services continue to be important during the recovery phase, but the nature of the services demanded differs from the emergency response phase. During the recovery phase, many people turn to self-employment for the first time in their lives due to a lack of other employment opportunities. To succeed, they need support in identifying viable self-employment activities and developing their business skills. In communities that are emerging from years of war, literacy training, basic health education, agricultural extension services and conflict resolution skills might all be needed. MFIs can opt to provide some of these services themselves through an integrated model such as Credit with Education (see Box 12.3 in the chapter on non-financial services) or by creating linkages to other service providers and support organizations that make these services easily accessible to their clients.

During the recovery phase, clients should transition away from **grants** and towards credit and other financial services that enable them to function self-sufficiently in the post-crisis environment. Grants may still be available at this stage, but the potential for them to hinder rather than promote recovery intensifies. MFIs that feel the need to integrate grants into their product portfolio should take great care to follow the guidelines for effective grant design provided in Chapter 13. Grants might be linked, for example, to a leasing or asset replacement loan product as described in Box 13.4. They could also form part of a start-up or graduation model that assists clients in launching their own income-generating activities (refer to Boxes 13.1 and 13.2).

In contrast to credit, there is no consensus on the degree of demand for **savings** services during the recovery phase. Some practitioners have found that people in conflict-affected areas are actually more inclined to save than to invest (Doyle, 1998). Others find that ongoing insecurity, lack of trust in institutions, and high transaction costs restrict the demand for savings long after a crisis ends. Certainly, clients who invest in their businesses and begin to generate income will need ways to manage their cash flows and risks, and accessible voluntary savings products could assist them with this challenge. In countries where lump-sum cash grants are distributed by aid agencies or large-scale cash-for-work programmes are initiated, savings accounts can serve the same purpose for a very different clientele (see Box 18.9).

Box 18.9 Can MFI Clients Save Even after a Major Disaster?

Yes! The poor can save soon after a disaster in both financial and non-financial forms. Whether or not savings are deposited with an MFI depends on clients' trust of the MFI, transaction costs and accessibility. MFIs operating in tsunami-affected areas of Sri Lanka reported larger total savings balances in March 2005 compared with March 2004. They also recorded larger total savings balances in December 2005 compared with December 2004. An assessment in Batticoloa district showed that around 35 per cent of cash grants and cash-for-work (CFW) payments received by beneficiaries were saved in MFIs (Aheeyar, 2006). In Aceh, Indonesia, Mercy Corps implemented a CFW programme in tsunami-affected areas that benefited nearly 18,000 participants and disbursed over US$4.5 million in direct payments. The programme began on 7 January 2005 and was gradually phased out by 31 July 2005 in favour of other programmes aimed at building livelihoods and more sustainable sources of income. Exit surveys of CFW participants showed that 29 per cent of households had deposited cash savings.

Source: Nagarajan, 2006.

18.5 Delivering a Post-crisis Product Portfolio

Although the range of products that an MFI can incorporate into its portfolio during both the emergency response and recovery phases is significant, this does not mean that it will be able to deliver any of those products effectively. As described in Section 18.2, the post-crisis environment complicates microfinance service delivery in many ways. Six of the major challenges that MFIs must overcome to succeed in a crisis-affected market are briefly explored below: communication, liquidity management, security, cost and risk management, motivating on-time repayment, and neutrality.

Communication

MFIs face three main communication challenges in a post-crisis environment. The first is public relations. MFIs often do not have much experience in this area, but their ability to function after a crisis depends, in large part, on the attitudes and impressions that clients and other members of the public form about them. If an institution is viewed as safe, sound and compassionate, people will trust it and do their best to maintain their relationship with it, even if the repayment of outstanding loans is difficult. When an institution is viewed as unstable, or interested only in recuperating its funds, the public is more likely to abandon it.

The second communication challenge is to manage expectations. An MFI will have to convey to clients that the crisis situation necessitates a different approach than usual (for example, relief grants or loan rescheduling), and that this approach is temporary. It needs to give clients information about the options available to them, and the policies and procedures the institution intends to follow – for instance, that loans will not be forgiven, that grace periods and loan rescheduling will depend on individual circumstances, that clients needing help should come to the branch office to discuss their situation, and so on.

The third main communication challenge is internal. An MFI's employees need to know how to assess the situation on the ground, and channel information about the impact of the crisis on staff and clients to decision-makers as quickly as possible. They also need to know how to respond to client requests for information. They must know what the new or revised policies are so they can give clients consistent, accurate information. They should also be encouraged to provide feedback on customer complaints and suggestions, and on their ideas for accommodating client needs better. As discussed in Section 18.6, having a crisis response plan in place, and training staff on the contents of that plan, can help to facilitate better internal communication during a crisis.

Liquidity Management[41]

Crises put pressure on an MFI's liquidity from a variety of angles: current borrowers may not be able to make loan repayments on time or at all; depositors will want access to their savings; additional reserves will need to be set aside if outstanding loans are rescheduled; both current and potential customers will seek emergency and reconstruction loans; and the MFI's own expenses will increase due to infrastructure or other types of damage. To survive the aftermath of a crisis, MFIs must ensure that they have access to sufficient funds to meet these needs.

[41] This section is adapted from Chu and Miehlbradt (1999b).

Box 18.10 Fast and Fair Distribution of Emergency Funds in Poland

Fundusz Mikro, a Polish MFI, established a disaster loan fund after the 1997 floods, financed by a donor grant. To ensure rapid loan disbursement, it assigned partial responsibility for damage assessment and total responsibility for emergency loan disbursements to the clients. Fundusz Mikro provided a standardized loan amount to groups of affected individuals, and the group members divided the loan amount on the basis of the losses suffered by each of them. This was a simple way of ensuring that only affected clients received emergency loans, as group members were unlikely to provide part of the capital to someone who did not need it. Through random checks Fundusz Mikro disqualified any group that submitted an application with a non-eligible person to ensure compliance with the emergency lending policy. Applications for emergency loans were considered from the smallest to the largest amount requested, thus discouraging people to ask for more than they needed.

Source: Miamidian et al., 2005.

As soon as an MFI can get a handle on its post-crisis situation, it should make daily projections of recoveries, income, expenses and loan disbursements for the current month and at least two months thereafter. It can then take steps to access the additional liquidity it will need. MFIs can expect to find liquidity from their required cash reserves and funds committed for new loan outlays. In addition, they can seek out loans (perhaps from commercial banks with which the MFI has a long-term relationship) and grants (usually through international fund-raising efforts and emergency requests to donors). Donor disaster response monies usually require several weeks to access, which will be too late for clients' immediate emergency needs, but they can help during the recovery phase.

Some MFIs working in chronic disaster areas have developed internal disaster funds that can be quickly accessed to solve (or at least reduce) a short-term liquidity crisis. After violent political conflicts and flooding in 2004, for example, the Haitian MFI Fonkoze began taking a monthly provision, apart from its loan loss provision, to prepare better for losses from unexpected events, including disaster, conflict and theft (Werlin and Hastings, 2006).

Disaster loan funds can also be capitalized by an initial donor grant and serve one MFI (as in the case described in Box 18.10) or many MFIs. CARE established a disaster loan fund, for example, that serves 22 smaller MFIs in Bangladesh (Brown and Nagarajan, 2000). The primary purpose of these funds is typically to meet affected households' immediate demand for cash rather than to cover any unexpected losses experienced by MFIs.

Security

MFIs' options for dealing with the insecurity present in post-crisis environments depend to some degree on the availability of commercial bank infrastructure to hold and move money. If commercial banks are operating and located nearby, MFIs can store money there rather than leave it in their own offices. They can also make special arrangements for clients to make payments and deposits into the MFI's account at a commercial bank. In Uganda, some MFIs avoid cash disbursements by giving clients individual cheques that can be cashed at their convenience. In South Africa, MFIs issue loans on automatic teller machine (ATM) cards, and clients use them to withdraw their funds and make repayments at commercial bank ATMs. Although this shifts security risk to clients, clients usually have more knowledge and flexibility about the safest time to access their cash, and may prefer this option to others that leave risk in the hands of the MFI but raise the cost of the service.

Regardless of whether they have access to commercial bank infrastructure, MFIs can take many other precautions in post-conflict areas to increase security and safety. For example:

- Avoid falling into patterns of behaviour. Vary the days of the week and locations for repayment meetings so most people are unaware when employees will be travelling with large sums.
- Reduce the frequency of disbursements and repayment, and/or open satellite offices to reduce the amount of travel necessary.
- Travel in pairs or in groups. In several Cambodian programmes, four to six staff members will go to the field, scatter, and meet up again before returning to the central office. This "safety in numbers" practice can also be used when clients are responsible for carrying payments.
- Equip frontline staff with radios for communication purposes.
- Maintain a low profile. Do not advertise the presence of branch offices, and do not have employees wear uniforms.
- Hire security companies that supply armed guards and/or armoured vehicles when large amounts of cash need to be transferred between central locations and outlying offices. Inform only staff who need to know that a transfer will take place.
- Purchase transit insurance policies and/or fidelity guarantee policies if available.
- Break repayments down into smaller, less tempting amounts by dividing large groups into smaller subgroups. These subgroups can then designate a member to collect and deposit members' payments, possibly outside group meetings.
- On the day of repayment, groups can randomly choose the member who carries payments to the MFI or partner bank. This helps prevent "inside jobs", in which a member would collude in advance with an outsider to stage a theft.
- Use traditional informal structures for transferring money to branches. In Afghanistan, for example, the Save the Children office in Kabul gives money to a Kabul-based family member, who in turn instructs a family living near the branch office to give the amount (less a fee) to the local Save branch.

Managing Risks and Costs

Many of the strategies described in this chapter to decrease the risk of operating in a post-crisis environment also increase costs. For instance, reducing the size of borrower groups might facilitate better repayment, but it also lowers loan officer productivity. Armed guards can increase staff and client safety, but their salaries must be paid. The provision of subsidized or interest-free emergency loans can lower political and reputation risk, but it also decreases revenue.

Although subsidized funds may be available to help an MFI operate in a post-crisis environment, such funding is limited and is by no means guaranteed. Ultimately, MFIs have to charge interest rates that cover their costs. If a post-conflict environment generates higher expenses, then interest rates there will need to be higher than in normal environments. Since natural disasters usually increase costs on a temporary basis, and generate a need for urgent access to funds when the crisis occurs, MFIs can charge an interest rate before the crisis that allows reserves to be set aside for use in the event of a crisis, as discussed previously.

MFIs that want to operate in a post-crisis environment need to prioritize risks and focus on those that represent the greatest potential loss. They must ask themselves whether each risk-reducing initiative is worth its associated costs, or they will quickly price themselves out of the market (or eat away at their capital). Higher risk tolerance combined with the flexibility to act quickly when adjustments are needed to keep risk within a tolerable range seems important to success.

Motivating On-time Repayment

Although it will be difficult for many borrowers to repay their loans on time after a crisis, it will be possible for others. Providing incentives that motivate clients to maintain their relationship with the institution and to make the extra effort to pay on time even if others cannot will help MFIs to control both costs and risks. For example, MFIs can reward on-time repayment during the emergency response phase with access to additional products or better terms during the recovery phase. Banco Solidario in Ecuador improved its on-time payment statistics during a period of extreme financial crisis by making new loans available only to people who had kept to their established repayment schedules (Magill, 2003). Refugees who repay their loans from the American Refugee Committee in West Africa are issued certificates with their names, loan information, and credit ratings that they can use as proof of credit history at lending organizations established by the American Refugee Committee when they return home (Mitten, 2007).

The early and regular presence of MFI staff in the field is also an important motivator. The visits signal to clients that the institution has not forgotten about them, and the compassion shown by employees when they visit can have a powerful psychological impact. A few encouraging words can help clients muster the confidence to face the future, and if staff are able to take the time to understand a client's situation and suggest a way forward, their visits can quickly produce results.

Neutrality

MFIs need to enter the post-crisis environment as a neutral third party. If they or their donor/investor base are seen to support one side of the conflict, one political party, one ethnic or religious group, or other similar division, they are likely to encounter resistance, and perhaps even attack from local entities. For instance, after US forces toppled Saddam Hussein, CHF (a US-based NGO formerly known as the Cooperative Housing Foundation) quickly discovered the need to disconnect itself from the US military in Iraq. The staff spent much of its first few months in Baghdad meeting with top Iraqi opinion-makers – Muslim clerics, business leaders, bankers, and appointed government officials – to disavow all connections with the so-called coalition forces. CHF believes that if it had not done this, it would never have succeeded in providing microcredit for the poor of that country (Woodworth, 2006).

18.6 Preparing Clients and Institutions for Crisis [42]

The options available to clients and institutions in a post-crisis environment will be influenced by the degree to which they were prepared for the crisis. Even in the case of rapid-onset disasters such as floods and earthquakes, minimal preparation on the part of clients and institutions can significantly increase their ability to survive and recover from a crisis. This section explores some of the actions MFIs can take to help prepare their clients and themselves to manage the risks and costs of a conflict or disaster.

Preparing Clients

There are six main ways that MFIs can assist clients to prepare for a crisis:

1. **Offer a voluntary savings product and encourage clients to use it.** Especially in regions that are prone to natural disasters, appropriate savings services can help households set asides reserves to deal with a crisis when it occurs. Unlike fixed assets, savings can be quickly liquidated if necessary to move to another location or to cope with the immediate aftermath of a crisis.
2. **Set up an emergency fund** within the institution or, if the MFI uses a large group delivery methodology, within borrower groups to provide clients with a financial safety net. If the MFI manages the fund, it needs to be kept liquid (and not used as loan capital) so that the funds are immediately accessible when a crisis strikes. If community or borrower groups manage the fund, they may choose to use the accumulated capital as a short-term emergency loan fund that covers individual emergencies as well as community-level crises.
3. If the potential for disaster is well known or predictable (for example, in regions that flood on an annual basis, or if tensions leading up to an election suggest the possibility of post-election violence), MFIs can **adjust the timing or terms of their loans** to limit risk exposure during the potential crisis period. In Bangladesh, for instance, some MFIs have adjusted their loan repayment schedules to reduce required repayments during the flood season. They also time loans for livestock so that animals can be raised to maturity and sold before the rainy season.
4. **Provide a commitment savings or housing loan product** and encourage clients to use these products to build more durable housing, to move to safer areas, or to invest in risk-reducing measures such as water-harvesting devices in drought-prone areas. One of the greatest risks to households in chronic disaster areas is poorly constructed housing, which is prone to extensive damage in winds or floods. In addition, clients continuing to reside in high-risk locations (such as within known flood zones or where mudslides are possible) are at greater risk than those living in safer areas.
5. **Explore the possibility of offering clients insurance products** that respond to aggregate (community-wide) crises. Providing this kind of insurance is a risky undertaking for MFIs, even if payment into the plan is mandatory. Still, some MFIs are experimenting with insurance products for disaster response, in some cases turning to the reinsurance market to spread aggregate risks more broadly. The Self-Employed Women's Association (SEWA) in India has created one deposit-linked insurance scheme, which compensates clients for business losses and deaths caused by fire or flood. The programme has been plagued with

42 This section is adapted from Chua and Miehlbradt (1999c and 1999d).

Box 18.11 Disaster Planning at Grameen Bank

As part of its disaster response plan, the Grameen Bank raises staff awareness about the incoming flood season by talking about the flood and how to combat it at the beginning of June each year. Employees urge members to save more during the normal months to deal with shortage during and after the flood. They advise the borrowers to immunize their livestock and poultry, as well as store feed for them, and to buy and store vegetables that have long shelf life, such as winter watermelon and squash. Members are also urged to prepare their houses to deal with flood, for example by building a loft where they can take shelter and store valuable items in the face of rapidly rising water.

Source: Dowla, 2007.

difficulties in getting the partner institution – a state insurance company – to make timely payments to clients. Vaigai Vattara Kalanjiyam in India, working with PRADHAN, also links an insurance fund to the state insurance company. In this scheme, clients may request payouts of up to four times the amount of premiums paid, once in a five-year period. Index insurance, discussed in Chapter 20 on rural microfinance, may be another option.

6. Beginning with the most at-risk client groups, MFIs can **create opportunities to discuss preparation and coping strategies with clients** before a crisis occurs. In addition to imparting specific technical information, these meetings mentally prepare clients for unexpected events and help them build a sense of personal and community empowerment to respond to crises. Meetings might include the following topics: household emergency coping strategies; the role of accessible savings; diversification of income-earning activities into disaster-resistant activities; the financing of seed or grain banks; preventive health practices; and sources of disaster relief services (see, for example, Box 18.11). MFIs can provide these non-financial services on their own, or in partnership with other government or non-governmental actors.

Preparing the Institution

Strengthening clients' ability to cope with crisis will benefit an MFI through increased customer retention and more productive use of the MFI's products and services. However, there are many other actions that an MFI can take to improve its own ability to operate in a post-crisis environment. The initiatives described below cannot fully prepare or protect an MFI from a crisis, but they can lessen its shock on the institution and its staff, and hasten the return to normal MFI operations. According to Abramovitz (2001), every dollar spent on disaster preparedness will save seven dollars in recovery efforts.

Identification of potential crises and measurement of potential losses. Once an MFI gathers this information, it can put cost-effective plans in place to mitigate the impact of a crisis. For example, field staff can help MFI management create a "risk map" that identifies which clients (by location, type of activity, or type of shelter) are at extreme, moderate, or minimal risk in the event of a natural disaster. The MFI can then identify what percentage of the current loan portfolio is held by at-risk clients and estimate the potential effect of the disaster on cash flow and financial returns, should the at-risk clients temporarily halt repayments or request emergency loans. On the savings side, the MFI can identify the amount of liquidity required to provide the at-risk population access to voluntary or compulsory savings, assuming that loan repayment inflows in a disaster situation will slow to zero. These figures can help management decide whether to increase liquidity reserves, to provision more for losses, or to change lending policies.

Participatory rapid appraisal tools, such as those developed by *MicroSave* for microfinance institutions, can assist MFIs in understanding their target market's experiences with crisis. Table 18.3 provides sample output from the Time Series of Crisis Tool, which can be used to identify disaster trends, the coping mechanisms typically used by clients, and the implications for MFIs.[43]

Table 18.3 Sample output from Time Series of Crisis Tool for drought

Explanation	Trends	Coping mechanisms	Institutional implications / opportunities
• "From 1970 to 1991, it was too rampant. Even people died, others migrated." • "Cows die or devalue (thinner), and are sold on a take-away price." • "I prefer to get rid of the animals at any price before they die."	• Drought is seasonal (Nov to Apr), every year, and sometimes in August as well. It is considered the major crisis because of the recurrent financial burden it creates in the community. • This group perceived that widespread famine could hit the community in the near future – 5 years. (Although Kayunga looks green in May...)	• Cut on food. "Black coffee, no sugar." "Skip meals." "Since it arouses famine, we ration the little food we have to take us through the day spell." • Some families sell their assets (animals) and/or mortgage land. "Some people sell household property to access cash." • Resort to savings in terms of food that they conserve for dry seasons. • Go to cities, such as Jinja and even Soroti, to buy food. • Borrow from family members and friends. • "When friends are not willing to give money, what do you do? YOU SUFFER." • Participants clearly said that they prefer not to borrow money from MFIs during drought periods, being afraid that they will not be able to pay back."People prefer borrowing from friends than MFIs." "The strict policies of lending are maintained even during hard times." "They can be tough on you, police is involved." • ROSCAs/ASCAs were not mentioned.	• Although there was considerable probing, participants are not willing to borrow from MFIs during crises. • The issue is not lack of supply of MFIs (UMFI and UWFT do have presence in the area) or of a specific loan product in times of emergencies. • Reluctance to borrow from UMFI is related to the "red marks" on their records when the client fails to pay on time. It makes them feel embarrassed. • UMFI might want to consider introducing a "yellow card" to warn clients. "The red mark comes too quickly." Participants suggested a 2-day consideration period before applying red marks for late payment, especially to good clients. "If you could not go ... you see, we come from Jinja." • UMFI should let clients know clearly that one red mark is allowed (according to loan officers), and afterwards, the amount for the next loan is lower. "The red mark still applies when the loan period has expired." They said it always affects access to higher loan amounts. • UMFIs repayment is flexible (bi-weekly or monthly) and is fine to them. However, UMFI might also want to consider the different nature of businesses for repayment schemes (farmers vs. market). • UMFI might want to open a branch in Jinja as clients need to travel long distances. • (And/or) UMFI should increase the number of loan officers in the Kayunga branch. There are 3 loan officers for a total of 2,400 clients (equivalent to approx. 300 groups of 5 to 10 clients each).

Source: MicroSave, as presented in Miamidian et al., 2005

[43] For more information on *MicroSave's* market research tools, visit: www.microsave.org.

Backing up client and financial records. Crisis response and post-crisis MFI recovery are often crippled by loss of client records. In disaster-prone areas, records should be regularly updated, duplicated, and stored away from disaster zones. At a minimum, MFI files can be stored in airtight, durable, fire- and water-resistant containers. MFIs with computerized information systems can store a backup of their files and software at an offsite location that is not likely to be affected by the same disaster or conflict that the institution might face.

Geographic and sector diversification. Rarely will a crisis affect all areas of a country simultaneously and with equal severity. Geographic diversification can allow branches unaffected by a crisis to provide bridge funding to affected regions. Similarly, sector diversification helps limit the number of clients that are likely to be affected by a given crisis. MFIs that serve only agricultural clients, for example, are particularly vulnerable to the effects of natural disaster.

Policies and procedures. A crisis response plan, or contingency plan, is essential for a rapid and effective response to crisis (refer to Box 18.12 and the case study at the end of this chapter for examples). The plan can describe:

- the policies and procedures that will take effect in the event of a crisis (for example, will emergency loans be made available, will clients be allowed to withdraw compulsory savings, will the MFI provide or refer any emergency relief activities to affected communities, will clients' outstanding loans be rescheduled);
- what will trigger the implementation of these policies and procedures (for example, government declaration of disaster, loss of homes);
- what criteria will be used to determine to whom the procedure applies;
- who will implement the policies (for example, which decisions can be taken by field officers, branch managers, or the head office);
- what mechanism(s) will be used to communicate with staff and clients,
- how staff will be rewarded for making the extra effort to contact clients and keep the programme intact, even when their own families may be affected by the crisis.

Each policy should include some flexibility in its parameters: different types and sizes of crisis will require different levels of response, and even for a specific event the effect on individual branches will vary. These differences may lead to dissimilar policies by area: for example, severely affected branches may have a longer rescheduling period than those that are only moderately affected. When developing the parameters for response, MFIs should undertake a "what-if" analysis (in other words, risk scenario planning) to ensure that they have sufficient resources to carry out the chosen policy for different levels of disaster, and to identify the effects of these policies on their financial standing.

Backup liquidity. As discussed above, the greatest problem facing an MFI after a sudden disaster is liquidity. Building an internal disaster fund, or arranging backup liquidity from commercial banks or donors in advance of a crisis, will speed an MFI's access to cash immediately after the crisis.

Partnerships. MFIs can identify government programmes and non-governmental organizations that provide emergency services such as food grants, medical supplies and services, clean water, and temporary shelters; pinpoint their areas of operation; and perhaps develop

Box 18.12 Disaster Planning at ACODEP in Nicaragua

ACODEP has developed a comprehensive disaster preparedness plan that includes modifications to the delivery of its products and services during a disaster, as well as the introduction of emergency and recovery products. In addition to a flexible credit policy for disaster emergency and recovery, ACODEP created a disaster loan fund to help the institution prepare better for possible cash flow demands and to control credit and liquidity risks. The MFI stops collecting payments during the emergency period, allows clients to withdraw compulsory savings deposits (which are normally used as collateral), stops lending, and on the basis of a field damage assessment, prepares loan restructuring and refinancing plans. In addition, it offers short-term loans of one or two months with special interest rates for household needs in cases of severe emergencies. ACODEP loans are restructured when clients lose their homes, but not their productive assets. Loans are also restructured for those clients that are severely injured. Loans may be refinanced when productive assets are completely lost.

Source: Pantoja, 2002, as cited in Miamidian et al, 2005.

partnerships that can channel relief to clients in the event of a crisis. MFIs can also develop relationships with institutions that track weather patterns and predict storms or floods, to provide staff and clients with early warning of a possible crisis.

Training. Staff can be trained in crisis response policies and procedures, or at least be given clear written guidelines to follow if crisis strikes. They can learn how to provide pre-disaster information to clients; techniques for working with clients during the crisis without damaging the MFI's "business" reputation; techniques for managing and accounting for relief funds; and ways to coordinate effectively with relief and emergency workers. Since crises frequently destroy communication and transportation links, leaving field staff cut off from the head office, it is important that these staff be capable of making critical crisis-response decisions.

Crisis mitigation team. Larger MFIs may establish a crisis mitigation task force made up of eight to ten mid-level and senior managers from across the institution. During normal times, the task force would be responsible for: 1) developing a comprehensive plan for disaster response; 2) undertaking pre-disaster projections for financial planning; 3) assigning disaster response responsibilities by department; and 4) identifying preventive measures to make the MFI less vulnerable to a sudden disaster. Once disaster strikes, the task force would serve as a forum for the smooth flow of activities and information. Each task force member would be assigned a disaster response task, such as communicating with branch offices to assess damages, liaising with donors and commercial banks, providing post-disaster accounting information, providing emergency services for staff or clients, or identifying and coordinating with emergency service providers.

Taken as a whole, the initiatives described above help to ensure that an MFI is forewarned about impending crises and has the necessary elements – including a plan, trained staff, and sufficient financial resources – to respond quickly and efficiently.

Main Messages

1. Microfinance can be an appropriate intervention immediately after a crisis.
2. MFIs that choose to operate in a post-crisis environment must be willing and able to experiment, and be sufficiently flexible to manage changing circumstances.
3. In post-crisis settings, it is more effective and less risky to offer microfinance services to a mixed clientele rather than to target any particular subgroup.
4. Prepare clients and the institution to manage crises before they occur.

Case Study: SFI Responds to Natural and Man-made Crises in the Philippines

Serviamus Foundation Incorporated (SFI) was established in 1998 in Mindanao, Philippines, as a non-profit NGO, with support from Catholic Relief Services (CRS). Its main product at the start of operations was a group loan based on the Grameen Bank model. As of December 2008, it was reaching 9,439 clients with 76 total staff, a gross loan portfolio of US$826,492 and savings of US$471,223.

In 1999 and 2000, Mindanao was hit by two major crises. In February 1999, the region was severely affected by flooding, caused mainly by the El Niño phenomenon. Approximately 650 families were displaced and more than 300 houses were destroyed. Then, in March 2000, fighting broke out between the Armed Forces of the Philippines and the Moro Islamic Liberation Front in the province of Lanao del Norte. This conflict led hundreds of people to flee from the province.

Both events affected the microfinance operations of SFI, and led the organization to react. On the one hand, SFI adapted its existing services to the changed circumstances and on the other hand, it created new products and services to meet the needs of its clients better in times of crisis.

Immediately after the flooding, SFI staff visited affected families in evacuation centres to assess their situation and provide some counselling. Overall, due to a high influx of private donations, well-functioning solidarity mechanisms, the quick receding of the water and a relatively small number of directly affected clients, SFI's microfinance operations were not seriously harmed by the floods. Therefore the loan policies were not changed and no rescheduling of loans took place. SFI did develop new products to correspond to the special needs of its clients, however. With the help of emergency assistance funds provided by CRS, SFI provided emergency loans and a few grants to especially affected families, mostly for house reconstruction.

The emergency loans had the following characteristics:

- payable within a maximum of three years (reduced in 2000 to one year);
- zero per cent interest rate; 2 per cent service charge;
- loan amount dependent on clients' capacity to pay and the severity of the damage;
- repayment incorporated in the weekly amortization of the regular loan;

- client eligible depending on the personal need for assistance and after submitting a basic questionnaire, including a breakdown on the desired use of funds.

As a rule, emergency loans had to be repaid first. During the repayment of the emergency loans, the repayment of other outstanding loans stopped. Clients therefore benefited from a de facto moratorium on pre-existing loans.

The impact of armed violence in 2000 was worse. At least 230 clients and their families were directly affected by the conflict, houses were burnt, shops destroyed and a few people killed. Adding to the general economic crisis in the area, the conflict led to the collapse of businesses and consequent repayment difficulties among SFI clients. In response, SFI granted its clients a three-week grace period and encouraged them to maintain their membership even if they could not continue repayment at that time. Depending on clients' individual situation, loans were rescheduled and grace periods of up to six months were permitted. SFI monitored client groups closely and allowed them to move to new loan cycles even if one member had failed to repay due to the conflict.

In sum, SFI introduced flexibility into the management of its outstanding loan portfolio to account for the difficult situations of its clients. Although client participation in meetings dropped significantly immediately after the crisis, it had recovered to its former level only two months later. The biggest loss to the organization occurred due to the flight of around 160 client families from the area, out of which only half repaid their outstanding loan. SFI had to write off this amount, but was able to absorb the loss due to its loan loss reserve.

Besides the direct effects of the armed violence on the clients, the elevated security threats also severely affected microfinance operations. In response, SFI set up a 24-hour guard in front of its office, purchased a vehicle to pick up collections at centres, varied the schedule of centre collections, and, whenever possible, deposited collected funds with the bank immediately. It also made a concerted effort to spread the word that SFI is a pro-poor organization and any attack on it would hurt the community.

Clients' feedback on the microfinance programme suggests that they were generally satisfied with SFI's crisis response. They expressed the need for even more flexibility in times of crisis, however, advocating for shorter loan terms, more flexible repayment schedules, and the waiving of penalties on overdue loans.

The long-term strategy of SFI for a better crisis response and mitigation included plans to provide disaster preparedness training for staff and clients, diversify its client base (geographically and by sector), develop insurance products, promote savings as self-insurance, and collaborate more closely with donors to speed up emergency loan disbursement after an event of crisis.

This case study was adapted from Seller (2002) with data provided by the MIX (www.mixmarket.org).

Recommended Reading

- Alidri, P.; van Doorn, J.; El-Zoghbi, M.; Houtart, M.; Larson, D.; Nagarajan, G.; Tsilikounas, C. 2002. *Introduction to microfinance in conflict-affected communities* (Geneva, ILO and UNHCR), at: http://www.ilo.org/public/libdoc/ilo/2002/102B09_320_engl.pdf
- Brown, W.; Nagarajan, G. 2000. *Disaster loan funds for microfinance institutions: A look at emerging experience* (Bethesda, Microenterprise Best Practices), at: http://www.microfinancegateway.org/gm/document-1.9.29690/3784_file_03784.pdf
- Chua, R.; Miehlbradt, A. 1999. *Rapid onset natural disasters technical briefs* (Bethesda, Microenterprise Best Practices), at: http://www.microlinks.org/ev_en.php?ID=7488_201&ID2=DO_TOPIC
- Doyle, K. 1998. *Microfinance in the wake of conflict: Challenges and opportunities* (New York, SEEP Network), at: http://www.microfinancegateway.org/p/site/m//template.rc/1.9.28945
- Foundation for Development Cooperation. 2006. *Training resources on microfinance and disaster management* (Queensland, Banking with the Poor Network), at: http://www.bwtp.org/arcm/mfdm/training.html
- Larson, D.; Pierce, M.; Graber, K.; Doyle, K.; Halty, M. 2004. *Technical briefs on post-conflict microfinance* (Bethesda, Microenterprise Best Practices), at: http://www.microlinks.org/ev_en.php?ID=7465_201&ID2=DO_TOPIC
- Magill, J. 2003. *The first 30 days: A practical guide to managing natural disasters for microfinance institutions* (Bethesda: Development Alternatives, Inc.), at: http://www.microfinancegateway.org/p/site/m//template.rc/1.9.42070
- Miamidian, E.; Arnold, M.; Burritt, K.; Jacquand, M. 2005. *Surviving disasters and supporting recovery: A guidebook for microfinance institutions*, Disaster Risk Management Working Paper Series No. 10 (Washington, DC, World Bank), at: http://www.microfinancegateway.org/gm/document-1.9.25290/23882_file_23882.pdf
- SEEP Network. 2009. *Minimum standards for economic recovery after crisis* (Washington, DC, SEEP), at: http://communities.seepnetwork.org/econrecovery/node/821

19 Islamic Microfinance[44]

Islamic microfinance represents the confluence of two rapidly growing industries: microfinance and Islamic finance. It has the potential to not only respond to unmet demand but also to combine the Islamic social principle of caring for the less fortunate with microfinance's power to provide financial access to the poor. Unlocking this potential could be the key to providing financial access to millions of Muslim poor who currently reject microfinance products that do not comply with Islamic law. ~ Karim et al. (2008)

The Islamic world is enormous, with 1.6 billion people, representing 23 per cent of an estimated world population of 6.8 billion (Pew Research Center, 2009). Except for a handful of countries in Southeast Asia and the Middle East, there are high and rising poverty levels in both urban and rural parts of most Muslim countries. In Indonesia alone, with the world's largest Muslim population, over half of the national population (about 129 million people) are poor or vulnerable to poverty with incomes less than US$2 a day. It is estimated that ten Islamic countries account for more than 600 million of the world's poor (Islamic Research and Training Institute, 2008).

Combine these statistics with research from Honohan (2007) that estimates 72 per cent of people living in Muslim-majority countries do not use formal financial services and the potential for microfinance in the Islamic world becomes clear. Even when financial services are available, some people do not use them because they view conventional products as incompatible with the financial principles set forth in Islamic law. In recent years, a few microfinance institutions have stepped in to serve low-income Muslim clients who demand products consistent with Islamic financial principles – leading to the emergence of Islamic microfinance as a new market niche.

This chapter explores the characteristics of Islamic microfinance and the strategies being used to serve this market segment. It addresses the following four questions:

1. What is Islamic finance?
2. What is the market for Islamic microfinance?
3. What products could Islamic microfinance offer?
4. What are the challenges inherent in serving this market?

19.1 What Is Islamic Finance?

Islamic finance refers to a system of finance based on Islamic law (commonly referred to as Sharia). It prohibits practices that are considered to be unfair or exploitative. The most widely known characteristic of Islamic finance is the strict prohibition on giving or receiving any fixed, predetermined rate of return on financial transactions. This ban on interest, agreed upon by a majority of Islamic scholars, is derived from two fundamental Sharia precepts:

[44] This chapter was adapted from Karim, N.; Tarazi, M. and Reille, X, Islamic microfinance: An emerging market niche, CGAP Focus Note No. 49 (Washington, DC, CGAP, 2008); and Islamic Research and Training Institute, *Islamic microfinance development: Challenges and initiatives*, Policy Dialogue Paper No. 2, (Jeddah, IRTI, 2008).

- **Money has no intrinsic worth.** Money is not an asset by itself, and can increase in value only if it joins other resources to undertake productive activity. For this reason, money cannot be bought or sold as a commodity, and money not backed by assets cannot increase in value over time.
- **Fund providers must share the business risk.** Providers of funds are not considered creditors (who are typically guaranteed a predetermined rate of return), but rather investors (who share the rewards as well as the risks associated with their investment). "Depositors" in Islamic banks are really shareholders who earn dividends when the bank turns a profit, or lose a portion of their savings if it turns a loss (Zaher and Hassan, 2001).

Islamic finance, however, extends beyond the ban on interest-based transactions. Additional key financial principles include the following:

- **Material finality.** All financial transactions must be linked, either directly or indirectly, to a real economic activity. In other words, transactions must be backed by assets, and investments may be made only in real, durable assets. This means that financial speculation, and activities such as short selling, are considered violations of Sharia.
- **Investment activity.** Activities deemed inconsistent with Sharia, such as those relating to the consumption of alcohol or pork, gambling or weapons production, cannot be financed. In broader terms, Sharia prohibits the financing of any activity that is considered harmful to society as a whole.
- **No contractual exploitation.** Contracts are required to be by mutual agreement, and must stipulate exact terms and conditions. Additionally, all involved parties must have precise knowledge of the product or service that is being bought or sold.

The body of law used to engineer Sharia-based financial contracts is complex. Scholars must complete several years of training before becoming certified to issue financial rulings. The industry's most prominent Islamic finance scholars are in general agreement on the basic set of financial precepts listed above. However, there is no centralized Sharia finance authority, and consequently there can be conflicting views on specific principles and on the implementation of these principles in designing and delivering Islamic financial products.

19.2 What Is the Market for Islamic Microfinance?

In a 2007 global survey on Islamic microfinance, the Consultative Group to Assist the Poorest (CGAP) collected information on over 125 institutions and contacted experts from 19 Muslim countries. The survey and a synthesis of other available data revealed that Islamic microfinance has a total estimated global outreach of only 380,000 customers and accounts for only an estimated 0.5 per cent of total microfinance outreach. The supply of Islamic microfinance is very concentrated in a few countries, with the top three (Indonesia, Bangladesh and Afghanistan) accounting for 80 per cent of global outreach (see Table 19.1).

Among the institutions that offer Islamic microfinance products, non-governmental organizations (NGOs) are the dominant players in terms of breadth of outreach, with just 14 institutions reaching 42 per cent of clients. Commercial banks (represented by only two institutions: Yemen's Tadhamon Islamic Bank and Bangladesh's Islami Bank Bangladesh Limited) have

Table 19.1 Outreach of Islamic microfinance

Region	No. of included institutions	% Female (avg.)	Total no. of clients	Total outstanding loan portfolio (US$)	Average loan balance (US$)
Afghanistan	4	22	53,011	10,347,29	162
Bahrain	1	n/a	323	96,565	299
Bangladesh	2	90	111,837	34,490,490	280
Indonesia*	105	60	74,698	122,480,000	1,640
Jordan	1	80	1,481	1,619,909	1,094
Lebanon	1	50	26,000	22,500,000	865
Mali	1	12	2,812	273,298	97
Pakistan	1	40	6,069	746,904	123
West Bank and Gaza**	1	100	132	145,485	1,102
Saudi Arabia	1	86	7,000	586,667	84
Somalia	1	n/a	50	35,200	704
Sudan	3	65	9,561	1,891,819	171
Syria	1	45	2,298	1,838,047	800
Yemen	3	58	7,031	840,240	146
TOTAL	126	59	302,303	197,891,882	541

**Micro and rural banks only.*
*** There were seven MFIs in the West Bank and Gaza that offered, with the help of training and funding facilities offered by the Islamic Development Bank, a total of 578 Islamic loans between 2005 and 2006. Data on only one of these seven are displayed in the table, because the remaining six MFIs were disbursing Islamic loans with average loan sizes higher than 250 per cent of the region's gross domestic product per capita.*

Source: Karim et al., 2008.

the second largest outreach, with over 87,000 clients. Interestingly, 105 Sharia-compliant rural banks in Indonesia account for 25 per cent of total clients, but 62 per cent of the outstanding loan portfolio because of their significantly higher average loan size and their focus on small and microenterprise financing.

Like conventional microfinance, Islamic microfinance tends to focus on female clients – a majority of Islamic MFI clients according to the CGAP survey were women (59 per cent on average, but up to 90 per cent in Bangladesh). Overall, the percentage of female clients using Islamic microfinance products is comparable to those using conventional microfinance products (65.7 per cent globally, and 65.4 per cent in the Arab world) (Microfinance Information eXchange, 2007).

Despite the relatively low outreach of Islamic microfinance to date, demand for Islamic microfinance products seems strong. Surveys in Jordan, Algeria and Syria, for example,

revealed that 20–40 per cent of respondents cite religious reasons for not accessing conventional microloans. This is not to say that conventional microfinance products have not been successful in Muslim majority countries. The Grameen Bank, one of the earliest microfinance programmes, originated in Bangladesh, and had 8 million clients at the end of 2009. Both Indonesia and Pakistan have vibrant microfinance industries. Approximately 44 per cent of conventional microfinance clients worldwide reside in Muslim countries.

Yet conventional microfinance products do not fulfil the needs of many Muslim clients. Just as there are mainstream banking clients who demand Islamic financial products, there are also many poor people who insist on these products. Indeed, Sharia compliance in some societies may be less a religious principle than a cultural one – and even the less religiously observant may desire Sharia-compliant products.

There is also a category of Muslim clients who use conventional microfinance products because that is what is available, but would prefer Islamic ones. Practitioners in Muslim-majority countries indicate that in Afghanistan, Indonesia, Syria and Yemen, some conventional microborrowers switch over once Islamic products become available. At the same time, however, anecdotal evidence suggests that survey respondents may verbally express a preference for Islamic products simply to demonstrate piety, but when given a choice in practice will opt for a lower-priced conventional product. Consequently, despite indications of demand for Islamic microfinance products, further research is needed to ascertain the nature and extent of the demand, and how to meet this demand in a cost-effective manner.

19.3 What Products Could Islamic Microfinance Offer?

Islamic microfinance services take the form of contracts. This section briefly describes seven basic types of contract, which can be used in different ways, and even combined, to create a variety of products:

1. *murabaha*;
2. *ijara*;
3. *mudaraba*;
4. *musharaka*;
5. *takaful*;
6. *qard hasan*;
7. *wadiah*.

Murabaha *(Cost-plus Financing)*

The most widely offered Sharia-compliant contract is *murabaha*, an asset-based sale transaction used to finance goods needed as working capital. Typically, the client requests a specific commodity for purchase, which a financial institution buys directly from the market and subsequently resells to the client, after adding a fixed "mark-up" for the service provided. Payment is deferred to a future date. In order for a *murabaha* sale to be Sharia-compliant, three main conditions must be met:

- The financial institution must own the commodity before selling it.
- The commodity must be tangible.
- The client must agree to the purchase and resale prices, as well as the frequency and number of repayments.

It is permissible for the financial institution to appoint the client as an "agent" (by means of another type of contract) to procure the commodity directly from the market on its behalf. However, ownership of the commodity (and the risks that come with ownership) lie strictly with the financial institution until the client has paid fully. It is this risk-bearing by the financial institution that legitimizes its profits from the perspective of Sharia. The mark-up is distinct from interest, because it remains fixed at the initial amount, even if the client repays past the due date.

Murabaha contracts are the easiest for microfinance institutions and their clients to manage, because they are well defined, they allow repayments in equal instalments, and they do not require clients to keep detailed accounting records. One example of a successful scheme is described in Box 19.1.

Box 19.1 Murabaha Financing in Syria

In Jabal al-Hoss, one of the poorest areas in Syria, self-reliant local financial institutions called *sanadiq* (literally "savings box") provide local financing through *murabaha* contracts. For instance, a *sanduq* might buy ten sheep and sell them to a member, to be repaid in instalments with a fixed mark-up (profit margin) of 2.5 per cent per month. At the end of the year the profit made by a *sanduq* is shared between the members and the *sanduq* as a source of growth.

The *sanadiq* are self-managed and autonomous in their decision-making. Their start-up is self-financed through member share capital, from which small loans are given for up to three months. The first *sanadiq* were created in the year 2000, with initial community mobilization and training being provided by the Rural Community Development Project (RCDP), a joint effort between the Ministry of Agriculture and Agrarian Reform and the United Nations Development Programme (UNDP). Once a *sanduq*'s financial operations were satisfactory, it gained access to refinancing from a *sanduq markazi*, or central fund, which was financed by the project.

Between September 2000 and December 2002, 22 *sanadiq* were established, comprising 4,691 members, with shareholder equity of US$ 130,000. The repayment rate as of 31 December 2002 was 99.7 per cent. Return on average equity was 17 per cent, almost half of which (46 per cent) was paid to shareholders; the balance (54 per cent) was retained as capital. During the second phase of RCDP, the Japanese Government and UNDP provided assistance to expand the *sanadiq* network and formalize its legal status. As of June 2006 there were 32 village-based *sanadiq* with 7,360 shareholders, 47 per cent of them women, most of whom were illiterate.

Source: Adapted from Imady and Seibel, 2003, and Seibel, 2007.

Ijara *(Leasing)*

Ijarah is a leasing contract that can be used to finance income-generating equipment, such as small machinery, tools, carts or rickshaws. The client receives the benefits associated with ownership of the asset in exchange for predetermined rental payments. The duration of the lease and its related payments must be determined in advance to avoid any speculation. The lessor (in this case, the financial institution) continues to be the owner throughout the *ijara* period, so that the risks associated with ownership of the asset remain with the institution. The cash flows are structured in a way that covers the cost of the asset and provides for a fair return to the financial institution. At the end of the lease the institution can donate the asset or transfer ownership to the client via a sale contract at a nominal price.

An important Sharia rule governing *ijara* as a tool of microfinance is that the risk and liabilities emerging from the ownership of the asset remain substantially with the lessor so that its profits are deemed legitimate. In a conventional financial lease the lessor transfers to the lessee the risks and rewards related to ownership of the leased asset, even though the title of the asset may or may not eventually be transferred to the lessee. The complete transfer of risk makes the financial lease unacceptable from the Sharia point of view.

With *ijara* contracts there is no compensation in case of destruction of asset value, except when the loss is caused by the negligence of the lessee (the client). A lessor can mitigate this risk by making the lessee specifically liable for damages, theft and/or loss on destruction of assets except in the case of force majeure. Further, specific risks of the lessor relating to the physical damage, theft and/or loss or destruction of the leased asset may be covered by Islamic insurance (refer to the discussion below on takaful). The lessor may include the cost of takaful premium in the *ijara* rental.

Musharaka *and* Mudaraba *(Profit and Loss Sharing)*

Profit- and loss-sharing schemes are the Islamic financial contracts most encouraged by Sharia scholars. *Musharaka* is equity participation in a business venture, in which the parties share the profits or losses according to a predetermined ratio. In the example provided in Figure 19.1, the investor (Partner A) contributes 60 per cent of the capital, receives 30 per cent of the profit and absorbs 60 per cent of any loss, while the client (Partner B) contributes 40 per cent of the capital, receives 70 per cent of the profit and absorbs 40 per cent of any loss. These percentages vary from one partnership to another. *Musharaka* is viewed by many as the purest form of finance because all parties share the underlying risk. It can be used for assets or for working capital.

A variant of this contract, known as the diminishing *musharaka*, has great potential for Islamic MFIs. Whereas a classical *musharaka* aims to involve the MFI as a permanent partner in the venture, in a declining *musharaka* the MFI's share in the equity is diminished each year through partial return of capital. The MFI receives periodic profits based on its reduced equity share that remains invested during the period. The share of the client in the capital steadily increases over time, ultimately resulting in complete ownership of the venture.

Mudaraba denotes trustee financing, in which one party acts as financier by providing funds, while the other party provides the managerial expertise in executing the project. As illustrated

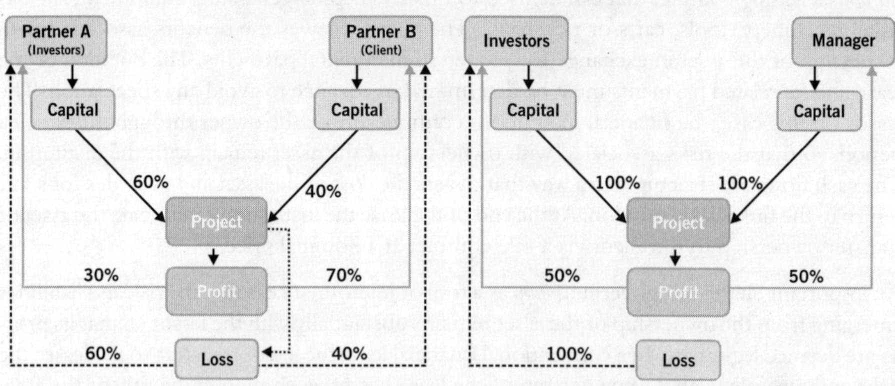

in Figure 19.2, profits are shared according to a predetermined ratio (50-50 in the example provided here), but financial losses are borne entirely by the financier (the manager loses time and effort). *Mudaraba* may be one of two types: restricted or unrestricted. In a restricted *mudaraba* the MFI specifies a particular business in which investments may be undertaken. In an unrestricted *mudaraba* the capital can be invested in any business that the client deems fit.

Although promoted strongly by Sharia, *musharaka* and *mudaraba* contracts are not popular among MFIs or clients. This is due to several factors. First, since the profit-sharing ratio is predetermined, but the profit is not, both *musharaka* and *mudaraba* schemes require vigilant reporting and a high level of transparency for profits and losses to be distributed justly. Clients often lack the necessary skills to do this, or are simply unwilling to report their profits and losses to the MFI on an ongoing basis. Second, the uncertainty about profits and the variability of profits from one week to the next make it very difficult for MFIs to predict cash flows. Finally, the repayment schedule is difficult for both loan officers and borrowers to understand. Even in a hypothetical situation in which profits are known, the borrower has to repay a different amount each period (and the loan officer has to collect a different amount each period). This lack of simplicity – relative to the equal repayment instalments provided under a *murabaha* contract – is a source of confusion for borrowers and loan officers.

Takaful *(Mutual Insurance)*

The equivalent of Islamic insurance, *takaful* is a mutual insurance scheme. The word originates from the Arabic word *kafala*, which means guaranteeing each other or joint guarantee. Each participant contributes to a fund that is used to support the group in times of need, such as death, crop loss, or accidents, and the premiums paid are invested in a Sharia-compliant manner. Mainstream insurance companies can work with MFIs as agents to offer *takaful* to their clients, as demonstrated by the case of Indonesia (see Box 19.2).

Box 19.2 *Takaful* and *Microtakaful* Insurance in Indonesia

Most of the insurance companies in Indonesia are either developing or have developed *takaful* insurance products, and even *takaful* divisions, to respond to and develop the growing demand from the Islamic community.

In Indonesia, *takaful* insurance is governed by the Ministry of Finance and its Insurance Directorate, but licensing and continued operation as a *takaful* insurer or *takaful* division are dependent on the approval of the National Sharia Board. The 18 members of the National Sharia Board must approve requests for new *takaful* products before the Insurance Directorate will begin their approval process. This process involves a review of several aspects of the product in order to confirm conformity with Sharia law. This includes how transactions are managed, how investments are made, into which investments Sharia premiums will be placed, and how earnings will be distributed.

In order to ensure continued compliance, the Board requires a three-member Sharia committee to be housed within the insurance company to review regular transactions and policies, and to guide management in their product and process decision-making regarding Sharia aspects of operations.

Another factor that must comply with Sharia law is the investment of insurance contributions and savings. In the past, this has been a limiting factor. How insurance is sold is also a factor in developing a Sharia-compliant product. *Takaful* insurance can be sold by an intermediary as long as three criteria are met:

1. The intermediary must charge a fee, not a commission.
2. Buyers must understand that the intermediary is only a pass-through to move their premiums to the Sharia insurer more efficiently.
3. Any proceeds (premiums) must be held in a separate account and not commingled with other intermediary funds.

The beginnings of *microtakaful* can be traced to 2006, when Germany's Allianz introduced a microinsurance version of its *takaful* policies in the country. After a 16-month pilot phase, a credit life programme, *Payung Keluarga* (meaning "Family Umbrella"), was introduced in January 2008, featuring options that included Islamic-law-compliant policies and co-insurance for spouses. By the end of 2008, Allianz had insured over 183,000 micro-credits, covering debtors of 21 partner MFIs (including four cooperatives, 11 social foundations, four rural banks and two commercial banks) against natural and accidental death, for an average premium of US$0.73. To keep premiums low, *Payung Keluarga* is a compulsory product; to reduce complexity, the MFI centrally decides on the product benefits on behalf of its customers.

Domestic insurance providers have also jumped onto the *microtakaful* bandwagon. In late 2006, PT Asuransi Takaful Keluarga (ATK), Takmin Working Group and Sharia microfinance institutions (LKMS) collaborated under the partner-agent model to launch *Takaful Micro Sakinah*, a Sharia-compliant credit insurance programme for microenterprises and poor families in Bogor. In 2008, ATK partnered with the National Alms Board (Baznas) to develop a *microtakaful* scheme for alms receivers. The policy costs Rp 50,000 (US$5) and will consist of reciprocal assistance funds managed by ATK and donation funds managed by Baznas. The latter distributes Rp 2,500 from each policyholder's premiums to worthy receivers. The policies pay out Rp 5 million for deaths resulting from natural causes and Rp 25 million for those caused by accidents.

Source: Hogarth, 2009; McCord et al., 2006; and Tan, 2008.

Qard Hasan[45]

Qard hasan is a loan granted without expectation of any return on the principal. These zero-return loans are loans that the Quran exhorts Muslims to make to "those who need them". Borrowers are allowed and even encouraged to return more than the amount borrowed, but the excess is viewed as a gift, and is permissible only if it is not demanded by the lender.

From the standpoint of a microfinance institution, a *qard hasan* contract can be used both as an instrument of savings mobilization and as an instrument of financing. This is because a *qard hasan* may or may not have a date of redemption. The absence of a specific date of redemption gives a lender the right to call for repayment at any time. Thus, when a deposit contract is modelled as a *qard hasan* contract, depositors (as the lenders) can take back their deposits with the microfinance institution at any time. Clients may find it attractive to place their surplus funds with an MFI on a *qard hasan* basis, even if there is no nominal return on their savings, because it allows them to store their savings in a safe place, while keeping them accessible in case of emergency and enabling them to perform an Islamic duty of helping the have-nots at the same time. This logic underlies the establishment of Qard Hasan Funds in Iran (see Box 19.3)

Box 19.3 Qard Hasan Funds in Iran

Qard Hasan Funds have been operating in the Iranian informal financial sector for the past two to three decades. It is estimated that currently more than 3,000 funds of this type are operating in urban and rural areas of the country. Qard Hasan Funds can be divided into at least four categories: Family Qard Hasan Funds, Workplace Qard Hasan Funds, Community or Village Qard Hasan Funds and large Qard Hasan Funds. In principle, all forms of Qard Hasan Fund are non-profit institutions in which members of a community set up a savings and loans society. Members deposit their savings with the fund in order that other members who need some loan for a short period can be helped from this fund. In essence, it is a mutual support fund – a depositor at one time may become a borrower at another time, and vice versa.

Members are free to withdraw some or all of their deposits if and when they want. No depositor demands or receives any amount in addition to his/her capital. As the members are known to each other and are trustworthy, there is little room for default on loans. The operations of the society are run by volunteers, using some free office space.

Other overheads, such as costs for stamps, stationery, transport, communication and so on, are covered in some Qard Hasan Funds through engagement of funds in business activities. In most of the others the borrowers have to pay the costs. Therefore, even though the capital is cost-free, the loan is not. It is interest-free but not cost-free.

Studies show that the average amount of savings deposits in Qard Hasan Funds is larger than those of banks. Loan applicants of *qard hasan* usually request loans for needs such as marriage, health, or housing. Depending on the size of the loan and borrowers' ability to pay, borrowers have between one and two years to repay the *qard hasan* loans. To be eligible for a *qard hasan* loan, a borrower must be in urgent need, have at least one referee or guarantor, and demonstrate sufficient ability to repay the loan.

Source: Adapted from Asgary, 2007.

[45] This section is adapted from Obaidulla (2008).

As a financing mechanism, the *qard hasan* contract also has some advantages. Unlike other Islamic finance contracts, it can place cash in the hands of a borrower that may be used for consumption as well as productive purposes, which makes it more useful for serving the very poor. In addition, MFIs can charge borrowers a service fee to cover the administrative expenses of handling the loan, provided that the fee is not related to the amount or term of the loan.

However, *qard hasan* contracts have several important disadvantages as well. First, they do not protect depositors from the harmful effects of inflation. According to Seibel (2007), depositors in Iran lost about half the value of their deposits each year during the mid-1990s, when inflation rates were around 50 per cent. Second, they are often considered a form of charity, because they are typically forgiven in the event of default. Thus MFIs who use this contract to finance entrepreneurs may have difficulty getting their loans repaid, and if other clients are effectively financing these loans through *qard hasan* deposits, they risk losing their savings. Third, outreach through *qard hasan* loans will be limited by the MFI's ability to raise *qard hasan* deposits, although this last challenge might be met by leveraging *zakat* (funds donated pursuant to the Muslim obligation to pay alms), as discussed in Section 19.5 below.

Wadia

Wadia is a contract whereby a person leaves valuables with someone for safekeeping. The keeper can charge a fee, even though in Islamic culture it is encouraged to provide this service free of charge or to recover only the costs of safekeeping without any profit. Under this mechanism, deposits can be held in trust and utilized by an MFI at its own risk. Any profit or loss resulting from the investment of these funds accrues entirely to the microfinance institution. One type of *wadia* contract, *wadiah yad dhammanah* (keeping valuable goods by guarantee), when combined with *qard hasan*, can form the basis for pawn lending, which is common in both Malaysia and Indonesia (see Box 19.4).

Using Islamic Finance Contracts to Mobilize Funds

It has already been discussed above how *wadia* and *qard hasan* can be used to capture deposits, but there are actually many ways to combine Islamic finance contracts to create Sharia-compliant savings accounts, as illustrated by the range of savings products offered by Bank Muamalat (see Box 19.5).

Mudaraba-based accounts allow customers to deposit money in a financial institution and share in the profits and risks of the institution's use of that money. However, since *mudaraba*-based savings products involve considerable downside risk (a loss by the institution would have to be absorbed by the depositor), they are rarely offered by Islamic microfinance institutions. A variant of this product is based on the notion of revenue-sharing instead of profit-sharing, and is reasonably commonplace in the case of Indonesian microfinance institutions (see Table 19.2 for a few examples).[46]

[46] It should be noted that when savings products are remunerated on the basis of revenue-sharing rather than profit-sharing, the underlying Shariah mechanism is no longer the classical *mudaraba* but rather a type of agency contract under which the depositor appoints the microfinance institution to manage its funds.

Box 19.4 *Murtahin* (Islamic Pawnbroking)

Pawnshops are one of the many types of institution providing Islamic microfinance. In Indonesia there are approximately 744 branches and 14 regional head offices, all of which are state-owned and run by Perum Pegadaian (PP). In 2001, PP established a Sharia Pawn Service Unit Division for implementing pawning practices based on Sharia pursuant to Article 7 of Government Regulation No. 103 of 2000.

Through the Sharia Pawn Service Unit Division, pawnshops provide fast loans based on collateral in the form of physical assets (for example, jewellery, precious metals or electronic devices) which do not require complex procedures to operate. During the lending period, pawnshops provide a place for safekeeping the pledged assets and, in turn, charge the borrowers a fee for costs related to their maintenance and safekeeping. Upon maturity, pawnshops have the right to sell or auction the pledged assets upon giving notice to the borrowers, unless the borrowers repay the debt and reclaim the pledged assets.

In Malaysia, the inclusion of Sharia regulation in the banking system in 1983 led to the establishment of Ar Rahnu in 1993. Ar Rahnu offers short-term, interest-free loans that require collateral, which is valued at current prices. During the lending period, the lender will charge a fee for safekeeping the collateral. At the end of the period, financing must be repaid and the collateral reclaimed. As in Indonesia, if the loan is not repaid within the agreed duration, the lender reserves the right to seize and auction the collateral to recover its financing costs, with any remaining balance returned to the borrower.

Source: Allen and Overy, LLP, 2009.

Box 19.5 Savings Products at Bank Muamalat in Indonesia

Bank Muamalat, Indonesia's first Sharia commercial bank, borrows money from the public using the following instruments.

- **Ummat Savings – Tabungan Ummat.** A savings account from which money can be withdrawn at any time from any Muamalat office or ATM. Customers share in the bank's revenue. Ummat Savings customers also receive life insurance and the opportunity to win a free Umrah pilgrimage to Mecca.
- **Trendi Savings – Tabungan Trendi.** A savings account for teenagers and students. Besides accident insurance coverage, it offers special prizes for highly ranked students and one-year scholarships for 50 students.
- **Ukhuwah Savings – Tabungan Ukhuwah.** A savings account conducted in cooperation with Dompet Dhuafa Republika for convenience in making regular and automatic payment of *zakat*, *infaq*, and *shadaqat* in three packages: Rp 25,000, Rp 50,000, and Rp 100,000. This savings account also gives the depositor an ATM card, shopping discounts at certain shops, and accident insurance coverage.
- **Arafah Savings – Tabungan Arafah.** A savings account designed specifically for the *hajj* pilgrimage. The saving scheme will help customers in planning their *hajj* in accordance with their financial capability and intended *hajj* date. Life insurance is also provided. The depositors are also eligible for prizes.
- **Fulinves Deposits – Deposito Fulinves.** A time deposit with a revenue-sharing package available for various terms and with a chance to win prizes. Life insurance is provided to those with longer-term deposits.
- **Wadi'ah Current Account – Giro Wadi'ah.** A current account providing chequing and allowing some profit sharing.
- **Muamalat Financial Institution Pension Fund – Dana Pensiun Lembaga Keuangan.** A pension fund for those who make regular deposits. The bank intends to add a variant that provides life insurance.

Source: Timburg, 2003.

Table 19.2 Deposit products in five Islamic rural banks (BPRS)

BPRS	Total amount (in million Rp)	Number of products	Savings accounts*		Time deposits*	
			Revenue-sharing client bank	Average return in % p.a.	Revenue-sharing client bank	Return in % p.a.
1 Alwadi'ah	3,796	4	50:50	6	70:30	10
2 Artha Fis.	619	4	30:70	12	40:60	18
3 Harum Hik.	4,018	3	40:60	8.8	65:35	14
4 Wakalumi	6,040	12	35:65	7.09	56:44–66:34	11.35–13.37
5 Bangka	5,622	n/a	40:60	7.5	55:45	11.5
Mean	4,019	5.75	40:60	8.3	60:50	13

** By comparison, BMI, an Islamic commercial bank, reports yields to depositors of 6–7 per cent p.a. on savings accounts and 7–9 per cent on term deposits.*

Source: Seibel, 2005.

Takaful can also operate as a savings product if premiums are invested in a Sharia-compliant manner and then disbursed at the end of an agreed term, regardless of any insurance claim. *Musharaka* contracts are not useful for capturing deposits, but they can be used to mobilize equity, as was seen in the case of the *sanadiq* described in Box 19.1. Villagers bought shares and became owners of self-reliant financial institutions.

Islamic microfinance instruments cannot be directly compared with conventional microfinance products because they combine commercial and financial transactions. Nevertheless, it is useful to note the range of instruments through which Islamic MFIs can meet the needs that conventional MFIs meet through microcredit, microleasing, microinsurance and microsavings (see Table 19.3).

19.4 What Are the Challenges Inherent in Serving this Market?

Although Islamic microfinance could potentially expand access to finance to unprecedented levels throughout the Muslim world, it does face several challenges: 1) ensuring and communicating authenticity; 2) finding a sustainable business model; 3) diversifying the product offering; 4) leveraging funds; and 5) establishing effective standards and supervision.

Authenticity

Sharia compliance is the differentiating factor between a conventional and an Islamic finance institution. Not only must Islamic finance institutions conform to Sharia in all their products, processes and activities; clients must also perceive them to conform.

Table 19.3 Comparing conventional microfinance and Islamic microfinance

Conventional microfinance products	Islamic microfinance options
Microcredit	• *Murabaha* (cost-plus financing) • *Musharaka* (equity participation) • *Mudaraba* (trustee financing) • *Qard hasan* (zero-return loans to clients) • *Murtahin* (pawnbroking) • *Bai al salam* (purchase with deferred delivery)
Microleasing	• *Ijara* (leasing)
Microinsurance	• *Takaful* (mutual insurance)
Microsavings	• *Wadia* (storage of valuables for safekeeping) • *Qard hasan* (zero-return loans from clients to MFI) • *Mudaraba* (clients place their deposits in trust with the MFI and share profits/loss) • *Murabaha* (clients help finance the MFI's *murabaha* contracts with other clients for a specific term and receive part of the fee) • *Takaful* (if premiums are invested and disbursed at end of term)

Source: Authors.

Islamic finance sometimes suffers from the perception that it is simply a "rebranding" of conventional finance, and not truly reflective of Islamic principles. Critics suggest that the pricing of some products offered as Sharia compliant parallels too closely the pricing of conventional products. For example, some institutions offer *murabaha* where interest appears to be disguised as a cost mark-up or administration fee.

Mainstream Islamic financial institutions provide comfort to their stakeholders that they conform to Islamic finance principles by setting up Sharia supervisory boards (SSBs). The members of SSBs are usually distinguished scholars who confirm the compliance of financial products and consistency of operations with Sharia. For Islamic MFIs this approach would be costly, so alternatives have to be considered. For example, institutions could approach Sharia scholars on a transaction-by-transaction basis or in relation to a particular product, as Islamic investment and financial cooperatives (IIFCs) did in Afghanistan (see Box 19.6). Islamic MFIs could also pool their resources and form associations, which could then set up a joint SSB.

According to Allen and Overy, LLP (2009), a key consideration when appointing a Sharia board is its composition. MFIs should strive to appoint experienced scholars that are well known in the area where they operate. They should also make sure that the board is made up of Sharia scholars who represent a range of Islamic schools of thought, as this will help reduce the risk of disagreements as to whether a particular product or transaction is Sharia compliant or not.

Box 19.6 WOCCU Expands Islamic Microfinance in Southern and Eastern Afghanistan

Since 2004, WOCCU has worked with local leaders across Afghanistan to establish the country's first fully Sharia-compliant financial institutions, which operate according to Islamic principles of finance. After five years of development, 16 member-owned IIFCs with 11 full service branches are currently bringing financial services to approximately 47,000 members across the country. Despite a harsh operating environment, three of the IIFCs are already self-sufficient, and overall membership is increasing by approximately 1,000 new members each month.

After just a few years of operation, the IIFCs have transformed the financial landscape in rural Afghanistan. The institutions have tested a new leadership model that places tribal elders on the boards of directors, a move that has significantly improved local acceptance of the IIFCs while helping maintain very low loan delinquency rates. The IIFCs have also obtained decrees from local religious leaders known as *fatwas*, indicating approval of the institutions' financial products.

The IIFCs' cooperative spirit of member service, reflective of the humanistic principles of Islam, is evident through a wide variety of community projects they support. IIFC activities include rebuilding mosques destroyed in conflict, offering individual development accounts (IDAs) for educating young bombing victims and their siblings, establishing tailoring and embroidery centres for women, and coordinating the delivery of basic health services in IIFC communities. In conflict-ridden areas where opium poppy production is widespread, including the provinces of Helmand, Kandahar, Kunar and Uruzgan, 90 per cent of IIFC loans are used for the production of alternative agricultural crops.

WOCCU's programme will continue to expand the IIFC network by adding an additional 15 IIFCs and seven branches in the south and east. It will also support the creation of a national association that will provide supervision, technical assistance and loan capital to the IIFCs to help grow Afghanistan's financial cooperative movement.

Source: Adapted from WOCCU, 2009.

Setting up an SSB will not, by itself, solve the authenticity challenge. Greater efforts can be made to encourage the exchange of experiences among religious leaders (particularly those serving poor populations at the local level) relating to the Sharia compliance of microfinance products, and to educate low-income populations, in collaboration with local religious leaders, on how microfinance products comply with Islamic law.

Sustainable Business Model

In *murabaha* and *ijara* transactions, which are the contracts being used most to date, MFIs purchase a commodity (such as equipment or inventory) and resell or lease it to a user with a mark-up. The costs associated with purchasing, maintaining, selling and leasing a commodity are significant. Credit officers are required to prepare a detailed feasibility study for every client, which then serves as the basis for financing. They must go to the market to purchase the commodity, and when they go, they must carry large amounts of cash, which leaves the MFI vulnerable to theft. To minimize this risk, some MFIs require more than one staff person to be present for certain levels of cash disbursement; others restrict the number of disbursements that can be made at once, thereby limiting the amount of cash that can be carried. Supervisors monitor purchases and sales to make sure the financing process is Sharia compliant and the MFI's ownership of all commodities is properly documented. Each of these controls increases the institution's costs and lowers staff productivity.

In addition to increasing costs, the design of Islamic financing contracts lowers effective portfolio yield and puts pressure on MFIs' revenue. When a *murabaha* loan is issued, the service charge is based on a fixed loan term and instalment schedule. When these parameters are violated by clients, the MFI has no recourse in terms of penalty to compensate for the fact that its loan is outstanding longer than expected, or that the loan instalment is late. The outstanding funds are not generating revenue for the MFI, yet the MFI will have to expend resources in an effort to get its capital back.

These challenges will not be overcome easily, but they must be overcome if Islamic MFIs are to be sustainable. To date, MFIs have responded by diluting the Islamic mode of financing. Rather than accompany a client who may want a particular kind of good that is sold in a far-off market, MFIs may give the money directly to the client to purchase the good, or delegate someone else to buy it. Institutions have reduced their monitoring of Sharia compliance and, in at least one documented case, this has resulted in an MFI giving out standard financing amounts rather than catering the financing to the asset being financed. This dilution of the Islamic mode of financing is contributing to the authenticity issue described above.

One way to overcome the challenges of *murabaha* and *ijara* transactions is to use other profit-sharing modes of financing instead, but they have their own problems. The main one is the moral hazard problem arising from the under-reporting of profit. This problem can be mitigated by supervising the operations and monitoring accounts of clients, but supervision and monitoring are costly. Perhaps partnerships can be formed and alternative delivery channels tested to allay some of the costs. User-owned models of service delivery may also provide a way forward, as seen in the Syria and Afghanistan cases described in Boxes 19.1 and 19.6. Having sufficient financing to offer additional services and/or larger loans following on-time repayment can also provide incentives for performance.

Some have suggested that Islamic MFIs should be able to draw more from the social capital that comes from being part of the Islamic community with shared values and principles. According to Ahmed (2002), Muslim employees should have an incentive to work hard for the betterment of the lives of the poor in an Islamic financial institution, and Islamic teachings should increase solidarity among clients and thereby improve the quality of social collateral. Furthermore, the moral teachings of Islam should make clients better debtors, as they consider repayment of debt a religious obligation. By tapping into this social capital more effectively, Islamic MFIs might be able to increase staff productivity and reduce defaults.

Product Diversity

Islamic for-profit microfinance remains highly *murabaha*-centric. The CGAP survey referred to in Section 19.2 above found that over 70 per cent of the products offered by Islamic MFIs are *murabaha*. Even *ijara* has not witnessed many takers among Islamic MFIs. Profit and loss sharing, though highly acclaimed as "ideal", is hardly used. Voluntary savings, deposits services, insurance, remittance and other fee-based services are generally not offered. By concen-

trating primarily on asset financing, the Islamic microfinance industry lacks the product diversification necessary to serve the various financial needs of the poor.

The entry of more commercial finance institutions into the low-income market should, with time, increase the diversity of products offered. A case in point is Allianz Global Investors' expansion of its microinsurance offering to India, Egypt, Colombia, Senegal, Cameroon, Côte d'Ivoire and Madagascar, no doubt influenced by the success of Allianz Life Indonesia. Noor Islamic Bank and Emirates Post Holding Group have announced plans to establish a company that will offer Sharia-compliant microfinance products, including microcredit, insurance, debit cards, remittance and currency exchange, and salary payments to the low-income segment of the United Arab Emirates population. Each entry by a corporate giant provides opportunities for MFIs to form innovative partnerships that can enable their clients to access a broader range of Sharia-compliant services affordably.

Leveraging Zakat and Islamic Funds

Throughout the Muslim world, microfinance (Islamic or otherwise) is still seen as a philanthropic activity rather than a business enterprise. Consequently, in the context of Islamic microfinance, there is a growing tendency to view *zakat* (funds donated pursuant to the Muslim obligation to pay alms) as a source of funding. Indeed, given the underlying principle of Islamic finance to promote the welfare of the community, *zakat* funds appear ideally suited to support Islamic microfinance. However, a heavy reliance on charity is not necessarily the best model for the development of a large and sustainable sector, and more reliable, commercially motivated streams of funding should be explored.

Managers at Islamic MFIs attest that there are certain problems in obtaining funds from external sources. First, the Islamic educational content of Islamic MFIs deters some external sources from funding them. Second, although some funds are available from government agencies, they impose terms and conditions that not only limit flexibility in the operations of MFIs, but may also be contrary to Islamic principles. For example, the funds are given on interest, and the MFIs are required to get a certain fixed rate of return on their investments to ensure repayment. As a result, certain Islamic modes of financing (such as *mudaraba* and *musharaka*) cannot be used to employ funds received from these sources.

One strategic use of *zakat* funds may come in the form of a guarantee fund, since *zakat* may legitimately be used to pay off unpaid debt of the poor. Credit guarantee schemes can be a strategic way to increase the attractiveness of microfinance to commercial banks, as illustrated by the success of the Grameen-Jamil Initiative in helping an Egyptian MFI leverage funding in local currency from a local bank (see Box 19.7). This kind of product can be made Sharia compliant, but if *zakat* funds are to be used, care would have to be taken to ensure that the coverage of the scheme is restricted to the extremely poor only.

Standards and Supervision

Islamic financial services originally operated in an unclear regulatory landscape. However, as they expanded, they presented several regulatory challenges that governments have attempted to address to various degrees. One approach has been to proactively encourage, even mandate, Islamic financial services by law. Northern Sudan, for example, adopted Sharia-compliant

Box 19.7 A Guarantee Product by Grameen-Jameel Initiative

The Grameen-Jameel Initiative, an innovative collaboration between Grameen Foundation and the Abdul Latif Jameel Group to fight poverty in the Arab World through microfinance, provided as its first transaction a US$2 million guarantee to Dakahlya Businessmen Association for Community Development (DBACD), a leading microfinance institution, enabling it to secure a local currency loan of US$2.5 million from BNP Paribas. With this new funding, DBACD can provide much-needed loans to 16,000 poor Egyptians. This deal negotiated by the Grameen-Jameel Initiative utilizes a US$1 million guarantee from Grameen Foundation's Growth Guarantee Programme. The other US$1 million guarantee comes from the Mohammad Jameel Guarantee Fund, established in favour of the Grameen-Jameel Pan Arab Initiative. Both the Grameen Foundation Growth Guarantees Programme and the Jameel Fund provide guarantees for MFIs to receive local currency financing from local commercial banks.

The guarantees of US$1 million each were issued by Citibank and Banque Saudi Fransi. In another first, this transaction is the only one to date where an Egyptian MFI has received leveraged funding from a commercial bank. Historically, banks in Egypt have required a 100 per cent guarantee. By providing credit enhancement and with the partial guarantee, Grameen-Jameel was able to interest international banks in lending to DBACD for its microfinance programmes.

Source: Islamic Research and Training Institute, 2008.

regulatory frameworks for the entire banking sector in 1984. Indonesia broke new ground in the realm of Islamic finance by creating in 1992 a formal, regulated Sharia banking sector alongside, and not instead of, its conventional banking sector. New regulations in Malaysia, Brunei and Pakistan have also supported the expansion of an Islamic finance industry alongside conventional financial services.

A second regulatory approach has been to address the growth of Islamic finance by separately regulating unique aspects of Islamic banking, such as the SSBs. For example, several countries (such as Kuwait, Jordan, Lebanon and Thailand) have regulated the competence and composition of SSBs, as well as related rules governing the appointment, dismissal and qualifications of SSB members (Grais and Pellegrini, 2006). However, no country is known to regulate the Sharia jurisprudence to be used by SSBs in judging Sharia compliance.

In parallel with increased attention by regulatory authorities, international organizations have also been created to set and encourage compliance with Islamic finance standards. For example:

- The Islamic Financial Services Board (IFSB), based in Malaysia, issues prudential standards and guiding principles for institutions offering Islamic financial services. The principles address the areas of risk management, capital adequacy, corporate governance, and the conduct of business, among others (for details, refer to http://www.ifsb.org).
- The Accounting and Auditing Organization for Islamic Financial Institutions (AAOIFI), based in Bahrain, prepares accounting, auditing, governance, ethics and Sharia standards for Islamic financial institutions and the industry (for details, refer to http://www.aaoifi.com).
- The Islamic Development Bank (IDB), a multilateral body headquartered in Saudi Arabia, fights poverty and promotes economic development in Islamic country members. It promotes microfinance and poverty alleviation programmes through its Islamic Solidarity

Fund for Development (ISFD), which recently committed US$500 million to microfinance development through its Microfinance Support Programme (MFSP).

Despite a shared core of Islamic values, these institutions often diverge from national regulators (and each other) over Sharia standards. It would be helpful if the IDB, IFSB and AAOIFI were to develop global financial reporting standards adapted to microfinance to build the infrastructure for transparency in the global Islamic microfinance sector. This infrastructure would entail comprehensive disclosure guidelines on Islamic microfinance accounting principles, pricing methodologies, financial audits and, eventually, rating services.

Main Messages

1. Sharia compliance is the differentiating factor between a conventional and an Islamic microfinance institution.
2. Islamic microfinance institutions must not only conform to Sharia in all their products, processes and activities; they must also be perceived to conform by their clientele.
3. Despite indications of demand for Islamic microfinance products, further research is needed to ascertain the nature and extent of the demand, and how to meet it in a cost-effective manner.
4. More creativity is required in the way MFIs combine Islamic contracts to diversify the portfolio of products being offered to clients.
5. MFIs should look for ways to partner with for-profit and not-for-profit entities that will enable their clients to access a broader range of Sharia-compliant services affordably.

Recommended Reading

- Ahmed, H. 2002. "Financing microenterprises: An analytical study of Islamic microfinance institutions", in *Islamic Economic Studies*, Vol. 9, No. 2 (Jeddah, Islamic Research and Training Institute (IRTI), Islamic Development Bank), at: http://www.microfinancegateway.org/gm/document-1.9.25170/41189_file_H_Ahmed_Financing_M.pdf
- Allen & Overy, LLP. 2009. *Islamic microfinance report* (Rome, International Development Law Organisation (IDLO)), at: http://www.microfinancegateway.org/p/site/m//template.rc/1.9.34511
- Islamic Research and Training Institute (IRTI). 2008. *Islamic microfinance development: Challenges and initiatives*, Policy Dialogue Paper No. 2 (Jeddah, IRTI), at: http://www.microfinancegateway.org/p/site/m//template.rc/1.9.30288
- Karim, N.; Tarazi, M.; Reille, X. 2008. *Islamic microfinance: An emerging market niche*, CGAP Focus Note No. 49 (Washington, DC, CGAP), at: http://www.cgap.org/gm/document-1.9.5029/FN49.pdf

- Maysami, R.; Kwon, W. *An analysis of Islamic Takaful Insurance – A cooperative insurance mechanism*, at: http://www.takaful.coop/doc_store/takaful/analysis%20of%20Islamic%20Takaful%20Insurance.pdf
- Obaidullah, M. 2008. *Introduction to Islamic microfinance* (International Institute of Islamic Business and Finance), at: http://www.microfinancegateway.org/gm/document-1.9.30212/08.pdf
- Obaidullah, M.; Latiff, H. (eds). 2008. *Islamic finance for micro and medium enterprises* (International Institute of Islamic Business and Finance and Centre for Islamic Banking, Finance and Management, Universiti Brunei Darussalam), at: www.imad.in/obaidullah-micro4.pdf
- Wieland, R. 2008. *Supporting credit union development in Afghanistan: An overview of issues important to the development of Shari'a-Compliant Cooperative Finance* (Madison, WI, WOCCU), at: http://www.microfinancegateway.org/gm/document-1.9.27299/46362_file_2008AfghanistanReport.pdf

20 Rural Microfinance

With rural poverty accounting for 63 per cent of poverty worldwide, the importance of making microfinance services available beyond city limits is clear. The rural poor constitute both the greatest unmet need and the largest unserved market for microfinance services.
~ Manndorff (2004)

Both government and non-government actors have been trying for decades to make financial services available to rural populations as a tool for economic growth, food security and poverty reduction. Yet some 900 million people living in rural areas still survive on less than US$1.08 per day, and the vast majority of rural households still lack access to financial services (World Bank, 2007).

Past efforts to provide access to financial services in rural areas focused on credit, which was often subsidized or directed towards particular agricultural sectors or groups, and this limited the number of people who could benefit from these services. Subsidized credit became highly politicized, and specialized agricultural finance institutions often failed. Private sector investment in rural financial markets was largely crowded out; non-agricultural and non-credit needs were rarely addressed; and when the subsidies could no longer be sustained, even access to credit dried up.

The current approach to rural finance recognizes that rural populations – like urban populations – demand a variety of financial services to support their economic activities, smooth their income flows, and mitigate their risks. It also recognizes that services need to be priced at a level that will cover their costs. However, the institutions that are attempting to provide these services are still struggling to develop and deliver products that are appropriate and affordable for rural clients.

This chapter will summarize the factors that make the rural market so challenging. It will also explore some of the products and strategies that different types of institution are using to serve this market effectively. The chapter will address the following four themes:

1. What is rural microfinance?
2. The challenges of rural financial service provision
3. Serving the rural market
4. An appropriate product mix for rural microfinance

20.1 What Is Rural Microfinance?

Rural microfinance is defined here as the provision of financial services to poor and low-income people in rural areas. It includes financial services that support agricultural activities as well as those that do not. As shown in Figure 20.1, rural finance is not the same as agricultural finance, because agricultural finance supports all agriculture-related activities including those of processors, distributors and exporters who may be located in urban and peri-urban areas and will not necessarily be low-income. Rural finance is provided only in rural areas, but supports a wide range of economic activities and households of various income levels.

Figure 20.1 Relationship between rural, agricultural and microfinance

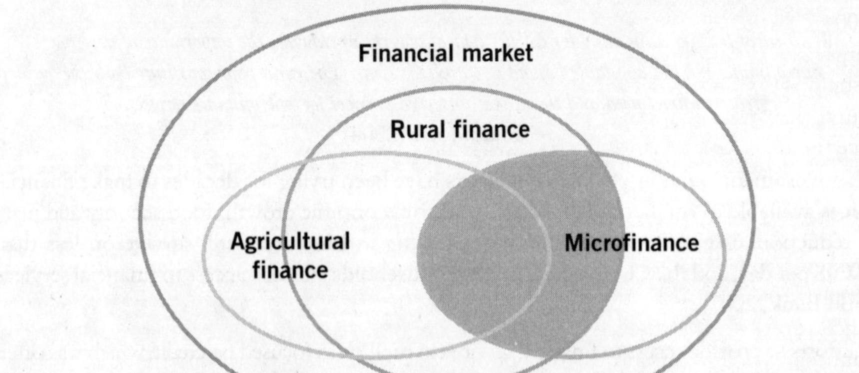

Source: IFAD, 2010.

The definition of a "rural area" varies from one country to another. According to the International Fund for Agricultural Development (IFAD, 2001), rural areas are commonly defined as having a population of 5,000 persons or less living in farmsteads or in groups of houses separated by farmland, pasture, trees or scrubland. The Small Enterprise Education and Promotion Network (SEEP, 2010a) provides an alternative definition, which has been accepted by MFIs in a wide range of countries: "an area in which the primary economic activities are small-scale agriculture and livestock rearing, although it also includes small-scale trade, service, and manufacturing activities. It is also characterized, in relative terms, by geographic isolation, low population densities, poorly developed infrastructure, underdeveloped market for goods and services, and high poverty concentration."

The SEEP definition suggests some of the challenges posed by the rural environment, which will be discussed in more detail in the following section, as well as some of the reasons for which financial services are demanded. In rural environments, financing may be needed to purchase agricultural inputs such as fertilizers, seeds, tools and equipment; to obtain veterinary services; to maintain buildings or fences; to contract labour for planting and harvesting; to transport goods to the market; and to do all of these things at the right time so as to improve product quality, efficiency and income. Payments need to be made and received. Income during peak agricultural seasons has to be managed in a way that can cover expenses during low-income periods. Investments have to be made in education, shelter and health. Emergencies need to be dealt with and environmental risks need to be managed. In principle, savings, credit, leasing, insurance, money transfers and non-financial services could all be of value to the rural market.

20.2 The Challenges of Rural Financial Service Provision[47]

In 2004, Calvin Miller presented 12 key challenges to rural financial service provision, which he organized into four categories: vulnerability constraints, operational constraints, capacity constraints and political/regulatory constraints. Although many other analyses of the challenges to rural financial service provision exist, his framework is a useful one for viewing at a glance the range of challenges that any MFI must face if it wishes to serve the rural market.

Vulnerability Constraints

1. **Systemic risk.** Rural incomes, especially among agriculturalists, are highly susceptible to similar risks at the same time (in other words, the risks are covariate). Weather is the most uncontrollable and often devastating risk, but disease, plagues and pests are also important. Failures in agriculture affect not only farmer households and their production and marketing linkages, but also the rural non-farm economies that revolve around and depend upon agricultural income flows.
2. **Market risk.** The prices of agricultural commodities fluctuate due to variations in weather and local production as well as "outside forces" such as political price controls, subsidies and globalization. The unpredictability of prices, combined with a lack of communications infrastructure which would enable buyers and sellers to access updated pricing information, increases the risk of rural economic transactions.
3. **Credit risk.** In rural areas, property rights are often undefined, land and movable property registries may not exist, and credit bureaus typically do not operate. Collateral substitutes such as mandatory savings or peer lending can be problematic, since clients with covariate and seasonal cash flows will have trouble making a deposit or assisting other group members with loan repayment during months of little or no income.

Operational Constraints

4. **Investment returns.** Rural capital revolves slowly, with often one or sometimes two crops per year. Profit margins are also low, which leaves less room for error and less capacity to pay for high-cost financial services.
5. **Lack of assets.** The relative poverty in rural areas causes common crises to become major crises due to the lack of an asset "cushion". Any loss of expected income through sickness or lower production has a significant impact. To compensate for this, traditional networks and the minimization of production risk tend to be more important than the maximization of profit, which results in lower levels of investment. The small asset base in rural areas also reduces savings and borrowing capacity, thus constraining economies of scale in the use or provision of services.
6. **Geographical dispersion.** In many countries, rural areas are characterized by low population density and high dispersion. This increases the per-client cost of service delivery. It is harder for loan officers to develop and be responsible for a large number of loans. It can also make financial service access difficult for clients who must travel long distances and spend significant time away from their business or household in order to conduct a financial transaction.

[47] This section is adapted from Miller (2004).

Capacity Constraints

7. **Infrastructure.** Poor communication, bad roads, unequipped schools and limited health services lower the efficiency of rural operations, discourage new investment in the area, and encourage many of the most talented and resourceful persons to migrate out of rural communities.
8. **Technical skills.** A relatively unskilled rural population is less prepared for employment, and may be less willing to adopt new technologies and ways of doing things. Illiteracy can be high, marketing skills can be weak, and poor handling of goods during harvest, processing or transportation can limit productivity and competitiveness. Financial service providers may need to invest more in training for staff and clients.
9. **Social exclusion.** Cultural, linguistic, gender, racial, religious and educational barriers affect market and financial integration. To the extent that rural populations consist of minority groups that are not fully integrated into mainstream civil society, additional effort may be required to build trust-based relationships between the community and a financial institution.
10. **Institutional capacity.** The management, technical, and risk-bearing capacity of institutions in rural areas is often weaker than in urban areas. One major exception to this general constraint is at the micro level, where social ties are strong and usually sufficient for the level of operations undertaken at that level.

Political and Regulatory Constraints

11. **Political and social interference.** Loans can be forgiven and credit can be subsidized to garner political support or to pursue developmental objectives. Although such interference occurs in urban areas, it is more common in rural areas, and when it occurs, it creates market distortions that make it difficult for financial institutions to operate sustainably.
12. **Regulatory framework.** Regulations and/or their lack of enforcement can hinder rural as well as urban environments. Land tenure regulations, contract enforcement provisions, banking laws, interest rate caps, exchange rate manipulation and tax considerations are examples of constraints that can hinder the viability of microfinance operations in rural areas.

These challenges translate into higher operating costs for the suppliers of financial services, higher transaction costs for clients who wish to access financial services, and greater risk of failure for everyone involved. Rural clients may have trouble generating sufficient or sufficiently reliable revenue from their income-generating activities to purchase financial services at the prices being offered or to make regular payments on the loans, leases or insurance policies they have already obtained. Financial service providers may not generate enough revenue to cover their costs, especially if external events such as a natural disaster or political interference generate substantial losses. These higher costs and higher risks have kept most microfinance institutions out of the rural market, but some are serving rural areas successfully. The next section of this chapter explores how.

20.3 Serving the Rural Market[48]

The microfinance institutions that are serving rural areas with some degree of success are not following a common approach or methodology. However, their models have some of the same features in common. Thirteen of these features are explored below. Few if any MFIs have adopted all of these strategies, but all of the strategies have contributed to the success of multiple institutions. Together, they constitute what may be an emerging model for successful outreach to the rural market, including those households that are dependent on agriculture as their primary source of income.

1) Base Lending Decisions on Household Repayment Capacity

Successful rural MFIs recognize that most rural households have multiple sources of income from which they can make loan payments. Even farming households diversify their sources of income by engaging in a variety of farm and non-farm activities. According to Christen and Pearce (2005), the average share of non-farm household income is highest in Africa (42 per cent) and Latin America (40 per cent), but is also significant in Asia (32 per cent). Household members engage in trading, rudimentary agricultural processing, day labour and livestock husbandry, in addition to producing staple foods and cash crops. They may travel to other parts of the country for seasonal employment on farms or employment in cities, or even go abroad and send back earnings. This is particularly true for households with smaller farms; those with larger farms tend to depend more on farming income.

This variety of income-generating activities can provide relatively steady cash flow for rural households, making it possible for them to make regular loan payments even when they borrow to invest in activities such as agriculture or livestock rearing, which have highly irregular cash flows. By basing lending decisions on household repayment capacity and not the cash flow of a specific income-generating activity, MFIs can recognize the fungibility of money and their clients' money management skills, and set the expectation that repayment is required regardless of whether a particular crop or non-farm activity turns out as planned.

2) Facilitate Access to a Broad Range of Financial Services

As discussed in Chapter 1, a broad range of products helps institutions meet client needs, expand outreach, increase retention, diversify sources of income and funding, and reduce risk. This is true in rural areas just as in urban areas. By offering a diversity of products – business loans as well as agricultural loans, savings and money transfer services, perhaps even leasing and insurance – MFIs can attract a larger client base from a given geographical area, thus increasing the productivity of rural branches (see Box 20.1).

In rural areas, access to remittance and deposit services is particularly important. Households that are dependent on a single crop and do not have many non-farm economic activities will have limited access to credit, and will need savings vehicles to self-finance both their agricultural activities and their household requirements during periods of little or no income. Even households that have access to credit will use savings and remittance monies to meet household needs prior to the harvest, as well as to manage the risk of unplanned expenditures and

48 This section is adapted from Christen and Pearce (2005).

Box 20.1 Diversification as a Rural Penetration Strategy in Uganda

When Uganda Microfinance Union (UMU), now Equity Bank Uganda, expanded into rural areas, its approach was to serve everybody within a certain distance from the branch office. While most MFIs financed only microentrepreneurs, UMU, as an integral part of its rural penetration strategy, also served rural schools, health posts, and different types of association. Point-of-sale devices for rural merchants and savings and money transfer services further complemented its strategy to turn every rural branch into a viable and profitable unit.

Source: Manndorff, 2004.

lower-than-expected agricultural or non-agricultural incomes. In many countries only licensed and regulated financial institutions are able to offer deposit services, but credit-only MFIs may be able to offer their clients greater access to these services by linking to regulated financial institutions, as described in point 8 below.

3) Allow Flexibility in Meeting Collateral Requirements

The challenges associated with asset registration in rural areas have led MFIs working in those areas to be quite flexible about their collateral requirements for agricultural loans. They accept a combination of personal guarantees and pledges on household and enterprise assets, rather than rely on land and property titles. Uganda's Centenary Bank, for example, accepts livestock, personal guarantees, land without titles, household items and business equipment as loan collateral. Caja Los Andes in Bolivia takes pledged assets, but measures their value to the borrower rather than the recovery value to the bank. In rural areas, loans for less than US$7,500 can be collateralized with farm or household assets, and unregistered land titles can be deposited with the bank as collateral for up to half of the value of a loan (Pearce and Reinsch, 2005b). Opportunity International Bank Malawi (OIBM) is considering acceptance of a letter from the local tribal chief to verify land ownership in lieu of a registered land title (Kalanda and Campbell, 2008). MFIs that are getting involved in value chain financing are finding inventories, accounts receivable and warehouse receipts to be useful collateral alternatives in rural areas.

For larger, longer-term investments such as borrowing to finance agricultural equipment purchases, a leasing product can provide a solution to a borrower's lack of usable collateral, since the lender maintains ownership of the asset until the loan is repaid. Although the challenges of microleasing (described in Chapter 10) have deterred most financial service providers from offering this product in rural areas, experiences like the one in Madagascar suggest conditions under which it may be feasible (see Box 20.2).

4) Bring Specialized Agricultural Knowledge Into the Credit Process

Traditional agricultural lenders have long employed specialized staff with training in crop and livestock production. Similarly, the few microfinance programmes that have expanded into agricultural activities have found it desirable to hire agronomists and veterinarians to support loan decisions and methodologies, either as in-house experts at the head office, or as field

Box 20.2 Microleases for Agriculture in Madagascar

The Savings and Agricultural Credit Banks of Madagascar, a network of more than 150 local banks and credit unions in rural Madagascar, has managed to overcome challenges common in agricultural microleasing. Its microleases finance capital equipment for agriculture, livestock rearing, rural crafts and domestic production (such as sewing). In 2001, the network had 1,800 leaseholders, with an average lease of US$450. The network has avoided problems associated with leasing to small farmers by:

- using flexible repayment schedules that fit clients' production cycles;
- requiring larger down payments on new equipment than is common in leasing arrangements (40 per cent, instead of 20 per cent); and
- leasing and re-leasing used equipment, rather than trying to sell it in thin secondary markets.

In addition, the network uses group mechanisms for client analysis and monitoring. The membership-driven nature of cooperatives and credit unions appears to make them willing to take greater risks (or make greater efforts to mitigate risks) to meet the financing needs of their members.

Sources: Wampfler and Mercoiret, 2001, World Bank, 2004, FAO, 2003, as cited in Christen and Pearce, 2005.

staff with knowledge of the agriculture sectors in their geographic area of operation. Just as urban microenterprise loan officers can quickly tell how well a small shop is managed, specialized staff in rural areas can ascertain how well a farming activity is pursued without generating a complex, thorough production model for a specific activity. Specially trained loan officers can optimally adjust the terms and conditions of an agricultural microfinance loan to the investment opportunity presented and the income flows of the farming household to minimize risk to the lender. This need for specialized training is one of the main reasons why many ACCION partners end up creating a separate rural sales team (Manndorff, 2004).

In addition to hiring the right people, MFIs can develop information systems that facilitate consistent analysis and inform loan officer decisions. For example, Centenary Bank trained loan officers in agriculture and agribusiness to help them understand farming as a business and thus monitor farmer clients more effectively. Such skilled staff can then develop sophisticated tools to support the credit decision process. The Economic Credit Institution, an MFI in Bosnia and Herzegovina that holds about half its portfolio in agriculture, developed spreadsheets for key agricultural products that are used to conduct cash-flow analyses of proposed agricultural activities. It complements this analysis with its experience in various agricultural sectors (cattle breeding, agriculture, apiculture) to evaluate potential loans. PRODEM followed a similar approach in Bolivia, as illustrated in the case at the end of Chapter 6 on microenterprise loans.

5) Adjust Loan Terms and Conditions to Cash Flows

Rural economic activities can produce cyclical cash flows, determined by crop production or animal husbandry schedules, as well as bulky cash flows. Lump sums of cash may be needed at staggered points in the production cycle, for example to finance the purchase of seeds and fertilizer early in the season, and to hire labour or transport at harvest time. Revenues may be delayed for some time, as with tree crops and feed cattle, and when they arrive, they may arrive in large lump sums, such as after a harvest or the sale of livestock. Finally, the value of most capital assets that might be acquired in rural areas tends to be much larger than a household's annual income, unlike in urban areas. Purchase of a traction animal or an irrigation pump could provide immediate income for the owner, but a loan to buy such an asset would likely take more than a year to pay back.

For all these reasons, MFIs that operate successfully in rural areas have found it necessary to research cash flow cycles closely, and to tailor loan procedures and products to those cash flows. They have integrated crop-based analysis into their wider client analysis, as discussed above, and have adjusted repayment schedules to take into account seasonal income cycles. For example:

- In El Salvador, Banco Pro Credit El Salvador uses bimonthly, trimester, semester, annual, end-of-crop-cycle and even irregular repayment schedules to match household cash flows for a range of agricultural activities (Pearce et al., 2004).
- Banco Los Andes Pro Credit takes a similar approach, but also offers loans in up to three instalments to fit the flow of farmers' income and expenses better.
- As discussed in Chapter 6, PRODEM was successful by customizing repayment schemes for each small farmer in a solidarity group. Some payments consisted of interest only, and some contained lump sum payments of principal, but no single payment exceeded 60 per cent of the loan amount.
- In Georgia, Constanta abolished prepayment fees for agricultural loans in order to encourage farmers to pay back their loans as early as possible if they sell their produce earlier than originally expected.

A few MFIs have been able to meet clients' longer-term investment needs through leasing and/or multi-year loans that are funded by the institution's equity or, occasionally, by long-term credit lines. In Nepal, for example, Small Farmer Cooperatives, Ltd (SFCLs) offers long-term loans which are financed by a mix of internal savings and long-term credit lines from the Agricultural Development Bank (see Box 20.3). At Sicredi in Brazil (see Box 20.5), short-term loans are financed by deposits, while longer-term loans are financed by loans from the National Development Bank.

6) Diversify

As discussed in point 2 above, MFIs that offer a range of products and services that appeal to different market segments can generate a larger client base and increase the productivity of each rural branch. They can also reduce risk by generating revenue from sources other than the loan portfolio. On the lending side of the business, MFIs can diversify in three main ways:

- **By lending only to diversified households.** Many MFIs that have developed a stable agricultural lending portfolio minimize risk by excluding households that rely on a single crop and have no off-farm income. The Pro Credit Banks generally follow this approach, as does PRODEM.

Box 20.3 SFCLs Tailor Long-term Loan Products to Agricultural Activities in Nepal

SFCL Prithvinagar is a small farmer cooperative located in a tea-growing area of Nepal near the Indian border. Previously, its loan products were not sufficiently large or long term to allow members to invest in tea production. So, it introduced an eight-year loan that covers three-quarters of the average cost of starting a small tea farm (0.6 hectares) and has a grace period of three years. Interest payments are made every three months between the third and fifth years of the loan term, while principal instalments are made every six months between the sixth and eighth years. The cooperative also offers tea farmers marketing services to help ensure loan repayments and higher prices for harvests. Tea leaves are collected from the farmers and marketed collectively, and the sales proceeds are returned to them after deducting loan payments.

An SFCL in Bhumistan offers a similar loan for the purchase of buffalo. The loan has a term of three years, with principal instalments paid every three months for the first nine months and the fourth payment required two years later, when the three-month schedule begins again. This gap in the repayment schedule allows the buffalo to have calves, during which time the borrower would not earn any money from the animal.

Sources: Wehnert and Shakya, 2001, and Staschen, 2001, as cited in Christen and Pearce, 2005.

- **By lending in different geographic and ecological areas and financing different types of crop and economic activities.** This helps MFIs protect themselves from external risks that are beyond their control, particularly weather-related risks and fluctuations in the price of certain crops. It also helps smooth the uneven workload and cash flows caused by the seasonality in agricultural lending. Without diversification, staff would be extremely busy during certain months, while in others, staff and cash would be underutilized. In Tajikistan, for example, IMON offsets its exposure in the fruit and vegetable subsector by offering loans for livestock, other rural-based enterprises, storage of products, and leasing services for farm equipment. Its rural portfolio performed well during the financial/economic crisis that began in 2007, which balanced the weaker performance of its portfolio in urban areas.
- **By limiting the volume and percentage of agricultural loans in the overall portfolio and in specific zones.** The rural portfolios of ACCION International's partners all contain a large percentage of loans for trade activities and small-scale off-farm production, with agricultural finance making up between 20 and 50 per cent of the entire rural portfolio (Manndorfff, 2004). When Confianza diversified its portfolio in Peru (see Box 1.1 in the chapter on understanding diversification), it set a target percentage for agricultural lending at 30 per cent of its overall portfolio. In Uganda, Centenary Bank took a similar approach, setting its upper limit at 25 per cent. In general, MFIs tend to limit agricultural lending to less than one-third of their portfolios. Some apply that limit to each economic sector within their agricultural portfolio as well.

7) Pay Attention to Value Chains

Miller and da Silva (2007) define a value chain as "the set of actors and the sequence of value-adding activities involved in bringing a product from production to the final consumer". In an agricultural value chain, these actors might include input suppliers, farmers, producer groups, local traders, processors, wholesalers and exporters. It can also include those who provide support services to the chain, as depicted in Figure 20.2.

Value chains should be of interest to MFIs for at least two reasons. First, they can help institutions identify market opportunities. Since a significant percentage of the financial services reaching small farmers and rural residents is provided by value-chain actors and not by regulated financial institutions (Fries and Akin, 2004), value-chain analysis can help an MFI understand the degree to which financial service needs are already being met within a particular chain, and where financial service delivery can still be improved. An MFI may be able to provide different services to different actors, thus expanding its own outreach while strengthening the overall performance of the chain.

Often the financial services provided within a value chain are limited in scope, short-term and conditional (in other words, tied to a specific crop, product, buyer or supplier). The businesses that provide credit within the chain frequently do not have the systems to monitor lending activities well, and provide loans only because they feel they must do so in order to secure a sufficient supply of decent-quality product, or to cover the seasonal cash shortages of their clients. They may welcome the chance to pass responsibility for financial service provision to someone else, or to enter into a relationship with an MFI that would make it easier for them to provide those services (for example, through a credit line that helps them manage

Figure 20.2 Value chain actors

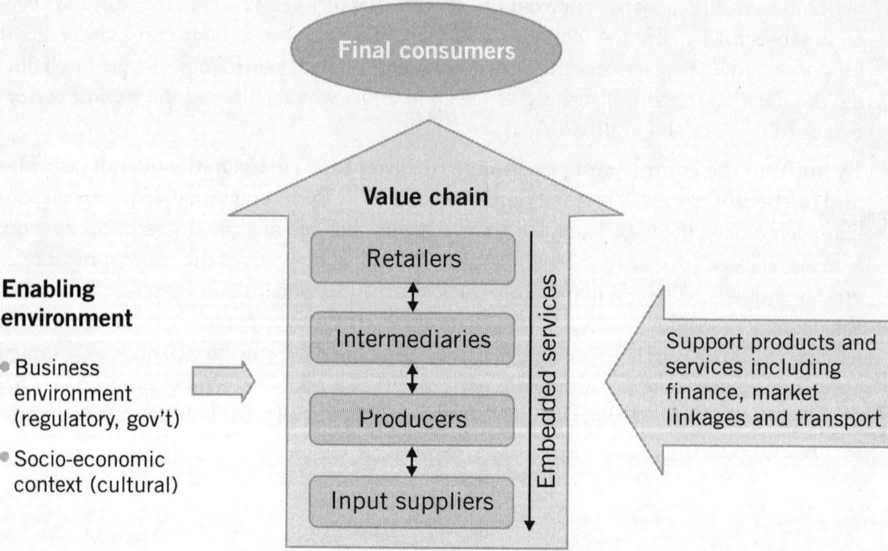

Source: Miehlbradt and Jones, 2007, as presented in Miller and Jones, 2010.

their own liquidity). Depending on their capacity, MFIs might be able to offer value-chain actors more flexible and longer-term loans as well as a broader range of financial services than those available within the value chain. An overview of the different kinds of product being used to finance agricultural value chains is provided in Table 20.1.

The second reason why value chains should be of interest to MFIs is their utility as a source of information and infrastructure that can lower risk and improve efficiency within an MFI's operations. By understanding the value chains within which clients operate, MFIs can increase the accuracy and perhaps even the speed of their loan appraisals. Value-chain actors can provide information on applicants' character and management ability, local crop cycles and yields, cash and commodity flows, as well as market demand and prices. Buyers may be able to offer small producers guaranteed market access or a certain level of guaranteed income through contractual arrangements, which would decrease the risk of lending to those producers. In the case of Hortifruti in Central America, even implicit contractual arrangements between small producers and a major supermarket chain were able to increase producers' access to credit (Gonzales et al., 2006). Some buyers provide warehouse receipts that small producers can use as collateral.

Value-chain actors also have networks for distributing inputs (which often includes the distribution of input credit) and collecting produce (as well as repayments) from farmers. These networks can be much more extensive than MFI branch networks, and could be used to channel other financial services. An MFI might be invited by a sugar cane company to open satel-

Table 20.1 Agricultural value-chain finance instruments

Category	Financing instruments
Product financing	• Commercial trader credit • Input supplier credit • Business agent / wholesaler (marketing company credit) • Lead company financing / contract farming
Receivables financing	• Sale of accounts receivable • Factoring • Forfaiting
Physical asset collateralization	• Credit guarantees (warehouse receipts) • Repurchase agreements (repos) • Financial lease (lease-purchase)
Risk mitigation	• Insurance • Forward contracts • Futures and hedging
Financial enhancements	• Securitization • Loan guarantees • Joint venture finance

Source: Summary of a detailed framework provided by Miller and Jones, 2010.

Box 20.4 Linking Banks, Small Farmers and an Input Provider in India

Mahindra Shubhlabh is part of the Mahindra empire (the world's third-largest tractor maker) and runs commercial agriculture support centres all over India. These centres and smaller franchises at the village level serve as one-stop shops where (mostly paddy) farmers can receive loans and technical assistance, rent specialized equipment (harvesters, tillers and the like) and buy seed and other inputs. Loans range from Rps 15,000 (about US$350) to Rps 100,000 (about US$3,000) per season, with an average loan of slightly more than US$500. Mahindra Shubhlabh facilitates farmers' access to credit by acting as an agent for banks, including ICICI Bank (India's second largest) and recommending that the banks provide loans to farmers to whom it is providing other services. Agribusiness buyers are also involved, with a three-way agreement whereby Mahindra Shubhlabh recommends a client to ICICI for credit, and the client (farmer) receives inputs on (ICICI) credit from Mahindra Shubhlabh after pledging its produce to a buyer. The buyer repays the loan at the end of the season out of the sale proceeds from the farmer's output. Mahindra Shubhlabh receives 1.5 per cent of the loan value for its loan processing and supervision services, dependent on the loan being repaid. In early 2004, this arrangement was used by 45 Mahindra Shubhlabh outlets with 5,600 active clients.

Source: Christen and Pearce, 2005.

lite offices at its mills to serve outgrowers, for example. Contractual arrangements can guarantee loan repayment if they require a buyer to deduct any amount owed to the MFI by a producer before making payment to the producer for the goods purchased. This was the arrangement between Sinokrot Food Company and Alrafah Microfinance Bank that was presented in Box 10.7 in the chapter on leasing.

In addition to supplying delivery infrastructure, value chain actors may also provide supportive infrastructure, such as timely access to appropriate inputs or equipment, storage facilities, certification services, technical advice on input use or crop varieties that will meet market demands, and so on. These non-financial services mitigate production risks and increase the likelihood that small producers will be able to repay an MFI's loan. By collaborating with, or even financing, larger actors in the value chain, MFIs can facilitate the timely provision of these services, as described in the case of Mahindra Shubhalabh found in Box 20.4.

8) Leverage Others' Infrastructure

Attaching the delivery of financial services to infrastructure already in place in rural areas reduces transaction costs for lenders and borrowers alike, and creates the potential for sustainable rural finance, even in remote communities. Financial institutions can partner with other financial entities, such as banks, or with non-financial entities, such as clinics, schools, lottery outlets, post offices, pharmacy chains, or agricultural input suppliers. The holder of the local infrastructure can gain additional revenue as a result of the financial services being channeled through its outlets, while the financial service provider avoids the investment and operational costs associated with setting up a dedicated network.

Compartamos in Mexico and Constanta in Georgia both use rural bank infrastructure to facilitate disbursements and repayments, thus keeping their own branch networks relatively small and costs low. Union Bank in Jamaica linked up with post offices to use their outlets to offer

deposit services to more than 75,000 depositors in rural areas at a reduced cost (Owens, 2003). The Bolivian MFI FIE operates teller windows within the rural branches of the NGO Pro Mujer with a similar objective (Wise, 2004). Hatton National Bank works through schools to make financial services available to youth in rural areas of Sri Lanka, and El Comercio partners with silos in Paraguay to provide small loans to single-crop soybean farmers (see Box 22.1 in the chapter on partnerships). As discussed in Box 13.11 in the chapter on grants, Equity Bank uses POS devices and retail agents to deliver cash transfers to remote areas in Kenya, while in rural India, financial institutions piggyback onto a network of more than 800,000 long-distance telephone booths to connect head offices quickly with mobile agents to provide remittance services (Nagarajan and Meyer, 2005). The range of possibilities for partnership is seemingly endless.

MFIs can also work with and through existing rural associations (for example, farmer groups, producer cooperatives, or informal savings and loan groups). Such membership-based organizations have a mixed track record in managing financial services, but they can be viable even in remote areas by making use of voluntary or semi-voluntary staff, drawing on community knowledge when making loan assessments, using community peer pressure to ensure loan repayments, and relying on low-level institutional systems and infrastructure. MFIs can work through such organizations to expand rural access to financial services, as rural banks have done with self-help groups in India, and as CRDB has done with rural savings and credit cooperatives (SACCOs) in Tanzania. In Ethiopia, Nyala Insurance Company is working through farmers' unions to deliver weather index insurance products (Meherette, 2009).

Working through existing associations can facilitate an MFI's work in several ways. If the MFI lends directly to an association's members, the association might be able to provide meeting facilities, communication channels, and information on the character and repayment capacity of loan applicants. It might even conduct marketing campaigns or initial client screening on behalf of the MFI. Even if it provides none of this, the association may facilitate clients' access to agricultural inputs and markets, thus increasing the likelihood that clients will generate enough income from their agricultural activities to repay the MFI's loans.

If an MFI provides financial services directly to the association, it will minimize its own transaction costs while significantly increasing the size of its average transaction. It may be able to help associations (or networks of associations) provide higher-quality service to members by providing services that they would not be able to access on their own (see Box 20.5). In Mexico, AMUCSS supports a network of informal microbanks in remote and difficult rural areas that provide members with access to remittance monies transferred through the formal banking system. Their service of transferring funds from bank branches in towns to microbanks in small rural communities substantially lowers the cost, time and risk involved in accessing the remittances (Pearce et al., 2004).

9) Deliver Services Through Groups

To serve small farmers and farmers in remote or marginal rural areas, group-based savings and lending techniques may be essential to mitigate risk, reduce operating costs and enforce repayment. In addition to working through existing associations and producer groups as mentioned above, MFIs that work successfully in rural areas often use large-group delivery methodologies to maximize the number of customers that they can serve at one time.

Box 20.5 Sicredi Provides Second-tier Support for Cooperatives in Brazil

Sicredi is a system of savings and loan cooperatives for small farming households in Brazil. It specializes in agricultural lending, primarily for the production of rice, wheat, beef, fodder, fish and vegetables, and for agricultural equipment. Sicredi follows consistent, agriculture-focused lending practices, and pools and manages liquidity risk at the system level. Uniform, system-wide standards are strictly enforced. To use the Sicredi name and logo, credit unions must meet stringent financial, policy and product quality standards. The financial details of all members are shared among the system to ensure peer enforcement of these standards. The high risks associated with narrow dependence on agricultural lending are managed by limiting the percentage of assets in such lending, financing long-term loans with borrowings from the National Development Bank and buying crop insurance (through Proagro, the national crop insurance programme).

Being part of a system is central to the success of Sicredi cooperatives; they can obtain refinancing, offer a wider range of services than the range they could offer if they were stand-alone entities, benefit from the system-level management of liquidity risks, and associate with a brand that requires commitment to high standards. The Sicredi council develops policies and products, and provides training services. A cooperative bank (Bansicredi) enables members to issue credit cards, offer Internet banking, issue trade credits (including letters of credit) and supply insurance (life, non-life and rural). Members can also facilitate forward sales, notably by coffee growers, through the Cedula de Producto Rural instrument. In addition, Sicredi's participation in the Proagro crop insurance programme, which adds a premium of 3.9 per cent to loan rates, enables its members to provide agricultural insurance.

Source: Christen and Pearce, 2005.

In Malawi, for example, when OIBM began serving rural areas and found it necessary to reduce the size of its loans, it maintained profitability by increasing the size of its borrower groups to 15–20 people (rather than 7–10 as in urban areas). It also took advantage of the very strong social cohesion found in rural areas by organizing rural groups into clusters where five to eight groups meet on a monthly basis in a central location to avoid loan officers travelling to visit each group. In some cases, the terms of agreement for the mutual guarantee have been adjusted so that enforcement is at this cluster level rather than at the group level (Kalanda and Campbell, 2008). A different version of the cluster approach enabled United Georgian Bank to reach rural areas of Georgia successfully using an individual lending model (see Box 20.6).

10) Use Technology to Reduce Transportation and Communication Costs

Technology can facilitate rural outreach by significantly increasing the efficiency and lowering the costs of financial service providers operating in rural areas. Among the most practical and increasingly affordable of these technologies are automatic teller machines (ATMs), smart cards, debit cards, personal digital assistants, handheld computers and cellular phones.

ATMs, smart cards and debit cards can provide flexible payment options and more convenient access to client accounts. They can also reduce branch infrastructure and employee costs, and facilitate financial services in areas with poor communications and electricity supplies. In Bolivia, PRODEM extended its branch network by installing ATMs in rural as well as urban areas. Its machines are equipped with fingerprint readers for client verification, and they provide audio instructions in three languages to make financial services more accessible

Box 20.6 Using a Cluster Approach to Provide Individual Loans in Rural Georgia

While most successful agricultural microlenders in other countries work with groups or as cooperatives, United Georgian Bank (UGB) had no choice but to go for individual lending. The Georgian mentality is rather individualistic, there are hardly any farmer organizations in the country, credit unions have failed, and farmers have no good memories of being forced into cooperative farming during the Soviet period. Individual lending proved very expensive in rural areas, however. In the beginning, UGB loan officers spent a lot of time travelling to individual clients for site visits. Later, a cluster approach was introduced, and this is what made agricultural lending feasible.

The basic idea of the cluster approach is simple. The bank selects larger villages with good agriculture potential and talks to the responsible village headman, a political administrator elected by the people, about the loan scheme. Then the village headman spreads the word in the village and organizes a farmer meeting in the village hall. At these meetings loan officers and unit managers inform the farmers about UGB's agricultural loan products, and interview applicants on the spot. In many cases the farm inspection can also be done the same day.

Apart from the obvious marketing advantage, the cluster approach has improved almost all operations in the credit cycle:

- The application-to-disbursement ratio has been increased from 10:2 to 10:9, because loan officers have trustworthy informants in the villages who can give references about applicants.
- Since most farmers in one village do more or less the same type of farming, loan appraisals are much easier to prepare, and different farmers can be compared with each other.
- Credit committee members find it easier to take decisions when there are several appraisals from the same village that can be compared.
- Disbursement and repayment are streamlined; most farmers of one village get their loans on the same day and have to repay on the same dates. This makes it easier for the loan officer to monitor repayment, and several or all farmers of one village can send their money with one villager to the next town's bank branch.
- Monitoring visits are scheduled according to the farming cycle, for example on days when farmers in the village harvest their crops and loan officers can visit ten or more clients in one trip.
- In case of delinquency the loan officer can talk to the client and his personal guarantors or other farmers in the village during one visit, putting pressure on the delinquent farmer by threatening to stop future lending to the entire village.

Source: Derflinger et al., 2006.

to illiterate and semi-literate clients, and to those who do not speak Spanish. Because the ATMs are linked to smart cards (which contain information on client accounts and previous transactions), they have to update data from the central processing site only twice a day, saving about US$ 800,000 a year in Internet access charges.

Personal digital assistants can streamline the work of loan officers and speed decision-making as long as a financial institution's loan analysis and client monitoring systems are sufficiently developed. Chile's Banco del Estado has used the technology with great success in generating agricultural loans at the farmstead based on hour-long visits. In the Dominican Republic, ADEMI (Asociación para el Desarrollo de Microempresas, Inc.) has developed a credit-scoring system linked to laptops and PDAs (personal digital assistants), which it estimates will substantially reduce loan disbursement time in rural areas (Pearce et al., 2004).

Cellular telephones offer tremendous potential for extending financial services in developing countries, including rural areas, as cellular networks are extended. In Kenya and the Philippines phones are being used to disburse loans, check loan balances and repayment schedules, facilitate remittance transfers and payments, save electronically and make cash withdrawals via local merchants and agents. As of November 2009, M-PESA (Kenya's most popular mobile money service) had 8.6 million users (one-quarter of Kenya's population), had approximately 15,000 agents (more than six times the number of ATMs and bank branches in the entire country), and was making person-to-person transactions worth more than US$320 million per month (Agrawal, 2010). Registration and cash deposits are free, there is no monthly fee, and a payment to another M-PESA subscriber costs just 30 Kenyan shillings, or approximately $0.35 (www.safaricom.co.ke). M-PESA is even being used to facilitate the sale of insurance (see Box 20.7).

Other technologies such as internet kiosks (see Box 20.8) and mobile branches can also be attractive technologies for facilitating the delivery of financial (and in the case of kiosks, non-financial) services. Specially equipped vehicles have been used to reach remote and mountainous areas successfully in Viet Nam, Kenya, Brazil and Georgia, for example, but mobile banks' ability to reach remote areas in a cost-effective manner is highly context specific. Indeed, a key lesson learned among microfinance institutions is that for any technology to add value, an institution must first conduct careful market research and cost–benefit analysis and then ensure that its information systems can provide data in the form and at the time the new technology requires.

Box 20.7 Technology Facilitates Insurance Scheme for Farmers in Kenya

Kilimo Salama, which in Kiswahili means "safe farming", uses a combination of mobile phones and 30 automated solar-powered weather stations to provide crop insurance. It has been set up by UAP Insurance of Kenya, Safaricom (Kenya's biggest mobile-network operator), and the Syngenta Foundation for Sustainable Agriculture, part of a big Swiss agribusiness group. After a successful trial with 200 farmers in 2009, Kilimo Salama expanded to serve 9,500 farmers by October 2010.

Farmers pay an extra 5 per cent of the value of a bag of seed, fertilizer or herbicide to insure it against crop failure. MEA Fertilizers and Syngenta East Africa, two agribusinesses hoping to benefit from higher sales of their products, match the farmers' investment to meet the full 10 per cent cost of the insurance premium. Local agents register a policy with UAP by using a camera-phone to scan a bar code on each bag sold. A text message confirming the policy is then sent to the farmer's handset. Farmers are registered at their nearest weather station, which transmits data over the mobile network. If weather conditions deteriorate, a panel of experts uses an index system to determine whether crops will no longer be viable. At that point, payouts are made directly to the handsets of farmers in the affected areas using Safaricom's M-PESA mobile-money service.

Source: Adapted from The Economist, 2010, and Ogodo, 2010.

Box 20.8 Using Internet Kiosks to Improve Information and Lower Costs

The first set of six *e-choupals* was pioneered in June 2000 by one of India's largest exporters of agricultural commodities, Indian Tobacco Company's International Business Division (ITC-IBD). Dubbed as a click-and-mortar business model, the system constitutes an Internet-enabled kiosk in a village, which is operated by a local farmer familiar with computers, known as the *choupal sanchalak.* Setting up each *e-choupal* entails an investment of US$2,500 to US$7,000. The *sanchalak* operates the kiosk, stays in touch with company representatives, and guides other farmers in the use of the technology. Farmers can use the kiosks to check the current market prices of their commodities, access market data, and obtain information on local and global weather and best farming practices. By 2002 some 1,200 Internet kiosks had been installed in 6,000 villages across 18 states in India, and were used to procure soybeans, coffee, shrimp, wheat, rice and lentils directly from farmers, saving time and money.

Currently, more than 2,600 *e-choupals* are in operation. There are plans to upgrade the system to become a one-stop shop for farmers, enabling them not only to sell farm products but also to buy inputs and consumer products on cash and credit. For instance, ITC has teamed up with Monsanto and the Seeds Corporation in Madhya Pradesh to sell seeds, and has teamed up with BASF (Badische Anilin- und Soda-Fabrik) to sell fertilizers. ITC charges a 10 per cent commission on sales transacted through the *e-choupals*, half of which is passed on to the *sanchalak* for executing the sale. Some farmers have begun to track soy futures on the Chicago Board of Trade, and most of them are bypassing local auction markets to sell their crops directly to ITC for about US$6 more per ton (Prahalad, 2005). There are opportunities for rural financial institutions to develop ties with such operations. For example, Megatop in India is offering a microinsurance programme for farmers in Andhra Pradesh and Madhya Pradesh through the *e-choupals* (Waterfield, 2004).

Source: Nagarajan and Meyer, 2005.

11) Increase Risk Exposure Gradually

Successful organizations build their capacity for rural, and especially agriculture, microfinance slowly and carefully. Banco del Estado de Chile spent two years adapting its microenterprise lending techniques before expanding into farming activities. Banco Pro Credit El Salvador is one of many MFIs that began by developing a rural portfolio from neighbouring branches, so that the new portfolio was relatively easy to access and monitor. MiCredito in Nicaragua and IMON in Tajikistan limited the crops that could be financed initially to focus on those that were most successful and marketable (Andrews, 2006). El Comercio finances only the last three months of the six-month soy production cycle, which limits its exposure to risks present in earlier months. Perhaps with time, as it increases its knowledge of the soybean value chain and as the chain itself is strengthened, it will expand its services to include the full cycle.

If an MFI segments its rural market, it can enter rural areas targeting low-risk clients in low-risk regions growing low-risk crops. Later, as it gains more knowledge about a particular crop or region, it can broaden its outreach. ADOPEM and Women's World Banking developed a Regional Selection Tool (see Table 20.2) that guided ADOPEM through an evaluation of different agricultural regions to determine the one with the most potential. The tool provides a useful example of how a criteria scoring model can be used to prioritize a market segment for development (for more information on criteria scoring models, refer to Chapter 2).

Table 20.2 Regional selection tool

Dimension	Variable	Indicator	Rate	Weight	Total value
Agricultural potential of the region	**Accessibility**	Distance to the closest branch		3%	
		Travel time		3%	
	Soil and weather	Transport options		3%	
		Main crops in the region		5%	
		Percentage of farms with access to irrigation		6%	
		Number of crop cycles per year		5%	
	Crop diversification	Rain level and distribution throughout the year		4%	
		Max, min and average temperatures / year		3%	
		Main weather risk in the region		4%	
		Type of soils		4%	
		Percentage of farming land / total land		4%	
Subtotal				**44%**	
Region's demographic characteristics	**The region has strong presence of small farmers**	Region's total population		4%	
		Number of farmers in the region		4%	
		Percentage of small farmers / total farmers		5%	
		Average area planted		3%	
		Technological level of small farmers		2%	
Subtotal				**18%**	
Productive infrastructure of the region	**Access to technical services**	Presence of agricultural input dealers		4%	
		Presence of technology transfer agencies		4%	
		Supply of crop insurance		2%	
	Access to financial services	Number of banks in the region		4%	
		Number of cooperatives in the region		3%	
		Percentage of farmers with access to financial services		3%	
		Types of financial product available		3%	
		Type of guarantees required		1%	
	Commercialization channels	Number of farmers' markets in the region		4%	
		Supermarkets and retailers in the region		4%	
		Agroindustries in the region		4%	
		Price and demand information available		2%	
Subtotal				**38%**	
Total				**100%**	

Source: Dellien and Lynch, 2007.

12) Consider Index Insurance to Protect Against Production and Price Risks[49]

Rural communities would love to find affordable protection from agricultural production risks. Unfortunately, crop and livestock insurance have proven extremely challenging to deliver, for a number of reasons. Perhaps the biggest one is moral hazard – farmers are less likely to take steps to reduce losses and more likely to take more risks (such as planting crops in marginal areas or paying less attention to livestock) when they know their losses will be covered (at least in part) by an insurance payout. Farms are often physically remote, which makes it hard for an insurer to check whether insured farmers are taking diligent care of their crops or animals. Remoteness also creates opportunities for fraud. A farmer could slaughter livestock and fraudulently claim they were stolen. Risk events that affect crops and livestock (for example, droughts, pests, epidemics) are likely to affect many farmers at the same time. Finally, since crop and livestock losses can be caused by a combination of insured and non-insured events, establishing the cause, extent and value of the insured loss can be a difficult and expensive exercise.

Together, these factors make agricultural insurance a very costly business, which is difficult to make profitable. Roth and McCord (2008) note that hardly any agricultural insurance programmes anywhere in the world cover their costs from premiums. Almost all have to be subsidized, which does not bode well for MFIs that wish to offer relevant insurance products in rural areas. As discussed in Chapter 9, property insurance that is tied to loan products can be viable, but stand-alone insurance for crops or livestock requires partnerships with donors or governments that are willing and able to provide sufficient subsidies to bring premiums to a level that is affordable for low-income clients.

Index insurance offers an alternative to traditional crop and livestock insurance that seems to have potential, because it eliminates many of the risks and costs that make those products unprofitable. Unlike traditional crop and livestock insurance, it is defined at a regional level, and is provided against specific events that are independent of the behaviour of the insured farmers. For example, weather-related insurance policies can be linked to rainfall or temperatures in a defined area, and provide payouts to policyholders when the relevant index falls below (or rises above) a certain level. Price-related policies provide payouts based on international crop prices.

With index insurance, moral hazard is eliminated, because no one can control the index (for instance, how much rain will fall). Therefore a farmer with insurance possesses the same economic incentives to manage his or her crop as an uninsured farmer. Payout is made to all insured clients within a geographically defined space, so there is no need to verify individual policyholders' claims of loss. Benefits can be paid out as soon as the size of the local rainfall deficiency is known. These features dramatically reduce administrative expenses, and can allow rural residents who are not farming or raising livestock, but whose income sources would be affected by crop or livestock losses (for example, landless labourers), to also benefit from the scheme.

Index-based insurance has the potential to reduce the risk of losses for financial service providers as well as individual farmers. Not only will farmers be in a better position to repay their loans despite livestock or crop losses, but MFIs can use index-based hedging instruments to manage their own potential losses from weather or price risks (see, for example, Box 20.9). Since index insurance is based on an independently verifiable index, it can also be reinsured, which allows

49 This section is adapted from Christen and Pearce (2005) and Roth and McCord (2008).

Box 20.9 Making the Most of Index Insurance in Tanzania

Area-based index insurance has only recently been extended to institutions that lend to or buy from small farmers, and successful examples are still rare. An emerging example involves the Kilimanjaro Native Cooperative Union, a large Tanzanian coffee cooperative of small farmers that trades about 11 per cent of national coffee production. The cooperative has had some success in reducing its exposure to negative coffee price movements by buying "put" options that allow it to maintain an agreed floor purchase price with farmers during the trading season. It borrows from a domestic bank, the Cooperative and Rural Development Bank (CRDB), to pay for the hedging contract premiums (the put options). Thus the cooperative has reduced its exposure to price fluctuations and falls in the value of coffee stocks held during processing or while awaiting sale.

Brokers can help financial service providers assess and price the risks in their agricultural portfolios and the risks of expanding agricultural lending, as well as negotiate insurance and hedging arrangements. Although brokers would ideally come from the private sector, the Kilimanjaro Native Cooperative Union and CRDB received such assistance from the World Bank's Commodity Risk Management Group, which helped the cooperative develop its risk management strategy and negotiate the put options. The group also trained CRDB staff in assessing price risks and providing advice on hedging trends. The group envisages this facilitating role to be performed in the future through a private broker, requiring only temporary donor or government support.

Source: Christen and Pearce, 2005.

insurance providers to transfer part of their risk to international markets, as Nyala Insurance Company of Ethiopia has done via Swiss Re (Hazell et al., 2010; Meherette, 2009).

Index insurance will not be viable in all markets, however. It is costly in marginal farming areas, in areas where weather trends are changing rapidly, and in areas where a particular risk event occurs frequently. Hazell et al. (2010) suggest as a practical rule of thumb that events that occur more frequently than once every seven years are likely to be too costly for most farmers to insure without a subsidy. The viability of index insurance is also dependent on the degree to which accurate, timely and comprehensive databases (for instance, on national or regional rainfall levels and commodity prices) are available for insurers to use to value instruments for weather and price risks. Data collection infrastructure can be an additional challenge. In Ethiopia, for example, most weather stations collect data manually on a daily basis, which is sent once a month by mail to regional offices and to the central office in Addis Ababa, where they are checked for inconsistencies and entered into a computer. To pilot weather insurance there, investments had to be made in automated weather stations.

All this attention to information and infrastructure is necessary to manage basis risk, the potential mismatch between the payout received by a policyholder (as triggered by the index) and the actual losses suffered. If, for example, a policyholder's farm lies too far from the rainfall gauge, if the gauge is inaccurate, or if the farm is located in a microclimate, the farm may receive very little rainfall while the gauge indicates that rainfall has been adequate, and the farmer receives no payment. Significant up-front investment is usually required to build a network of weather stations that can send sufficiently frequent, local and reliable data to manage basis risk. Basis risk can also make index insurance difficult to sell, and may be part of the rea-

> **Box 20.10 Using Weather Insurance to Unlock Rural Credit**
>
> MicroEnsure, one of the pioneers in weather index insurance, launched its first products in 2004 in Malawi, working with the World Bank. The original motivation for these products was that smallholder farmers in Malawi were excluded from obtaining credit for purchasing inputs such as fertilizer and seeds owing to lenders' concerns over drought. When weather index insurance became available to mitigate the climatic risk, lenders were willing to advance credit to the farmers, who in turn purchased better inputs and increased their yields (in some cases by 300 per cent). The experience of MicroEnsure has been that farmers' main motivation for purchasing weather insurance is to unlock rural credit; there has been minimal success in selling weather insurance as stand-alone products. Over the past few years MicroEnsure has developed index products using a range of triggers, including drought, typhoon and excess rain, and for a range of crops and countries, including India, the Philippines, Rwanda and Tanzania, as well as continued work in Malawi. The focus has always been to use weather index insurance to unlock rural credit for groups of farmers rather than to cover whole countries.
>
> *Source: Leftley, 2009.*

son why it has been marketed more successfully as a tool for unlocking credit to farmers than as a stand-alone product (see Box 20.10).

13) Take Steps to Mitigate Political Risk

Whether persistent or unpredictable, government and donor intervention in agricultural markets and lending is perhaps the greatest source of risk for rural lenders. MFIs working in rural areas cannot entirely avoid or transfer this risk, but they can take steps to mitigate its impact. Three strategies commonly adopted by MFIs that regularly confront political risk are briefly described below.

- Communicate the institution's neutrality clearly and regularly to clients and staff, so that the MFI is not associated with any particular political group or source of power. Staff can be asked to remain neutral in their public interactions, and clients can be warned that repayment will be expected no matter which politician says otherwise. The MFI can use this communication as an opportunity to re-articulate its mission and vision, and the benefits clients can access in the long term by supporting the institution's sustainability.
- Work together with other financial service providers, perhaps through a national association of microfinance institutions, to raise awareness among government officials of how much more sustainable rural financial institutions can contribute to rural development and food security as compared with short-term subsidies.
- Diversify geographically. Political interference is often localized in one district or province, so if an MFI has operations in many districts, a political crisis in one can be overcome with the support of operations in others.

20.4 An Appropriate Product Mix for Rural Microfinance

As argued earlier in this chapter, a broad mix of financial services is relevant in rural areas, just as it is in urban areas. Savings, credit and money transfer services will almost certainly be demanded if their design is right. It is a challenge to provide affordable and convenient savings services in rural areas, but technology, large-group methodologies and partnerships are making this possible, as discussed above and in Chapter 4 on savings. The options for providing rural money transfers are similar, with technology and partnerships that piggyback on the infrastructure of others providing the most cost-effective solutions, as explored in Chapter 11.

With credit, risk management is the key challenge. Agricultural lending is possible, but MFIs must have the systems in place to manage the additional risks associated with this kind of lending, and they must be able to implement them at a cost that is sustainable for both MFIs and clients. Many of the strategies mentioned in this chapter are complex, and require a particular set of inputs and/or the coordination of multiple actors to succeed. The greater the difference between an MFI's standard urban or working capital lending and the requirements for agricultural lending, the greater the need for caution. Market segmentation and the scoring models presented in Chapter 2 can help institutions expand slowly, at a pace that matches their capacity. However, focusing only on particular subsegments or value chains can bring its own problems, namely concentration risk and a lack of outreach among populations that are harder to serve.

Larger and longer-term loans are very much needed to facilitate investment and increase household income in rural areas, but these continue to be the most difficult products for MFIs to finance, in part because of institutions' own lack of long-term financing, but also because of the increased risk inherent in these products, and the more sophisticated financial management skills and systems required to manage those risks.

Insurance, leasing and non-financial services also require specialized skills: actuarial expertise in the case of insurance, equipment maintenance providers in the case of leasing, and agronomists and marketing specialists in the case of non-financial services. The requirements for developing and delivering these products may seem daunting, but financial service providers can collaborate with other actors and build on their knowledge and infrastructure to collectively manage risk, develop appropriate products and increase competitiveness. The experiences of Drumnet in Box 20.11 and IMON (in the case at the end of this chapter) provide examples of what might be possible in the future.

Box 20.11 DrumNet's Value Chain Management System

In Kenya, the key players required for a vibrant smallholder agricultural sector are present – commercial banks, large-scale produce buyers, farm input suppliers, transporters, and the smallholder farmers themselves. However, a critical factor inhibiting development is the absence of a platform that facilitates the flow of information and financial transactions among those actors. DrumNet, a pilot project of PRIDE AFRICA, was launched in March 2003 as a rural value-chain management system that facilitates these transactions.

The business model is straightforward. DrumNet facilitates and brokers services to a value chain where certified farm groups stand on the producing/selling side, a reputable buyer on the buying side, and certified input suppliers and a commercial bank in the middle. A large and reputable agro-processing company, the "buyer", signs a fixed-price purchase contract with the farmer groups under a master contract managed by DrumNet. The DrumNet master contract represents the roles, rights and obligations of all parties in the value chain. Subcontracts between parties define the obligations of each specific actor. The contract's sales proceeds flow through the bank to repay all production credit and fees owed by the producer.

On the finance side of the model, DrumNet stepped back from the traditional microfinance approach of being a supplier of credit, and concentrated on working with a commercial bank to structure credit and banking services to producer groups based on the sales proceeds paid by the buyer that flow through the bank. DrumNet's information communication technology system provides the internal controls to monitor transactions and contract compliance, and to report on all the movements of factors and funds within the value chain. DrumNet also partners with other organizations to provide capacity building in farmer group dynamics, training and certification to assure the buyer of the quality required. For its brokerage, administrative and transactional services, DrumNet charges fee shares from its value-chain partners and members.

Although smallholder farmers are DrumNet's target market, all parties in its model benefit from participation. Farmers gain increased income and liquidity. Buyers gain access to trained and reliable farmers who can deliver a timely and predictable quantity and quality of goods. Input suppliers gain increased sales while avoiding credit risk. Banks gain additional revenue, an expanded deposit base, cash management and quality control systems that mitigate credit risk, and access to a virtually untapped wholesale client base that provides cost-effective risk diversification.

Source: Adapted from Campaigne, 2010.

Main Messages

1. Rural populations – like urban populations – demand a variety of financial services to support their economic activities, smooth their income flows, and mitigate their risks.
2. Measure rural household cash flows and adjust loan terms and conditions to match them.
3. Diversify by region, ecology and economic activity.
4. Pay attention to value chains.
5. Build on the knowledge and infrastructure of others to overcome the challenges of the rural environment.

Case Study: Integrated Agricultural Programming in Tajikistan

Background. Tajikistan is a mountainous landlocked country in Central Asia with more than 70 per cent of the population living in rural areas. Since 1991, when the country became an independent state, civil war, economic collapse, floods, landslides and a major drought in 2000–2001 have reduced 84 per cent of Tajikistan's population to poverty (GDP per capita in 2001 was US$161). Northern Tajikistan is known for its fruits and vegetables, which provide a rich opportunity for effective agricultural programming. The fruits and vegetables are generally grown by smallholder farmers, some of whom are also microprocessors who prepare their horticultural outputs for local markets using traditional means (for example, pitting, cutting and shaping their produce with labour-intensive hand tools).

In 2004, Mennonite Economic Development Associates (MEDA) began implementing a four-year agricultural development programme in Northern Tajikistan that focused on the horticulture subsector. Prior to the start of the programme, farmers did not have access to credit to purchase inputs, improve stock or upgrade irrigation. The limited credit available in the region was available mainly to traders. Producers often had only limited access to external markets and larger processors, so they sold their goods at local markets or to traders. As a result, waste was high, with quoted figures ranging from 25 per cent to 50 per cent spoilage in 2001.

Programme design. MEDA designed a programme with two levels of intervention. First, it would assist smallholder farmers in adapting to and growing within a globalizing market economy by: 1) providing access to traditional and new production knowledge; 2) supporting the adoption of up-to-date technologies, improved inputs and better services; 3) strengthening farmers' ability to work cooperatively and take collective action; and 4) establishing a viable rural credit programme that would continue to serve farmers after the programme ended. Second, the programme would advance the creation and growth of small and medium enterprises (SMEs) to process and market the rural agricultural output of the region, filling a current gap in the value chain. The main activities at this level included business development, technical assistance and technology transfer, association formation, and SME finance.

MEDA partnered with the Association of Business Women (ABW), a multi-purpose NGO, to implement the programme. ABW was already operating in Northern Tajikistan, it dem-

onstrated a strong willingness to expand into rural and agricultural finance, and it committed management time above and beyond programme funding. It had been implementing a microcredit programme in close partnership with Mercy Corps since 1999, but served primarily urban clients. Shortly after the partnership with MEDA began, ABW separated its lending activities from the rest of its operations, first creating a microfinance foundation in 2004, and in 2007 transforming itself into the commercial microlending organization, IMON International, LLC.

Implementation. MEDA and ABW/IMON conducted a baseline survey to define the indicators that would serve as a basis for the development and implementation of their activities. The survey collected information on household income and expenses, on agricultural activities and markets, and also on credit. The results showed that one-third of interviewees had some experience with credit, but mostly from informal sources without interest or a real repayment schedule. Eighty per cent of respondents were interested in taking a loan. About half were interested in a short-term loan of US$300–$1,500 for agricultural inputs or equipment rental. The other half were interested in longer-term loans for larger amounts (above US$1,500) for investment in irrigation systems or equipment purchase. Survey participants understood interest rate concepts, and had ideas about how much they would be willing to pay: for short-term credit, between 2 and 4 per cent monthly, and for long-term credit between 1 and 3 per cent monthly.

Building on the survey results, ABW's knowledge of the local environment, and MEDA's experiences with rural credit in other countries, the two organizations designed four products, the terms of which are summarized in Table 20.3.

Table 20.3 Product offering included in ABW/IMON's business plan

	General WC	Ag loan	Leasing – fixed assets	Specialty products
Use	Working capital loan or small fixed assets – traders, processsors	Production inputs, fertilizer, etc.	All types of fixed assets	For example, irrigation
Amout (min–max)	C$0–1,300	C$150–1,650	C$650–5,000	Max. C$5,000
Term (min–max)	3–6 months	6–9 months	6–18 months	To be decided
Payment frequency	2 weeks or monthly	Interest monthly, principal in 2–4 payments at end	Monthly	Monthly
Grace period	None	3–6 months	0–2 months	To be decided
Interest range	3–3.5%	3–3.5%	2.5–3%	To be decided
Fees	1–4%	2–3%	2–3%	To be decided
Penalty	1%	1%	1%	To be decided
Collateral	None required but is accepted	Contribute 30% of need	Organization owns item until paid for	To be decided

Source: Jones, 2007.

A major challenge for the programme was to coordinate the sharing of information between value-chain development actors and rural financial service providers so that data on agricultural cycles and risks would inform product design, loan appraisal, balanced portfolio growth, and other rural finance decisions. At the country level, managers for the value chain development component and the financial services component came together for weekly coordination meetings, while at the district level, loan officers and extensionists shared offices, so they were able to exchange information with regard to clients and loan applications on a daily basis.

Results and lessons learned. As of October 2006, 3,557 loans had been disbursed totalling US$1,414,734. IMON was able to cover the operating costs of the agricultural loan portfolio from interest earned within 18 months, and reported almost no default (see Table 20.4). IMON's total portfolio grew from US$1.3 million at the beginning of 2004 to nearly US$8 million at the end of 2006, and it had become the leader in rural finance in Tajikistan. During the programme period loans were mainly for working capital, such as production inputs, but, in the off-season, lending for livestock, produce storage and winter crops kept the portfolio active. Both group and individual loans were successful. Agro-leasing was not developed as planned, owing to the absence of local suppliers, but a microleasing product with longer terms and larger amounts was later introduced by IMON.

Table 20.4 Performance of the MEDA/IMON loan portfolio as of October 2006

Operating efficiency and portfolio quality	MEDA agricultural loan fund portfolio	IMON (ABW) total portfolio
Portfolio at risk (PAR) 1 day	0.10%	0.65%
Operating expense ratio	15.23%	21.61%
Average outstanding loan size	US$1,055	US$1,733
Return on assets	31.5%	10.5%
Return on equity	n/a	24.4%

Source: Jones and Pasricha, 2007.

The use of extensionists to train and advise loan officers has been so successful that IMON replicated the model in other branches. Having extensionists who could not only advise on general agricultural issues, but also knew specific clients and situations greatly reduced the risk to the portfolio. In addition, agriculture extension clients were able to apply improved techniques and adopt new technologies more rapidly because of their access to the loan fund. Nevertheless, extensionists initially spent a lot of time referring clients to the loan officers and reviewing loan applications, which meant that they had less time for setting up their own training and technical assistance programmes than desirable. Overall, it was viewed as a positive trade-off during the start-up period, but later extensionists were encouraged to focus more on agricultural training and technical assistance, and in some cases were moved to separate offices.

This case study was adapted from Jones (2007) and Jones and Pasricha (2007).

Recommended Reading

- Buchenau, J.; Meyer, R. 2007. *Introducing rural finance into an urban microfinance institution: The example of Banco Procredit, El Salvador*, Paper presented at the International Conference on Rural Finance Research: Moving Results into Policies and Practice (Rome, FAO), at: http://www.fao.org/ag/rurfinconference/docs/papers_theme_3/introducing_rural_finance.pdf
- Christen, R.; Pearce, D. 2005. *Managing risks and designing products for agricultural microfinance: Features of an emerging model*, CGAP Occasional Paper No. 11 (Washington, DC, CGAP), at: http://www.cgap.org/gm/document-1.9.2705/OP11.pdf
- Dellien, H.; Lynch, E. 2007. *Rural finance for small farmers: An integrated approach*, WWB Focus Note (New York, NY, Women's World Banking), at: http://www.swwb.org/files/pubs/en/rural_finance_for_smaller_farmers_e.pdf
- Doran, A.; McFadyen, N.; Vogel, R. 2009. *The missing middle in agricultural finance: Relieving the capital constraint on smallholder groups and other agricultural SMEs* (Oxford, Oxfam), at: http://www.oxfam.org.uk/resources/policy/trade/downloads/research_agricultural_finance.pdf
- Fries, R.; Akin, B. 2004. *Value chains and their significance for addressing the rural finance challenge*, USAID MicroReport No. 20 (Washington, DC, USAID), at: http://www.microlinks.org/ev_en.php?ID=7098_201&ID2=DO_TOPIC
- Hazell, P.; Anderson, J.; Balzer, N.; Hastrup Clemmensen, A.; Hess, U.; Rispoli, F. 2010. *The potential for scale and sustainability in weather index insurance for agriculture and rural livelihoods* (Rome, International Fund for Agricultural Development and World Food Programme), at: http://www.microfinancegateway.org/gm/document-1.9.43862/Weather_insurance_scale_and_sustainability_IFAD-WFP_WRMF.pdf
- IFAD. 2010. *IFAD decision tools for rural finance* (Rome), at: www.ifad.org/ruralfinance
- Miller, C. 2005. *Development partners perspective: Global perspectives in rural finance and poverty alleviation*, 4th AFRACA Microfinance Forum, Kampala, Uganda, at: www.ruralfinance.org
- Miller, C.; Jones, L. 2010. *Agricultural value chain finance: Tools and lessons* (Rugby, Practical Action Publishing and FAO).
- Nagarajan, G.; Meyer, R. 2005. *Rural finance: Recent advances and emerging lessons, debates, and opportunities*, Reformatted version of Working Paper AEDE-WP-0041-05, (Columbus, Ohio State University, Department of Agricultural, Environmental, and Development Economics), at: http://www.microfinancegateway.org/gm/document-1.9.29202/27421_file_FINALPDF.pdf
- Roth, J.; McCord, M. 2008. *Agricultural microinsurance: Global practices and prospects* (Appleton, WI, The MicroInsurance Centre), at: http://www.microinsurancenetwork.org/publication/fichier/Agriculture_Microinsurance__Global_Practices_and_Prospects.pdf
- Rural Finance Learning Centre, at: www.ruralfinance.org
- USAID Rural and Agricultural Finance Seminar Series, at: www.microlinks.org

21 SME Finance

Microcredit can help the poor subsist from day to day, but in order to lift them out of poverty, larger loans are needed so that the poor can expand their productive activities and thereby increase their assets. ~ World Bank (2009b)

According to the World Bank, the global volume of financing for small and medium enterprises (SMEs) is estimated at US$10 trillion. Seventy per cent of this financing is concentrated in high-income OECD (Organisation for Economic Co-operation and Development) countries. The median ratio of SME loans to GDP in those countries is 13 per cent, compared with only 3 per cent in developing countries (CGAP, 2010b).

SMEs need access to a range of financial services just as microenterprises and large corporate enterprises do. Yet, for them, accessing credit has been much more difficult than access to other financial services. The International Finance Corporation (IFC) recently reported that 70–76 per cent of the formal SMEs in emerging markets already have a banking relationship via deposit and checking accounts, while only about 30–35 per cent have access to credit (IFC, 2010). Certainly, more can be done to expand SME access to savings, insurance, money transfer and leasing services, but the challenges inherent in doing so are not that different from the challenges inherent in expanding outreach to mainstream microfinance clients, as discussed in Part II of this book.

This chapter will, therefore, focus on credit and the associated services that MFIs might provide in an attempt to increase their outreach to small and medium enterprises. It will address the following five topics:

1. Defining the SME market
2. Why serve SMEs?
3. Why does the SME finance gap exist?
4. The right kind of finance for SMEs
5. Delivering the right kind of finance

21.1 Defining the SME Market[50]

Definitions of micro, small and medium enterprise vary greatly across countries. However, most definitions are based on a handful of the same criteria. A recent study by the IFC found that financial regulators in 68 countries base their SME definition on one or more of the following three criteria: number of employees, sales volume, or loan size. Frequently, the definition relies on multiple criteria, and varies by industry. In Pakistan, for example, SME refers to an entity that employs no more than 250 persons in the manufacturing or service sectors or 50 persons in the trade sector, with sales up to US$590,000 for trade and industry firms, US$1.2 million for manufacturing firms, and no more than US$3.5 million for any industry of operation.

If loan size or sales volume are used as criteria, they are often expressed in relation to some base amount rather than in absolute terms, for example sales not exceeding 1,000 times mini-

[50] Unless otherwise specified, the data in this section of the chapter come from International Finance Corporation (2010).

mum salaries or income per capita. This is particularly true in countries with high inflation or in fast-growing economies. Unfortunately, even when the maximum cut-off value is expressed as a ratio, it does not translate into a common point of reference that can be used to distinguish SMEs from larger businesses worldwide. For instance, the cut-off sales value for an SME in Azerbaijan represents 23 times income per capita, whereas in South Africa it represents more than 8,000 times income per capita.

For the purposes of this chapter, micro, small and medium enterprises are differentiated using the criteria provided in Table 21.1. The table can help MFIs identify the general differences between the SME segment and others, but institutions that wish to serve SMEs will need to profile the segment more accurately using national measurement criteria.

Commercial banks serve some SMEs; however, they mostly target businesses with collateral, a relatively solid bottom line, and the capacity to absorb larger sums. These businesses are usually located in urban areas. MFIs also serve some SMEs, although not always with the amount or type of financing that they desire. Most MFIs have limited ability to accompany clients' businesses as they grow. The end result is an SME finance gap that is sometimes referred to as the "missing middle" (see Figure 21.1). Some industry sources estimate that 60 to 80 per cent of small businesses in low-income countries remain underserved (CapitalPlus Exchange, 2010).

Table 21.1 SME characteristics in relative terms

	Micro	Small and medium	Large
Number of employees	1–4; often family	5–250	> 250
Entrepreneur's orientation	Income stabilization / growth	Growth / profit	Profit / growth
Average loan size required[51]	< US$10,000; in developing countries, generally below US$1,000	> 250% per capita gross national income < US$ 1million	> US$1 million
Degree of formality	Often without a business licence; rarely with fixed place of business separate from home	Formal business license; fixed place of business either owned or leased	Often incorporated; may have multiple fixed locations
Access to finance	Often have no access to formal finance	Lack access to the right kind of finance	Financing is not a major barrier
Record-keeping	Business and household funds co-mingled; little or no record-keeping	Separate, but often basic, business and household records and financial management	Professional accounting and financial management
Management skills	Generally low	Developing	Sophisticated

Source: Adapted from Deelen and Molenaar, 2004, and Sia and Nails, 2008.

51 The parameters for average loan size are roughly described here on the basis of two international guidelines: 1) the World Bank's definitions of small enterprise (one that requires a loan between US$10,000 and US$100,000) and medium enterprise (one that requires a loan between US$100,000 and US$1 million); and 2) the MicroBanking Bulletin's definition of the small business peer group to include MFIs that have an average loan balance per borrower that is greater than 250 per cent of per capita gross national income.

Figure 21.1 Generalized illustration of the "missing middle"

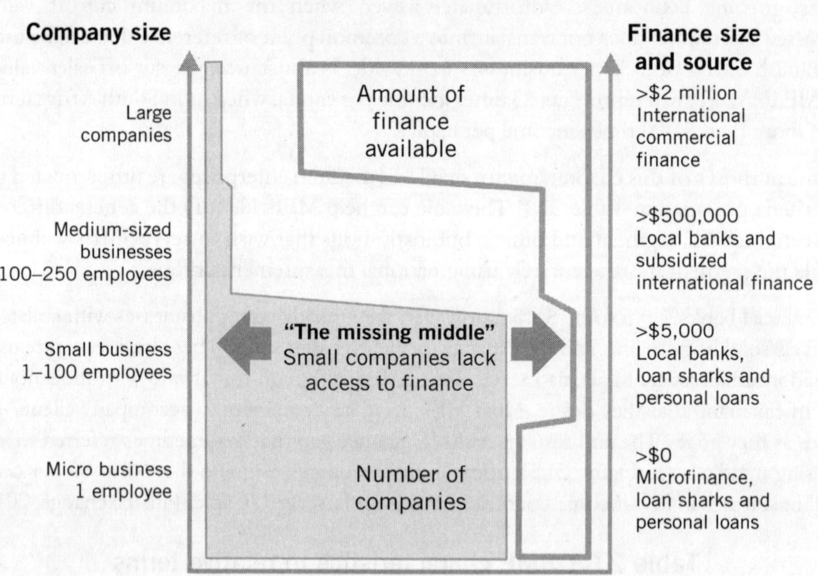

Source: Sanders and Wegener, 2006.

21.2 Why Serve SMEs?

An increasing number of commercial banks are attempting to move into the SME market (often referred to as "downscaling") as more and more MFIs consider moving up (often referred to as "upscaling"). There are several characteristics of the SME market that are making it attractive from both sides:

- **Potential demand.** A recent IFC-McKinsey study estimates that there are between 36 and 44 million formal SMEs operating worldwide, 25–30 million of which are located outside OECD countries. Approximately 45–55 per cent of formal SMEs in emerging markets need credit but do not have access to it, and another 21–24 per cent have access to some credit, but identify financing as a constraint (IFC, 2010).
- **Potential for growth.** Small and medium businesses contribute an average of 51.5 per cent of the GDP in high-income countries, but only 15.6 per cent in low-income countries (Ferranti and Ody, 2007). SMEs in developing countries are probably capable of producing much more output than is currently possible.
- **Potential for financial services to alleviate SME growth constraints.** In the World Bank's *World Business Environment Survey* of more than 10,000 firms in 80 countries, SMEs worldwide named financing constraints, on average, as the second most severe obstacle to their growth (after taxes and regulation) (Ferranti and Ody, 2007). Beck (2007) reports that smaller firms' financing obstacles have almost twice the effect on their growth as larger firms' capital constraints.

> **Box 21.1 Job Creation by SMEs vs. Microenterprises**
>
> According to an impact study by Asian Credit Fund, a Mercy Corps' SME credit programme in Kazakhstan, a typical microcredit client in Kazakhstan employs on average three workers and invests less than 50 per cent of net profit back into the business. At the same time, a typical small business client employs on average 50 workers and retains on average 80 per cent of the net profit in the business.
>
> *Source: Asian Credit Fund, 2006.*

- **Potential for profit.** In 2009, the IFC reported that leading banks in emerging markets are reporting return on assets (ROA) of 3–6 per cent for their SME operations compared with 1–3 per cent bank-wide (Fernandez and Sene, 2010).
- **Development impact.** SMEs typically create more jobs than large firms or microenterprises (see, for example, Box 21.1), and the jobs they create are often filled by poor, unskilled people. This is important, given that many poor people prefer a stable source of employment income to being self-employed. The fact that most SMEs are locally owned and operated is also significant; SMEs tend to develop local products and services for local needs using local resources (Sanders and Wegener, 2006). One review of ten case studies in Latin America and Central and Eastern Europe found that every dollar invested in a small enterprise generated an average of ten dollars of economic activity in the local economy (SEAF, 2004).
- **Innovative nature.** SMEs often work in new industries, find alternative ways to deliver existing products, advance new ideas, and serve new niches.

In sum, the SME market provides an opportunity for increasing outreach, profit and impact. It is becoming an increasingly attractive option as competition increases and profit margins decrease for both banks and MFIs in their traditional markets.

21.3 Why Does the SME Finance Gap Exist?

Although the SME market segment has clear potential, there are many reasons why neither banks nor microfinance institutions are serving it effectively. The principal reasons relate to: 1) the higher risk of lending to this market; 2) the differences between the SME market and financial institutions' traditional markets, which necessitate significant operational changes; and 3) the cost of delivering loan products that can effectively meet SME needs. Each of these factors is explored below.

SMEs Are a Riskier Market

Credit risk in the SME market is greater for both downscaling banks and upscaling MFIs. Banks have much less information available to them when analysing SMEs than they would for larger enterprises, which increases the possibility of lending to a borrower who will not be able or willing to repay the loan. MFIs are accustomed to making loans without audited financial statements or a verifiable credit history, but the larger amounts and longer terms of SME loans increases their exposure. If a bad decision is made, the loss will be greater.

SMEs usually have more to offer in the way of collateral than microenterprises, but their assets are likely to be movable (for example, livestock, machinery or vehicles), have low market value or be hard to liquidate. They may not be registered, and they may not be sufficient to meet banks' collateral requirements, which in some cases amount to three times the loan value (Sanders and Wegener, 2006).

For downscaling banks, entry into the SME market can decrease **concentration risk**, because more loans of a smaller size are being made to businesses in different sectors. However, for upscaling MFIs, entry into the SME market usually increases concentration risk, because larger loans are being made to a smaller number of businesses, and those businesses may be clustered in a limited number of sectors. Sometimes this is demand driven, as certain sectors have a larger number of SMEs than others, but it can also be supply driven. MFIs sometimes decide to focus their financing on a small number of sectors or value chains so they can use their limited resources to understand them well.

SMEs are **more vulnerable to the business environment**. They often lack the capacity of larger firms to work through the complexities of regulatory and bureaucratic procedures (IFC, 2010). They have fewer resources to fall back on in the event of a shock. Unlike microenterprises, which can be flexible in managing their business activities and change quickly from one business to another if market conditions change, SMEs make investments in their business and in the acquisition of skills that limit their flexibility. Since the cost of switching activities is higher, they are more likely to remain where they are and have to absorb the impact of changes in the environment around them. Thus financial institutions that serve them are more exposed to external risk.

Finally, SMEs often possess **inadequate knowledge and/or skills** to manage the increasing complexity and size of their operations effectively. Microentrepreneurs can handle their small-scale operations and small loan amounts with a relatively low level of skill, and large companies can hire specialists to design and manage their accounting systems, business planning, market research and other activities necessary to manage large-scale operations. SME managers find themselves in the difficult position of having to perform a wider range of tasks themselves without having accessed the type of education that would have prepared them to carry out these responsibilities. Low levels of financial literacy can also prevent SMEs from adequately assessing and understanding different financing options.

Major Market Differences Necessitate Major Changes

Table 21.1 illustrated some of the main differences between the microenterprise, SME and large enterprise market segments, namely the number of employees, amount of financing needed, business orientation, degree of formality, quality of record-keeping and strength of management skills. Interestingly, these differences impact on financial institutions in distinct ways, depending on the type of market they traditionally serve. For banks that serve primarily large businesses, the SME sector is challenging because of the relatively small loan amounts being requested, the poor quality of information available, the lack of attractive collateral, and weak management skills. Nearly the opposite is true for MFIs, which find it challenging to make larger loans for longer terms that are flexible enough to meet the needs of borrowers' businesses (see Figure 21.2).

Figure 21.2 Differing perceptions of the SME challenge

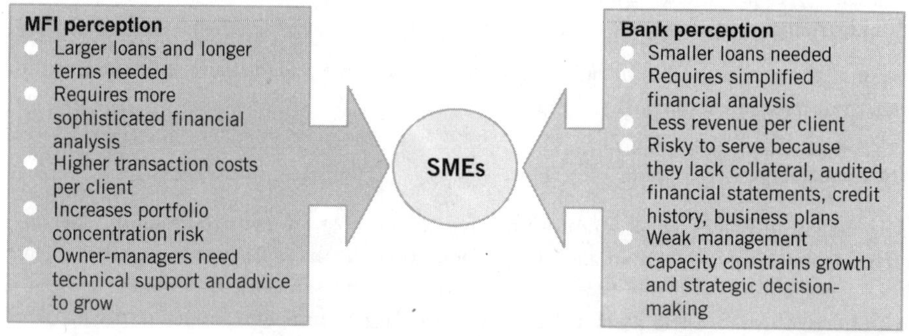

Source: Authors.

These differences make it necessary for financial institutions that want to serve SMEs to make significant changes in their operations. For example:

- **Methodology.** SME loan sizes are small relative to the transaction costs of delivery. The methods used to assess the creditworthiness of large companies will be too expensive or impractical to be effective in the SME market, while those used to assess the creditworthiness of microenterprises will not sufficiently protect an MFI against loss. Thus new methodologies must be developed, and systems must be put in place to support them.
- **Staff development.** Staff must be hired or developed who understand the SME market and are capable of analysing its capacity and risks. Staff with the appropriate profile are often difficult to find and, for MFIs, more expensive to retain.
- **Organizational structure.** Given the different skill sets and methodologies required for SME finance, institutions may need to reorganize the way they distribute people and functions to provide an appropriate balance of autonomy, support and accountability.
- **Incentive schemes.** The longer-term and tailored nature of SME loans makes individual incentive schemes harder to design fairly. If loan officers are rewarded under a generic scheme, they may avoid the SME market or try to shortcut certain procedures, since the appraisal and monitoring of SME loans take longer than for microenterprise loans, and generate less income than larger enterprise loans. The existing scheme may have to be adjusted, or a new one created.
- **Cultural change.** To serve such a different market segment effectively, institutions must introduce new values, habits and/or attitudes. This is rarely easy. The shift from one way of doing things to another can create resistance among staff. It can also create tension between employees who serve different client groups, especially if there are perceived inequities in the way they are treated. In MFIs, for example, SME loan officers will typically carry a smaller caseload; have greater access to technology; and earn higher salaries than microenterprise loan officers. Institutions must find a way to minimize this tension and resistance.
- **Financial management.** This is an area of particular concern for MFIs, which often have limited access to long-term funds for on-lending. SME demand for finance is also harder to predict than microfinance demand, because the latter is largely dependent on

seasonal working capital needs, whereas SMEs may have irregular and quite diverse financing requirements. To serve this market, MFIs must secure longer-term financing and strengthen their capacity to manage liquidity.

Together, these changes can be quite intimidating, and can easily discourage financial institutions from trying to serve SMEs.

Higher Costs

SME finance involves small amounts relative to the cost of each transaction. Although microfinance involves even smaller sums, methodologies have been developed to deliver these sums at an acceptable level of cost and risk. The same methodologies are not as cost-effective in the SME market, because of the larger sums and longer terms involved. Additional steps must be taken to analyse a business's ability to generate sufficient cash flow to service a loan, because if something goes wrong, clients will typically lack the capacity to solve the problem using household assets or other income sources.

For banks, costs are higher because of the extra effort required to gather information about a potential borrower's creditworthiness. Business records may not exist, or if they do, they may be incomplete or unreliable. Financial statements may not be prepared according to standard accounting practices; some operations may be omitted or recorded incorrectly, and auditing them can be labour and time intensive. Even if SME borrowers have collateral and reliable business and financial records, their relatively smaller loans generate less revenue, potentially resulting in losses.

Thus a major challenge for SME finance is finding a way to cover costs. A recent study by the IFC and Oliver Wyman suggests that about 80 per cent of the SME finance gap can be attributed directly to the cost of distributing credit (IFC, 2010). Unlike in microfinance, products cannot be completely standardized, and institutions cannot charge whatever price is necessary to cover costs because the profit margins of most SMEs are relatively low and there is a limit to how much they can afford to pay. The higher the interest rate set, the greater the likelihood that financial institutions will attract only riskier borrowers who have the potential to generate a return that is large enough to service a loan financed at that rate. Instead, financial institutions must find a way to lower costs.

21.4 The Right Kind of Finance for SMEs

Whereas microentrepreneurs often lack any access to formal finance, small and medium enterprises typically lack access to the right kind of formal finance. What SMEs typically need is a combination of capital to grow and a trusted advisor who can provide access to information that helps them make optimal choices about what kind of financing to seek, when, and under what terms, as well as opportunities to develop their management skills and market. They need tailored products that respond to the particular needs of their business, and they need to interact with people who understand their business well enough to identify potential areas of weakness as well as strategies for addressing those weaknesses. MFIs such as BRAC Bank in Bangladesh (see Box 21.2) that have been able to provide this mix at an appropriate cost and level of risk are seeing the SME side of their business flourish.

Box 21.2 BRAC Bank's Recipe for Success in the SME Market

BRAC Bank Ltd was established in 2001 with a focus on the small business sector, operating with a "double bottom-line" agenda: a combination of profit and social responsibility. Its small business banking model emphasizes relationship banking and collateral free lending up to US$14,000. The SME Banking unit goes beyond traditional banking and works as a business partner to entrepreneurs, building awareness, providing training, and arranging roadshows to support and develop their businesses. BRAC Bank is the premier small business bank in Bangladesh in terms of small business loans outstanding, with nationwide coverage, 44 per cent of which is in rural areas. It serves more than 100,000 SMEs, with an average loan of US$4,136.

Source: IFC, 2010.

Tailored Products

SME loans are more likely to be successful when the timing and repayment terms are tied to the financing need. Traditional microenterprise loan products that start small and gradually increase in size with each subsequent borrowing, or require all borrowers in a group to borrow roughly the same amount at the same time, will not meet the needs of most SME clients. A first-time borrower who needs an equipment loan could easily require a larger amount and a longer term than a repeat borrower who needs seasonal working capital.

Although any of the basic loan features described in Chapter 6 can vary from one SME loan product to the next, there are two features that define the main product options for SMEs: loan term and collateral. Since SMEs need to finance specific expenditures as well as recurring expenditures in the short and long term, the four main types of loan product can be succinctly presented in a matrix such as the one in Table 21.2. Each type of finance is briefly described below:

1. **Temporary working capital loans** finance a business's periodic need for cash in its daily operations (for example, to purchase inventory or to cover cyclical business fluctuations). They can be provided in the form of credit cards, bank overdrafts or revolving lines of credit. Funds can be advanced when needed, paid down when cash is available, then re-advanced when needed again. The maximum amount varies greatly, depending on a borrower's credit history; interest rates usually float; and a borrower pays interest only on the outstanding balance. Loans in this category are often unsecured, although they may be backed by accounts receivable or inventory.

Table 21.2 Four main types of SME finance

Nature of business need	Recurring expenditure	Specific expenditure
Short-term	Temporary working capital	Short-term commercial loans
Long-term	Permanent working capital	Long-term commercial loans

Source: Authors.

2. **Short-term commercial loans** differ from lines of credit in that a fixed sum is borrowed for a specific expenditure (for example, to purchase a particular piece of equipment or pay a specific debt) and for a set time, with interest paid on the lump sum. These loans are sometimes used to finance the same type of operating costs as a temporary working capital loan, but the structure of the loan is fundamentally different. Funds are accessed once and repaid on an agreed-upon schedule. They are usually less expensive than a line of credit, especially if the loan is secured by some type of collateral, because the lender's risk exposure is more limited.
3. **Long-term commercial loans** are also given for a specific expenditure and with a set repayment period and interest, but they are repaid over a period of more than one to three years. Since the term is longer, the risk to the lender is higher, so collateral requirements and/or the interest rate will be higher than for short-term loans. This kind of product is generally used to finance fixed assets.
4. **Permanent working capital** is a long-term loan that supports a rapidly growing business's frequent need for cash. This type of financing is typically extended in a term loan that allows a business to increase its base level of current assets quickly and repay the debt incurred over a number of years.

The type of loan product that will be appropriate for a particular SME at a particular point in time will vary greatly, depending on its maturity and the sector in which it operates. For example, a wholesale business may require a larger loan with a shorter term for funding its inventory than a retail business. A young enterprise may need permanent working capital, whereas a mature one may need only temporary working capital in the form of a revolving line of credit.

An SME's operating cycle will also influence loan product structure. The operating cycle is the time that it takes for a business to convert cash into revenue through the production of some good or service. For instance, if a farmer borrows cash to buy seeds and fertilizer to grow crops that will eventually be sold to a wholesaler, then the farmer's operating cycle is the length of time between his purchase of inputs and the sale of his crop. Working capital loans for small producers will generally require longer terms than those for service providers, because producers use their loan to buy raw material that may take many months to convert into a product that can be sold.

By understanding an SME's operating cycle and the factors that influence it, a financial institution gains important information about the nature and amount of financing needed, the appropriate sources of repayment, the timing of repayment, and the risks associated with repayment. By providing the right amount of financing at the right time, financial institutions can help SMEs make more efficient use of their resources, turn their assets and receivables over more quickly (or with higher quality), and generate more income. For instance, a farmer may need a large loan with a long term and a grace period for the purchase of raw materials at the beginning of its operating cycle, but require a small loan for a short term when it is time to transport goods to a wholesaler.

One aspect of loan design that was not mentioned in Chapter 6, and which becomes important in SME finance because of the tailored nature of loan contracts, is covenants. A loan covenant is a clause in the lending contract that requires one party (the borrower) to do, or refrain from doing, certain things. **Protective covenants** are actions that a borrower agrees to take during

the life of a loan. They may include maintaining a minimum level of working capital, carrying adequate insurance, adhering to certain repayment schedules, or supplying the lender with regular financial statements and reports. **Restrictive covenants** are provisions that aim to prevent certain events. They might prohibit a borrower from selling the business during the loan term, or exceeding a certain leverage ratio. The three most common restrictive covenants involve repayment terms, the use of collateral, and periodic reporting (Wilmington Trust, 2010).

Financial institutions can use covenants to create loan contracts that are less risky for the borrower as well as the MFI. They can be particularly useful with SMEs whose management skills may not be strong enough to recognize the importance of maintaining certain ratios or behaviour.

Business Advice

Given that SMEs are focused primarily on growth, yet tend to lack a solid base of skills with which to manage that growth, their ability to make effective use of financial services will be heavily influenced by their ability to access capacity-building opportunities. Loan officers, either deliberately or not, can provide guidance during the appraisal and monitoring of loans that helps borrowers understand what they need to pay attention to, how to analyse their current situation, and how to plan for the future. At ACLEDA Bank (Cambodia), K-Rep Bank (Kenya) and SOA Kredit (Azerbaijan), loan officers often assist and guide prospective borrowers in completing their business plans and other documents to support their loan request (Sia and Nails, 2008). Loan contract covenants can also provide useful guidance, although their impact in terms of developing SMEs' management skills is limited.

SME clients face ongoing challenges that financial institutions will not be able to address through the lending process alone. Those that want to support their clients' growth (and protect their own investment) may want to provide additional advisory services, either directly or by linking clients to providers of business development services (see Chapter 12 on non-financial services). Some of the ways that financial institutions have directly provided business advice are:

- distributing pamphlets or posting articles on branch bulletin boards with information on legal and regulatory issues, marketing strategy, and other topics;
- offering financial education or training workshops (for example, on business plan development, the preparation of financial statements, or how to present a financial plan to potential investors);
- providing business strategy tips in marketing campaigns;
- arranging a roadshow or trade fair;
- hosting "after hours" seminars at their office, with special guests who are experienced in a given area of SME management.

This kind of assistance can be particularly useful for empowering female entrepreneurs, who tend to be more cautious about the amount of risk they are willing to take on, and are more likely to identify the lack of management training as a constraint on their business growth (Powers and Magnoni, 2010). The many reasons for which female entrepreneurs might lack the skills or confidence to grow are discussed in Chapter 17 on microfinance for women, but the result is clearly reflected in studies such as the one conducted by EA Consultants in early 2010 with six Bolivian MFIs that collectively serve just over 400,000 microcredit clients and 10,000 SME clients. Approximately 51 per cent of the MFI's microcredit clients are women, compared with only 36 per cent of SME clients. According to Powers and Magnoni (2010), these results are similar to those seen in the rest of Latin America. Business training and mentoring along the lines of that envisaged by the Strengthening Women Entrepreneurship in Peru (SWEP) project (see Box 21.3) might enable more female entrepreneurs to take advantage of business expansion opportunities, including SME finance.

21.5 Delivering the Right Kind of Finance

The million dollar question in SME finance is how to deliver tailored loan products and business advice to SMEs at an affordable cost and acceptable risk. This section explores eight of

Box 21.3 Building Women Entrepreneurs' Capacity for Growth in Peru

Women entrepreneurship is a powerful force in Peru, one of only two countries in the world in which women are more likely to start a business than men (the other is Japan). Moreover, women in Peru own and operate a significantly higher percentage of businesses (38.5 per cent of all enterprises) than do women in other Latin American countries. However, a growing body of research suggests that this entrepreneurship potential is constrained by low levels of business capacity.

In one-on-one interviews and focus group discussions, Peruvian women microentrepreneurs recently told a research team from Harvard University that they need training on a variety of basic business management issues, such as setting prices, stabilizing costs, separating personal from business finances, conducting market research, and improving customer service. Most of them sought to expand their businesses, but felt lost about how to determine the amount they could afford to take out in loans, the revenue they needed to pull in to make a profit, and the amount they needed to reinvest. The research results are informing the design of the Strengthening Women Entrepreneurship in Peru (SWEP) project, which has two components, each targeting a distinct group of women.

The first component, called "Proyecto Salta" (*salta* means jump in Spanish), is a large-scale, country-wide training programme focused on women microentrepreneurs. It includes seminars, mentoring, and other resources to help 100,000 women microentrepreneurs grow their businesses. Training sessions are held in urban and rural locations, and stress practical methods for improving business processes, building self-esteem, and getting access to resources.

The second component is part of the Goldman Sachs 10,000 Women programme, a business certificate programme for women small business owners. The purpose of this programme is to provide 700 women with access to advanced business education, international networks, mentoring, and capital. Women receive extensive classroom instruction conducted by the Universidad del Pacifíco in Lima and other cities in Peru. In addition to classroom time, the women receive personal business mentoring by Peruvian and international women executives.

Source: Adapted from Downing and Murphy, 2010, and Thunderbird School for Global Management, 2010.

the most prevalent strategies being adopted by upscaling MFIs and downscaling banks to overcome the challenges discussed in Section 21.3. They are: placing more emphasis on cash flow analysis, using credit scoring to help streamline the decision-making process, renovating the organizational architecture, drawing from microfinance best practice in the area of relationship lending, making use of alternative credit instruments, balancing standardization and customization, cross-selling, and partnering.

Focusing Analysis on Capacity

The creditworthiness of any borrower is generally assessed through an analysis of the "5 Cs": character, capacity, capital, collateral and conditions.[52] All five factors are important, but the emphasis placed on each varies with the type of loan being requested. Microenterprise lending focuses primarily on character, while mortgage lending focuses heavily on collateral. SME lenders have been successful by making capacity the highest priority for analysis.

In microlending, the analysis of a client's character outweighs other factors, because loan amounts are small and clients' demand for credit is great. Borrowers strive to repay loans even if things go wrong in their business, because they want to maintain their access to credit. They often rely on other sources of income to repay their loans, which may have been used to smooth household cash flows and not to invest in a business. In SME lending, larger loan sizes make character a necessary but insufficient screening criterion. No matter how much borrowers may want to pay, they are much more likely to not be able to pay if their investment in the business does not generate sufficient cash flow to service the loan.

Since many SMEs lack attractive, registered collateral and work in environments where collateral seizure is both time consuming and expensive in relation to the average SME loan size, lenders prefer not to rely heavily on collateral guarantees to ensure their loans get repaid. Instead, they focus on assessing the business's capacity to generate cash flow, both now and in the future.

Microloans also require some analysis of cash flows and business needs; however, the analysis is simpler, and focuses on the ability of a business to generate cash in the short term. Recognizing that most microborrowers do not separate their business and household finances, MFIs tend to mitigate the risk that borrowers will not invest their loan fully in their business by assessing current cash flow only, and do not take into account the additional income that might be generated if the loan is invested in the business.

In SME lending, cash flow analysis is more sophisticated, and forecast over a longer period. A term loan for equipment, for instance, may require a monthly cash flow analysis for at least two years and then annually for the remainder of the loan term (Hsu, 2009). This need to project cash flows into the future makes the assessment of business conditions more important in SME lending than in microlending. Upscaling MFIs pay more attention to the size of an SME's market and market share, its business strategy, its relationships with other actors in its value chain, its management and organization, and the sensitivity of its cash flows to potential external threats.

52 This analysis is discussed in more detail in the first volume of the *Making Microfinance Work* series. Refer to Churchill and Frankiewicz (2006).

For downscaling banks, the challenge is to match the sophistication of financial analysis to the size of loan requested. Such financial institutions have the skills and the tools to conduct a detailed assessment of an SME's capacity, but these assessments will usually be too expensive to be covered by the revenue that the loan might generate, especially if the SME's financial statements are either non-existent or unreliable. Instead, SME lenders focus their loan analysis on cash pressure points. For example:

- Will sales go up as projected?
- How quickly are accounts receivables collected?
- What are the long-term cash drivers of the business (for instance, gross margin, operating expenses as a percentage of sales), and how does the performance of this business compare with that of competitors and industry benchmarks?

SME lenders often develop their loan officers' ability to work with clients to complete a simplified income or cash flow statement template jointly with the borrower when audited financials are not available. They may analyse deposit and withdrawal patterns in the business's current account or mobile wallet. Some institutions develop guidelines on acceptable performance so that loan officers can quickly determine whether a potential borrower is a viable client (Sia and Nails, 2008). At the Kazakhstan Small Business Programme, loan officers are trained to insist on inspecting firms' parallel internal books and to use those accounts, together with their own calculations of sales figures, to arrive at a realistic assessment of capacity to repay the loan (Malhotra et al., 2006).

Since cash flow projections are critical to assessing repayment capacity and structuring appropriate financing for SMEs, financial institutions invest considerably in training loan officers to develop and analyse financial projections. This training goes beyond the simple calculation of ratios, and explores how to understand a business through its financial statements. Mentoring programmes are often put in place so that more experienced loan officers can assist junior officers in developing their analysis skills.

Credit Scoring[53]

Credit scoring is a mathematical technique that uses historic credit data to predict a future outcome, typically the probability of a potential client defaulting. More commonly used in retail/consumer credit, the methodology has been adapted successfully by institutions such as Wells Fargo in the United States (see Box 21.4) to objectively measure risk and establish the credit worthiness of SMEs using a minimum of data that can be easily validated.

Instead of conducting extensive analysis of financial statements, credit scoring uses a combination of simple predictive variables, such as length of time in business, nature of business, length of time with the financial institution, and so on, to generate a score that represents the probability of future repayment. While it is unlikely that SME lenders would rely solely on a credit score to make a lending decision, credit-scoring models can be effectively used as a pre-screening tool to identify which loan applications should be investigated more thoroughly and which can be rejected without investing in more detailed analysis. Credit scoring can actually improve the overall quality of lending decisions in environments where experienced credit

53 This section is adapted from IFC (2010) and Caire (2004).

Box 21.4 Credit-scoring SMEs at Wells Fargo

Wells Fargo, founded in 1852, is the largest SME bank in the United States in terms of total dollar volume. By 2004, it had a US$6.3 billion outstanding SME loan portfolio, of which 94 per cent was unsecured. The average loan balance is US$15,000, and median deposits are US$7,000. Wells Fargo manages SME credit risk through a total portfolio approach instead of the more traditional individual loan approach, making use of statistical methods that tolerate losses similar to consumer lending. Automation is a key to its efficient cost management and fast customer response: credit reports and scoring, a large percentage of credit decisions, and customer communication are automated.

The bank has developed a robust credit-scoring system for its small business lending. It collects an extensive range of data, and uses a scorecard for loan origination that includes elements such as number of years in business, years as a bank customer, credit history of the business owner or owners, average bank deposit balance, business location, financial assets, and liabilities of the owner or owners. Its dedicated SME Business Direct division obtains approximately 100 pieces of information from consumer credit bureaus every month on every customer, including their credit score, number of accounts, and open commitments. Business Direct also employs statistical models for targeted marketing to attract low-risk small business borrowers, for customer management, and for loan collection. Ongoing assessments of the risks of each account are conducted and necessary actions are taken at the first sign of trouble. Pricing is increased for risky behaviours such as frequent delinquency and over-limit. At the same time, automatic or conditional line increases are granted for good customers.

Use of the credit-scoring model enables Wells Fargo to accept loan applications by mail or telephone. No collateral, financial statements or tax returns are required. Two-thirds of all decisions are made automatically, based on the scorecard, and the remaining one-third through 15-minute reviews. As a result, Wells Fargo's costs for processing small business loans of US$30 per loan are among the lowest in the industry.

Source: Adapted from Malhotra et al., 2006, and IFC, 2010.

analysts are hard to find or afford. As such, it can play an important role in reducing the average time to process applications and therefore the cost of client acquisition, two key factors that deter lenders from serving the SME market.

However, the methodology has its limitations, not the least of which is the availability of historical data from which to build the models. Most lenders are unlikely to have sufficient portfolio data, in particular the requisite number of bad accounts, for the model-building process to be statistically reliable. In these circumstances, one option is to use a generic model that has been proven to work in a similar environment, and then fine-tune the variables and points allocation over time in the light of experience.

Another option is to create a judgemental scorecard. This kind of scorecard uses a mathematical model based on an institution's credit policy, market knowledge and risk preferences. It can be created without any historical data, so it can even be applied to new segments. A very simple judgemental scorecard might be a checklist of minimum criteria a potential borrower must meet, while a more sophisticated card would combine and weight all key underwriting criteria such that scorecard decisions generally agree with those made by credit officers. An example of a simple variable weighted judgemental scorecard is provided in Table 21.3.

Table 21.3 Simple variable weighted judgemental scorecard

Variable	Scoring		
1. Loan to collateral value	> 70%	50– 0%	< 50%
	0	1	2
2. Annual turnover to loan value	< 3×	3–5×	> 5×
	0	1	2
3. Years in business	< 1	2–4	> 4
	–2	1	2
4. Current ratio	< 0.5	0.5–1	> 1
	0	1	2
5. Total assets	< 100,000	100,000 – 500,000	> 500,000
	0	1	2

Source: Caire, 2004.

Because judgemental scorecards rely more on human expertise and organizational knowledge than on statistical relationships, building them usually requires more time and input from senior management. Since they are not statistically reliable, they are used primarily as a screening device, to channel potential SME clients into different categories of follow-up, and not as the sole basis for a credit decision (see, for example, the case of BRI in Box 21.5).

Drawing from Microfinance Best Practice in Relationship Lending[54]

According to Malhotra et al. (2006), the key characteristic cutting across developing-country commercial banks that apply microfinance principles to SME finance is that they have

Box 21.5 Credit Scoring at Bank Rakyat Indonesia (BRI)

BRI subjects all small loan applications to an internally developed credit scorecard. However, unlike the credit-scoring system used in more advanced environments, BRI's credit scorecard is not used as a credit decision-making tool in lieu of the conventional financial analysis, but essentially as a credit-screening tool. The credit scorecard has a number of predetermined attributes against which a specific score is tabulated. The specific attributes are not weighted according to their relative importance. The scoring system considers both non-financial and financial factors on a 54 per cent to 46 per cent basis. The total score determines how the credit evaluation is to proceed. A range of scores is assigned a certain colour: white, black or grey. Accounts whose aggregate score results in a "white" category are considered good, and can therefore be processed by the credit officer proposing the loan. If the total score lands within a "grey" range, processing can continue, but must be done by a higher group of analysts and not by the proposing credit officer. Those falling in the "black" category will not be processed further.

Source: Sia and Nails, 2008.

[54] This section was adapted from Sia and Nails (2008).

focused on relationship-intensive banking rather than more traditional transactions banking. The relationship lending model is based on qualitative information, with an emphasis on the character and reliability of business owners gathered from informal sources such as suppliers and community leaders, whereas the transactions lending approach is based primarily on hard quantitative data that can be observed and verified.

Some of the practices demonstrated in microfinance that have been applied successfully to serve SMEs are:

- Financing smaller, shorter-term needs first and then offering larger amounts and longer terms for well-performing borrowers. Although this approach limits financial institutions' ability to meet SMEs' needs early on, it can facilitate the establishment of a relationship that becomes more productive over time.
- Developing simplified and standardized operating procedures with accompanying guidelines on standard times for completion. This might include a checklist of required documents to minimize the possibility of errors, disbursing loans into borrowers' bank accounts, or recording standardized procedures in operating manuals.
- Streamlining the underwriting process so that it focuses on the most important elements of small business evaluation, such as the first form of repayment (cash flow), the second form of repayment (collateral or guarantors), character analysis, and a site visit.
- Using technology to avoid repetitive steps in the processing of transactions, and to monitor risk by sector, type of business, and geographic area. This becomes even more important in SME lending than in microlending, owing to the increased exposure to portfolio concentration risk.
- Conducting personal as well as professional character assessments. On a personal basis, loan officers might visit the borrower's residence, or cross-check with community leaders and neighbours to assess the borrower's standing. On a professional basis, they might verify a borrower's relationships with suppliers (for example, the volume of purchases, payment habits, the length of the relationship), or even employees. In instances where the place of business is rented, the lease payment history of the borrower can also be verified.
- Monitoring loans through monthly site visits that build an ongoing relationship with borrowers, and assess changes in their internal and external conditions.

Renovating the Organizational Architecture

When banks approach SMEs, they tend to do so through a dedicated small business unit. Institutions such as BRI, BRAC Bank, Inecobank (Armenia), SOA Kredit and K-Rep Bank take this approach and find that it allows them to design tailored policies and guidelines, portfolio management tools, marketing strategies and staff training (Sia and Nails, 2008). They also tend to divide staff by specialization, so that client officers are responsible for marketing and managing the client relationship, while credit analysts take primary responsibility for managing risk (see Figure 21.3). Credit analysts often work cooperatively with client officers to raise their risk awareness so that loan applications have a higher likelihood of not being rejected later on in the process (IFC, 2010).

Figure 21.3 Risk management practices of banks serving SMEs

Percentage
90
80
70
60
50
40
30
20
10
0

40 0 Largely automated
40 83 Done by risk credit analyst
80 83 Separate from sales
75 67 Done primarlly at headquarters

Developed countries
Developing countries

Source: IFC, 2010.

Some larger institutions have created business centres that service various branches within a geographic area. This helps them reduce costs by centralizing some functions that are subject to economies of scale, such as back-office functions. The account manager in a branch reaches out to new SMEs and manages the ongoing relationship.

Smaller institutions, poverty-focused organizations and institutions that do not serve a wide spectrum of business enterprises tend not to have separate units exclusively for small business lending. In Pakistan, Asasah experimented with specialized small enterprise lending officers, but then decided to keep its approach simple enough for existing staff to handle. Afghanistan Rural Microfinance Programme (ARMP) plans to hire separate loan officers when it begins making loans above US$3,000, but will not create a separate unit to manage them (Chen and Weiss, 2007).

For institutions that are interested primarily in serving graduating microenterprise clients, this approach might be strategic, because it takes advantage of existing staff's knowledge and client relationships. However, for it to be successful, staff must be well trained to manage both types of lending, and avoid confusion between the two. Some ProCredit banks involve higher-level staff (a credit manager or experienced client relationship manager) early in the SME loan origination process rather than rely on loan officers to manage the complete loan cycle as they do for microloans. This lets the bank set the tone with the client, and gives support to the loan officer (McDonald, 2009).

Alternative Credit Instruments

The risks and costs of traditional SME lending have led some financial institutions to explore other types of contract that can make lending to small and medium enterprises viable, namely leasing, factoring and credit guarantee schemes. Discussed in detail in Chapter 10, **leasing** can provide SMEs with access to long-term finance for investment in capital equipment. It reduces a financial institution's risk, because the leased asset itself serves as collateral.

Factoring provides a source of working capital finance for SMEs. In a factoring transaction, an SME sells its creditworthy accounts receivable at a discount to a financial intermediary

(referred to as "the factor") and receives immediate cash (see Box 21.6). The SME benefits from transferring and prematurely cashing invoices that may not be payable for another month or more. The financial intermediary, besides getting a service fee, is able to face the credit risk of the buyer rather than the seller. Since the seller is often a higher-risk small firm while the buyer is a larger enterprise that is more likely to have a reputable credit history and audited financial statements, factoring can be a risk-containing strategy for a financial institution (Bebczuk, 2009).

Credit guarantee schemes are arrangements under which a third party commits to partially or totally cover a lender's losses in the event that a borrower defaults. The guarantor can be a public or private entity. Credit guarantee schemes can serve as a substitute for collateral, and enable financial institutions to lend more or for longer terms than they would be willing to otherwise. Unfortunately, many guarantee schemes have had poor results in the past. This is due to several reasons, namely banks becoming lax in monitoring the SME portfolio because of the overly comfortable safety cushion of the guarantee, and lack of assurance of the financial sustainability of the guarantee funds (Malhotra et al., 2006). Table 21.4 summarizes two public schemes that are currently seen as promising. Both have low net loss rates, and have demonstrated the ability to facilitate access to financing for SMEs that would not have had it otherwise. Major microfinance networks such as ACCION International and Women's World Banking have also provided successful credit guarantee funds to their member institutions, although these were not specifically focused on SME lending.

Box 21.6 Nacional Financiera's Factoring Programme

Nacional Financiera (NAFIN), a state-owned development bank in Mexico with 32 branch offices nationwide, developed a so-called productive chains programme to link large, creditworthy buyer firms with small, risky firms unable to access formal finance. Participating in the factoring programme are 190 big buyers and more than 70,000 SME suppliers. Twenty domestic banks and finance companies act as the factors.

The NAFIN factoring programme operates an electronic platform that provides factoring services online. The web site has a dedicated page for each big buyer, and small suppliers are grouped into chains with the big buyers with whom they have business relationships. The suppliers and NAFIN sign an agreement allowing the electronic sale and transfer of receivables. Once a supplier delivers goods and its invoice to the buyer, the buyer posts a negotiable document equal to the amount that will be factored on its NAFIN web page. In general, this is equal to 100 per cent of the value of the receivable. The supplier is then able to access its buyer's NAFIN web page and see all factors that are willing to factor this particular receivable, along with their quotes for interest rates. Picking the one it deems has the most favourable terms, the supplier clicks on the name of the factor, and the amount of the negotiable document less interest is transferred to the supplier's bank account. When the invoice is due, the buyer pays the factor directly. The efficiency of the electronic platform means that small suppliers typically have money within one business day. NAFIN is spreading this model into Venezuela, and possibly into other Latin American countries as well, in the near future.

Source: Malhotra et al., 2006.

Table 21.4 Two examples of partial credit guarantees

	FOGAPE	Small Business Financing Programme
Country	Chile	Canada
Outreach (per year)	30,000 guarantees issued (1,800 per million people)	10,000 guarantees issued (300 per million people)
Sustainability	Net loss rate = 1.5%	Net loss rate = 3%
Additionality	Increases probability for firms to get credit by 14 percentage points	74% of firms using the guarantee would not have been able to get a loan otherwise
Design	• Targeted to small firms (low ceilings) • Portfolio approach • Variable coverage ratio (70–80%), higher for investment loans • Unique bidding procedure • Reasonable risk-based fees (1–2%), depending on default rates	• Targeted to small firms (low ceilings) • Investment loans • Portfolio approach • Lower coverage ratio for larger loans (maximum 85% of eligible loss) • Reasonable fees (2%) • Strict payment rules

Source: IFC, 2010.

Balancing Standardization and Customization

Since tailoring is important yet expensive, SME lenders tend to offer a mix of standardization and customization. They do this in several different ways. First, they offer some products that are tailored to individual SME needs, and others that are standardized. Second, they give more importance to tailoring as the size of the firm, and the size of the financing requested, increase. Third, they design products that are tailored to SMEs with similar needs, such as fishing companies or agricultural producers. Individual SMEs perceive these products as being tailored to their specific needs, even though they are frequently the same product with some degree of customization. Fourth, loan products are priced on a client-by-client basis, but a grid with ranges of interest rates for clients of similar risk profiles guides the pricing decision. Finally, account managers act as the personalized point of contact. Even if they deliver mostly generic products, they select a combination of products that can collectively meet SME needs.

Cross-selling

Financial institutions that serve SMEs effectively rarely focus on the provision of credit alone. They cross-sell their clients a variety of products and services, such as deposit accounts, investment products, factoring, leasing and international trade financing, among others. A recent report by the IFC (2010) presented research results which indicate that banks offer their SME clients an average of five to ten different deposit products, nine to 18 credit products and seven to 16 transactional products (see Table 21.5). SMEs purchase several of these products, in different categories, and their use of deposit, account management and other

Table 21.5 Products used by SMEs and revenue generated

	Developed countries	Developing countries
Average number of products offered to SMEs		
Deposit products	5.3	10.6
Credit products	9.4	18.7
Transactional products	7.7	16.9
Number of products used per SME client		
Deposit products	2.7	2.3
Credit products	3.3	2.4
Breakdown of revenue from SME segment by product type (% of revenue)*		
Credit	32	38
Deposit and account management	42	29
Other	24	32

Source: IFC, 2010.

financial services generates significantly more revenue than their use of credit. Clearly, by diversifying the product portfolio and cross-selling a useful mix of services, financial institutions can increase the profitability of the SME market segment.

Partnerships

Providing linkages to other sources of financial or non-financial services is often a more efficient and effective strategy for helping SMEs meet their varied needs than trying to meet all of those needs alone. For example, an MFI's term loan can be complemented by short-term trade credit from business suppliers, or its working capital loan might be complemented by a leasing product from a leasing company. If an MFI faces financial constraints, it can negotiate a service agreement with a bank through which the bank provides financing and the MFI manages the client relationship and loan monitoring. An MFI might also negotiate with a government agency, donor organization or association network to access a guarantee mechanism that would enable the MFI to offer SMEs longer-term loans.

Financial institutions can seek out partners that are willing to transfer knowledge or skills that are needed to enter the SME market or develop new products to meet their needs. Most of the banks profiled by Malholtra et al. (2006) received high-quality technical assistance from expert practitioners that allowed them to build their successful SME finance businesses. Peer learning and knowledge exchange networks such as the one launched by CapitalPlus Exchange Corporation in Ethiopia (see Box 21.7) provide additional opportunities to collaborate with others to serve SMEs better.

As discussed in Chapter 22, the options for partnership are nearly endless, but two others are important to mention in the context of SME finance. First, financial institutions can enter into

Box 21.7 Global Network Aims to Serve Small Businesses

The Small Business Banking Network (SBBN) is an initiative of CapitalPlus Exchange Corporation (Exchange). Founded and launched on 1 November 2010 in Addis Ababa, Ethiopia, SBBN is the world's first global network for leaders and senior executives of financial institutions committed to serving the small business market in emerging economies. It relies upon an interactive online community and international forums, combined with on-site capacity-building to advance the effectiveness of small business banking operations. The initiative builds on Exchange's seven years of experience using peer learning and knowledge exchange networks to develop the capacity of its partner banks. The SBBN's advisory board includes CEOs and senior managers who represent the following leading banks: Equity Bank (Kenya), BRAC Bank (Bangladesh), Planters Development Bank (Philippines), Diamond Bank (Nigeria) and Standard Bank (South Africa). For more information, refer to: http://shorecapexchange.stage.smallworldlabs.com/about.

Source: CapitalPlus Exchange Corporation, 2010.

partnerships with other financial institutions, with industry associations, or with civic organizations to lobby for changes in the enabling environment for SME lending, such as improved credit bureaus, asset registries, or laws permitting the collateralization of movable assets. Second, they can partner with non-financial service providers to facilitate SME access to training, technical assistance, mentoring and other support services that can strengthen their management skills and enhance their capacity to make effective use of financial services.

21.6 Conclusion

SME finance constitutes an attractive market segment for financial institutions that make a strategic decision to invest in the institutional changes that are necessary to serve the market effectively. New methodologies, skills, incentive systems, attitudes and financing may be necessary, but the benefits of investing in this segment can far outweigh the costs. SME finance, particularly when complemented by appropriate business advice, can alleviate growth constraints and enable SMEs to create more jobs, develop local markets and stimulate innovation, while also generating revenue for lending institutions.

To fill the SME finance gap, institutions must find a way to serve small and medium enterprises at an acceptable cost and level of risk. This is challenging, but pioneering banks and MFIs are demonstrating that it is possible, through adjustments in credit analysis, streamlined processes and organizational restructuring, credit scoring, the standardization of customizable products, alternative credit instruments, cross-selling and partnerships.

For MFIs, targeting SMEs will increase staff and management requirements and add complexity to institutions' operational systems, but this can be a positive challenge. MFIs can upgrade their systems, improve their qualifications and strengthen their financial and client relationship management, while opening up a new market segment with large and growing needs.

Main Messages

1. By investing in SMEs, MFIs can fuel job creation, innovation and local economic development.
2. SMEs need access to a broad portfolio of financial products, just as micro and large enterprises do.
3. In SME lending, the purpose of the loan should determine its repayment source and loan structure.
4. SMEs typically need a combination of capital to grow and access to capacity-building opportunities.
5. SME lenders must match the sophistication of financial analysis to the size of loan requested.

Case Study: SME Lending at ProCredit Bank Mozambique

ProCredit Mozambique is a part of ProCredit Holding,[55] which currently has 22 banks in different countries in Eastern Europe, Latin America and Africa. In Mozambique, ProCredit is registered as a commercial bank and is the largest of the four commercial banks dedicated to microfinance. It currently has 21 branches in seven of Mozambique's 11 provinces with a total of 626 employees, out of which 72 per cent are located in the branches. By June 2010, ProCredit had 24,957 loan clients, 137,399 depositors and a credit portfolio of US$ 28,488,322.

From its inception in the year 2000, ProCredit Mozambique has been continuously developing products. At present, the bank offers a wide range of products, including current accounts, term deposits, savings accounts, business loans, home improvement loans, agricultural loans, domestic and international wire transfers, overdraft facilities, bank guarantees and e-banking.

SME Loan

ProCredit's SME loan is a type of business loan. What distinguishes it from other business loans is primarily the amount, which starts at US$30,000. However, there are other fundamental differences: the terms are longer (up to five years); there is a three-month grace period; the interest rate is lower, and it is negotiable, depending upon the perceived risk involved. It can be as low as 2 per cent per month,[56] whereas microloans can be provided at a rate of 6.5 per cent, depending on the loan amount (the lower the amount, the higher interest rate). Additionally, SMEs are required to provide financial statements and proof of revenues and/or expenses.

55 http://www.procredit-holding.com and http://www.bancoprocredit.co.mz

56 Interest rates for other commercial banks not dedicated to microfinance are between 20 and 22 per cent per annum, the equivalent of 1.7–1.8 per cent per month.

Drivers for the Introduction of an SME Loan

The decision to introduce an SME loan product was taken in 2007 – in other words, after seven years of operation in the Mozambican market. This decision was based on microcredit clients' feedback related to the need for larger loans to finance their business growth. It was also based on a careful analysis of internal and external secondary sources of information. An analysis of the portfolio revealed that the pace of growth was slowing down, suggesting the need for product development. At the same time, ProCredit realized that there was a market segment that was not being served – neither by other MFIs, which were providing relatively smaller loans than ProCredit, nor by banks, which tend to serve medium to large companies that can satisfy bank requirements for collateral, financial statements, business plans, and so on. Another driver for the development of an SME loan was the fact that competition among MFIs, mainly in the capital city Maputo, was increasing. There was a need to offer a range of products that would increase clients' loyalty to the institution.

SME Loan Product Development and Implementation

ProCredit Mozambique does not have a product development department, so products are developed by their respective areas – in other words, banking services, cards, payments, and so on. Instead of developing a new product from scratch, ProCredit decided to bring in an internal consultant who had been involved in SME product development for ProCredit affiliates in other countries. By doing so, it was able to benefit from lessons learned by other members. This was facilitated by the fact that all network members used the same information technology (IT) platform.

The consultant, in close collaboration with the marketing, IT and legal departments, and after some consultation with potential clients, developed a product for the Mozambican context. An SME coordinator was nominated, and over the course of a year the consultant conducted a specific training programme for the team that dealt with the SME loan product and performance monitoring. At the beginning, the product was offered only in Maputo, in a branch that was established to serve SME clients exclusively, to which staff were recruited internally and externally. Training on the product methodology and SME loan assessment was delivered by in-house trainers. As a general rule, ProCredit uses only trainers from its internal network, because it considers training events to be an important opportunity to reinforce institutional values and culture.

As the main vehicle for marketing the product, ProCredit sent letters to several SMEs that were identified through an official SME database published by the Mozambican government's national institute of statistics. It believed that for this segment direct marketing would be much more effective than other sales strategies.

About 18 months later, the product was gradually expanded to other provinces, not only because clients were demanding a similar product but also because it is ProCredit's philosophy to offer the same package of products in different locations where it operates. Again, selected branch staff were recruited internally and externally and trained to deliver the product.

Over the years, ProCredit has introduced small modifications to the product based on client feedback. The feedback is obtained during frontline staff interaction with clients, and during meetings that branch managers and product managers hold regularly with clients. Some of the refinements that were made include the reduction of paperwork and lowering of the interest rate; at the moment, the bank is considering extending the term up to ten years. Apart from the SME loan, other products and services have been introduced to benefit SME clients, namely guarantee letters, an overdraft facility, wire transfers, and e-banking.

The Results

As of June 2010, the SME loan accounted for approximately 38 per cent of ProCredit's portfolio. Due to the success of this product, the bank decided to increase its focus on the SME market and, in February 2010, it increased its minimum loan amount to US$1,000.

This case study was adapted from Hunguana, 2010, with information provided by ProCredit Bank Mozambique.

Recommended Reading

- Caire, D. 2004. *Building credit scorecards for small business lending in developing markets* (London, Bannock Consulting), at: www.microfinance.com/English/Papers/Scoring_SMEs_Hybrid.pdf
- Doran, A.; McFadyen, N.; Vogel, R. 2009. *The missing middle in agricultural finance: Relieving the capital constraint on smallholder groups and other agricultural SMEs* (Oxford, Oxfam), at: http://www.oxfam.org.uk/resources/policy/trade/downloads/research_agricultural_finance.pdf
- International Finance Corporation (IFC). 2010. *Scaling-up SME access to financial services in the developing world*, Financial Inclusion Experts Group, SME Finance Sub-Group (Washington, DC, IFC), at: http://www.ifc.org/ifcext/media.nsf/Content/SMEFinancialAccessReport_Nov2010
- Malhotra, M.; Chen, Y.; Criscuolo, A.; Fan, Q.; Hamel, I.; Savchenko, Y. 2006. *Expanding access to finance: Good practices and policies for micro, small, and medium enterprises* (Washington, DC, World Bank), at: http://info.worldbank.org/etools/docs/library/236032/SMEAccessToFinance_Final_083106.pdf
- Sanders, T.; Wegener, C. 2006. *Meso-finance: Filling the financial service gap for small businesses in developing countries* (Amsterdam, NCDO), at: www.bidnetwork.org/download.php?id=40005
- Sia, M.; Nails, D. 2008. *Winning strategies for successful small business lending*, Exchanging Views Series #6 (Chicago, ShoreCap Exchange), at: http://www.microfinancegateway.org/p/site/m//template.rc/1.9.31173
- USAID. 2009. *Lending at the intersection of micro and SME finance: Compilation document* (Washington, DC, USAID), at: www.microlinks.org/sc/micro2SMEfinance

As of June 2010, the SME [illegible] approximately [illegible] per cent of [illegible] [illegible]. Due to [illegible] [illegible] the [illegible] [illegible] [illegible] 2010 [illegible] [illegible] [illegible] US$1,000 [illegible]

[illegible]

Recommended Reading

[illegible] (2004) [illegible] [illegible] (London: [illegible])

[illegible]

[illegible]

[illegible]

[illegible]

[illegible] http://[illegible]

[illegible]

[illegible]

[illegible]

[illegible]

IV

Diversifying Successfully

Part IV: Diversifying Successfully

The last three chapters of this book return to the management agenda that was introduced in Chapters 1, 2 and 3. How can the opportunities and risks of diversification be managed so as to generate maximum value for MFIs and their clients?

Drawing from microfinance as well as mainstream business management literature, Chapters 22 to 24 tackle the principal implementation challenges that MFIs face as they attempt to offer a more diverse mix of products in a greater variety of markets. Chapter 22 focuses on partnership management. Chapter 23 tackles cultural, staffing, motivation, communication, systems and change management issues. Chapter 24 explores how product portfolio management can help MFIs focus their diversification so that it supports their mission and objectives in an optimal manner. Together, these three chapters aim to demonstrate how proactive, ongoing management of the diversification process can enable MFIs to achieve greater outreach.

IV Diversifying Successfully

22 Building and Managing Partnerships

The choice of… with whom to make alliances… is among the most important that any firm ever makes…. Collaborative ventures are partly defensive innovations in that they are aimed at reducing or sharing risks and costs. They are also offensive innovations in that they extend the skill base of the firm and the range of knowledge available to it and thereby improve its ability to compete. Because specialist knowledge is produced, collaboration can be a source of sustained competitive advantage because it is difficult to imitate. ~ *Robinson et al. (2000)*

Partnerships have been referred to frequently in this book as a strategy for overcoming an MFI's constraints and weaknesses as well as an opportunity for expanding outreach. The enthusiasm surrounding partnerships as a business strategy is not unique to microfinance. In 2006, Pricewaterhouse Coopers interviewed leaders of 339 of the fastest-growing companies in the United States and found that 57 per cent considered alliances, including joint ventures and contractual partnerships, to be somewhat (30 per cent) or very (27 per cent) important for reaching their business objectives. Thirty-seven per cent believed that such alliances would be very important in the next three years (Pricewaterhouse Coopers, 2006). According to Dyer et al. (2001), the top 500 global businesses have an average of 60 major strategic alliances each.

Attractive as partnerships may be, building and managing them effectively is not necessarily easy. This chapter will explore the different types of partnership currently being used in microfinance, and analyse what makes those partnerships worthwhile. It will also draw from the experiences of financial as well as non-financial institutions to identify techniques for negotiating and maintaining effective partnerships. It will focus on the following five themes:

1. Defining partnership
2. Benefits and risks of partnership
3. The partnering process
4. Partnership agreements
5. Communicating for success

22.1 Defining Partnership

The word "partnership" describes a range of different relationships. It is often used interchangeably with terms such as alliance, collaboration or linkage. In microfinance, it is also frequently used to describe commercial and contractual relationships that fail to meet the criteria of most definitions of partnership. This is problematic, because MFIs and their partners sometimes make assumptions about their relationship based on differing interpretations of "partnership", which later result in miscommunication or conflict. Thus one of the first steps that MFIs can take to build an effective partnership is to ensure that all parties have a clear understanding of the nature of the relationship into which they are entering (Bedson, 2008).

Dictionaries define **partnership** in two main ways: 1) as a legal relationship between two or more persons contractually associated as joint principals in a business; and 2) as a cooperative relationship between people or groups who agree to share responsibility for achieving some

specific goal.[57] MFIs work with a wide variety of organizations (see Table 22.1) to meet their objectives, and many of these relationships can be classified as partnerships according to the second definition. For example:

- **Referrals and endorsements.** One partner provides information about another which allows clients to become familiar with that organization on informal terms. MFIs often use this option to raise awareness about non-financial services that their clients might find useful, for example health care, counselling or business training. As discussed in Chapter 14, some MFIs rely on referrals to identify potential clients in underserved market segments, such as persons living with a disability or HIV/ADIS.
- **Supplier–buyer relationships.** One partner supplies a product or service to another on a preferential basis, or becomes an integral part of the buyer's operation through extensive cooperation. For instance, Financiera El Comercio in Paraguay works with soybean silo owners to reach soybean producers with new financial products linked to the soybean value chain (see Box 22.1).
- **Development partnership.** One partner contributes more resources than it expects to recover through the partnership in exchange for certain developmental outcomes, for instance, women's empowerment or outreach to underserved communities. Essentially, this is a type of supplier-buyer relationship, although it may be that no purchase is made. A partner may provide grants, technical assistance or client services without expecting to generate revenue through the partnership to cover the cost of those contributions.

Table 22.1 Snapshot of MFI partner diversity

Partner type	Examples
Banks	• Constanta in Georgia uses bank infrastructure for loan disbursements and repayments. • BancoSolidario in Ecuador collaborates with commercial banks in Spain to provide remittance services to Ecuadorian migrants in Spain. • AMEEN promotes, evaluates, approves, tracks and collects microenterprise loans for three commercial bank branches in Lebanon.
Other financial service providers	• SEWA and BASIX serve as agents for Unit Trust of India Asset Management Company. • Gatsby Trust and DCLU Leasing in Uganda partnered to increase outreach in rural areas. • Swadhaar FinServe Pvt. Ltd (a non-banking finance company offering microcredit services) collaborates with its sister organization, Swadhaar FinAccess (a non-profit company), to offer clients "credit plus" activities including financial education and savings facilitation as a business correspondent for two banks. • Jamaica Cooperative Credit Union League partnered with a local money transfer company to bundle four foreign money transfer companies into a service under its own proprietary brand. • Polish credit unions work with TUW SKOK to offer a savings completion product. • ICICI Bank partners with more than 27 MFIs to serve self-help groups in India. • CRDB in Tazania serves rural areas by working through rural savings and credit cooperatives (SACCOs).

[57] The definitions in this chapter are taken from Princeton University's WordNet, available at http://wordnet.princeton.edu

Table 22.1 (continued)

Partner type	Examples
Post offices	• Union Bank in Jamaica, Zakoura Foundation in Morocco and Wizzit Payments Ltd in South Africa use post office outlets to offer deposit services.
NGOs	• The private financial fund FIE operates teller windows within the rural branches of the NGO Pro Mujer in Bolivia. • Fundo de Credito Comunitario in Mozambique partnered with non-governmental agencies to provide in-kind grants to clients in the wake of a natural disaster. • In Ghana, Sinapi Aba Trust collaborates with Planned Parenthood to raise awareness about HIV/AIDS and to offer clients confidential testing, health referrals and support. • XacBank worked with the Mongolian Education Alliance to design and deliver financial education curricula for girls.
Educational institutions	• Equity Bank partners with Mayanja Memorial Training Institute to provide education loans in Kenya, and Hatton National Bank works through schools to make financial services available to youth in Sri Lanka.
Information and communication technology companies	• In rural India, financial institutions piggyback onto a network of 800,000 long-distance telephone booths to connect quickly with mobile agents to provide remittance services. • Vodafone and First Microfinance Bank in Afghanistan offer loan disbursements and repayments via a mobile money platform.
Retailers and consumer goods companies	• Caixa Economica Federal offers loan, savings and payment services in all of Brazil's 1,600 municipalities through more than 12,000 agents, 75% of which are lottery ticket outlets and 25% are merchants such as pharmacies or supermarkets. • Fincomun in Mexico partners with the bread company BIMBO to market Fincomun's products among its clients, preselect potential borrowers, and collect loan payments through BIMBO delivery truck drivers. • ACCESS Microfinance Alliance (a loose federation of about 110 NGO MFIs) partners with Hindustan Unilever to sell water filters in India. • SEEDS in Sri Lanka partners with international solar companies to help clients acquire an alternative energy source.
Agribusiness actors	• ICICI Bank partners with input suppliers and buyers to offer credit to farmers in India. • El Comercio and soybean silo owners facilitate credit to soybean farmers in Paraguay.
Apex organizations and federations	• The 27 members of FENACOAC, a federation of savings and credit cooperatives in Guatemala, have access to each other's points of service, jointly developed products, liquidity facilities and technical assistance.
Government agencies	• OIBM in Malawi and Equity Bank in Kenya have partnered with government agencies to facilitate the distribution of public assistance in remote areas.
Funders	• As of December 2010, the MIX Market listed 166 funders providing loans, debt securities, equity investments, grants and/or guarantees to MFIs.

Source: Authors.

Box 22.1 Financiera El Comercio and Paraguayan Silo Owners

El Comercio analysed the soybean value chain to understand the financial relationships among agribusinesses and farmers. It saw an opportunity to leverage the existing contract farming relationships between silos and farmers. Farmers receive a loan in the form of seeds and fertilizer from the silos. When a farmer needs additional cash, the silo refers the farmer to El Comercio. A loan officer from El Comercio visits the farmers and evaluates their credit viability. The farmer signs a traditional credit contract with El Comercio, accepts the loan conditions, and repays after harvest. Collateral for the loan is the contract for the purchase of soybeans with the silo, which acts as a guarantee from the silo. In about one-fourth of the linkages, the silo automatically discounts both the cost of inputs and loan repayment (for the loan to El Comercio) from the sale of the crop when the farmer brings the harvest to the silo. When this occurs, the silo repays El Comercio on behalf of the farmers.

Source: Diaz and Hansel, 2005.

- **Joint research, development or marketing.** Partners may exchange information in the joint development of a product or technology that will be used by one or more partners. Examples include FINCA's partnership with HSBC Mexico (a commercial bank) to offer prepaid bank cards to its clients (refer to the case study at the end of this chapter), and Hewlett-Packard's collaboration with ten public and private sector partners in Uganda, including three MFIs, to create an open source information technology for MFIs.
- **Outsourcing.** One partner transfers a business function to another. This type of relationship is found between CREDIFE and Banco del Pichincha in Ecuador. CREDIFE provides loan origination and credit administration services to Banco del Pichincha, which disburses the loans and records them on its books. When MFIs work as agents for insurance or money transfer companies, the companies typically outsource their sales and payment functions to MFIs, which receive a fee for their services.
- **Franchising.** One partner (as the franchisor) can grant territorial rights for the use of its trademarks and technologies to another partner (as franchisee), which pays a fee to the franchisor. XacBank offers a franchise product to rural credit and savings cooperatives in Mongolia, and ICICI Bank is testing a credit franchisee model with equipment dealers in India (see Box 22.2).
- **Equity investment.** One partner invests in another, thus owning a part of that entity's equity. Telenor Pakistan (a mobile phone operator) acquired 51 per cent of Tameer Microfinance Bank, the MFI with which it collaborates to offer the *easypaisa* branchless banking service (Owens, 2009).
- **Joint venture.** Partners become joint owners of a new legal entity. In Ghana, HFC Bank and CHF International, with assistance from USAID and UN Habitat's Slum Upgrading Facility, created a non-financial service company, Boafo, which services housing loans that are kept on the balance sheet of the bank. HFC acts as a joint venture managing partner and minority shareholder (Hokans, 2008). In Bangladesh, the Grameen Group and Groupe Danone entered into an agreement to form a company called Grameen Danone Foods to supply nutritious food to poor children using a community-based business model. Grameen Bank offers working capital financing; Danone provides technical expertise; and GAIN, an NGO, leads the social marketing efforts (George, 2009).

Box 22.2 Credit Franchisees in India

ICICI Bank and International Development Enterprises-India (IDEI) partnered to develop a franchisee model with irrigation dealers, reducing the cost of lending to farmers and enabling them to purchase drip irrigation. Under the model, irrigation dealers in IDEI's network can become credit franchisees if they work in an area not served by ICICI, and are willing to enter into a risk-sharing arrangement with the bank to provide farmers with access to financial services. Instead of paying a certain sum of money for the right to become a franchisee, dealers make an equity contribution (providing a first loss default guarantee) of at least US$11,000, which they can leverage up to ten times through ICICI to lend to farmers.

Credit franchisees conduct loan appraisal, determine loan sizes, and process, manage and collect loan repayments from farmers. The loans are on the books of ICICI Bank, and the bank trains the credit franchisees in credit appraisal. The loan appraisal process is designed to take two days, and the repayment period varies according to crop cultivation cycles, with a maximum two-year loan term. The interest rate is 14 per cent per year, which includes a 3 per cent margin for franchisees, who decide whether or not to pass the margin on to the farmer. ICICI Bank receives interest income in lieu of royalties or a management fee.

Source: Adapted from Magleby-Lambert, 2006, and Diaz and Hansel, 2007.

These different types of partnership are summarized in Figure 22.1 along a continuum of engagement. Referrals require very little loss of autonomy or control, whereas joint ventures bind partners together fully in pursuit of their joint objective. The partnerships on the left-hand side of the continuum tend to be used for more limited or low-risk collaboration, whereas those on the right-hand side tend to be used for more high-risk, ambitious and typically long-term objectives.

By definition, a partnership must involve shared responsibility for achieving a specific objective. If an MFI purchases property insurance for its own premises, or borrows money from a commercial bank on market terms, it is not entering into a partnership. It is conducting an arm's length transaction to implement its own agenda, and it should not expect any special treatment from the entity that is selling the good or service it is purchasing.

Figure 22.1 Types of partnership by degree of engagement

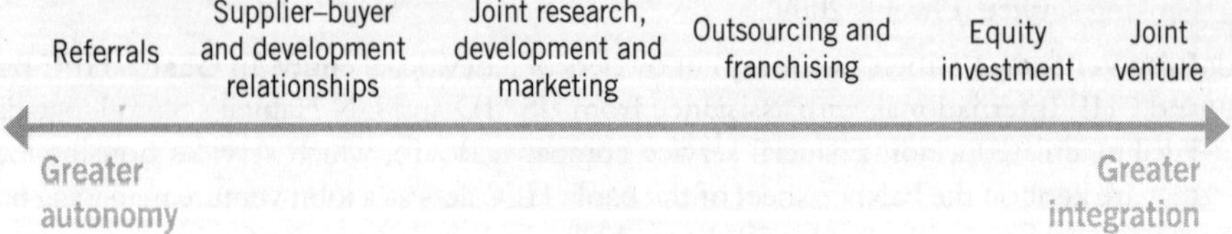

Source: Authors.

If, however, an MFI enters into agreement with a commercial bank to expand the quality or nature of the services provided to clients, this can be considered a partnership. In Guatemala, for instance, the Cooperative for Rural Development of the Western Region (CDRO)'s partnership with Banrural gave it access to additional funds for on-lending, but it also gave CDRO's clients access to safe and convenient savings and payments services through Banrural. Of course, relationships that begin as commercial transactions can develop into more strategic partnerships over time. Tulay Sa Pag-Unlad Development Corporation (TSPI), a Philippine NGO, first obtained small credit lines from local banks, then it negotiated access to larger credit lines and to the banks' ATMs in selected locations, and now it hopes to arrange for its clients to access the banks' savings and money transfer services (Gallardo et al., 2006).

Although partnership can be defined in relatively broad terms, a successful partnership is more difficult to characterize. It requires careful attention to the way responsibility is shared, and to the processes and infrastructure that are put in place to ensure that the objective(s) of the partnership are met. Box 22.3 presents one definition of an idealized microfinance partnership, which provides a useful reference point for this chapter's discussion. Two aspects of the definition are worth highlighting, as they have been identified as characteristics that distinguish partnerships from other types of inter-organizational relationship (Brinkerhoff, 2002):

- **Comparative advantage.** Each partner brings a distinctive feature or capability to the relationship that others can leverage to achieve something they would not have been able to achieve on their own.
- **Mutuality.** The partners in the relationship respect and are accountable to each other, making sure that each one benefits from the relationship.

The remainder of this chapter explores how MFIs can build partnerships that enable them to leverage the strengths of others, and manage those partnerships so as to maximize the potential benefits of the relationship.

Box 22.3 Defining Successful Partnership

An idealized, multi-stakeholder partnership in microfinance can be defined as follows: an alliance among two or more diverse parties – which may include banks, other businesses, public agencies, MFIs, NGOs or community groups – in which partners commit resources to achieve a specific purpose. This purpose would address key challenges that have not successfully been addressed by any one organization acting alone. Partners combine their resources and competences in a complementary and synergistic way, based on what they do best. Partnerships are based on principles of equity and transparency. Importantly, they imply a sharing of both risks and benefits, and achievement of the partnership goals in a way that is mutually beneficial to each of the partners and their clients.

Source: Greener, 2006.

22.2 Benefits and Risks of Partnership

Although the benefits of partnership have been mentioned in different parts of this book, it is worthwhile to summarize them here and to consider them in comparison with the risks of partnership.

Benefits of Partnering

MFIs engage in partnerships for a variety of reasons, namely to reduce risk, to overcome constraints, to speed the pace at which objectives can be achieved, and to expand the scope of what can be accomplished. The major benefits that can be gained through partnership are briefly described below:

- **Risk reduction.** Although partnerships expose an institution to several risks, they can reduce many others. For instance, MFIs can leverage the information, expertise and relationships that partners possess to improve the quality of their loan appraisal, to manage delinquency more effectively, to develop products that meet the needs of different market segments, and to monitor and respond to risks better in the external environment. Partnerships can also help MFIs provide services that enable clients to manage their own risks better .
- **Greater technical capacity.** Partnerships can facilitate an MFI's access to infrastructure or systems, to expertise outside its areas of competence, and to opportunities for transferring knowledge or skills to staff. Chapters 5 and 9, for example, illustrate how MFIs collaborate with insurance companies to access actuarial and asset management expertise, reinsurance, and sales training for staff.
- **Improved efficiency.** By leveraging partners' core competences, MFIs can achieve their objectives faster and/or at a lower cost than if they act alone. For instance, input suppliers and buyers can expedite an MFI's assessment of producers' willingness and capacity to repay loans. Established banks can give MFI clients access to a nationwide network of ATMs and point-of-sale devices much faster than an MFI could build one. Through partnerships, MFIs can "inherit" already-proven products and business processes, thus avoiding the financial and opportunity costs of learning through trial and error.
- **Access to financial resources.** Partners may be able to provide MFIs with additional capital, liquidity or guarantees that they can use to expand outreach beyond what would be possible on their own.
- **More diverse product portfolio.** By capturing some of the above benefits, MFIs may be able to offer products and services through partnerships that they would not be able to offer otherwise. Many MFIs are actually prohibited from providing certain services that their clients need because of their legal status (for example, savings, insurance, remittances). All ten of the chapters in Part II of this book provide examples of partnerships that have enabled MFIs to expand their product portfolio.
- **Regulatory compliance.** Financial service providers that are not able to meet regulatory requirements on their own can sometimes do so through partnerships. This is true not only for MFIs that wish to diversify their product offering, but also for commercial banks in countries such as India which are required to lend at least 40 per cent of their portfolio in the so-called "priority sector", which includes microcredit.

- **Stronger customer relationships.** By enabling MFIs to offer a greater variety of products, more appropriate products, more affordable prices and/or better quality service, partnerships can improve customer satisfaction and contribute to greater customer loyalty.
- **Stronger brand.** A partnership with a well-known and highly regarded partner can enhance an MFI's reputation and increase its visibility in a given market.
- **Outreach to new markets.** Partners can bring clients to an MFI or help an MFI reach out to a new market segment through their infrastructure, credibility, or knowledge of a particular customer group. MFIs may also be able to help partners reach new markets through their distribution systems and customer base.
- **Competitive advantage.** Partnerships can enable MFIs to innovate and do something differently than the competition. Tameer Microfinance Bank's partnership with Telenor Pakistan, for instance, distinguishes it from all other MFIs in Pakistan today.
- **Greater impact.** Partnerships can enable MFIs to contribute in a more holistic way to poverty reduction, economic development and improved quality of life for their clients. They make it possible for all types of financial service provider to offer both productive and protective microfinance services. They can also help clients to access non-financial services that enable them to make better use of financial services, as discussed in Chapters 14 to 17.

Risks of Partnering

Despite the long list of benefits, there are four main challenges that often deter MFIs from entering into partnerships. First, when an MFI enters a partnership, it loses control over the implementation of certain activities and exposes itself to **counterparty risk** – the possibility that the organizations with which the MFI has joined forces might fail to perform in some way that is harmful to the MFI. This can range anywhere from failure to deliver a stationery order on time to engaging in unlawful practices that bring disrepute to the MFI through association. Client relationships can be seriously damaged by a partner that treats clients with disrespect, or provides poor quality service.

Second, it can be difficult for an MFI to estimate the resources required to engage in a successful partnership. Even in a relatively simple relationship involving two partners that work in the same sector and possess similar motivations, it can be hard to predict the cost of building and managing the partnership. The technical requirements of collaboration can be itemized and budgeted for with relative ease, but it is difficult to know how much time it will take to negotiate the partnership, to understand the partner's culture and systems, to maintain effective communication, to resolve differences and misunderstandings, and to jointly take decisions that affect the partnership. When a partnership involves a larger number of organizations with diverse backgrounds or motivations (such as a commercial bank, an NGO and a government safety net programme; or an MFI, retail stores and a technology vendor), the cost and capacity required to build and manage the relationship can easily be underestimated.

Third, it is possible that the people, technical capacity or unique knowledge that one partner brings into the partnership can be used by another partner in a way that impacts negatively on its market share. Either during or after the period of collaboration, partners could become competitors.

Finally, there is the risk that resources will be wasted on an ineffective partnership. Studies indicate that anywhere between 30 and 70 per cent of strategic alliances fail (Reuer, 2004). Assuming that the microfinance industry is no better at managing partnerships than other industries, one-in-three MFI partnerships is unlikely to justify the time and money invested in it. These are intimidating odds, particularly for partnerships that require significant effort and resources.

Managing Partnership Risks

Although the risks described above cannot be eliminated, they can be mitigated, both during the initial formation of a partnership and in the way the relationship is maintained over time. Many of the causes of partnership failure can be avoided through: 1) a systematic partnering process; 2) a clear partnership agreement; and 3) clear communication. These three strategies are discussed in the remaining sections of this chapter.

22.3 The Partnering Process

As with product and market development, partnership development can benefit from a systematic approach. The partnering process, or cycle, has four main phases: 1) exploring; 2) building; 3) managing and maintaining; and 4) evaluating and moving on. It is a cycle because the assessment of an existing partnership may result in a decision to sustain, expand or reformulate the partnership, which would send the parties involved back to a previous phase in the process (see Figure 22.2). Steps that MFIs take in each of these stages can help them maximize the benefits gained through partnership and minimize the risks, as discussed below.

Phase 1: Exploring

In the first phase of the partnering cycle, an institution explores the idea of partnership. It might be approached by a potential partner, or it might consider initiating a partnership itself to capture some of the benefits discussed in Section 22.2. Regardless, its first step should be to assess whether a partnership would support its business strategy cost-effectively and, if so, what type of partnership would likely be most effective. This is the time to explore the partnership options that are legally available, and to become familiar with typical partnership risks and challenges.

An MFI's main activity during this phase is an internal assessment of its operations, capacity, needs and objectives to determine what benefits it wants to seek from a partnership, what characteristics or competences it might want to look for in a partner, and what capabilities it can offer others. It must assess whether it has the resources, skills and commitment to develop a partnership. Do the people who will need to be involved in the partnership have the time to be involved?

Figure 22.2 The partnering cycle

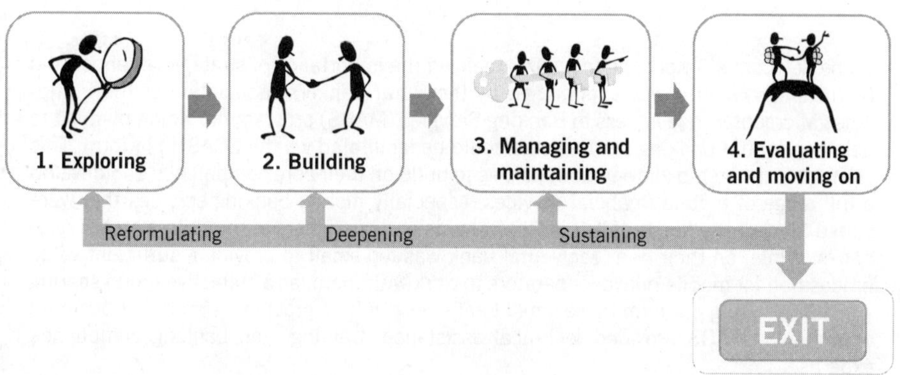

Source: Authors.

MFIs that lack the scale or resources to negotiate a useful partnership might be better off looking for ways to achieve their objectives through the simple purchase of goods or services that can supplement their areas of weakness. For example, where carrier services are available, MFIs can send and receive electronic payments using a standard money transfer service without investing in partnership negotiations with money transfer companies that are unlikely to bring better terms. Both Smart in the Philippines and M-PESA in Kenya now provide a corporate portal as part of their standard business service that would enable MFIs to track payments made into their account, prepare batch payments, and originate bulk SMS alerts (Ketley, 2010).

Alternatively, MFIs can spend time in this first phase looking for additional partners that might be able to strengthen their negotiating position. Third parties are involved in a wide range of microfinance partnerships. Often it is a project or donor that plays the role of partnership broker in the hope of demonstrating the viability of a partnership that can expand microfinance outreach. In the Philippines, the Microenterprise Access to Banking Services (MABS) programme played this role in negotiations between rural banks, Globe Telecom, and the Bangko Sentral ng Pilipinas (Central Bank) to expand rural access to financial services using mobile telephones (see Box 22.4). In Viet Nam, when microfinance was an unknown sector for insurers, the International Labour Organization organized a workshop to bring MFIs and insurance companies together to explore opportunities for collaboration.

Essentially, the first phase of the partnering process explores the business case for partnership. An MFI assesses roughly how it might benefit from a particular type of collaboration, and at what expense and level of risk, and then decides whether it wants to engage potential partners to examine the case in detail. This phase prepares an MFI to enter into negotiations from a confident and fully informed position. If the MFI understands the importance of the proposed partnership to its overall business strategy, and the likely costs and benefits relative to its next best alternative, it will know how much it can give away in the negotiation. It will also know which risk exposures must be controlled and which benefits are non-negotiable. MFIs that skip this step and rush into negotiations with a potential partner put themselves in a weaker negotiating position, and miss out on the first major opportunity to mitigate partnership risk.

Box 22.4 Multi-stakeholder Partnership Carries More Weight in the Philippines

Globe Telecom's G-Xchange Inc. (GXI) realized the importance of strategic alliances and partnerships when it was approached by the Rural Bankers Association of the Philippines Microenterprise Access to Banking Services (MABS) programme, which planned to help banks offer banking services that could be facilitated via the GCASH platform. This strategic partnership allowed both parties to build on their core competence and develop a full range of mobile financial services, especially mobile banking services that were suited to meet the needs of low-income clients and customers of multiple member rural banks. While, on their own, each rural bank was too small to provide a sufficient value proposition for mobile network operators to work with them, as a collective group sharing a mobile banking platform these small banks were able to provide a significant business opportunity. MABS provided technical assistance, training, and banking compliance expertise.

Five rural banks were able to register over 70,000 clients and employees for mobile phone banking services in more than 50 communities. In one small town, the Rural Bank of Cantilan was able to register over 1,200 mobile phone banking clients using the GCASH platform. With a total population of only 26,500 and approximately 6,000 households, the bank was able to help create and establish a fairly widespread mobile payment and mobile phone banking ecosystem that benefited both the bank and GXI.

Source: Adapted from Owens, 2009, and Bedson, 2008.

Phase II: Building

In the second phase of the partnering cycle, institutions select their partners and build their working relationships. There are a number of important activities that take place in this phase, each of which is described below, although not in any particular order, because many activities can be implemented at the same time.

Partner selection. As mentioned above, an MFI might be invited to join a partnership, or it might invite others to partner with it. In both cases, the institution should carefully evaluate not only the idea of partnership, but also with which organization(s) the MFI should partner. This will require a bit of research, to avoid making inaccurate assumptions about potential partners' history, capacity or expectations. An MFI might look at a potential partner's annual reports, browse its web site, request a site visit, or ask others who know the organization for their views. Box 22.5 provides a list of some of the questions institutions can seek the answers to as they assess the attractiveness of a potential partner.

Of all the issues MFIs could pay attention to at this point in the process, the experiences of financial and non-financial institutions that have entered into partnerships suggest that two in particular are worth highlighting: culture and flexibility. Shared values strengthen a partnership. Indeed, there are certain values, such as respect, transparency and mutual benefit, that seem universally important for success. Yet differences in partner values or ways of doing things will not necessarily prevent success; potential partners can still identify mutual objectives and create a shared partnership vision (Bedson, 2008). For instance, a commercial bank seeking to maximize profits can have an effective partnership with a socially oriented

Box 22.5 Assessing Partner Capacity

- **Strategic fit.** Does the potential partner understand the MFI's vision of the partnership? Are its mission and culture compatible with those of the MFI? Does it respect the MFI, even if it is larger or more powerful? Could a partnership with this entity be mutually beneficial?
- **Financial stability.** How stable is the organization? What is its financial performance over the past three years? If it depends on donor subsidies, how constant is its access to donor money? Are its contracts long term?
- **Reputation.** What is the reputation of the potential partner? How is it perceived in the market? How is it perceived by the MFI's staff?
- **Experience.** What are the organization's competence and track record in the area in which the MFI wants to collaborate? Has it worked with clients with characteristics similar to those of the MFI?
- **Flexibility.** Is the organization interested in serving the MFI's market? Is it open to learning about the MFI's clients, and willing to adjust its products/services to their needs?
- **Capacity.** Does the potential partner have the capacity to meet the MFI's needs? How has it demonstrated this capacity? Does it have the resources to meet the MFI's timing and quality requirements?
- **Competition.** Will the partnership be exclusive? Can the organization engage in similar partnerships with the MFI's competitors? What is the organization's market share, and who are its main competitors in the MFI's area?
- **Transparency.** Is the organization forthcoming about answering questions? Does it provide open and honest responses? Does it volunteer additional information as relevant?
- **Partnership history.** Has the organization been successful in partnering with other institutions? What do these organizations have to say about the potential partner?
- **Commitment.** Is there sufficient buy-in from key staff who will be engaged in the partnership? Is there a champion who will provide a focal point for the partnership? Is the organization willing to contribute a comparable amount of resources?

Source: Adapted from Liber and Gommans, 2007, and Green, 2008.

but professional NGO MFI. What is important is for partners to understand their cultural differences, and to make a conscious decision about whether they can work together effectively in spite of those differences.

MFIs that are building relatively high-cost or high-risk partnerships might consider adopting an approach used by the pharmaceutical company Eli Lilly & Co. Lilly integrates a cultural assessment into its standard due diligence process for potential partners. The assessment examines a potential partner's corporate values and expectations, organizational structure, reward systems and incentives, leadership styles, decision-making processes, patterns of human interaction, work practices, history of partnerships, and human resources practices (Dyer et al., 2001). The information gathered is used to screen potential partners, as well as organize and structure the partnership if it moves forward.

MFIs that are building less risky or more informal partnerships are unlikely to find this approach useful, but simply being alert to cultural similarities and differences during the search for potential partners can help institutions make less risky choices. In general, the more partners have culturally in common, the easier and less costly it will be to manage the partnership. If an MFI is concerned about a particular risk, it can observe potential partners' behaviour during the screening and negotiation process, and select those who demonstrate most respect for managing that risk, or have a culture with values that protect against that risk.

A second cultural characteristic worth screening for is flexibility. To what extent is the potential partner, particularly its senior management, willing to work with the MFI to meet its needs and those of its clients? Is it willing to adjust its product design or terms of service? Is it willing to test new processes or approaches? Or is it determined to stick with its standard recipe? Potential partners that are open to the possibility of experimentation are less risky, since they are more likely to adapt as necessary during the partnership to achieve the agreed-upon objectives.

If an MFI is the one selecting partners, it has two main options for approaching candidates: directly or through a competitive tender. The case study of FINCA presented at the end of this chapter provides one example of the direct method. Box 22.6 gives two brief examples of MFIs that used the tender approach. Obviously, both techniques can be successful. An MFI's choice of technique is likely to depend on the number of potential partners available and their expected level of interest in collaborating with the MFI. The fewer the options, and the more partners have to be coaxed to consider the idea of partnership, the more the direct approach will be attractive.

Negotiation. Once an MFI identifies the organization(s) with which it would like to partner, it must negotiate the terms of a partnership that will benefit everyone involved. Often referred

Box 22.6 Two Examples of the Tender Approach to Client Selection

CARE conducted supply and demand research into offering microinsurance through rural banks in Ghana. It then brought all interested rural banks and insurers together for a one-day workshop to explain the results and the product concept itself. After this, CARE sent a tender offer out to all insurers. The interested insurers responded with their premium rates for the products demanded (as well as other specific requirements). CARE then used an assessment grid to select their ultimate choice – Gemini Life Insurance of Ghana (GLICO). The process generated much interest from the insurers – 12 insurers and brokers attended the original meeting, and eight submitted responses to the tender offers – and this enabled CARE to get the product it wanted under the most appropriate conditions.

ASA in India also used the tender method, and sought insurers that would allow it to conduct the claims verification and pay clients directly, since it had experienced significant problems with late and rejected claims with previous insurance partners. It sent out an invitation letter to a dozen insurance companies and received bids from almost all of them. Interestingly, ASA chose to work with three insurers with nearly identical products, each covering a different geographical area. Although managing the three relationships involved more work, ASA preferred this solution because it created competition among the insurers. If one was underperforming, the MFI could seamlessly phase it out and transfer those clients to one of its other insurance partners.

Source: McCord, 2006.

to as interest-based negotiation, this step of the process is less about getting the best deal possible and more about drawing out the underlying interests of all parties and discussing them in a way that builds consensus around the goals, objectives and core principles of the partnership, as well as the division of responsibilities among partners. The definition of a common vision can be particularly important, as it helps partners focus on the overall effort rather than on the narrow achievement of their individual goals. Once an agreement has been reached, it can be documented as described in Section 22.4. This formalizes the consensus, and facilitates communication and monitoring of the partnership.

Interest-based negotiation is best served when those involved listen carefully, ask open-ended questions, summarize what has been said to ensure understanding, exercise patience and tact, and agree to disagree when necessary in order to move the discussion forward (Tennyson, 2003). Risk assessment is also important, although it is often ignored in the enthusiastic search for partnership benefits. One of the ways that partners can help to ensure mutual benefit is to encourage risk assessment early in their collaboration, and to address any concerns in an open and non-judgemental atmosphere. Actions taken to help control each other's risk exposure can contribute to the next activity, building trust.

Building trust. Partners must depend on each other if they are to leverage each other's strengths. If any party cannot trust the others to fulfil their commitments, the partnership will not move forward. Thus the building of trust is a key activity in the second phase of the partnering process, and can be pursued in four main ways:

1. **By identifying common traits**, values or history that enable partners to understand and perhaps even predict each other's needs, preferences and reactions. The more partners understand each other, the more capable they become of acting in each other's best interest. The more connections they build, the easier it is to relate to each other, and the more comfortable they become in the relationship.
2. **By sharing information**, particularly with respect to motivations and expectations, so that partners can understand better the rationale behind each other's demands. Honesty and transparency help banish the idea that partners are hiding their true intentions, or behaving irrationally. The more partners know about each other, the less they worry about being unpleasantly surprised.
3. **By demonstrating respect for difference** – not just respect for each other's differences, but respect for others who think and do things differently. This reassures partners that if differences arise between them in the future, they should be able to resolve them or work around them.
4. **Through successful joint action.** The screening and selection process helps MFIs identify partners that will be easier to trust, but it is the joint activity of developing the terms of a partnership agreement that makes the roots of the partnership begin to grow. Partners are able to demonstrate their respect for each other, their willingness to be transparent, and their ability to make decisions that benefit each other. Yet the trust will still be fragile until partners begin to implement the agreement and prove through their actions that they are willing and able to deliver what they promise.

Given the importance of being able to deliver on early commitments, successful partnerships often begin with a testing period or a limited degree of collaboration that offers the possibility for expansion if the initial cooperation is successful. IDEI and ICICI Bank, for example, started their partnership with a six-month pilot that financed just one product, an irrigation system that IDEI was already marketing. The partners agreed that if a credit franchisee managed that product effectively, it could then add other products to its portfolio. Negotiating an early agreement for limited partnership reduces risk, and makes it more likely that partners will have built sufficient trust during the screening and negotiation process to implement a successful partnership. Hopefully, the act of implementing an initial partnership successfully will build more trust and make it possible to undertake more ambitious initiatives later.

Planning the partnership's activities. Often, the partnership agreement will work out the principles of partnership, and then the practical details of how the partners will implement those general commitments are defined later in a joint work plan or activity agreement. Even if an exit plan is not included in the partnership agreement, it should at least be discussed during this phase. It may seem negative to talk about the end of the partnership at its beginning, but doing so can help relieve pressure, facilitate contingency planning, protect partners from counterparty risk, and inspire the definition of incentives for sustaining a partnership beyond the pilot phase.

Putting systems, infrastructure and resources in place to implement the plan. Partners must decide how they want to organize their partnership and then source the necessary human, financial and infrastructure resources to begin implementation. Two issues warrant particular attention here: governance and accountability.

Experience has shown that it is critical to find a champion for each partnership at the senior management level. This champion drives the partnering process and helps secure the necessary resources to build and maintain the alliance. Yet putting too much power or responsibility in the hands of a champion will expose the MFI to risk. The partnership needs to have sufficient support from others in the institution to ensure that the partnership can be sustained even without the champion. Few MFIs will have sufficient scale or number of partnerships to warrant a dedicated partnership management function, but a partnership manager located in the operations or business development department could provide continuity and assist with communication, knowledge management, monitoring and evaluation, and internal coordination of an MFI's external relationships.

Partners need to be accountable to their own organizations, but they must also be accountable to each other to ensure that the partnership generates benefits for all. Management information systems (MIS) need to be compatible, and interfaces may need to be built to enable partners to communicate with each other. For AMEEN and its partner banks in Lebanon, compatible MIS were key to effective financial and portfolio management (Green and Estévez, 2005). Some MFIs in India have a computer in their head office that is linked to the MIS of their partner so that they can enter data directly into its system. Unfortunately, the compatibility of information systems is often overlooked and causes huge problems, typically increasing costs and sometimes resulting in the failure of partnerships that do not build strong enough systems to support collaboration prior to implementation.

Phase III: Management and Maintenance

Once resources are in place, the implementation process begins. Partners ideally work to a pre-agreed timetable to deliver specific results. They communicate regularly to monitor progress and identify solutions to unanticipated challenges. They measure the effectiveness of the partnership in achieving its objectives, as well as the impact of the partnership on the partner organizations, and make adjustments as appropriate to increase efficiency, output or the quality of interaction.

The biggest mistake that an MFI can make during this phase of the partnering cycle is to assume that the partnership will manage itself. Even if collaboration begins with a solid foundation, trust can be quickly destroyed if one or more partners do not fulfil their commitments at the time of implementation. MFIs need to actively manage each partnership to ensure that they deliver what they promise, when they promise, and with the level of quality promised. This will not necessarily be easy. In the partnership between FIE and Pro Mujer, the heavier workload faced by cashiers that were assigned to work at Pro Mujer affected both customer service and staff morale negatively. It took more than a year for the institutions to build an effective partnership at the operational level (Antezana and Pérez, 2007). In SKS's partnership with a mobile phone company, clients blamed it for user interface difficulties and repeated technical problems. SKS had to confront these problems, because they overwhelmed staff and created client dissatisfaction with its loan product.

Partnerships will not always run smoothly, but that does not mean that things will end badly. If partners are actively managing their relationship, they can identify problems early when they are still small; they can find ways to build each other's capacity in areas of weakness; they can learn from their mistakes; and the partnership can ultimately meet its objectives. Partners need to be attentive and flexible in order to respond effectively to changes in partners' capacity, the demands of the market, and the external environment.

Ultimately, partnerships are relationships and, just like any relationship, they require attention, care, and regular communication to remain strong. Section 22.5 offers several practical examples of mechanisms MFIs have put in place to maintain good communication and to strengthen their relationship over time.

Phase IV: Evaluating and Moving On

Some partnerships are designed to be temporary. They exist to implement a specific project, such as researching a new market or demonstrating the viability of a technology, and when the project is over, the results are evaluated (see Box 22.7) and the partnership ends. In such cases, the fourth and final phase of the partnering process consists of transferring lessons learned from the partner organizations to others who can use them and, perhaps, transferring activities that were launched by the partnership to a sustainable home.

Most partnerships are not intended to be temporary, or if they are, their end date is not clearly defined. The partnership is periodically evaluated, and, depending on the results, partners may decide to sustain, deepen, reformulate or terminate their collaboration.

Sustaining the partnership. This option is typically chosen if a partnership is performing relatively well and implementation is on track, but objectives have not yet been achieved. Part-

Box 22.7 Evaluating a Partnership

Partnerships can usefully be evaluated from four perspectives:

1. **Impact.** Did the partnership achieve its goals?
2. **Strategy.** Was partnership the most effective or efficient way to achieve these goals?
3. **Value added.** Did all partners benefit from their involvement in the partnership?
4. **Mechanics.** What could have made the partnership more successful?

Lessons learned in all of these areas can inform an MFI's decision about how to proceed with a particular partnership, as well as improve its overall partnership management in the future.

Source: Adapted from The Partnering Initiative, undated.

ners return to the managing and maintenance phase and continue active pursuit of their objectives.

Deepening the partnership. This option is commonly chosen when partners achieve one set of targets and decide they want to continue working together to achieve even more. They may expand the geographic coverage of their partnership, the number of customers served or the range of products offered, but the nature of their collaboration remains similar enough that they can build on their current methods of doing business. In this case, partners return to the building phase to define what it is they want to do next.

Reformulating the partnership. This option may be chosen for a variety of reasons. Partners may achieve their original objective, and decide to continue working together in a different way. They may have trouble meeting their objective, and decide they have to bring in another partner with competence in their area of weakness. One partner may exit the partnership, making it necessary to find another to fill its shoes. Or the environment can change, making the partners' original objective irrelevant. Any of these scenarios can bring a partnership back to the first stage of the partnering cycle, in which the remaining partners explore their options and build a somewhat different relationship.

Terminating the partnership. Not all partnership agreements have a fixed termination or expiration date. However, the option to terminate the partnership is generally a mutual right enjoyed by all parties to an agreement (Green, 2008). In some cases, written notice must be provided before a termination goes into effect. In others, a party can call for the immediate termination of partnership without giving notice, provided that such termination is with cause (for example, if another party failed to perform an obligation in the partnership agreement, or if extraordinary circumstances make it improbable that the party will be able to fulfil its obligations in the agreement).

If a partnership fails, exiting will require skilful and sensitive management to minimize damage. This will be easier to implement if exit options were considered as part of the partnership agreement. If the agreement provides no guidance on how parties' duties and obligations should be unwound, the potential for conflict, losses and tarnished reputations increases.

If, on the other hand, a partnership is successful, this should be a cause for celebration, both internally and externally. Internal celebration recognizes and appreciates the efforts of all who contributed to making the partnership a success. It boosts morale and confidence, and builds support for future partnerships. External celebration can strengthen each partner's brand by raising the institution's visibility, distinguishing it from the competition, and communicating success.

22.4 Partnership Agreements

As noted at the beginning of the chapter, there are many types of partnership that involve various degrees of engagement. Depending on the degree of engagement, the parties in a partnership may express their decision to collaborate in one of the following ways:

- **"Gentlemen's" agreement:** an informal agreement between two or more parties that may be written, verbal, or simply understood as part of an unspoken agreement by convention or through mutually beneficial etiquette. It relies upon the honour of the parties for its fulfilment, rather than being in any way enforceable.
- **Letter of intent:** a document that expresses an intention to take (or forgo) some action. It is often used to declare officially that partners are negotiating a larger or more formal agreement. It can also clarify key points or create "big picture" consensus on a proposed relationship, and provide safeguards in the event that a deal collapses during negotiation. Letters of intent are usually not binding in their entirety, but they may contain provisions that are binding, such as a confidentiality agreement, or a promise not to negotiate similar agreements with other parties unless certain conditions are met.
- **Term sheet:** very similar to a letter of intent in that it is a preliminary, mostly non-binding document that is used to record two or more parties' intentions to enter into a future agreement based on specified (but incomplete or preliminary) terms. The difference between the two is mostly a matter of style. A letter of intent is typically written in letter form, and focuses on the parties' intentions; a term sheet skips most of the formalities, and lists deal terms in bullet-point or similar format.
- **Memorandum of understanding (MOU):** a written, but non-contractual, agreement between two or more parties to take a certain course of action. It is similar to a letter of intent, although a letter of intent can express a single party's intentions towards another, whereas an MOU must be signed by both parties to be valid. It differs from a term sheet in that it usually is not a preliminary document. Depending on the exact wording, an MOU can be legally binding. To avoid confusion, it is a good idea for an MOU to clearly state whether its signatories intend for the document, or specific provisions, to be legally binding.
- **Legal agreement or contract:** a binding agreement between two or more parties that is enforceable by law or by binding arbitration. There are numerous types of legal agreement including agency agreements, co-brand agreements, collaboration agreements, franchise agreements, investment agreements, joint venture agreements, licensing agreements, outsourcing agreements, underwriting agreements, and more. The specific format of these agreements can vary from one country to another depending on local contract law.

When collaboration with another entity is limited, low-cost and low-risk, MFIs often use a gentlemen's agreement to quickly bring the partnership to life. This is the case with most referral relationships, for example, which are established on the basis of an informal verbal promise. Even these partnerships expose an MFI to risk, however, and a written partnership agreement can be a valuable tool for mitigating that risk. It can help clarify the purpose of cooperation, the resources each party will contribute, how long the relationship will last, and so on. It can also help protect an MFI's intellectual property and its client relationships. When CDRO negotiated its partnership with Banrural, for example, the partners agreed that the bank would not provide services that CDRO was already providing (Gallardo et al., 2006). Many MFIs make sure they are the only ones to interact directly with the client so that they can reduce the possibility that entrepreneurial partners will be able to steal their clients in the future.

The larger the number of partners involved, and the greater the differences between them, the more important a partnership agreement will be in managing the risks inherent in collaboration. In general, the more critical a partnership is to the success of an MFI's business strategy, the more seriously it will want to consider types of partnership and partnership agreement that legally bind the two entities. The general advantages and disadvantages of more informal and formal partnership agreements are presented in Table 22.2.

If an MFI chooses to enter into a written partnership agreement, it can use the following checklist to identify issues that might usefully be addressed in that agreement. The checklist is compiled from a literature search on good partnership practice, but draws heavily from two sources in particular, Lee (2006) and Green (2008):

- ✓ Purpose and objectives of the partnership
- ✓ Roles and responsibilities of each partner
- ✓ Resources being contributed by each partner
- ✓ Allocation of risks and revenues between partners
- ✓ Structure for managing the partnership
- ✓ Joint work plan encompassing activities, timing and performance indicators
- ✓ Measures to strengthen partners' capacity to implement their commitments
- ✓ Process for problem solving and the resolution of conflicts
- ✓ Provisions to protect each organization's proprietary information and human resources from inappropriate use or solicitation
- ✓ Strategies for dealing with staff turnover or succession
- ✓ Measures to mitigate external risks and threats to the partnership
- ✓ Guidelines for communicating with the public about the partnership
- ✓ Procedures for monitoring performance
- ✓ Exit and termination provisions

Table 22.2 General comparison of formal and less formal partnership agreements

	Less formal	More formal
Advantages	• Greater freedom to explore ideas and intentions • Flexible and non-bureaucratic • Lawyers not usually involved • Lower administrative costs	• Increased authority and capacity to influence • More focused activities • Enhanced ability to mobilize and manage large-scale resources • Greater chances of sustainability
Disadvantages	• Not taken seriously enough by parties outside the partnership • Key players too easily diverted by other priorities • Not structured enough to manage large resources	• Subject to legislative restrictions • Tendency to become over-bureaucratic and impersonal • Higher administrative costs

Source: Adapted from Tennyson, 2003.

22.5 Communicating for Success

As illustrated in Table 22.3, communication is a core activity in each phase of the partnering process. It is critical for building trust, negotiating effectively, making joint decisions, keeping implementation on track, and solving problems as they occur. Yet communication is not only an ingredient for success; it can also be the cause of failure. McManus and Tennyson (2008) argue that "partnering is above all a communication challenge." If partners have weak communication skills, they will have difficulty completing any of the activities in Table 22.3 effectively.

With no intention to be exhaustive, this section describes some of the steps that MFIs can take to strengthen their communication at each stage of the partnering process.

Table 22.3 Communication activities in the partnering process

Exploring	Building	Managing and maintaining	Evaluating and moving on
• Raising awareness of partnership as an option • Assessing internal capacity • Contacting potential partners • Motivating potential partners to engage • Mobilizing resources	• Screening potential partners • Building trust • Clarifying expectations • Negotiating commitments • Defining an agreement • Establishing communication channels	• Monitoring progress • Keeping others up to date • Gathering and responding to feedback • Solving problems • Negotiating adjustments • Demonstrating that commitments have been met	• Evaluating results • Documenting and disseminating lessons learned • Discussing next steps • Celebrating success • Transitioning • Informing stakeholders of results and future plans

Source: Authors.

Phase I: Exploring

- Articulate a vision for the partnership that can help motivate internal and external support for the idea of collaboration.
- Before approaching potential partners, list in order of priority the specific characteristics or competences that you seek in a partner. Also list the strengths that you can offer a partner in return.
- Learn the language of the partners with which you want to negotiate.
- When approaching potential partners, avoid using vocabulary or jargon that might be incomprehensible or alienating.
- Consider recruiting a third party to open up communication with potential partners in areas that are unfamiliar to you, or in sectors where your institution, or microfinance in general, lacks visibility or credibility.
- Avoid making assumptions about potential partners. Research potential partners' history, values and capabilities, and be proactive about sharing information that can help potential partners clarify their preconceived ideas about you.

Phase II: Building

- During the screening process, pay attention to how effectively a potential partner communicates and not just what they communicate.
- Create a culture within the relationship where it is okay to say "I do not understand," "I do not know," or "Can you explain?"
- Know what you want, and know your next best alternative to partnership, before you begin negotiations.
- In negotiations, try to trade instead of concede, and use traded movement to eventually close the deal (Khan, 2004).
- Build support for the idea of partnership internally as well as externally. Articulate how a partnering approach will benefit your organization and your clients.
- Invite potential partners into the field so that they can understand your work and target market better.
- Make the partnership agreement as clear as possible to minimize the possibility of misunderstandings, inadequate performance, disputes and uncertainty. Include definitions of important or complex terms in the agreement.
- Choose good communicators to represent your organization in the partnership, or develop communication skills in the key players who need it.
- Make regular partner communication someone's responsibility early on. If it will be the responsibility of multiple staff members, identify a focal point who will manage the partnership.
- Ask partners for training to help staff understand who they are, what they do, and how they can support the partner through their own work. La Equidad, a Colombian insurer, developed a two-day special programme to train the credit analysis of its agent Women's World Foundation (McCord, 2006).

- Set up communication systems that facilitate one partner's accountability to the others. Identify what kind of information and reporting each partner requires, and design a system that can provide it.
- Agree on an external communication approach. When or under what circumstances do partners want to communicate with the public? With whom do they want to make sure they communicate effectively? Can partners use each other's logos and trademarks?

Phase III: Managing and Maintaining

- Make sure clients are well informed about the roles and services of the partner.
- Demonstrate when partner commitments are fulfilled, either in verbal or written progress reports; this builds trust and confidence.
- Communicate regularly with partners to stay abreast not only of partnership activities, but also of relevant changes in their business and environment. Knowledge of such changes enables partners to respond with flexibility and understanding.
- Create conducive environments for learning conversations to take place between partners. Twice each year, the Polish insurer TUW SKOK holds a retreat with the managers of major credit unions, and uses that opportunity to inform them of upcoming plans, to solicit feedback on product design and customer service, and to cultivate sales competition between credit unions (Churchill and Pepler, 2004).
- Set service standards. This can help communicate to staff and partners what level of quality is required.
- Provide training for staff of partner institutions to understand the roles and rationale of the partnership. Include an introduction to partner organizations as part of new staff orientation.
- Gather feedback from clients and staff on each partner's performance.
- Ensure that an appropriate complaints and suggestion system is in place and working effectively. In addition to quarterly meetings and weekly conference calls, the Microdevelopment Finance Team that developed the Remote Transaction Solution in Uganda established a web site through which people could share comments, ideas and innovations (Greener, 2006).
- When a problem arises, replace finger-pointing with dispassionate analysis of how both parties contributed to it, and what each can do to improve it (Hughes and Weiss, 2007). Since claims processing tends to be one of the most contentious issues in insurance partnerships, the Indian insurer Shepherd formed a review committee with representatives from the MFI, insurer and clients that meets quarterly (or more often if necessary) to improve claims processes (Churchill and Roth, 2006).
- It can take time for partnerships to achieve their objectives, so assess factors that will affect ultimate performance (for example, response time, percentage of claims rejected) and not just the achievement of targets.
- Ensure that information is agreed to by all partners before it is put in the public domain.
- Keep good records. Not everything that happens in a partnership needs documenting, but good record-keeping helps to ensure transparency, to hold partners accountable for commitments made, and to capture the partnership's history.

Phase IV: Evaluating and Moving On

- Treat the periodic evaluation of your partnerships more as a "health check" than as a judgement of success or failure.
- Jointly discuss the results of the evaluation to ensure that the partnership is enabling all partners to achieve their objectives.
- If a partnership is meeting its objectives, use the evaluation to explore how partners might be able to do what they do even better, or perhaps, how they might expand the scope of their collaboration.
- Internalize lessons learned through the evaluation by adjusting in-house capacity-building to demonstrate effective and discourage ineffective behaviours.
- Organize events to celebrate and publicize partnership achievements.
- Recognize and reward individuals' contributions to the success of a partnership.
- If a partnership is not effective in its current form, explore whether it can transform into something that can be effective, rather than abandon it as a failure.

Table 22.4 Partnership risks revisited

Risk	Description	Mitigation strategies
Counterparty risk	The organizations with which an MFI partners might fail to perform in some way that harms the MFI	• Thoroughly pre-screen partner(s) • Define a common vision for the partnership, with clear goals, roles, responsibilities, objectives and ground rules established • Use a written partnership agreement to articulate clearly the limits of engagement (e.g., timeframe, resource commitment), options for exit, and legal recourse • Ensure that each party brings a core competence to the relationship that others do not want to lose access to • Plan for ongoing capacity-building • Monitor partnership performance; set performance standards • Communicate clearly with clients about the partnership; help clients protect themselves from partner non-performance
Competition risk	One partner might "steal" the knowledge, staff or customers of another partner for competitive gain	• Include client confidentiality and intellectual property provisions in the partnership agreement • Negotiate for the MFI to maintain frontline contact with the customer • Build a transparent, trusting relationship, with incentives for sustaining collaboration
Strategic risk	Poor decision-making or resource allocation could result in partnership failure	• Assess internal capacity to manage a partnership before approaching potential partners • Screen potential partners carefully for strategic fit • Know what you want and your next best alternative to partnership before entering negotiations • Develop a budget that accounts for various contingencies • Select a partner that can contribute comparable resources

Source: Authors.

22.6 Conclusion

Partnership is a broad term that is used to describe a wide range of relationships between MFIs and others who agree to share responsibility for achieving some specific goal. These relationships can enable MFIs to diversify the product portfolio and expand outreach in ways that would be impossible otherwise.

Partnerships will not necessarily be successful, however. They require commitment and communication among all players to ensure that partners achieve their own as well as the partnership's common objectives. They also require careful management of some major partnership risks, namely counterparty risk, competition risk and strategic risk, which includes the possibility of underestimating the cost of engaging in a successful partnership and the possibility that the partnership will fail in helping the MFI to achieve its objectives. Table 22.4 summarizes some of the key strategies that have been identified in this chapter for mitigating these major risks.

Main Messages

1. Partnerships do not manage themselves.
2. A systematic partnering process can help MFIs mitigate the risks of partnership.
3. Use a partnership agreement to set clear expectations about objectives, roles and responsibilities.
4. Start small and build on success.
5. Communicate regularly to ensure that each partner benefits from meeting the partnership's objectives.

Case Study: FINCA's Partnering Process for Prepaid Cards in Mexico

Founded in 1989, FINCA in Mexico provides small loans, averaging US$408, to over 116,738 of Mexico's lowest-income entrepreneurs (96 per cent of whom are women). For years, it had relied on an expensive, inconvenient cheque system for loan disbursements. After studying local markets, as well as reviewing the options available within the microfinance industry, FINCA identified a prepaid card system as the best option for improving its services and reducing its costs. Unlike a debit card, which is linked to an individual current account, a prepaid card is electronically "loaded" with cash derived from a single pooled account managed by the card issuer. FINCA believed the card would provide increased flexibility and security to clients by enabling them to withdraw loan disbursements in multiple tranches, rather than in one lump sum. It also hoped that it could use the card's technology to deliver other products, such as remittances and savings, in the future.

Since FINCA lacked the resources to offer prepaid cards on its own, it sought a partner locally to offer them. After analysing its own capacity, its challenges and its strategic priorities, FINCA decided it needed a partner that:

- operated in the same geographical areas as FINCA clients;
- had a good reputation for service;
- had access to large electronic card networks in Mexico, such as Visa; and
- could use Internet-based connections in rural areas.

Planning Phase

Figure 22.3 below outlines a framework for FINCA's decision-making process and the activities it undertook to identify potential partners and pursue eventual negotiations.

Figure 22.3 Step-by-step planning process for an MFI–bank partnership

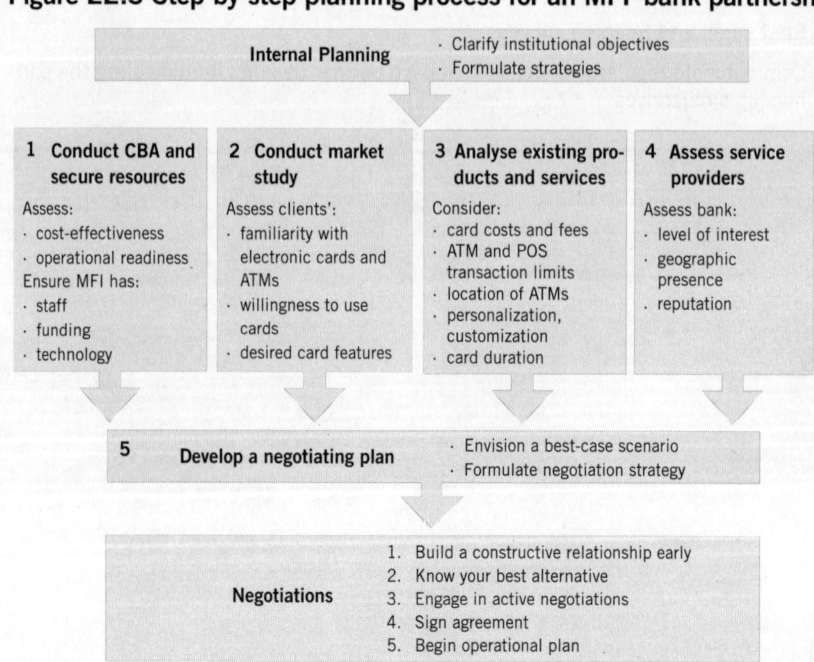

Source: Muñoz et al, 2009.

Conduct cost–benefit analysis (CBA) and secure necessary resources. It is important that an MFI assesses whether it will be able to implement a bank partnership successfully, and especially whether it has the necessary internal buy-in. FINCA's first step was to ensure that the benefits of a card-based system outweighed the costs of implementation. After establishing the feasibility of the new product, FINCA had to secure the required resources for development.

Conduct a market study. In May 2007, FINCA contracted a specialized research firm to conduct a market study to analyse various factors that would impact on card uptake by region. Based on its findings, the study recommended that FINCA make the transition from cheques to prepaid cards gradually, starting in regions of least resistance, with an interim period of mixed disbursement systems (cheques and cards). The results of this market study later enabled FINCA to approach banks with a concrete concept of client expectations for a card-based product.

Analyse existing consumer products and services. It is critical for an MFI to have a thorough understanding of the consumer products and services available in the marketplace, as well as the attributes of these products and services. This information helps MFIs learn about different options, consider what clients would like, and understand the competition. It also informs their negotiations with potential partners. FINCA analysed several options for cards, based on a number of key attributes, including cost of the physical card, cost per transaction, withdrawal limits, ATM locations and card personalization. Once these specific variables were reviewed, and the various institutions compared side by side, product qualities and institutional leaders emerged.

Assess service providers. After determining which type of product or service it most likes, an MFI should assess the different providers that offer the product. FINCA's goal in Mexico was to expand its services to rural and underserved populations, so partnership with HSBC Mexico was appealing, because it offered significant rural coverage through correspondent agents. Customization and personalization of the cards were also high priorities for FINCA. HSBC agreed to allow the MFI to add its own design and print client names on its card, whereas the other banks did not.

Develop a negotiating plan. Once an MFI has completed the steps above, it should develop a best-case scenario and a negotiation plan. At a minimum, this plan should inform management of what is reasonable, realistic and desirable from a potential partnership. By the end of its planning phase, FINCA knew its priorities for negotiating with banks: a customized, personalized, prepaid card product offered by a reputable bank that had sizable rural outreach.

Negotiation Phase

By analysing the market and clarifying its priorities, an MFI can prepare itself to work much more effectively with a potential partner. FINCA's experience provides a number of important lessons:

1. **Start by building a constructive relationship.** Trying to convince uncommitted banks to negotiate can waste resources and time. Serious, committed banks will provide timely follow-up, point out mutual interests, be flexible in negotiations, and be transparent. FINCA started by talking to banks it already knew, thanks to previous arrangements that allowed its clients to cash MFI cheques. It then forged positive, personal relationships with key personnel at the partner bank. FINCA selected staff experienced in banks and card products to spearhead the negotiations; it ensured that management was involved; it had three points of contact at HSBC, met with high-level executives, and provided feedback on time.
2. **Know your best alternative to a negotiated agreement (BATNA).** As with any negotiation, MFIs must specify what they seek from a bank partnership, what their priorities are, and what their "walk-away" situation is. A BATNA is essentially the next-best thing an MFI could do without the particular partnership. It implies knowing what other products, services and competition are in the market, and helps an MFI negotiate, because

Figure 22.4 FINCA's Carta Inteligente

Source: Muñoz et al., 2009.

it can weigh a bank's offered terms against these alternatives. Prior to negotiations, FINCA knew the few key areas critical to the success of the project, and aimed to secure the most favourable terms possible for these areas during the negotiations.

3. **Engage in active negotiations.** In bank–MFI partnerships, negotiation typically begins when a bank presents a detailed business proposition for the new product. The MFI must accept, reject or negotiate the terms. The length of the negotiation depends on the number and complexity of issues to be discussed, and on the readiness of both parties to reach and implement an agreement. The negotiations between FINCA and HSBC took over 16 months; the timeline was delayed by other responsibilities of FINCA staff, the hesitancy of HSBC to meet FINCA's varied technical requests, and the need for Visa Inc. to approve all issues relating to the production or appearance of the cards. Key issues successfully negotiated with HSBC included a reduced cost per card and lower cost per transaction, an extension of the cards' validity from 24 to 30 months, a redesigned card that features the MFI's logo, colours, and clients' names (which was important because clients perceive the card as a status symbol), and client confidentiality (which helped lower the risk of HSBC using the data to target FINCA clients). FINCA's key bargaining chip was making a strong business case – demonstrating to the bank the potential of issuing perhaps more than 60,000 cards. FINCA also committed to purchasing the first 20,000 cards, in exchange for securing their personalization.
4. **Sign agreement.** If negotiations are successful, an MFI and bank sign an agreement or contract. This agreement is usually developed by the bank, and outlines product offerings, the processes required of each party, and other general rights and obligations. In this case, HSBC submitted to FINCA a standard contract for prepaid card clients. Both parties modified the document through two rounds of negotiation. An additional, legally binding agreement, to be renewed annually, laid out the specific terms of the product as negotiated (such as those involving personalization and data security).
5. **Begin operational plan.** Once an agreement is signed, MFI managers and operations staff formulate a timeline for implementing the new product or service. The same FINCA staff members who were involved in the negotiations continued to work on the project during implementation; the MFI's senior managers also remained intimately involved in supervising the rollout. The operational work plan included a detailed timeline for training FINCA staff and clients, piloting and evaluating the cards, and establishing benchmarks for client uptake.

Results

Preliminary data on the partnership between FINCA and HSBC have been promising. From the bank's side, HSBC has a new source of revenue, and has achieved name recognition among previously unbanked clients (through ATMs). For FINCA, recent estimates show that the MFI has experienced cost savings with prepaid card clients in either the fifth loan cycle (with the cost of training included) or the third loan cycle (without training costs). For customers, out of 100 prepaid card clients who were surveyed, 86 found the card cheaper than the cheque and 93 planned to use it for their next loan cycle.

This case study was adapted from Muñoz et al. (2009).

Recommended Reading

- Achola, P.; Jones, L.; Meissner, L.; Ratcliff, C. 2009. *Partnering to achieve economic impact in HIV and AIDS-impacted communities: A partnership toolkit for microenterprise development* (New York, SEEP Network), at: www.seepnetwork.org/Resources/Tool_BASICS_Partnership.pdf
- Bedson, J. 2008. "Microfinance partnerships: Capacity building", in *ADB Finance for the poor*, Vol. 9, No. 2 (Asian Development Bank), available at: www.adb.org/documents/periodicals/microfinance
- Development Alternatives, Inc. 2007. *Commercial bank and MFI linkages: Tools for assisting MFIs in partnering with commercial banks, A guide for assisting microfinance institutions in negotiating service agreements with commercial banks* (Washington, DC, USAID), at: http://www.microlinks.org/ev_en.php?ID=23966_201&ID2=DO_TOPIC
- Diaz, L.; Hansel, J. 2007. *Practitioner-led action research: Making risk-sharing models work with farmers, agribusinesses and financial institutions* (Washington, DC, The SEEP Network), at: http://communities.seepnetwork.org/system/files/Making+Risk+Sharing+Models+Work.pdf
- Gallardo, J.; Goldberg, M., Randhawa, B. 2006. *Strategic alliances to scale up financial services in rural areas*, World Bank Working Paper No. 76 (Washington, D.C., World Bank), at: http://siteresources.worldbank.org/INTACCESSFINANCE/Resources/StrategicAlliances.pdf
- ITCILO. *The Synergies Project*, at: http://p31.itcilo.org/entdev/synergies/en
- Khan, M.S. 2004. *Tools for pro-poor public private partnerships* (New York, NY, Public Private Partnerships for the Urban Environment, UNDP), at: http://www.margraf-publishers.com/UNDP/PPPUE/index.html
- Liber, D.; Gommans, C. 2007. *Partners and action: Financial institutions and health and AIDS risk management* (Dakar, AfriCap Microfinance Fund), at: http://www.microfinancegateway.org/p/site/m//template.rc/1.9.25583
- McManus, S.; Tennyson, R. 2008. *Talking the walk: A communication manual for partnership practitioners* (London, International Business Leaders Forum (IBLF), at: http://thepartneringinitiative.org/publications/Toolbooks/Talking_The_Walk.jsp
- Tennyson, R. 2003. *The partnering toolbook* (London, International Business Leaders Forum (IBLF), Global Alliance for Improved Nutrition (GAIN)), at: http://thepartneringinitiative.org/publications/Toolbooks/The_Partnering_Toolbook.jsp

23 Delivering a Diverse Product Portfolio

Although it is easy to describe the ideal product array, it is very difficult to deliver it.
~ Rhyne and Otero (2006)

Delivering one product is relatively easy. All of an MFI's people and systems can be organized to support that one product. There is a clear focus and unity of purpose, so all staff can feel part of the same delivery chain. With each addition to an MFI's portfolio, delivery becomes more complex. Resources have to be divided among products. Systems must be designed to support multiple products. Unity of purpose does not come naturally; it has to be created.

This chapter explores the challenges of delivering a diverse mix of products. As institutions seek to integrate new products or markets into their ongoing operations, what issues should they pay attention to, and what strategies can they use to manage the challenges effectively? The chapter addresses six core issues:

1. Adapting the institutional culture
2. Deciding who should deliver what
3. Empowering staff to deliver multiple products
4. Communicating with clients
5. Reengineering systems to manage greater complexity
6. Managing change

23.1 Adapting the Institutional Culture

As MFIs diversify, they introduce new things. They might introduce an entirely new product or a new way of delivering old products to a new market. These changes can have a profound impact on an institution, not only because they require new systems and procedures, but also because they may require staff to take on new responsibilities and manage multiple workflows. Learning how to operate new systems and follow new procedures can be hard enough, but diversification usually requires employees to adopt new attitudes and values as well, and this is much more difficult. Consider a few examples of the cultural challenges MFIs have faced:

- When postal savings banks in East Africa decided to introduce loan products, staff that used to passively accept deposits from the public and then invest them in low-risk treasury bills suddenly had to learn how to make loans and be proactive about getting them back.
- The strength of FINCA International's brand as a lending organization, exemplified by its tagline "Small loans, big changes", initially constrained diversification. MFIs in its network had to reinvent themselves in order to introduce savings services successfully.
- Delta Life in Bangladesh completely separated its microinsurance and conventional insurance staff, both in the field and in the head office, to create distinct working environments. The conventional insurance agents work on a commission basis and fulfil primarily a sales function, while the microinsurance field workers, known as "organizers", manage the entire relationship with the policyholder, including premium collection, loans and loan

repayments and claims. They act as advisors instead of salespersons, helping low-income households to recognize what risks it would be appropriate to manage through insurance (Churchill and Leftley, 2006).

- A group-based loan product typically values community and consensus, requires fairly large rooms or outside spaces for meetings, and depends on peer support and pressure for on-time repayment. By contrast, an individual loan product values independence and privacy, requires small meeting spaces and/or one-on-one consultation at the client's place of business, and depends on qualified appraisal, collateral and the client's capacity for on-time repayment. SHARE India found the culture and work approach needed to deliver group and individual loans to be so different that it created an entirely new network of branches in urban areas that were exclusively dedicated to individual lending (refer to the case study at the end of this chapter).
- By August 2002 the Grameen II "methodology" had officially replaced classic Grameen in all of the Grameen Bank's 1,200 or so branches. Nevertheless, as of February 2006, there were still components of the new methodology, such as variable instalment payments and special savings withdrawals, that field staff were choosing not to make available to members (Rutherford, 2006b).
- At G & T Continental, the second largest bank in Guatemala, entry into the microfinance market required a paradigm shift – a shift in understanding and attitude among the bank's executive management and an adaptation of its traditional front office services to connect with clients in low-income neighborhoods (Vance, 2008).

Introducing a new product or market into an MFI's existing operations can create a clash between the "old" and "new" ways of doing things. If new employees are hired to deliver the new product or serve the new market, they may possess a very different set of skills and attitudes than employees who have been working with the institution for years. They may be treated differently, perhaps receiving more attention from senior management, or access to newer technology and equipment. These differences can create resentment, impede teamwork and harm morale.

The success of an MFI's diversification efforts depends on its ability to integrate what is new and what is old, in line with the institution's business strategy. It is not an easy task, since different products may require different cultures, but there are many things MFIs can do to encourage integration once they realize it is important and requires attention. A common error is to underestimate the importance of culture to successful diversification and, as a result, to omit cultural considerations from the product or market development plan.

The strategies discussed in Sections 23.3 and 23.6 for empowering staff and managing change can be useful to MFIs that want to improve their employees' ability and willingness to do things differently. If adopted, such strategies can indirectly shape an institution's culture to make it more supportive of diversification. However, MFIs can also take direct and deliberate steps to make their culture a more powerful tool for managing diversification.

Shaping a Culture that Supports Diversification

In the first volume of the *Making Microfinance Work* series (Churchill and Frankiewicz, 2006), institutional culture was described as the "set of values, attitudes and behaviours that are shared consistently throughout an organization". Culture can be found in an MFI's formal policies and procedures, in the unwritten rules that guide employee behaviour, in the institution's goals and reward systems, in its structures and communications, and so on. Because culture is found in so many different places, MFIs that wish to shape it in support of diversification must identify not only the values, attitudes or behaviours they want to change, but also the actions they will take to introduce, strengthen or remove those elements from their culture.

The best way to avoid the potential for conflict between old and new products (and the people and systems that deliver them) is to shift the institution's cultural focus away from the delivery of specific products and to concentrate on meeting the needs of each client instead. If lifelong relationships with clients are valued more than product-based relationships, conflicts between old and new can be resolved in favour of whatever approach most strengthens the relationship between MFI and client. Old and new staff, old and new systems, and old and new products can work together in pursuit of that goal.

Shifting an institution's culture to focus on the needs of each client rather than the delivery of specific products is a major shift, and will require action on many fronts to change the way the institution's systems and people interact with clients, and the way they prioritize the issues raised in those interactions. Some of the strategies MFIs can implement are listed below.

- Build consensus among staff with respect to who the institution is trying to serve and why. Help them understand the profiles of different market segments, how the needs and preferences of one segment differ from another, and how the MFI's various products can work together to meet their different needs.
- Identify a set of core institutional values that should be respected in the delivery of all products, and incorporate those values in staff recruitment, orientation, training, performance evaluation and reward systems. When Uganda Women's Finance Trust began offering voluntary savings services as well as loans to both women and men, it changed its name to U-Trust and began working with staff to build client relationships that prioritized the value of trust.
- Make customer service one of the core values that is prioritized and reinforced. Consider making explicit commitments to all clients through a customer service charter such as the one in Box 23.1. Then monitor and reward performance against those commitments.
- Highlight the institution's core values in marketing materials, and look for external partners that possess similar values.
- Create structures that support clients' use of multiple products. Look for ways to ease customers' transition from one product to another, and from one part of the MFI's office to another, for example through signage, information desks or customer service officers.
- Organize the institution's information by customer as well as by product so that staff can understand the nature of the MFI's relationship with each client over time, and not just his or her current use of one product in particular.
- Monitor overall customer satisfaction and loyalty in addition to product satisfaction and loyalty. Disseminate the results.
- Provide incentives that motivate customer service and teamwork, and not just the achievement of particular products' outreach objectives.

Box 23.1 Customer Service Charter of Al Rajhi Bank, Saudi Arabia

Mandate

Our goal is to provide outstanding customer service by following up customer enquiries and requests in a quick and efficient manner. We believe that excellent customer relationships are the result of us working together by:

- Developing trust through open, honest and simple communication
- Being approachable and listening to customer views
- Treating our customer with fairness and respect, exhibiting friendliness
- Ensuring ease, expertise and efficiency when a customer deals with Al Rajhi Bank
- Strict adherence to Islamic principles
- Our customer service levels are measured each year through our customer satisfaction survey. Our customer's involvement in this is critical for both the customer and the bank.

Our service goals

- Make Al Rajhi Bank the customer's first choice for all their banking needs
- To be available to help, Saturday to Wednesday, from 8:00 am to 5:00 pm in branches and offices. In addition, we will aim to provide 24-hour, 7-day access to Internet and telephone banking and a network of automatic teller machines
- Provide the customer with clear, concise information about our products, services and the facilities suitable to them, the benefits, expectations, fees and charges that are applicable and delivery channels within our bank
- Have well-trained, helpful and friendly staff, that work for ultimate customer satisfaction
- Respond quickly and efficiently to customer requests
- Provide accessible premises, services and suitable auxiliary aids to customers with disabilities
- Provide assistance and service if customers are unable to speak English/Arabic

Getting things right

We value our customer's feedback deeply, both positive and negative. If a customer has a complaint about something that has gone wrong, we want to know so we can make it right, and reduce the chance of it happening again. Our goal is to respond within 24 hours if a concern, complaint or compliment about any of our products and services is made. With more complex issues, we will inform our customers about the estimated time it may take to resolve.

Source: Al Rajhi Bank, 2010.

Although a customer-focused culture will support an MFI's diversification efforts, it can create conflicts between staff who serve different market segments. It can also be resisted by staff who worry about the impact that it will have on their workload. Thus additional actions must be taken to minimize the potential for conflict and resistance. For example:

1. Embrace participatory planning processes. As discussed in Chapter 2, the more employees are involved in product development, the more they will understand what is happening and why it is happening. They will have more opportunities to share product development suggestions that can fuel diversification, and to ask questions that might resolve their concerns about it. If diversification ideas are vetted by a product management committee that represents various departments of the institution, support for diversification will be built across departments before any idea is approved. If the committee meets regularly, then conflicts between products or markets can be brought to the institution's attention as they appear, and be addressed before they create major problems.
2. Sell the benefits of product diversification to internal customers (in other words, to employees) each time it happens. Demonstrate how product diversification has increased customer satisfaction in the past or, if this is the first time the MFI is diversifying, articulate how diversification will enable staff to meet customer needs better in the future, thus improving customer satisfaction, retention or repayment and, subsequently, the quality of work for staff.
3. Provide staff with regular performance reports that communicate how each market segment is contributing to the achievement of the MFI's vision, mission and strategic objectives.
4. Conduct cultural audits both before and during the diversification process to identify attitudes or behaviours that are interfering or could interfere with successful diversification, and then take steps to remove those barriers.
5. Cultivate greater openness among staff to new ways of doing things. This openness can be nurtured in a variety of ways: for example, by making change a habitual part of daily operations, by creating a desire to find new ways of doing things in pursuit of an objective, or by communicating the positive impact of changes when an institution makes them. The founders of Uganda Microfinance Union (now part of Equity Bank Ltd) made change the institution's "supreme value" with the explicit purpose of preventing staff from becoming too comfortable with any one way of doing things (Churchill et al., 2002). Regardless of how an MFI does it, if employees become more open to doing things differently, then the changes brought by product diversification will be more easily accepted. If change is made part of an institution's culture and expertise is built in managing it, then the changes brought by diversification also have a much better chance of being effectively implemented.

Diversification plans will often need to include actions that discourage staff from maintaining certain old habits, as well as actions to encourage new habits. MFIs that have not yet incorporated customer service or continuous improvement into their culture, or are looking for ways to eliminate an existing behaviour or stereotype, may find Table 23.1 useful. The strategies listed there provide examples of actions MFIs have taken take to accomplish these objectives.

Protecting the Institution's Cultural Core

As an MFI diversifies, there will be certain things that it will not want to change. It is dangerous, however, to assume that those things will not change just because the MFI does nothing deliberate to change them. The new people, systems, products and markets that enter the institution's operating environment will bring new behaviours, attitudes and values. If the

Table 23.1 Strategies for shaping the institutional culture

To introduce a new component	To strengthen an existing component	To remove an unwanted component
• Review and then adjust existing policies and procedures to include or respect the new component • Launch a campaign or competition to encourage staff to try it • Announce the new component in the context of the MFI's mission or strategic objectives • "Sell" the new component; explain why it is a good idea • Lead by example • Recruit new employees who demonstrate the value	• Recruit employees and external partners who value it • Set an internal standard and monitor performance against it • Recognize staff who meet or exceed the standard • Develop capacity to meet the standard as part of staff and department performance plans • Post visible reminders • Create an institutional ritual that celebrates it • Provide coaching for mentors so they can demonstrate it more effectively	• Articulate why it no longer supports the MFI's mission or strategic objectives • Adjust policies and procedures to eliminate or discourage it • Communicate the changes so that every employee gets the message • Provide incentives for changing behaviour • Ask clients to tell the MFI if they encounter it • Make an extra effort to change the behaviour of opinion leaders

Source: Adapted from Churchill and Frankiewicz, 2006.

institution provides no clear guidance, cultural elements that the institution wants to retain could be weakened by others. The MFI could begin to see inconsistencies in the way its products are delivered. In the worst-case scenario, a gap could appear between what the institution says it wants to achieve and what it actually achieves.

To prevent undesirable changes in culture, an MFI must be proactive about protecting the parts of its culture that are most important to it. These elements are usually articulated in the institution's mission statement, but not always. If an MFI is trying to develop a new competence to give it competitive advantage in certain key markets, it may want to make a special effort to maintain the values, attitudes and behaviours that will help it build competence in that area.

Once an MFI has identified the cultural elements it wants to safeguard, it can take steps to defend them. Some of the strategies that were presented in Table 23.1 for introducing or strengthening a cultural component are also useful here. MFIs can deliberately recruit employees and partners who value these components, regularly reinforce them in staff meetings and publications, set internal standards that support them, and reward performance against those standards. As mentioned in Chapters 2 and 3, institutions can screen their diversification ideas and avoid products and markets that might steer them away from their stated mission.

Some MFIs, such as Kenya Women's Finance Trust (KWFT), set measurable limits on how much a new product or market should be allowed to influence its operations (see Box 23.2). Its experience shows how revisions to the mission statement and/or key policy statements can help an institution articulate a core commitment more clearly. It also illustrates the usefulness of identifying a measurable indicator that can be used to track changes in the value, atti-

Box 23.2 Protecting a Core Cultural Component

Kenya Women's Finance Trust (KWFT) wanted to make sure that it would retain its focus on helping very poor women, even if it introduced an individual loan product that served the needs of a higher-income clientele, so it revised its mission statement to incorporate a provision that 75 per cent of its portfolio value would be allocated to clients whose income is below the Kenyan GDP per capita.

Source: Dellien et al., 2005.

tude or behaviour that an MFI wants to protect. In KWFT's case, the indicator (percentage of the portfolio allocated to clients with income below the national average) was used to set a standard, but such indicators can also be used by MFIs to monitor the impact that diversification might have. Actions would not have to be taken prior to the launch of a new product, but they could be triggered if the new product started to negatively affect something that the MFI holds dear.

Measurable indicators can also make it easier for internal auditors to get involved in monitoring the extent to which core elements of the institution's culture are being respected. MFIs that derive competitive advantage from a particular cultural element such as innovation or triple bottom line performance (commercial, social, environmental) might find it useful to include culture risk among the priority risks that are monitored on a regular basis.

One additional strategy for protecting the core elements of an institution's culture is to cultivate in-house leadership. Leaders that are born within the institution will have lived and breathed its culture for many years. They will be more likely to understand what it is, how it has developed, how it has contributed to institutional success over time, and how it needs to be nurtured than leaders who are recruited from the outside. It will be easier for them to perpetuate the culture through their own example, because the institution's values, attitudes and behaviours will already be ingrained within them (provided these leaders were well selected and developed over time). Leaders brought in from outside will need time to learn the institution's culture, and may be quite tempted to change it based on their experiences elsewhere. This is not necessarily bad, but it will threaten the MFI's traditional way of doing things. Thus the decision to recruit externally should be deliberate, and supportive of the institution's business strategy.

23.2 Deciding Who Should Deliver What

The second major challenge that MFIs face when diversifying their product portfolio is how to organize themselves to deliver that portfolio. Should each staff member be able to meet all client needs? If staff specialize, should they specialize in the delivery of a specific product, product line or function? Will the institution need to create new positions that were not required in the past? Will outside partners be involved, and if so, who will build and maintain a successful relationship with those partners?

The Organization of Frontline Staff

Frontline staff of a multi-product MFI can be organized in three different ways: by client, product or function. Each of these options has advantages and disadvantages.

If an MFI chooses to organize its service delivery by **client**, then each frontline staff member attempts to meet all of a customer's financial needs. This approach can facilitate high-quality customer service and strong relationships. It can also facilitate cross-selling (see Section 23.4 below) and a life-cycle approach to portfolio management, since staff members can suggest different products and services in response to a customer's needs over time. Staff can focus on the delivery of services to a specific market segment, and can be recruited and trained with the needs and preferences of that market segment in mind. Banks such as Banco Economico in Bolivia often choose this option when downscaling into microfinance, because the profile of this market segment differs substantially from that of its existing clientele. The success of Banco Economico's "Mi Socio" product line has been partly attributed to its front office staff, who have a substantially different profile from that of the bank's other employees.

Organizing service delivery by client poses some challenges, however. It can be difficult to keep staff well informed about all of the products in a portfolio, and to recruit individuals who possess the varied skill set necessary to deliver them. For example, as described in Chapter 6, the skills to manage group loans are quite different than for individual loans. Integrated systems will be needed to enable frontline staff to access all of a client's accounts. Fraud and human resource risks are also greater under this approach, since so much control over the client relationship is vested in a single individual. Clients may become loyal to the particular staff member who provides the institution's services rather than to the institution itself.

From a product portfolio management perspective, there are two other disadvantages to organizing frontline staff by client. First, staff may push the products they like or know best at the expense of other products, and leave the MFI with an incorrect impression of the true demand for its available services. Appropriate incentives and support need to be provided to motivate and empower staff to communicate effectively and deliver the entire portfolio. Second, when one employee is delivering multiple products it becomes more difficult to determine how much staff time is consumed by each product, and therefore how much each product costs.

If an MFI chooses to organize its service delivery by **product**, then each frontline staff member will specialize in a specific product. This allows each staff member to focus on one thing, which can facilitate higher-quality delivery of that particular product, since staff have more opportunity to practise and refine their delivery of that service. It may be easier and less expensive to recruit staff to fill product-focused positions, since the skill set required is narrower. Simple products can be provided by less skilled and less expensive staff.

Organizing service delivery by product is problematic, however, because no one in particular takes responsibility for building the overall customer relationship. Cross-selling is more difficult, because staff are less knowledgeable about the other products offered by the institution, and lack a mandate to deliver them. Even when cross-selling is successful, extra care must be taken to help customers transition from one product to another.

A hybrid of the client- and product-focused approaches organizes service delivery so that frontline employees deliver all products in a certain category or product line (for example, loan products). This option blends the advantages and disadvantages of the two approaches, and is quite popular among MFIs. However, it is not particularly customer friendly, and has been rejected by many other service industries for this reason. It is hard to imagine a restaurant, for example, that requires customers to order their appetizer, main course, drinks and dessert from four different people. MFIs that want to deliver a diverse mix of products that responds to client needs are likely to find a structure that organizes staff by product to be the most limiting.

The third main option for organizing frontline service delivery is by **function**. An MFI that chooses this option might have different staff take responsibility for promoting the institution's products, greeting clients when they enter the institution, opening or closing accounts, processing loan applications, accepting payments, collecting on past due loans, and so on. Organizing service delivery by function is advantageous, because it is easier to recruit and build specific technical or operational competence. It is also easier to outsource functions that are highly specialized, are rarely needed, or can be offered more cost-effectively by an external partner (see, for example, Box 23.3). It facilitates risk management, particularly in the delivery of loan products, since different staff will take responsibility for different steps in the process, and it will be difficult for any one staff member to defraud the institution. Organizing staff by function also makes it possible to focus more on processes, and for staff to invest time and energy in making those processes as efficient as possible. The "credit factory" approach used by many consumer lenders is an example of function-based service delivery.

As with the other two options, there are disadvantages to distributing frontline staff responsibilities by function. Most importantly, it makes it difficult for the institution to ensure a customer's seamless passage from one step of the product delivery process to another. Since individual staff members may see their responsibilities end when their particular part of the process is completed, they may not pay sufficient attention to the transitions between steps in the process, or to the customer's overall experience with the service. Documents could be misplaced without anyone taking responsibility for them, and an application could be delayed for days before anyone realizes it has happened. Minor delays at various steps of the process might be unrecognizable to individual staff members, but might add up to something

Box 23.3 Construction Assistance Staffing Considerations

Construction assistance for housing microfinance, even at minimal levels, may require a potentially different staff profile than what is required for other credit products. Many organizations have combined the role of loan officer with the technical knowledge and skills required to evaluate construction plans and budgets. In the case of CHF International's housing finance operation in Gaza, engineers and architects have taken on the responsibilities normally associated with a loan officer in terms of evaluating not only the repayment capacity of the potential client but also the technical strength of the proposed construction.

Alternatively, this assistance can be contracted out to individuals or institutions with greater construction knowledge. FUNHAVI, for example, contracts a certified architect to review the construction budgets and plans developed by its technical staff. While the MFI views this level of review as critical to its loan assessment process, the amount of work was not sufficient to maintain this level of expertise in-house.

Source: Tilcock, 2004.

Table 23.2 Options for distributing frontline staff responsibilities

Distribution of responsibilities	Benefits	Challenges
By client	• High-quality customer service • Helps build lifelong customer relationships • Can focus on meeting the needs of specific market segments • Facilitates cross-selling	• Keeping staff well informed about all products • Integrating systems • Cost of recruiting or developing staff with the necessary skill set • Fewer points of contact with each customer increases fraud risk • Clients may be more loyal to individual staff than to the MFI • More complex product costing
By product	• Quality product delivery • Easier and less expensive to recruit and develop staff with appropriate skills	• No one in particular takes responsibility for building the overall customer relationship • Cross-selling; helping clients make optimal use of the MFI's services • Client transitions between products
By function	• Easier to recruit and develop staff with specific technical competence • More opportunities for outsourcing • Risk management • Efficient processes	• Client transitions between steps in the process • Lack of attention to the overall customer relationship • Systems that facilitate communication

Source: Authors.

substantial by the time the service is delivered to the client. Systems are needed to facilitate communication between different staff so that each is well informed when picking up responsibility for a customer from the other, and regular monitoring is required to avoid inefficiency and ensure overall customer satisfaction.

The benefits and challenges associated with organizing frontline service delivery by client, product and function are summarized in Table 23.2.

Given the pros and cons of each option, how are MFIs to choose amongst them? There are several factors that can influence the choice:

1. **Skills required.** Are the skills needed to manage the various products in the MFI's mix similar or quite different? Can staff be easily trained to have those skills? If the skills are similar or can be easily built, a client-focused structure becomes feasible. If the skills are quite distinct or are difficult to acquire, a product or functional focus will make more sense. For example, the decision by ACCION partners to create a separate rural loan officer force was driven by the distinct skill set required for success in their urban and rural markets (see Box 23.4).

Box 23.4 A Separate Rural Loan Officer Force?

Some ACCION partners expanding from urban to rural areas have initially resisted building a separate rural loan officer force, holding that a unified corporate identity should be maintained and staff should be able to move from one department to the next. Yet experience has shown that urban loan officers transferred to rural areas have not performed as well as loan officers that have been hired specifically for rural areas. In fact, often successful rural loan officers have an entirely different background and skill set than urban loan officers. In many cases, educational backgrounds in agronomy have proven to be more valuable for rural loan officers than formal education in finance or business administration, primarily because financial skills can be taught more easily to agronomists than agronomy can be taught to graduates with finance degrees.

Source: Manndorff, 2004.

2. **Product culture.** As mentioned in the previous section, it is important for MFIs to shift their cultural focus away from the delivery of individual products and towards overall customer service. Nevertheless, products have distinct cultures, which often reflect the nature of the relationship that needs to be built with clients purchasing that product. As illustrated by SHARE's experience, individual and group loan products can have substantially different cultures. So can credit and insurance. Delta Life attempted to diversify into microcredit but failed, because the culture associated with collecting timely loan repayments differed too much from that of collecting insurance premiums. In the latter case, Delta Life was asking clients to let it hold their money, so it was inappropriate for staff to be aggressive if a payment was not made on time. In the case of loans, clients were holding Delta Life's money, and field agents needed to assume responsibility for getting it back (McCord et al., 2006a). If an MFI's portfolio contains products with significantly different cultures, it might be useful to organize frontline staff by product (or by product cluster, if multiple products can be supported by a similar culture).
3. **Labour costs.** Are the individuals who perform more sophisticated tasks significantly more expensive than those who perform semi-skilled tasks? Are they available? If a labour market has many skilled and affordable persons available for employment, then organizing staff by client can make sense. Employees will be more capable of handling the complexity associated with the delivery of a diverse product portfolio. If, however, better-skilled or better-educated employees are expensive and difficult to find, then hiring staff to deliver only one product or fulfil one function may be more strategic.
4. **Size of branch, institution and portfolio.** Economies of scale are usually necessary to justify specialization. Smaller institutions tend to organize their service delivery by client, since there is not enough volume to support specialists who deliver distinct products or functions. As institutions grow, specialization becomes more viable. For example, when credit unions collaborating with TUW SKOK (Mutual Insurance Company of Cooperative Savings and Credit Unions) in Poland and La Equidad in Colombia generate a certain number of insurance policies per year, a staff member is hired to work exclusively on insurance, which tends to increase the rate of sales growth (Churchill and Leftley, 2006).

5. **Degree of geographic isolation.** The more difficult it is to physically reach customers, the more attractive it will be to organize service delivery by client. Challenging terrain, low population density and weak infrastructure can increase the amount of time and money that must be spent each time a staff member and a client wish to interact. Under these conditions, it is usually more cost-effective for one staff member to deliver all of an MFI's services at a location that is near to where customers work or live than to have multiple staff members make the journey, each to offer a different product or service. MFIs that use large group lending methodologies, such as SEWA (Self-Employed Women's Association) in India or FINCA Azerbaijan, often organize their service delivery by client, because it is more efficient for one staff member to travel for 2 hours and meet 40 clients' needs than for 40 clients to come to the institution.
6. **Market segment.** Different market segments may prefer different delivery channels, or demand a substantially different product mix. For example, women in some cultures prefer to be served by female staff. Entrepreneurs with larger businesses are more likely to demand leasing, trade finance, longer-term loans and cash flow management advice than entrepreneurs with smaller businesses. As discussed in Box 1.2 in the chapter on understanding diversification, the systems and relationships that must be built to serve low-income salaried clients differ substantially from those needed to serve microentrepreneurs. MFIs that are trying to serve multiple market segments with significantly different characteristics may find it useful to allocate different staff to serve different market segments – in other words, to distribute responsibilities by client.
7. **Degree of product integration.** If the products in an MFI's portfolio have little connection to each other, such as a housing loan and a school fees savings product, organizing staff by product can be strategic. Employees can be recruited with a particular set of skills and focus on delivering a particular product or product category well. However, if products "piggyback" on top of each other or use the same delivery channel, organizing frontline staff by client or function may be more strategic. At Taytay sa Kauswagan, Inc. (TSKI) in the Philippines, for example, all insurance products are tied to loan products, and can therefore be sold with relative ease by loan officers.
8. **Technology.** MFIs with a robust, computerized information system and networked branches will find it easier to adopt a client- or function-based approach than those who do not. Institutions with manual systems can implement a client-based approach, especially when they have a limited or highly standardized product offering, but the more products an MFI wishes to offer, and the more flexible it wants to be, the more important technology will become. A function-based structure depends heavily on technology to facilitate cost-effective transitions from one process and person to another, so it is unlikely to be attractive to MFIs that lack the computerized systems to support it.
9. **Pace of institutional growth.** An MFI's growth rate will influence whether it is in a position to motivate and develop staff through promotions, or whether job enrichment is a more important strategy for this purpose. If job enrichment is important, then a client-based approach that can help push each employee to become more capable of delivering a quality, integrated service may be preferable.

New Positions, Functions and Expertise

Product diversification may require that MFIs staff new positions, introduce new functions or acquire new expertise. Much of the drive for additional capacity will be product driven; in other words, the specific positions, functions or expertise required will vary, depending on the particular product being introduced. A savings product may require that tellers be hired, for example. Insurance products may require underwriting expertise. A mobile phone-based money transfer service will require new technology and the capacity to maintain it.

As discussed in Chapter 22, diversification brings a wealth of opportunities for partnering with other entities to acquire additional capacity. This can be strategic when the expertise that is required is expensive, difficult, or time-consuming to develop. A straightforward cost–benefit analysis that includes an assessment of partnership risk can help MFIs decide whether they should fulfil a particular function in-house or outsource it.

Beyond these product-specific needs, there are three areas of expertise that diversifying institutions may want to develop in-house: product management, partnership management and customer relationship management.

Product management. As discussed in Chapter 2, a product management committee can greatly facilitate the development and maintenance of a diverse product portfolio by bringing together key staff from different parts of the institution to define product strategy, guide implementation and monitor performance. The committee can be supported by product managers – individuals who monitor the performance of a particular product and coordinate actions that ensure the institution gets as much value out of that product as possible (refer to Chapter 24 for more detail). Product managers can monitor competition and other risks that might impact on their product, and be the contact person for staff queries or requests for support related to the product.

Partnership management. The more important partnerships become to an MFI's business strategy, the more seriously it will want to take the partnership management function. It could assign product managers the responsibility for managing the partnerships associated with their product or product category. Alternatively, it could identify a specific person within the MFI to take on the role of partnership manager. This individual would possess the negotiation and communication skills necessary to create and maintain healthy alliances and outsourcing relationships with the institution's partners. This person could also be charged with monitoring the external environment to identify new partnership opportunities that could support the institution's outreach objectives.

Customer relationship management. MFIs that adopt a product- or function-based organizational structure often create the position of customer service officer at the branch level to provide the cross-product and cross-function support that can be lacking in those structures. Customer service officers can greet clients when they first enter the institution, answer any general queries they might have, point them in the right direction for accessing the service they need, and follow up on the quality of the service received. If these officers are hired from the communities being served, they can also help bridge the differences that may exist between an MFI's culture and that of its market.

Box 23.5 What is CRM?

Customer relationship management (CRM) is a broadly recognized, widely implemented strategy for managing and nurturing a company's interactions with customers. The overall goals are to find, attract and win new clients, retain those the company already has, entice former clients back into the fold, and reduce the costs of marketing and client service (Wikipedia, 2010).

True CRM brings together information from all data sources within an organization (and, where appropriate, from outside the organization) to give one, holistic view of each customer in real time. This allows customer-facing employees in such areas as sales, customer support and marketing to make quick yet informed decisions on everything from cross-selling and up-selling opportunities to competitive positioning tactics.

Once thought of as a type of software, CRM has evolved into a customer-centric philosophy. It is a strategy that is used to learn more about customers' needs and behaviours in order to develop stronger relationships with them.

Source: Adapted from destinationCRM.com, 2010.

Beyond this, MFIs may want to make a specific individual or department at the head office responsible for the customer relationship management function (see Box 23.5). A customer-centric business strategy will require that customer-centric processes and technology be implemented throughout an institution, but having someone encourage and coordinate this effort can be useful as diversification increases the complexity of customer relationships. Typically developed within the marketing department, the customer relationship management (CRM) function can improve an MFI's ability to identify and profile market segments; track clients' changing needs, product usage and satisfaction; and mine that data to support ongoing product development, cross-selling and customer loyalty programmes.

23.3 Empowering Staff to Deliver Multiple Products

The diversification of a product portfolio has implications for all staff, regardless of how an institution decides to distribute functions and responsibilities amongst employees. Certainly, delegating responsibility for some portion of the delivery process is part of what gives staff the power to act, but improving employees' capacity and motivation to deliver a more complex product offering is even more critical to success. There are three main strategies through which MFIs can empower their staff to deliver multiple products: 1) training; 2) supportive infrastructure; and 3) incentives.

Training

The more an MFI diversifies, the more complex its training needs become. A diversifying MFI will typically need to strengthen its training function, and budget additional resources to prepare staff to deliver a more diverse portfolio. This will involve both product-specific training and general training to support the delivery of a diverse product portfolio. The latter category is often neglected.

Product-specific training. If a new product is introduced, everyone in the institution needs to know that it is being introduced, why it is being introduced, whose needs it is designed to serve, and how it is designed to meet those needs. They must also understand how the new product will work together with other products in the portfolio to achieve the institution's objectives. Without this context, product-specific training may teach staff how to deliver a new product without convincing them that it *should* be delivered.

Ideally, all staff would receive enough information about the product that if they were asked about it on the street, they could explain it well enough to attract potential customers to visit the MFI in search of more information, or to make a purchase. Role-plays in the training room can give staff practice in answering questions that are likely to be asked by prospective clients. Sharing the results of the MFI's competition analysis and highlighting areas in which the product performs well relative to the competition can also help staff to communicate the value of the product. Of course, employees who are assigned responsibility for actual delivery of the product will need more detailed training on the product's features and processes, as well as the specific tasks they must implement.

If an existing product is changed in some way, all staff need to be informed that changes have been made, and why. They may not need to know the details of those changes, but they need to be aware that a change has been made, or they may misinform clients in the future. Keeping staff informed about the changes being made also helps to create a culture of continuous improvement, which is an important ingredient in quality service provision and effective change management. Typically, only major product design changes are conveyed through classroom training; others can be communicated effectively through written circulars and face-to-face meetings. To ensure that staff receive this communication as it was intended, employees can be asked to sign a circular once they have read and understood it, or to take periodic quizzes that assess whether their product knowledge is up to date.

General training to support diversification. When new employees enter the institution, they need to be introduced to the overall product mix, the type of value it is designed to deliver, how each product can serve the needs of the target market, and how the different products in the portfolio fit together by market segment. They will also need to know where they can get additional information or find reference material about the institution's various products. This is true even if the employee will deliver only a subset of all products, because a broad understanding of the overall product portfolio will enable that staff member to cross-sell other products, to have basic answers to customers' queries, and to know how to find information about other products and how to refer customers appropriately.

It may be desirable to include on-the-job training in each product during the probation period, or to have a policy of rotating staff across products, so that each new employee learns about the institution's product offering through experience. This is especially true for management trainees who will need to oversee staff who are delivering different products. Knowledge gained through this kind of hands-on training is much more likely to be retained than information gathered in a classroom.

To support diversification over time, staff may need occasional training in other areas:

- **Customer service:** to develop specific skills that will improve the quality of service delivered to customers; to communicate new customer service priorities or standards; or to introduce new technologies (or new ways of using old technologies) to serve customers better.

- **Time management:** to assist employees in balancing the demands of multiple products.
- **Cross-selling:** to help employees understand how clients' use of the MFI's products is evolving, perhaps due to changes in the external environment or in the needs of the market segments being served.
- **Analysis:** to help middle managers, in particular, to interpret performance reports and use them to set priorities for their staff in a way that enables the team to achieve its objectives.
- **Risk management:** to raise awareness of risks that need to be managed; to develop the ability to implement new controls; to strengthen skills that are needed to implement existing controls more effectively.
- **Change management:** to assist staff in reorienting to the needs of a new customer group, or in adapting their systems to incorporate a new product or partner.

Improving the effectiveness of training. Although training is important, it can be costly, both financially and in terms of opportunity cost, since staff must be removed from their operational environment to attend the training. Because of these costs, MFIs often make a grave mistake and forgo training. However, investments in training are critical to successful product diversification. The following suggestions illustrate actions that an MFI can take to ensure that it generates a significant return on its training investment:

1. **Set clear objectives.** This will focus both trainers and trainees on what they need to do. If the objectives describe results that the MFI wants to see in the work environment and not only in the training room, they will guide both trainers and trainees to produce results beyond the training room.
2. **Hold trainers responsible for delivering a curriculum that will achieve agreed-upon objectives.** MFIs can ask trainers to deliver certain key messages, or enable staff to develop certain skills and compensate the trainer on the basis of how well those tasks are performed. For example, the MFI and the trainer could agree in advance on the content of an exam that would be given to employees attending the course, and the trainer would receive a base fee plus a bonus based on the percentage of trainees who pass the exam. The exam could take the form of a product knowledge test, a percentage reduction in the employee's error rate, an on-the-job demonstration of a process or procedure as monitored by a supervisor, or a variety of other formats.
3. **Hold staff accountable for meeting the learning objectives and not just attending the training.** Using the examples provided in the previous point, staff could be required to pass an exam before the end of their probationary period, or in order to be eligible for a promotion. Alternatively, participation in a training course could be integrated into an employee's annual performance plan. It could be designed to improve the employee's skills in a particular area, and those skills would be evaluated on the job as part of the annual performance review.
4. **Assess results three months after the training.** Letting trainers, trainees and supervisors know that learning will be assessed not only on the last day of the training, but also at some later point in time, will encourage everyone to take steps to ensure that what is learned is not immediately forgotten. Of course, the assessment then needs to take place when the MFI said it will take place, or the strategy will fail to motivate performance in the future.

5. **Introduce supportive infrastructure.** Giving trainees information about resources and systems that can support them when they return to their work environment can increase their confidence and willingness to implement what they have learned outside the training room.
6. **Recycle product development tools.** Tools that were created during a product's development can be used to communicate with staff long after the product is launched. Process maps, for example, may have been created during the product's design phase, but they can be used to explain the details of a process to anyone who needs to be involved with it. They communicate who is supposed to carry out which steps; how long each step should take; where documents should be received, passed and filed; and how risks should be managed. The maps are particularly good training tools, because they contain visual diagrams of what is supposed to happen, and not just text. Another tool that can be useful is the 8P Framework (see Section 23.5 below). The details of a product are often laid out according to this framework to facilitate competition analysis, or the design of marketing messages. Trainers could recycle that summary to efficiently explain a product's features to employees who are not yet familiar with them.
7. **Create training opportunities that are not classroom-based.** Learning can be more efficient if staff can access new information or experiences without having to be absent from work. There are many ways to do this, most of which fall into the category of on-the-job training, but opportunities for distance learning are increasing, given the development of Internet, videoconferencing and chat technologies, as well as the infrastructure that makes these technologies accessible at a reasonable price. Organizations such as the Rural Finance Learning Centre, echange, and the SEEP (Small Enterprise Education and Promotion) Network have already developed CD-ROM and Internet-based distance learning courses on topics that are relevant for diversifying MFIs: liquidity management, agricultural lending, market research, customer service, and more. MFIs might also consider developing their own simple PowerPoint® presentations with embedded audio and video links to help introduce staff to a new product or market segment, or to refresh employee knowledge of the overall product mix for the purposes of cross-selling.
8. **Be more systematic about peer-to-peer learning.** On-the-job training will be more cost-effective if it is planned so that those who will be doing the training can be prepared for it. MFIs such as Equity Bank in Kenya plan, for example, to have staff who are involved in piloting a new or improved product be the ones who will train others to roll out the product in new locations. Staff who will be doing the coaching can receive training in how to be an effective coach. They may need to strengthen certain skills, such as listening, questioning, or giving constructive criticism. Both trainees and coaches can be given guidelines with respect to the knowledge that should be communicated, the behaviours and processes that should be modelled, and the skills that should be observed and developed once the trainee begins to implement tasks. Feedback can then be provided on the performance of the coach and the trainee according to the guidelines provided. Peer-to-peer learning also can also be facilitated in contexts other than one-on-one coaching, as demonstrated by the training credit committees used at Mi-Bospo in Boznia-Herzegovina (see Box 23.6).

Box 23.6 Training through Credit Committees

As part of its training programme, MI-BOSPO established training credit committees through which applications were discussed before passing to the formal credit committee for final loan decisions. The training credit committee provided a sort of laboratory of learning for both loan officers and managers. They enabled detailed discussions on a range of issues and dilemmas presented by different types of application, and avoided turning formal credit committees into training sessions.

Source: Dellien et al., 2005.

Supportive Infrastructure

Training is not the only way to increase employees' capacity and motivation to deliver a more diverse portfolio. In fact, the infrastructure that an MFI does or does not provide to support employees' delivery of its products can have a much larger impact on which products they choose to deliver, and on the quality and consistency with which they deliver those products. Four components of a supportive infrastructure are described below: reference sources, feedback and learning systems, leadership and direction, and decentralization.

Reference sources. Product manuals, brochures, process maps and frequently asked question sheets can remind staff of product details, and assist in troubleshooting when a customer asks a question to which the staff person does not know the answer. These materials can be made available in hard copy or via an intranet-based reference system that might include a searchable database of product questions or a blog through which staff can communicate more informally. In addition to written materials, product managers can serve as "help desks", offering employees one-on-one assistance with issues that are not addressed elsewhere. Once a new issue is raised and resolved, the product manager can institutionalize the learning by updating other reference materials, for example by adding the question and its solution to the frequently asked questions database, or adjusting relevant process maps to clarify a procedure.

Feedback systems. Although feedback and learning systems are important for mono-product institutions, they become even more important for multi-product institutions as a tool for safeguarding the customer relationship and overall customer satisfaction. They can channel compliments, complaints and suggestions about the overall product mix, as well as about individual products, to a place where action can be taken. Project management software with issue-tracking features can enable MFIs to track customer service issues and ensure that they are responded to. Feedback systems should channel input from both internal and external clients, giving staff a way to share their challenges and learning with others in the institution, and giving others a chance to respond. Weekly meetings at the branch level, performance evaluations, internal audit reports, market research initiatives, hotlines and suggestion boxes are all potential components of such a system.

Leadership and direction. Regardless of how a diversified MFI chooses to divide responsibilities amongst its frontline staff, it needs to clarify what it expects from each employee, and it needs to guide employees' allocation of time and effort. Organizational charts and job descriptions are powerful tools for communicating responsibility. A job description can make employees aware that cross-selling is something they should be doing, for example, and an

Box 23.7 Sample Quality Standards

- Cash deposit: time at counter less than 1.5 minutes
- Account opening: time at account opening desk 10 minutes
- Customer enquiries: 80 per cent of enquiries at enquiries desk less than 5 minutes
- Number of transactions per teller per day: 350
- Accuracy of processing: more than 97.5 per cent
- Score on product knowledge exam: 85 per cent

Source: Adapted from Wright et al., 2005.

organizational chart can help staff understand to whom they must be accountable, and from whom they can expect regular guidance with respect to institutional and team priorities. Supervisors are usually the ones to communicate which products employees should promote, and how much time they should spend on one product versus another, but there are other tools that can provide guidance as well.

For years, ASA (Association for Social Advancement) in Bangladesh used blackboards in its branches to focus field officers on the repayments and savings they were expected to bring back each day after visiting their groups (Rutherford et al., 2008). Quality standards can be used to communicate the level of effort that staff should invest in delivering a service or fulfilling a particular function (see Box 23.7). Incentives, as discussed below, can encourage staff to focus their time or effort on a specific set of priorities.

Decentralization. If an MFI's structure provides clear leadership and direction, but concentrates decision-making power at the head office, frontline staff can become frustrated and disillusioned with what they perceive to be bureaucratic, uninformed or time-consuming approval processes. As long as sufficient controls are in place to facilitate decisions at the field level, frontline staff will have more opportunity to take ownership and pride in their service delivery. They will have more freedom to do what needs to be done to achieve institutional objectives.

Incentives

When employees are asked to deliver multiple products, they have to make daily decisions about how much time and energy they will spend on each product, which transactions they will process first, which products they will recommend to clients, and so on. There is a natural tendency to prioritize those products that are easiest or least risky to deliver, but not necessarily the ones that generate the greatest value for the institution, or for the client (see, for example, Box 23.8).

Box 23.8 Working Capital Loans vs. Housing Microfinance

In a joint study of ten MFIs offering housing microfinance, ACCION International and Habitat for Humanity International found that loan officers at most MFIs are responsible for marketing and evaluating both working capital microenterprise loans and housing microfinance, given that the general characteristics and delivery methods of the loan products are quite similar. However, the two additional steps of the credit evaluation unique to the housing loan product (evaluation of project budget and sketch of proposed housing improvements) have discouraged active selling of housing microfinance by loan officers concerned with meeting productivity goals.

Source: Mesarina and Stickney, 2007.

Incentives are a valuable management tool, because they can influence these decisions. They can be used to communicate an MFI's priorities, and to motivate staff to spend more time on products or functions that they might otherwise not prioritize. For instance, if an MFI wants to focus staff on customer service rather than the delivery of specific products, it can build a financial incentive scheme that measures customer satisfaction, processing time and client retention, or offer an employee of the month award based on the same indicators.

Incentive schemes can also facilitate decentralization and self-management by aligning employees' self-interest with an MFI's core values or strategic objectives (see, for example, Box 23.9). Incentive schemes that use simple, measurable indicators make it easy for employees to identify what their institution wants, and to regularly gauge whether they are delivering what is expected.

Although incentives are powerful, they will not necessarily support diversification. When Al Amana in Morocco first introduced business training as a non-financial product, loan officers undersold it, because their incentive scheme did not reward them for spending time on the product. Sometimes MFIs are tempted to use their incentive schemes to encourage sales of

Box 23.9 Grameen Bank's Five-Star Incentive System

Grameen Bank rates its branches according to a five-star system designed to promote core Grameen values, notably savings, prudence and education. Branches are awarded stars of different colours based on their achievements against the following five benchmarks: 1) Green Star – a 100 per cent repayment rate; 2) Blue Star – profitability; 3) Violet Star – deposits exceed loans outstanding; 4) Brown Star – all children of borrowers attend school; 5) Red Star – all borrowers have crossed over the poverty line. Branch staff can wear the stars as a badge of honour and display their stars in the branch stationery to show their achievement.

According to Mohammed Yunus, Grameen Bank's founder, the system "has generated a burst of energy all around. [Staff] are not doing it for any monetary benefit, they are doing it in the spirit of competition – to be ahead of their peers, to create a record for his branch, or area, or zone, to make a personal contribution in changing the economic and social condition of the poor families he is working for, and, above all, to prove their worth to themselves."

Source: Adapted from Yunus, 2002, and O'Reilly, 2008.

their most profitable products. This can generate short-term returns for the MFI, but it can also discourage staff from placing clients' needs at the forefront of their marketing activities, and can weaken the long-term customer relationship.

It is not easy to create an incentive scheme that motivates exactly the kind of performance an MFI is looking for. If managers wish to take advantage of this tool, they need to take care in its design and maintenance. Some of the issues worth taking into account in the context of diversification are:

- **Simplicity.** Incentive schemes need to be simple enough for staff to understand and find motivating. If an MFI tries to offer one incentive scheme that rewards something different about every product, the scheme will be too complex to be useful. MFIs that organize their service delivery by client are better off choosing the products that most warrant attention, and selecting a few indicators on which to base the incentive scheme. MFIs that organize their service delivery by product and do not have many products could offer a different incentive scheme for each product, and focus them on a limited number of indicators. The more complex the product menu becomes, the more simple it will be to reward overall performance based on profitability or customer satisfaction, with occasional targeted competitions to emphasize specific issues in the short term.
- **Delivery channel clustering.** If staff deliver more than one product but can be grouped by delivery channel, a separate scheme could be developed for each delivery channel. For example, one group of field officers might work on the outskirts of town, providing group loans, a voluntary savings service and a mandatory insurance service through monthly group meetings. Another group of field officers might serve individual clients at the branch office premises. Each could have its own incentive scheme.
- **Fairness.** If frontline staff have distinct product responsibilities, offering a reward for one product's performance and not another can create animosity and poor morale among those who work with the unrewarded product. The same is true for staff serving different market segments. Not all segments have the same potential for growth, so branch-based incentives need to be benchmarked to the market potential of the area being served.
- **Graduation.** If one product is meant to be a stepping stone to another, and the same employee cannot deliver both products, employees who support a client's transition to the next product should receive a reward when the client graduates. If there is no reward, staff will be less likely to encourage graduation. This is what happened at FINCA Uganda when it introduced its new Small Enterprise Partnership product. Some credit officers opposed the new product, because the transfer of high-value clients to the new product affected their bonus payments (Cracknell et al., 2002).
- **Risk.** Incentives should always balance quantity with quality. Incentive schemes for loan products, for example, should measure delinquency levels, whereas those for insurance products should look at the quality of claims processing and the percentage of policy renewals.
- **Testing.** Given the positive and negative effects that an incentive scheme can have on a new product's introduction, it is a good idea to observe the impact of incentives during the product's pilot test. If a new incentive scheme will be introduced along with the new product, the scheme should be tested as part of the pilot so that adjustments can be made as necessary to ensure the effectiveness of the scheme before rollout.

> **Box 23.10 Prizma's Use of Individual and Group Performance Goals**
>
> In Bosnia-Herzegovina, Prizma uses a combination of individual and group-based incentives, to include depth of outreach, service quality and the financial health of the MFI as a whole. Loan officers are rewarded monthly for performance on a few select indicators, including client caseload, dropout rates, portfolio at risk, loans disbursed, and depth of outreach. In addition, all branch staff receive a percentage of Prizma's annual surplus as a profit-sharing bonus. This is measured with varying weights set by the Board annually and based on the team's aggregate score across its six core performance areas:
>
> 1. Productivity – number of clients per staff
> 2. Breadth – growth in number of active clients
> 3. Depth – number of new, very poor clients, as measured by its Poverty Scorecard
> 4. Efficiency – administrative efficiency ratio
> 5. Dropouts – dropout rate over 90 days
> 6. Write-offs – annual write-off rate
>
> Prizma's headquarters staff are also eligible for annual profit-sharing bonuses, based on average branch performance. This gives them an incentive to ensure the sound functioning of the MFI's operations as a whole.
>
> *Source: Campion and Linder, 2008.*

- **Adjustability.** MFIs need to be able to change their incentives periodically to emphasize different priorities. For instance, if an institution is short of funds, it can have a special competition for savings mobilization; if it then becomes overly liquid, it can switch priorities to lending. If incentives are not regularly adjusted to motivate specific performance, they can lose their power as a management tool and come to be perceived as an entitlement.
- **Group vs. individual.** Individual incentives can be appropriate when revenue (or a measurable social return) is generated by specific individuals. They can work for many loan, leasing, insurance and money transfer products, but with savings products it is difficult to identify and reward individual contributions. MFIs that offer both savings and loans sometimes use a combination of individual and group incentives, as Prizma has done in Bosnia-Herzegovina (see Box 23.10). One of the most powerful reasons for diversified MFIs to use group-based incentives is to motivate teamwork and cross-selling.

23.4 Communicating with Clients

Effective communication of the value of each product becomes more difficult as the number of products in the portfolio grows. Previous sections of this chapter have already identified several actions that MFIs can take in an attempt to reduce the risk of confusion among clients:

- Divide frontline staff responsibilities by customer rather than product.
- Create customer service representatives who take special responsibility for client communication.

- Provide training, reference systems and other support infrastructure to help all staff understand and be able to communicate the overall product mix.

There are, however, six other steps that institutions can take to help clients identify the right products for their varied needs, and to ensure that the expanding product portfolio strengthens rather than threatens customers' relationship with the MFI. These are:

1. Make sure that products are clearly differentiated from each other and from the competition.
2. Craft clear messages with a customer focus.
3. Build a brand that connects each product to an overarching MFI–customer relationship.
4. Tailor the product mix and communications strategy to meet the needs of different market segments.
5. Bundle and cross-sell products.
6. Provide or facilitate access to financial education opportunities so that clients can understand better how to make use of diverse product options.

Product Differentiation

The more clearly distinct one product is from another, the easier it will be for staff to explain what each product has to offer, and the easier it will be for clients to identify which product(s) might be able to meet their needs at a particular point in time. The more products an MFI introduces into its portfolio, the more difficult it can become to distinguish one from another. Even two relatively different loan products – one group-based and one for individuals – can be confused and even misused by clients if the features of the products overlap. SHARE in India made certain that there would be no confusion between its three loan products by establishing mutually exclusive ranges for the loan amounts for each product, as illustrated in Table 23.3.

One of the most useful tools for differentiating products is the marketing framework known as the "8 Ps". This framework is useful because it breaks the components of a product into eight parts, which are summarized in Table 23.4. These eight parts describe different aspects of the core, actual and augmented product that were introduced in Chapter 1, and can help institutions design products that are unique. Although two products may be similar in many respects, a different design in one of the 8P areas can differentiate them. In MFIs that have a large product portfolio, tables that analyse and compare products along the 8P framework can be used for internal training purposes to assist staff in understanding which product is more appropriate to meet which client needs, and why.

Table 23.3 Product differentiation at SHARE (India)

Product	Loan Amount
Group loan	Up to Rs 10,000
Individual loan with simplified cash flow appraisal	From Rs 10,001 to Rs 20,000
Individual loan with complete appraisal process	Above Rs 20,000

Source: Dellien et al., 2005.

Table 23.4 The 8 "P"s of marketing

The "P"	Details of the "P"
Product design	Specific features such as minimum balances, loan terms; also ancillary aspects such as disbursement times, collateral or guarantees, amortization schedules, repayment structures (e.g. balloon payments or interest-free grace periods).
Price	Interest rate, withdrawals costs, loan fees, prepayment penalties, prompt payment incentives, transaction costs, etc. The price needs to be considered fair by the customer, given the benefits provided by the other 7 Ps, while generating enough revenue to cover the institution's costs of providing those benefits.
Promotion	Advertising, public relations, publicity, and all aspects of sales communication.
Place	Distribution, making sure that the product/service is available where and when it is wanted. This includes such options as outreach agents, mobile bankers and ATMs. From the customer's perspective, place refers to convenience and accessibility of the product or service being offered.
Positioning	Is the MFI occupying a distinct competitive position in the mind of the target customer? This could be in terms of low transaction cost, low price, high quality, security of savings, quick turnaround time, professional service, etc. It is a perception. The positioning of products needs to be consistent with the overall positioning of the institution.
Physical evidence	Makes the MFI and its intangible services visible. It includes the presentation of the product, how the branch looks, whether it is tidy or dirty, newly painted or decaying, the appearance of the brochures, posters and passbooks, etc.
People	How are clients treated by the MFI's staff? Are they treated with the courtesy and attention befitting a customer? Are they made to feel welcome? etc.
Process	The way in which product and services are delivered: how the transaction is processed and documented, the queues, the forms to be filled, etc.

Source: Frankiewicz et al., 2004.

MFIs can also use the 8P framework to identify differences between their existing products and those of the competition (see Table 24.4 in the chapter on product portfolio management). If frontline employees understand those differences, it can help them explain to customers what makes each of their products unique. When an MFI's product features are relatively similar to those of the competition, the 8P analysis can help staff identify how their MFI's delivery of the product is more attractive than that of the competition. Finally, for MFIs that have many products in their portfolio, the analysis enables staff to hone in on an area of relative strength, which can help them make a sale.

Creating Clear Messages with a Customer Focus

Once an MFI knows what differentiates the individual products in its portfolio, communicating that information to customers is not as straightforward as it might at first appear. The language and format that an institution uses to describe a product internally are usually not the same kind of language or format that customers would find attractive or helpful. To create a clear message for customers' consumption, MFIs should pay attention to five things in particular: benefits, language, graphics, competitive advantage and transparent pricing.

Benefits. Much more important than the list of product features is an explanation of what the product or product portfolio can do for the customer. Why should anyone buy it? What problems can it help customers solve, or what opportunities can it help them take advantage of?

Language. One of the more difficult parts about communicating with customers is getting the word choice right. Literally, an MFI's customers may speak different local languages, or they may use local expressions within a national language. They will probably use a more basic vocabulary than the head office staff who typically design an MFI's marketing messages. Testing messages with frontline staff and with customers before using them in a major campaign can be very helpful in ensuring that customers will understand and respond to a message in the way an MFI hopes.

Graphics. In written communication, pictures can be worth a thousand words. A colourful, attractive design with photographs of people who resemble an MFI's target clients will deliver a "this MFI is for you" message much more powerfully than the words by themselves. A brochure for an MFI that serves 95 per cent women and wants to continue serving primarily women should look different from that of an MFI that aims to serve a balanced number of women and men. Similarly, a brochure for owners of small and medium enterprises should look different from a brochure for microenterprises. Maps with branch locations, and tables or charts with product information, can be much easier to understand than text.

Competitive advantage. Customers are aware of an MFI's competition – sometimes more aware than the institution itself. They will often shop around, or at least gather information from family and friends about what others have to offer, before making a decision about whether to buy from any particular institution. The information clients gather may be true or misguided, and MFIs have little control over that. However, they can help to shape potential clients' perceptions of their institution by clearly stating what their institution's advantage is over the competition. How is their product better than other similar products available in the market?

Pricing. Detailed information on pricing is often omitted from marketing messages in order to focus customers on the benefits of a product rather than its costs, to avoid having to reprint expensive brochures every time a product's price changes, and to make it more difficult for competitors to understand the MFI's product strategy. This decision is rational, but there are some clear disadvantages:

- The more difficult it is for potential clients to determine the true cost of a product, the longer it will take them to make a purchase decision. They may decide it is not worth the effort to purchase the product, or they may choose to purchase from a competitor that is easier to understand.
- Clients may purchase the product and then be upset afterwards when they discover "hidden" fees or transaction costs that they did not initially perceive. If this happens, an MFI may succeed at getting the initial sale, but at the expense of a long term relationship.
- A lack of transparency around prices makes it easier for unscrupulous competitors to take advantage of the poor. They can offer products that look simple but deliberately hide fees, charges or conditions that increase the cost of borrowing, limit insurance benefits, or erode the amount clients save or transfer.

The more clearly an MFI communicates its pricing policy and helps potential clients understand the pricing considerations that deserve attention, the easier it will be for them to assess the true value of the MFI's offering, and to protect themselves from predatory financial service providers. This does not mean that MFIs must provide detailed price information in their first communication with clients, or that it must be printed in their brochures. It can, for example, be provided as a black-and-white insert to the brochure, or be shared during client orientation sessions. MFIs that wish to assess the transparency of their current pricing policies can refer to the guidelines and indicators recently developed by the Smart Campaign (see Box 23.11).

Box 23.11 Transparent and Responsible Pricing as a Client Protection Principle

Transparent and Responsible Pricing is one of the six client protection principles that have been endorsed by over 450 organizations – including hundreds of retail microfinance providers, networks, associations, support organizations, and close to 90 investors and donors – participating in the Smart Campaign. Listed below are the seven indicators that are currently used by providers to assess the degree to which they are translating the commitment to transparent pricing into action:

1. Prices, terms and conditions of all financial products are fully disclosed to the client prior to sale, including interest charges, insurance premiums, minimum balances, all fees, penalties, linked products, third-party fees, and whether those can change over time.
2. Staff are trained to communicate effectively with all clients, ensuring that they understand the product, the terms of the contract, their rights and obligations. Communications techniques address literacy limitations (for example, reading contracts out loud, materials in local languages).
3. Multiple channels for disclosing clear and accurate information about the product are used, such as brochures, orientation sessions, meetings, posting information in the branch, or web sites.
4. The financial institution follows truth-in-lending laws and required annual percentage rates (APR) or effective interest rate calculation formulae. In the absence of industry-wide requirements, information is provided that shows the total amount that the client pays for the product.
5. Loan contracts show an amortization schedule that separates principal, interest, fees; define the amount, number and due dates of instalment payments and include fees and conditions for early repayment, late payments and default. Debt-collection practices are revealed to the borrower prior to the time of sale.
6. Clients are given adequate time to review the terms and conditions of the product, and have an opportunity to ask questions and receive information prior to signing contracts.
7. Clients regularly receive clear and accurate information regarding their accounts (for example, account statements, receipts, balance inquiries).

Questions for measuring an MFI's performance in each area, as well as indicators for assessing how responsible an MFI's pricing may be can be found in the Smart Campaign publication "Conducting Client Protection Assessments: A Guide" available at: http://www.smartcampaign.org.

Source: Adapted from Smart Campaign, 2010.

Branding

Although the differentiation of individual products is important, so is the identity of the institution and the relationship that an MFI builds with each client independent of the individual products that a client is using at a particular point in time. The products in an MFI's portfolio need to support and strengthen that relationship, rather than eclipse it. A product can eclipse an institution if it becomes so popular that clients know the service by the name of the product and the person who delivers it, rather than by the name of the institution. If this happens, it will be more difficult for the MFI to cross-sell other products or to adjust product strategy in the future.

Branding refers to the actions that an MFI takes to build an identity or personality in the marketplace that communicates what the institution stands for – what it is good at, or what distinguishes it from the competition. The key to successful branding of a diversified portfolio is to build an identity that unifies the product mix and, to the extent possible, to create product brands that reflect the institutional brand, so that each product can be easily recognized as a product of the MFI.

Although detailed guidance on how to build a brand is beyond the scope of this chapter, there are four techniques worth discussing here because of their usefulness in helping to communicate to customers that an MFI's individual products are part of a larger package of services.

1. Elements of the MFI's name, logo, tagline or colours can be incorporated into the name, logo, tagline or colours of each product. Three examples of this technique are provided in Figure 23.1.
2. Customers can be provided with more than one channel for communicating with the institution, at least one of which is not product-specific. A customer service representative at the branch level or a hotline answered by staff in the head office are two examples of such channels.
3. An MFI can identify what it is that binds its product portfolio together, and highlight that element in all of its marketing materials. For example, if an institution has focused its product portfolio around meeting the needs of women throughout their life cycle, each product brochure could explain how that particular product could be useful to a woman at different moments in her life. If an MFI focused on a core competence such as convenience, then each product's brochure could highlight what makes the product convenient.
4. An MFI can find a way to refer to other products in its portfolio, even when the primary purpose of the communication is to highlight one product in particular. For instance, the institution with a product portfolio that focuses on meeting the needs of women throughout their life cycle could include a diagram on the back page of each product's brochure that positions all the products offered by the MFI along a timeline according to when in a woman's life those products might be useful. In the MFI that focuses on convenience, there could be a tagline that says, for example, "...just one of the many products that Microbank can bring to your door".

Figure 23.1 Product branding at BancoSol, Mibanco and Tameer Micro Finance Bank

Source: www.bancosol.com.bo, www.mibanco.com.pe, and www.tameerbank.com.

No matter what kind of identity an MFI decides to create in the marketplace, it is important that it can deliver what it promises. If it communicates to customers that what makes it special is its ability to deliver what customers need faster than anyone else, then it must be able to deliver its products quickly. If it does not, customers will lose trust in the institution.

The drive for consistency does not require that an MFI deliver exactly the same product mix in every branch, or to every market segment. However, it does require consistent messages about what the MFI is delivering, where, to whom, and why. As mentioned earlier in this chapter, staff training, reference sources, customer service standards and incentive schemes can help frontline staff know what messages to communicate and be motivated to deliver those messages when they interact with customers. In addition to this, an MFI might want to communicate directly with customers, perhaps through a customer service charter that it displays on the walls of its branches or attaches to its product contracts (refer back to Box 23.1), or perhaps through an annual event at which a member of the senior management team meets with customers at each branch and updates them on what will change and what will not in the coming year. The particular channel of communication is less important than making sure customers are informed when changes are made to products. In the midst of such changes, it can be helpful for customers to be reminded of what will not change, so that their relationship with the MFI is firmly rooted in a core commitment to service that transcends any particular product.

Tailoring the Mix

There are several reasons why an MFI might not want to offer the same mix of products in every location or communicate in the same way with every customer.

- Not all products will be relevant for each market segment. Agricultural loans and livestock insurance are likely to be of little use to households living in urban areas, while loan products that require collateral or business records are unlikely to be of use to the poorest.
- Not all products will be profitable in all market segments. Door-to-door deposit collection might be feasible in densely populated communities, but not in areas of low population density.
- Not all market segments use the same channels of communication. Newspapers, billboards and bus signage can be cost-effective marketing channels in urban areas, but radio and roadshows will usually be more effective in rural areas, especially if there is a high level of illiteracy.
- Not all market segments look the same, speak the same language, or value the same things. Youth and pensioners, for example, are likely to relate to very different vocabulary, pictures and examples.

Diversified MFIs can improve the effectiveness of their client communication by tailoring the content of messages and the selection of communication channels to the needs and characteristics of different market segments. This will make product messages more attractive and easier to understand, as well as more cost-effective to deliver.

Since some sales strategies are more effective with certain products, MFIs will want to modify their communications messages and channels as the product portfolio changes. Personal selling is critical for the sale of insurance, for example, because customers usually have little experience with insurance, and must be coaxed into considering its possible utility. By contrast, public relations is an important strategy for the sale of a savings product, because people must believe in an MFI's desire and ability to serve the community over the long term before they will trust the MFI with their funds. With money transfer products, sales campaigns are needed for both senders and receivers, as illustrated by the case in Box 23.12.

Table 23.5 summarizes the five main sales strategies, along with examples of some of the mechanisms that can be used to implement those strategies. Choosing the right combination of strategies to sell the products in a portfolio to a particular market segment is an art more than a science, but cost–benefit analysis can help MFIs to choose their mix strategically. A simple analysis of the number of customers who are recruited by each sales mechanism, as illustrated in Table 23.6, can facilitate this analysis. The information to complete this analysis can be gathered at the time each product is sold, either through a question on the account opening form, such as "How did you hear about this product?", or through a verbal question asked by the officer providing a fee-based service. Cost data can be provided by the department in charge of marketing the institution's products.

Box 23.12 Send-side Marketing by Fonkoze in Haiti

Send-side marketing is crucial to the success of money transfer services in recipient countries, but it can be easily overlooked. The Haitian MFI Fonkoze learned this lesson when it launched its own low-cost money transfer service in cooperation with a commercial bank in the United States. Although it negotiated attractive terms with the bank, and generated a break-even transaction volume, the new transfer product did not produce sufficient profits to invest in improving the service.

Consequently, Fonkoze formulated a send-side marketing campaign targeted at the Haitian community living in the United States. At first, Fonkoze planned to produce public service announcements, purchase targeted radio and print advertisements, and conduct radio interviews in US cities with large Haitian populations. However, the MFI quickly realized that this type of expensive marketing was better at producing market awareness than at changing client behaviour. Because Fonkoze's original money transfer service worked quite differently from a typical money transfer company (a customer mails a check to the US bank partner of Fonkoze, which then sends the funds to the Haitian MFI), it needed a marketing campaign that could convince potential clients to do things differently, rather than simply change service providers.

The MFI also needed to overcome the image of unreliability that small institutions offering low-cost services often suffer from among many Haitians abroad. The result was an innovative campaign of "family days" at Fonkoze branches in Haiti, during which the institution rented out cybercafés and gave customers a free five-minute phone call to the United States. Fonkoze also gave non-clients free phone calls, provided they took the money they would have spent on a call and opened an account with the MFI. Using this technique, the first event generated 100 new accounts in a single day. The MFI controlled costs by not paying for individual calls, but by purchasing them in bulk at a deep discount by paying the cybercafé's daily rate. During the calls, grateful clients almost invariably mentioned Fonkoze to their relatives, producing a referral from a trusted source – the best kind of publicity the institution could generate.

The calls also produced a targeted list of clients who already send money to Fonkoze clients regularly, representing an ideal market for its money transfer service. The MFI concluded that this focused strategy yielded better customer conversion rates than the expensive, untargeted media placements used in the past.

Source: Isern et al., 2008.

Bundling and Cross-selling

Cross-selling refers to the raising of awareness among users of one product that other products are available from the same institution which might be able to meet their other financial needs. Cross-selling can make an MFI's communication more efficient, since it enables all frontline staff to help disseminate information about all products. If cross-selling is done well, staff will share information about relevant products at the right time to an appropriate subset of clients, which increases the likelihood that time spent on a sales pitch will actually result in a sale. As loan officers get to know their borrowers, for example, they can find out who has children approaching school age, and speak with them about the MFI's school fees savings product. If customers approach an MFI to open a commitment savings product, they can be asked whether they would also like to also purchase savings completion insurance, so that their savings goal will be met in the event of accidental death or disability.

Table 23.5 Sales strategies

Personal selling	Direct marketing	Public relations	Advertising	Sales promotions
• Sales teams visiting markets, companies etc. • Cross-selling to existing clients • Letters to clients • Enquiries desks • Kiosk marketing	• Targeted press advertising • Radio – direct response • Direct mail • Telephone marketing • Roadshows • Kiosk marketing	• Press releases/ coverage • Speeches at functions/events • Special events • Written materials – annual reports/ newsletters etc. • Endorsements • Sponsorship • Public service activities	• Posters • Brochures • Signage • Radio • Newspapers • Roadshows • Tapes in branches	• Product rate reductions • Lotteries • Give-aways • Roadshows • Competitions

Source: McCord et al., 2004.

Table 23.6 Simple sales strategy cost–benefit analysis

Sales strategy	Cost	Number of clients recruited by product				Cost per client
		Individual loan	Group loan	Insurance	Total	
Radio	7,500	860	1,440	203	2,503	3.00
Posters	200	102	15	9	126	1.59
Billboards	1,000	150	90	105	345	2.90
Pamphlets	500	43	180	22	245	2.04
Personal selling to new clients	2,500	521	1,025	213	1,759	1.42

Source: Authors.

Cross-selling can be efficient for customers as well. Frontline staff can help clients sort out which of the MFI's products might be useful to them, so they do not have to sort through all of the products themselves. MFIs with a diverse product portfolio can potentially provide a "one-stop shopping" experience for customers by fulfilling all their financial service needs and making it unnecessary for them to go anywhere else. Cross-selling is actually a useful strategy for communicating that the MFI is interested in developing a multifaceted, lifelong relationship with clients, and not just a transaction-based product relationship.

Bundling refers to the sale of products or services as a packaged deal – in other words, for a single price. As an MFI diversifies, and its product portfolio becomes complex, bundling offers an opportunity to simplify the product menu for different market segments and make it easy for clients to identify services that have been designed specifically to meet their needs.

Bundling also reduces the per-product cost of acquiring and maintaining a customer (see Box 23.13). Thus the price that can be set for a bundle of products is usually lower than the price of buying each product independently. If customers need all of the products in a bundle, this can provide tremendous value. However, if they are forced to purchase a product that they do not need, simply to have access to the one that they want, dissatisfaction can result. A bundled approach can result in customers paying for services or benefits that they do not even know they have. As discussed in previous chapters, MFIs often bundle loan products with compulsory savings, credit life insurance or non-financial services, but this does not always increase outreach, especially when the purchase of the bundle is mandatory.

Bundling and cross-selling can be combined, and one of the best reasons to do so is to introduce a new product. Health insurance, for example, can be offered to clients who currently hold a life insurance policy at a bundled premium that is lower than the premium charged for purchasing both products separately. New products can also be bundled with coupons or discount incentives linked to an existing product. For instance, a text-a-payment mobile phone money transfer service could be sold to existing borrowers, who would receive one free payment per month for each on-time loan repayment made via the text-a-payment service.

Client Education

A final strategy for improving communication with clients that is particularly relevant for diversifying MFIs is client education. Clients may not be familiar with the new products that MFIs are introducing, such as insurance, leasing, micropensions and long-term savings. They may not perceive the need for such services, and the product concepts themselves can be complicated to understand. Even familiar products such as liquid savings accounts and money transfer services can be made more attractive to clients if they understand better how the products work, why they can be trusted, and how they can be used to help manage their financial lives.

Client education is an excellent example of a non-financial service that could be bundled with an existing financial service to increase the potential for cross-selling. Financial literacy training can help clients assess their financial situation, plan for the future, set financial goals, and

Box 23.13 Banks and Price Bundling

There are three reasons why banks are a good example of the type of consumer service business for which price bundling is effective. First, banks are characterized by a high ratio of fixed to variable costs. Once an individual establishes an account relationship with a bank, the marginal costs associated with selling and delivering additional services to the individual are generally low compared with the bank's total costs. Second, bank services entail a high degree of cost-sharing, such that the same facilities, equipment and personnel are used to provide multiple services to the customer. Third, bank services are interdependent in terms of demand. That is, financial services are designed to satisfy related customer needs, so that customers are often potential buyers of a range of financial services. In addition, price bundling has been shown to reduce competitive rate shopping, and is perceived as a way to help banks avoid costly rate wars.

Source: Hayes and Eduardo, 2003.

identify how an MFI's financial services can help them meet those goals. One-on-one coaching or consultation with staff during a periodic visit to a customer's home or business could reinforce this training. Other types of client education, such as the explanation of a new technology being introduced by the MFI (see, for example, Box 23.14), can serve the dual purpose of getting clients excited about the way the MFI is growing and innovating to serve them better, and facilitating clients' productive use of the technology.

The experience of Banco Popular in Colombia provides an example of how insufficient client education can have the opposite effect, creating additional costs (see Box 23.15). If the bank had communicated more clearly upfront how clients could manage the new technology effectively, it could have helped clients engage in behaviour that would have significantly reduced its cost of delivering the product.

23.5 Strengthening Systems to Manage Greater Complexity

The more an MFI diversifies, the more capable its systems must be of managing complexity. As discussed above, performance management systems must be adjusted to prioritize multiple objectives and provide staff with reference material, feedback, incentives and other support to guide and motivate their delivery of a complex product portfolio. Client communication systems must also be improved to help customers understand the product menu, and how they can use different products to meet their needs over time. In addition to these changes, product diversification will typically require that financial, information and risk management systems be strengthened as well.

Financial Management

In general, diversification shifts the focus of financial management from accounting practices to more sophisticated financial analysis. Proper accounting remains vital, and becomes more complex with each additional product, but new challenges appear with respect to the management of assets, liabilities and earnings.

Asset and liability management. Differences in the terms of an MFI's assets (primarily loans to clients) and liabilities (primarily customer deposits and loans made to the MFI) expose it to three types of risk: interest rate risk, exchange rate risk and liquidity risk.

- **Interest rate risk** arises from differences between the interest rate that an MFI pays for its financing and the rate that it receives for the loans (and perhaps leases) that it extends to clients. Financial institutions deliberately create differences in these rates in order to generate revenue, but interest rates on liabilities tend to change more frequently and more unexpectedly than the interest rates MFIs charge for their loans, which can decrease revenue and harm profitability.
- **Exchange rate risk** arises from differences in the price of currencies that an MFI may use to fund its operations or to deliver its services. Even if the quantity of a particular currency in its possession does not change, the value of that currency can rise or fall on a daily basis, which will affect the real value of the assets and liabilities that an MFI holds in that currency.
- **Liquidity risk** arises primarily from differences in the maturity of assets and liabilities. For instance, clients with demand deposits can ask to withdraw their savings at any time,

Box 23.14 Client Education Facilitates New Product Acceptance at FINCA Mexico

FINCA initiated a partnership with HSBC to offer its clients the "Cheque Inteligente", a customized prepaid card that allows access to loans at ATMs, merchant point-of-sale (POS) terminals, and Telecomunicaciones de México outlets throughout the country. For many FINCA clients, the Cheque Inteligente represents their first contact with the formal banking sector. About 65 per cent of clients surveyed prior to implementation had no experience using electronic banking cards or ATMs.

To overcome this obstacle and assuage clients' anxieties about using the prepaid cards, FINCA, with support from USAID, developed a comprehensive set of training materials to teach clients how to use the cards. These included a model ATM for simulating transactions, and two printed mini-guides with step-by-step instructions on how and where to use the Cheque Inteligente. Clients can test transactions using the mini-guides and the practice ATM at their village bank meetings before initiating real transactions at functional automated terminals. Commenting on the model ATM, Giset Galindo, a credit officer and training facilitator in Cuautla in Morelos, says, "You can really see the clients' confidence rise as they use [it]."

Overall satisfaction with the programme is very high. Of clients surveyed, 93 per cent intended to use the card again for their next loan disbursement. Furthermore, 99 per cent claimed that the training and materials they received proved useful. María Ortiz in San Juan Bautista Cuicatlán says, "[The card] motivated us a lot. We want to take advantage of these new products."

Source: Muñoz et al., 2009.

Box 23.15 The Impact of Insufficient Client Education

In Colombia, banks delivering Familias en Accion unexpectedly found that using prepaid cards cost twice as much (US$4.9) as making transactions at branch teller windows (US$2.5) (Marulanda, 2008). Banco Popular's social payments programme had to replace clients' prepaid cards five times as often as the bank's prepaid Visa cards for wage payments. Poor customer education was one of the prime reasons for these increased expenses. Some clients had laminated their debit cards – making them unusable – because they were told that the magnetic strip should be protected. Further, because cards were not personalized, they needed to be reissued whenever PINs were lost – this occurred more frequently than anticipated. These examples underscore how important it is to educate customers on how to use their cards so that electronic delivery options are well executed and competitive with, if not cheaper than, branch-based transactions.

Source: Pickens et al., 2009.

while clients whose loans are funded with that savings may not repay their loans for many months. In the broadest sense, liquidity risk refers to the possibility that an MFI will not have sufficient cash on hand to meet its financial obligations as they come due. This includes being able to fulfil withdrawal requests, make bill and remittance payments, fund new loan disbursements, and respond to emergencies.

The function of asset–liability management is to measure and control the level of these risks. Diversification makes the job more difficult by increasing the number of products – each with its own terms – whose cash flows, currencies and financing needs must be balanced. As long as an MFI works in one currency and offers a limited number of short-term loan products that are financed by equity and compulsory savings, asset–liability management is relatively simple. Once voluntary savings, longer-term loans or money transfer products are added to the mix, the risk of not having sufficient cash on hand to meet customers' demands increases significantly. The risk of having excess cash also increases, and MFIs need to invest that cash wisely or their earnings will suffer.

To control these risks, diversifying MFIs must strengthen their capacity to analyse, understand and manage more complex asset and liability relationships. Some of the strategies institutions use to accomplish this are described below.

- **Augment the human resource base.** MFIs can recruit new employees who already have experience managing the assets and liabilities of a diversified financial institution, or they can invest in developing these skills among current staff through training and professional education. Regulatory authorities may actually require that key financial managers hold certain degrees or qualifications in order for an MFI to be licensed to offer a new type of product, such as savings or insurance.
- **Decentralize certain tasks** to more junior staff or hire an assistant. As cash management becomes more time consuming, for example, an MFI may want to recruit a treasury manager to take responsibility for the institution's overall liquidity position (see Box 23.16), freeing up the chief financial officer to spend more time on analysis and other responsibilities.
- **Enhance oversight.** Diversifying MFIs often establish an asset and liability committee (ALCO) at the board and/or senior management levels to monitor the evolving structure of the MFI's balance sheet, discuss anticipated interest rate and market changes, review policies, and recommend or set new policies in response to those changes.
- **Use more tools to project and monitor the MFI's current position.** There are many tools at an MFI's disposal for analysing its current asset–liability situation. Each one increases managers' understanding of the risks being faced, which puts them in a better position to control those risks. Daily **cash forecasting**, for example, estimates the size and timing of cash inflows and outflows based on historical data (modified to take into account an MFI's current activities), which helps an MFI determine how much cash it needs to have on hand to meet its daily obligations. Longer-term **cash flow budgeting** is part of the annual planning process. It anticipates liquidity needs based on an institution's assumptions about future operations, and helps the MFI develop plans that can be adequately funded. **Sources-and-uses analysis** examines the cost of each source of funds, and the revenues from each use of funds, to determine whether funds are being used in the best way possible. A **gap management report** helps MFIs analyse the degree to which their risk-sensitive assets and liabilities are matched (Biety, 2005).
- **Analyse ratios.** Ratios are another tool for helping MFIs understand their current asset–liability situation, and the kind of changes that may need to be made. MFIs can set a target for each ratio and then monitor actual performance against those targets. Depending on the degree to which performance falls above or below a desired ratio, an MFI

Box 23.16 Roles and Responsibilities of a Treasury Manager

The function of the treasury manager is to manage the institution's overall liquidity position. This includes ensuring adequate liquidity levels at branches and head office, adhering to reserve requirements and other liquidity ratios mandated by the central bank, minimizing the cost of forgone earnings on idle funds and avoiding the cost of emergency borrowing, maximizing the return on investments outside the loan portfolio, and managing the interest rate spread between loans and deposits. Key responsibilities include the following:

- Review cash holdings at branches on a consistent basis, and facilitate transfer and pricing of excess to branches with cash shortfalls.
- Monitor balances on bank accounts to evaluate availability of idle cash for investment.
- Monitor interest rate risk, liquidity risk, foreign exchange risk (if applicable).
- Prepare liquidity reports required in normal operations, for treasury management meetings, for ALCO meetings, or to meet compliance reporting requirements.

Source: Ledgerwood and White, 2006.

would take different actions. For example, an institution can monitor its ratio of liquid assets to total demand deposits, and if the actual ratio falls below the target ratio, managers will know that they need to increase the institution's cash position. The Microfinance Reporting Standards Initiative provides guidance on recommended financial management ratios for MFIs (see Box 23.17).

- **Establish sources of backup liquidity.** This makes it possible for MFIs to avoid holding large amounts of cash that earn little or no interest. Some MFIs access backup liquidity by establishing lines of credit or overdraft facilities with commercial banks. Others, such as FECECAM in Benin, access a liquidity pool through a credit union federation or other second-tier organization. Still others arrange for another MFI or cooperative to serve as a liquidity pool. Even demand deposits in another financial institution can provide backup liquidity in the event of a crisis. One of the reasons why Fonkoze was able to begin operating so soon and so widely after the January 2010 earthquake in Haiti was its ability to quickly access US$2 million from its account at the City National Bank in New Jersey.
- **Improve cash management.** Cash that is held on-site by an MFI earns no return, so MFIs make an effort to minimize the amount of time that cash is not "working" or earning interest. They may coordinate loan disbursements with the receipt of client savings deposits; pay expenses only on their due date; or place excess funds in demand-deposit and short-term time deposit accounts with other financial institutions or other highly liquid investments, among other strategies (Biety, 2005).
- **Develop new products.** Although new products should not be developed solely for the purpose of asset–liability management, it may be that a mismatch in an MFI's asset–liability balance can be improved by introducing a new product that customers find valuable. If, for example, an MFI obtains long-term financing in a foreign currency that is used as legal tender in its country, it could introduce a loan product in that currency to bal-

Box 23.17 Microfinance Reporting Standards Initiative

Over the past decade, there has been an industry-wide effort to identify and implement financial reporting standards for microfinance institutions. The objective is to provide uniform financial information for all MFIs, regardless of size, maturity or geographic location, to managers and stakeholders, including investors, donors, raters, MIS software developers and associations. This promotes transparency, facilitates comparability, improves decision-making, and increases investment by making it easier to observe and understand an MFI's financial health.

After extensive industry collaboration, the SEEP Network released a milestone document in 2005: *Measuring performance of microfinance institutions: A framework for reporting, analysis, and monitoring (the Framework).* The Microfinance Reporting Standards Initiative seeks to keep the Framework up to date with the evolving microfinance landscape. Its "Secretariat" is hosted by the SEEP Network. Practitioner involvement is facilitated by the Financial Services Working Group (FSWG), with input provided by representatives from a range of microfinance industry stakeholders. The reporting standards adoption process follows a multi-stage model, based upon that of the International Accounting Standards Board (IASB), which allows for public input and transparency.

The most recent set of standards produced by the Initiative includes 35 ratios and four asset-liability management tables. They are consistent with International Financial Reporting Standards (IFRS), a set of global accounting standards increasingly adopted throughout the world, and with the Basel II framework. Additionally, all financial statement line items are aligned with the standardized nomenclature developed for global financial reporting called eXtensible Business Reporting Language (XBRL). The ratios and the asset-liability tables can be downloaded free of charge from the Initiative's web site:
http://seepnetwork.org/Pages/Initiatives/FinancialReportingStandardInitiative.aspx.

Source: Adapted from SEEP Network, 2010b.

ance its foreign currency exposure on the liability side of the balance sheet. A successful long-term savings product could make it possible for an MFI to introduce a longer-term loan product such as housing loans. Variable-rate loan products are often not attractive to microfinance clients, but if they were introduced successfully, they could help MFIs to manage interest-rate risk.

- **Forge partnerships.** Some products, such as insurance and international money transfers, can greatly complicate an MFI's asset–liability management if it attempts to offer the product on its own. Partnership with an insurance company or global money transfer company such as Western Union or Money Gram can simplify its asset–liability management challenge by transferring foreign exchange risk or certain assets and liabilities to the partner.

Profitability. Diversification can affect an MFI's earnings in a number of ways. As discussed in Chapters 1 and 2, it can increase an institution's revenue and diversify its risk, but it can also increase costs and make the MFI vulnerable to new risks that could result in losses. Many strategies for capturing the opportunities and minimizing the threats presented by diversification have already been discussed, for example cross-selling and building lifelong customer relationships to generate more revenue from each client, using performance management sys-

tems to increase efficiency and productivity, and engaging all employees in a robust risk-management system. A few other strategies for increasing revenue while controlling costs and risks merit attention here:

- **Access rules.** For products that are in high demand, but are riskier or more difficult to deliver, MFIs can give preferential access to loyal or high-performing customers only. This provides an incentive for clients to use the MFI's other products in a way that will "earn" them access to premium products, and it limits the degree of the MFI's exposure to the risks inherent in the product.
- **Activity-based costing.** Product costing helps MFIs avoid pricing products at a level that is unprofitable. It gives institutions the information they need to bundle products effectively, and to evaluate the feasibility of various pricing strategies. Although activity-based costing is more demanding than allocation-based costing, it is particularly valuable for MFIs with a diverse product portfolio, because it calculates the cost of activities as well as products. With this information, MFIs can assign costs to market segments in addition to products. They can also identify processes that are relatively expensive and/or affect more than one product and prioritize these for cost reduction, thus increasing the profitability of multiple products in the portfolio at once.
- **Product and customer profitability analysis.** By putting systems in place to allocate costs and revenues to specific products and/or market segments (see Box 23.18), MFIs can identify which are profitable and which are not. They can then use this information to design pricing, marketing and product development strategies that promote profitable products, target profitable market segments, divest from unprofitable markets, and strengthen (or eliminate) unprofitable products.
- **Pricing strategy.** Once an MFI knows how much each product costs to deliver, it can set a price for each product that takes into account market demand, the price being offered by competitors, the stage of the product's life cycle (see Chapter 24), and the institution's mission. It can charge a higher mark-up on products with high demand and no competition, and a lower mark-up on products that must compete with many similar offerings. It can even accept losses on a particular product or market segment, as BRAC and Hatton National Bank have done (see Boxes 23.19 and 23.20), as long as it knows that those losses can be covered by revenue generated by other more profitable products. Pricing strategy can also be used to reward or encourage certain behaviour. For example, India's VimoSEWA offers a discount to members who enrol their whole family in an insurance policy, and Bangladesh's Grameen Kalyan charges a lower insurance premium to clients of its sister company, Grameen Bank, than to the general public.

Maximizing the profitability of a product portfolio does not necessarily mean maximizing the profitability of each product in the portfolio. One less profitable product might benefit clients in ways that competitors' products do not, and result in customers being more loyal and purchasing other, more profitable products that they would not have purchased otherwise. A less profitable product might also draw new clients into a relationship with the MFI who might otherwise not have been interested, and the MFI can broaden and deepen that relationship over time.

Box 23.18 Customer Profitability Analysis

Institutional understanding of customer profitability tends to be limited in microfinance. Profitable customers are often lost through overpricing, and unprofitable customers are won by underpricing, or are subsidized by more profitable customers (Richebacher, 2003). Very few MFIs have a clear understanding of the connection between customer types, or particular market segments, and costs. Methods to further this understanding range in complexity from simple analysis, such as using percentages of sales, to developing complicated allocation methods based on actual activities that incur costs. In general, these approaches are derived from product profitability analysis – the unit profitability of each product is multiplied by the number of units sold to a particular customer (Falletti, 2002).

Implementing customer profitability models requires an MFI to allocate costs by customers. Such an allocation needs to be coupled with a move away from the more traditional product management focus to a customer management focus. In the product management model, for example, one manager handles mortgages, another term deposits, and another working capital loans. The managers do not necessarily know how any one customer interacts with the entire MFI. For any one product, a customer may be a low-value customer, but she or he may be very valuable if considered across the organization. Yet, because the product managers cannot know this, they may underinvest in the customer. If the MFI followed a customer management model, the customer's true value would be apparent, and could be managed accordingly.

Source: Ledgerwood and White, 2006.

Information Management

Diversification complicates the flow of information into, within and out of an institution. Not only is there more information to process, but there is a greater variety of information to process, and there are more stakeholders who need access to different subsets of that information. The insurance company with which an MFI is partnering might want data on the policies sold each day; regulators might want a weekly liquidity report; product managers might want product performance reports by market segment; and so on. As the number of products being purchased by the average client increases, the information system becomes a critical tool for managing customer relationships at all levels of the institution.

In general, an MFI's information system serves four main functions: 1) it collects information; 2) it organizes information so that users can efficiently find what they need; 3) it processes information to facilitate user analysis and decision-making; and 4) it channels reporting and communication. For an MFI to diversify successfully, its information system must become capable of handling greater volume and complexity as it fulfils each of these functions.

The volume challenge is typically a hardware challenge that institutions address during the new product or market development process. However, it is not always possible to predict hardware challenges, or the stress that a new product will place on an existing information system. If a new product is much more successful than predicted, for example, business volume can quickly overwhelm system capacity. Thus installing scalable systems or having a plan for how system capacity can be scaled up if necessary is important.

Box 23.19 Start-up Subsidies for Customers at BRAC

At BRAC in Bangladesh, initial loans to new customers were so small – just Tk2,500 (approximately US$38) – that BRAC lost money servicing them at the given interest rate (15 per cent charged on a flat basis, roughly equivalent to a 30 per cent per year effective interest rate). At loan sizes of Tk4,000 and more, BRAC recovered costs with interest earnings, but not at Tk2,500. BRAC calculated that it cross-subsidized at a rate of Tk225 on a Tk2,500 loan, suggesting that BRAC would have needed to raise effective interest rates by about nine percentage points for small loans. BRAC's management feared that effective interest rates of 40 per cent would be unaffordable for the poorest borrowers, and could undermine social goals. By charging new clients borrowing small amounts the same price as other clients, the subsidies (actually "cross-subsidies" in this case) were not associated with "cheap credit" and all of the negative trappings that entails. Instead, they were strategically deployed and targeted to aid the poorest customers. They allowed the customers to begin the first stages of a relationship that ultimately was sustainable.

Source: Morduch, 2005.

Box 23.20 Cross-subsidies at Hatton National Bank in Sri Lanka

In a 2007 interview, Chandula Abeywickrema, Deputy General Manager of Hatton National Bank, described intentional strategies to cross-subsidize products:

"We recently developed a senior citizen banking product. We pay one per cent extra interest to senior people saving with us. This older clientele also appreciate our free health insurance product, by which they can receive reimbursement of hospitalization expenses. At the other end of the life cycle, we have developed infant savings products. We are offering this product in our partner hospitals. As soon as a baby is born there, the parents can open a bank account in the name of the infant with a minimum of US$10 deposit. In Sri Lanka, it is considered a good omen to offer valuables to the baby on the day of birth. With this infant account, parents and relatives are incentivized to place money in the child's account instead of offering other gifts.

"For the moment, neither the senior citizen product nor the infant account product is profitable per se. What we do is we cross-subsidize these products with other, more profitable products. We developed all these targeted savings products because part of our vision at Hatton is to cover all segments of the society. And in the long term, we believe the infant accounts will probably bring us the same benefits as the children's accounts, while the senior citizen programme already gives a very positive image of the bank."

Source: Adapted from De Montesquiou, 2007.

The complexity challenge is more severe, and addressing it often requires a combination of hardware, software and human resource investments. To face the challenge, MFIs must first identify the human and technological components of their information system, and assess the extent to which they are capable of meeting the needs of various stakeholders. An information system audit along the lines of that described in Chapter 24 might be helpful at this point. Process mapping can also be useful, particularly when trying to integrate a new product's information needs into an existing system.

Once an MFI understands the strengths and weaknesses of its current system, it can make changes as necessary to increase the system's capacity to carry out each of the functions illustrated in Figure 23.2 with a greater degree of complexity. Some examples of the changes MFIs might make are described below.

Collecting information. MFIs can assign specific individuals or teams the responsibility for collecting specific kinds of information. They can change the frequency with which data is collected and/or the channels that are used to collect it. They can programme their computer systems to track product usage by market segment, or adjust data collection forms to facilitate segmentation (for example, by creating a space on complaint and suggestion forms so that customers and staff can clearly identify which product is being referring to). They can also make an effort to motivate staff to collect quality information in a timely manner using the strategies discussed in Chapter 2.

Organizing information. MFIs can make changes in the way information is sorted or the locations where it is stored. They can define different levels of access and assign permissions so that employees are given access to information on a "need-to-know" basis. They can build the capacity to identify and profile market segments, to track their needs, product usage, satisfaction or other characteristics, and to update those profiles on a regular basis. A relationship management database could provide integrated information about a client's use of all the institution's products, and costs could be assigned to specific products or customer groups to facilitate profitability analysis.

Analysing information. An MFI's system can be designed to process some types of information automatically, and to trigger alarms when performance against the indicators falls outside the range considered normal. For example, all members of the asset and liability committee could be notified if cash reserves as a proportion of total demand deposits fall below 20 per cent. The system could also allow managers to request their own dashboard to monitor the performance of a particular individual, team, product or customer group. The capacity to generate charts and graphs that illustrate trends in pictures instead of numbers can also be useful.

Figure 23.2 Four functions of an information management system

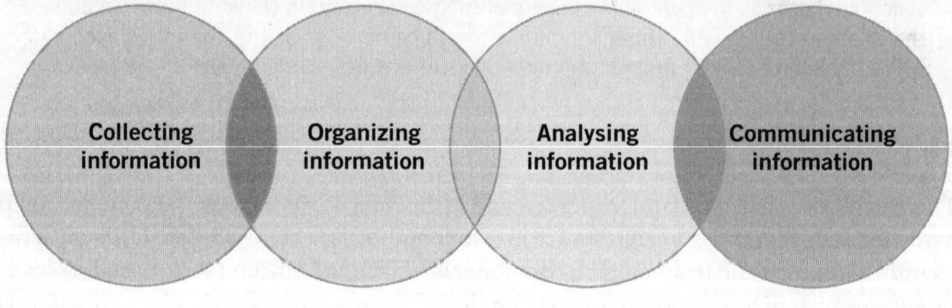

Source: Authors.

Communicating information. Automated messages and standardized reports can guarantee that certain types of information are channelled to the individuals who need to use it. Guidance can be provided to staff on how to select communication channels strategically, depending on the type of information that needs to be sent, to whom, and with what level of urgency. Interfaces may need to be put in place for the exchange of electronic data with partners or regulators. Cross-functional communication channels will also be needed to support customer relationship management, and feedback loops will have to be monitored regularly to ensure channels remain open and useful.

As they diversify, MFIs usually find it necessary to create an information technology (IT) department, or at least the position of IT manager, so that the institution does not depend entirely on outsourced services to manage its information system. The IT manager can take responsibility for building and maintaining a system that supports all departments, overseeing hardware and software procurement and installation, developing system documentation, training staff on hardware and software, and so on.

Risk Management

As discussed in Chapter 2, the development of new products and markets both exposes MFIs to new risks and increases their exposure to familiar risks. This is often the case with asset and liability management, for example, and information systems risk, as discussed above. Institutions are also more vulnerable to fraud. As an MFI's operations become complex, it is more difficult to create effective controls and monitor compliance. Warning signs can be drowned out by the sheer volume of information that managers must process on a daily basis.

MFIs can take several steps to make their risk management systems more capable of handling the complexity that comes with diversification:

- **Make risk management part of the institution's culture.** Any of the strategies mentioned in Section 23.1 can be used to increase staff awareness of the risks in their environment. Incorporating risk considerations into basic management systems such as record-keeping, quality control, training or performance evaluation, and communicating clearly with each staff member about the role they can and should play in helping to manage risk, can help everyone contribute to effective risk management.
- **Take a systematic approach.** In an MFI with complex operations, it is critical to adopt a systematic approach to identify, measure, control and monitor the many different types of risk to which an MFI is exposed. This should include an analysis of the risks associated with specific products and market segments.
- **Task a specific entity with supervising risk management.** This could be a risk manager, department or committee (see Box 23.21), depending on the size and complexity of the MFI. XacBank in Mongolia, which offers a diverse menu of more than 30 different products, has both a risk management committee and an integrated risk management division (XacBank, 2009). Regardless of who does the supervising, holding a specific entity responsible for overall risk management can help an MFI organize its various risk management activities and reduce the likelihood that some risk exposures will be left unidentified or uncontrolled.

Box 23.21 Risk Management Committee

The risk management committee (RMC) is a small committee that unites principal senior managers in an internal risk management review team that focuses on the institution's most important risks and controls. It is an early and effective mechanism for anticipating and managing new and ongoing risks across the various business departments. The RMC assigns responsibility for measuring, managing and prioritizing the institution's risks. Most importantly, it generates strong, open communication among the senior managers of the different business units, fostering a more collaborative approach to risk management.

The RMC receives reports from various parts of the institution (refer to the table below for examples), and monitors risk exposure against approved tolerance limits. It maintains a risk assessment report that summarizes the institution's risks and serves as input to the internal audit team, which tests and adjusts this assessment with findings reviewed by the committee. The RMC circulates summaries of its meeting minutes quarterly to the board, which serves as the check on its performance.

Sample reports submitted to the RMC

Report name	Prepared by	Frequency of preparation	Frequency of distribution
1. Non-performing loans report	Credit Department	Monthly	Quarterly
2. Environmental scanning report	Marketing Unit	Quarterly	Quarterly
3. Cash and liquidity policy exceptions report	Finance Department	Monthly	Quarterly
4. Customer survey report	Marketing Unit	Biannual	Biannual
5. Regulatory violation report	Internal Control Department	Upon receipt from regulatory authorities	Quarterly
6. Fraud and malpractices report	Internal Control Department	Monthly	Quarterly
7. Audit exceptions report	Internal Control Department	Monthly	Quarterly
8. Legal liability report	External lawyers	Upon receipt from lawyers	Quarterly

In addition to the responsibilities noted above, the RMC evaluates all new products to ensure they do not pose undue risk to the institution (in other words, the "risk–return" trade-off is in balance). It also conducts a centralized review of all risk management policies on an annual basis to make sure they are effective, and are updated regularly.

Source: Adapted from Schneider-Moretto, 2005, and Triodos Facet, 2009.

- **Prioritize risks.** Since the resources for managing risks are limited, prioritization is necessary to ensure that the most dangerous risks are addressed first. Each department has a natural tendency to prioritize the risks that affect it most, so the entity that supervises risk management can help establish priorities that are strategic for the MFI as a whole.
- **Create a committee of the board of directors that focuses specifically on risk management.** As the complexity of operations increases, it can become unwieldy for all members of the board to invest the time necessary to provide effective oversight of risk management. ALCO and credit committees can develop or recruit the expertise necessary to provide clear guidance on the level of financial risk that can be tolerated, and ensure that management is implementing the procedures and controls necessary to keep risk below that level. A risk management committee of the board can play a similar role with respect to overall risk management by reviewing current exposure and compliance in all risk categories, and adjusting limits and controls as necessary.
- **Enhance internal audit capacity.** The workload of the internal audit team will increase each time a new product is introduced. There will be more policies and procedures to check compliance against, more reports to review, greater variety of transactions to test for accuracy, and more potential for irregularities and complaints from internal and external customers that might have to be investigated. Consequently, the more an MFI diversifies, the more manpower the internal audit function will need to do its job effectively.
- **Audit the MFI's information system from the perspective of risk,** and make sure the right people are getting the information they need to make decisions and produce reports in a timely manner.
- **Client education.** If an MFI trains clients so that they know what procedures should be followed, and who they can contact in the event of any deviation from those procedures, clients can help an MFI manage its risks as well.

23.6 Managing Change

Diversification requires change. As illustrated above, it can require a large number of changes, a large variety of changes, and large-scale changes that affect entire systems. This is a potential problem according to Brand (1998b), since "the most common source of institutional product failure is succumbing to internal resistance to change." What can managers do, therefore, to plan, organize, lead and control change in a way that minimizes resistance and produces successful results?

Planning

Successful product diversification requires a plan, which is usually articulated in the form of product strategies or product marketing plans for each product in an MFI's portfolio, and an overall product portfolio strategy, which is usually articulated in an MFI's business plan (see Chapter 24). Coordinating and motivating the successful implementation of product development activities without such a plan is difficult, if not impossible. Different departments will inevitably pursue distinct objectives, communicate divergent priorities, make disparate assumptions or set varying timelines for implementation. A plan provides a roadmap, and a common focus.

The process through which an institution's plans are developed is also important. As mentioned in Chapter 2, one of the most effective strategies for motivating staff to embrace new products and the changes that come with them is to involve employees in the development of those products. If employees are part of the process, they will be better informed and have less reason to fear or resist changes that they do not understand or control.

Another way to minimize resistance to change is to think in advance about who the change is likely to affect, and what can be done to facilitate specific employees' or clients' acceptance of the change. Strategies can be designed to get the buy-in of key staff or opinion leaders, or to help clients become comfortable with a new way of doing things, as FINCA did when it introduced ATMs (see Box 23.15).

Finally, MFIs can resist being overly ambitious, and ensure that resources remain to deal with the unexpected complications that are certain to occur during the diversification process. Plans that allocate human or financial resources too tightly can generate high levels of stress and lead not only to resistance but, potentially, product failure.

Organizing

Once an MFI has a plan, getting the right resources in place at the right time to implement diversification is largely a function of communication and coordination. Many of the strategies discussed in Section 23.3 can assist MFIs in empowering staff to deliver a diverse portfolio: for example, making sure everyone understands what their roles and responsibilities are, providing supportive infrastructure and training to make implementation easier, and ensuring that communication channels are open and feedback is encouraged. This last item is particularly important, because the amount of information that is communicated and the way it is communicated can have a major impact on the degree to which employees resist a change. Even if mistakes are made and resistance appears, functioning feedback loops can help an MFI identify what is wrong and what is needed for the resisters to feel comfortable moving forward or be willing to make the change (see Box 23.22, for example).

Leading

As discussed in Section 23.3, the simple fact that a plan and the resources to implement it are in place does not mean that anyone will be motivated to achieve the targets set out in the plan. Change can be intimidating and uncomfortable, and it requires effort. Most employees will resist making that effort unless someone gives them a good reason to do so.

Successful diversification requires leaders who can articulate for each staff member why they should support change. Why is their institution introducing a new product? Why this particular product? How will the product help the institution achieve its mission? What difference will it make in a client's life, and how will it benefit employees themselves?

Leadership is also important for maintaining momentum. As Kanter et al. (1992) argue, "Any new strategy, no matter how brilliant or responsive, no matter how much agreed on and admired, will probably fail without someone with power pushing it." Resistance can be more a battle against inertia than an outright rejection of a new idea or objective. One motivating speech from the CEO in support of product diversification is unlikely to create enough energy

Box 23.22 Creating Resistance

In one institution, a modern technology savings product was introduced into a branch where all other transactions used old technology. Three people were trained on the product (teller, branch manager, and regional marketing officer) and then it was launched.

At first, transaction volume was slow, and the teller simply sat in the transactions window and did little while other staff members were variably busy. No effort was made to teach the other staff about the product.

This system created very serious animosity among the staff, for several reasons:

- The "new technology" teller had a very easy workload while the others felt they were overworked.
- The "old technology" staff saw themselves potentially without a job as the more efficient product eventually took over all the business.
- The "old technology" staff were not trained on the new product, and they felt left out (this exacerbated their concerns about losing their jobs).
- There was no communication to the whole staff about the place of this new product in the product mix and the institution's plans for the future. This allowed people to imagine the worst for themselves.

This led to serious resentment by the "old technology" staff, who made every effort to sabotage the new product. The result was extremely slow growth. When several small changes were made, including basic training for all staff, placement of brochures in the lobby, an effort to bring the staff together as a team, and the periodic rotation of the "new technology" teller with the others, it was reported that product growth doubled in less than a month by the number of customers that they had previously managed to gather in five months.

Source: McCord et al., 2004.

to sustain employees as they struggle to learn how to deliver a new product or build relationships with a new market segment. Regular messages are needed to signal the institution's high-level commitment to change, to remind staff of the vision and benefits that will be realized through the new product or market, to praise local efforts at implementation, and so on.

Much of this leadership needs to be provided by an MFI's top management or product champion, but some of it must be provided by each manager who supervises employees who are expected to contribute to the change. It is their regular communication of targets, willingness to support learning, and discipline in keeping their team on track that makes implementation ultimately successful.

Controlling

Successful change does not occur overnight. Performance must be monitored and actions taken to ensure objectives are met. Human resource management systems need to hold staff accountable for implementing agreed-upon changes, rewarding those who do and putting pressure on those who do not.

As with planning, the more that staff are involved in monitoring their own performance as well as that of the product portfolio, the better they will understand the status quo, and the more likely it is that they will understand why change is necessary. If, for example, employees are aware that their branch receives at least one request for an individual loan product every day, they will not be surprised if the head office eventually decides to introduce one. In fact, they will probably support the new product as a necessary and desirable change.

Having everyone involved in monitoring and controlling the risks in their environment also facilitates successful change. Staff in different departments and at different levels of an institution recognize discrete risks and have distinct sources of information that can shed light on the potential impact of each risk. If risks are identified locally when they are small, they can usually be controlled more quickly and at a lower cost than when they are large enough to attract the attention of the head office.

Having everyone involved, however, does not mean that all of an MFI's employees can sit around the same table to make a decision. Staff will be involved in product development changes in a variety of ways, and at various levels. Having an entity such as a product management committee that can take the lead in planning, organizing and controlling all this involvement can be a critical factor in success. Essentially, this is the product portfolio management function, which is topic of the next and final chapter of this book.

Main Messages

1. Do not underestimate the importance of culture for successful diversification.
2. Build an organizational structure that recognizes customers' varied needs and facilitates easy access to appropriate products for meeting those needs.
3. Empower staff to be capable of and motivated to deliver a diverse product mix.
4. Diversify marketing strategies to communicate clearly with different market segments.
5. Strengthen financial, information and risk management systems to handle the complexity that comes with diversification.
6. Diversification requires change. Plan, organize, lead and control it to produce successful results.

Case Study: A Specialized Delivery Structure for Individual Lending at SHARE

SHARE initially launched individual lending by making only minor adjustments to its existing group loan delivery processes. It assumed that the same staff would be able to handle both products, and that branch and area managers would be able to monitor both products with little extra effort. Six months after the introduction, management realized that loan officers and branch managers were not able to handle both products, and that the staff profiles for the two products should be differentiated to respond better to the new requirements of the individual loan product.

SHARE has an army of well-trained group lending staff that is very effective in following guidelines and procedures; however, they faced specific challenges in integrating individual lending because of its more complex lending processes. While the strong culture of following clear and simple guidelines with light analytical decision-making by loan officers provided good results for the group loan product, it is not a working culture that is conducive to implementing individual lending. Individual lending requires an objective analysis of the client's risks and repayment capacity, and promotes and encourages critical thinking among staff. Although group lending staff might be able to develop the skills required for individual lending, SHARE branch managers determined that the culture and work approach that were being used to deliver group loans were incompatible with the delivery of individual loans through the same loan officer.

SHARE's director opted for an entirely new network of branches in urban areas to be exclusively dedicated to individual lending. This approach eliminated a variety of integration issues, and provided a tidy solution for avoiding the organizational challenges of transforming an institution of 2,000 employees and 200 offices. New staff and managers were recruited, with a special individual lending manager at the head office managing operations in the units. Given the large-scale scope of operations and anticipated demand for individual lending in urban centres, this was a feasible option from a cost-effectiveness perspective.

However, SHARE is now grappling with the integration of individual lending services into its rural offices where, owing to lower densities and credit demand patterns, the decision has been made to offer individual loans alongside group loans. SHARE's alternative approach illustrates how implementing individual lending is a process shaped by the specific market environment and institutional circumstances of each MFI.

This case study was adapted from Dellien et al. (2005).

Recommended Reading

- Bankakademie. 2000b. *Liquidity management: A toolkit for microfinance institutions.* (Eschborn, Deutsche Gesellschaft fur Technische Zusammenarbeit (GTZ), at: http://www2.gtz.de/dokumente/bib/00-0974.pdf
- Churchill, C.; Frankiewicz, C. 2006. *Making microfinance work: Managing for improved performance* (Geneva, ILO).
- Dellien, H.; Burnett, J.; Gincherman, A.; Lynch E. 2005. *Product diversification in microfinance: Introducing individual lending* (New York, Women's World Banking), at: http://www.microfinancegateway.org/gm/document-1.9.28060/27432_file_ind_lend.pdf

- Ledgerwood, J.; White, V. 2006. *Transforming microfinance institutions: Providing full financial services to the poor* (Washington, DC, World Bank).
- Pikholz, L.; Champagne, P.; Mugwang'a, T.; Moulick, M.; Wright, G.; Cracknell, D. 2005. *Institutional and product development risk management toolkit* (Nairobi, *MicroSave*, Shorebank Advisory Services), at: http://www.microsave.org/toolkit/institutional-and-product-development-risk-management-toolkit
- Schneider-Moretto, L. 2005. *Tool for developing a financial risk management policy* (New York, Women's World Banking).
- Wright, G.; Cracknell, D. 2005. *Strategic marketing toolkit* (Nairobi, MicroSave), at: http://www.microsave.org/toolkit/strategic-marketing-toolkit
- Triodos Facet. 2009. *SMARTRAC Public Tools Series for Risk Management and Sustainability* (Zeist, Triodos Facet and Triodos Investment Management), at: http://www.triodosfacet.nl/content/view/45/89/lang,english/

24 Product Portfolio Management

Resources are simply too scarce to allocate to the wrong projects. The consequences of poor portfolio management are evident: you squander scarce resources on the wrong projects and as a result starve the truly deserving ones. ~ Cooper and Edgett (1999)

Regardless of how, when or why an MFI decides to diversify, the maintenance of a successful product portfolio over time is a challenge that all diversified institutions face. It requires ongoing monitoring of the target market's evolving needs and preferences, regular evaluation of the portfolio's ability to meet market expectations, and frequent adjustments in the delivery and, at times, the composition of the product mix in order to achieve institutional objectives.

This last chapter provides a framework for understanding the product portfolio management function and organizing the activities that need to be carried out by those who take responsibility for this function. It also explores tools and approaches that can be used to carry out these responsibilities effectively. The chapter addresses six main themes:

1. What is product portfolio management?
2. Product strategy
3. Strategy implementation
4. Portfolio review
5. Removing a product from the mix
6. How many products is too many products?

24.1 What Is Product Portfolio Management?

Though there are many definitions of product portfolio management, an eloquently concise one comes from the consulting firm Oliver Wyman (2010): "focusing product development activity on the areas that deliver the greatest incremental value to the business".

Two aspects of this definition are worth noting. First, the use of the verb "to focus" emphasizes that product portfolio management is all about resource allocation (Cooper and Edgett, 1999). An institution's existing products and new product or market ideas compete for limited resources in terms of management attention, staff time, marketing budget, and so on. Decisions about which and how many resources to invest in a particular product fall within the product portfolio management function.

The second key element of the definition is its focus on value. Product portfolio management aims to allocate resources across products in a way that delivers the greatest possible benefit for a given level of expenditure. The benefits sought by MFIs vary, depending on their mission, vision and strategic objectives. Some seek to maximize profit; others want to maximize outreach to those who do not yet have access to financial services; some aim to facilitate asset building among members of a particular community or market segment. Regardless of the specific benefits sought, the product portfolio management function should focus resources on the products and activities that generate the greatest returns for the institution and its target market.

The product portfolio management function consists of three main activities: 1) product strategy; 2) product development; and 3) portfolio review. Although product development has been discussed at length throughout this book, little has been said about how to make sure that product development proceeds as planned and achieves the desired results. Thus this chapter will focus on the definition of a strategy, the monitoring of its implementation, and the analysis of results to facilitate strategic decisions for the future.

24.2 Product Strategy

Product strategy needs to be defined at two levels:

1. What products will an MFI offer to which markets?
2. How will each product be developed to best support the institution's goals for the period?

The answer to the first question is defined by an MFI's product portfolio strategy, while the answer to the second is defined by individual product marketing strategies. Both types of strategy are discussed below.

Product Portfolio Strategy

Product portfolio strategy is usually established as part of an institution's business planning process. Decisions about what products an institution will offer to which markets are generally taken by top managers, because these decisions lie at the heart of an institution's overall strategy. The quality of their decisions is greatly affected, however, by the quality of data and analysis that informs those decisions.

As shown in Figure 24.1, strategy should be shaped by an institution's mission, vision and values, as well as an analysis of its strengths, weaknesses, opportunities and threats (SWOT). The former defines the institution's outreach priorities while the latter defines its current position. Four types of analysis inform the SWOT:

1. **Market analysis** investigates the MFI's current and potential markets. Who is the institution serving? Is that who it is supposed to be serving? What customer needs is the MFI meeting? Which unmet needs are most important to the target market? Are there other markets that the MFI could serve? What are the needs, preferences, values and priorities of these markets?
2. **Competitor analysis** clarifies who an MFI's competitors are and what its position is relative to the competition. Where does it face the most competition and why? Where does it have an advantage over the competition? What kind of value is each competitor trying to offer the market? How is the competitive environment changing?
3. **Institutional analysis** examines the MFI's capacity and the strengths and weaknesses of its current performance. It assesses physical assets as well as intangible assets such as knowledge, institutional culture, reputation, systems and product brands.
4. **PEST analysis** explores the political, economic, social (including legal and environmental) and technological environment within which an MFI operates.

With one eye on the institution's mission, vision and values, and the other eye on its SWOT analysis, an MFI's leadership can define its overall strategy for the coming period. Usually,

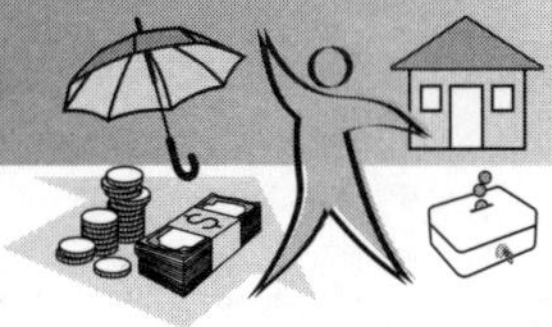

Figure 24.1 Strategy formulation

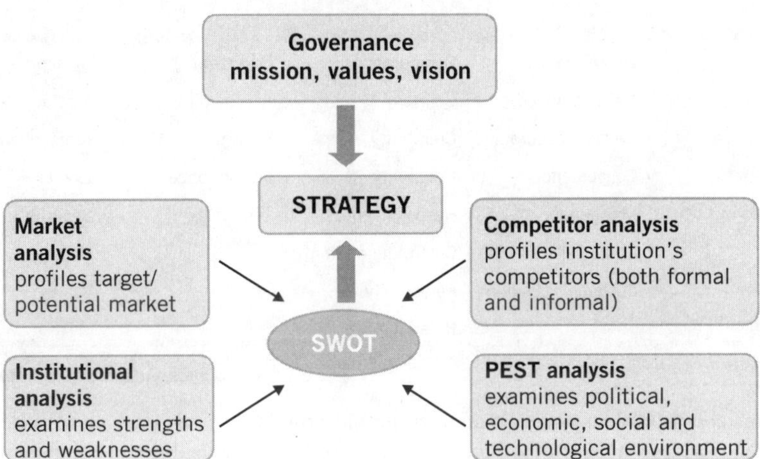

Source: Wright et al., 2007.

that strategy can be defined more effectively by focusing on strengths rather than weaknesses (Wright et al., 2007). In other words, how can an institution use its strengths to pursue market opportunities, protect itself against threats, and improve areas of weakness? As part of their SWOT analysis, MFIs may find it helpful to actually rank their strengths (and weaknesses, opportunities and threats) in order of importance using a simple ranking exercise to help them identify the issues they most want to address in their strategy.

In a competitive environment, it is particularly important to evaluate strengths relative to the competition so that strategy is built on the basis of a competitive advantage. MFIs should ask themselves not only what they do well, but also what they do better than the competition. The strengths that are unique and hard to copy will be the best ones to focus on, because they will enable the institution to offer value over time that no one else is able to provide.

If an institution cannot identify an existing competitive advantage, then its strategy will need to create one, by:

- matching an existing strength with an opportunity in the market environment to offer benefits to customers in the future that no competitor is currently providing; or
- converting a weakness into a strength that can then be matched with an opportunity to offer benefits to customers in the future that no competitor is currently providing; or
- converting a threat into an opportunity, which can then be matched with an existing strength to offer benefits to customers that no competitor is currently providing (Ennew et al., 1995).

The search for competitive advantage is a search for difference. What does an MFI have that others do not have, or what can it do that others are not doing, to meet customers' current needs and desires better than the competition? Some of the ways that MFIs can distinguish themselves from the competition are summarized in Table 24.1.

Table 24.1 Differentiation variables

Product	Services	Personnel	Channel	Image
Features	Ordering ease	Competence	Coverage	Symbols
Price	Delivery speed	Courtesy	Accessibility	Media
Performance	Delivery accuracy	Credibility	Expertise	Atmosphere
Reliability	Convenience	Reliability	Performance	Events
Innovation	Maintenance	Responsiveness	Technology	Security
Variety	Customer training	Communication		Heritage
Flexibility	Customer consulting	Personality		Values
Design		Relationships		

Source: Adapted from Kotler, 2000.

Decisions about product portfolio strategy should flow fairly easily once an MFI defines its outreach priorities and its competitive advantage. An MFI's leadership can compare the available growth options (see Chapter 1) and decide which one(s) will enable the institution to achieve more of the kind of outreach it wants to achieve with the resources available, at an acceptable level of risk.

Consider, for example, the three different kinds of institution presented in Table 24.2. National Bank offers a broad range of products, and has recently entered several new markets where it faces little competition. It has decided that its priority is to increase breadth (the number of clients served) by penetrating the markets where it is already operating with its existing product portfolio. InnovaBank also offers a significant range of products, but it faces intense competition from a market leader with a massive branch network. InnovaBank's competitive advantage is its reputation as an innovator, so it has decided that its priority should be new product development for existing markets. Mikra Savings and Loan is a non-bank financial institution that is trying to reach a more disadvantaged market segment than it currently serves. It knows that its existing products are not meeting the needs of that market segment, so it has prioritized new product development.

Since it has little competition, National Bank can afford to target a broad market. It will take a life-cycle approach to its product mix, which should make it easy to communicate its broad range of products to customers. It will also bundle products together to serve customers' needs during a particular phase of life, and aim to increase revenue through cross-selling. InnovaBank would be unlikely to survive with this strategy, since its major competitor also has many products, and cross-sells effectively. Instead, it will build on its reputation as an innovative financial service provider to develop new products that take advantage of its new MIS capabilities, and explore various e-banking technologies. It must be efficient, because it does not have the resources to develop and maintain an increasing number of products, so it will allow new products to cannibalize and replace the weakest old products. Mikra Savings and Loan does not want to eliminate any products – it has only three: a basic group loan, an individual loan and a basic savings product. It wants clients to be able to continue using these services, but it will add a product to the mix to enable those who do not qualify for the group lending programme to enter into a relationship with the institution.

The composition, strengths and weaknesses of an MFI's current product portfolio will influence its strategic planning for the coming period. However, once strategic objectives have been defined, it is those objectives that should shape the future composition of the portfolio and the development of the individual products contained within it.

The products with most potential to advance or hinder the achievement of an institution's objectives should receive the most attention. To give a straightforward example, if an MFI decides that it wants to be the most profitable in the country within the next three years to prepare for an initial public offering (IPO), it would want to review each of its products for profitability. The most profitable products would then be given the largest budgets for marketing and expansion while the least profitable ones would be eliminated, replaced, or redeveloped to become more profitable.

Table 24.2 Sample strategies

	National Bank	InnovaBank	Mikra Savings and Loan
Summary of current position	Commercial bank with many products; recently established in several new markets with low competition	Commercial bank with many products; faces intense competition from a massive network	Non-bank financial institution with three basic products; wants to reach more disadvantaged segment
Outreach priority	Breadth	Worth	Depth
Target market	Low-income households	Two segments: 1) younger generation that will become mass market of the future 2) successful micro-entrepreneurs who want their bank to grow with them	Poorest of the poor
Competitive advantage	Product range	Energetic, creative young staff Technology	Customer relationships
Market growth strategy	Penetrate existing markets with existing products	New products for existing markets	New product for a new market
Strategy towards competition	Set the lowest price in the market for a few highly demanded products to attract customers and then offer them bundled products. Increase revenue through cross-selling	Use MIS for data mining and profile target market Constantly assess their needs and priorities through ongoing market research and adjust product offering in response New and modified products should build on e-technology platform.	Main competition comes from government subsidized programmes and grants that are not sustainable. MFI will seek to partner with government and donors for financing of a sustainable approach
Implications for product portfolio strategy	Life-cycle approach Maintain broad product range Portfolio must have coherence to make cross-selling easy	Market segment combined with core competence approach New products should cannibalize old	Developmental approach Maintain current portfolio but add product that will enable poorest to enter into a relationship with the MFI

Source: Authors.

If an MFI can identify actions to improve a product's performance, then modifying the product will usually be the best way to proceed. After all, significant resources will have already been invested in the product, and the clients who use it may be quite attached to it. If, however, a product is in decline (see Section 24.3 below), if the cost of fixing it is greater than the revenue that the product is likely to generate in the future, or if competition is fierce and resources for growth are extremely limited, then the institution will want to seriously consider dropping the weak product so that its resources can be put to better use elsewhere.

According to Argouslidis (2003), there are nine factors that financial institutions take into account when evaluating weak services. Listed in order of importance, the factors are:

1. Impact on the relationship with customers
2. Impact on the corporate image
3. Impact on the sales of other services
4. Impact on the profitability of other services (cross-selling)
5. Impact upon a full-line policy (namely, a policy to offer a full range of services)
6. Extent to which a similar service exists to satisfy customer needs
7. Likelihood of an organized intervention if the product is eliminated (for example, an adverse government reaction or negative media attention)
8. Impact on human resources and employee relationships
9. Benefits that competitors can develop as result of the service being eliminated

Financial institutions tend not to drop products that are gateways to other, more profitable products. One example of this is student accounts, which make little or no immediate profit for an institution, but can help build loyal relationships with clients who are likely to be profitable once they graduate and find employment. A basic savings account may not generate much revenue either, but it can be a window through which other more profitable services can be sold. Westley and Palomas (2010) found, for example, that small savers generate profits of over 400 per cent of the small-saver deposit balances at Centenary Bank in Uganda and over 1,000 per cent of the small-saver deposit balances at ADOPEM in the Dominican Republic.

Financial institutions also tend not to drop products if doing so would negatively affect their image in the market. Because of the intangible nature of financial services, and the need to build trust-based relationships with clients, institutions will be reluctant to remove a product if they think it would create the impression of impermanence ("being here today and gone tomorrow"). This risk can be mitigated by phasing in a new product at the same time as the old one is phased out, thus creating the impression of rejuvenation rather than scaling back, or by launching a personal sales campaign that helps clients understand how other products offered by the institution can meet their needs better (see Section 24.5 for more details).

Product Marketing Strategy

The other level at which product strategy needs to be defined is the level of individual products. Once an MFI has decided what products it wants to offer, and in which markets it wants to offer them, it must define a plan for developing and delivering each of the products in its

portfolio so that it meets client and institutional needs as effectively as possible. Even if an MFI's portfolio strategy is simply to sell more of an already existing product in markets it is already serving, the institution will have to clarify how it plans to do that.

The process for defining each product's strategy is similar to that used in defining the product portfolio strategy as a whole. The same packages of information described in Figure 24.1 can be used to conduct SWOT analyses for specific products, and to identify each product's competitive advantage. It is important to do this analysis at the product level and not just at the institutional level, because each product's market situation will be different. Products can face different levels of competition from different types of competitor depending on the regulatory environment, the financial landscape, and the newness of the product. What provides an institution with a general competitive advantage (for example, its broad diversity of products) may not be enough to convince customers to use a particular product (for example, a term deposit) if that product is offered by many other institutions at a more favourable rate. If an MFI wanted to attract longer-term savings to finance its much more popular and unique loan products, it would need to define a strategy for increasing sales of the term deposit.

The target market's needs and priorities can also differ from one product to the next. Clients may not care much about convenience when they are borrowing, and have only to visit the MFI once per month to pay their loan instalment. However, when they consider opening a passbook savings account to manage their cash flow on a much more frequent basis, they will pay more attention to how far they have to travel to access the account. Even the target market itself may differ from one product to another. Although XacBank aims to serve a relatively broad market, its savings product for girls must meet the needs of a substantially different market segment than the rest of its products designed for adults. The features, delivery mechanisms and communication channels for that product differ from others.

There are two tools that can help MFIs understand a product's current position, and identify actions to improve its performance. The first is product life-cycle analysis. The **product life cycle** is a simple concept based on the assumption that products have a limited lifetime. They are born when they are introduced to the market, they grow, they mature, and eventually they die. Some products last for decades while others last only a few months. Some fail and never make it past the introductory phase.

As shown in Figure 24.2, each phase of the product life cycle has different sales and profit characteristics. MFIs face different opportunities and challenges with respect to product delivery, depending on which phase a particular product is in. The four phases of the product life cycle are briefly described below.

- In the **introduction** phase, a product generates many expenses and little revenue. There are few customers, and new staff and systems have to be prepared for growth. Promotion and pricing strategies are designed to raise awareness of the product, and to encourage potential customers to try it. If the product is new for the market, there may be little competition as other institutions watch to see how the market reacts.
- In the **growth** phase, the market is aware of the product, and sales volume increases, often quite rapidly. More new customers are using the product, and previous customers, if satisfied with the service, are coming back as repeat buyers. In her 1998b publication on product design, Monica Brand referred to this as the "easy money phase", since it is the time

Figure 24.2 Product life cycle

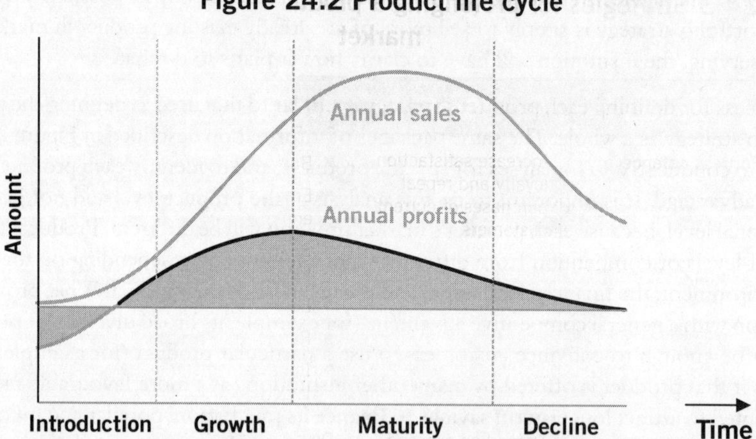

Source: Management and Development Centre, 2009.

when an institution can quickly gain the accounts of people living or working nearby without having to make much effort to recruit those accounts. Competition may be increasing, but the institution has an advantage, since its growth facilitates economies of scale which reduce unit costs and increase profitability. There is still a great deal of unmet demand. Profit begins to decline towards the end of this phase as the institution tries to expand to more distant or more difficult-to-reach markets, and as competition intensifies.

- In the **maturity** phase, the product is well established and, if it has been successful, competitors have introduced similar products. The product is still profitable, but the easy-to-serve markets are becoming saturated, most buyers are repeat buyers, and market share is more difficult to maintain. Competition becomes intense, leading to aggressive promotional and pricing programmes, which lead to smaller profit margins. More deliberate marketing, cross-selling and cost reductions are needed to survive in this stage.
- In the **decline** phase, prices fall, the product becomes less profitable, and sales stagnate or decline as buyers move on to other products that can meet their changing needs better. Intense rivalry exists among the institutions that continue to offer the product. If actions are taken to revive interest in the product, sales may begin to grow. Otherwise, revenue continues to fall, and the product eventually becomes unprofitable.

By analysing information about a product's performance, an MFI can roughly determine the life-cycle phase in which that product is currently located. It can then identify actions that might speed, for example, the product's entry into the growth phase, or prolong the amount of time it spends in the growth and maturity stages (see Table 24.3). If the analysis of product performance suggests that a product is entering the decline phase, management will need to decide whether to invest in refreshing the product or remove the product from the mix so that its resources can be spent more effectively elsewhere.

Table 24.3 Strategies for prolonging a product's life cycle in a competitive market

	Strategy	Goal	Activities
FOR THE MARKET LEADER	**Fortress defence**	Increase satisfaction, loyalty and repeat purchases of current customers	• Build on existing MFI strengths • Emphasize quality and product enhancement • Stress uniqueness and superiority of product features • Loyalty programmes • Reminder advertising • Improvements in after-sales service and logistics
FOR THE MARKET LEADER	**Flanker defence**	Defend an exposed weakness (or flank)	Develop a second product brand (either higher quality, higher price, or lower quality, lower price)
FOR THE MARKET LEADER	**Market expansion**	Establish strong market positions in different market segments	• Develop line extensions, new brands or alternative product forms using similar technology to appeal to different market segments • Build specialized distribution networks that give access to underserved segments • Design multiple promotion campaigns for different segments
FOR THE MARKET LEADER	**Contraction or strategic withdrawal**	Focus on strongest markets	Reduce or even stop marketing efforts in some segments and focus on the most promising ones where a sustainable relative advantage can be created or sustained
FOR THE MARKET LEADER	**Confrontation**	Challenge competitive offerings	• Improve the product • Increase promotional efforts or lower prices • Invest in improving processes to lower unit costs • Develop new products with superior features which represent better value for money
FOR THE MARKET FOLLOWER	**Frontal attack**	Directly challenge a competitor in its areas of strength	• Develop superior products • Spend more on promotion and distribution than competitors • Provide better customer service
FOR THE MARKET FOLLOWER	**Flanking attack**	Catch the market leader off guard by attacking an area of weakness	• Develop a unique or superior product which satisfies unmet customer needs • Build more appropriate distribution channels for accessing underserved segments
FOR THE MARKET FOLLOWER	**Encirclement**	Attack competitor on several fronts at once	Same as flanking but in multiple segments

Table 24.3 (continued)

	Strategy	Goal	Activities
FOR THE MARKET FOLLOWER	**Bypass or leapfrog**	Avoid the competitor's main market	• Diversify into unrelated products • Diversify into new geographical markets • Surpass existing products with new technologically advanced products
	Guerrilla attack	Harass the market leader by disrupting its plans and diverting some of its resources and attention	• Sudden and sporadic sales promotion schemes • Short-term price reductions • Segment-specific advertising campaigns
FOR LEADERS AND FOLLOWERS	**Extensive penetration**	Convert current non-users to users in a market already served	• Increase the value of the product by adding new features or services • Enhance distribution coverage through innovative networks • Sales promotions in the form of coupons, bundling and sampling
	Use expansion	Increase current customers' use of the product	• Provide reminder communications • Make the product easier or more convenient to use • Reduce the undesirable consequences of frequent use • Develop positive associations with use occasions • Develop new product uses • Promote product use at different locations or for different purposes

Source: Adapted from Avlonitis and Papastathopoulou, 2006.

As suggested by Table 24.3, the list of potential strategies for expanding the sales and/or profitability of a product is long. To identify which actions an MFI might want to take, a second tool can be helpful. The **product competition analysis framework** presented in Table 24.4 combines the concept of the core, actual and augmented product (discussed in Chapter 1) with the 8 Ps of the marketing mix (discussed in Chapter 23) to create a framework for comparing an MFI's product offering against client demands and the competition's supply. After the last three columns of the table are completed, an MFI can identify where it is meeting customer needs, where it is not, where it is strong versus the competition and where it is weak.

Table 24.4 Product competition analysis framework

Product	Clients	Competition	Our MFI
Core product:			
Needs **Wants**	What is the unmet need or want?	How are these needs being met by others?	How are we addressing this need/want, if at all?
Actual product:			
Product design **Price** **Physical evidence (passbook, statement, etc.)**	What terms and conditions do the clients want?	What products compete with ours? What are their terms and conditions?	How does our product compare with the others offered by our MFI?
Augmented product:			
Promotion **Place** **Positioning** **Physical evidence (branch appearance, etc.)** **People** **Process**	How do clients want us to interact with them? Are they literate, geographically concentrated, what do they value, etc.?	How do competitors reach the target market? What is their image and the image of their product(s) in the market?	How do we currently sell our product (e.g. marketing, incentives, etc.)? How are we perceived in the market? How is our current product perceived by clients (and non-clients)?

Source: MicroSave, as presented in Frankiewicz et al., 2004.

As was the case with product portfolio strategy, MFIs can use the results of their competition analysis to identify options for using their strengths to take advantage of opportunities in the market environment. For example:

- They can craft marketing messages that focus on their strengths, highlighting in particular the ones that address priority customer needs and desires, because that is where they offer better value than the competition.
- They can plan how to use one of their strengths (or convert a weakness into a strength) to respond to a demand from their existing market that neither they nor their competition are effectively meeting.
- They can plan how to reach new market segments that want what the MFI already delivers well.
- They can plan how to strengthen areas where the competition is performing well but they are not, and this is resulting in a loss of market share.

After weighing the various options, MFIs should choose a handful of the most promising strategies to implement in the coming period. The decision about which strategies are most promising will be shaped by each MFI's overarching objectives for the period. Returning to the example posed earlier in this chapter, if an institution prioritizes profitability, then the strategies that will be deemed most promising are the ones that are likely to generate the greatest increase in profitability. If, however, an MFI's strategic objective for the period is to reach

Figure 24.3 Value analysis from the clients' perspective

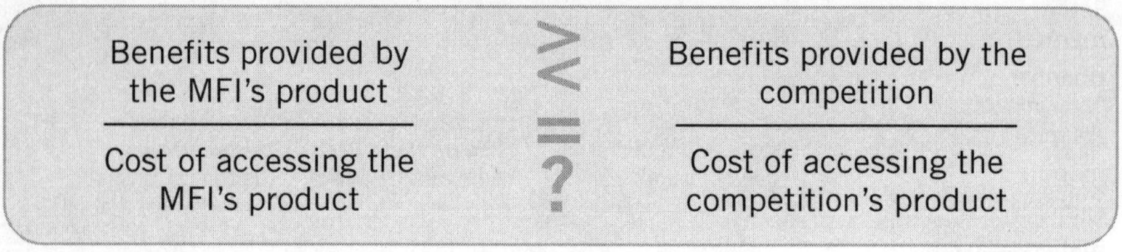

Benefits provided by the MFI's product / Cost of accessing the MFI's product	>< = ?	Benefits provided by the competition / Cost of accessing the competition's product

Source: Authors.

a more disadvantaged clientele, then the most promising options will be the ones that make the product more accessible to that market.

It is worth stressing the importance of using product competition analysis to define a shortlist of options that would be valuable from the customer's perspective, before using the institution's priorities to decide which strategies should be pursued. Recalling that value is a relationship between benefits and costs (see Figure 24.3), MFIs need to identify options that will either benefit customers more or cost them less than the competition's offering.

Although MFIs could do the opposite and consider the institution's priorities first, this would put the cart before the horse. An institution exists to serve its customers, and not vice versa. In addition, and on a more practical level, starting with the institution's priorities would vastly increase the number of options an MFI would have to consider. With all the tools that exist today to improve institutional performance and marketing, the problem is rarely not having enough options, but rather deciding which of the available options would make the best use of limited resources. By identifying customer priorities in the context of the competition's current offering first, an MFI can quickly focus its attention and decision-making resources on a smaller set of options for maximizing value.

Towards a Quality Product Strategy

In order for the strategic decisions that are taken at both the portfolio and the individual product levels to become useful, they need to be put in writing and communicated to the staff who will be expected to implement them. If an MFI follows a participatory planning process that involves all staff in its decision-making, there will already be broad understanding and support for decisions by the time they are made, but implementation will still require that the selected strategies be clearly recorded in a central location so they can be easily referenced and guide consistent product delivery.

Product portfolio strategy is usually articulated in an MFI's business plan and/or strategic marketing plan, while individual product strategy can be summarized in a product marketing plan. The contents of these plans need not be complex, but they should include strategic

objectives, measurable indicators that can be used to track progress, targets that indicate the expected level of performance, a list of the specific initiatives or activities that will be implemented to achieve the objectives, a timeline, and resource assignments (both human and financial).[58]

As mentioned in Chapter 23, product marketing plans can also summarize key product information to guide staff who will be taking the MFI's products to the market. A description of each product's features (perhaps using the 8 Ps framework), its most important market segments, and the main messages to be communicated to each could be helpful to those trying to sell the product.

24.3 Strategy Implementation

Effective strategy implementation is considered by many to be much more difficult than effective strategy design. In a frequently cited *Fortune Magazine* cover story, Charan and Colvin (1999) estimated that 70 per cent of CEOs' failures result not from poor strategy but rather from poor execution. So what can MFIs do to try to make sure that the product development strategies they carefully design are actually implemented in a way that produces the desired results?

Kaplan and Norton (2001) place much of the blame for strategy failure on the weak or non-existent link between budgets and strategy. They make a distinction between operational budgeting, which deals with the ongoing expenses that support recurring operations, and strategic budgeting, which authorizes expenses that enable an organization to develop new products and capabilities. Because of the large base of products, infrastructure and customers that are usually maintained from one year to the next, most of an institution's spending will be found in its operational budget (see Figure 24.4). However, Kaplan and Norton argue, some portion of its resources should be allocated to a budget that funds strategic activities, and the implementation of that budget should be monitored separately from the implementation of ongoing activities. What often happens is that institutions try to implement strategy through their ongoing activities, squeezing time out of already busy people and scraping funding together from slack in the operating budget. In their opinion, inadequate staffing and financial support cause strategic initiatives to fail.

One of the most important things that an MFI can do in support of effective strategy implementation is to make sure that its strategic objectives have adequate resources earmarked for their implementation. It is better to implement two strategic objectives successfully with the resources available than fail at achieving five because no initiative received the support necessary for success. MFIs may find it helpful to create a separate budget for strategic initiatives, and to monitor performance against that budget on a regular basis, as Kaplan and Norton suggest.

[58] Refer to *MicroSave*'s Product Marketing, Strategic Marketing and Business Planning toolkits (available at www.microsave.org) as well as www.balancedscorecard.org for publicly available tools that MFIs can use to guide their product strategy processes.

Figure 24.4 Operational and strategic budgets

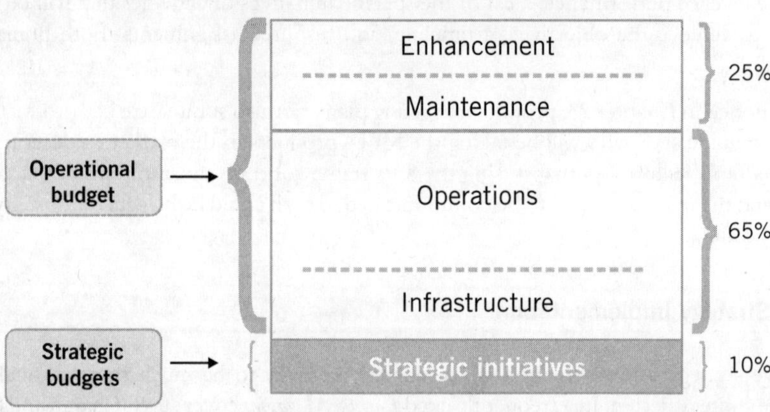

Source: Kaplan and Norton, 2001.

A second reason for strategy failure that is frequently cited is lack of follow-up. According to Mankins and Steele (2005), whose company collaborated with the Economist Intelligence Unit to survey executives from 197 companies worldwide, "Less than 15% of companies make it a regular practice to go back and compare the business's results with the performance forecast for each unit in its prior years' strategic plans…. Indeed, the fact that so few companies routinely monitor actual vs. planned performance may help explain why so many companies seem to pour good money after bad – continuing to fund losing strategies rather than searching for new and better options." Continuous monitoring is one of the seven recommendations they make for more successful strategy implementation (see Box 24.1).

If MFIs regularly monitor the implementation of their strategic plans and the extent to which the planned initiatives are producing the desired results, they will be able to make adjustments as necessary along the way to make sure that their objectives are achieved. Creating a culture of accountability is also important. Simply asking about the status of a plan's implementation can help to communicate that it is still a priority and keep staff focused on its execution.

Box 24.1 Closing the Strategy-to-Performance Gap

1. Keep it simple, make it concrete.
2. Debate assumptions, not forecasts.
3. Use a rigorous framework, speak a common language.
4. Discuss resource deployments early.
5. Clearly identify priorities.
6. Continuously monitor performance.
7. Reward and develop execution capabilities.

Source: Mankins and Steele, 2006.

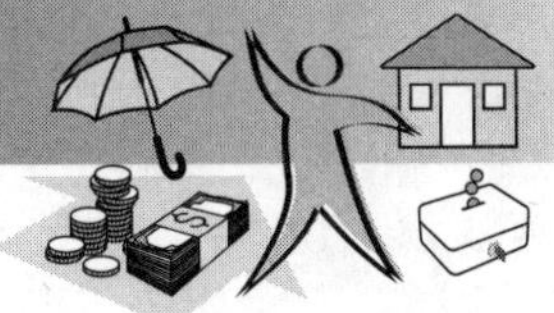

The Challenge of Effective Monitoring

As discussed in Chapter 2, if each department understands its contribution to the product development process and has systems in place to gather, process, analyse and/or channel information effectively, it will be relatively easy for members of a product management committee to bring knowledge about internal and external trends to the table to inform product development decisions, and to monitor the implementation of those decisions. Of course, if appropriate systems are not in place, or if no one in particular is tasked with gathering product and market information, then the chances of that knowledge being brought to the table to inform strategic decisions are slim.

The time to think about what information needs to be gathered and who should gather it is now, before the information is needed to make business decisions. This is one of the critical investments that undiversified institutions can make to prepare themselves for diversifying successfully. For institutions that have already diversified, investing in stronger information systems could be the key to maintaining a strategic portfolio over time. As noted in Chapter 23, the development of information systems refers to more than just the input and processing of data by the institution's computerized management information system. It refers to the entire array of formal and informal channels that people use to pass information from one part of the institution to another.

Table 24.5 provides an illustrative example of a tool that could be used to organize an information system audit. The table assesses the degree to which information is available for six kinds of analysis: competition, market, PEST, performance, communication channel effectiveness and risk. In the first column, staff would describe the information they need in order to contribute effectively to the product development process. Someone (perhaps a consultant, customer service officer or information officer) could then investigate who is gathering that information, how it is being channelled, and whether it is being channelled to those who need it. This person (or team) could also recommend actions to strengthen the system in areas of weakness.

MFIs can reap three main benefits through an information audit. First, the process can help raise awareness amongst all staff of the information they need to be gathering in order to make their contribution to product development. Second, it can help everyone think through how and when information should be passed to those who will analyse or apply it. Third, it can highlight opportunities for improving the effectiveness of the systems and channels through which information flows.

The Role of the Product Management Committee

If a product management committee exists, it can take responsibility for organizing an information audit from a product development perspective. It can advocate recommended improvements to be made, and follow up on any agreed-upon changes. It can also serve as a focal point for product development updates.

Table 24.5 Sample framework for an information system audit

Area of analysis	Who needs what information	Who collects the information, how, how often	How information is channelled
COMPETITION	• Sales staff: our strengths and competitors' weaknesses • Marketing: actions the competition is taking • Senior management: how is the competitive environment changing	• Ongoing field staff observation • Quarterly customer advisory board • Marketing staff monitors press • *Recommend introduction of quarterly mystery shopping*	• Field staff provide input via branch managers during weekly meetings *but meetings are not held regularly and input is not encouraged in some locations* • *No reliable mechanism for channelling market intelligence gathered by Head Office*
MARKET	• Everyone: who is the target market? What are their needs, priorities, opinions about us? • Operations: estimated future demand • Business development and finance: new markets with potential	• Marketing creates annual segment profiles • Customer service officers conduct exit interviews • Suggestion box (ongoing) • Hotline (ongoing) • Field observation (ongoing) • Application data entered into MIS (ongoing)	• Field staff provide input via branch managers during weekly meetings *but meetings are not held regularly and input is not encouraged in some branches* • Market segment profiles exist at Head Office only • Staff newsletter showcases one client per month
PEST	Everyone: what political, environmental, social or technological risks must be managed? What trends might create opportunities?	• Field staff observation • Finance manager monitors economic indicators • Marketing staff monitors press • *Need better monitoring of legal and technology developments*	• Intranet and staff newsletter provide channel, *but poorly organized* • Annual "state of our world" presentation by CEO • Weekly staff meetings
PERFORMANCE	• Product management committee: product and market segment performance • All staff: progress towards personal, unit and MFI objectives • Partners: product sales, customer profiles	• Product manager gathers monthly data on product performance • Finance reports on segment, branch and product profitability • *URGENT need for product costing* • Human resources department organizes annual staff performance appraisals	• Monthly PMC meetings • Monthly management reports track progress against growth targets and budget • Performance appraisals are conducted in 360 degree format • *Periodic product knowledge tests could give staff and supervisors feedback on message content*

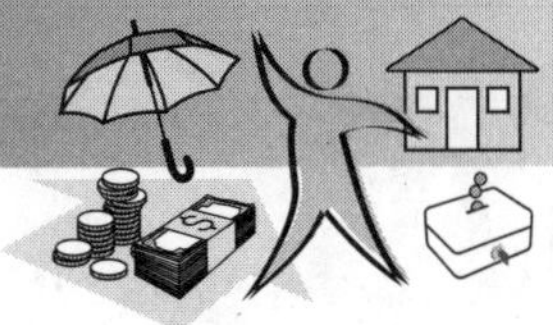

Table 24.5 (continued)

Area of analysis	Who needs what information	Who collects the information, how, how often	How information is channelled
COMMUNICATION CHANNELS	• CEO: what (dis)incentives for communication exist? • Supervisors: where in my unit is information getting stuck? • Information officer: are channels being used, timely, accurate, secure, accessible, overburdened?	• Annual staff survey and feedback loop review conducted jointly by an external consultant and the customer service department • Staff observation • Technology helpline	• Informal feedback from supervisors to remove blockages and disincentives. *Audit report submitted only after four months – delay is too long* • Technology helpline reacts to calls but issue patterns are not being tracked
RISK	• Product management committee: signs of product cannibalization, relevance of and compliance with product policies and procedures, staff attitude towards products • Clients: accurate product information • Regulators: compliance with policies and legislation	• Head of Marketing analyses monthly data on product performance • Internal and external audit • Supervisors conduct spot checks on an irregular basis • Rotating field representative sits on PMC	• Auditors report directly to Board but share product related observations with PMC • *Setting minimum standards of performance on periodic product knowledge tests could help ensure accuracy of information given to clients*

Source: Authors.

Perhaps most importantly, the committee can create a space for discussing strategy rather than day-to-day operations. It can facilitate regular monitoring of product strategy implementation, and provide periodic opportunities for different parts of the institution to share information and resolve conflicts on product issues. This can help everyone stay on track and lessen resistance to strategy implementation that may arise over time. If a product management committee does not exist, then making another entity responsible for these tasks can help strategy implementation succeed.

24.4 Portfolio Review

Portfolio review is the third main activity within the product portfolio management function. It involves the evaluation of information that has been gathered throughout the product development process to determine the health of the product portfolio. Of course, if the required information has not been gathered through ongoing product development activities, then the review may involve information collection and analysis in addition to evaluation.

In general, the portfolio review should help an institution understand where its product portfolio is strong, where it is weak, and whether a change in strategy is needed. The specific questions that the review can answer include the following:

1. Is the product portfolio enabling the institution to achieve its objectives? Which products are contributing most to the achievement of outreach priorities? Which products contribute the least?
2. Is each product in the portfolio achieving the targets that were set for it? If not, why not? If so, how much more potential does each product have for growth?
3. Are resources allocated in a way that maximizes returns for a given level of risk? Could resources that are currently allocated to poorly performing products be better allocated to other products or to new product opportunities?
4. Is the portfolio appropriately balanced in terms of risk?
5. Are customers satisfied with the product mix? Is there a new or growing need that the existing product portfolio is not meeting well?
6. Is the existing product portfolio capable of meeting anticipated challenges from the competition?

To answer these questions, large amounts of data may have to be processed to make it possible to draw conclusions. Spreadsheets are commonly used to present summaries of actual versus projected growth in customer numbers or portfolio volume, levels of expenditure, portfolio at risk, and so on. But the amount of data presented in the spreadsheets can become overwhelming, and some aspects of product performance are not communicated clearly in a spreadsheet. So what other tools might an MFI use to analyse product performance and identify the products that deserve the most attention? This section briefly describes three options that MFIs can apply with relative ease.

Dynamic Rank-ordered List

To use this tool, an MFI must identify a small number of criteria that it considers important in evaluating product performance. It then ranks products according to their performance in those areas. In the example provided in Table 24.6, an MFI's products are ranked on the basis of three criteria: 1) strategic importance (contribution to the achievement of the institution's strategic objectives for the period); 2) profitability; and 3) growth potential. The passbook savings product, for instance, is ranked first in terms of strategic importance but last in terms of profitability.

Table 24.6 Dynamic rank-ordered list

Product	Strategic importance	Profitability	Potential for growth	Score (ranking)
Passbook savings	1	6	1	2.7 (1)
Individual microenterprise loan	3	2	4	3.0 (2)
Consumption loan	6	1	2	3.0 (2)
Life insurance	2	5	3	3.3 (4)
Group microenterprise loan	4	3	5	4.0 (5)
Term savings	5	4	6	5.0 (6)

Source: Authors.

After ranking the products' performance in each area, an overall product ranking is created by averaging the products' rankings across all criteria. In the example above, passbook savings had the highest average score, which suggests that it was the MFI's best-performing product, whereas term savings was the weakest. This identification of relative strength and weakness can guide an MFI's future resource allocation, and also draw attention to products that may need a new strategy. One disadvantage of this technique is that it gives each criterion equal importance, which may not reflect reality, and may mislead decision-makers.

Scoring Models

Scoring models are similar to rank-ordered lists in that they evaluate product performance against specific criteria, and then amalgamate the results to produce a score that can be used to identify relatively strong and weak products. However, they are more precise than rank-ordered lists, because they allow MFIs to establish specific measurement indicators for each criterion, and to weight the value of each. Examples of scoring models that were used for the purpose of screening diversification options were presented in Chapter 2 (see Table 2.5) and Chapter 20 (see Table 20.2). Obviously, the criteria used to review product performance would differ from those used to screen new product ideas, but the process of building and using the model to score products and product ideas would be the same.

The indicators that MFIs could include in a product review scoring model include:

- Percentage growth in number of customers
- Percentage growth in average account balance
- Volume of loans disbursed or savings mobilized
- Percentage of claims rejected
- Client turnover
- Average customer satisfaction score
- Size of the product's potential market
- Percentage of this product's customers who use at least one other product of the MFI
- Net present value of the product's revenues less all expenses for the next three years

Scoring models can be quite useful for comparing products within the same product line. When comparing performance across product lines, however, the model can be difficult to design. Savings, credit, insurance and money transfer products have very different performance indicators, so their results can be directly compared only in a limited number of areas, such as the average customer satisfaction score. With some indicators it may be necessary to measure performance differently for different product lines, but a score can be generated that has a common meaning across products. For example, client turnover might be measured differently for borrowers and insurance policyholders, but whatever is considered "excellent performance" in the two scenarios could generate a score of 5, while the weakest level of performance could generate a score of 1.

Visual Charts

Portfolio maps, bubble diagrams, pie charts and histograms are created using much of the same data as the other techniques explored above, but the visual way in which the results are presented makes them useful not only for identifying strong and weak products, but also for analysing the degree to which there is appropriate balance in a product portfolio. This is their primary strength.

Visual charts can provide a great deal of information in a single picture, but that information must be interpreted by decision-makers. Whereas the ranking and scoring tools described above list products in order of strength, charts such as the risk vs. reward bubble diagram in Figure 24.5 suggest no particular action. Interpreting the chart requires some understanding of the institution's objectives and tolerance for risk. If the team interpreting the chart lacks this understanding, the data will not be very useful, although the chart could help the team define objectives or risk tolerance levels for the future.

Visual charts can also help facilitate discussions about the allocation of resources. In the example provided in Figure 24.5, the size of each bubble corresponds to the resources being spent on that product this year. An MFI can look at the distribution of resources and ask itself whether that is the right distribution for the future. If it wants to introduce a new product and has to finance it using existing resources, it can use the chart to help it decide where it might draw those resources from.

Figure 24.5 Sample risk vs. return bubble diagram

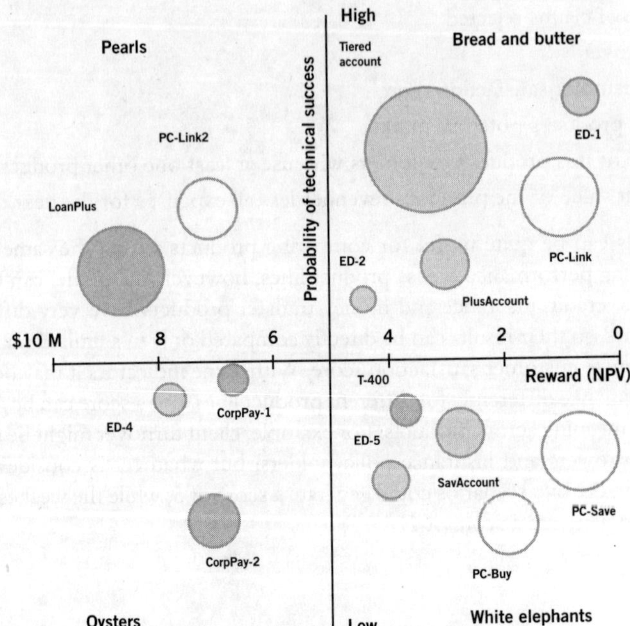

Source: Cooper and Edgett, 1999.

Figure 24.6 Clients served **Figure 24.7 Accounts opened per month**

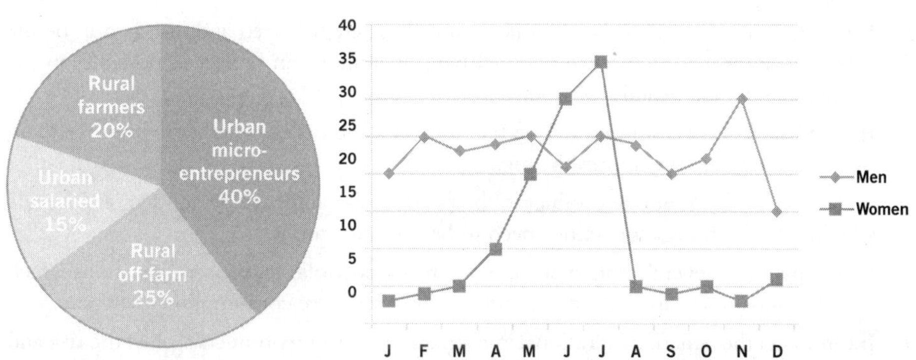

Source: Authors. *Source: Authors.*

There are many types of chart that MFIs can create to review the performance of their product portfolio. The risk vs. reward bubble chart is a popular one for financial institutions. Charts that plot products according to their competitive strength and market attractiveness are also popular (see Chapter 3). Pie, bar and line charts are the ones used most by MFIs, perhaps because they are generated from information contained in a spreadsheet. These charts can, however, be more useful than a spreadsheet in highlighting important information and illustrating trends (see, for example, Figures 24.6 and 24.7).

Dynamic charts (those that describe performance over a period of time) are generally more helpful than **static charts** (those that describe performance at one point in time), because they provide a context within which to interpret current performance. To know that 40 per cent of an institution's clients are urban microentrepreneurs is interesting, but is this a larger or smaller percentage than in the previous period, and how close is that percentage to the institution's target for the period?

The main disadvantage of visual charts is that an institution can produce too many of them, overwhelming decision-makers with data rather than facilitating their analysis of product portfolio performance. It is generally recommended to use a carefully selected, relatively small number of charts that can facilitate discussions about resource allocation and future strategy. A good place to start is with the institution's priorities. What did the MFI want to achieve during this period, and to what extent did the institution's different products help to achieve those goals?

Using the Review to Inform Strategy

Regardless of the specific method used for evaluating the product portfolio, the review should produce information that enables senior managers to make decisions about an appropriate strategy for moving forward. MFIs can, and often do, define their product strategy without conducting a portfolio review, but doing so leaves them exposed to inefficiency risk and mission drift, among other things. By evaluating all of the products in its portfolio at once, an MFI can gain the following benefits:

- It can clearly identify the strongest or most promising products, and make sure it gives them the support they need.
- It can determine whether its portfolio is appropriately balanced and, if it is not, define actions to improve the balance that will have as minimal an impact as possible on the strongest and most promising products.
- It can identify the weaker products in the portfolio, and decide whether to improve them or perhaps remove them from the mix.
- It can discern whether one product in the portfolio is cannibalizing another, and decide whether this is strategic or actions need to be taken to stop it.
- If resources are severely constrained, it can make portfolio-level decisions about which products most merit investment and how to limit resource consumption elsewhere.
- It can weigh the benefit of additional investments in existing products against the risk and return projections of new product ideas.
- It can consider the impact that changes to one product might have on others.
- It can analyse the coherence of the product portfolio. Does the approach that has been used to communicate the portfolio in the past still make sense for the future, given changes in products and, perhaps, the composition of the overall mix?
- It can segment product performance by market and analyse the trends. If certain market segments are performing poorly across products, then the institution can consider leaving those segments, or developing products to serve them better. If one product is performing poorly in a particular market but other products are doing well, the experiences of those working with other products can be brought to bear on a strategy for improving the one product's weaknesses.
- It can analyse the degree to which products are being cross-sold. Are certain products being used by the same types of client? If so, are there opportunities for bundling the two products that would increase customer satisfaction or decrease the institution's cost of delivering those products?
- It can compare trends in customer satisfaction with individual products and satisfaction with the product portfolio as a whole. Are clients rejecting a particular product or the entire institution? Are they rejecting the institution because of a particular product, and if so, what should be done about that? If clients love a particular product but not the institution, this may signal latent loyalty that the MFI can leverage in future product development.
- Finally, if the review is conducted by a cross-functional team such as the product management committee, it can help create consensus among department heads, each of whom has control over a certain percentage of the institution's resources, about the degree of investment and attention that each of the MFI's products should receive in the coming period. Future strategy, and support for future strategy implementation, can emerge as a natural outcome of the review process.

By using the portfolio review to accomplish such activities, MFIs can better prepare themselves to define a strategy for the next period that does not just carry on with business as usual, but rather, proactively manages resources to maximize the value being created for the institu-

tion and its clients. Products can be prioritized and resources can be allocated on the basis of performance rather than on the basis of a certain percentage growth over the previous year. Managers will be cognizant of which products are contributing most to the achievement of the institution's mission, and they can do their best to support and protect those products in the face of crisis and the daily challenges of strategy implementation.

24.5 Removing a Product from the Mix

If, as a result of the portfolio review process, an MFI decides that it wants to remove a product from its mix, how can it go about doing that? A study conducted by Argouslidis (2004) in the United Kingdom's financial services market revealed ten different strategies, listed below in order of use:

1. Eliminate the service to new customers, leaving the existing customers unaffected
2. Eliminate the service to new customers; existing ones cannot purchase additional units
3. Drop immediately
4. Service simplification (elimination of some features of the service)
5. Phase out slowly
6. Service merging
7. Eliminate the service for some segments and keep it open for others
8. Eliminate the service, but use its brand name in another service
9. Eliminate and sell out
10. Drop from standard range and offer it only as a "special"

Argouslidis' study corroborated the results of other research that identified elimination of the service to new customers while leaving existing customers unaffected as the most frequently used exit strategy. Although this strategy requires that an institution maintain the infrastructure to deliver the product, it can keep existing customers happy while not allowing the product to expand. This may be a reasonable compromise, given the importance of healthy customer relationships to the long-term success of a financial institution.

The second strategy on Argouslidis' list might be more useful for MFIs, at least where loan products are concerned, since the infrastructure to deliver the product would have to be maintained only for a certain period of time. Customers would have time to adjust to the idea that they need to transition to another product, and the institution would have time to convince them that a different product could meet their needs as well as, if not better than, the old product. The strategy is less attractive for liquid savings products, since there is no defined end date for the contract. Customers could, if they wanted to, keep their accounts open indefinitely.

The fifth strategy is similar to the second in that it eliminates a product over some period of time, although in this case it is the customer who usually decides when the service will be discontinued, and not the MFI. There are many ways that an institution could encourage customers to voluntarily stop using a product. It could offer customers a new product that fixes things they did not like about the existing product. It could reduce its marketing of the undesirable product and/or increase its price to make it less attractive than other product options. In a slow phase-out, cannibalization is often deliberately pursued as a business strategy (see Box 24.2).

The sixth option on Argouslidis' list, service merging, is essentially the path that the Grameen Bank chose when it consolidated more than a dozen loan products into three in 2001. As Mohammed Yunus (2007) wrote: "We wanted to simplify life for our borrowers." Existing loans were converted to "basic" loans or "flexi" loans over the course of approximately one year. New loans (with the exception of housing) were given out as "basic" loans. MFIs that find their product portfolio has proliferated beyond what they or their customers can manage may find service-merging an approach worth pursuing.

There is one more strategy that MFIs are beginning to find useful, and that is number seven on Argouslidis' list. This strategy is often referred to as a niche or concentration strategy. Under this approach an institution aims to strengthen the position of its product in one or only a few market segments that are particularly promising, and it stops trying to offer the product to others. This is the approach being taken by some MFIs in the area of agricultural lending (see Chapter 20). Rather than make loans available to all farmers growing all kinds of crop, they make loans available to farmers growing specific crops that are part of an identified

Box 24.2 Cannibalization as a Business Strategy

Cannibalization, the depletion of one product in favour of another within the same institution, is not necessarily a negative thing (at least when it comes to financial products). What determines the benefit or detriment is the level of efficiency of operations of the new product versus that of the old, or cannibalized, product. Where you have a new product that is significantly more efficient, as in a computerized product versus a manual product, cannibalization can have a very positive effect in moving clients from a time-consuming, expensive product to a cheaper, more efficient product. Simply the transfer of significant numbers of the old accounts to the new has the potential to dramatically improve the institution's profitability.

However, where the two products are essentially equivalent in terms of efficiency and costs, then cannibalization effectively wastes the efforts of staff as customers close one account to open another, or simply withdraw some of what is in one to deposit in another without increasing the value of their transactions with the MFI. This kind of cannibalization can obscure the real impact of the new product if the institution recognizes its growth without realizing that it is coming at the expense of the health of an existing product. The only reason to risk cannibalization in this case is if the new product has significant potential to appeal to a larger or different market than the existing product.

Under these circumstances, MFIs can try to minimize cannibalization by focusing their marketing efforts on attracting new customers, highlighting benefits specifically focused on them. Special promotions could be made to attract new customers to the new account while other promotions entice existing customers to hold on to their existing account (for example, balance maintenance awards, raffles or longevity premiums). Promotional posters and other such advertising could be primarily focused and placed outside the MFI's offices to have a lesser impact on current customers.

Source: Adapted from McCord et al., 2004.

value chain. Institutions that adopt a concentration strategy often adapt their product to make it more appealing to the targeted segment(s).

Obviously, the longer it takes to remove a product from the portfolio, the longer an institution will have to bear the costs of delivering that product. The more competitive the environment, the more likely institutions will be to drop a product quickly so that they can free resources for use elsewhere. MFIs will probably find it helpful to have a timeline for migrating clients off the product they want to discontinue so that as many customers as possible can make the choice voluntarily, but also the institution can move its people, infrastructure and financial resources onto more productive products with relative efficiency. The more time goes by, and the less money and energy an institution invests in a weak product, the more it will become a liability. The quality of service delivered will eventually drive remaining clients away, and the institution's reputation could be damaged in a way that affects other products as well.

Whatever strategy an MFI chooses, it is important that the decision be communicated clearly to staff so that they understand what is happening well enough to be able to communicate effectively with clients. Clients will need to be encouraged and supported to make the transition away from the discontinued product to another product that can meet the same need. If this is not done, the client is likely to transition to the competition instead. MFIs should also be careful to comply with contractual agreements and, if a contract allows for negotiation, seek customers' acceptance of the new terms. This may not be legally necessary, but it can help the MFI to preserve the customer relationship throughout the product transition. For the same reason, any costs borne by customers in order to make the transition to the new product should, whenever possible, be reimbursed by the MFI, perhaps through a rebate or special "transition offer" on the price of the product.

As demonstrated by the Grameen Bank example, product elimination can be a complex process that takes months or even years to complete. As such, it needs to be managed, just as other more productive product development activities need to be managed, to ensure that it achieves the desired results.

24.6 How Many Products Is Too Many Products?

Once an institution begins to diversify, one of the questions it will eventually want to consider is when to stop diversifying. As discussed in Chapter 1, the options for diversification are seemingly endless, and it is very tempting to offer a broad array of products, some of which are only slightly different from each other, for marketing purposes (see Box 24.3). The problem with this strategy is that every new product adds complexity to an MFI's operations, and eventually the cost of that increased complexity will outweigh the benefits generated by adding one more product.

If a strategic product mix will not proliferate endlessly, how can an MFI know when enough is enough? There is no absolute answer to this question. As shown in Table 24.7, some of the world's most successful MFIs offer as many as 18 products and others as few as three. This rudimentary analysis provides some indication of the scale of diversification that can be effective, but ultimately, the question must be answered by each institution depending on its own

> **Box 24.3 Product Proliferation**
>
> Product proliferation is increasingly common amongst many financial institutions that try to tailor products to respond to individual market segments with specific needs. These institutions can find themselves offering many slightly different products. At one extreme *MicroSave* once worked on product costing with a bank that discovered that it was offering 89 different products – some with only a handful of customers using them!
>
> *Source: Wright, 2000b.*

internal capacity and business strategy. What products does it need to offer to fulfil its mission, and how much complexity is it able to handle at a particular point in time?

If an MFI's monitoring system is working well, then the institution will gather information during its daily operations that will help it identify whether its product portfolio is appropriately diverse, whether clients have important financial needs that are not being met, whether the MFI's staff or systems are already strained trying to deliver the current product portfolio, and so on (see Chapter 2). Through the product portfolio management function, MFIs can use this information to shape their future strategy – not only with respect to which products to add and which to remove, but more importantly, how to focus resources on the products and activities that will generate the greatest returns for the institution and its target market.

Table 24.7 Scale of diversification among a sample of successful MFIs[59]

Institution	Country	Number of products
ASA	Bangladesh	18
Bandhan	India	3
Crediamigo	Brazil	6
FMM Bucaramanga	Colombia	8
FONDEP Micro-Credit	Morocco	3
ACSI	Ethiopia	7
Compartamos	Mexico	5
Al Amana	Morocco	3
FMM Popayan	Colombia	7
WWB Cali	Colombia	9
EKI	Bosnia and Herzegovina	5
Partner	Bosnia and Herzegovina	10
Grameen Koota	India	6
CMAC Cusco	Peru	14
BRAC	Bangladesh	7

Source: Authors, compiled from listed MFI web sites, 2009.

[59] This table lists a sample of 15 of the top 21 MFIs on *Forbes Magazine*'s list of the world's top 50 microfinance institutions (Swibel, 2007). The 15 MFIs listed are those whose web sites clearly identified the products being offered to clients as of July 2009. Twelve out of 15 of these MFIs are also on the 2008 Global 100 Composite produced by the Microfinance Information eXchange (MIX).

Main Messages

1. Focus product development activity on the areas that deliver the greatest incremental value.
2. Monitor the performance of individual products as well as the product portfolio.
3. Link strategies to budgets.
4. The process of product elimination needs to be managed just like any other product development activity.

Recommended Reading

- Avlonitis, G.; Papastathopoulou. 2006. *Product and services management* (Thousand Oaks, CA, and London, Sage Publications).
- Cooper, R. G.; Edgett, S. J. 1999. *Product development for the service sector: Lessons from market leaders* (Cambridge, MA, Perseus Books).
- Gorchels, L. 2003. *The product manager's field guide: Practical tools, exercises, and resources for improved product management* (New York, NY, McGraw-Hill).
- Mankins, M.; Steele, R. 2005. "Turning great strategy into great performance", *Harvard Business Review*, July-August, at: www.hbr.org
- Wright, G.; Pawlak, K.; Tounitsky, W.; Parrott, L.; Cracknell, D.; Arunachalam, R. S. 2007. *Strategic business planning for market-led financial institutions toolkit* (Nairobi, *MicroSave*), at: http://www.microsave.org/toolkit/strategic-business-planning-toolkit

1. Focus product development activity on the items that deliver the greatest incremental value.

2. Monitor the performance of individual products as well as the entire portfolio.

3. Link strategies to budget.

4. The process of product [illegible] needs to be managed just like [illegible] product development activity.

Recommended Reading

Adams, C., Hayes [illegible] (2010) [illegible]. Thousand Oaks, CA, and London: Sage Publications.

Cooper, R. G., Edgett, S. J. [illegible]. Cambridge, [illegible]: Perseus Books.

Gorchels, L. 2000 [illegible]. New York: McGraw-Hill.

Madhav[illegible], M. S., [illegible], R. 200[illegible]. [illegible]

[illegible]

Bibliography

Bibliography

Abed, F. H.; Matin, I. 2007. "Beyond lending: How microfinance creates new forms of capital to fight poverty", in *Innovations*, Vol. 2, Issue 1–2, pp. 3–17 (Cambridge, MA, MIT Press Journals), at: http://www.microfinancegateway.org/gm/document-1.9.29516/16.pdf

Abeywickrema, C. 2009. *The role of the Hatton National Bank in creating access to financial services for youth in Sri Lanka*, Youth-Inclusive Financial Services Linkage Program Case Study #1(Washington, DC, Making Cents International and Colombo, Hatton National Bank), available at: http://www.makingcents.com/products_services/resources.php

Abramovitz, J. 2001. N. *Unnatural disasters*, World Watch Paper 158 (Washington, DC, World Watch Institute).

Achola, P.; Jones, L.; Meissner, L.; Ratcliff, C. 2009. *Partnering to achieve economic impact in HIV and AIDS-impacted communities: A partnership toolkit for microenterprise development* (New York, SEEP Network), at: www.seepnetwork.org/Resources/Tool_BASICS_Partnership.pdf

Adam, S. 2003. *Final report on promotion of destitute women under TIDP* (Eschborn, Deutsche Gesellschaft für technische Zusammenarbeit (GTZ)).

Agnes, Y. 2002. *Engendering microfinance services: Beyond access*, Paper presented at the workshop: Women's Empowerment or Feminisation of Debt? Towards a New Agenda in African Microfinance, London, March 2002, available at: http://www.genfinance.info/Case Studies/CEEWU.pdf

Agrawal, M. 2010. *M-Pesa: Transforming millions of lives,* Telecom Circle, at: http://www.telecomcircle.com/2010/01/m-pesa/#ixzz0vmblw5Zs

Aheeyar, M. 2006. *Cash grants and microfinance in livelihood recovery in Tsunami affected areas of Sri Lanka*, Humanitarian Policy Group Background Paper (London, Overseas Development Institute), at: http://www.odi.org.uk/hpg/papers/BGP_SriLanka_cash_mfinance.pdf

Ahmed, H. 2002. "Financing microenterprises: An analytical study of Islamic microfinance institutions", in *Islamic Economic Studies*, Vol. 9, No. 2 (Jeddah, Islamic Research and Training Institute (IRTI), Islamic Development Bank), pp. 27–64, at: http://www.microfinancegateway.org/gm/document-1.9.25170/41189_file_H_Ahmed_Financing_M.pdf

Ahmed, M.; Islam, S.; Quashem, M.; Ahmed, N. 2005. *Health microinsurance: A comparative study of three examples in Bangladesh*, CGAP Working Group on Microinsurance, Good and Bad Practices Case Study No. 13 (Washington, DC, CGAP Working Group on Microinsurance), at: http://www.microfinancegateway.org/gm/document-1.9.25418/27889_file_Bangldesh_Health_Go.pdf

—; Ramm, G. 2006. "Meeting the special needs of women and children", in Churchill, C. (ed.), 2006, pp. 130–144 (Geneva, ILO)

Al Rajhi Bank. 2010. *Customer Service Charter*, at: http://www.alrajhibank.com.sa/Business/CBG/CustomerService/Pages/default.aspx

Alexandria Business Association (ABA). 2010. *Alexandria Business Association Small and Micro Enterprise Development Project*, at: http://www.aba-sme.com/index.htm

Aliber, M. 2001. "Rotating savings and credit associations and the pursuit of self discipline", in *African Review of Money, Finance and Banking*, pp. 51–73.

Alidri, P.; van Doorn, J.; El-Zoghbi, M.; Houtart, M.; Larson, D.; Nagarajan, G.; Tsilikounas, C. 2002. *Introduction to microfinance in conflict-affected communities* (Geneva, ILO and UNHCR), at: http://www.ilo.org/public/libdoc/ilo/2002/102B09_320_engl.pdf

Allen & Overy, LLP. 2009. *Islamic microfinance report* (Rome, International Development Law Organisation (IDLO), at: http://www.microfinancegateway.org/p/site/m//template.rc/1.9.34511

Alles, S. M. 1999. *The Small Economic Activities Development (SEAD) Program for Liberian refugees and poor Ivorian families* (Abidjan, Côte d'Ivoire, International Rescue Committee).

Andrews, M. 2006. *Microcredit and agriculture: How to make it work* (Waterloo, MEDA), at: http://www.microcreditsummit.org/papers/Workshops/22_Andrews.pdf

Anker, R. 2005. *Women's access to occupations with authority, influence and decision-making power*, Working Paper No. 44 (Geneva, International Labour Organization (ILO), Policy Integration Department), available at: http://www.ilo.org/wcmsp5/groups/public/—-dgreports/—-integration/documents/publication/wcms_079178.pdf

Antezana, S.; Pérez, J. 2007. *Sistematización del apoyo de PROFIN al instrumento de alianzas estratégicas* (La Paz, PROFIN), at: http://www.microfinanzas.org/uploads/media/alianzas-estrategicas.pdf

Argouslidis, P. 2003. *Factors to consider prior to eliminating a financial service: empirical evience from the British financial services sector*, Working Paper (Athens, University of Economics and Business).

—. 2004. "An empirical investigation into the alternative strategies to implement the elimination of financial services", in *Journal of World Business*, Vol. 39, No. 4, pp. 393–413.

Armendáriz, B.; Roome, N. 2008. *Empowering women via microfinance in fragile states*, Working Paper No. 08/001 (Brussels, Centre Emile Bernheim Research Institute in Management Sciences, Université Libre de Bruxelles), at: http://www.microfinancegateway.org/gm/document-1.9.24892/19.pdf

Asgary, A. 2007. "Informal microfinance institutions: Case of qard hasan funds in Iran ", in Habib, A. (ed.): *Non-Bank Financial Institutions: Islamic Alternatives* (Jeddah, Islamic Research and Training Institute, IDB).

Asian Credit Fund. 2006. *Client survey results.*

Asociación Nacional Ecuménica de Desarrollo (ANED), www.aned.org

Associated Press. 2010. "Medals for Haiti recovery, Little for homeless," Port-au-Prince, Haiti, July 12, 2010, at: http://abcnews.go.com/Entertainment/wireStory?id=11148267

Athmer, G. 2004. *Gender audit*, CETZAM Zambia.

Austrian, K.; Ngurukie, C. 2009. *Safe and smart savings products for vulnerable adolescent girls in Kenya & Uganda*, Youth-Inclusive Financial Services Linkage Program Case Study #3 (Washington, DC, Making Cents International; New York, Population Council and Nairobi, MicroSave Consulting Ltd.), available at: http://www.makingcents.com/products_services/resources.php

Avlonitis, G.; Papastathopoulou, P. 2006. *Product and services management* (Thousand Oaks, CA, and London, Sage Publications).

Banco FIE. 2010. *Microjusticia*, available at: http://www.bancofie.com.bo/transparencia-y-compromiso-social/microjusticia/

Banco Solidario. 2002. *En operación la mayor red de servicios para migrantes*, at: http://www.banco-solidario.com/noticia.php?notID=61

Bankakademie. 2000a. *Marketing for microfinance depositories: A toolkit* (Eschborn, GTZ), at: http://www2.gtz.de/dokumente/bib/00-1782.pdf

—. 2000b. *Liquidity management: A toolkit for microfinance institutions.* (Eschborn, Deutsche Gesellschaft fur Technische Zusammenarbeit (GTZ), at: http://www2.gtz.de/dokumente/bib/00-0974.pdf

Banking with the Poor Network (BWTP). 2006a. *Microleasing in livelihood restoration following a natural disaster*, BWTP Brief No. 5 (Singapore), at: http://www.microfinancegateway.org/p/site/m//template.rc/1.9.42077

—. 2006b. *Grants and loans in livelihood restoration following a natural disaster* (Singapore), at: http://www.bwtp.org/arcm/mfdm/Web Resources/Briefs/Brief_3.pdf

Banthia, A.; Johnson, S.; McCord, M.; Mathews, B. 2009. *Microinsurance that works for women: Making gender-sensitive microinsurance programs* (Geneva, ILO), at: http://www.ilo.org/public/english/employment/mifacility/download/mpaper3_gender.pdf

— ; Shell, B. 2009. "The youth frontier in microfinance: Savings and financial education for girls in Mongolia", *Microfinance Insights*, Vol. 15 (Nov/Dec), pp. 46–47, at: http://www.swwb.org/files/mfinsights_issue15.pdf

Barbados Youth Business Trust. 2007. *Annual Report 2005/2006* (St. Michael, Barbados), at: http://www.youthbusiness.bb/cms/files/stories/annual_reports/BYBT_Report.pdf

Barrientos, A.; Scott, J. 2008. *Social transfers and growth: A review*, Brooks World Poverty Institute Working Paper No. 52 (Manchester, University of Manchester), available at: http://www.bwpi.manchester.ac.uk/resources/Working-Papers/bwpi-wp-5208.pdf

Barringer, B.R.; Ireland, R.D. 2005. *Entrepreneurship: Successfully launching new ventures* (Upper Saddle River, NJ, Prentice Hall).

Barua, D. 2006. *Five cents a day: Innovative programs for reaching the destitute with microcredit, no-interest loans, and other instruments: The experience of Grameen Bank*, Paper presented at Global Microcredit Summit in Halifax, Nova Scotia, Canada, at: http://www.microfinancegateway.org/gm/document-1.9.28368/36737_file_Barua.pdf

BASIX Academy for Building Lifelong Employability Ltd. (B-ABLE). 2010. *About us*, at http://www.b-able.in/aboutus.php

Bauer, S.; Finnegan, G.; Haspels, N.; Deelen, L.; Seltik, H.; Majurin, E. 2008. *GET ahead for women in enterprise: Training package and resource kit*, 2nd edition (Geneva, ILO), available at: http://www.ilo.org/wcmsp5/groups/public/—-ed_emp/—-emp_ent/documents/publication/wcms_116100.pdf

Bebczuk, R. 2009. *SME access to credit in Guatemala and Nicaragua: Challenging conventional wisdom with new evidence*, Documento de Trabajo Nro. 80, Centro de Estudios Distributivos, Laborales y Sociales (Buenos Aires, Universidad Nacional de La Plata), at: http://www.microfinancegateway.org/p/site/m/template.rc/1.9.34606/

Beck, T. 2007. *Financing constraints of SMEs in developing countries: Evidence, determinants and solutions*, paper prepared for the KDI conference on "Financing Innovation-Oriented Businesses to Promote Entrepreneurship" Development Research Group (Washington, DC, World Bank), at: http://arno.uvt.nl/show.cgi?fid=95654

Bedson, J. 2008. "Microfinance partnerships: Capacity building", in *ADB Finance for the Poor*, Vol. 9, No. 2 (Asian Development Bank), available at: www.adb.org/documents/periodicals/microfinance

Berenbach, S.; Guzmán, D. 1992. *The solidarity group experience worldwide* (Washington, DC, ACCION International), at: http://resources.centerforfinancialinclusion.org/

Bezard, G. 2003. *Global money transfers: Exploring the remittances gold mine* (Boston, MA, Celent Communications).

Bhatt, O. P. 2010. *Chairman's speech, State Bank of India*, at: http://www.moneycontrol.com/annual-report/statebankindia/chairmans-speech/SBI

Biety, M. 2005. "Liquidity management", in Hirschland, M. (ed.), 2005, pp. 275–300.

Biswas, 2003. "Housing is a productive asset: Housing finance for self-employed women in India" in *Small Enterprise Development*, Vol. 14, No. 1, pp. 49–55 (Warwickshire, Practical Action Publishing), at: http://www.ingentaconnect.com/content/itpub/sedv/2003/00000014/00000001/art00009

Blume, J.; Breyer, J. Forthcoming. *Microfinance and child labour*, Employment Working Paper (Geneva, ILO).

Boston Consulting Group. 2003. *Preparing for the endgame: Global payments 2004* (London).

Boucher, S.; Summerlin, R.; Martinez, M. 2010. *Poverty targeting and measurement tools in microfinance: Progress out of poverty index and the poverty assessment tool* (Social Performance Task Force), at: http://sptf.info/page/user-reviews-of-sp-tools

BRAC. 2010. *BRAC social enterprises*, at: http://www.brac.net/content/social-enterprises-0

Branch, B. 2002. "Savings product management: Establishing the framework" in Branch, B.; Klaehn, J. (eds.), 2002, pp. 63–112.

—; Klaehn, J. (eds.). 2002a. *Striking the balance in microfinance: A practical guide to mobilizing savings* (Washington, DC, Pact Publications and World Council of Credit Unions), available at: http://www.woccu.org/publications/savings

—; Klaehn, J. 2002b. "The keys to striking the balance: An introduction to savings mobilization", in Branch, B.; Klaehn, J. (eds.), 2002, pp. 1–28.

Brand, M. 1998a. *New product development for microfinance: Evaluation and preparation*, Microenterprise Best Practices (MBP) Project, Technical Note Number 1 (Bethesda, MD, MBP Development Alternatives Inc., USAID), at: http://www.microlinks.org/ev02.php?ID=7478_201&ID2=DO_TOPIC

—. 1998b. *New product development for microfinance: Design, testing and launch*, Microenterprise Best Practices (MBP) Project, Technical Note Number 2 (Betheda, MD, MBP, Development Alternatives Inc., USAID), at: http://www.microlinks.org/ev_en.php?ID=7477_201&ID2=DO_TOPIC

—. 2001. *The MBP guide to new product development*, Microenterprise Best Practices (MBP) Project (Bethesda, MD, Development Alternatives Inc., ACCION, USAID), at: http://www.microlinks.org/ev_en.php?ID=7501_201&ID2=DO_TOPIC

—. 2003. *Market intelligence: Making market research work for microfinance* (Boston, MA, ACCION), at: http://publications.accion.org/publications/InSight_7__162.asp

Breyer, J. 2006a. *Financial arrangements in informal apprenticeships: Determinants and effects, findings from urban Ghana*, Social Finance Programme Working Paper No. 49 (Geneva, ILO), at: http://www.ilo.org/wcmsp5/groups/public/—-ed_emp/documents/publication/wcms_106332.pdf

—. 2006b. Interview with Nelson Agyemang.

Brinkerhoff, J.M. 2002. "Assessing and improving partnership relationships and outcomes: A proposed framework", in *Evaluation and Programme Planning*, Vol. 25, Issue 3, pp. 215–231.

Brown, W.; Churchill, C. 1999. "Providing insurance to low-income households. Part I: A primer on insurance principles and products", *New Products for Microfinance*, Review Paper 1 (Bethesda, MD, USAID MBP Project), at: http://www.microfinancegateway.org/gm/document-1.9.26877/2459_file_02459.pdf

—; —. 2000. "Insurance provision in low-income communities. Part II: Initial lessons from micro-insurance experiments for the poor", *New Products for Microfinance*, Review Paper 2 (Bethesda, MD, USAID MBP Project), at: http://www.microfinancegateway.org/gm/document-1.9.28683/2460_file_02460.pdf

—; Garcia, A. 2002. "Micasa: Housing financing in Peru" in *CIVIS*: *Shelter Finance for the Poor Series*, Issue 4ii (Washington, DC, Cities Alliance), at: http://www.citiesalliance.org/ca/civis

—; Nagarajan, G. 2000. *Disaster loan funds for microfinance institutions: A look at emerging experience* (Bethesda, Microenterprise Best Practices), at: http://www.microfinancegateway.org/gm/document-1.9.29690/3784_file_03784.pdf

Brusky, B., 2004. *Housing microfinance,* CGAP Donor Brief No. 20 (Washington, DC, CGAP), at: http://www.cgap.org/gm/document-1.9.2395/DonorBrief_20.pdf

Buchenau, J.; Meyer, R. 2007. *Introducing rural finance into an urban microfinance institution: The example of Banco Procredit, El Salvador*, Paper presented at the International Conference on Rural Finance Research: Moving Results into Policies and Practice (Rome, FAO), at: http://www.fao.org/ag/rurfinconference/docs/papers_theme_3/introducing_rural_finance.pdf

Bundred, F.; Penner, J.; Achola, P. 2007. *Responding to HIV/AIDS within MFIs in Mozambique: Lessons learned from an action research project*, microREPORT #80 (Washington, DC, USAID), at: http://www.microlinks.org/ev_en.php?ID=18264_201&ID2=DO_TOPIC

Bwire, F.; Mukasa, G.; Mersland, R. 2008. *Access to mainstream microfinance services for persons with disabilities: Lessons learned from Uganda*, Report presented at the UN Convention on the Rights of Persons with Disabilities: A Call for Action on Poverty, Lack of Access and Discrimination, 19–22 May 2008, Addis Ababa, Ethiopia, at: http://papers.ssrn.com/sol3/papers.cfm?abstract_id=1101701

Caire, D. 2004. *Building credit scorecards for small business lending in developing markets* (London, Bannock Consulting), at: www.microfinance.com/English/Papers/Scoring_SMEs_Hybrid.pdf

—; Barton, S.; de Zubiria, A.; Alexiev, Z.; Dyer, J.; Bundred, F.; Brislin, N. 2006. *Handbook for developing credit scoring systems in a microfinance context*, MicroREPORT #66 (Washington, DC, USAID), at: http://www.microfinancegateway.org/gm/document-1.9.29619/37251_file_34.pdf

Camfed International. 2008. *Youth financial services case study: Camfed International Zambia* (Washington, DC, Making Cents International and Cambridge, Camfed International), at: http://www.makingcents.com/pdfs/resources/0809/YFS_Case_Study_Financial_Services.pdf

Campaigne, J. 2010. "Case Study 4. DrumNet and technological innovations", in Miller, C.; Jones, L., 2010, pp. 126–137.

Campion, A.; Linder, C.; with Knotts, K. 2008. *Putting the "social" into performance management: A practice-based guide* (Brighton, University of Sussex, Institute of Development Studies), at: http://www.microfinancegateway.org/p/site/m//template.rc/1.9.30448

Canadian International Development Agency (CIDA). 2010. *CIDA's policy on gender equity* (Gatineau, CIDA), available at: http://www.acdi-cida.gc.ca/acdi-cida/acdi-cida.nsf/eng/EMA-218123616-NN9

CapitalPlus Exchange Corporation. 2010. *CapitalPlus Exchange commemorates global launch of its Small Business Banking Network in Addis Ababa, Ethiopia*, Press Release, 1 November, 2010 (Chicago, CapitalPlus Exchange Corporation), at: www.shorecapexchange.org/system/files/PressRelease-SBBN.pdf

CARE Foundation. 2010. *Insuring primary care: A sustainable financing solution for rural primary health*, Learning Journey (Geneva, Microinsurance Innovation Facility), at: http://www.microinsurancefacility.org/knowledge-center/learning-journeys

Carothers, R.; Foad, M.; Denomy, J. 2009. "Improving working conditions through microfinance programming," in *African Newsletter on Occupational Health and Safety: Accident prevention – a safe workplace*, Vol. 19, No. 1, pp. 20–22 (Helsinki, Finnish Institute of Occupational Health), at: http://www.ppic-work.org/download/publications/AfricanNewsletter12009.pdf

CFED. 2010. *Individual development accounts: IDA basics* (Washington, DC, CFED), at: http://cfed.org/programs/idas/ida_basics/

CGAP Savings Information Resource Center. 2006. *Poor peoples' savings: Q&As with experts* (Washington, DC, CGAP), at: http://www.microfinancegateway.org/p/site/m//template.rc/1.9.30272

Champagne, P.; Pikholz, L.; Arunachalam, R. S.; Baron, C.; Sempangi, H.; Cracknell, D.; Wright, G. 2008. *A toolkit for process mapping for MFIs* (Nairobi, *MicroSave*), at: http://www.microsave.org/toolkit/process-mapping-and-risk-analysis-toolkit

Chandani, T.; Twamuhabwa, W. 2009. *A partnership to offer educational loans to nursing students in Uganda*, Youth-Inclusive Financial Services Linkage Program Case Study #4 (Washington, DC, Making Cents International and Banyan Global; Nairobi, Equity Bank), available at: http://www.makingcents.com/products_services/resources.php

Charan, R.; Colvin, G. 1999. "Why CEOs fail", in *Fortune*, Vol. 139, No. 12, 21 June (New York, NY, Time Inc.).

Chaturvedi, H.; Kumar, D.; Singh, R. (eds.). 2005. *India Insurance Report*, Series I (Greater Noida, Birla Institute of Management Technology).

Chemonics, 2006. *Catching the technology wave: Mobile phone banking and text-a-payment in the Philippines* (Washington, DC, Chemonics International Inc.), available at: http://www.kiwanja.net/database/document/report_tech_wave.pdf

Chen, M.A.; Snodgrass, D. 2001. *Managing resources, activities and risk in urban India: The impact of SEWA Bank* (Washington, DC, AIMS), at: pdf.usaid.gov/pdf_docs/PNACN571.pdf

—. 2005. *Towards economic freedom: The impact of SEWA* (Ahmedabad, SEWA), at: http://www.sewaresearch.org/Impact.PDF

Chen, G.; Weiss, K. 2007. "Lessons from South Asian MFIs moving up market", in *Enterprise Development and Microfinance*, Vol. 18, No. 4, pp. 328–341 (New York, NY, Practical Action Publishing) at: http://practicalactionpublishing.org/publishing/SED_18-4

Chen, S. 2009. *Learning from pilots: The case of ShoreBank International/AMPER in Pakistan* (Washington, DC, SEEP Network, and ShoreBank International Ltd.), at: http://www.seepnetwork.org/Resources/Maternity_pilot_Case_Shorebank.pdf

Cheston, S.; Kuhn, L. 2002. *Empowering women through microfinance* (New York, NY, UNIFEM), at: http://www.microcreditsummit.org/papers/empowerintro.htm

CHF International. 2001. *So, you want to do housing microfinance? A guide to incorporating a home improvement loan program into a microfinance institution* (Silver Spring, MD, CHF International), at: http://www.chfinternational.org/node/32902

Child Wise. 2004. *Child wise choose with care: A handbook to build safer organisations for children* (Melbourne, Child Wise).

Choudhury, S. 2006. *Better serving the multitude institutional action plan* (Dhaka, ASA), at: www.asabd.org

Christen, R. 2004. "Foreword", in F. Daphnis; B. Ferguson (eds.), 2004, pp. ix–xiv.

—; Mas, I. 2009. "It's time to address the microsavings challenge, scalably", in *Enterprise Development and Microfinance*, Vol. 20, No. 4, pp. 274–285 (New York, NY, Practical Action Publishing) at: http://practicalactionpublishing.org/publishing/SED_20-4

—; Pearce, D. 2005. *Managing risks and designing products for agricultural microfinance: Features of an emerging model*, CGAP Occasional Paper No. 11 (Washington, DC, CGAP), at: http://www.cgap.org/gm/document-1.9.2705/OP11.pdf

—; Srinivasan, N.; Voorhies, R. 2005. "Managing to go down market", in Hirschland, M. (ed.), 2005, pp. 93–116.

Chua, R.; Miehlbradt, A. 1999a. *Loan rescheduling after a natural disaster*, Rapid Onset Natural Disaster Brief No. 1, (Bethesda, Microenterprise Best Practices), at: http://www.microfinancegateway.org/p/site/m//template.rc/1.9.28770

—; —. 1999b. *MFI liquidity problems after a natural disaster*, Rapid Onset Natural Disaster Brief No. 5 (Bethesda, Microenterprise Best Practices), at: http://www.microfinancegateway.org/p/site/m//template.rc/1.9.28835

—; —. 1999c. *Pre-disaster planning to protect microfinance institutions*, Rapid Onset Natural Disaster Brief No. 6 (Bethesda, Microenterprise Best Practices), at: http://www.microfinancegateway.org/p/site/m//template.rc/1.9.28507

—; —. 1999d. *Pre-disaster planning to protect microfinance clients,* Rapid Onset Natural Disaster Brief No. 7, (Bethesda, Microenterprise Best Practices), at: http://www.microfinancegateway.org/p/site/m//template.rc/1.9.28504

Churchill, C. 1999. *Client-focused lending: The art of individual microlending* (Washington, DC, Calmeadow), at: http://resources.centerforfinancialinclusion.org/

—. 2003. "Emergency loans: The other side of microcredit", in *ADB Finance for the Poor*, Vol. 4, No. 3 (Asian Development Bank), available at: www.adb.org/documents/periodicals/microfinance

—. (ed.). 2006. *Protecting the poor: A microinsurance compendium* (Geneva, ILO), at: http://www.munichre-foundation.org/StiftungsWebsite/Projects/Microinsurance/2006Microinsurance/Microinsurance_Compendium.htm

—; Cohen, M. 2006. "Marketing microinsurance", in Churchill, C. (ed.), 2006, pp. 174–196.

—; Costner, D. 2001. *CARE's microfinance risk management handbook* (Atlanta, GA, CARE).

—; Frankiewicz, C. 2006. *Making microfinance work: Managing for improved performance* (Geneva, ILO).

—; Guérin, I. 2004. *Microfinance-led strategies to eliminate bonded labour*, Independent paper, at: http://ilo-mirror.library.cornell.edu/public/english/employment/finance/download/churchguer.pdf

—; Hirschland, M.; Painter, J. 2002. *New directions in poverty finance: Village banking revisited* (Washington, DC, The SEEP Network), at: http://www.seepnetwork.org/Resources/637_file_New_Directions_in_Poverty_Finance.pdf

—; Leftley, R. 2006. "Organization development in microinsurance", in Churchill, C. (ed.), 2006, pp. 270–287.

—; Liber, D.; McCord, M.; Roth, J. 2003. *Making insurance work for microfinance institutions: A technical guide to developing and delivering microinsurance* (Geneva, ILO).

—; Pepler, T. 2004. *TUW SKOK, Poland.* CGAP Working Group on Microinsurance Good and Bad Practices Case Study No. 2 (Washington, DC, CGAP), at: http://www.ilo.org/wcmsp5/groups/public/—-ed_emp/documents/publication/wcms_122457.pdf

—; Roth, J. 2006. "Microinsurance: Opportunities and pitfalls for microfinance institutions", in Churchill, C. (ed.), 2006, pp. 452–468 (Geneva, ILO), at: http://www.munichre-foundation.org/StiftungsWebsite/Projects/Microinsurance/2006Microinsurance/Microinsurance_Compendium.htm

Cilimkovic, S.; Jahic, S. 2009. *Youth inclusive financial services: A case study from Bosnia*, Youth-Inclusive Financial Services Linkage Program Case Study #11 (Washington, DC, Making Cents International and Tuzla, Partner Microcredit Foundation), available at: http://www.makingcents.com/products_services/resources.php

Clearline International. 2010. *A new concept in health care financing*, at: http://www.clearlinehmo.com/index.php

Coetzee, G.; Kabbucho, K.;Mnjama, A. 2002.*Understanding the re-birth of equity building society in Kenya* (Nairobi, MicroSave), at: http://www.microsave.org/research_paper/understanding-the-re-birth-of-equity-building-society-in-kenya

Cohen, M. 2003. *The impact of microfinance*, CGAP Donor Brief No. 13 (Washington, DC, CGAP), at: http://www.cgap.org/gm/document-1.9.2407/DonorBrief_13.pdf)

—; Sebstad, J. 2003. *Financial education for the poor*, Financial Literacy Project Working Paper Number 1 (Washington, DC, Microfinance Opportunities), at: http://www.globalfinancialed.org/documents/WP1_FinEd4Poor.pdf

—; Stack, K.; McGuinness, E. 2003. *Financial education: A win-win for clients and MFIs* (Washington, DC, Microfinance Opportunities), at: http://www.ruralfinance.org/servlet/BinaryDownloaderServlet?filename=1123071437399_Financial_Education_WinWin_Clients_MFIs.pdf

Collins, D., Morduch, J., Rutherford, S.; Rothven, O. 2009. *Portfolios of the poor: How the world's poor live on $2 a day* (Princeton, NJ, Princeton University Press).

Comstock, M.; Iannone, M.; Bhatia, R. 2009. *Maximizing the value of remittances for economic development*, at: http://www.microfinancegateway.org/p/site/m//template.rc/1.9.40864

Conklin, S.; Torres, V.; Derdari, B.; Akhmisse, L. 2008. *Linking youth with knowledge and opportunities in microfinance (LYKOM) project, Morocco: A youth livelihoods program case study* (Washington, DC, The SEEP

Network and Save the Children), at:
http://www.microlinks.org/ev_en.php?ID=32768_201&ID2=DO_TOPIC

Consultative Group to Assist the Poorest (CGAP). 2002. *Savings are as important as credit: Deposit services for the poor*, Donor Brief No. 4 (Washington, DC), at:
http://www.cgap.org/gm/document-1.9.2435/DonorBrief_04.pdf

—. 2010a. *Policy glossary*, at:
http://www.microfinancegateway.org/p/site/m/template.rc/1.11.48251/1.26.9205/

—. 2010b. *Financial access 2010: The state of financial inclusion through the crisis* (Washington, DC, CGAP), at:
http://www.cgap.org/gm/document-1.9.46570/FA_2010_Financial_Access_2010_Rev.pdf

Cooper, R.G., de Bretani, U. 1984. "Criteria for screening new industrial products" in *Industrial Marketing Management*, Vol. 13, No. 3, pp. 149–156 (Oxford, Elsevier, Ltd.)

—; Edgett, S. J. 1999. *Product development for the service sector: Lessons from market leaders* (Cambridge, MA, Perseus Books).

Counts, A.; Collins, L.; Octavio, G.; Rai, V. 2005. *Recovery from the tsunami disaster: Poverty reduction and sustainable development through microfinance*, A Special Report (Washington, DC, Grameen Foundation USA), at:
http://www.grameenfoundation.org/sites/default/files/pdf/Recovery-from-Tsunami-Disaster.pdf

Cracknell, D. 2006. "Understanding and preventing the failure of new products", in *Small Enterprise Developm*ent, Vol. 17, No. 3, pp. 54–62 (Warwickshire, Practical Action Publishing).

—; Sempangi, H.; Wright, G.; Mutesasira, L.; Mukwana, P.; McCord, M. 2002. *Lessons from MicroSave's Action Research Programme 2001*, MicroSave Briefing Note No. 10 (Nairobi, MicroSave), at:
http://www.microsave.org/briefing_notes/briefing-note-10-lessons-from-imicrosavei%E2%80%99s-action-research-programme-2001

—; —; —. 2004. *Costing and pricing of financial services: A toolkit* (Nairobi, *MicroSave*), at:
http://www.microsave.org/toolkit/costing-and-pricing-toolkit.

Daniels, A.; Jeans, A. 2009. "Integrated approaches to enabling the most vulnerable to participate in markets", in *Enterprise Development and Microfinance*, Vol. 20, No. 2, pp. 139–157 (Rugby, Practical Action Publishing), at
http://www.ingentaconnect.com/content/itpub/edm/2009/00000020/00000002/art00006

Daphnis, F. 2004a. "Housing microfinance: Toward a definition", in Daphnis, F.; Ferguson, B. (eds.), 2004, pp. 1–14.

—. 2004b. "Elements of product design for housing microfinance", in Daphnis, F.; Ferguson, B. (eds.), 2004, pp. 84–114.

—; Ferguson, B. (eds.). 2004. *Housing microfinance: A guide to practice* (Bloomfield, CT, Kumarian Press, Inc.).

Daru, P.; Churchill, C.; Beemsterboer, E. 2005. "The prevention of debt bondage with microfinance-led services", in *The European Journal of Development Research*, Vol. 17, No. 1, pp. 132–154 (Basingstoke, Palgrave Macmillan).

Dawit, K. 2010. *Leasing product development at African Village Financial Services*, unpublished ILO case study.

Deelen, L.; Dupleich, M.; Othieno, L.; Wakelin, O. 2003. *Leasing for small and micro enterprises: A guide for designing and managing leasing schemes in developing countries* (Geneva, ILO), at:
http://www.microfinancegateway.org/gm/document-1.9.29539/13819_13819.pdf

—; Molenaar, K. 2004. *Guarantee funds for small enterprises: A manual for guarantee fund managers* (Geneva, ILO), at:
www.ilo.org/public/libdoc/ilo/2004/104B09_435_engl.pdf

Dellien, H.; Burnett, J.; Gincherman, E.; Lynch, E. 2005. *Product diversification in microfinance: Introducing individual lending* (New York, NY, Women's World Banking), at:
http://www.swwb.org/product-diversification-in-microfinance-introducing-individual-lending

—; Leland, O. 2006. *Introducing individual lending*, WWB how-to guide (New York, NY, Women's World Banking), at: http://www.microfinancegateway.org/gm/document-1.9.29474/33826_file_Individual_20Lending_20How_to_20Guide.pdf

—; Lynch, E. 2007. *Rural finance for small farmers: An integrated approach*, WWB Focus Note (New York, NY, Women's World Banking), at: http://www.swwb.org/files/pubs/en/rural_finance_for_smaller_farmers_e.pdf

DeMarco, D.; Mills, G.; Ciurea, M. 2008. *Assets for independence evaluation: Process study final report* (Cambridge, MA, Abt Associates Inc.), at: www.acf.hhs.gov/programs/ocs/.../AFI_Final_Process_Study_ES.pdf

De Montesquiou, A. 2007. *Banking on the future: An interview with Chandula Abeywickrema from Hatton National Bank in Sri Lanka* (Washington, DC, CGAP), at: http://www.microfinancegateway.org/gm/document-1.9.29510/49615.pdf

Department for Families and Communities. 2007. *Child safe environments: Principles of good practice* (Adelaide, Government of South Australia), at: http://blogs.dfc.sa.gov.au/m/dfcweb_fsa/755/download.aspx

Dercon, S. 2009. "Risk, poverty and insurance", Brief 3, in Hill, R.; Torero, M. (eds.): *Innovations in insuring the poor*, Focus 17 (Washington, DC, IFPRI), at: www.ifpri.org/publication/innovations-insuring-poor

Derflinger, K.; Ivaniychuk, O.; Grossmann, H. 2006. *Myth and reality of agricultural micro-lending: Experiences from a commercial bank in Georgia* (Frankfurt, Frankfurt School of Finance & Management).

destinationCRM.com. 2010. *What is CRM ?* (New York, NY, CRM Media), at: http://www.destinationcrm.com/Articles/CRM-News/Daily-News/What-Is-CRM-46033.aspx

Deutsche Gesellschaft für Technische Zusammenarbeit (GTZ). 2000. *A risk management framework for microfinance institutions* (Eschborn, GTZ, Division 41 Financial Systems Development and Banking Services), at: http://www.gtz.de/en/dokumente/en_risk_management_framework_for_MFI.pdf

Development Alternatives, Inc. 2007. *Commercial bank and MFI linkages: Tools for assisting MFIs in partnering with commercial banks, A guide for assisting microfinance institutions in negotiating service agreements with commercial banks* (Washington, DC, USAID), at: http://www.microlinks.org/ev_en.php?ID=23966_201&ID2=DO_TOPIC

Diaz, L.; Hansel, J. 2005. *The missing link in the value chain: Financing rural farmers and Microentrepreneurs – Strategic alliances for financial services and market linkages in rural areas* (Washington, DC, SEEP Network and USAID), at: http://communities.seepnetwork.org/edexchange/system/files/Missing+Link+in+Value+Chain+Financing+for+Rural+Farmers.pdf

—; Hansel, J. 2007. *Practitioner-led action research: Making risk-sharing models work with farmers, agribusinesses and financial institutions* (Washington, DC, The SEEP Network), at: http://communities.seepnetwork.org/system/files/Making+Risk+Sharing+Models+Work.pdf

Donahue, J.; Kabbucho, K.; Osinde, S. 2001. *HIV/AIDS – Responding to a silent economic crisis among microfinance clients in Kenya and Uganda* (Nairobi, *MicroSave*), at: http://www.microsave.org/research_paper/hivaids-responding-to-a-silent-economic-crisis-among-microfinance-clients-in-kenya-an

Doran, A.; McFadyen, N.; Vogel, R. 2009. *The missing middle in agricultural finance: Relieving the capital constraint on smallholder groups and other agricultural SMEs* (Oxford, Oxfam), at: http://www.oxfam.org.uk/resources/policy/trade/downloads/research_agricultural_finance.pdf

Dowla, A. 2004. "Microleasing: The Grameen Bank experience", in *Journal of Microfinance*, Vol. 6. No. 2, pp. 138–160 (Provo, UT, Brigham Young University), at: http://contentdm.lib.byu.edu/cdm4/document.php?CISOROOT=/Microfinance&CISOPTR=228&REC=1

—. 2007. *Helping hand instead of handouts: Social safety net provision by Grameen Bank*, Poverty and Capital Conference, University of Manchester, 2–4 July 2007, at: http://www.sed.manchester.ac.uk/research/events/conferences/povertyandcapital/dowla.pdf

Downing, S.; Murphy, L. 2010. *Microenterprise development in Peru: Will a women-targeted, one-size-fits-all training effectively serve Peru's female microenterpreneurs?* (Cambridge, MA, Harvard Kennedy School), at: http://www.innovations.harvard.edu/cache/documents/11053/1105305.pdf

Doyle, K. 1998. *Microfinance in the wake of conflict: Challenges and opportunities* (New York, SEEP Network), at: http://www.microfinancegateway.org/p/site/m//template.rc/1.9.28945

Dunford, C. 2001. *Building better lives: Sustainable integration of microfinance and education in child survival, reproductive health, and HIV/AIDS prevention for the poorest entrepreneurs* (Washington, DC, Microcredit Summit Campaign), at: http://www.microcreditsummit.org/papers/BBLcomplete.pdf

Dupleich, M. 2000. *Programa de leasing de ANED* [also available in English: *ANED – The microleasing programme*] (La Paz, Asociación Nacional Ecuménica de Desarrollo – ANED).

—. 2003. *El Microleasing: Una nueva alternativa financiera para el desarrollo del pequeño agricultor rural y la microempresa* (La Paz, Asociación Nacional Ecuménica de Desarrollo – ANED), at: http://www.microfinanzarural.org/articulos/cap03art05.pdf

Dyer, J.; Kale, P.; Singh, H. 2001. "How to make strategic alliances work", in *MIT Sloan Management Review*, Vol. 42, No. 4, at: http://sloanreview.mit.edu/the-magazine/articles/2001/summer/4243/how-to-make-strategic-alliances-work/

The Economist. 2010. "Microfinance for students", 9 September, available at: http://www.economist.com/node/16996791?story_id=16996791&fsrc=rss

EDUCA-PRO. 2010. *Preguntas frecuentes*, at: http://www.educapro.org.bo/

El-Zoghbi, M.; de Montesquiou, A.; with Hashemi, S. 2009. *Creating pathways for the poorest: Early lessons on implementing the graduation model*, CGAP Brief (Washington, DC, CGAP), at: http://www.cgap.org/gm/document-1.9.41162/BR_Creating_Pathways_Poorest.pdf. Hunger Safety Net Programe: http://www.hungersafetynet.org

Ennew, C.; Watkins, T.; Wright, M. 1995. *Marketing financial services*, 2nd ed., (Oxford, Butterworth-Heinemann).

Epstein, K.; Smith, G. 2007. "The ugly side of microlending: How big Mexican banks profit as many poor borrowers get trapped in a maze of debt", *Business Week*, 13 Dec. 2007, at: http://www.businessweek.com/magazine/content/07_52/b4064038915009.htm

Escobar, A.; Merrill, S. 2004. "Housing microfinance: The state of the practice", in F. Daphnis; B. Ferguson (eds.), 2004, pp. 33–68.

Falletti, P. 2002. "Financial management", in McNaughton, D.; Carlson, D. (eds.), *Banking institutions in developing markets: Building strong management and responding to change*, Vol. 1, pp. 64–83 (Washington, DC, World Bank).

Farlex Financial Dictionary, 2009. http://financial-dictionary.thefreedictionary.com/Nonfinancial+Services and http://financial-dictionary.thefreedictionary.com/Investment.

Ferguson, B. 2004. "The key importance of housing microfinance", in F. Daphnis; B. Ferguson (eds.), 2004, pp. 15–32.

Fernandez, J.; Sene, L. 2010. *Investing in Africa: Defining the "missing middle"*, at: http://www.huffingtonpost.com/j-skyler-fernandes/investing-in-africa-defin_b_534767.html

Fernando, N. 2003. "Pawnshops and microlending: A fresh look is needed", in *ADB Finance for the Poor*, Vol. 4, No. 1 (Asian Development Bank), at: www.adb.org/documents/periodicals/microfinance

Ferranti, D.; Ody, A. 2007. *Beyond microfinance: Getting capital to small and medium enterprises to fuel faster development*, Policy Brief No. 159 (Brookings Institution), at: http://www.brookings.edu/~/media/Files/rc/papers/2007/03development_ferranti/pb159.pdf

Finextra Research. 2005. *ICICI Bank to deliver kiosk-based ebanking to rural India*, at: http://www.finextra.com/news/fullstory.aspx?newsitemid=13834

Finscope South Africa. 2007. *Technical overview: Financial service measures*, at: http://www.finscope.co.za/technicaloverview.html

FMO. Undated. *Environmental & social risk management tools for MFIs*, at: http://www.fmo.nl/smartsite.dws?id=531

Fonseca, D. 2008. *The neighborhood bank: CrediAmigo – award for excellence in microfinance*, at: http://www.iadb.org/mif/microenterpriseamericas/2008/articledetail.cfm?artid=5341&language=En

Food and Agriculture Organization of the United Nations (FAO). Undated. *Women and food security*, at: http://www.fao.org/FOCUS/E/Women/Sustin-e.htm

—. 2003. *Term financing in agriculture: A review of relevant experiences*, FAO Investment Centre Occasional Paper No. 14 (Rome), at: http://www.fao.org/docrep/008/ae373e/ae373e00.HTM

Foundation for Development Cooperation. 2006. *Training resources on microfinance and disaster management* (Queensland, Banking with the Poor Network), at: http://www.bwtp.org/arcm/mfdm/training.html

Frank, C. 2008. *Stemming the tide of mission drift: Microfinance transformations and the double bottom line*, WWB Focus Note (New York, Women's World Banking), at: http://www.swwb.org/files/pubs/en/stemming_the_tide_of_mission_drift_microfinance_transformations_and_the_Double_Bottom_Line.pdf

Frankiewicz, C. 2001. *Building institutional capacity: The story of Prodem 1987–2000* (Toronto, Calmeadow).

—. 2006. *Costs and benefits of market research and pilot testing for new product development in microfinance* (Nairobi, *MicroSave*), at: http://www.microsave.org/research_paper/costs-and-benefits-of-market-research-and-pilot-testing-for-new-product-development-i

—; Wright, G; Cracknell, D. 2004. *Product marketing toolkit* (Nairobi, *MicroSave*), at: http://www.microsave.org/toolkit/product-marketing-toolkit

Fraslin, J. 2003. *CECAM: A cooperative agricultural financial institution providing credit adapted to farmers' demand in Madagascar*, Paper presented at "Paving the Way Forward for Rural Finance: An International Conference on Best Practices", Washington, DC, 2–4 June 2003.

Freedom from Hunger. 2010. *Technical Resources and Services – for the Public and Practitioners*, at: http://www.ffhtechnical.org

Fries, R.; Akin, B. 2004. *Value chains and their significance for addressing the rural finance challenge*, USAID MicroReport No. 20 (Washington, DC, USAID), at: http://www.microlinks.org/ev_en.php?ID=7098_201&ID2=DO_TOPIC

Gallardo, J.; Goldberg, M., Randhawa, B. 2006. *Strategic alliances to scale up financial services in rural areas*, World Bank Working Paper No. 76 (Washington, DC, World Bank), at: http://siteresources.worldbank.org/INTACCESSFINANCE/Resources/StrategicAlliances.pdf

Garand, D. 2005. *VimoSEWA, India*, CGAP Working Group on Microinsurance, Good and Bad Practices Case Study No. 16 (Washington, DC, CGAP Working Group on Microinsurance), at: http://www.microfinancegateway.org/gm/document-1.9.25692/28653_file_VimoSEWA_English.pdf

George, M. 2009. "Partnerships for greater scale and impact", in *Microfinance Insights*, Vol. 10, Jan/Feb, pp. 24–26, at: www.microfinanceinsights.com

Gepaya, L.Y. 2009. *Youth inclusive financial services: Marketing and delivery is what matters*, Youth-Inclusive Financial Services Linkage Program Case Study #6 (Washington, DC, Making Cents International and Panabo

City, Panabo Multi-Purpose Cooperative), available at: http://www.makingcents.com/products_services/resources.php

Global Financial Education Program. 2009. *Young people: Your future your money*, Content Note (Washington, DC, Microfinance Opportunities, Citi Foundation, Freedom from Hunger), at: http://www.globalfinancialeducation.org/documents/Youth%20Module%20Content%20Note.pdf (Washington, DC, Microfinance Opportunities and Davis, Freedom from Hunger).

Gobezie, G. 2010. *Product development at ACSI*, unpublished ILO case study.

Gonzalez, A. 2008. "Sources of revenue and assets allocation at MFIs", in *MicroBanking Bulletin*, Issue 17, pp. 17–18 (Washington, DC, the MIX), at: http://www.themix.org/microbanking-bulletin/mbb-issue-no-17-autumn-2008

—. 2009. *Consumption, commercial or mortgage loans: Does it matter for MFIs in Latin America?* MIX Data Brief No. 3 (Washington, DC, Microfinance Information eXchange, Inc.), at: http://www.themix.org/publications/consumption-commercial-or-mortgage-loans-does-it-matter-mfis-latin-america

Gonzalez-Vega, C.; Chalmers, G.; Quiros, R.; Rodriguez-Meza, J. 2006. *Hortifruti in Central America: A case study about the influence of supermarkets on the development and evolution of creditworthiness among small and medium agricultural producers*, microREPORT #57 (Washington, DC, USAID), at: http://www.microlinks.org/ev_en.php?ID=12564_201&ID2=DO_TOPIC

Gorchels, L. 2003. *The product manager's field guide: Practical tools, exercises, and resources for improved product management* (New York, NY, McGraw-Hill).

Grais, W.; Pellegrini, M. 2006. *Corporate governance in institutions offering Islamic financial services*, World Bank Policy Research Working Paper 4052 (Washington, DC, World Bank).

Grameen Foundation. 2008a. *Progress out of Poverty Index pilot training participant guide*, at: http://www.progressoutofpoverty.org/piloting-ppi

—. 2008b. *Negros Women for Tomorrow Foundation (NWTF)*, Progress out of Poverty Index Case Study Series, at: http://www.progressoutofpoverty.org/casestudies

—. 2010. *Progress out of Poverty Index (PPI) indicators and lookup tables for the Philippines*, at: http://www.progressoutofpoverty.org/philippines

Green, C. 2008. *Microfinance and HIV/AIDS: Strategic partnerships*, Microfinance and HIV/AIDS Note 2 (Washington, DC, USAID), at: http://www.microlinks.org/ev_en.php?ID=22387_201&ID2=DO_TOPIC

—; Estévez, I. 2005. *Opening markets through strategic partnerships: The alliance between AMEEN Sal and three Lebanese commercial banks*, USAID microREPORT #40 (Washington, DC, USAID), at: http://www.microlinks.org/ev02.php?ID=10620_201&ID2=DO_TOPIC

Greener, P. 2006. *Partnerships in microfinance: A discussion primer* (Brisbane, Foundation for Development Cooperation, Banking with the Poor Network, Citigroup Foundation), at: http://www.microfinancegateway.org/gm/document-1.9.26202/41748.pdf

Grosh, M.; del Ninno, C.; Tesliuc, E.; Ouerghi, A. 2008. *For protection and promotion: The design and implementation of effective safety nets* (Washington, DC, World Bank), available at: http://siteresources.worldbank.org/SAFETYNETSANDTRANSFERS/Resources/ProtectionandPromotion-Overview.pdf

Hakobyan, A. 2006. *Coping with the "unexpected": The experience of ACBA Leasing in Armenia*, USAID microNOTE #35 (Washington, DC, USAID), at: http://www.microfinancegateway.org/gm/document-1.9.29363/07.pdf

Halder, S.R. 2003. "BRAC's business development services – do they pay?", in *Small Enterprise Development*, Vol. 14, No. 2, pp. 26–35 (Warwickshire, Practical Action Publishing), at: http://www.ingentaconnect.com/content/itpub/sedv/2003/00000014/00000002/art00006

Hamed, Y. 2010. *Lending to youth: The experience of Al Amal Microfinance Bank in Yemen*, unpublished case study (Geneva, ILO).

Handicap International. 2006. *Good practices for the economic inclusion of people with disabilities in developing countries* (Lyon, Handicap International), at:
http://www.handicap-international.org/uploads/media/goodpractices-GB-2coul.PDF

Harper, M. 2002. *Grameen bank groups and self-help groups: What are the differences?* (Filigrave, ITDG Publishing), at: http://www.microfinancegateway.org/gm/document-1.9.27267/3249.pdf

Hashemi, S.; Rosenberg, R. 2006. *Graduating the poorest into microfinance: Linking safety nets and financial services*, CGAP Focus Note No. 34 (Washington, DC, CGAP), at:
http://www.cgap.org/gm/document-1.9.2586/FN34.pdf

Hassen, F.; Sulaiman, M. 2007. *How sustainable is the grain in food consumption of the CFPR/TUP beneficiaries?*, CFPR working paper, No. 18 (Dhaka, BRAC Research and Evaluation Division and Aga Khan Foundation Canada).

Hatch, J.; Hatch, M.S. 1989. *Village bank manual for leaders and promoters*, Preface (Washington, DC, FINCA).

—; Levine, S.; Penn, A. 2002. *Innovations from the field: A daringly brief summary of a huge phenomenon* (Washington, DC, Microcredit Summit Campaign) at: http://www.microcreditsummit.org/papers/innovations.pdf

Havers, M. 1999. "Microenterprise and small business leasing: Lessons from Pakistan", in *Small Enterprise Development*, Vol. 10, No. 3, pp. 44–51 (Warwickshire, Practical Action Publishing), at:
http://www.ingentaconnect.com/content/itpub/sedv/1999/00000010/00000003/art00006

Hayes, J.B.; Eduardo, M. 2003. "An economic decision-making framework for price bundling of retail banking services", in *Academy of Marketing Studies Journal*, Vol. 7, No. 2, pp. 27–38 (Candler, NC, Allied Academics).

Hazell, P.; Anderson, J.; Balzer, N.; Hastrup Clemmensen, A.; Hess, U.; Rispoli, F. 2010. *The potential for scale and sustainability in weather index insurance for agriculture and rural livelihoods* (Rome, IFAD and WFP), at:
http://www.microfinancegateway.org/gm/document-1.9.43862/Weather_insurance_scale_and_sustainability_IFAD-WFP_WRMF.pdf

Heisey, J. Undated. *Our partnership for inclusive development: Trickle Up Program* (New York, Trickle Up), at:
http://www.miusa.org/idd/resourcecenter/moving-towards-inclusion/chapter4

Helms, B. 2006. *Access for all: Building inclusive financial systems* (Washington, DC, CGAP), at:
http://www.cgap.org/gm/document-1.9.2715/Book_AccessforAll.pdf

Herrera, C.; Miranda, B. 2004. *Columna, Guatemala*, CGAP Working Group on Microinsurance, Good and Bad Practices Case Study No. 5 (Washington, DC, CGAP Working Group on Microinsurance), at:
http://www.microfinancegateway.org/gm/document-1.9.27410/24120_file_COLUMNA_English.pdf

Hickson, R. 1999. *Reaching extreme poverty: Financial services for very poor people*, Office for Development Studies, UN Development Programme (New York, NY, UNDP), at:
http://www.microfinancegateway.org/gm/document-1.9.26895/2853_file_02853.pdf

Hirschland, M. 2000. *Guidelines for developing microsavings services: A desk review for Freedom from Hunger*, Unpublished paper.

—. (ed.). 2005. *Savings services for the poor: An operational guide* (Sterling, VA, Kumarian Press, Stylus Publishing, LLC).

—. 2005a. "Savings products", in Hirschland, M. (ed.), 2005, pp. 137–158.

—. 2005b. "Beyond full-service branches", in Hirschland, M. (ed.), 2005, pp. 159–192.

—. 2009. *Youth savings accounts: A financial service perspective*, USAID microREPORT #163 (Washington, DC, USAID), at: http://www.microlinks.org/ev02.php?ID=43511_201&ID2=DO_TOPIC

Hishigsuren, G.; Husseini, H. 2007. *Study on options, management and enforcement of collateral for microfinance loans in the West Bank and Gaza Strip* FIELD Report No. 4 (Washington, DC, USAID), at: http://www.microfinancegateway.org/gm/document-1.9.31154/21.pdf

Hogarth, R. 2009. *Microinsurance client base of Allianz Life Indonesia grows four-fold in 2008*, at: http://www.microcapital.org/microcapital-story-microinsurance-client-base-of-allianz-life-indonesia-grows-four-fold-in-2008/

Hokans, J. 2008. *Maximizing choice: Diverse approaches to the challenge of housing microfinance*, USAID microREPORT #97 (Washington, DC, USAID), available at: http://www.microlinks.org/ev01.php?ID=23323_201&ID2=DO_TOPIC

Honohan, P. 2007. *Cross-country variations in household access to financial services*, Presented at the World Bank Conference on Access to Finance, Washington, DC, 15 March (Washington, DC, The World Bank) at: http://siteresources.worldbank.org/INTFR/Resources/Cross_Country_Variation_In_Household_Access.pdf

Hossain, I. 2005. *Financial performance: MicroSave briefing notes on Grameen II #4* (Nairobi, *MicroSave*), at: http://www.microsave.org/briefing_notes/grameen-ii-4-financial-performance.

Hossain, M.; Lab-oyan, G.; Larcombe, K.; Sapkota, K. 2005. "Developing or strengthening savings operations", in Hirschland, M. (ed.), 2005, pp. 63–92.

Hsu, A. 2009. "Day 1 posting", in: *USAID: Lending at the intersection of micro and SME finance: Compilation document*, at: www.microlinks.org/sc/micro2SMEfinance

Huda, K.; Simanowitz, A. 2009. "A graduation pathway for Haiti's poorest: Lessons learnt from Fonkoze", in *Enterprise Development and Microfinance*, Vol. 20, No. 2, pp. 86–106 (Warwickshire, Practical Action Publishing), at: http://www.ingentaconnect.com/content/itpub/edm/2009/00000020/00000002/art00003

Hughes, J.; Weiss, J. 2007. "Simple rules for making alliances work", *Harvard Business Review*, at: http://www.bnet.com/cp/simple-rules-for-making-alliances-work/173987

Hunger Safety Net Programe: http://www.hungersafetynet.org

Hunguana, H. 2010. *SME lending at ProCredit Bank Mozambique*, unpublished case study for the Making Microfinance Work training curriculum.

Imady, O.; Seibel, H. 2003. "Sanduq: A microfinance innovation in Jabal Al-Hoss, Syria", in NENARACA Newsletter Sept. 2003 (Amman, NENARACA).

ImpAct. 2003. *Microfinance and poverty: Developing systems for monitoring depth of poverty outreach and impact* (Brighton, ImpAct), at: http://www.microfinancegateway.org/gm/document-1.9.26659/17.pdf

Inter-American Development Bank (IADB). 2007. *Emerging link: Remittances and microfinance* (Washington, DC), at: http://www.iadb.org/features-and-web-stories/2007-12/english/emerging-link-4315.html

International Finance Corporation (IFC). 2010. *Scaling up SME access to financial services in the developing world*, Financial Inclusion Experts Group, SME Finance Sub-Group (Washington, DC), at: http://www.ifc.org/ifcext/media.nsf/Content/SMEFinancialAccessReport_Nov2010

International Fund for Agricultural Development (IFAD). 2001. *Rural poverty report 2001* (New York, Oxford University Press Inc.), at: www.ifad.org/poverty

—. 2010. *IFAD decision tools for rural finance* (Rome), at: www.ifad.org/ruralfinance

International Labour Office (ILO). 2005. *A global alliance against forced labour* (Geneva), at: http://www.ilo.org/wcmsp5/groups/public/—-ed_norm/—-declaration/documents/publication/wcms_081882.pdf

—. 2006. *The end of child labour: Within reach* (Geneva).

—. 2007a. *Microfinance for decent work: Taking action* (Geneva).

—. 2007b. *A manual for gender audit facilitators* (Geneva), at: http://www.ilo.org/dyn/gender/docs/RES/536/F932374742/web%20gender%20manual.pdf

—. 2008. *Microfinance for decent work: An action research programme*, Social Finance Programme Announcement (Geneva).

—. 2010a. *Global Social Trust: A project of international solidarity between Luxembourg and Ghana, Information paper* (Geneva), at: http://www.ilo.org/public/english/protection/secsoc/gst/

—. 2010b. *Global employment trends for youth* (Geneva).

International Programme on the Elimination of Child Labour (IPEC). 2008. *Global child labour developments: Measuring trends from 2004 to 2008* (Geneva, ILO).

Isern, J.; Deshpande, R.; van Doorn, J. 2005. *Crafting a money transfers strategy: Guidance for pro-poor financial service providers*, CGAP Occasional Paper No. 10 (Washington, DC, CGAP), at: http://www.cgap.org/gm/document-1.9.2704/OP10.pdf

—; Donges, W.; Smith, J. 2008. *Making money transfers work for microfinance institutions: A technical guide to developing and delivering money transfers* (Washington, DC, CGAP), at: http://www.cgap.org/p/site/c/template.rc/1.9.3003/

Iskenderian, M. 2010. "Women's World Banking brings credit to the third world," at *Knowledge@Wharton*, at: http://www.forbes.com/2010/07/12/womens-world-banking-microfinance-entrepreneurs-finance-wharton.html

Islam, S. 2006. *Introducing voluntary savings services: A how-to guide* (Washington, DC, Women's World Banking), at: http://www.microfinancegateway.org/p/site/m//template.rc/1.9.35040

Islamic Research and Training Institute (IRTI). 2008. *Islamic microfinance development: Challenges and initiatives*, Policy Dialogue Paper No. 2 (Jeddah, IRTI), at: http://www.microfinancegateway.org/p/site/m//template.rc/1.9.30288

Ivatury, G. 2005. *Brazil's banking correspondents*, CGAP Note (Washington, DC, CGAP).

—; Mas, I. 2008. *The early experience with branchless banking*, CGAP Focus Note No. 46 (Washington, DC, CGAP), at: http://www.cgap.org/gm/document-1.9.2640/FN46.pdf

Jamii Bora. 2006. *About Jamii Bora's housing program*, at: http://www.jamiibora.org/housing.htm (last accessed 14 December 2010).

Jaramillo, M. 2008. *Challenges and opportunities for banking remittances: Key elements needed to develop a strategy to bank recipients of remittances*, ACCION Insight #25 (Boston, MA, ACCION International), at: http://resources.centerforfinancialinclusion.org/publications/InSight_25_238.asp

Johnson, S. 2000. "Gender impact assessment in microfinance and microenterprise: Why and how", *Development in Practice*, Vol. 10, No. 1, pp. 89–93 (Oxford, Routledge), at: http://www.informaworld.com/smpp/content~db=all~content=a713660375~frm=titlelink?words=johnson&hash=2078388641

—. 2004. "Taking stock: A new gender agenda for microfinance?" in *Small Enterprise Development*, Vol. 15, No. 1, pp. 10–11 (Rugby, Practical Action Publishing), at: http://www.ingentaconnect.com/content/itpub/sedv/2004/00000015/00000001/art00004

Jones, L. 2007. *Reducing borrower and lender risk through context sensitive product and portfolio design: The case of "integrated" agricultural development in Tajikistan*, Paper presented at the International Conference on Rural Finance Research: Moving Results into Policies and Practice, Rome, FAO Headquarters (Rome, FAO, Ford Foundation, IFAD), available at: http://www.ruralfinance.org/servlet/BinaryDownloaderServlet/46799_Paper_2.pdf?filename=1175154776548_reducin_borrower_and_lender_risk.pdf&refID=46799

—; Pasricha, N. 2007. "Reducing borrower and lender risk through context-sensitive product and portfolio design: The case of complementing agricultural development with microfinance in Tajikistan", in

Enterprise Development and Microfinance, Vol. 18, No. 2, pp. 126–142 (Rugby, Practical Action Publishing).

—; Snelgrove, A. 2006. "From behind the veil: Industry-level methodologies and the implications for disadvantaged communities, the case of sequestered women in Pakistan", in *Small Enterprise Development Journal*, Vol. 17, No. 2, pp. 47–54 (Rugby, UK, ITDG Publishing), at: http://www.meda.org/web/images/stories/ML/Case-of-Sequestered-Women.pdf

Kalanda, A.; Campbell, B. 2008. *Banking rollout approaches to rural markets: Opportunity International Bank of Malawi*, White Paper No. 8 (Oak Brook, IL, Opportunity International), at: http://www.opportunity.net/Publications/CaseStudies/

Kanter, R.M.; Stein; B.; Jick, T. 1992. *The challenge of organizational change* (New York, NY, The Free Press).

Kaplan, R.; Norton, D. 2001. *The strategy-focused organization: How balanced scorecared companies thrive in the new business environment* (Boston, MA, Harvard Business School Press).

Karim, N.; Tarazi, M.; Reille, X. 2008. *Islamic microfinance: An emerging market niche*, CGAP Focus Note No. 49 (Washington, DC, CGAP), at: http://www.cgap.org/gm/document-1.9.5029/FN49.pdf

Karlan, D.; Valdivia, M. 2006. *Teaching entrepreneurship: Impact of business training on microfinance clients and institutions*, at: http://karlan.yale.edu/p/TeachingEntrepreneurship.revision.final.pdf

—; Morduch, J. 2010. "Access to finance," in Rodrik, D.; Rosenzweig, M. (eds.): *Handbook of development economics*, Vol. 5, pp. 4707–4777 (Amsterdam, North-Holland), at: http://www.microfinancegateway.org/gm/document-1.1.4153/Access%20to%20Finance%20Ideas%20and%20Evidence_Credit.pdf

Kashfi, F. 2009. *Youth financial services: The case of BRAC and the adolescent girls of Bangladesh*, Youth-Inclusive Financial Services Linkage Program Case Study #5 (Washington, DC, Making Cents International and Dhaka, BRAC), available at: http://www.makingcents.com/products_services/resources.php

Ketley, R. 2010. *Mobile payments: Rethinking partnership strategies?* Briefing Note #83 (Nairobi, MicroSave), at: www.microsave.org

Khan, M.S. 2004. *Tools for pro-poor public private partnerships* (New York, NY, Public Private Partnerships for the Urban Environment, UNDP), at: http://www.margraf-publishers.com/UNDP/PPPUE/index.html

Kisaame, J. 2003. *Case study of DFCU Leasing Company – Uganda*, Paper presented at "Paving the Way Forward for Rural Finance: An International Conference on Best Practices", Washington, DC, 2–4 June 2003: Washington, DC, at: http://pdf.usaid.gov/pdf_docs/PNADF022.pdf

Kotler, P. 1999. *Kotler on marketing: How to create, win, and dominate markets* (New York, NY, Free Press).

—. 2000. *Marketing management: Millennium edition*, 10th Edition (Upper Saddle River, NJ, Prentice Hall).

—; Andreasen, A. 1996. *Strategic marketing for non-profit organizations* (Upper Saddle River, NJ, Prentice Hall).

—; Keller, K. 2006. *Marketing management*, 12th Edition (Upper Saddle River, NJ, Prentice Hall).

Kring, T. 2005. *A strategy for the use of microfinance in the Pakistan Time-Bound Programme*, unpublished ILO consultant report.

Kruize, A. 2007. *Habitat for humanity: Vietnam partnering with MFIs to improve housing for the poor*, USAID microNOTE #35 (Washington, DC, USAID), at: http://www.microlinks.org/ev_en.php?ID=20522_201&ID2=DO_TOPIC

Kumar, K.; McKay, C.; Rotman, S. 2010. *Microfinance and mobile banking: The story so far*, Focus Note No. 62 (Washington, DC, CGAP), at: http://www.microfinancegateway.org/p/site/m/template.rc/1.9.45556/

Larson, D.; Pierce, M.; Graber, K.; Doyle, K.; Halty, M. 2004. *Environmental preconditions for successful post-conflict microfinance*, Microenterprise Best Practices (MBP) Microfinance Following Conflict Brief No. 4 (Bethesda, MBP), at: http://www.microfinancegateway.org/gm/document-1.9.26284/14557_14557.pdf

Leatherman, S.; Christensen, L.; Holtz, J. 2010. *Innovations and barriers in health microinsurance*, Microinsurance Paper No. 6 (Geneva, ILO), at: http://www.ilo.org/public/english/employment/mifacility/download/mpaper6_health_en.pdf

Ledgerwood, J. 1998. *Microfinance handbook: An institutional and financial perspective*, Sustainable banking for the poor (Washington, DC, World Bank), at: http://www.microfinancegateway.org/p/site/m//template.rc/1.9.30882

—; White, V. 2006. *Transforming microfinance institutions: Providing full financial services to the poor* (Washington, DC, World Bank).

Lee, N. 2000. *Client-based market research: The case of PRODEM* (Toronto, ON, Calmeadow).

Lee, S. 2006. *Public-private partnerships for development: A handbook for business* (Washington, DC, USAID, Committee for Economic Development), at: http://www.ced.org/images/library/reports/intl_econ/usaid_partnership06.pdf

Leftley, R. 2005. *Technical assistance for the promotion of microinsurance: The experience of Opportunity International*, CGAP Working Group on Microinsurance, Good and Bad Practices Case Study No. 11 (Washington, DC, CGAP Working Group on Microinsurance), at: http://www.microfinancegateway.org/gm/document-1.9.26910/27601_file_cstudy11.pdf

—. 2009. "Innovations in insuring the poor for food, agriculture, and the environment," *Innovations in Insuring the Poor*, Focus 17, Brief 4, at: http://www.ifpri.org/sites/default/files/publications/focus17_04.pdf

Liber, D.; Gommans, C. 2007. *Partners and action: Financial institutions and health and AIDS risk management* (Dakar, AfriCap Microfinance Fund), at: http://www.microfinancegateway.org/p/site/m//template.rc/1.9.25583

Lindert, K.; Linder, A.; Hobbs, J.; de la Brière, B. 2007. *The nuts and bolts of Brazil's Bolsa Família Program: Implementing conditional cash transfers in a decentralized context*, Social Protection Discussion Paper No. 0709 (Washington, DC, World Bank).

Littlefield, E.; Morduch, J.; Hashemi, S. 2003. *Is microfinance an effective strategy to reach the millennium development goals?*, CGAP Focus Note No. 24 (Washington, DC, CGAP), at: http://www.cgap.org/gm/document-1.9.2568/FN24.pdf

Lunde, S.A.; Sheldon, T.; Waterfield, C. 2006. *Using Microfin 4: A handbook for operational planning and financial modeling* (Washington, DC, CGAP), at: http://www.microfin.com/download.htm

Lyman, T.; Pickens, M.; Porteous, D. 2008. *Regulating transformational branchless banking: Mobile phones and other technology to increase access to finance*, Focus Note No. 43 (Washington, DC, CGAP), at: http://www.cgap.org/gm/document-1.9.2583/FN43.pdf

Lynch, E. 2009. *Transforming the landscape of leadership in microfinance: Maintaining the focus on women* (New York, NY, Women's World Banking), at: http://www.swwb.org/files/pubs/en/transforming_the_landscape_of_leadership_in_microfinance_e.pdf

Maes, J.; Foose, L.; Hishigsuren, G. 2006. *Microfinance and non-financial services for very poor people: Digging deeper to find keys to success*, SEEP Technical Note (New York, NY, SEEP, Poverty Outreach Working Group), at: http://www.seepnetwork.org/Resources/4661_file_POWG_Microfinance_and_Non_Financial_Services.pdf

Magill, J. 2003. *The first 30 days: A practical guide to managing natural disasters for microfinance institutions* (Bethesda: Development Alternatives, Inc.), at: http://www.microfinancegateway.org/p/site/m//template.rc/1.9.42070

Magleby-Lambert, R. 2006. *ICICI Bank credit franchise initiative*, Presentation of the Small Enterprise Finance Centre of the Institution for Financial Management and Research, available at: http://www.ifmr.ac.in/pdf/creditFranchiseSEFC.pdf

Mahajan, V. 2005. *From microcredit to livelihood finance* (Hyderabad, BASIX), at: http://www.microfinancegateway.org/gm/document-1.9.25359/34431_file_06.pdf

Making Cents International. 2009. *State of the field in youth enterprise, employment and livelihoods development: Market-driven approaches; monitoring, evaluation, and impact assessment; and youth-inclusive financial services* (Washington, DC, Making Cents International), at: http://www.makingcents.com/products_services/resources.php

—. 2010a. *State of the sector*, at: http://www.yfslink.com/resources/state-of-the-sector

—. 2010b. *State of the field in youth enterprise, employment and livelihoods development: Programming and policymaking in youth enterprise, employment, and livelihoods development; and youth-inclusive financial services* (Washington, DC, Making Cents International), at: http://www.makingcents.com/products_services/resources.php

Malhotra, M.; Chen, Y.; Criscuolo, A.; Fan, Q.; Hamel, I.; Savchenko, Y. 2006. *Expanding access to finance: Good practices and policies for micro, small, and medium enterprises* (Washington, DC, World Bank), at: http://info.worldbank.org/etools/docs/library/236032/SMEAccessToFinance_Final_083106.pdf

Management and Development Centre. 2009. available at: http://d25846573.e241.egysign.net/Pages/Operation%20Management/Production%20&%20Operation%20Management/Operation%20Startegy/Operation%20Startegy.asp (accessed on January 11, 2010).

Mankins, M.; Steele, R. 2005. "Turning great strategy into great performance," in *Harvard Business Review*, July-August, at: www.hbr.org

Manndorff, H. 2004. *ACCION's experiences with rural finance in Latin America and Africa*, ACCION Insight No. 11 (Boston, ACCION International), at: http://resources.centerforfinancialinclusion.org/publications/InSight_11_180.asp

MarketVision Research. 1998. *Market segmentation: A guide to conducting segmentation research* (Cincinnati, OH, MarketVision Research, Inc.), at: http://www.marketvisionresearch.com/pdf/Segment.PDF

Martin, C. 2008. *Going to scale with housing microfinance: The role of commercial banks*, USAID microREPORT #92 (Washington, DC, USAID), at: http://www.microlinks.org/ev_en.php?ID=22878_201&ID2=DO_TOPIC

Marulanda, B. 2008. *Social protection payments: A case study of familias en Accion in Colombia*, Presentation at DFID–CGAP G2P and Financial Inclusion seminar, South Africa, 3–4 November.

Mas, I. 2009. "Reframing micro-finance: Enabling small savings and payments, everywhere", in *Financing for Development*, Commonwealth Heads of Government Meeting, Republic of Trinidad and Tobago, 27–29 November (Henley Media Group) at: http://www.microfinancegateway.org/p/site/m//template.rc/1.9.40878

—; Radcliffe, D. 2010. *Mobile payments go viral: M-PESA in Kenya* (Seattle, Bill and Melinda Gates Foundation), at: http://www.microfinancegateway.org/p/site/m/template.rc/1.9.43376/

Match Savings, http://www.matchsavings.org

Matin, I. 2005. *Delivering the "fashionable" [inclusive microfinance] with an "unfashionable" [poverty] focus: Experiences of BRAC*, Presentation to the Asian Development Bank, at: http://www.adb.org/Documents/Events/2005/ADB-microfinance-week/presentation-day1-03-matin.pdf

—; Halder, S. 2004. *Combining methodologies for better targeting of the extreme poor: Lessons from BRAC's CFPR/TUP programme*, CFPR-TUP Working Paper Series No. 2 (Delhi, BRAC), at: http://www.microfinancegateway.org/gm/document-1.9.29043/35030_file_55.pdf

—; Sulaiman, M.; Rabbani, M. 2008. *Crafting a graduation pathway for the ultra poor: Lessons and evidence from a BRAC programme*, CPRC Working Paper No. 109, BRAC Research and Evaluation Division (Manchester, The Chronic Poverty Research Centre (CPRC)), at: http://www.microfinancegateway.org/gm/document-1.9.29364/16.pdf

Matul, M.; Durmanova, E.; Tounitsky, V. 2006. *Market for microinsurance in Ukraine: Low-income household needs and market development projections* (Warsaw, Microfinance Centre for Central and Eastern Europe and the New Independent States), at: http://www.mfc.org.pl/images/pliki/06.pdf

—.; Szubert, D.; Cohen, M.; McGuinness, E. 2006. *Attracting the unbanked: Preliminary guidelines for maximizing existing infrastructure through serving untapped markets* (Washington, DC, Microfinance Opportunities and Microfinance Center for Central and Eastern Europe and the New Independent States), at: http://www.microfinancegateway.org/gm/document-1.9.29432/36678_file_06.pdf

—; —; Vardanyan, G.; Lalayan, M.; Tomilova, O. 2006. *Entering new markets: How market research can inform new product development*, MFC Spotlight No. 13 (Warsaw, Microfinance Centre for Central and Eastern Europe and the New Independent States), at: http://www.mfc.org.pl/doc/Research/ImpAct/SN/SN13.pdf

Max New York Life Insurance Company, Ltd. 2010. *Max Vijay: Rajat, Swarna, Heera*, at: http://www.maxvijay.com/products_rajat.aspx

Mayoux, L. 1999. "Questioning virtuous spirals: Micro-finance and women's empowerment in Africa", in *Journal of International Development*, Vol. 11, No. 7, pp. 957–984 (Hoboken, NY, John Wiley & Sons, Ltd).

—. 2005. *Road journeys*, at: http://www.lindaswebs.org.uk/Page3_Orglearning/PALS/PALSIntro.htm

—. 2006. *Gender questions for product market research*, at http://www.genfinance.info/MktResPALS/Gender%20Sensitive%20Product%20Market%20Research.pdf

—. 2008. *Women ending poverty: The WORTH program in Nepal: Empowerment through literacy, banking and business, 1999–2007* (Kathmandu, Valley Research Group), at: http://www.pactworld.org/galleries/worth-files/Nepal_Final_Report_Letter_0825_PDF.pdf

—; Hartl, M. 2009. *Gender and rural microfinance: Reaching and empowering women*, Guide for practitioners (Rome, IFAD), at: www.ifad.org/gender/pub/gender_finance.pdf

Maysami, R.; Kwon, W. *An analysis of Islamic Takaful Insurance: A cooperative insurance mechanism*, at: http://www.takaful.coop/doc_store/takaful/analysis%20of%20Islamic%20Takaful%20Insurance.pdf

McCarter, E. 2006. "Women and microfinance: Why we should do more", *University of Maryland Law Journal of Race, Religion, Gender and Class*, Vol. 6, No. 2, pp. 352–366.

McCarty, M.Y. 2007. *Marketing for microfinance* (New York, NY, Women's World Banking), at: http://www.swwb.org/files/pubs/en/marketing_for_microfinance_e.pdf

McCord, M. 2006. "The partner-agent model: Challenges and opportunities", in Churchill, C. (ed.), 2006, pp. 357–377.

—; Buczkowski, G. 2004. *CARD MBA: The Philippines*, CGAP Working Group on Microinsurance, Good and Bad Practices Case Study No. 4 (Washington, DC, CGAP Working Group on Microinsurance), at: http://www.microfinancegateway.org/gm/document-1.9.25204/23881_file_card_good_and_bad_case_study_no._4.pdf

—; —; Saksena, P. 2006. "Premium collection: Minimizing transaction costs and maximizing customer service", in Churchill, C. (ed.), 2006, pp. 197–215.

—; Ramm, G.; McGuinness, E. 2006b. *Microinsurance demand and market prospects: Indonesia* (Munich, Allianz AG, GTZ and UNDP), at: https://www.allianz.com/static-resources/en/about_allianz/sustainability/media/documents/microinsurance_indonesia.pdf

—; Wright, G.; Cracknell, D. 2003. *A toolkit for planning, conducting and monitoring pilot tests* (Nairobi, *MicroSave*), at: http://www.microsave.org/toolkits/2/16.

—; —; Sempangi, H.; Cracknell, D.; Mgwang'a, T.; Mithika, M. 2004. *Product rollout: A toolkit for expanding a tested product* (Nairobi, MicroSave), at: http://www.microsave.org/toolkit/product-roll-out-a-toolkit-for-expanding-a-tested-product-throughout-the-market

McDonald, J. 2009. "Day 2 posting", in: *USAID: Lending at the intersection of micro and SME finance: Compilation document*, at: www.microlinks.org/sc/micro2SMEfinance

McDonald, M.; Dunbar, I. 2004. *Market segmentation: How to do it, how to profit from it* (Oxford, Elsevier Butterworth-Heinemann).

McGuinness, E. 2005. *Research on the institutionalization of market-led microfinance: A case study of XacBank, Mongolia* (Washington, DC, Microfinance Opportunities, USAID).

McKay, C.; Pickens, M. 2010. *Branchless banking 2010: Who's served? At what price? What's next?* Focus Note No. 66 (Washington, DC, CGAP), at: http://www.cgap.org/gm/document-1.9.47614/FN66_Rev1.pdf

McKee, K. 2005. "Prerequisites for intermediating savings", in Hirschland, M. (ed.), 2005, pp. 27–42.

McManus, S.; Tennyson, R. 2008. *Talking the walk: A communication manual for partnership practitioners* (London, International Business Leaders Forum (IBLF), at: http://thepartneringinitiative.org/publications/Toolbooks/Talking_The_Walk.jsp

MEDA. 2004. *Business plan for rural credit program for the Association of Business Women of Tajikistan* (Waterloo, Mennonite Economic Development Associates).

—. 2010. *Moroccan youth learn, earn through YouthInvest training*, at: http://100hourstochange.blogspot.com/2010/10/moroccan-youth-learn-earn-through.html (last accessed 9 November 2010).

Meherette, E. 2009. "Providing weather index and indemnity insurance in Ethiopia", *Innovations in Insuring the Poor*, Focus 17, Brief 8, at: http://www.ifpri.org/sites/default/files/publications/focus17_08.pdf

Mersland, R. 2005. *Microcredit for self-employed disabled persons in developing countries* (Oslo, Atlas Alliance), available at: http://mpra.ub.uni-muenchen.de/2068/1/MPRA_paper_2068.pdf

Mesarina, N.; Stickney, C. 2007. *Getting to scale in housing microfinance: A study of ACCION Partners in Latin America*, ACCION InSight No. 21 (Boston, MA, ACCION International), at: http://resources.centerforfinancialinclusion.org/insight/InSight_21_221.asp

Meyer, J.; Zimmerman, J.; Boshara, R. 2008. *Child savings accounts: Global trends in design and practice, Global Assets Project* (St. Louis, Washington University and Washington, DC, New America Foundation), at: www.newamerica.net/files/nafmigration/Global_CSAs_printFINAL_0.pdf

Miamidian, E.; Arnold, M.; Burritt, K.; Jacquand, M. 2005. *Surviving disasters and supporting recovery: A guidebook for microfinance institutions*, Disaster Risk Management Working Paper Series No. 10 (Washington, DC, World Bank), at: http://www.microfinancegateway.org/gm/document-1.9.25290/23882_file_23882.pdf

Micra Indonesia, 2010. *Promoting female migrant workers' access to finance through the PNPM*, at: www.micra-indo.org/content/view/71/72/en/

Microfinance Information eXchange (MIX), http://www.themix.org

—. 2003. *The MicroBanking Bulletin*, Issue No. 9 "Focus on savings" (Washington, DC) at: http://www.themix.org/microbanking-bulletin/mbb-issue-no-9-2003-focus-savings

—. 2006. *MicroBanking Bulletin: 2005 Benchmarks*, Issue 19 (Washington, DC), available at: http://www.themix.org/publications/microbanking-bulletin/2006/08/anniversary-issue-microbanking-bulletin-autumn-2006-issue

—. 2007. *MicroBanking Bulletin: 2006 Benchmarks*, Issue 15 (Washington, DC), at: http://www.themix.org/publications/microbanking-bulletin/2007/09/2006-benchmark-tables

—. 2008. *MicroBanking Bulletin: 2007 Benchmarks*, Issue 19 (Washington, DC), available at: http://www.themix.org/publications/microbanking-bulletin/2008/09/2007-mfi-benchmarks

—. 2009. *MicroBanking Bulletin: 2008 Benchmarks*, Issue 19 (Washington, DC), at: http://www.themix.org/publications/microbanking-bulletin/2009/12/2008-mfi-benchmarks

Microfund for Women. 2010. *Microfund for Women continues at the forefront of innovation and pioneers region's first gender-sensitive microinsurance product*, Press Release, at: http://www.microfund.org.jo/PublicNews/Nws_NewsDetails.aspx?lang=2&NewsID=479&site_Id=1&M=%208 (last accessed 14 December 2010).

MicroSave. Undated. *Market research for microfinance toolkit*, available at: http://www.microsave.org/toolkit/market-research-for-microfinance-toolkit

—. 2004. *Market research for microfinance toolkit* (Nairobi, *MicroSave*), at: http://www.microsave.org/toolkit/market-research-for-microfinance-toolkit

—. 2005. *Customer service toolkit* (Nairobi, *MicroSave*), at: http://www.microsave.org/toolkit/customer-service-toolkit

Miehlbradt, A.; Jones, L. 2007. *A market research toolkit for value chain initiatives – Information for action: A toolkit series for market development practitioners* (Waterloo, MEDA), at: http://www.meda.org/web/images/stories/ML/Market_Research_Toolkit.pdf

McVay, M. 2002. "Developing commercial markets for business development services: Are 'how-to-do-it' recipes possible?", Seminar Reader (Turin, ITCILO), at: http://www.bds-forum.net/bds-reader/theory/2-bds-reader-turin-2002.pdf

Miller, C. 2004. *Twelve key challenges in Rural Finance*, Unpublished paper presented at the FAO Rural Finance Workshop, SEEP Pre-event in Washington, DC, 28 October 2004, available at: http://www.seepnetwork.org/Resources/2062_Twelve_Key_Challenges_in_Rural_Finance.doc

—. 2005. *Development partners perspective: Global perspectives in rural finance and poverty alleviation*, 4th AFRACA Microfinance Forum, Kampala, Uganda, at: www.ruralfinance.org

—; da Silva, C. 2007. "Value chain financing in agriculture", in *Enterprise Development and Microfinance*, Vol. 18, No. 2, pp. 95–108 (Rugby, Practical Action Publishing).

—; Jones, L. 2010. *Agricultural value chain finance: Tools and lessons* (Rugby, Practical Action Publishing and FAO).

Mills, G.; Lam, K.; DeMarco, D.; Rodger, C.; Kaul, B. 2008. *Assets for Independence Act evaluation: Impact study: Final report* (Cambridge, MA, Abt Associates Inc.), at: www.acf.hhs.gov/programs/ocs/afi/AFI_Final_Impact_Report.pdf

Mitten, L. 2007. *Conflict-affected states*, RAFI Note No. 10 (Washington, DC, USAID), at: http://www.microfinancegateway.org/gm/document-1.9.29361/11.pdf

Morawczynski, O. 2009. "Saving through the mobile phone: The case of M-PESA", in *MicroBanking Bulletin*, Issue 19 (Washington, DC, MIX) at: http://www.themix.org/publications/saving-through-mobile-phone

Morduch, J. 2005. "Smart subsidy for sustainable microfinance", in *Finance for the Poor*, Vol. 6, No. 4 (Manila, Asian Development Bank), at: http://www.adb.org/Documents/Periodicals/Microfinance/finance-200564.pdf

Mosley, P. 2009. *Assessing the success of microinsurance programmes in meeting the insurance needs of the poor*, DESA Working Paper No. 84 (New York, United Nations Department of Economic and Social Affairs), at: http://www.un.org/esa/desa/papers/2009/wp84_2009.pdf

Moulick, M.; Mutua, A.; Muwanguzi, M.; Ngurukie, C.; Onesimo, M.; Wright, G. 2008. "Cash, children or kind? Developing old age security for low-income people in Africa", in Matthaus-Maier, I.; von Pischke, J. D. (eds.): *New partnerships for innovation in microfinance*, pp. 265–278 (Berlin, Springer-Verlag).

Mugwang'a, T.; Cracknell, D. 2005. *Microfinance institutions and salary based consumer lending*, *MicroSave* Briefing Note No. 45 (Nairobi, *MicroSave*), at: http://india.microsave.org/briefing_notes/briefing-note-45-microfinance-institutions-and-salary-based-consumer-lending

Muñoz, R.; Galicia, G.; Benet, M.; Poulton, D.; Buick, S. 2009. *Bank-microfinance alliances: FINCA's pilot program for prepaid credit cards in Mexico* (Washington, DC, SEEP Network and FINCA International), at: http://www.microlinks.org/ev_en.php?ID=41346_201&ID2=DO_TOPIC

Murray, I. 2005. *Understanding the customer through market segmentation*, Presentation at the Second Annual Conference of Sanabel Microfinance Network of Arab Countries.

Murray, U.; Boros, R. 2002. *A guide to gender sensitive microfinance*, Socio-Economic and Gender Analysis Programme – SEAGA (Rome, FAO, Gender and Population Division), at: http://www.fao.org/sd/seaga/downloads/en/microfinanceen.pdf

Mutalima, I. 2006. *Microfinance and gender equity: Are we getting there?* http://www.microcreditsummit.org/papers/Workshops/28_Mutalima.pdf

Mutangadura, G. 2004. *Women and land tenure rights in Southern Africa: A human rights-based approach* (Lusaka, United Nations Economic Commission for Africa – Southern Africa Office), at: http://www.iied.org/pubs/pdfs/G00173.pdf

Mutesasira, L.; Osinde, S.; Mule, N. 2001. *Potential for leasing products: Asset financing for micro- and small businesses in Tanzania and Uganda* (Nairobi, *MicroSave* Africa) at: http://www.microsave.org/research_paper/potential-for-leasing-productsasset-financing-for-micro-small-businesses-in-tanzania-

NABARD. 2008. *Status of Microfinance in India 2007-2008*, at: www.nabard.org

Nagarajan, G. 2001. *Looking into the gift horse's mouth: Implications of cash grants for disaster response by microfinance institutions in Mozambique*, MBP Project (Washington, DC, USAID), at: www.microlinks.org/ev_en.php?ID=8082_201&ID2=DO_TOPIC

—. 2004. "Microbanking with adolescent youth," in *ADB Finance for the Poor*, Vol. 5, No. 4 (Manila, Asian Development Bank), at: http://www.adb.org/documents/periodicals/Microfinance

—. 2005. *Microfinance, youth and conflict: Emerging lessons and issues*, microNOTE # 4 (Washington, DC, USAID), at: http://www.microlinks.org/ev_en.php?ID=7123_201&ID2=DO_TOPIC

—. 2006. *Savings for risk mitigation and crisis recovery*, Brief No. 6 (Singapore, Banking with the Poor Network), at: http://www.microfinancegateway.org/p/site/m/template.rc/1.9.42076/

—; Meyer, R. 2005. *Rural finance: Recent advances and emerging lessons, debates, and opportunities*, Reformatted version of Working Paper AEDE-WP-0041-05 (Columbus, Ohio State University, Department of Agricultural, Environmental, and Development Economics), at: http://www.microfinancegateway.org/gm/document-1.9.29202/27421_file_FINALPDF.pdf

Nair, A.; Kloeppinger-Todd, R. 2006. *Buffalo, bakeries, and tractors: Cases in rural leasing from Pakistan, Uganda, and Mexico*, Agriculture and Rural Development Discussion Paper 28 (Washington, DC, World Bank) at: http://vle.worldbank.org/bnpp/files/TF053594BuffaloBakeriesandTractorsCaseStudiesinRuralLeasing.pdf

—; —; Mulder, A. 2004. *Leasing: An underutilized tool in rural finance*, Agriculture and Rural Development Discussion Paper 7 (Washington, DC, World Bank), at: http://www.microfinancegateway.org/gm/document-1.9.29537/23470_file_23470.pdf

Narayan, D; Petesch, P. (eds.). 2007. *Moving out of poverty, Volume 1, Cross-disciplinary perspectives on mobility* (Basingstoke, Palgrave Macmillan and Washington, DC, World Bank), at: http://siteresources.worldbank.org/INTMOVOUTPOV/Resources/9780821369913.pdf

Nelson, C.; Garber, C.; MkNelly, B.; Lippold, K.; Edgcomb, E.; Horn, N.; Gaile, G.; Beard, B. 2000. *Learning from clients: Assessment tools for microfinance practitioners* (Washington, DC, USAID, AIMS, SEEP Network), at: http://www.seepnetwork.org/Resources/646_file_aimstools.pdf

Nguyen, V; Duong, L. 2010. *Enhancing communication with men to better reach women*, unpublished ILO case study.

Nourse, T.; Gerstle, T.; Snelgrove, A.; Rinck, D.; McVay, M. 2006. *Market development in crisis-affected environments: Emerging lessons for achieving pro-poor economic reconstruction* (New York, SEEP Network), at: http://www.microfinancegateway.org/p/site/m//template.rc/1.9.42056

Nulty, M.; Nagarajan, G. (eds.). 2005. *Serving youth with microfinance: Perspectives of microfinance institutions and youth serving organizations* (Washington, DC, USAID), http://pdf.dec.org/pdf_docs/Pnadf315.pdf

O'Reilly, M. 2008. *Unintentional messages… a window into real microfinance,* Posting on Microfinance Practice listserve, 12 December 2008.

Obaidullah, M. 2008. *Introduction to Islamic microfinance* (International Institute of Islamic Business and Finance), at: http://www.microfinancegateway.org/gm/document-1.9.30212/08.pdf

Obaidullah, M.; Latiff, H. (eds.). 2008. *Islamic finance for micro and medium enterprises,* (International Institute of Islamic Business and Finance and Centre for Islamic Banking, Finance and Management, Universiti Brunei Darussalam), at: www.imad.in/obaidullah-micro4.pdf

Ogodo, O. 2010. "Texting program helps Africa farmers fight drought", *National Geographic News,* 29 October, at: http://news.nationalgeographic.com/news/2010/10/101029-kenya-microinsurance-farming-science-environment/

Oliver Wyman. 2010. *Product portfolio management,* at: http://www.oliverwyman.com/cn/2522.htm

One World Action. 2010. *Visibility and voice – Organising women construction workers in Delhi,* Making a difference: Citizens and their organisations and networks contributing to change, OWA PPA 2009-10: Case study 53, at: http://www.oneworldaction.org/papers_documents_archives/case_studies/asia

Opoku, L.; Foy, D. 2008. "Pathways out of poverty: Innovating banking technologies to reach the rural poor", in *Enterprise Development and Microfinance,* Vol. 19, No. 1, pp. 46–58 (Rugby, Practical Action Publishing), at: http://www.ingentaconnect.com/content/itpub/edm/2008/00000019/00000001/art00005

Opportunity International. 2010. *Fund an apprentice,* at: http://www.opportunity.org.uk/Page.php?id=176 (last accessed 20 October 2010).

Organisation for Economic Co-operation and Development (OECD). 2008. *Gender and sustainable development: Maximising the economic, social and environmental role of women* (Paris, OECD), at: http://www.oecd.org/dataoecd/58/1/40881538.pdf

Orozco, M. 2006. *International flows of remittances: Cost, competition and financial access in Latin America and the Caribbean – toward an industry scorecard* (Washington, DC, Inter-American Development Bank), at: https://www.thedialogue.org

—; Hamilton, E. 2008. "Remittances and MFIs: Issues and lessons from Latin America", in Matthaus-Maier, I.; von Pischke, J.D. (eds.): *New partnerships for innovation in microfinance* (Berlin, Springer-Verlag), pp. 129–146.

Owens, J. 2003. "The partner savings plan of the Workers Bank, Jamaica: Lessons in microsavings from ROSCAs," in Wenner, M. et al. (eds.): *Promising practices in rural finance: Experiences from Latin America and the Caribbean,* Chapter 9 (Washington, DC, IADB), at: www.ruralfinance.org

—. 2006. *Text-a-Deposit: Expanding mobile phone banking to include savings services* (Washington, DC, CGAP), at: http://www.microfinancegateway.org/gm/document-1.9.25123/49626_Text-A-Deposit%20Expanding.pdf

—. 2009. *The role of partnerships and strategic alliances to promote mobile phone banking at the bottom of the pyramid,* Briefing Note #68 (Nairobi, MicroSave), at: http://www.microfinancegateway.org/p/site/m//template.rc/1.9.31228

Palaniswamy, V. 2005. *The complementary use of loans and grants* (New York, Trickle Up), at: http://www.microfinancegateway.org/gm/document-1.9.26791/54.pdf

Pamilyang OFW Savers and Wellness Club. 2010. *Benefits and FAQs*, at: http://www.ofwsaversclub.com/global/index.php

Pantoja, E. 2002. *Microfinance and disaster risk management: Experiences and lessons learned* (Washington, DC, World Bank), at: http://www.proventionconsortium.org/themes/default/pdfs/microfin_DRM.pdf

Parker, J.; Nagarajan, G. 2001. *Technical tool briefs for natural disaster response* (Bethesda, MD, Microenterprise Best Practices), at: www.microfinancegateway.org

—.; Pearce, D. 2002. *Microfinance, grants, and non-financial responses to poverty reduction: Where does microcredit fit?*, CGAP Focus Note No. 20 (Washington, DC, CGAP), at: http://www.cgap.org/gm/document-1.9.2565/FN20.pdf

The Partnering Initiative. Undated. *Reviewing: A three-fold approach*, PowerPoint slide, at: http://thepartneringinitiative.org/areas_of_work/Review_and_Evaluation.jsp

Pearce, D.; Goodland, A.; Mulder, A. 2004. *Microfinance institutions moving into financing for agriculture*, CGAP Information Note on Microfinance and Rural Finance No. 2 (Washington, DC, CGAP), at: http://www.microfinancegateway.org/gm/document-1.9.27438/21653_006.pdf

—; Reinsch, M. 2005a. *Confianza in Peru overcomes adversity by diversifying its loan portfolio*, CGAP Agricultural Microfinance Case Study No. 1 (Washington, DC, CGAP), at: http://www.microfinancegateway.org/gm/document-1.9.29637/29789_file_Confianza_in_Peru.pdf

—; —. 2005b. *Caja Los Andes (Bolivia) diversifies into rural lending*, CGAP Agricultural Microfinance Case Study No. 3 (Washington, DC, CGAP), at: http://www.microfinancegateway.org/gm/document-1.9.27797/29792_file_Caja_Los_Andes.pdf

Pearson, R.; Kilfoil, C. 2007. *Dowa emergency cash transfer (DECT) wider opportunities evaluation and recommendations: Solid lessons and a promising vision*, DECT Wider Opportunities Report (Johannesburg, Siana Strategic Advisors (Pty) Ltd.), at: http://www.odi.org.uk/hpg/papers/resources/DECT Wider Opportunities Report-Final-v01.pdf

Pew Research Centre. 2009. *Mapping the global Muslim population: A report on the size and distribution of the world's population* (Washington, DC, Pew Forum on Religion and Public Life), at: http://pewforum.org/uploadedfiles/Topics/Demographics/Muslimpopulation.pdf

Phillips, M. 2007. "Raising the roof: In Africa, mortgages boost an emerging middle class Zambian experiment, with U.S. help, Aims to create a new suburb", in *Wall Street Journal*, 17 July, Page A1.

Pickens, M.; Porteous, D.; Rotman, S. 2009. *Banking the poor via G2P payments*, CGAP Focus Note No. 58 (Washington, DC, CGAP), at: http://www.cgap.org/gm/document-1.9.41174/FN58.pdf

Pikholz, L.; Champagne, P.; Mugwang'a, T.; Moulick, M.; Wright, G.; Cracknell, D. 2005. *Institutional and product development risk management toolkit* (Nairobi, *MicroSave*, Shorebank Advisory Services), at: http://www.microsave.org/toolkit/institutional-and-product-development-risk-management-toolkit

Pioneer Life Inc. 2008. *Big dreams blast off with SPARX, your smarter piggy bank*, at: http://www.sparx.com.ph/sparx/index.html

Porteous, D. 2006. *Assessing the potential of financial markets: Connecting low income borrowers*, KfW Symposium, Berlin, at: http://www.kfw-entwicklungsbank.de/EN_Home/Sectors/Financial_system_development/Events/Symposium_2006/Topic_introduction_papers_and_presentations.jsp

—; Collins, D.; Abrams, J.; Toniatti, D. 2008. *Segmenting the markets for savings among the poor across countries* (Somerville, MA, Bankable Frontier Associates), at: http://www.bankablefrontier.com/assets/pdfs/GF_SAVINGS_REPORT_v3_0-1.pdf

Powers, J; Magnoni, B. 2010. *A business call to her own: Identifying, analyzing and overcoming constraints to women's small businesses in Latin America and the Caribbean* (Washington, DC, Inter-American Development Bank), at: www.iadb.org/document.cfm?id=35327678

Prahalad, C.K. 2005. *The fortune at the bottom of the pyramid: Eradicating poverty through profits*, (Upper Saddle River, NJ, Wharton School Publishing).

Pricewaterhouse Coopers. 2006. *Alliances and acquisitions increasingly important for fast-growth* companies, Trendsetter Barometer, at: www.barometersurveys.com/production/BarSurv.nsf/vwResources/PR_PDF_Files_2006/$file/tb060516.pdf

Pro Mujer. 2010. *Health care support & training*, at: https://promujer.org/index.tpl?NG_View=39 (last accessed 17 October 2010).

QED Group LLC and International Resources Group. 2008. *Savings: The forgotten half of financial interventions – An online speaker's corner hosted by Madhurantika Moulik of MicroSave* (Washington, DC, USAID) at: http://www.microlinks.org/ev.php?ID=24986_201&ID2=DO_TOPIC

Quisumbing, A.; Pandolfelli, L. 2008. *Promising approaches to address the needs of poor female farmers*, International Food Policy Research Institute (IFPRI) Research Brief No. 13 (Washington, DC, IFPRI), at: www.landcoalition.org/pdf/08_IFPRI_Poor_female_farmers.pdf

Rabbani, M; Prakash, V.; Sulaiman, M. 2006. *Impact assessment of CFPR/TUP: A descriptive analysis based on 2002–2005 panel data,* CFPR/TUP Working Paper Series No. 12 (Dhaka, BRAC Research and Evaluation Division and Aga Khan Foundation Canada), at: http://www.bracresearch.org/workingpapers/impact_tup.pdf

Radermacher, R; Wig, N; Putten-Rademaker, O; Müller, V; Dror, D. 2005. *Yeshasvini Trust, Karnataka – India,* CGAP Working Group on Microinsurance Good and Bad Practices, Case Study No. 20 (Washington, DC, CGAP Working Group on Microinsurance), at: http://www.microfinancegateway.org/gm/document-1.9.25131/30774_file_Yeshasvini_Trust_Go.pdf

Ramírez, C.; García Domínguez, C.; Míguez Morais, J. 2005. *Crossing borders: Remittances, gender, and development* (Santo Domingo, United Nations International Research and Training Institute for the Advancement of Women (UN–INSTRAW), at: http://www.un-instraw.org/en/images/stories/remmitances/documents/crossing_borders.pdf

RBAP-MABS. 2010a. *Background on mobile phone banking and mobile commerce initiative*, at: http://www.mobilephonebanking.rbap.org/page/about_us

—. 2010b. *Mobile phone banking services*, at: http://www.mobilephonebanking.rbap.org/article/archive/15

Reavis, C. 2008. "Off the streets and into a 'good family'", in *Microfinance Insights*, Vol. 9, Nov/Dec 2008 (Mumbai, Intellecap), at: http://www.microfinancinsights.org

Reddy, D.N.; Kundu, A.; Sharma, A.N. Undated. *Report on vulnerability to debt bondage index (VDBI)* (New Delhi, ILO/Kathmandu and Institute for Human Development).

Rehman, A. 2007. "Towards Islamic microfinance: A primer", *Microfinance Voices*, at: http://www.microfinancegateway.org/p/site/m//template.rc/1.26.9091

Reinsch, M.; Ramirez, R. 2010. *Health savings: A technical note* (Davis, CA, Freedom from Hunger), at: http://www.microfinancegateway.org/p/site/m//template.rc/1.9.47106

responsAbility. 2008. *Consumer credits for the poor – Risk or opportunity* (Zurich, responsAbility Social Investments Ltd), at: http://www.microfinancegateway.org/gm/document-1.9.34460/11.pdf

Reuer, J. 2004. *Strategic alliances: Theory and evidence* (New York, Oxford University Press).

Rhyne, E.; Otero, M. 2006. *Microfinance through the next decade: Visioning the who, what, where, when, and how* (Boston, ACCION International), at: http://www.microfinancegateway.org/gm/document-1.9.28243/36423_file_Microfinance_through_the_Next_Decade.pdf

Richardson, D. 2000. "Unorthodox microfinance: The seven doctrines of success," in *Microbanking Bulletin*, No. 4, pp. 3–7 (Toronto, ON, Calmeadow, PACT Publications), at: http://www.microfinancegateway.org/gm/document-1.9.28497/2417_file_02417.pdf

—; Hirschland, M. 2005. "The keys to cost recovery", in Hirschland, M. (ed.): *Savings services for the poor: An operational guide* (Sterling, VA, Kumarian Press, Stylus Publishing, LLC), pp. 43–62 .

Richebacher, T. 2003. "The art of customer profitability analysis", in *destinationCRM.com* (New York, NY, CRM Media), at: http://www.destinationcrm.com/articles/default.asp?ArticleID=3038

Robinson, D.; Hewitt, T.; Harris, J. 2000. *Managing development: Understanding inter-organizational relationships* (Thousand Oaks, CA, Sage Publications).

Robinson, M. 2002. *The microfinance revolution, Volume 2: Lessons from Indonesia* (Washington, DC, World Bank).

Rosenberg, R. 2010. *Does microcredit really help poor people?,* CGAP Focus Note No. 59 (Washington, DC, CGAP), at: http://www.microfinancegateway.org/p/site/m//template.rc/1.1.4333

Roth, J. 1995. "Silence is golden for insurance sharks", in *Mail and Guardian* (South Africa), 3 Feb. 1995.

—; Athreye, V. 2005. *TATA-AIG Life Insurance Company Ltd., India*, CGAP Working Group on Microinsurance, Good and Bad Practices Case Study No. 14 (Washington, DC, CGAP Working Group on Microinsurance), at: http://www.microfinancegateway.org/gm/document-1.9.26900/28285_file_Tata_AIG_Good_and_Bad_Case_Study_14.pdf

—; Churchill, C.; Ramm, G.; Namerta. 2005. *Microinsurance and microfinance institutions: Evidence from India*, CGAP Working Group on Microinsurance, Good and Bad Practices Case Study No. 15 (Washington, DC, CGAP Working Group on Microinsurance), at: http://www.microfinancegateway.org/gm/document-1.9.25332/28334_file_MI_and_MFIs_in_Indi.pdf

—; Garand G.; Rutherford, S. 2006. "Long-term savings and insurance", in Churchill, C. (ed.), 2006, pp. 94–110.

—; McCord, M. 2008. *Agricultural microinsurance: Global practices and prospects* (Appleton, WI, The MicroInsurance Centre), at: http://www.microinsurancenetwork.org/publication/fichier/Agriculture_Microinsurance__Global_Practices_and_Prospects.pdf

—; McCord, M.; Liber, D. 2007. *The landscape of microinsurance in the world's 100 poorest countries* (Appleton, WI, MicroInsurance Centre), at: http://www.microinsurancecentre.org/UI/DocAbstractDetails.aspx?DocID=634

—; Rusconi, R.; Shand, N. 2007. *The poor and voluntary long term contractual savings: Lessons from South Africa*, Social Finance Working Paper No. 48 (Geneva: ILO), available at: http://www.ilo.org/employment/Whatwedo/Publications/lang—en/docName—WCMS_106331/index.htm

Rozner, S. 2006. *Rural leasing*, RAFI Notes Issue 11 (Washington, DC, USAID Offices of Agriculture and Microenterprise Development), at: http://www.microlinks.org/ev_en.php?ID=14604_201&ID2=DO_PRINTPAGE

Rutherford, S. 1995. *ASA: The biography of an NGO* (Dhaka, ASA).

—. 2005. "Why do the poor need savings services?", in Hirschland, M. (ed.), 2005, pp. 15–26.

—. 2006a. "The Grameen pension savings scheme", in *Finance for the poor: Quarterly Newsletter of the focal point for microfinance*, Vol. 7, No. 3 (Asian Development Bank), at: www.adb.org/Documents/Periodicals/Microfinance/finance-200603.pdf

—. 2006b. *GRAMEEN II: The first five years 2001–2005* (Nairobi, MicroSave), at: http://www.microsave.org/research_paper/grameen-ii-the-first-five-years

—. 2008. "Micropensions: Old age security for the poor?", in Matthaus-Maier, I.; von Pischke, J.D. (eds.): *New partnerships for innovation in microfinance* (Berlin, Springer-Verlag), pp. 241–264.

—. with Wright, G.; Sinha, S. K. 2008. *Managing growth of microfinance institutions: ASA Bangladesh single-minded growth* (Nairobi, MicroSave), at: http://www.microsave.org/research_paper/managing-growth-of-microfinance-institutions-asa-bangladesh-single-minded-growth

Sander, C. 2008. "Remittance money transfers, microfinance and financial integration: Of credo, cruxes, and convictions", in Matthaus-Maier, I.; von Pischke, J.D. (eds.): *New partnerships for innovation in microfinance* (Berlin, Springer-Verlag) pp. 113–128.

Sanders, T.; Wegener, C. 2006. *Meso-finance: Filling the financial service gap for small businesses in developing countries* (Amsterdam, NCDO), at: www.bidnetwork.org/download.php?id=40005

SBI Life Insurance Company, Ltd. 2010. *SBI Life – Grameen Shakti*, at: http://www.sbilife.co.in/sbilife/content/10_2878

Schiller, J. 2009. *Making financial services and business skills development available to African children and youth: Accomplishments and limitations of research and monitoring,* Youth-Inclusive Financial Services Linkage Program Case Study #12 (Washington, DC, Making Cents International and Woking, UK, Plan International), available at: http://www.makingcents.com/products_services/resources.php

Schneider-Moretto, L. 2005. *Tool for developing a financial risk management policy* (New York, Women's World Banking).

Schreiner, M.; Clancy, M.; Sherraden, M. 2002. *Saving performance in the American Dream Demonstration, a national demonstration of Individual Development Accounts* (St. Louis, MO, Center for Social Development), at: csd.wustl.edu/Publications/Documents/ADDReport2002.pdf

SEAF. 2004. *The development impact of small and medium enterprises: Lessons learned from SEAF investments*, Volume I: Main Report (Washington, DC, Small Enterprise Assistance Funds), at: http://seaf.com/images/reports/11/Volume%201%20Main%20Report.pdf

SEEP Network. 2006. *Consumer protection principles in practice: A framework for developing and implementing a pro-client approach to microfinance*, SEEP Progress Note No. 14 (Washington, DC, SEEP Network), available at: http://www.seepnetwork.org/Resources/4664_file_Progress_Note_14.pdf

—. 2008. *SEEP Network guidelines for microenterprise development in HIV and AIDS-impacted communities: Supporting economic security and health, Book 2 – For microenterprise development practitioners* (Washington, DC, SEEP Network), at: http://communities.seepnetwork.org/hamed/node/764

—. 2009. *Minimum standards for economic recovery after crisis* (Washington, DC, SEEP), at: http://communities.seepnetwork.org/econrecovery/node/821

—. 2010a. *Social Performance Glossary*, at: www.seepnetwork.org/files/4728_file_Soical_Performance_Glossary.pdf (last accessed Sep. 14, 2010).

—. 2010b. *Microfinance financial reporting standards: Measuring financial performance of microfinance institutions*, Draft for public comment dated May 2010 (New York, NY, SEEP Network), at: http://seepnetwork.org/Pages/Initiatives/FinancialReportingStandardInitiative.aspx

Seibel, H.D. 2005. *Islamic microfinance in Indonesia*, Sector Project Financial Systems Development Report, (Eschborn, Deutsche Gesellschaft für Technische Zusammenarbeit (GTZ)), at: http://www.gtz.de/de/dokumente/en-islamic-mf-indonesia.pdf.pdf

—. 2007. *Islamic microfinance: The challenge of institutional diversity*, University of Cologne Development Research Centre, at: http://www.uni-koeln.de/ew-fak/aef/12-2007/2007-5%20Seibel%20Islamic%20Microfinance%20-%20The%20Challenge%20of%20Inst.pdf

Seller, D. 2002. *Microfinance in natural and manmade disasters*, report prepared for the Microfinance Unit and the Emergency Response Team, Program Quality and Support Department (Baltimore, MD, Catholic Relief Services).

—. 2008. *Microfinance: An appropriate instrument after man-made and natural disasters?* Dissertation (unpublished), University of Vienna.

Sempangi, H.; Messan, H. 2005. *Microleasing: An alternative way of financing productive assets*, *MicroSave* Briefing Note # 35 (Nairobi, *MicroSave*), at: http://www.microsave.org/briefing_notes/briefing-note-35-microleasing-an-alternative-way-of-financing-productive-assets

SEWA. 2009. *SEWA Bank products* (Delhi, Self-employed Women's Association), at: http://www.sewa.org/images/pdf/new/product.pdf

Shahnaz, D.; Shankar, S. 2010. *Growth pangs of a microfinance institution, Bullock-Cart Workers Development Association (BWDA): Trying to speed ahead without going off-course* (Singapore, National University of Singapore).

Shell, B. 2009. *Product development for girls: Girls' savings and financial education*, Youth-Inclusive Financial Services Linkage Program Case Study #14 (Washington, DC, Making Cents International and New York, Women's World Banking), available at: http://www.makingcents.com/products_services/resources.php

Shrader, L.; Kamal, N.; Darmono, W.A.; Johnston, D. 2006. *Youth and access to microfinance in Indonesia: Outreach and options* (Jakarta, ImagineNations and the World Bank Group), at: http://www.imaginenations.org/documents/Microfinance%20in%20Indonesia%20Study.pdf

Shumann, R. 2004. *Developing housing microfinance products in Central America*, ACCION InSight No. 12 (Boston, MA, ACCION International), at: http://resources.centerforfinancialinclusion.org/publications/InSight_12_181.asp

Sia, M.; Nails, D. 2008. *Winning strategies for successful small business lending*, Exchanging Views Series #6 (Chicago, ShoreCap Exchange), at: http://www.microfinancegateway.org/p/site/m//template.rc/1.9.31173

Sievers, M.; Vanderberg, P. 2007. "Synergies through linkages: Who benefits from linking micro-finance and business development services?", in *World Development,* Vol. 35, No 8, pp. 1341–1398 (Oxford, Elsevier), at: http://p31.itcilo.org/entdev/synergies/en/category-2

Silicon Valley Community Foundation. 2007. *Families saving and building hope: 2007 report on graduates of the Assets for All Alliance* (San Jose, CA, Lenders for Community Development and Mountain View, CA, Silicon Valley Community Foundation), at: http://www.opportunityfund.org/social-impact/ida/impact

Simanowitz, A. 2003. *Appraising the poverty outreach of microfinance: A review of the CGAP Poverty Assessment Tool (PAT)*, Imp-Act Occasional Paper, at: www.imp-act.org (Brighton, Imp-Act).

—. 2008a. *Using microfinance to fight poverty, empower women and address gender-based violence and HIV*, IDS Research Summary (Brighton, University of Sussex, Institute of Development Studies), at: http://www.ids.ac.uk/go/microfinance

—. 2008b. *Combining microfinance and training on gender and HIV – A proven approach to reduce poverty and halve violence against women* (Brighton, University of Sussex, Institute of Development Studies), at: http://www.ids.ac.uk/go/microfinance

—. with Walter, A., 2002. "Ensuring impact: Reaching the poorest while building financially self-sufficient institutions, and showing improvements in the lives of poor women and their families", in Daley-Harris, S. (ed.): *Pathways out of poverty: Innovations in microfinance for the poorest families*, pp. 1–76 West Hartford, CT, Kumarian Press).

Smart Campaign. 2010. *Conducting client protection assessments: A guide* (Washington, DC, Center for Financial Inclusion), at:

http://www.smartcampaign.org/storage/documents/Tools_and_Resources/Conducting_Client_Protection_Assessments-A_Guide-The_Smart_Campaign.pdf

Staehle, M. 2005. "Flexible financial services for the poor: Experience of *Safe*Save, Bangladesh", in *Finance for the poor. Quarterly Newsletter of the focal point for microfinance*, Vol. 6, No. 3 (Asian Development Bank), at: http://www.adb.org/documents/periodicals/microfinance/

Standard Chartered. 2010. *Standard Chartered launches new website to help women entrepreneurs start and grow their businesses*, Press Release, 8 March 2010 (Singapore, Standard Chartered), at: http://www.standardchartered.com.sg/press-releases/en/_pdf/2010/press_100308.pdf

Staschen, S. 2001. *Financial technology of Small Farmer Cooperatives Ltd (SFCLs): Products and innovations*, Working Paper 2 (Kathmandu, Rural Finance Nepal).

Storm-Swire, L. 2009. *Exploring youth financial services: The case of Pro Mujer in Bolivia*, Youth-Inclusive Financial Services Linkage Program Case Study #13 (Washington, DC, Making Cents International and La Paz, Pro Mujer), available at: http://www.makingcents.com/products_services/resources.php

Sustainable Microfinance for Women's Empowerment, http://www.genfinance.info/

Swibel, M. 2007. "The world's top microfinance institutions", *Forbes Magazine*, 20 December 2007, at: www.forbes.com/2007/12/20/top-microfinance-philanthropy-biz-cz_ms_1220intro.html

Symbiotics. 2007. *Symbiotics closes the first series of its Subordinated Debt CDO programme to provide quasi capital financing to microfinance institutions*, 21 September (Geneva, Symbiotics), at: http://www.syminvest.com

Szubert, D.; Pawlak, K.; Matul, M. 2005. *Quantitative market research manual for MFIs* (Nairobi, *MicroSave*), at: http://www.microfinancegateway.org/p/site/m//template.rc/1.9.26888

—; Petric, B. 2005. *Market development through product refinement*, based on a case study of MikroCredit EKI (Nairobi, *MicroSave* and Warsaw, Microfinance Centre for Central and Eastern Europe and the New Independent States).

Tan, H. 2008. "The missing link in takaful", in: *Middle East Insurance Review*, July 2008 (Singapore, Ins Communications Pte Ltd), at: http://www.takaful.coop/doc_store/takaful/Microtakaful%20July%202008.pdf

Tennyson, R. 2003. *The partnering toolbook* (London, International Business Leaders Forum (IBLF), Global Alliance for Improved Nutrition (GAIN)), at: http://thepartneringinitiative.org/publications/Toolbooks/The_Partnering_Toolbook.jsp

Teskiewicz, A. 2007. *Modelos predictivos para cobranza y refinanciación* [Predictive modeling for collections and refinancing], First Collection Summit (Buenos Aires, Credit Management Solutions).

Thunderbird School for Global Management. 2010. *Thunderbird for good: Strengthening women entrepreneurship in Peru*, at: http://www.thunderbird.edu/about_thunderbird/thunderbird_good/peru/index.htm (last accessed 14 December 2010).

Tilock, K. 2004. "Construction assistance and housing microfinance", in F. Daphnis; B. Ferguson (eds.), 2004, pp. 115–122.

Timburg, T. 2003. *Islamic banking and its potential impact* (Madison, WI, Broadening Access and Strengthening Input Market Systems), at: http://www.microfinancegateway.org/p/site/m//template.rc/1.9.27287

Tran, N.; Yun, T.S. 2004. *TYM's Mutual Assistance Fund: Vietnam*, CGAP Working Group on Microinsurance, Good and Bad Practices Case Study No. 3 (Washington, DC, CGAP Working Group on Microinsurance), at: http://www.microfinancegateway.org/gm/document-1.9.24400/22460_TYM_Good_and_Bad_Case_Study_3.pdf

Trickle Up. 2010. *Our supporters* (New York, NY, Trickle Up), at: http://www.trickleup.org/about/Our-Supporters.cfm

Triodos Facet. 2009. *SMARTRAC Public Tools Series for Risk Management*, Tool 11 (Zeist, Triodos Facet and Triodos Investment Management), at: http://www.triodosfacet.nl/images/stories/smartrac/smartracpublictoolsseries_tool11.pdf

UN-Habitat. 2003. *The challenge of slums: Global report on human settlements 2003* (Nairobi, UN-Habitat), at: http://www.unhabitat.org/downloads/docs/GRHS.2003.0.pdf

—. 2005. *Global Report on Human Settlements 2005: Financing urban shelter* (Nairobi, UN-Habitat), at: http://www.unhabitat.org/pmss/listItemDetails.aspx?publicationID=1818

—. 2008. *Housing for all: The challenges of affordability, accessibility and sustainability* (Nairobi, UN-Habitat), at: http://www.unhabitat.org/pmss/listItemDetails.aspx?publicationID=2547

UNAIDS. 2009. *AIDS epidemic update 2009* (Geneva, UNAIDS/WHO).

United Nations. 2007. *Mainstreaming disability in the development agenda,* in Commission for Social Development, 46th session (New York, Economic and Social Council).

—. 2009a. *World population prospects: The 2008 revision population database* (New York, NY, United Nations, Department of Economic and Social Affairs, Population Division), at: http://esa.un.org/unpp

—. 2009b. *World survey on the role of women in development: Women's control over economic resources and access to financial resources, including microfinance* (New York, NY, United Nations, Department of Economic and Social Affairs, Division for the Advancement of Women), at: http://www.un.org/womenwatch/daw/ws2009/

United Nations Children's Fund (UNICEF). 2007. *Gender equality: The big picture* (New York, NY), at: http://www.onbeingfemale.com/wp-content/uploads/2010/03/legalequityunicef.pdf

United Nations Educational, Scientific and Cultural Organization (UNESCO). 2010. *Adult and youth literacy: Global trends in gender parity*, UIS Fact Sheet, September 2010, No. 3 (Montreal), at: http://unesco.org/education/ild2010/FactSheet2010_Lit_EN.pdf

United Nations Entity for Gender Equality and the Empowerment of Women, at: http://www.unwomen.org/

United Nations High Commissioner for Refugees (UNHCR). 2006. *Statistical Yearbook 2006: Trends in displacement, protection and solutions* (Geneva), at: www.unhcr.org/statistics.html

United Nations Population Fund (UNFPA). 2010. *Gender equality: Ending widespread violence against women* (New York, NY), at: http://www.unfpa.org/gender/violence.htm (last accessed 17 October 2010).

USAID. Undated. "Leasing", in *Module VI: Rural & Agricultural Finance Specialty Topic Series*, at: http://www.microlinks.org/ev_en.php?ID=13176_201&ID2=DO_TOPIC

—. 2008. *MD overview: Clients affected by HIV/AIDS* (Washington, DC, USAID), at: http://www.microlinks.org/ev02.php?ID=12666_201&ID2=DO_TOPIC

—. 2009. *Lending at the intersection of micro and SME finance: Compilation document* (Washington, DC, USAID), at: www.microlinks.org/sc/micro2SMEfinance

—. 2010. *Poverty assessment tools*, at: http://www.povertytools.org/index.html

USAID Rural and Agricultural Finance Seminar Series, at: www.microlinks.org

Uthira, D.; Manohar, H. 2009. "Economic implications and sustainability of micropensions in the era of pension reforms in India", in *International Research Journal of Finance and Economics*, Issue 24, pp. 36–47 (London, EuroJournals Publishing, Inc.), at: http://www.eurojournals.com/finance.htm

Van Doorn, J.; Churchill, C. 2004. *Microfinance against child labour*, ILO Technical Guidelines (Geneva, ILO, Social Finance Programme), at: http://www.oit.org.pe/ipec/documentos/microfinance_guideline.pdf

Vance, I. 2004. "Land and collateral issues", in F. Daphnis; B. Ferguson (eds.), 2004, pp. 123–150.

—. 2008. "Promising practices and lessons new distribution channels: Holistic housing finance services for the poor", in *Highlights: Housing finance for the poor*, Vol. 3 (Washington, DC, CGAP), at: http://www.habitat.org/housing_finance/pdf/CGAP_Housing_Finance_for_the_Poor_Newsletter_Spring_2008.pdf

Vyas, J. 2008. *Micro pension for informal sector women workers* (Ahmedabad, Shri Mahila SEWA Sahakari Bank Ltd.), at: http://www.microfinancegateway.org/gm/document-1.9.36474/12.pdf

Wagner, T. 2010. *Micro-financing allows everyone to be a philanthropist* (New York, NY, NY1 News), at: http://www.ny1.com/content/top_stories/112252/micro-financing-allows-everyone-to-be-a-philanthropist

Wall Street Journal. 2010. "Max New York Life's lesson in insuring a rural foothold", 4 May, at: http://online.wsj.com/article/SB127296921636786509.html?mod=WSJ_latestheadlines#articleTabs%3Darticle

Wampfler, B.: Mercoiret, M. 2001. *Microfinance and producers' organizations: Roles and partnerships in the context of liberalization* (Paris, Agricultural Research Centre for International Development).

Waterfield, C. 2004. *Virtual conference on electronic banking for the Poor, Conference held 16–24 February 2004 (final report)* (Nairobi, MicroSave), at: http://www.microfinancegateway.org/p/site/m//template.rc/1.9.26585

Wehnert, U.; Shakya, R. 2001. *Are SFCLs viable microfinance organizations?: A comprehensive financial analysis of 33 SFCLs*, Working Paper 1 (Kathmandu, Rural Finance Nepal).

Werlin, S.; Hastings, A. 2006. *Post-disaster and post-conflict microfinance: Best practices in light of Fonkoze's experience in Haiti* (Port-au-Prince, Fonkoze), at: http://www.microfinancegateway.org/gm/document-1.9.28056/37055_file_WerlinHastings.pdf

Westley, G. 2003. *Equipment leasing and lending: A guide for microfinance*, Sustainable Development Department Best Practice Series (Washington, DC, IADB), at: http://www.microfinancegateway.org/gm/document-1.9.26285/3772_file_03772.pdf.

—. 2004. *A tale of four village banking programs: Best practices in Latin America* (Washington, DC, IADB), at: http://www.microfinancegateway.org/gm/document-1.9.27393/22782_VB_BPP_FINAL.doc

—; Palomas, X.M. 2010. *Is there a business case for small savers?* CGAP Occasional Paper No. 18 (Washington, DC, CGAP), at: http://www.cgap.org/gm/document-1.9.47356/OP_18_Rev.pdf

Wieland, R. 2008. *Supporting credit union development in Afghanistan: An overview of issues important to the development of Shari'a-Compliant Cooperative Finance* (Madison, WI, WOCCU), at: http://www.microfinancegateway.org/gm/document-1.9.27299/46362_file_2008AfghanistanReport.pdf

Wikipedia. 2010. *Customer relationship management*, at: http://en.wikipedia.org/wiki/Customer_relationship_management.

Wilmington Trust. 2010. *Understanding loan covenants*, at: http://www.wilmingtontrust.com/wtcom/index.jsp?fileid=3000111 (last accessed 14 December 2010).

Wilson, T. 2001. *Microfinance during and after armed conflict: Lessons from Angola, Cambodia, Mozambique and Rwanda* (Durham, The Springfield Centre for Business in Development), at: http://www.microfinancegateway.org/gm/document-1.9.29223/14563_14563.pdf

Wilson, K.; Burpee, G. 2008. *Filling the blue box: Mutuelles, self-financing and financial services in the south of Haiti* (Boston, Feinstein International Center), at: http://www.microlinks.org/ev.php?ID=24196_201&ID2=DO_TOPIC

Wipf, J.; Garand, D. 2008. *Performance indicators for microinsurance: A handbook for microinsurance practitioners* (Luxembourg, ADA), at: http://www.microfinancegateway.org/p/site/m//template.rc/1.9.29234

Wise, H.M. 2004. *Cajas externas in Bolivia: A strategic alliance to increase savings in under-served markets*, Paper presented at the 2004 AGM SEEP Meetings at the Innovations in Rural Finance training session, 26 October 2004, at: http://www.seepnetwork.org/Resources/1061_FIE_ProMujer_Presentaci_n_de_Conclusiones_Eng.ppt.

Wisniwski, S. 1999. *Microsavings compared to other sources of funds*, Working Group on Savings Mobilization (Eschborn, Germany, CGAP), at: http://www.microfinancegateway.org/gm/document-1.9.28712/1756_file_01756.pdf

World Council of Credit Unions (WOCCU). 2009. *WOCCU expands Islamic financial services to southern, eastern Afghanistan*, at: http://www.woccu.org/press/releases?id=1645

Women's World Banking. 2003. *Asset building for old age security: A case for hybrid long-term savings micropension products* (New York, Women's World Banking), at: http://www.microfinancegateway.org/gm/document-1.9.38456/33.pdf

Woodworth, W. 2006. *Microcredit in post-conflict, conflict, natural disaster, and other difficult settings* (Provo, Brigham Young University), at: http://www.microfinancegateway.org/gm/document-1.9.26040/37054_file_Woodworth.pdf

World Bank. 2004. *Agriculture investment sourcebook* (Washington, DC).

—. 2007. *World Development Report 2008: Agriculture for Development* (Washington, DC).

—. 2008. *Finance for all? Policies and pitfalls in expanding access* (Washington, DC), at: http://siteresources.worldbank.org/INTFINFORALL/Resources/4099583-1194373512632/FFA_book.pdf

—. 2009a. *Gender in agriculture: Sourcebook* (Washington, DC), at: http://siteresources.worldbank.org/INTGENAGRLIVSOUBOOK/Resources/CompleteBook.pdf

—. 2009b. *Escaping poverty is possible when there are local opportunities for people with initiative*, Press Release No: 2009/250/PREM, available at: http://web.worldbank.org/WBSITE/EXTERNAL/NEWS/0,,contentMDK:22097477~pagePK:34370~piPK:34424~theSitePK:4607,00.html

—. 2010. *Migration and remittances*, Issue Brief (Washington, DC), at: http://siteresources.worldbank.org/TOPICS/Resources/214970-1288877981391/Annual_Meetings_Report_DEC_IB_MigrationAndRemittances_Update24Sep10.pdf

World Health Organization (WHO). 2009. *Women's health*, Fact sheet No. 334 (Geneva).

World Vision. 2010. *Structure and funding* (Monrovia, CA), at: http://www.wvi.org/wvi/wviweb.nsf/maindocs/39F905AE21E265C1882573750075074B?opendocument

Wright, G. 2000a. *Microfinance systems: Designing quality financial serices for the poor* (London, Zed Books).

—. 2000b. *Designing innovative products, processes and channels for the promotion of microfinance*, Prepared for the NABARD Workshop on "Microfinance: Future Policy Options" (Nairobi, MicroSave), at http://www.microsave.org/research_paper/designing-innovative-products-processes-and-channels-for-the-promotion-of-microfinance

—; Brand, M.; Northrip, Z.; Cohen, M.; McCord, M.; Helms, B. 2001. *Looking before you leap: Key questions that should precede starting new product development* (Nairobi, *MicroSave*), at: http://www.microsave.org/system/files/Looking_Before_You_Leap.pdf

—; Cracknell, D. 2005. *Strategic marketing toolkit* (Nairobi, MicroSave), at: http://www.microsave.org/toolkit/strategic-marketing-toolkit.

—; Cracknell, D.; Parrott, L. 2005. *Customer service toolkit* (Nairobi, *MicroSave*), at: http://www.microsave.org/toolkit/customer-service-toolkit

—; Christen, R; Matin, I. 2001. *ASA's culture, competition and choice: Introducing savings services into a MicroCredit institution* (Nairobi, *MicroSave*), at: http://www.microsave.org/system/files/ASA%E2%80%99s_Culture_Competition_and_Choice.pdf

—; Dondo, A. 2000. *Are you poor enough? Client selection by microfinance institutions,* MicroSave Briefing Note No. 07 (Nairobi, *MicroSave*), at: http://www.microsave.org/briefing_notes/briefing-note-7-are-you-poor-enough-client-selection-by-microfinance-institutions

—; Pawlak, K.; Tounitsky, W.; Parrott, L.; Cracknell, D.; Arunachalam, R. S. 2007. *Strategic business planning for market-led financial institutions toolkit* (Nairobi, *MicroSave*), at: http://www.microsave.org/toolkit/strategic-business-planning-toolkit

XacBank, LLC. 2009. *Audited financial statements, 31 December 2009*, at: http://www.mixmarket.org/sites/default/files/XacBank_AFS_09.pdf

Youth-Inclusive Financial Services Case Studies Series 2009, available at: http://www.makingcents.com/products_services/resources.php

Youth Save Consortium. 2010. *Youth savings in developing countries: Trends in practice, gaps in knowledge* (Westport, CT, Youth Save Initiative) at: http://www.microfinancegateway.org/gm/document-1.9.45704/youth%20savings.pdf

Yunus, M. 2002. *Grameen Bank II: Designed to open new possibilities* (Dhaka, Grameen Communications), at: http://www.grameen-info.org/index.php?option=com_content&task=view&id=30&Itemid=116

—; Jolis, A. 1999. *Banker to the poor: Micro-lending and the battle against world poverty*, 2007 edn. (New York, PublicAffairs).

Zaher, T.; Hassan, M. 2001. "A comparative literature survey of Islamic finance and banking", in *Financial Markets, Institutions and Instruments*, Vol. 10, No. 4, pp. 155–199 (Malden, MA and Oxford, Blackwell Publishers).

Zeller, M. 2004. *Review of poverty assessment tools*, Report submitted to IRIS and USAID as part of the Developing Poverty Assessment Tools Project (Washington, DC, IRS/USAID), at: http://www.microfinancegateway.org/p/site/m//template.rc/1.9.33305

Zimmerman, J.; Moury, Y. 2009. *Savings-linked conditional cash transfers: A new policy approach to global poverty reduction*, A Global Assets Project Policy Brief (Washington, DC, New America Foundation), at: http://www.newamerica.net/files/nafmigration/NAF_CCT_Savings_April09_Final.pdf

Index